GEOS

the pearson custom library for geography & geology

Elemental Geosystems
Westfield State University
GARP 0102

Cover Art: Courtesy of Photoubrary.com, Robert Harding World Imagery, Getty Images/Photodisc.

12 18

This special edition published in cooperation with Pearson Learning Solutions.

Printed in the United States of America.

Please visit our website at *www.pearsonlearningsolutions.com*.

Attention bookstores: For permission to return any unsold stock, contact
us at *pe-uscustomreturns@pearson.com*.

Pearson Learning Solutions, 501 Boylston Street, Suite 900, Boston, MA 02116
A Pearson Education Company
www.pearsoned.com

ISBN 10: 1-256-60682-0
ISBN 13: 978-1-256-60682-6

Table of Contents

Essentials of Geography

Essentials of Geography

Gough Island (40.2° S 9.5° W) is in the south Atlantic Ocean, about 425 km (264 mi) from the nearest settlement. This volcanic island of just 65 km^2 area (25 mi^2) is a wildlife reserve and has been a UNESCO World Heritage Site since 1994. Boat landings are not permitted and only a six-person remote weather station is occupied. Despite its remote location, this unique place is not immune to human impacts. In 2004, discovery of bird nest predation, by accidentally introduced house mice, launched scientific studies to control and eradicate the mice to protect endangered wildlife. To understand such a place, we see the value of the integrative science of physical geography. [Bobbé Christopherson.]

KEY LEARNING CONCEPTS

After reading the chapter, you should be able to:

- ***Define*** geography and physical geography in particular.
- ***Describe*** systems analysis, open and closed systems, and feedback information, and ***relate*** these concepts to Earth systems.
- ***Explain*** Earth's reference grid: latitude and longitude and latitudinal geographic zones and time.
- ***Define*** cartography and mapping basics: map scale and map projections.
- ***Describe*** remote sensing and the geographic information system (GIS), and ***explain*** how both tools are used in geographic analysis.

Where Is Four Corners, Exactly?

Amidst the high desert landscape of the American Southwest is the unique Four Corners landmark, where a monument marks the intersection of Colorado, New Mexico, Arizona, and Utah. This location is the only point in the United States where four states touch. It is a must-see destination for many visitors, a place where feet and hands can each be in a different state and families and friends can straddle the disk marking the precise location where state boundaries meet. The original surveyor, Chandler Robbins, marked the spot with a 2.1-m (7-ft) sandstone monument in 1875. The present monument and visitor plaza date to 1992 and are owned and operated by the Navajo Nation Parks and Recreation Department (Figure GN 1).

In the spring of 2009, news reports claimed that the location of Four Corners was in error, that in fact the monument was located 4 km (2.5 mi) west of the precise location. The reports claimed that new surveys by the National Geodetic Survey (NGS) using Global Positioning System (GPS) satellites and state-of-the-art mapping technology refuted the original 1875 surveys. For such an important landmark, this was shocking news. Did the monument now need to be moved, or was the news in error?

For the average visitor, such precise measurement details are unimportant. For the scientist, engineer, or natural resource professional, such an error has wide-ranging implications. Four Corners is an established benchmark in the western United States upon which other surveys and locations are based.

The question of accuracy relates to which meridian was used for the original survey. Congress ordered Chandler Robbins in 1875 to use the Greenwich meridian, London, which later became the official 0° prime meridian, from which we measure longitude west or east on Earth. However, in the late 1800s many western states were set with surveys using the Washington meridian, which is about 77° 3′ west longitude from Greenwich. If Robbins' survey had used the Washington meridian, the marker would be off as described by the media reports.

(a)

(b)

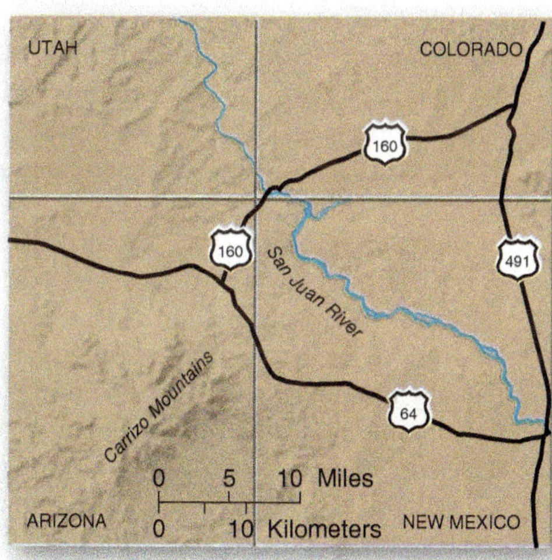

FIGURE GN 1 Four Corners landmark and benchmark.
(a) The Four Corners tourist plaza just off US Highway 160. (b) Survey benchmark 1992 replacement. (c) Map of the Four Corners region. [USGS.]

A few weeks later the news stories were corrected as the details of the original survey came to light. While the monument does appear to be offset from its intended location, the actual offset is only 548 m (1800 ft) to the east rather than the west. However, according to NGS, the monument is in the right spot. It turns out that the location of a physical monument is usually the ultimate authority in delineating a boundary.

Thus, once the Four Corners monument was established and accepted by all parties involved—in this case, the four territories and the U.S. Congress—it became the *exact* spot where the four states meet. The location, set for more than 125 years, is used in the modern National Spatial Reference System and is in the right place—36° 59′ 56.3150″ north latitude by 109° 02′ 42.6210″ west longitude (http://www.glorecords.blm.gov/).

At the heart of geographic science are such topics as place, location, latitude and longitude, the Greenwich prime meridian, and mapping. In this chapter, you work with these concepts, the "Essentials of Geography."

Welcome to the study of physical geography! We examine the powerful Earth systems that influence our lives and the many ways humans impact those systems. In this second decade of the 21st century, a century that will see many changes to the natural environment, we find ourselves in an exciting time to study physical geography, learning about the building blocks that form the landscapes, seascapes, atmosphere, and ecosystems upon which we depend.

Much has happened recently. Consider the following events, among many—and the questions they raise for the study of Earth's systems:

- The 2010 eruption of the Eyjafjallajökull volcano in Iceland disrupted airline schedules and global travel as prevailing winds spread ash over Europe and Asia. What atmospheric forces affected the ash movement from such a volcanic event?
- The 2010 *Deepwater Horizon* oil spill disaster in the Gulf of Mexico continues to unfold as scientists study and map crude oil and chemical dispersants. Spill oil persists on the floor of the Gulf and along coastal wetlands, continuing to harm marine life. How do ocean currents and hurricanes play a part in the oil's distribution?
- In Haiti, the January 2010 magnitude 7.0 earthquake literally brought one of the poorest countries on Earth to collapse, killing more than 200,000 people and leaving millions homeless. Estimates set the damage in Haiti at more than double the country's entire gross domestic product. Why do earthquakes occur in particular locations across the globe?
- The March 2011 magnitude 9.0 earthquake and 10-m to 20-m (33 to 66 ft) tsunami devastated Honshu Island, Japan—at $309 billion (USD), Earth's most expensive natural disaster. This caused the worst multiple nuclear power plant catastrophe in history, with 3 core meltdowns, releasing huge quantities of radioactivity onto the land, into the food web, and into the ocean and atmosphere. What causes a tsunami, and how far does it travel? How will prevailing winds and currents disperse the radiation across the globe?
- This past decade experienced the highest temperatures over land and water in the instrumental record. The year 2010 tied 2005 as the warmest year on record for global temperatures. In response, the extent of sea ice in the Arctic Ocean continues to decline to record lows. Intense weather events and flooding continue to increase. And, 2011 set tornado records, causing such devastation in Tuscaloosa, Alabama, Joplin, Missouri, and elsewhere.

Climate change science will be an overriding topic for the global society this century. The Intergovernmental Panel on Climate Change (IPCC; http://www.ipcc.ch/) completed its *Fourth Assessment Report* in 2007. The Climate Congress held an International Climate Change Conference in Copenhagen, Denmark, in March 2009, as an update to the IPCC with more than 80 countries and 2500 scientists (http://climatecongress.ku.dk/). The Climate Congress concluded:

> The *worst-case* IPCC (2007) projections, or even worse, are being realized. . . . Emissions are soaring, projections of sea-level rise are higher than expected, and climate impacts around the world are appearing with increasing frequency.

Financial data from 15 of the world's largest financial institutions estimated that annual weather-related damage losses (from drought, floods, hail, tornadoes, derechos, tropical systems, monsoon intensity, storm surges, blizzards and ice storms, and wildfires) could exceed $1 trillion by 2040 (adjusted to current dollars)—up from $210 billion in 2005 (Hurricane Katrina alone produced $125 billion in losses). Global climate change is driving this increasing total, at a pace that is accelerating. A new study published in 2011 found that flooding frequencies and extreme weather events more than doubled since 1970.

Imagine the challenge society as a whole and we in physical geography face to understand how Earth's systems operate and then to forecast changes. Physical geography uses a *spatial* perspective and gives you the tools to understand what is happening in specific locations and across the globe. This text presents updated science and information to help you understand our dynamic Earth systems.

Why does the environment vary from equator to midlatitudes, between deserts and polar regions? How does solar energy influence the distribution of trees, soils, climates, and lifestyles? Why are we experiencing record levels of wildfires? Why are earthquakes and volcanoes active in certain regions and what is the risk? What produces the patterns of wind, weather, and ocean currents? Why are global sea levels on the rise? How do natural systems affect human populations, and, in turn, what impact are humans having on natural systems? Why are record levels of plants and animals facing extinction? We explore those questions, and more, through geography's unique perspective. Welcome to an exploration of physical geography!

In this chapter: Our study of Earth systems begins with a look at the science of physical geography and the geographic tools we use. Physical geography is key to studying entire Earth systems because of its integrative spatial approach.

Physical geographers analyze systems to study the environment. Therefore, we discuss systems and the feedback mechanisms that influence system operations. We then consider location, a key theme of geographic inquiry—the latitude, longitude, and time coordinates that inscribe Earth's surface and the new technologies in use to measure them. Next, we examine maps as critical tools that geographers use to portray physical and cultural information. This chapter concludes with an overview of the technology that is adding exciting new dimensions to geography: remote sensing from space and computer-based geographic information systems.

The Science of Geography

Now is the era of **Earth systems science**. This science contributes to our emerging view of Earth as a complete entity—an interacting set of physical, chemical, and biological systems that produce a whole Earth. Physical geography is at the heart of Earth systems science as we answer the *spatial* questions concerning Earth's physical systems and their interaction with living things.

Geography (from *geo*, "Earth," and *graphein*, "to write") is the science that studies the relationships among natural systems, geographic areas, society, cultural activities, and the interdependence of all of these *over space*. The term **spatial** refers to the nature and character of physical space, its measurement, and the distribution of things within it.

For example, think of your own route to the classroom or library today or the way you get to work and how you used your knowledge of street patterns, traffic trouble spots, one-way streets, parking spaces, or bike rack locations to minimize walking distance. All these are spatial considerations that influence human actions.

To help in this definition, we separate geographic science into five spatial themes: **location**, **region**, **human–Earth relationships**, **movement**, and **place**, each illustrated and defined in Figure 1. *Elemental Geosystems* draws on each theme.

Geographic Analysis

Within these five geographic themes, a method rather than a specific body of knowledge governs geography. The method is **spatial analysis**. Using this method, geography synthesizes (brings together) topics from many fields, integrating information to form a whole-Earth concept. Geographers view phenomena as occurring in spaces, areas, and locations. The language of geography reflects this spatial view: space, territory, zone, pattern, distribution, place, location, region, sphere, province, and distance. Geographers analyze the differences and similarities among places.

Process, a set of actions or mechanisms that operate in some special order, is central to geographic analysis. As examples in *Geosystems*, numerous processes are involved in Earth's vast water–atmosphere–weather system, or in continental crust movements and earthquake occurrences, or in ecosystem functions, or in a river's drainage basin dynamics. Geographers use spatial analysis to examine how Earth's processes interact over space or area.

Therefore, **physical geography** is the spatial analysis of all the physical elements and process systems that make up the environment: energy, air, water, weather, climate, landforms, soils, animals, plants, microorganisms, and Earth itself. As with any science, physical geographers employ the **scientific method**. Focus Study 1 explains this essential process of science.

The Geographic Continuum

Geography is eclectic, integrating a wide range of subject matter from diverse fields; virtually any subject can be examined geographically. Figure 2 shows a continuous distribution—a continuum—along which the content of geography is arranged. Physical and life sciences are at one end, and human and cultural sciences are at the other. As the figure shows, various specialties within geography draw from these subject areas.

The continuum in Figure 2 reflects a basic duality, or split, within geography—*physical geography* versus *human/cultural geography*. Some societies parallel this duality. Humans at times think of themselves as exempt from physical Earth processes—like actors not paying attention to their stage, props, and lighting. We all depend on Earth's systems to provide oxygen, water, nutrients, energy, and materials to support life. The growing complexity of the human–Earth relationship requires that we shift our study of geographic processes toward the center of the continuum in Figure 2 to attain a more balanced perspective—such is the thrust of *Elemental Geosystems*. Such a synthesis is key to environmental planning and resource sustainability strategies.

Earth Systems Concepts

The word *system* is in our lives daily: "Check the car's cooling system"; "Is a broadband system available for my Internet browser?"; "How does the grading system work?"; "A weather system is approaching." *Systems analysis* techniques began with studies of energy and temperature (thermodynamics) in the 19th century and were further developed in engineering during World War II. Systems methodology is an important analytical tool.

Systems Theory

Simply stated, a **system** is any ordered, interrelated set of things and their attributes, linked by flows of energy and matter, as distinct from the surrounding environment outside the system. The elements within a system may be arranged in a series or interwoven with one another. A system comprises any number of subsystems. Within Earth's systems, both matter and energy are stored and retrieved, and energy is transformed from one type to another. (Remember: *Matter* is mass that assumes a physical shape and occupies space; *energy* is a capacity to change the motion of, or to do work on, matter.)

Open Systems Systems in nature are generally not self-contained: Inputs of energy and matter flow into the system, and outputs of energy and matter flow from the system. Such a system is an **open system**. Within a system, the parts function in an interrelated manner, acting together in a way that gives each system its operational

FIGURE 1 Five themes of geographic science.
Drawing from your own experience, can you think of several examples of each theme? [Photos by Karl Birkeland, except Movement by Ian Dagnall/Alamy; image NASA/GSFC.]

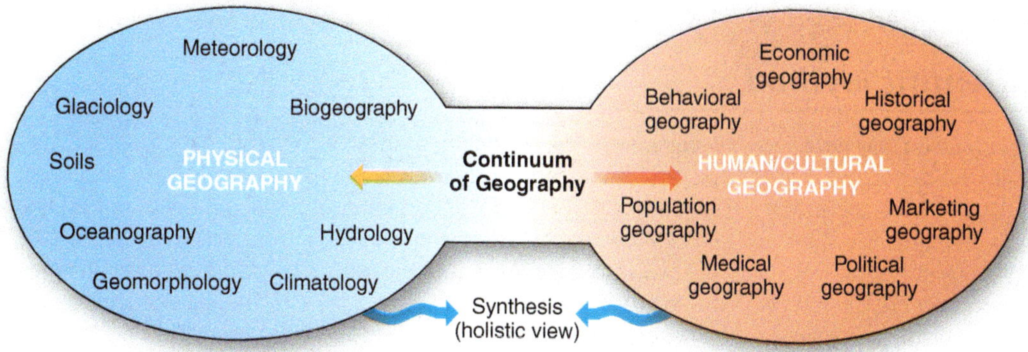

FIGURE 2 The content of geography.
Geography derives subject matter from many different sciences. The focus of this book is physical geography, but we also integrate some human and cultural components. Movement toward the middle of the continuum suggests a synthesis of Earth topics and human topics.

character (Figure 3). Earth is an open system in terms of energy because solar energy enters freely and heat energy leaves, going back into space. Most natural systems are open in terms of energy.

Earth systems are dynamic (energetic, in motion) because of the tremendous infusion of radiant energy from the Sun. This energy comes through the outermost edge of Earth's atmosphere to power terrestrial systems, being transformed along the way into various forms of energy, such as kinetic energy (of motion), potential energy (of position), or chemical or mechanical energy—setting the fluid atmosphere and ocean in motion. Eventually, Earth radiates this energy back to the cold vacuum of space as heat energy.

Closed Systems A system that is shut off from the surrounding environment so that it is self-contained is a **closed system.** Although such closed systems are rarely found in nature, Earth is essentially a closed system in terms of physical matter and resources—air, water, and material resources. The only exceptions are the slow escape of lightweight gases (such as hydrogen) from the atmosphere into space and the input of frequent, but tiny meteors and cosmic dust. The fact that Earth is a closed material system makes recycling efforts inevitable if we want a sustainable global economy.

System Example Figure 4 illustrates a simple open-flow system, using plant photosynthesis as an example. In photosynthesis, plants use sunlight as an

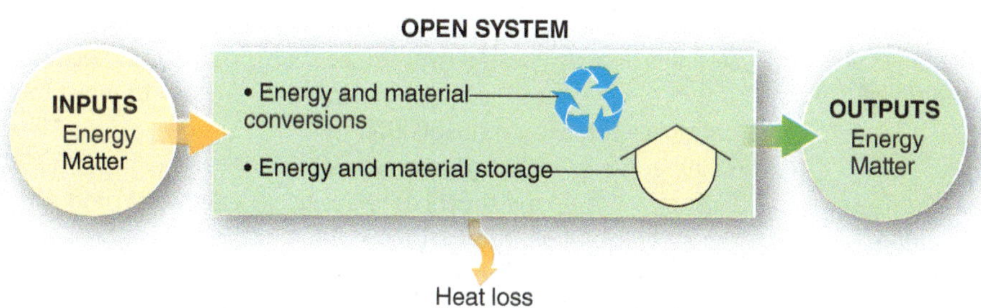

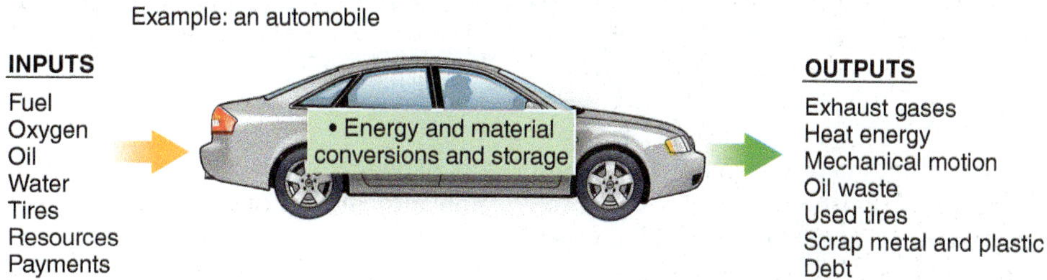

FIGURE 3 An open system.
In an open system, inputs of energy and matter undergo conversions and are stored as the system operates. Outputs include energy and matter and heat energy (waste) that flow from the system. See how the various inputs and outputs are related to the operation of a car—an open system. Expand your viewpoint to the entire system of auto production, from raw materials, to assembly, to sales, to car accidents, to junkyards. Can you identify other open systems that you encounter in your daily life?

The Scientific Method

The term *scientific method* may have an aura of complexity, but it shouldn't. The scientific method is simply the application of common sense in an organized and objective manner. A scientist observes, makes a general statement to summarize the observations, formulates a hypothesis, conducts experiments to test the hypothesis, and develops a theory and governing scientific laws. Sir Isaac Newton (1642–1727) developed this method of discovering the patterns of nature, although the term *scientific method* was applied later.

Complexity dominates nature, making several outcomes possible as a system operates. Science serves an important function in understanding such uncertainty. Yet the more knowledge we have, the more our awareness of and uncertainty about other possible outcomes and events increase. This, in turn, demands more precise and aggressive science.

Follow the scientific method illustration in Figure 1.1. The scientific method begins with our perception of the real world and a determination of what we know, what we want to know, and the many unanswered questions that exist.

Scientists who study the physical environment begin with the clues they see in nature.

Step 1 *Observe and measure.* The process begins as scientists figure out what data are needed and begin to collect those data. These observations are analyzed to identify coherent patterns that may exist. This search for patterns requires inductive reasoning, or the process of drawing generalizations from specific facts. This step is important in modern geographic science, in which the goal is to understand a whole functioning Earth, rather than isolated, small compartments of information. Such understanding allows the scientist to construct models of general operations of Earth systems.

Step 2 *Form and test a hypothesis.* If patterns are discovered, the researcher may formulate a *hypothesis*—a tentative explanation for the phenomena observed. Further observations are related to the general principles established by the hypothesis. More data gathering may support or disprove the hypothesis, or predictions made according to it may prove accurate or inaccurate. These findings provide negative feedback, requiring the researcher to adjust data collection and model building and to refine the hypothesis statement. Verification of the hypothesis after exhaustive testing may lead to its elevation to the status of a *theory.*

Step 3 *Formulate a theory.* The word *theory* can be confusing as used by the media and general public. A theory is constructed on the basis of several extensively tested hypotheses. Theories represent truly broad general principles—unifying concepts that tie together the laws that govern nature. Examples include the theory of relativity, theory of evolution, atomic theory, Big Bang theory, stratospheric ozone depletion theory, and plate tectonics theory. A theory is a powerful device with which to understand both the order and the chaos (disorder) in nature. Using a theory allows predictions to be made about things not yet known, the effects of which can be tested and verified or disproved through tangible evidence. The value of a theory is the continued observation, testing, understanding, and pursuit of knowledge that the theory stimulates. A general theory reinforces our perception of the real world, acting as positive feedback.

Pure science does not make value judgments. Instead, pure science provides people and their institutions with objective information on which to base their own value judgments. Social and political judgments about the applications of science are increasingly critical as Earth's natural systems respond to the impact of modern civilization. Scientist Jane Lubchenco, the first female administrator of the National Oceanic and Atmospheric Administration (NOAA), in her 1997 American Association for the Advancement of Science Presidential Address stated:

> Science alone does not hold the power to achieve the goal of greater sustainability, but scientific knowledge and wisdom are needed to help inform decisions that will enable society to move toward that end.

The growing awareness that human activity is producing global climate change places increasing pressure on scientists to participate in decision making. Numerous editorials in scientific journals have called for such applied science involvement.

energy input and material inputs of water, nutrients, and carbon dioxide. The photosynthetic process converts these inputs to stored chemical energy in the form of plant sugars (carbohydrates). The process also releases an output from the plant system: the oxygen we breathe.

Reversing the process, plants derive energy for their operations from respiration. In respiration, the plant consumes inputs of chemical energy (carbohydrates) and oxygen and releases outputs of carbon dioxide, water, and heat energy into the environment. Thus, a plant acts as an open system, in which both energy and materials freely flow into and out of the plant.

System Feedback As a system operates, it generates outputs that influence its own operations. These outputs function as "information" that returns to various points in the system via pathways, or **feedback loops**. Feedback information can guide, and sometimes control, further system operations. In the plant's photosynthetic system

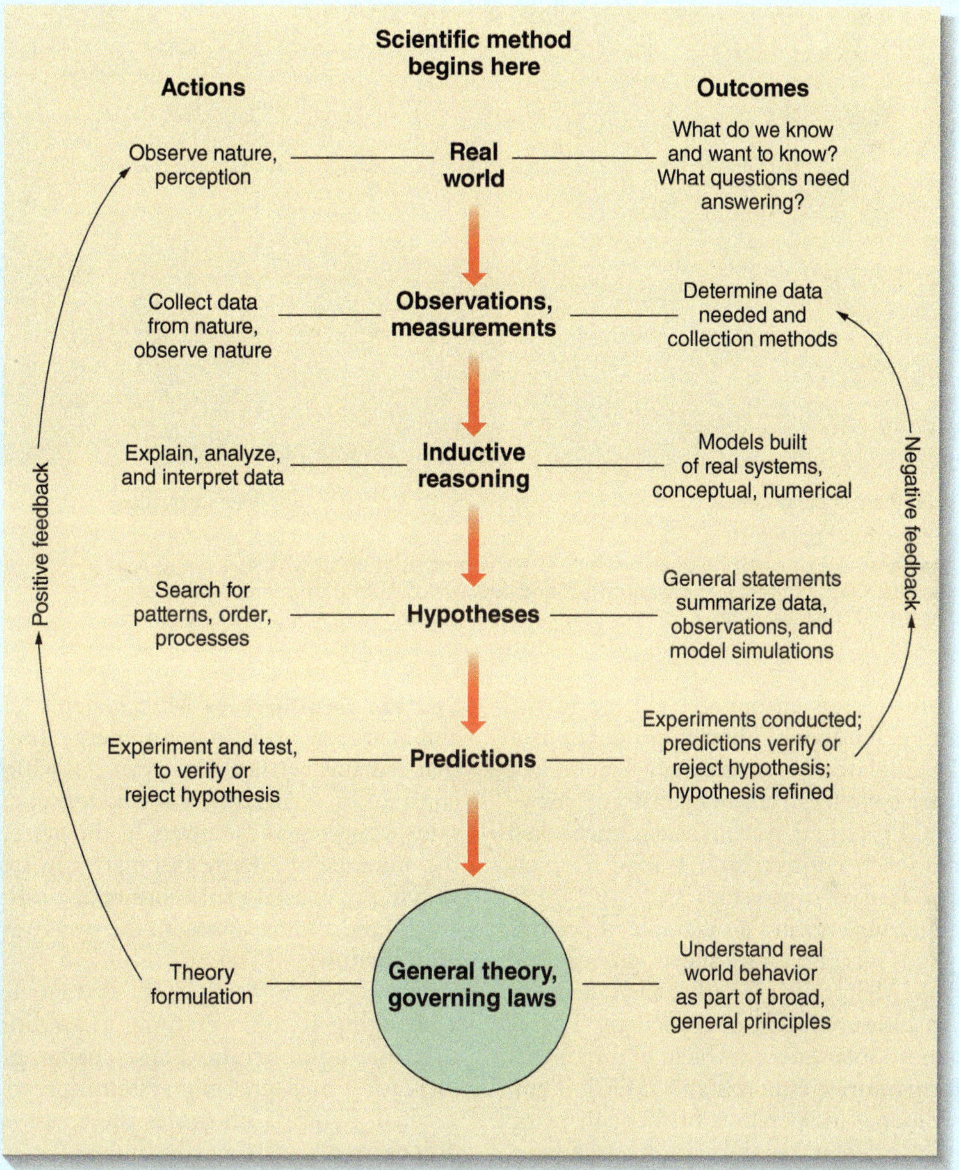

FIGURE 1.1 Scientific method flow chart.
The scientific method process: from perceptions, to observations, reasoning, hypothesis, and predictions, and possibly to general theory and natural laws.

(see Figure 4), any increase or decrease in daylength (sunlight availability), carbon dioxide, or water produces feedback that causes specific responses in the plant. For example, decreasing the water input slows the growth process; increasing daylength increases the growth process, within limits.

If the feedback information discourages change in the system, it is **negative feedback**. Further production of such feedback opposes system changes. Such negative feedback informs and causes self-regulation in a natural system, stabilizing the system. Negative feedback loops are common in nature, since they lead to stability. For example, the growth of riparian, or streamside, vegetation in a river system stabilizes the banks and inhibits erosion, providing a negative feedback. In many ecosystems, predator populations provide negative feedback for other animals; the size of the prey population tends to achieve a balance with the number of predators. If a predator population drops abruptly, prey populations increase and cause ecosystem instability.

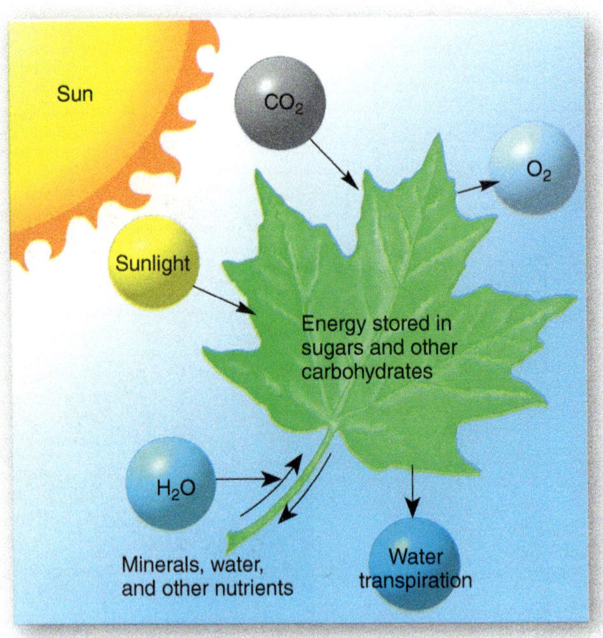

(a) Plant photosynthesis

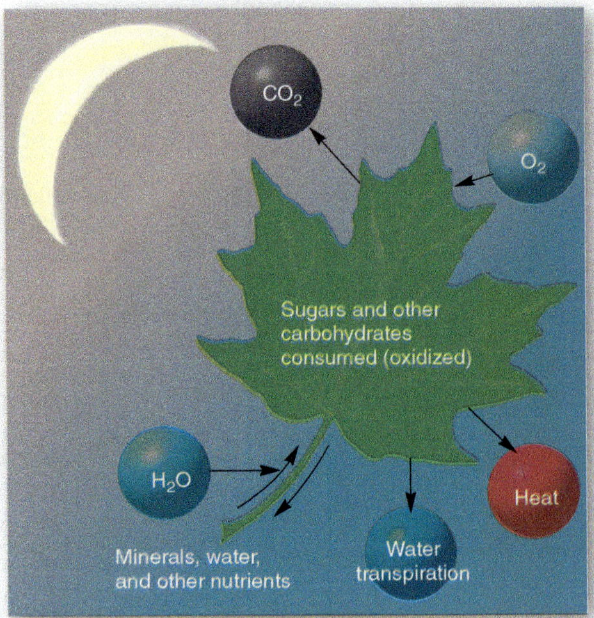

(b) Plant respiration

FIGURE 4 A leaf is a natural open system.
A plant leaf provides an example of a natural open system. (a) In the process of photosynthesis, plants consume light, carbon dioxide (CO_2), nutrients, and water (H_2O) and produce outputs of oxygen (O_2) and carbohydrates (sugars) as stored chemical energy. (b) Plant respiration, illustrated here at night, approximately reverses this process.

If feedback information encourages change in the system, it is **positive feedback**. Further production of positive feedback stimulates system changes. Unchecked positive feedback in a system can create a runaway ("snowballing") condition. In natural systems, such unchecked system changes can reach a critical limit, leading to instability, disruption, or death of organisms.

Global climate change creates an example of positive feedback as meltponds increase on ice sheets, glaciers, and ice shelves worldwide. Meltponds are darker and reflect less sunlight; they have a lower albedo, or reflectivity. Therefore, they absorb more solar energy, which, in turn, melts more ice, which forms more meltponds, and so forth. Thus, a positive feedback loop is in operation, further enhancing the effects of higher temperatures and warming trends.

Based on satellite images and aerial surveys, scientists determined a spatial increase in meltpond distribution of 400% across the Arctic since 2000. Overall ice-mass losses from Greenland more than doubled between 1996 and 2010. The meltponds are symptomatic of climatic warming. Likewise, as sea ice melts, the darker open water absorbs more sunlight, which produces increased air and water temperatures.

Think of the numerous devastating wildfires that occurred globally in the last decade, including record wildfires in terms of area burned in the western United States, Australia, and elsewhere, as examples of positive feedback. As the fires burned, they dried wet shrubs and green wood around the fire, thus providing more fuel for combustion. The greater the fire is, the greater the availability of fuel becomes, and thus more fire is possible—a positive feedback for the fire.

System Equilibrium Most systems maintain structure and character over time. An energy and material system that remains balanced over time, in which conditions are constant or recur, is in a *steady-state condition*. When the rates of inputs and outputs in the system are equal and the amounts of energy and matter in storage within the system are constant (or more realistically, as they fluctuate around a stable average), the system is in **steady-state equilibrium**.

However, a steady-state system may demonstrate a changing trend over time, a condition described as **dynamic equilibrium**. These changing trends of either increasing or decreasing system operations may appear gradual. Figure 5 illustrates these two equilibrium conditions, steady-state and dynamic.

Note that systems try to maintain their functional operations; they tend to resist abrupt change. However, a system may reach a **threshold**, or *tipping point*, where it can no longer maintain its character, so it lurches to a new operational level. This abrupt change places the system in a *metastable equilibrium*. An example of such a condition is a hillside or coastal bluff that adjusts after a sudden landslide. A new equilibrium is eventually achieved among slope, materials, and energy over time.

This threshold concept raises concern in the scientific community, especially if some natural systems reach their tipping-point limits. The relatively sudden collapse of ice shelves surrounding a portion of Antarctica, the sudden crack-up of ice shelves on the north coast of Ellesmere Island, Canada, and the recent extinctions of animal species serve as examples of systems at a threshold that are changing to a new status.

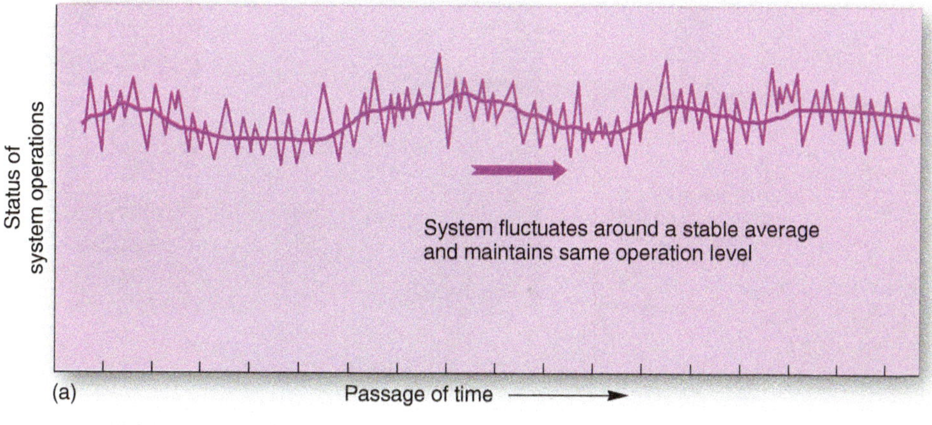

Coastal systems pass a threshold.

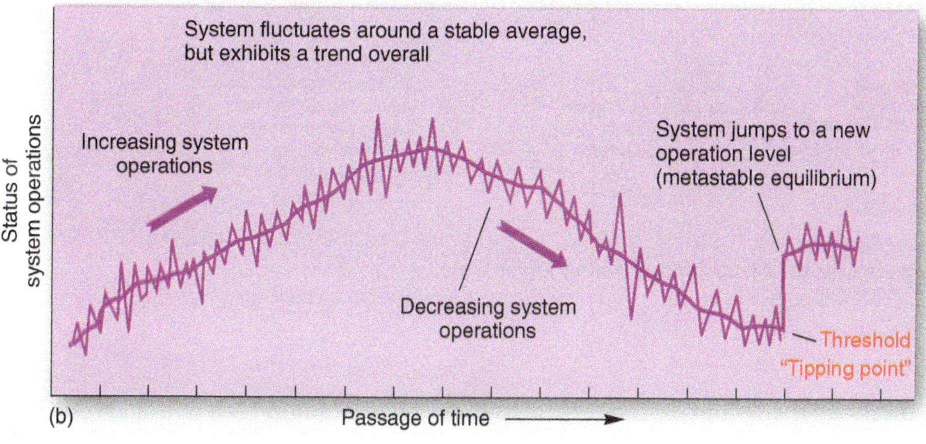

FIGURE 5 System equilibria: Steady-state and dynamic.
(a) A steady-state equilibrium over time; system operations fluctuate around a stable average. (b) A dynamic equilibrium condition, where system fluctuations show a trend over time. Landslides along the Pacific Coast south of San Francisco moved the cliff face some 30.5 m (100 ft) inland during January 2010. A threshold was reached and the bluffs collapsed. [Inset photo by Bobbé Christopherson.]

Thresholds can also be reached in plant and animal communities. The bleaching (death) of living coral reefs worldwide accelerated dramatically after 1997, when warming conditions in oceans combined with pollution to lead coral systems to a threshold. Today, about 50% of the corals on Earth are ailing or nearing collapse. Harlequin frogs of tropical Central and South America are another example of species reaching a tipping point, with increased extinctions since 1986 (Figure 6).

Systems Analysis and Species Extinction Scientists found that the key to understanding extinctions of harlequin frog (*Atelopus varius*) and golden toad (*Bufo periglenes*) species in the Monteverde Cloud Forest Reserve, Costa Rica, and elsewhere in Central and South America was a consideration of climate change and how this alters transmission of diseases and pathogens. One infectious agent, the *chytrid fungus* (*Bactrachochytrium dendrobactidis*), has spread as thermal-optimum conditions were reached in its mid-elevation range (1000 m to 2400 m; 3280 ft to 7874 ft) in the mountain-cloud forest.

Human-forced climate change is increasing the temperature of the ocean and atmosphere. Higher temperatures cause higher evaporation rates, which affect the condensation level. As the warm, moist air moves onshore and reaches the mountains, the air lifts and cools, and condensation occurs at higher elevations than before. Increased clouds affect the daily temperature range: Clouds at night, acting like insulation,

FIGURE 6 Harlequin frog extinction alarm.
About two-thirds of harlequin frog species went extinct over the last two decades as a result of climate change. This "rana dorado," or golden frog, survives only in captivity. [Dante Fenolio/ Photo Researchers.]

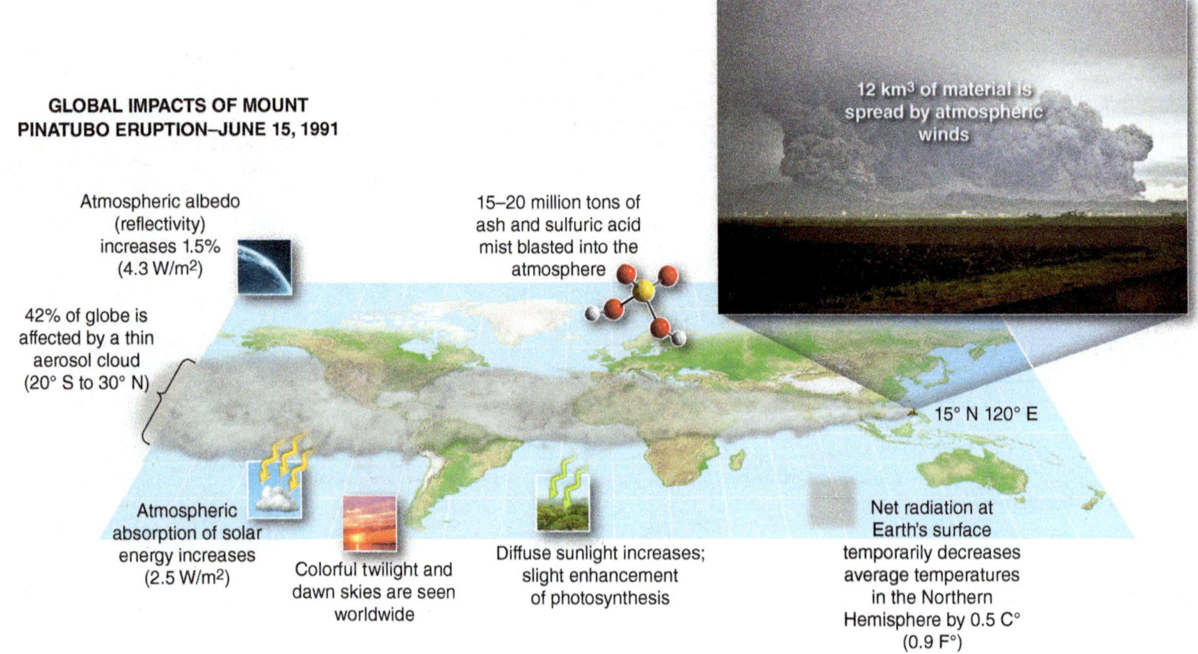

FIGURE 7 The eruption of Mount Pinatubo.
The 1991 Mount Pinatubo eruption affected the Earth–atmosphere system on a global scale. As you read *Elemental Geosystems*, you will find references to this eruption in many chapters. [Inset photo by Dave Harlow, USGS.]

raise nighttime minimum temperatures, whereas clouds during the day act as reflectors, lowering daytime maximum temperatures.

The *chytrid* fungus does best when temperatures are between 17°C and 25°C (63°F and 77°F). The new cloud cover keeps the daytime maximum below 25°C (77°F) at the forest floor. In these more favorable conditions, the disease pathogen flourishes. Harlequin frogs have moist, porous skin that the fungus penetrates, killing the frog. Between 1986 and 2006, approximately 67% of the 110 known species of harlequin frogs went extinct—extinction is forever.

From this example, can you see the power of systems analysis? Global warming intensifies the hydrologic cycle, raises air and water temperatures, and increases evaporation, all of which change the nature of cloud formations and alter daily temperature patterns.

Mount Pinatubo—Global System Impact A dramatic example of interactions between volcanic eruptions and Earth systems illustrates the strength of spatial analysis. Mount Pinatubo in the Philippines erupted violently in 1991, injecting 15–20 million tons of ash and sulfuric acid mist into the upper atmosphere (Figure 7). This was the second greatest eruption during the 20th century; Mount Katmai in Alaska (1912) was the only one greater. The eruption materials from Mount Pinatubo affected Earth systems in several ways, which are noted on the map. For comparison, the 2010 eruption of Eyjafjallajökull in Iceland was about 100 times smaller in terms of the volume of material ejected, with debris reaching only the lower atmosphere.

The story of Mount Pinatubo and its implications is woven through eight topics: systems theory, effects on energy budgets in the atmosphere, satellite images of the spread of debris by atmospheric winds, temporary effect on global atmospheric temperatures, volcanic processes, past climatic effects of volcanoes, and effects on net photosynthesis. Instead of simply learning about the eruption, we should see the linkages and global impacts of such a volcanic explosion.

GEO REPORT 1 *Amphibians at thresholds*

Amphibian species are a threatened group of animals, with approximately one-third of recognized species now at risk of extinction. According to the International Union for Conservation of Nature (IUCN) Amphibian Specialist Group, two new initiatives are aimed at stopping the amphibian decline: increased habitat protection for species that are found in only a single location and stepped-up efforts at testing antifungal drugs to halt the killer frog disease and ease the current amphibian extinction crisis (more at http://www.amphibians.org/).

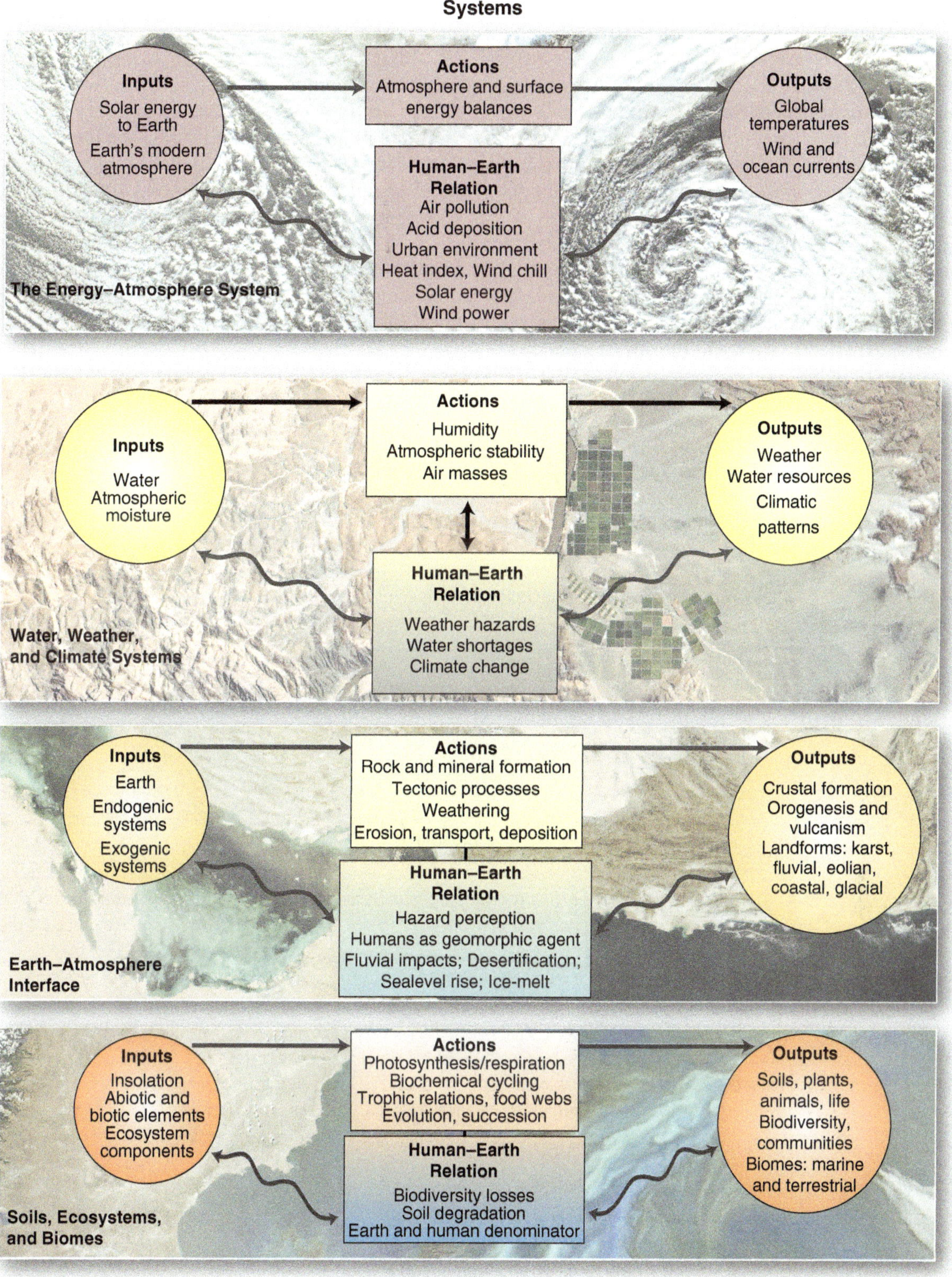

FIGURE 8 The systems.

Systems in *Elemental Geosystems*

To further illustrate the systems organization in this textbook, notice the flow of energy, materials, and information throughout the 4 parts and 17 chapters (Figure 8). This book presents subjects in the same sequence in which they occur in nature. In this way, topics follow a logical progression that unfolds according to the energy and material flows within individual systems or with time and the flow of events.

In Figure 8, you see the Sun begins. The energy flows across space to the top of the atmosphere and through the atmosphere to the surface and surface energy budgets. Then we look at the outputs of temperature and winds and ocean currents. Note the same logical systems flow in the other three parts.

Models of Systems A **model** is a simplified, idealized representation of part of the real world. Models are designed with varying degrees of generalization. In your life, you may have built or drawn a model of something that was a simplification of the real thing—such as a model airplane or model house.

The simplicity of a model makes a system easier to understand and to simulate in experiments (for example, the leaf model in Figure 4). A good example is a model of the *hydrologic system*, which models Earth's entire water system, its related energy flows, and the atmosphere, surface, and subsurface environments through which water moves.

Adjusting the variables in a model produces differing conditions and allows predictions of possible system operations. However, predictions are only as good as the assumptions and accuracy built into the model. A model is best viewed for what it is—a simplification to help us understand complex processes. Each of Earth's four "spheres" represents such a model of Earth's systems.

Earth's Four "Spheres" Earth's surface is a vast area of 500 million km^2 (193 million mi^2) where four immense open systems interact. Figure 9 shows a simple model

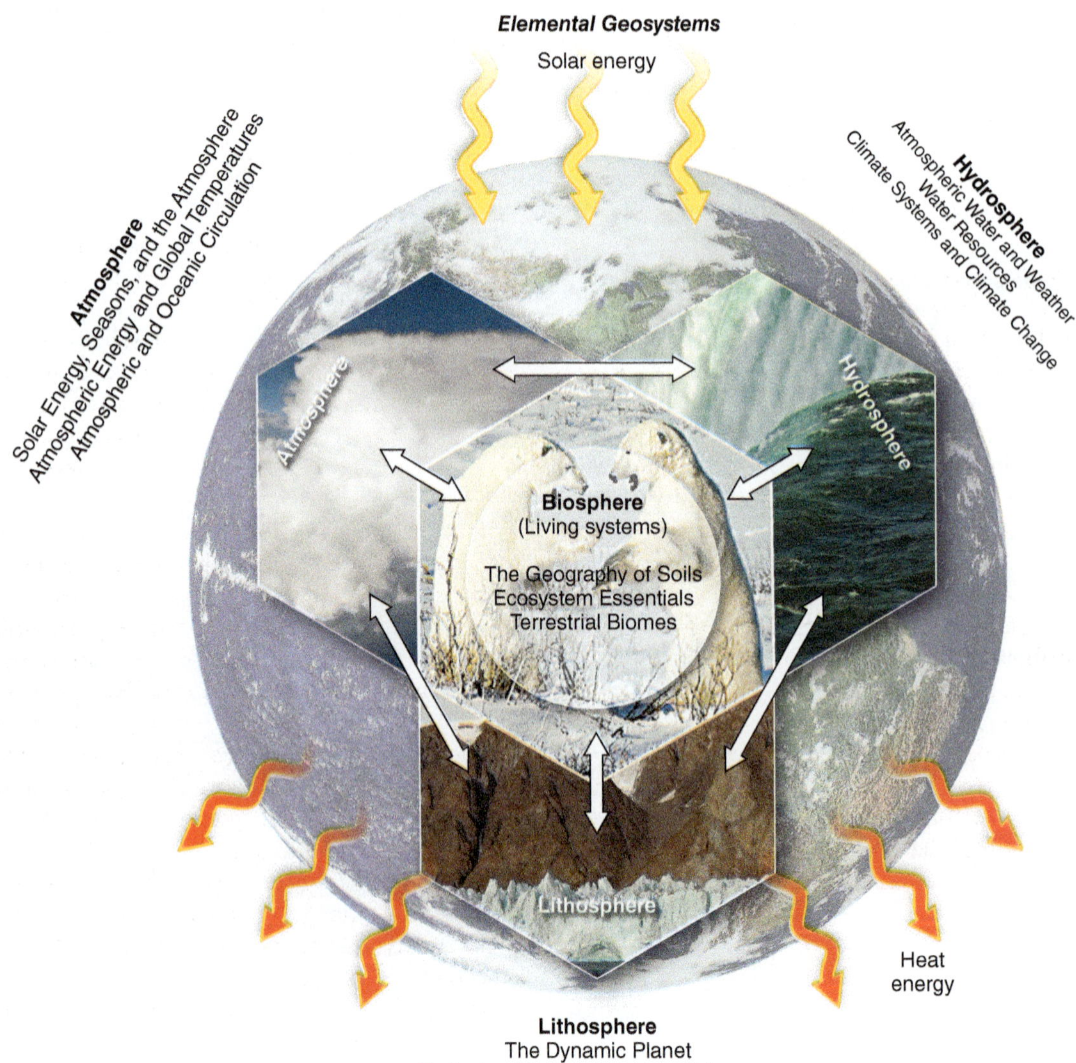

FIGURE 9 **Earth's four spheres.**
Each sphere is a model of vast Earth systems. [Inset photos by Bobbé Christopherson; whole Earth image NASA.]

of three **abiotic**, or nonliving, systems overlapping to form the realm of the **biotic**, or living system. The abiotic spheres are the *atmosphere*, *hydrosphere*, and *lithosphere*. The biotic sphere is the *biosphere*.

The various arrows in the figure show that content in each part interrelates as you build your knowledge of Earth's abiotic and biotic systems.

- **Atmosphere** The **atmosphere** is a thin, gaseous veil surrounding Earth, held to the planet by the force of gravity. Formed by gases arising from within Earth's crust and interior and the exhalations of all life over time, the lower atmosphere is unique in the Solar System. It is a combination of nitrogen, oxygen, argon, carbon dioxide, water vapor, and trace gases.
- **Hydrosphere** Earth's waters exist in the atmosphere, on the surface, and in the crust near the surface. Collectively, these waters form the **hydrosphere**. That portion of the hydrosphere that is frozen is the **cryosphere**—ice sheets, ice caps and fields, glaciers, ice shelves, sea ice, and subsurface ground ice. Water of the hydrosphere exists in all three states: liquid, solid (the frozen cryosphere), and gaseous (water vapor). Water occurs in two general chemical conditions, fresh and saline (salty).
- **Lithosphere** Earth's crust and a portion of the upper mantle directly below the crust form the **lithosphere**. The crust is quite brittle compared with the layers deep beneath the surface, which move slowly in response to an uneven distribution of heat energy and pressure. In a broad sense, the term *lithosphere* sometimes refers to the entire solid planet. The soil layer is the *edaphosphere* and generally covers Earth's land surfaces. In this text, soils represent the bridge between the lithosphere and biosphere.
- **Biosphere** The intricate, interconnected web that links all organisms with their physical environment is the **biosphere**, or **ecosphere**. The biosphere is the area in which physical and chemical factors form the context of life. The biosphere exists in the overlap among the abiotic, or nonliving, spheres, extending from the seafloor, the upper layers of the crustal rock, to about 8 km (5 mi) into the atmosphere. Life is sustainable within these natural limits. The biosphere evolves, reorganizes itself at times, faces extinctions, and manages to flourish.

A Spherical Planet

We all have heard that some people in the past believed Earth was flat. Yet Earth's *sphericity*, or roundness, is not as modern an idea as many think. For instance, more than two millennia ago, the Greek mathematician and philosopher Pythagoras (ca. 580–500 B.C.) determined through observation that Earth is spherical. We do not know what observations led Pythagoras to this conclusion. Can you guess at what he saw to deduce Earth's roundness?

He might have noticed ships sailing beyond the horizon and apparently sinking below the water's surface, only to arrive back at port with dry decks. Perhaps he noticed Earth's curved shadow cast on the lunar surface during an eclipse of the Moon. He might have deduced that the Sun and Moon are not just the flat disks they appear to be in the sky, but are spherical, and that Earth must be a sphere as well.

Earth's sphericity was generally accepted by the educated populace as early as the first century A.D. Christopher Columbus, for example, knew he was sailing around a sphere in 1492; this is one reason why he thought he had arrived in the East Indies.

Earth as a Geoid Until 1687, the spherical-perfection model was a basic assumption of **geodesy**, the science that determines Earth's shape and size by surveys and mathematical calculations. But in that year, Sir Isaac Newton postulated that Earth, along with the other planets, could not be perfectly spherical. Newton reasoned that the more rapid rotational speed at the equator—the equator being farthest from the central axis of the planet and therefore moving faster—produces an equatorial bulge as centrifugal force pulls Earth's surface outward. He was convinced that Earth is slightly misshapen into an *oblate spheroid*, or, more correctly, an *oblate ellipsoid* (*oblate* means "flattened"), with the oblateness occurring at the poles.

Earth's equatorial bulge and its polar oblateness are universally accepted and confirmed with tremendous precision by satellite observations. The "geoidal epoch" is our modern era of Earth measurement because Earth is a **geoid**, meaning literally that "the shape of Earth is Earth-shaped." Imagine Earth's geoid as a sea-level surface that extends uniformly worldwide, beneath the continents. Both heights on land and depths in the oceans measure from this hypothetical surface. Think of the geoid surface as a balance among the gravitational attraction of Earth's mass, the distribution of water and ice along its surface, and the outward centrifugal pull caused by Earth's rotation. Figure 10 gives Earth's average polar and equatorial circumferences and diameters.

Water in the Solar System

Among the planets in the Solar System, only Earth possesses surface water in such quantity, some 1.36 billion km^3 (0.33 billion mi^3), although subsurface water was discovered on the Moon in its polar areas, Mars, Jupiter's moon Europa, and Saturn's moons Enceladus and Titan. In the Martian polar region, remote spacecraft are studying ground ice and patterned ground phenomena caused by freezing and thawing water. In the Universe, deep-space telescopes reveal traces of water in nebula and distant planetary objects.

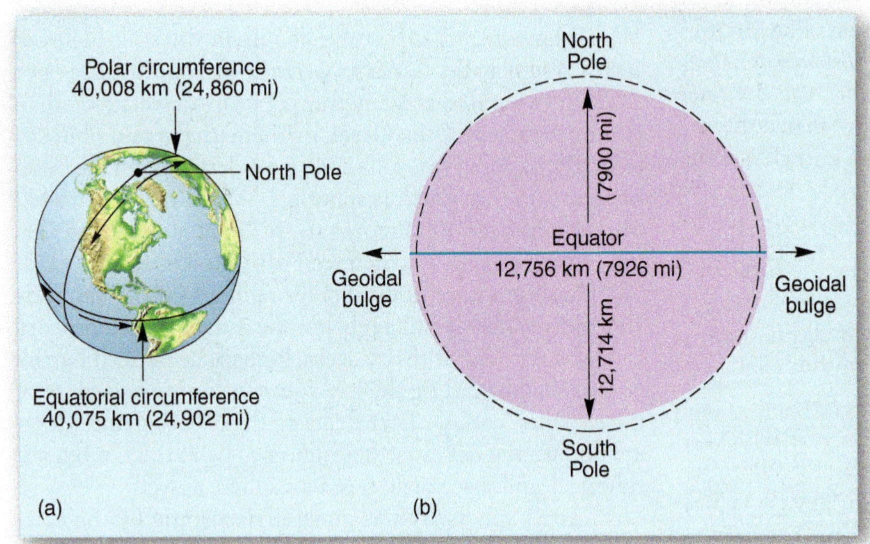

FIGURE 10 Earth's dimensions. Earth's (a) equatorial and polar circumference and (b) diameter. The dashed line is a perfect circle for reference to Earth's geoid.

Measuring Earth in 247 B.C.

Eratosthenes (ca. 276–195 B.C.) served as the librarian of Alexandria in Egypt during the third century B.C. He was a Greek geographer and astronomer in a position of scientific leadership. Alexandria's library was the finest in the ancient world. Among his achievements was calculating Earth's polar circumference to a high level of accuracy. Here's how he did it. As you read, follow along on Figure 11.

Travelers told Eratosthenes that on June 21 they saw the Sun's rays shine directly to the bottom of a well at Syene, the location of present-day Aswan, Egypt. This meant that the Sun was directly overhead on that day. North of Syene in Alexandria, Eratosthenes knew from his own observations that the Sun's rays never were directly overhead, even at noon on June 21. This day is when the noon Sun is at its northernmost position in the sky. He knew objects in Alexandria, unlike objects in Syene, always cast a noontime shadow on June 21. Using his knowledge of geometry, Eratosthenes conducted an experiment to explain the different observations.

In Alexandria at noon on June 21, he measured the angle of a shadow cast by an obelisk (a perpendicular column). Knowing the height of the obelisk and measuring the length of the Sun's shadow from its base, he solved the triangle for the angle of the Sun's noon rays, which he

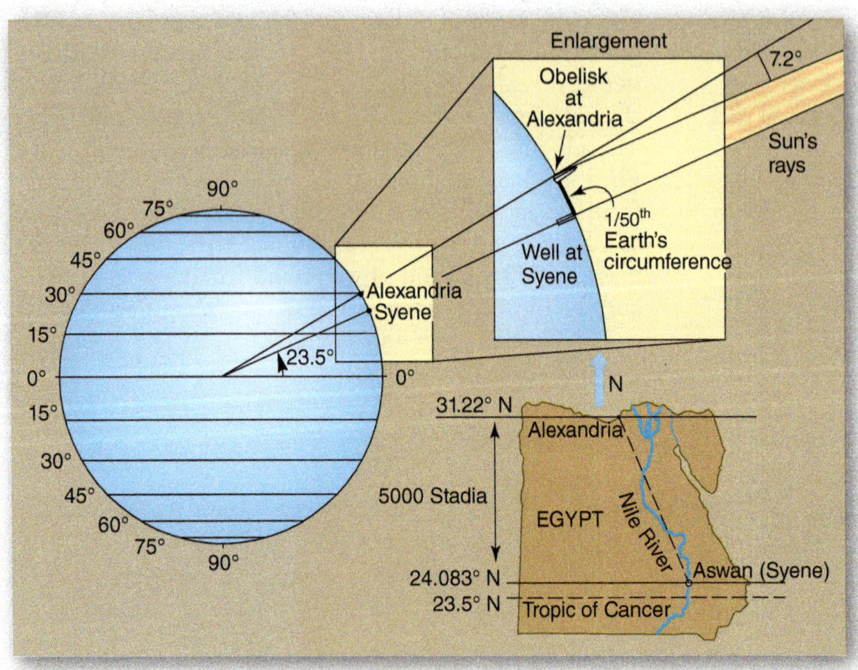

FIGURE 11 Eratosthenes' calculation. Eratosthenes' work teaches the value of observing carefully and integrating all observations. Calculating Earth's circumference required application of his knowledge of Earth–Sun relationships, geometry, and geography.

determined to be 7.2° off from directly overhead. However, at Syene on the same day, the angle of the Sun's rays was 0° from a perpendicular, arriving from directly overhead.

Eratosthenes knew from geometry that the distance on the ground between Alexandria and Syene formed an arc of Earth's circumference equal to the angle of the Sun's rays at Alexandria. Since 7.2° is roughly 1/50 of the 360° (360° ÷ 7.2° = 50) in Earth's total circumference, he knew the distance between Alexandria and Syene must represent approximately 1/50 of Earth's total polar circumference.

Next, Eratosthenes measured the surface distance between the two cities as 5000 stadia. A *stadium*, a Greek unit of measure, equals approximately 185 m (607 ft). He then multiplied 5000 stadia by 50 to determine that Earth's polar circumference is about 250,000 stadia. Eratosthenes' calculations convert to roughly 46,250 km (28,738 mi), which is remarkably close to the correct value of 40,008 km (24,860 mi) for Earth's polar circumference. Not bad for 247 B.C.!

Location and Time on Earth

Geographic science requires an internationally accepted, coordinated grid system to determine location on Earth. You can see the importance from the chapter-opening photo of Gough Island; or, in the photo at the end of this chapter, tracking the location of the subsolar point. The terms *latitude* and *longitude* were in use on maps as early as the first century A.D., with the concepts themselves dating back to Eratosthenes and others.

The geographer, astronomer, and mathematician Ptolemy (ca. A.D. 90–168) contributed greatly to the development of modern maps, and many of his terms are still used today. Ptolemy divided the circle into 360 degrees (360°), with each degree having 60 minutes (60′) and each minute having 60 seconds (60″) in a manner adapted from the ancient Babylonians. He located places using these degrees, minutes, and seconds. However, the precise length of a degree of latitude and a degree of longitude remained unresolved for the next 17 centuries.

Latitude

Latitude is an angular distance north or south of the equator, measured from the center of Earth (Figure 12a). On a map or globe, the lines designating these angles of latitude run east and west, parallel to the equator (Figure 12b). Because Earth's equator divides the distance between the North Pole and the South Pole exactly in half, it is assigned the value of 0° latitude. Thus, latitude increases from the equator northward to the North Pole, at 90° north latitude, and southward to the South Pole, at 90° south latitude.

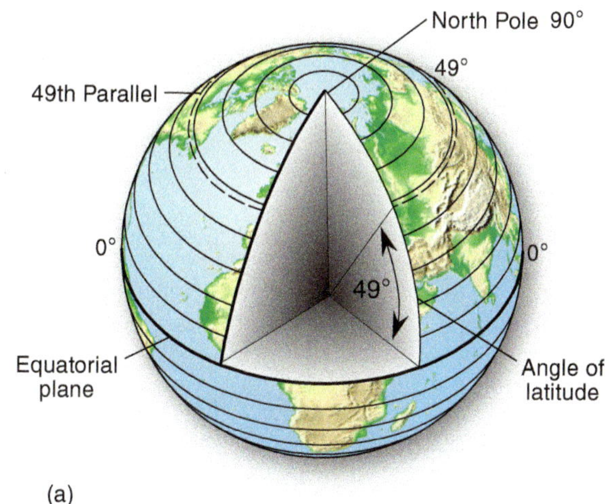

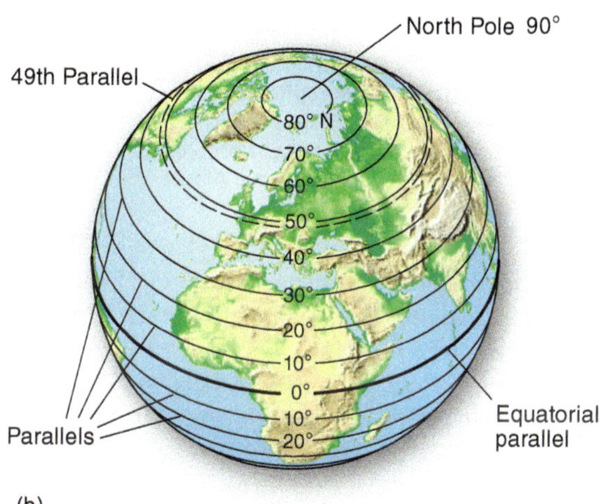

FIGURE 12 Parallels of latitude.
(a) Latitude is measured in degrees north or south of the equator (0°). Earth's poles are at 90°. Note the measurement of 49° latitude. (b) These angles of latitude determine parallels along Earth's surface. Do you know your present latitude?

A line connecting all points along the same latitudinal angle is a **parallel**. In the figure, an angle of 49° north latitude is measured, and, by connecting all points at this latitude, we have the 49th parallel. Thus, *latitude* is the name of the angle (49° north latitude), *parallel* names the line (49th parallel), and both indicate distance north of the equator.

Latitude is readily determined by observing *fixed celestial objects* such as the Sun or the stars, a method dating to ancient times. During daylight hours, the angle of the Sun

GEO REPORT 3 *The value of a stadium*

From the Greek *stade,* the value of a Greek stadium varied in time and place. For this calculation related to Eratosthenes' measurement, we used 185 m (607 ft) as a stadium length. This represents an average value in the Greek era. The word for the stadium measure was expanded to be the word to describe the arena in which foot races took place—thus our modern stadiums. Think of Eratosthenes' work when you see a stadium on campus.

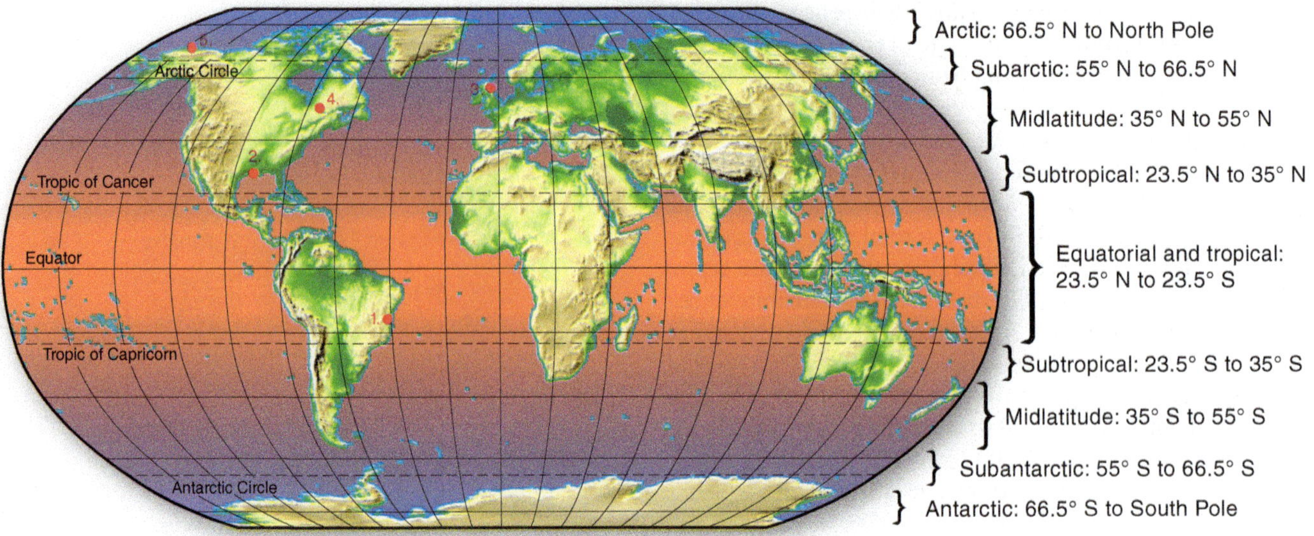

FIGURE 13 Latitudinal geographic zones.
Geographic zones are generalizations that characterize various regions by latitude. Think of these as transitioning into one another over broad areas. Noted cities: 1. Salvador, Brazil; 2. New Orleans, Louisiana; 3. Edinburgh, Scotland; 4. Montreal, Quebec; 5. Barrow, Alaska, see Critical Thinking 1 below.

above the horizon indicates the observer's latitude, after adjustment is made for the season and for the time of day. Because Polaris (the North Star) is almost directly overhead at the North Pole, persons anywhere in the Northern Hemisphere can determine their latitude at night simply by sighting Polaris and measuring its angle above the local horizon. The angle of elevation of Polaris above the horizon indicates the latitude of the observation point. Go to this chapter on our *MasteringGeography* web site to see an illustration of sighting on Polaris to determine latitude.

In the Southern Hemisphere, Polaris cannot be seen because it is below the horizon. Instead, latitude south of the equator is measured by sighting on a constellation that points to a celestial location above the South Pole. This indicator constellation is the Southern Cross (*Crux Australis*).

Latitudinal Geographic Zones Natural environments differ dramatically from the equator to the poles. These differences result from the amount of solar energy received, which varies by latitude and season of the year. As a convenience, geographers identify *latitudinal geographic zones* as regions. "Lower latitudes" are those nearer the equator, whereas "higher latitudes" are those nearer the poles.

Figure 13 portrays these zones, their locations, and their names: *equatorial* and *tropical*, *subtropical*, *midlatitude*, *subarctic* or *subantarctic*, and *arctic* or *antarctic*. These generalized latitudinal zones are useful for reference and comparison, but they do not have rigid boundaries; rather, think of them as transitioning one to another.

The *Tropic of Cancer* (about 23.5° north parallel) and the *Tropic of Capricorn* (about 23.5° south parallel) are the most extreme northern and southern parallels that experience perpendicular (directly overhead) rays of the Sun at local noon. When the Sun arrives overhead at these tropics, it marks the first day of summer in each hemisphere. The *Arctic Circle* (about 66.5° north parallel) and the *Antarctic Circle* (about 66.5° south parallel) are the parallels farthest from the poles that still experience 24 uninterrupted hours of night (including dawn and twilight) during local winter and continuous day during local summer.

CRITICAL THINKING 1

Latitudinal zones and temperature

Retrieve annual temperature data for five cities from near the equator to beyond the Arctic Circle. Note the geographic location for each of the five cities on the latitudinal geographic zone map in Figure 13. In which zone is each city located? To approximate locations use an atlas, web site, or encyclopedia. Roughly characterize changing temperature patterns through the seasons as you move away from the equator. Describe what you discover.

Longitude

Longitude is an angular distance east or west of a point on Earth's surface, measured from the center of Earth (Figure 14a). On a map or globe, the lines designating these angles of longitude run north and south (Figure 14b). A line connecting all points along the same longitude is a **meridian**. In the figure, a longitudinal angle of 60° E is measured. These meridians run at right angles (90°) to all parallels, including the equator.

Thus, *longitude* is the name of the angle, *meridian* names the line, and both indicate distance east or west of an arbitrary **prime meridian**—a meridian designated as 0° (Figure 14b). Earth's prime meridian passes through the old Royal Observatory at Greenwich, England, as set by an 1884 treaty—the *Greenwich prime meridian*.

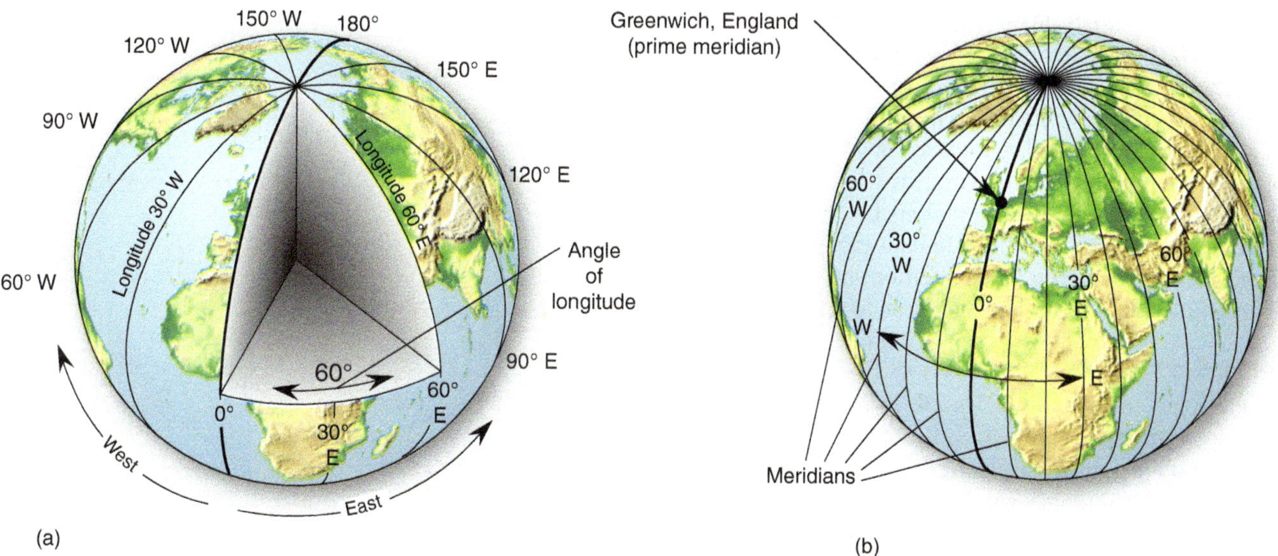

FIGURE 14 Meridians of longitude.
(a) Longitude is measured in degrees east or west of a 0° starting line, the prime meridian. Note the measurement of 60° E longitude. (b) Angles of longitude measured from the prime meridian determine other meridians. North America is west of Greenwich; therefore, it is in the Western Hemisphere. Do you know your present longitude?

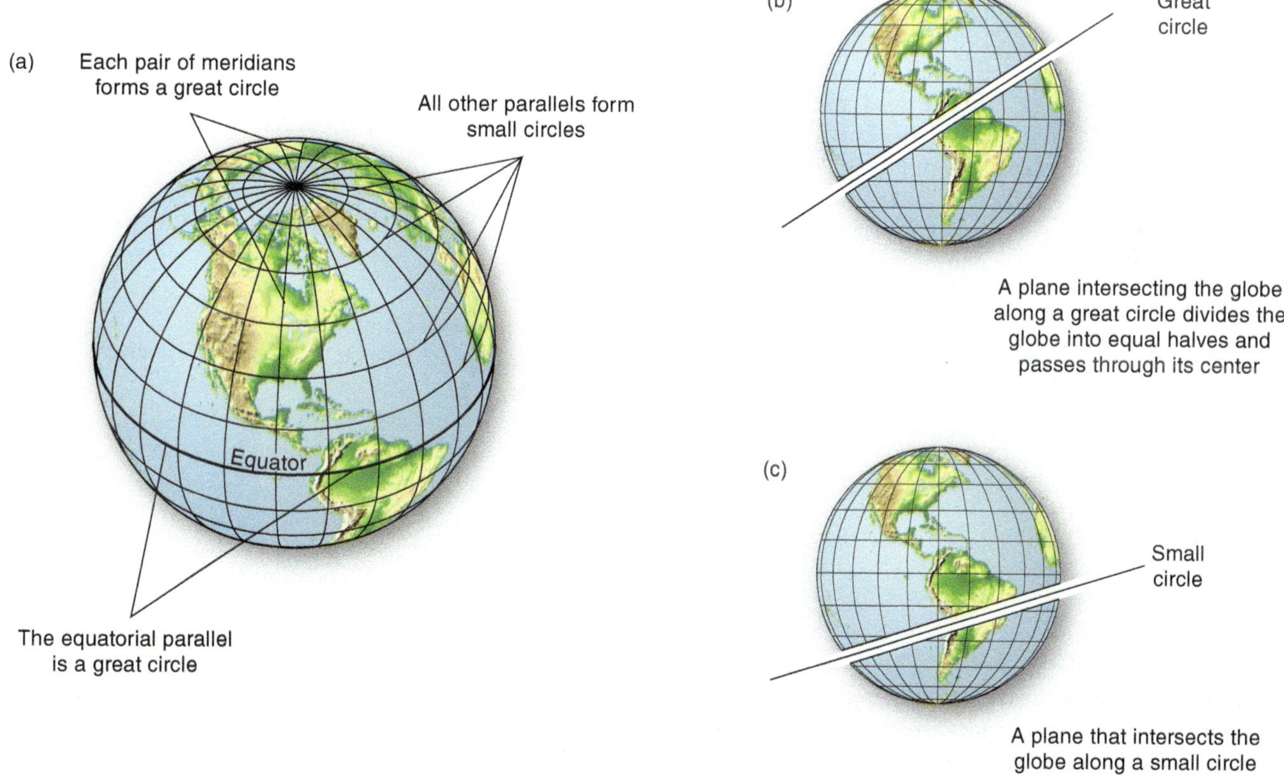

FIGURE 15 Great circles and small circles.
(a) Examples of great circles and small circles on Earth. (b) Any plane that divides Earth into equal halves intersects the globe along a great circle; this great circle is a full circumference of the globe and is the shortest distance between any two surface points. (c) Any plane surface that splits the globe into unequal portions intersects the globe along a small circle.

We noted that latitude is determined easily by sighting the Sun or the North Star or by using the Southern Cross as a pointer. In contrast, a method of accurately determining longitude, especially at sea, remained a major difficulty in navigation until after 1760. The key to measuring the longitude of a place lies in accurately knowing time and required the invention of a clock without a pendulum. In Chapter 1 on the *MasteringGeography* web site, you find an exciting chapter in human discovery focusing on the relationship between time and longitude called "The Timely Search for Longitude."

Great Circles and Small Circles

Great circles and small circles are important concepts that help summarize latitude and longitude (Figure 15). A **great circle** is any circle of Earth's circumference whose center coincides with the center of Earth. An infinite number of great circles can be drawn on Earth. Every meridian is one-half of a great circle that passes through the poles. On flat maps, airline and shipping routes appear to arch their way across oceans and landmasses. These are *great circle routes*, the shortest distance between two points on Earth (discussed on the *Mastering-Geography* web site).

In contrast to meridians, only one parallel is a great circle—the *equatorial parallel*. All other parallels diminish in length toward the poles and, along with any other non–great circles that one might draw, constitute **small circles**. These circles have centers that do not coincide with Earth's center.

Figure 16 combines latitude and parallels with longitude and meridians to illustrate Earth's complete coordinate grid system. Note the red dot that marks our measurement of 49° N and 60° E, a location in western Kazakhstan. Next time you look at a world globe, follow the parallel and meridian that converge on your location.

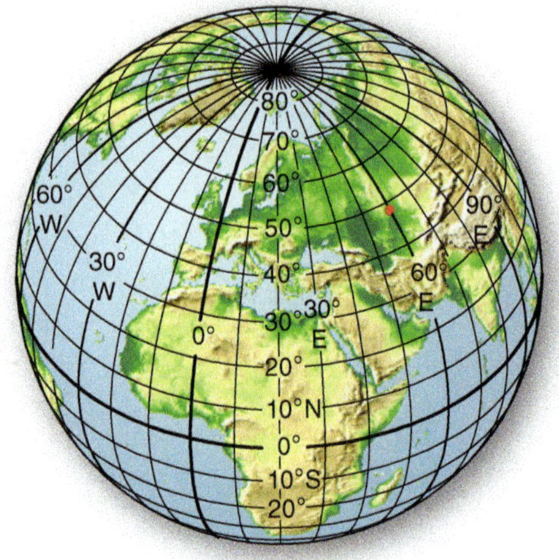

FIGURE 16 Earth's coordinate grid system.
Latitude and parallels and longitude and meridians allow us to locate all places on Earth precisely. The red dot is at 49° N latitude and 60° E longitude.

Every possible square meter of Earth's surface has its own address relative to the latitude–longitude grid.

A GPS receiver, now built into cell phones, digital cameras, and camcorders, senses signals from a minimum of three satellites for location and four satellites to measure the receiver's altitude. This is accomplished by calculating the distance between each satellite and receiver using clocks built into each instrument that time radio signals traveling at the speed of light between them (Figure 17). The receiver reports latitude, longitude, and elevation (Figure 18). Within *Differential GPS (DGPS)*, accuracy increases to 1 m to 3 m by comparing readings with another base station (reference receiver) for a differential correction.

CRITICAL THINKING 2

Where are you?

Select a location (for example, your campus, home, or workplace or a city) and determine the following: elevation, latitude, and longitude—including the coordinates in degrees, minutes, and seconds. Describe the resources you used to gather this geographic information, such as an atlas, web site, Google Earth™, or GPS measurement.

Global Positioning System

Today, using a handheld instrument that receives radio signals from satellites, you can accurately calibrate latitude, longitude, and elevation—and even know where your car is as you drive along, often with an electronic voice telling you where to turn.

The **Global Positioning System (GPS)** comprises 24 orbiting satellites, in six orbital planes, that transmit navigational signals for Earth bound use (backup GPS satellites are in orbital storage as replacements). Think of the satellites as a constellation of navigational beacons with which you interact to determine your unique location.

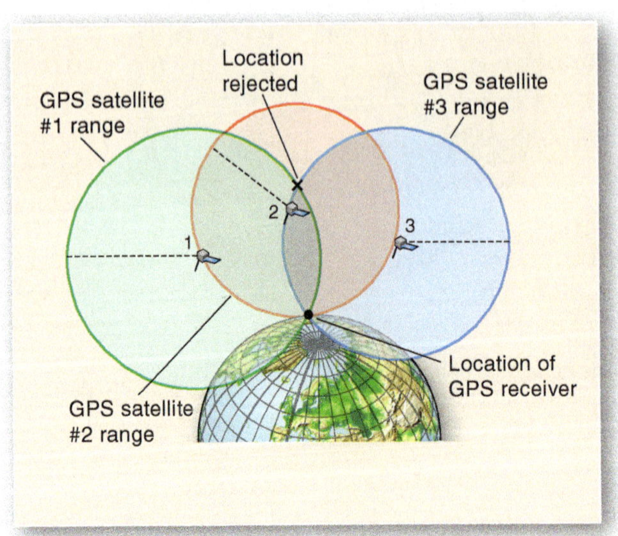

FIGURE 17 Using satellites to triangulate location through GPS.
Imagine a ranging sphere around each of three GPS satellites. These spheres intersect at two points, one easily rejected because it is some distance above Earth and the other at the true location of the GPS receiver. In this way, three satellites can determine location; adding a fourth satellite measures elevation.

FIGURE 18 GPS in action.
Location coordinates on a GPS unit in operation on a research ship as it crosses Earth's equator at 0° latitude. Locate these latitude and longitude coordinates on a globe or map. How far from the nearest land is the ship? What is the name of this ocean? [Bobbé Christopherson.]

FIGURE 19 GPS used to measure Everest's summit height.
Installation of a Trimble 4800 GPS unit at Earth's highest benchmark, only 18 m (60 ft) below the 8850-m (29,035-ft) summit. Previously, the height was set at 8848 m. Scientists using GPS data accurately analyzed the rate the mountain range is moving due to tectonic forces. [Photo and GPS installation by adventurer/climber Wally Berg, May 20, 1998.]

The GPS satellite measurements help refine our knowledge of Earth's exact shape and how this shape is changing. The GPS is useful for diverse applications, such as navigating on the ocean, surveying land, tracking small changes in Earth's crust, managing the movement of fleets of trucks, mining and mapping resources, tracking wildlife migration and behavior, carrying out police and security work, and conducting environmental planning. Outdoor recreationists and sportspersons commonly carry handheld GPS devices that allow them to track their own location. Commercial airlines use the GPS to improve accuracy of routes flown and thus increase fuel efficiency. Through GPS technology, modern cell phones know where they are on Earth.

Scientific applications of GPS technology are extensive. Relative to earthquakes in southern California, the GPS Observation Office monitors a network of 250 continuously operating GPS seismic stations—the Southern California Integrated GPS Network (SCIGN; http://www.scign.org/). This system can record fault movement as small as 1 mm (0.04 in.). In 1998, scientists used GPS technology to accurately determine the height of Mount Everest in the Himalayan Mountains (Figure 19), raising its elevation by 2 m (6 ft). GPS measurements of Mount Kilimanjaro in Africa lowered its summit from 5895 m to 5892 m (19,340 ft to 19,330 ft).

In *precision agriculture*, farmers use GPS devices to determine crop yields on specific parts of their farms. A detailed plot map is made to guide the farmer in the addition of more fertilizer, proper seed distribution, precise irrigation applications, or other work needed. A computer and GPS unit on board the farm equipment guide the work. This is the science of *variable-rate technology*, made possible by GPS technology.

The GPS is important to a locational, spatial geographic science because this precise technology reduces the need to maintain ground control points for location, mapping, and spatial analysis. Instead, geographers working in the field can easily determine their position, as well as boundaries and other data points, accurately as they work, reducing the need for traditional surveys.

Prime Meridian and Standard Time

Coordination of international trade, airline schedules, business and agricultural activities, and daily living depends on a worldwide time system. Today, we take for granted standard time zones and an agreed-upon prime meridian, but such a standard is a relatively recent development.

Setting time was not a great problem in small European countries, most of which are less than 15° wide. But in North America, which spans more than 90° of longitude

GEO REPORT 4 *GPS origins*

Originally devised in the 1970s by the Department of Defense for military purposes, GPS is now commercially available worldwide. In 2000, the Pentagon shut down its Pentagon Selective Availability security control, making commercial resolution the same as military applications. Additional frequencies were added in 2003 and 2006, which increased accuracy significantly to less than 10 m (33 ft). For a GPS overview, see http://www.colorado.edu/geography/gcraft/notes/gps/gps_f.html.

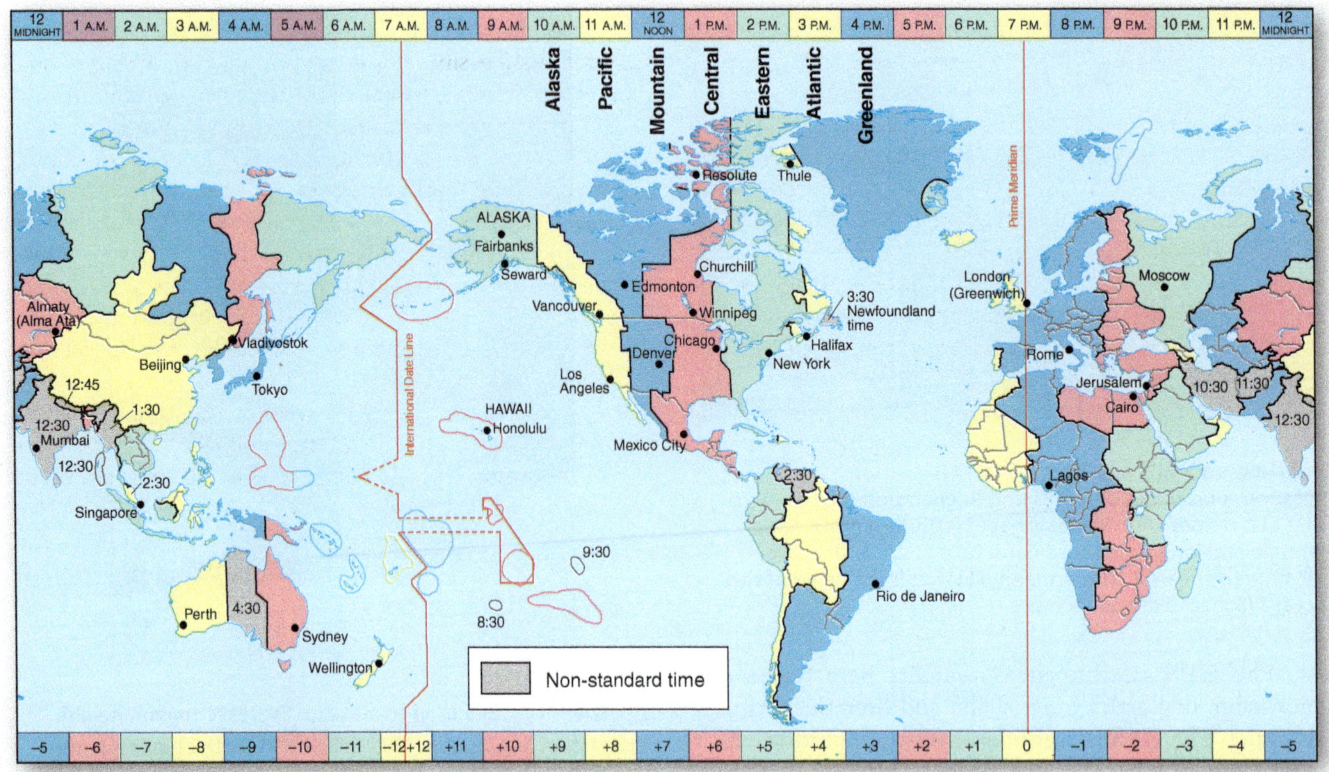

FIGURE 20 Modern international standard time zones.
Numbers along the bottom of the map indicate how many hours each zone is earlier (plus sign) or later (minus sign) than Coordinated Universal Time (UTC) at the prime meridian. If it is 7 P.M. in Greenwich, determine the present time in Moscow, London, Halifax, Chicago, Winnipeg, Denver, Los Angeles, Fairbanks, Honolulu, Tokyo, and Singapore. [Adapted from Defense Mapping Agency. See http://aa.usno.navy.mil/faq/docs/world_tzones.html.]

(the equivalent of six 15° time zones), the problem was serious. In 1870, railroad travelers going from Maine to San Francisco made 22 adjustments to their watches to stay consistent with local time.

In Canada, Sir Sanford Fleming directed the fight for standard time and for an international agreement on a prime meridian. His struggle led the United States and Canada to adopt a standard time in 1883. Twenty-seven countries attended the 1884 International Meridian Conference in Washington, DC, to set a global standard. Most participating nations chose the highly respected Royal Observatory at Greenwich, London, England, as the place for the prime meridian of 0° longitude for maps. Thus, a world standard was set—**Greenwich Mean Time (GMT)**—and a consistent Universal Time was established (see http://wwp.greenwichmeantime.com/).

The basis of time is that Earth revolves 360° every 24 hours, or 15° per hour (360° ÷ 24 = 15°). Thus, a time zone of 1 hour is established, spanning 7.5° on either side of a *central meridian*. Today, only three adjustments are needed in the continental United States—from Eastern Standard Time to Central, Mountain, and Pacific—and four changes across Canada.

Assuming it is 9:00 P.M. in Greenwich, then it is 4:00 P.M. in Baltimore (+5 hr), 3:00 P.M. in Oklahoma City (+6 hr), 2:00 P.M. in Salt Lake City (+7 hr), 1:00 P.M. in Seattle and Los Angeles (+8 hr), noon in Anchorage (+9 hr), and 11:00 A.M. in Honolulu (+10 hr). To the east, it is midnight in Ar Riyāḍ, Saudi Arabia (−3 hr). The designation A.M. is for *ante meridiem*, "before noon," whereas P.M. is for *post meridiem*, "after noon." A 24-hour clock avoids the use of these designations: 3 P.M. is stated as 15:00 hours; 3 A.M. is 3:00 hours.

As you can see from the modern international time zones in Figure 20, national boundaries and political considerations distort time boundaries. For example, China spans four time zones, but its government decided to keep the entire country operating at the same time. Thus, in some parts of China clocks are several hours off

GEO REPORT 5 *Magellan's crew loses a day*

Early explorers had a problem before the date-line concept. For example, Magellan's crew returned from the first circumnavigation of Earth in 1522, confident from their ship's log that it was Wednesday, September 7. They were shocked when informed by local residents that it was actually Thursday, September 8. Without an International Date Line, they had no idea that they must advance a day somewhere when sailing around the world in a westward direction. Imagine the confusion of the arriving crew.

from what the Sun is doing. In the United States, parts of Florida and west Texas are in the same time zone.

International Date Line An important corollary of the prime meridian is the 180° meridian on the opposite side of the planet. This meridian is the **International Date Line (IDL)**, which marks the place where each day officially begins (at 12:01 A.M.). From this "line," the new day sweeps westward. This *westward* movement of time is created by Earth's turning *eastward* on its axis. Locating the date line in the sparsely populated Pacific Ocean minimizes most local confusion.

At the IDL, the west side of the line is always one day ahead of the east side. No matter what time of day it is when the line is crossed, the calendar changes a day (Figure 21). Note in the illustration the departures from the IDL and the 180° meridian; this deviation is due to local administrative and political preferences.

Coordinated Universal Time For decades, Greenwich Mean Time (GMT) from the Royal Observatory's astronomical clocks was the world's Universal Time (UT) standard for accuracy. GMT was broadcast using radio time signals as early as 1910. Taking the initiative in 1912, the French government called a gathering of countries to better coordinate radio time signals. At this conference, GMT was made standard, and a new organization was set up to be the custodian of "exact" time—the International Bureau of Weights and Measures (BIPM; see http://www.bipm.org). Progress was made in accurately measuring time with the invention of a quartz clock in 1939 and atomic clocks in the early 1950s.

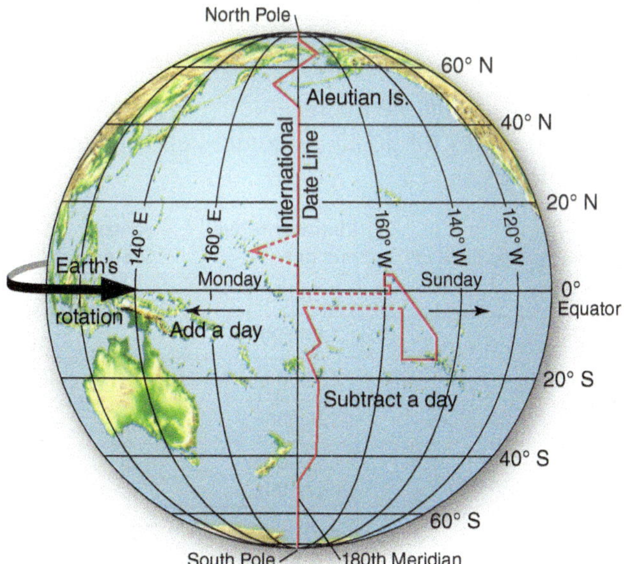

FIGURE 21 International Date Line.
International Date Line location is approximately along the 180th meridian (see the IDL location on Figure 20). Note the dotted lines on the map—island countries set their own time zones, but their political control extends only 3.5 nautical miles (4 mi) offshore. Officially, you gain 1 day crossing the IDL from east to west.

Accurate time is not a matter of simply keeping track of Earth's rotation, since it is slowing down from the tug of tidal forces and rearrangement of water. Note that 150 million years ago a "day" was 22 hours long, and 150 million years in the future a "day" will be approaching 27 hours in length.

The **Coordinated Universal Time (UTC*)** time-signal system replaced GMT universal time in 1972 and became the legal reference for official time in all countries. Although the prime meridian still runs through Greenwich, UTC is based on average time calculations from atomic clocks collected worldwide. You might still see official UTC referred to as GMT or Zulu time.

Time and Frequency Services of the National Institute for Standards and Technology (NIST), U.S. Department of Commerce, operates several of the most advanced clocks. For the time, call 303-499-7111 or 808-335-4363, or see http://nist.time.gov/ for UTC. In Canada, the Institute for Measurement Standards, National Research Council Canada, participates in determining UTC, English, 613-745-1578; French, 613-745-9426; for more see http://time5.nrc.ca/JavaClock/timeDisplayWE.shtml.

Daylight Saving Time In 70 countries, mainly in the temperate latitudes, time is set ahead 1 hour in the spring and set back 1 hour in the fall—a practice known as **daylight saving time**. The idea to extend daylight for early evening activities (at the expense of daylight in the morning), first proposed by Benjamin Franklin, was not adopted until World War I and again in World War II, when Great Britain, Australia, Germany, Canada, and the United States used the practice to save energy (1 less hour of artificial lighting needed).

In 1986 and again in 2007, the United States and Canada increased daylight saving time. Time "springs forward" 1 hour on the second Sunday in March and "falls back" 1 hour on the first Sunday in November, except in a few places that do not use daylight saving time (Hawai'i, Arizona, and Saskatchewan). In Europe, the last Sundays in March and October are used to begin and end the "summer-time period." (See http://webexhibits.org/daylightsaving/.)

Maps, Scales, and Projections

The earliest known graphic maps date to 2300 B.C., when the Babylonians used clay tablets to record information about the region of the Tigris and Euphrates Rivers (the area of modern-day Iraq). Today, the making of maps and charts is a specialized science as well as an art, blending aspects of geography, engineering, mathematics, graphics, computer science, and artistic specialties. It is similar in ways to architecture, in which aesthetics and utility combine to produce a useful product.

A **map** is a generalized view of an area, usually some portion of Earth's surface, as seen from above and greatly

*UTC is in use because agreement was not reached on whether to use the English word order, CUT, or the French order, TUC. UTC was the compromise and is recommended for all time-keeping applications; use of the term *GMT* is discouraged.

reduced in size. **Cartography** is that part of geography that involves mapmaking. Maps are critical tools with which geographers depict spatial information and analyze spatial relationships.

We all use maps at some time to visualize our location in relation to other places, or maybe to plan a trip, or to coordinate commercial and economic activities. Have you found yourself looking at a map, planning real and imagined adventures to far-distant places? Maps are wonderful tools! Understanding a few basics about maps is essential to our study of physical geography.

The Scale of Maps

Architects, toy designers, and mapmakers have something in common: They all create scale models. They reduce real things and places to the more convenient scale of a drawing; a model car, train, or plane; a diagram; or a map. An architect renders a blueprint of a structure to guide the building contractors, selecting a scale so that a centimeter (or inch) on the drawing represents so many meters (or feet) on the proposed building. Often, the drawing is 1/50 or 1/100 real size.

The cartographer does the same thing in preparing a map. The ratio of the image on a map to the real world is **scale**; it relates a unit on the map to a similar unit on the ground. A 1:1 scale means that a centimeter on the map represents a centimeter on the ground, although this is an impractical map scale, since the map is as large as the area mapped! A more appropriate scale for a local map is 1:24,000, in which 1 unit on the map represents 24,000 identical units on the ground.

Cartographers express map scale as a representative fraction, a graphic scale, or a written scale (Figure 22). A *representative fraction* (*RF*, or *fractional scale*) is expressed with either a colon or a slash, as in 1:125,000 or 1/125,000. No actual units of measurement are mentioned because any unit is applicable as long as both parts of the fraction are in the same unit: 1 cm to 125,000 cm, 1 in. to 125,000 in., or even 1 arm length to 125,000 arm lengths.

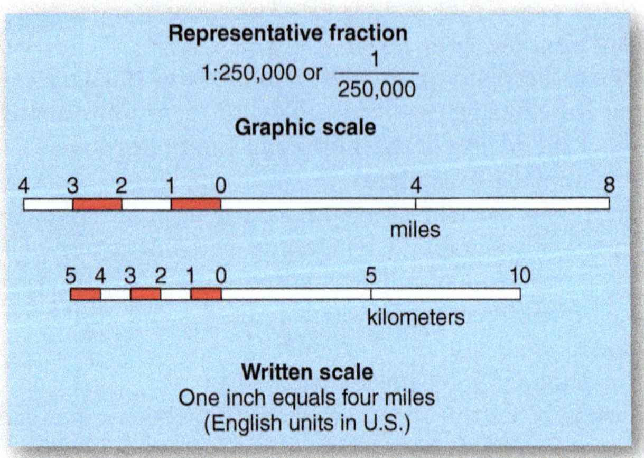

FIGURE 22 Map scale.
Three common expressions of map scale—representative fraction, graphic scale, and written scale.

A *graphic scale*, or *bar scale*, is a bar graph with units to allow measurement of distances on the map. An important advantage of a graphic scale is that, if the map is enlarged or reduced, the graphic scale enlarges or reduces along with the map. In contrast, written and fractional scales become incorrect with enlargement or reduction. As an example, if you shrink a map from 1:24,000 to 1:63,360, the written scale "1 in. to 2000 ft" will no longer be the correct. The new correct written scale is 1 in. to 5280 ft (1 mi).

Scales are *small*, *medium*, and *large*, depending on the ratio described. In relative terms, a scale of 1:24,000 is a large scale, whereas a scale of 1:50,000,000 is a small scale. The greater the denominator in a fractional scale (or the number on the right in a ratio expression), the smaller the scale and the more abstract the map in relation to what is being mapped. Examples of selected representative fractions and written scales are listed in Table 1 for small-, medium-, and large-scale maps.

CRITICAL THINKING 3
Find and calculate map scales

Find a globe or map in the library or geography department and check the scale at which it was drawn. See if you can find examples of fractional, graphic, and written scales on wall maps, on highway maps, and in atlases. Find some examples of small- and large-scale maps, and note the different subject matter they portray.

Look at a world globe that is 61 cm (24 in.) in diameter. (Use different values depending on the globe you are using.) We know that Earth has an equatorial diameter of 12,756 km (7926 mi), so the scale of such a globe is the ratio of 61 cm to 12,756 km. To calculate the representative fraction for the globe in centimeters, divide Earth's actual diameter by the globe's diameter (12,756 km ÷ 61 cm). (Hint: 1 km = 1000 m, 1 m = 100 cm; therefore, Earth's diameter of 12,756 km represents 1,275,600,000 cm; and the globe's diameter is 61 cm.) In general, do you think a world globe is a small- or a large-scale map of Earth's surface?

TABLE 1 Sample Representative Fractions and Written Scales for Small-, Medium-, and Large-Scale Maps

System	Scale Size	Representative Fraction	Written System Scale
English	Small	1:3,168,000	1 in. = 50 mi
		1:1,000,000	1 in. = 16 mi
		1:250,000	1 in. = 4 mi
	Medium	1:125,000	1 in. = 2 mi
		1:63,360 (or 1:62,500)	1 in. = 1 mi
	Large	1:24,000	1 in. = 2000 ft
System		**Representative Fraction**	**Written System Scale**
Metric		1:1,000,000	1 cm = 10.0 km
		1:25,000	1 cm = 0.25 km
		1:10,000	1 cm = 0.10 km

Map Projections

A globe is not always a helpful map representation of Earth. When you go on a trip, you need more-detailed information than a globe can provide. Consequently, to provide local detail, cartographers prepare large-scale *flat maps*, which are two-dimensional representations (scale models) of our three-dimensional Earth. Unfortunately, such conversion from three dimensions to two causes distortion.

A globe is the only true representation of *distance*, *direction*, *area*, *shape*, and *proximity*. A flat map distorts these properties. Therefore, in preparing a flat map, the cartographer must decide which characteristic to preserve, which to distort, and how much distortion is acceptable. To understand this problem, consider these important properties of a globe:

- Parallels always are parallel to each other, always are evenly spaced along meridians, and always decrease in length toward the poles.
- Meridians always converge at both poles and always are evenly spaced along any individual parallel.
- The distance between meridians decreases toward poles, with the spacing between meridians at the 60th parallel equal to one-half the equatorial spacing.
- Parallels and meridians always cross each other at right angles.

The problem is that all these qualities cannot be reproduced on a flat surface. Simply taking a globe apart and laying it flat on a table illustrates the challenge faced by cartographers (Figure 23). You can see the empty spaces that open up between the sections, or gores, of the globe. This reduction of the spherical Earth to a flat surface is a **map projection**. Thus, no flat map projection of Earth can ever have all the features of a globe. Flat maps always possess some degree of distortion—much less for large-scale maps representing a few kilometers; much more for small-scale maps covering individual countries, continents, or the entire world.

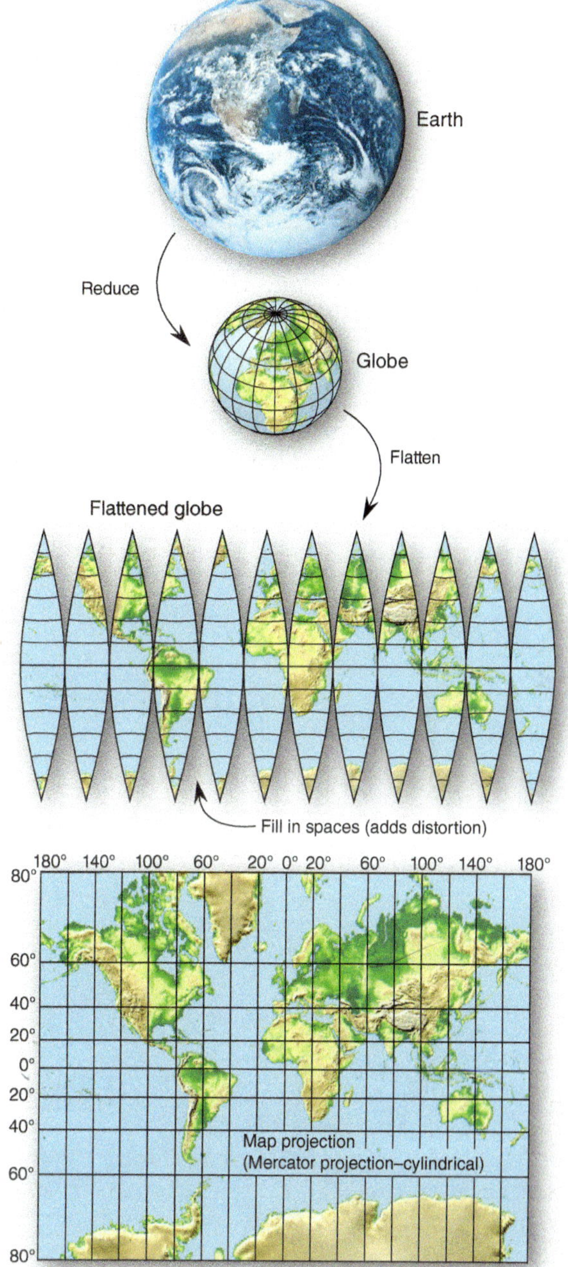

FIGURE 23 From globe to flat map. Conversion of the globe to a flat map projection requires decisions about which properties to preserve and the amount of distortion that is acceptable. [NASA astronaut photo from *Apollo 17*, 1972.]

Properties of Projections There are many map projections, four of which are shown in Figure 24. The best projection is always determined by its intended use. The major decisions in selecting a map projection involve the properties of **equal area** (equivalence) and **true shape** (conformality). A decision for one property sacrifices the other, for they cannot be shown together on the same flat map.

If a cartographer selects equal area as the desired trait—for example, for a map showing the distribution of world climates—then true shape must be sacrificed by stretching and shearing, which allow parallels and meridians to cross at other than right angles. On an equal-area map, a coin covers the same amount of surface area no matter where you place it on the map. In contrast, if a cartographer selects the property of true shape, such as for a map used for navigational purposes, then equal area must be sacrificed, and the scale will actually change from one region of the map to another.

The Nature and Classes of Projections Despite the fact that modern cartographic technology uses mathematical constructions and computer-assisted graphics, the word *projection* is still used. The term comes from times past, when geographers actually projected the shadow of a wire-skeleton globe onto a geometric surface. The wires represented parallels, meridians, and outlines of the continents. A light source then cast a shadow pattern of latitude and longitude lines from the globe onto various geometric surfaces, such as a *cylinder*, *plane*, or *cone*.

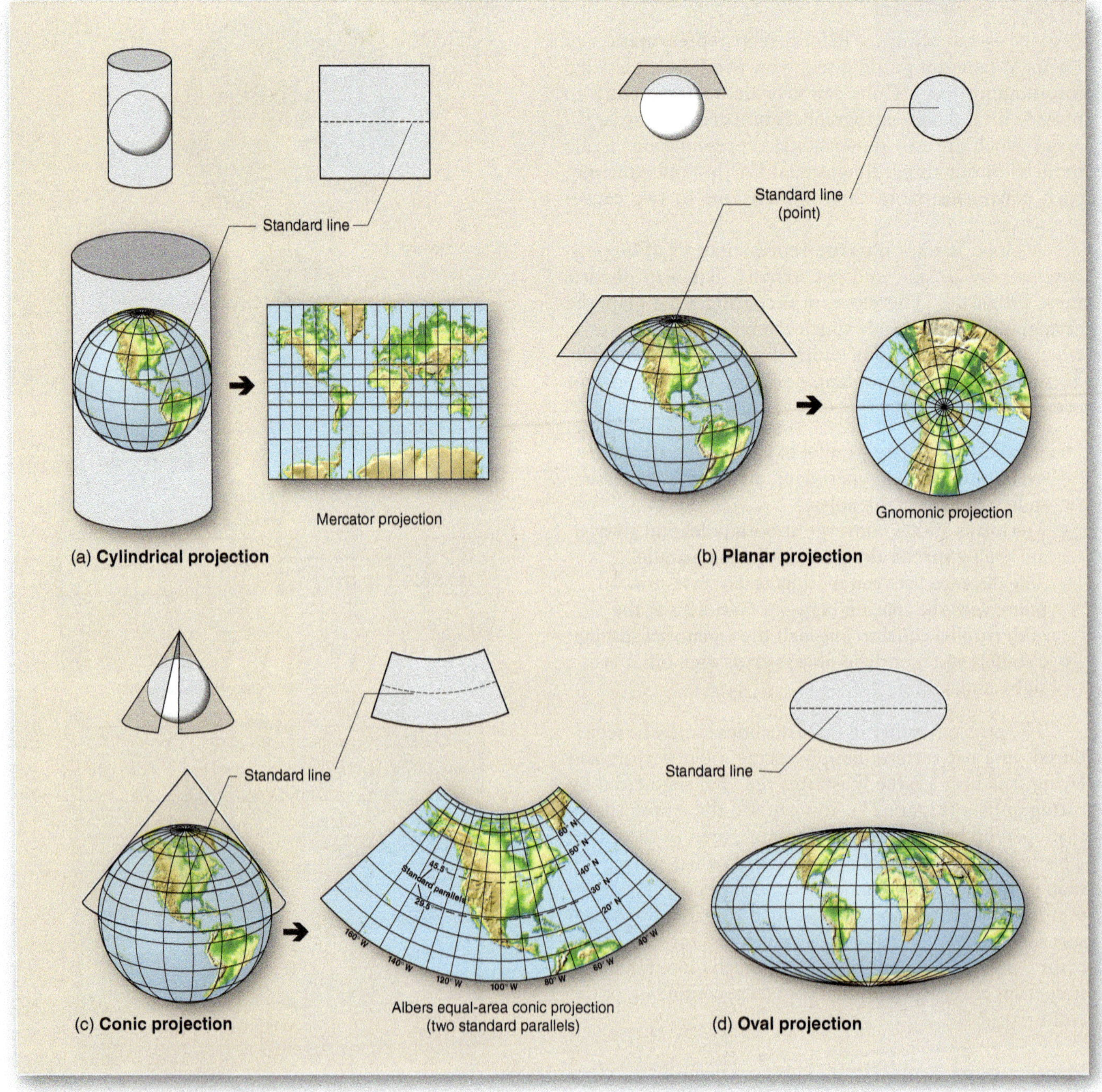

FIGURE 24 Classes of map projections.
Four general classes and perspectives of map projections—(a) cylindrical, (b) planar, (c) conic, and (d) oval projections.

Figure 24 illustrates the general classes of map projections and the perspectives from which they are generated. The classes shown include the cylindrical, planar (or azimuthal), and conic. Another class of projections, which cannot be derived from this physical-perspective approach, is the nonperspective oval shape. Still other projections derive from purely mathematical calculations.

With projections, the contact line or contact point between the wire globe and the projection surface—a *standard line* or *standard point*—is the only place where all globe properties are preserved. Thus, a *standard parallel* or *standard meridian* is a standard line true to scale along its entire length without any distortion. Areas away from this critical tangent line or point become increasingly distorted. Consequently, this line or point of accurate spatial properties should be centered by the cartographer on the area of interest.

The commonly used **Mercator projection** (from Gerardus Mercator, A.D. 1569) is a cylindrical projection (Figure 24a). The Mercator is a true-shape projection, with meridians appearing as equally spaced straight lines and parallels appearing as straight lines that are spaced closer together near the equator. The poles are infinitely stretched, with the 84th N parallel and 84th S parallel fixed at the same length as that of the equator. Note in

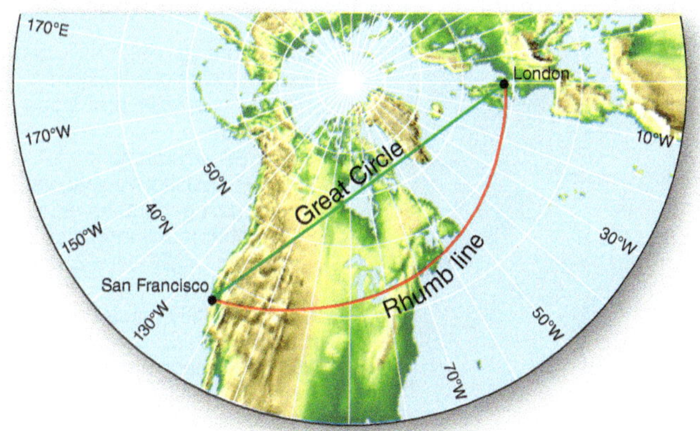

(a) Gnomonic Projection

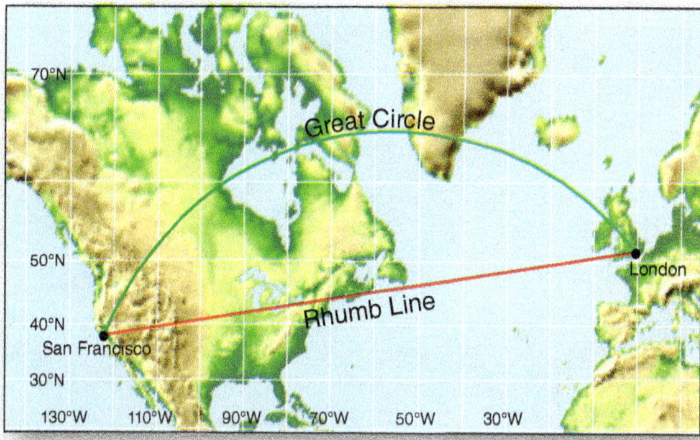

(b) Mercator Projection (conformal, true shape)

FIGURE 25 Determining great circle routes.
A gnomonic projection (a) is used to determine the shortest distance—great circle route—between San Francisco and London because on this projection the arc of a great circle is a straight line. This great circle route is then plotted on a Mercator projection (b), which has true compass direction. Note that straight lines or bearings on a Mercator projection—rhumb lines—are not the shortest route.

Figures 23 and 24a that the Mercator projection is cut around the 80th parallel in each hemisphere because of the severe distortion at higher latitudes.

Unfortunately, Mercator classroom maps present false notions of the size (area) of midlatitude and poleward landmasses. A dramatic example on the Mercator projection is Greenland, which looks bigger than all of South America. In reality, Greenland is an island only one-eighth the size of South America and is actually 20% smaller than Argentina alone.

The advantage of the Mercator projection is that a line of constant direction, known as a **rhumb line**, or *loxodrome*, is straight and therefore facilitates plotting directions between two points (Figure 25b). Thus, the Mercator projection is useful in navigation and is standard for nautical charts prepared by the National Ocean Service.

The *gnomonic*, or *planar, projection* in Figure 24b is generated by projecting a light source at the center of a globe onto a plane that is tangent to (touching) the globe's surface. The resulting severe distortion prevents showing a full hemisphere on one projection. However, a valuable feature is derived: All great circle routes, which are the shortest distance between two points on Earth's surface, are projected as straight lines (Figure 25a). The great circle routes plotted on a gnomonic projection then can be transferred to a true-direction projection, such as the Mercator, for determination of precise compass headings (Figure 25b).

Topographic maps are essential tools of landscape analysis. Geographers, other scientists, travelers, and anyone visiting the outdoors may use topographic maps. Perhaps you have used a "topo" map in planning a hike. U.S. Geological Survey (USGS) topographic maps are a staple.

Remote Sensing and GIS

Geographers probe, analyze, and map our home planet through remote sensing and geographic information systems (GIS). These technologies enhance our understanding of Earth. Geographers use remote-sensing data to study all the subjects in this text and the human activities that produce global change and impact Earth systems.

Remote Sensing

In this era of observations from orbit outside the atmosphere, from aircraft within it, and from remote submersibles in the oceans, scientists obtain a wide array of remotely sensed data (Figure 26). Remote sensing is nothing new to humans; we do it with our eyes as we scan the environment, sensing the shape, size, and color of objects from a distance, registering energy from the visible-wavelength portion of the electromagnetic spectrum. Similarly, when a camera views the wavelengths for which its film or sensor

GEO REPORT 6 *Mapping anniversary for the USGS*

December 2009 marked the 125th anniversary since Congress authorized the USGS to systematically map the country. The USGS National Mapping Program is complete for the lower 48 states, numbering 53,838 separate 7.5-minute quadrangles. *The National Map* (available at http://nationalmap.gov/), a collaborative effort by USGS and federal, state, and local agencies, provides downloadable digital topographic data for the entire United States. These data include aerial photographs, elevation, roads, geographic names, and land cover. The National Map is an important tool for scientists, teachers, students, and the public to access geographic information.

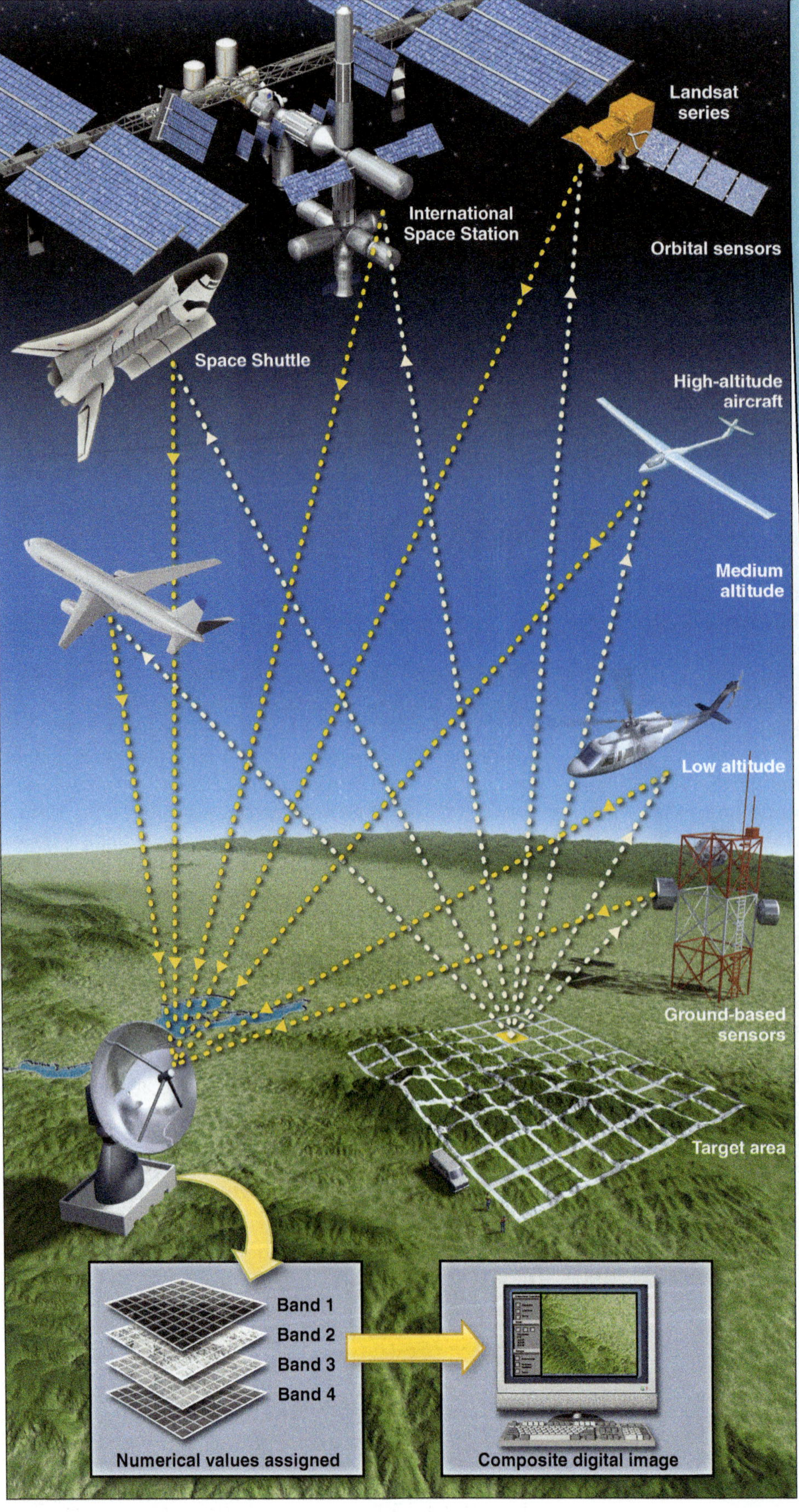

A sample of orbital platforms:

CloudSat: Studies cloud extent, distribution, radiative properties, and structure.

ENVISAT: ESA environment-monitoring satellite; 10 sensors, including next generation radar.

GOES: Weather monitoring and Forecasting; *GOES-11, -12, -13,* and *-14.*

GRACE: Accurately maps Earth's gravitational field.

JASON-1, -2: Measures sea-level heights.

Landsat: *Landsat-1* in 1972 to *Landsat-7* in 1999, provides millions of images for Earth systems science and global change.

NOAA: First in 1978 through *NOAA-15, -16, -17, -18,* and *-19* now in operation, global data gathering, short- and long-term weather forecasts.

RADARSAT-1, -2: Synthetic Aperture Radar in near-polar orbit, operated by Canadian Space Agency.

SciSat-1: Analyzes trace gases, thin clouds, atmospheric aerosols with Arctic focus.

SeaStar: Carries the *SeaWiFS* (Sea-viewing Wide Field-of-View instrument) to observe Earth's oceans and microscopic marine plants.

Terra and Aqua: Environmental change, error-free surface images, cloud properties, through five instrument packages.

TOMS-EP: Total Ozone Mapping Spectrometer, monitoring stratospheric ozone, similar instruments on *NIMBUS-7* and *Meteor-3.*

TOPEX-POSEIDON: Measures sea-level heights.

TRMM: Tropical Rainfall Measuring Mission, includes lightning detection and global energy budget measurements.

For more info see: **http://www.nasa.gov/centers/goddard/missions/index.html**

FIGURE 26 Remote-sensing technology.
Remote-sensing technology measures and monitors Earth's systems from orbiting spacecraft, aircraft in the atmosphere, and ground-based sensors. Various wavelengths (bands) are collected from sensors. Computers process the data to produce digital images for analysis. A sample of remote-sensing platforms is listed along the side of the illustration. The Space Shuttle is shown in its inverted orbital flight mode. (Illustration is not to scale.)

is designed, it remotely senses energy that is reflected or emitted from a scene.

Our eyes and cameras are familiar means of obtaining **remote-sensing** information about a distant subject without having physical contact. Cartographers have used aerial photographs for years to improve the accuracy of surface maps faster and more cheaply than can be done by on-site surveys. Remote sensors on satellites, the International Space Station, and other craft sense a broader range of wavelengths than can our eyes. They can be designed to "see" wavelengths shorter than visible light (ultraviolet) and wavelengths longer than visible light (infrared and microwave radar).

Following launch, satellites can be set in several types of orbits: geostationary, polar, and Sun-synchronous, illustrated in Figure 27. In a geostationary (geosynchronous) orbit, typically at an altitude of 35,790 km (22,239 mi), satellites pace Earth's rotation speed and therefore remain "parked" above a specific location, usually the equator (Figure 27a). This "fixed" position means that satellite antennas on Earth can be pointed permanently at one position in the sky where the satellite is located; the *GOES* weather satellite is an example.

Figure 27b shows a polar-orbiting satellite typically residing at an altitude between 200 km and 1000 km (124 mi and 621 mi) and passing over every portion of the globe as Earth rotates beneath it, completing each orbit in 90 minutes. Such satellites are good for difficult regions such as the poles, for environmental studies, and for spy surveillance; examples include *Terra* and *Aqua*.

Figure 27c demonstrates a Sun-synchronous orbit, shifting its 600 km to 800 km (373 mi to 497 mi) altitude, near-polar track, about 1° per day (365 days in a year, 360° in a circle), providing a surface below in constant sunlight for visible-wavelength images or in constant darkness for longwave radiation images.

Satellites do not take conventional-film photographs. Rather, they record images that are transmitted to Earth-based receivers in a way similar to television satellite transmissions or a digital camera. A scene is scanned and broken down into pixels (*pic*ture *el*ements), each identified by coordinates named *lines* (horizontal rows) and *samples* (vertical columns). For example, a grid of 6000 lines and 7000 samples forms 42,000,000 pixels, providing great detail. The large amount of data needed to produce a single image requires computer processing and data storage at ground stations.

Digital data are processed in many ways to enhance their utility: simulated natural color, "false" color to highlight a particular feature, enhanced contrast, signal filtering, and different levels of sampling and resolution. Active and passive are two types of remote-sensing systems.

Active Remote Sensing Active systems direct a beam of energy at a surface and analyze the energy reflected back. An example is *radar* (*ra*dio *d*etection *a*nd *r*anging). A radar transmitter emits short bursts of energy that have relatively long wavelengths (0.3 cm to 10 cm) toward the subject terrain, penetrating clouds and darkness. Energy reflected back to a radar receiver for analysis is known as *backscatter*. Several important radar satellites are in orbit at this time, such as *QuikSAT*, *RADARSAT-1* and *-2*, and *SCISAT-1*.

A synthetic aperture radar system aboard an aircraft imaged the San Andreas fault near San Mateo, California (Figure 28). The Jet Propulsion Laboratory (JPL), part of the National Aeronautics and Space Administration (NASA), developed systems to repeatedly capture detailed, three-dimensional images along this fault system to track

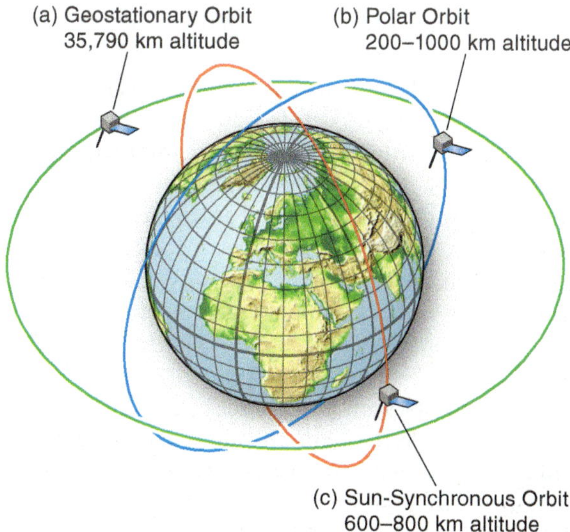

FIGURE 27 Three satellite orbital paths.

FIGURE 28 Radar image of active earthquake fault. Synthetic aperture radar image made from an aircraft repeatedly over time allows study of stress-accumulating portions of the fault. Can you see the fault rift area running from southeast to northwest in this 2009 false-color image, in the area filled with a reservoir? [UACSAR image by JPL/NASA; photo by Author.]

movement and areas that are building up energy for future earthquakes. Images collected in a time series allow scientists to make pixel by pixel comparisons in computers to detect even the slightest horizontal or vertical movement between images. This type of information identifies accumulating strain along the faults.

Passive Remote Sensing Passive remote-sensing systems record energy radiated from a surface, particularly visible light and infrared. Our own eyes are passive remote sensors, as was the *Apollo 17* astronaut camera that made the photograph (film) of Earth on the back cover of this book.

Passive remote sensors on *Landsat* satellites provide a variety of data, as shown in images of New Orleans before and after Katrina, and the Mississippi River. Two *Landsats* remain operational, *Landsat-5* and -7. See http://landsat.gsfc.nasa.gov/ for more information and additional links.

A number of satellites carry passive remote sensors for weather forecasting. The *Geostationary Operational Environmental Satellites*, known as *GOES*, became operational in 1994 and provide the images you see on television weather reports. The *NOAA-15* through *NOAA-19* satellites complete nearly polar orbits 14 times a day and provide data for long-term weather prediction. These are in Sun-synchronous orbits and carry the *advanced very high resolution radiometer* (*AVHRR*), which uses six sensors to detect different bands of radiation wavelengths. AVHRR images show the effects of the Mount Pinatubo eruption on the global atmosphere.

Key to NASA's Earth Observing System (EOS) is satellite *Terra*, which began beaming back data and images in 2000 (see http://terra.nasa.gov/), followed by another satellite in the series, *Aqua*. Five instrument packages observe Earth systems in detail. The image of Earth on the half-title page of this book includes a cloud snapshot from *GOES* added to *Terra* MODIS images.

GOES-11 is now above 135° W for western North America and eastern Pacific Ocean weather. *GOES-12* sits above 75° W longitude to monitor central and eastern North America and the western Atlantic. Think of these satellites as hovering over these meridians for continuous coverage, using visual wavelengths for daylight hours and infrared for nighttime views. For the future, *GOES-13* and *GOES-14* are parked in orbit and are ready when needed (Figure 29). See the Geostationary Satellite Server at http://www.goes.noaa.gov/. The *GOES* Project Science appears at http://rsd.gsfc.nasa.gov/goes/.

For a sampling of global remote-sensing coverage from a variety of satellite platforms, go to the USGS Global Visualization Viewer, select the satellite and click on the map for a location, and then watch (http://glovis.usgs.gov/). For more on active and passive remote-sensing platforms, see the section "Remote sensing status report" in this chapter on the *Mastering-Geography* web site.

FIGURE 29 ***GOES-14* first image.**
GOES-14 made its first image July 27, 2009; the improved technology in this satellite produces 1-km (0.62-mi) resolution. Can you find the cloud-free southwestern United States? Thunderstorms along the Texas–Oklahoma border? Two tropical waves are visible in the eastern Pacific Ocean. [NASA.]

Geographic Information Systems

Techniques such as remote sensing acquire large volumes of spatial data that must be stored, processed, and retrieved in useful ways. A **geographic information system (GIS)** is a computer-based, data-processing tool for gathering, manipulating, and analyzing geographic information. Today's sophisticated computer systems allow the integration of geographic information from direct surveys (on-the-ground mapping) and remote sensing in complex ways never before possible.

Through a GIS, Earth and human phenomena are analyzed over time. This can include the study and forecasting of diseases such H1N1 flu and West Nile virus, or the population displacement caused by Hurricane Katrina, or the destruction from the Haitian and Chilean earthquakes in 2010 and Japan in 2011, or interactive land-cover maps, to name a few examples (Figure 30b and c). Whereas printed maps are fixed at time of publication, GIS maps can be modified and evolve instantly.

The beginning component for any GIS is a map, with its associated coordinate system such as latitude–longitude. This establishes reference points against which to position data. The coordinate system is digitized, along with all areas, points, and lines. Increasingly, GPS units are now used to provide the basic mapping data needed for a GIS. Remotely sensed imagery and data are then added on the coordinate system. The resulting *digital elevation models (DEMs)* aid scientific analysis of topography, area–altitude distributions, slopes, and local stream-drainage characteristics, among many applications. The data then

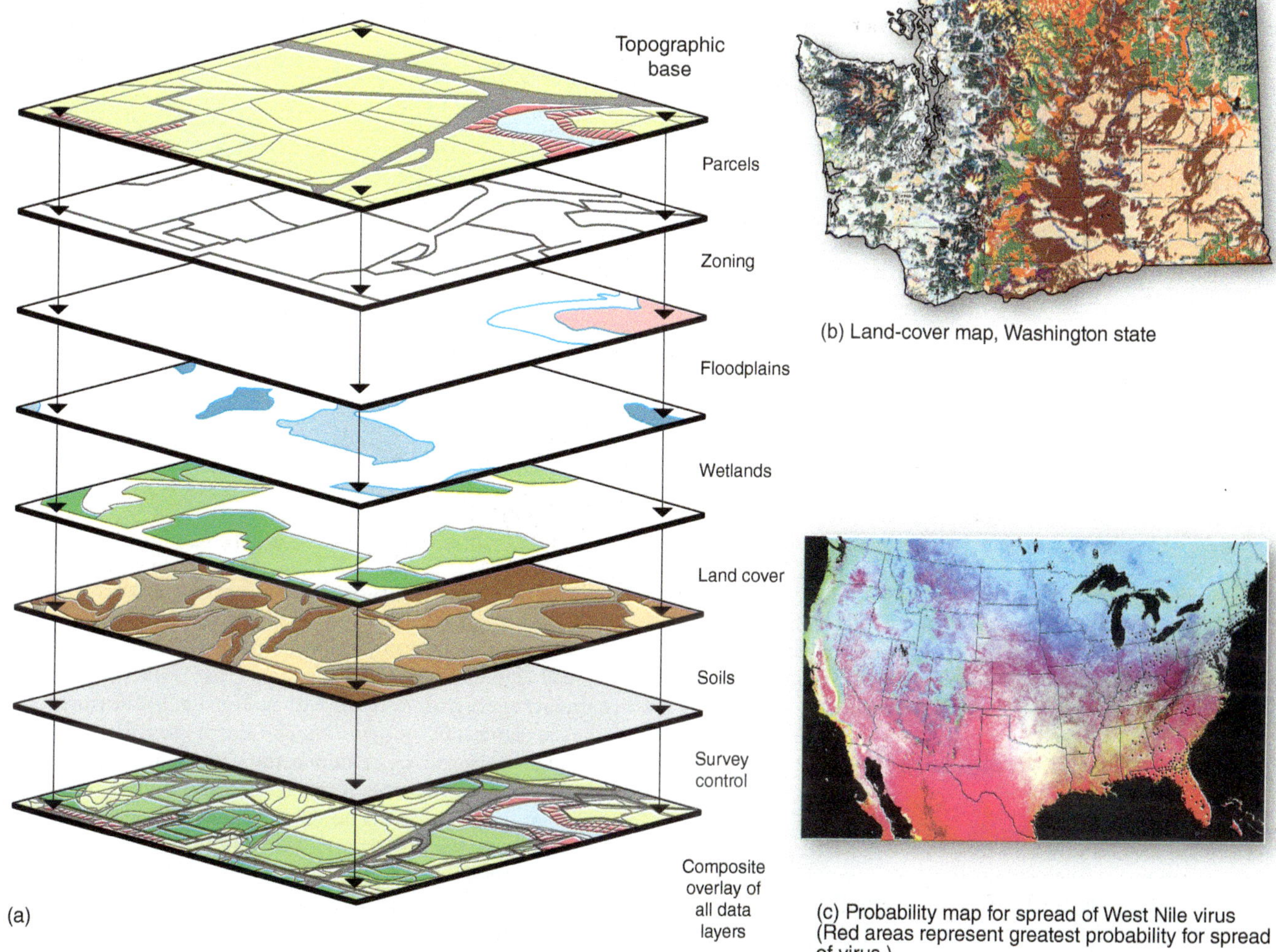

FIGURE 30 A geographic information system (GIS) model.
(a) Layered spatial data in a GIS format. (b) This comprehensive land-cover map is an important component of a statewide GIS analysis for Washington. The goal is to evaluate the protection of species and biodiversity. (c) A NASA GIS study uses satellite-derived temperature, humidity, and vegetation variables in a GIS overlay of environmental conditions for a probability map of the spread of West Nile virus. [(a) After USGS. (b) GIS map courtesy of Dr. Kelly M. Cassidy, *Gap Analysis of Washington State*, v. 5, Map 3, University of Washington. (c) NASA/GSFC.]

are available for computer manipulation, display, and GIS operations.

A GIS is capable of analyzing patterns and relationships within a single data plane, such as the floodplain or soil layer in Figure 30a. A GIS also can generate an overlay analysis where two or more data planes interact. When the layers are combined, the resulting synthesis—a *composite overlay*—is ready for use in analyzing complex problems. The utility of a GIS compared with that of a fixed map is the ability to manipulate the variables for analysis and to constantly change the map.

The applications of GIS are wide-ranging and cross many disciplines. Geographic Information Science (GISci) embodies the development, use, and application of GIS. An international conference series on GISci began in 2000 and continues biannually (see http://giscience.org/). These conferences bring together leading scientists from academia, industry, and government to explore emerging research across the disciplines and to seek applications in many fields. An important direction is toward more user-friendly GIS systems in the future.

Access to GIS is expanding with increased availability of numerous open-source GIS software packages. These are usually free, have on-line support systems, and are updated frequently (see http://opensourcegis.org/).

Programs for visualizing Earth, such as Google Earth™, provide three-dimensional viewing of the globe, as well as geographic information, in a program that can be downloaded from the Internet (http://earth.google.com/). Google Earth™ allows the user to "fly" anywhere on Earth and zoom in on landscapes and features of interest, using satellite imagery and aerial photography at varying resolutions. You can find where you live and your campus. Users can select layers, as in a GIS model, depending on the task at hand and the composite overlay displayed.

Career opportunities in GIS continue to increase. Regardless of your academic major, the ability to analyze data spatially is important. The annual ESRI (Environmental

Systems Research Institute) International Users Conference, whose attendance is approaching 15,000 people, continues to be the largest gathering of GIS professionals to share state-of-the-art applications of GIS technology (http://www.esri.com/).

GIS degree programs are available at many colleges and universities. GIS curriculum and certificate programs are now available at many community colleges. A consortium of three universities forms the National Center for Geographic Information and Analysis (NCGIA) for GIS education. These GIS centers are Department of Geography, University of California Santa Barbara, Santa Barbara; Department of Surveying and Engineering, University of Maine, Orono; and State University of New York–Buffalo, Buffalo. (See http://www.ncgia.ucsb.edu/.)

KEY LEARNING CONCEPTS REVIEW

To assist you, here is a review in handy summary form of the Key Learning Concepts listed on this chapter's title page. Each concept review concludes with a list of the key terms from the chapter, their page numbers, and review questions. Such summary and review sections follow each chapter in the book.

■ *Define* geography and physical geography in particular.

Human–Earth Relationships
Human–environment connections include resource exploitation, hazard perception, and environmental pollution and modification. A *Terra* satellite image of the *Deepwater Horizon* oil spill in the Gulf of Mexico, highlighted by a sunglint on the gulf's surface. This human-caused spill is the largest offshore drilling disaster in history.

Geography brings together disciplines from the physical and life sciences with the cultural and human sciences to attain a holistic view of Earth—physical geography is an essential aspect of the emerging **Earth systems sciences. Geography** is a science of method, a special way of analyzing phenomena over space; **spatial** refers to the nature and character of physical space. Geography integrates a wide range of subject matter, and geographic education recognizes five major themes: **location, region, human–Earth relationships, movement**, and **place**. Geography's method is **spatial analysis**, used to study the interdependence among geographic areas, natural systems, society, and cultural activities over space or area. **Process**—that is, analyzing a set of actions or mechanisms that operate in some special order—is central to geographic synthesis.

Physical geography applies spatial analysis to all the physical elements and process systems that make up the environment: energy, air, water, weather, climate, landforms, soils, animals, plants, microorganisms, and Earth itself. Understanding the complex relations among these elements is important to human survival because Earth's physical systems and human society are intertwined. The development of hypotheses and theories about the Universe, Earth, and life involves the **scientific method.**

Earth systems science
geography
spatial
location
region
human–Earth relationships
movement
place
spatial analysis
process
physical geography
scientific method

1. What is unique about the science of geography? On the basis of information in this chapter, define physical geography and review the geographic approach.
2. In general terms, how might a physical geographer analyze water pollution in the Great Lakes?
3. Assess your geographic literacy by examining atlases and maps. What types of maps have you used: Political? Physical? Topographic? Do you know what map projections they employed? Do you know the names and locations of the four oceans, seven continents, and most individual countries? Can you identify the new countries that have emerged since 1990?
4. Suggest a representative example for each of the five geographic themes and use that theme in a sentence, such as, atmospheric and oceanic circulation spreading radioactive contamination is an example of the movement theme.
5. Have you made decisions today that involve geographic concepts discussed within the five themes presented? Explain briefly.

■ ***Describe*** systems analysis, open and closed systems, and feedback information, and ***relate*** these concepts to Earth systems.

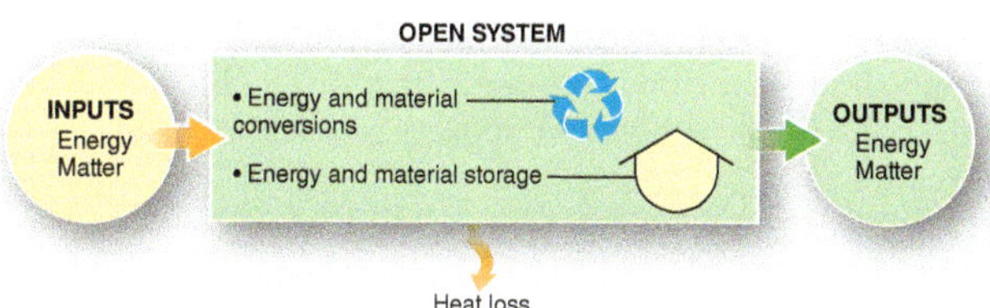

A **system** is any ordered, related set of things and their attributes, as distinct from their surrounding environment. Systems analysis is an important organizational and analytical tool used by geographers. Earth is an **open system** in terms of energy, receiving energy from the Sun, but it is essentially a **closed system** in terms of matter and physical resources.

As a system operates, "information" is returned to various points in the system via pathways of **feedback loops**. If the feedback information discourages change in the system, it is **negative feedback**. Further production of such feedback opposes system changes. Such negative feedback causes self-regulation in a natural system, stabilizing the system. If feedback information encourages change in the system, it is **positive feedback**. Further production of positive feedback stimulates system changes. Unchecked positive feedback in a system can create a runaway ("snowballing") condition. When the rates of inputs and outputs in the system are equal and the amounts of energy and matter in storage within the system are constant (or when they fluctuate around a stable average), the system is in **steady-state equilibrium**. A system that demonstrates a steady increase or decrease in system operations—a trend over time—is in **dynamic equilibrium**. A **threshold**, or tipping point, is the moment at which a system can no longer maintain its character, so it lurches to a new operational level, one that may not be compatible with previous conditions. Geographers often construct a simplified **model** of natural systems to better understand them.

Four immense open systems powerfully interact at Earth's surface: three **abiotic**, or nonliving, systems—the **atmosphere**, **hydrosphere** (including the **cryosphere**), and **lithosphere**—and a **biotic**, or living, system—the **biosphere**, or **ecosphere**.

system
open system
closed system
feedback loop
negative feedback
positive feedback
steady-state equilibrium
dynamic equilibrium
threshold
model
abiotic
biotic
atmosphere
hydrosphere
cryosphere
lithosphere
biosphere
ecosphere

6. Define systems theory as an organizational strategy. What are open systems, closed systems, and negative feedback? When is a system in a steady-state equilibrium condition? What type of system (open or closed) is the human body? A lake? A wheat plant?
7. Describe Earth as a system in terms of both energy and matter; use simple diagrams to illustrate your description.
8. What are the three abiotic spheres that make up Earth's environment? Relate these to the biotic sphere: the biosphere.

■ ***Explain*** Earth's reference grid: latitude and longitude and latitudinal geographic zones and time.

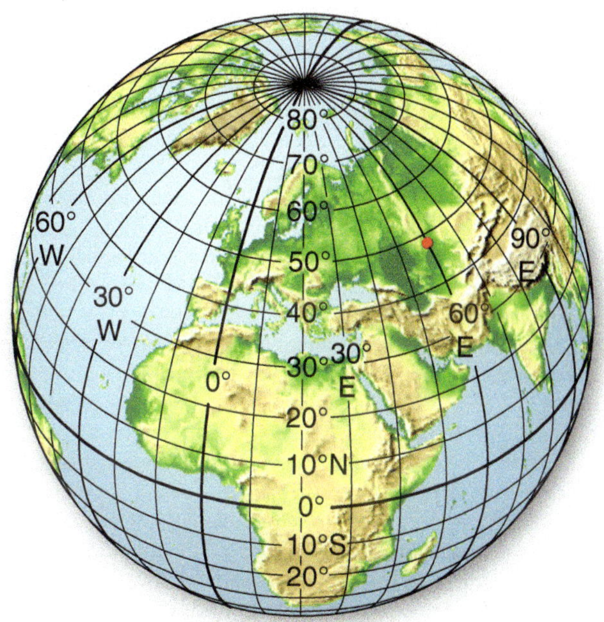

The science that studies Earth's shape and size is **geodesy**. Earth bulges slightly through the equator and is oblate (flattened) at the poles, producing a misshapen spheroid, a **geoid**. Absolute location on Earth is described with a specific reference grid of **parallels** of **latitude** (measuring distances north and south of the equator) and **meridians** of **longitude** (measuring distances east and west of a prime meridian). A historic breakthrough in navigation and timekeeping occurred with the establishment of an international **prime meridian** (0° through Greenwich, England) and the invention of precise chronometers that enabled accurate measurement of longitude. A **great circle** is any circle of Earth's circumference whose center coincides with the center of Earth. Great circle routes are the shortest distance between two points on Earth. **Small circles** are those whose centers do not coincide with Earth's center. Latitude, longitude, and elevation are accurately calibrated using a handheld **Global Positioning System (GPS)** instrument that reads radio signals from satellites.

The prime meridian provided the basis for **Greenwich Mean Time** (**GMT**), the world's first universal time system. A corollary of the prime meridian is the 180° meridian, the **International Date Line**, which marks the place where each day officially begins. Today, **Coordinated Universal Time** (**UTC**) is the worldwide standard and the basis for international time zones. **Daylight saving time** is a seasonal change of clocks by 1 hour in summer months.

geodesy
geoid

latitude
parallel
longitude
meridian
prime meridian
great circle
small circle
Global Positioning System (GPS)
Greenwich Mean Time (GMT)
International Date Line
Coordinated Universal Time (UTC)
daylight saving time

9. Draw a simple sketch describing Earth's shape and size.
10. How did Eratosthenes use Sun angles to figure out that the 5000-stadia distance between Alexandria and Syene was 1/50 of Earth's circumference? Once he knew this fraction of Earth's circumference, how did he calculate the entirety of Earth's circumference?
11. Define latitude and parallel and define longitude and meridian using a simple sketch with labels.
12. Define a great circle, great circle routes, and a small circle. In terms of these concepts, describe the equator, other parallels, and meridians.
13. Identify the various latitudinal geographic zones that roughly subdivide Earth's surface. In which zone do you live?
14. What does timekeeping have to do with longitude? Explain this relationship. How is Coordinated Universal Time (UTC) determined on Earth?
15. What and where is the prime meridian? How was the location originally selected? Describe the meridian that is opposite the prime meridian on Earth's surface.
16. What is GPS and how does it assist you in finding location and elevation on Earth? Give a couple of examples where GPS technology was utilized to correct heights for some famous mountains.

- ***Define*** cartography and mapping basics: map scale and map projections.

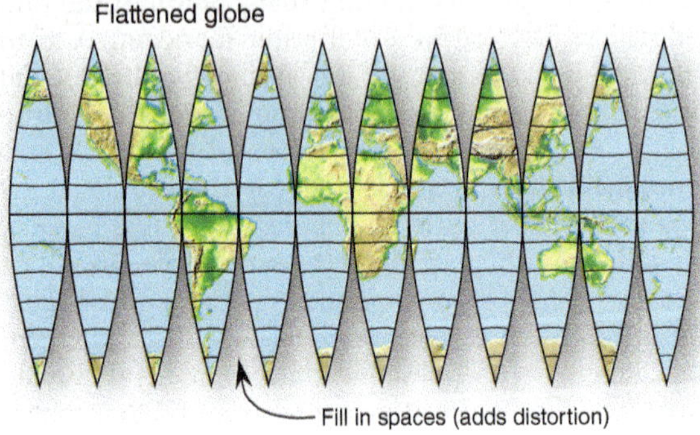

A **map** is a generalized view of an area, usually some portion of Earth's surface, as seen from above and greatly reduced in size. **Cartography** is the science and art of mapmaking. For the spatial portrayal of Earth's physical systems, geographers use maps. **Scale** is the ratio of the image on a map to the real world; it relates a unit on the map to an identical unit on the ground. Cartographers create a **map projection** for specific purposes, selecting the best compromise of projection for each application. Compromise is always necessary because Earth's round, three-dimensional surface cannot be exactly duplicated on a flat, two-dimensional map. **Equal area** (equivalence), **true shape** (conformality), true direction, and true distance are all considerations in selecting a projection. The **Mercator projection** is in the cylindrical class; it has true-shape qualities and straight lines that show constant direction. A **rhumb line** denotes constant direction and appears as a straight line on the Mercator.

map
cartography
scale
map projection
equal area
true shape
Mercator projection
rhumb line

17. Define cartography. Explain why it is an integrative discipline.
18. What is map scale? In what three ways may it be expressed on a map?
19. State whether the following ratios are large scale, medium scale, or small scale: 1:3,168,000; 1:24,000; 1:250,000.
20. Describe the differences between the characteristics of a globe and those that result when a flat map is prepared.
21. What type of map projection is used in Figure 13? In Figure 20?

- ***Describe*** remote sensing and the geographic information system (GIS), and ***explain*** how both tools are used in geographic analysis.

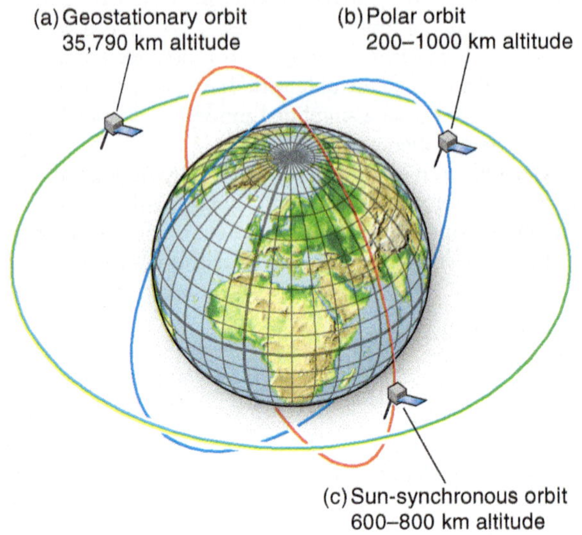

Orbital and aerial **remote sensing** analyzes the operation of Earth's systems. Satellites do not take photographs, but record images that are transmitted to Earth-based receivers. Satellite images are recorded in digital form for later processing, enhancement, and generation.

The mountain of data collected is put to work using **geographic information system (GIS)** technology. Computers process geographic information from direct surveys and remote sensing in complex ways never before possible. GIS methodology is an important step in better understanding Earth's systems and is a vital career opportunity for geographers.

The science of physical geography is in a unique position to synthesize the spatial, environmental, and human aspects of our increasingly complex relationship with our home planet—Earth.

remote sensing
geographic information system (GIS)

22. What is remote sensing? What are you viewing when you observe a weather satellite image on TV or in the newspaper? Explain.
23. Describe the *Terra*, *Landsat*, *GOES*, and *NOAA* satellites and explain them using several examples. Go to the NASA or ESA (European Space Agency) web site and view some satellite images.
24. If you were in charge of planning the development of a large tract of land, how would GIS methodologies assist you? How might planning and zoning be affected if a portion of the tract in the GIS is a floodplain or prime agricultural land?

MasteringGEOGRAPHY™

Visit http://www.masteringgeography.com/ for several figure animations, satellite loops, self-study quizzes, flashcards, visual glossary, case studies, career links, text reference maps, RSS Feeds, and an ebook version of *Elemental Geosystems*. Included are many geography web links to interesting Internet sources that support this chapter.

The Four Corners region featured in the *Geosystems Now* case study for this chapter, imaged by NASA's *Terra* Satellite. *Terra* is a polar-orbiting satellite that began service in 2000 and is managed by NASA at its Goddard Space Flight Center in partnership with the Jet Propulsion Laboratory. *Terra's* MODIS sensor captures true-color images and is an important tool in monitoring and analyzing Earth's systems. The more than 5-ton craft orbits at an average altitude of 670 km (416 mi). Clockwise from the upper-left in the scene is Utah, then Colorado, New Mexico, and Arizona. Checking a map of the region can you identify some of the features? [NASA/GSFC.]

Solar Energy, Seasons, and the Atmosphere

Solar Energy, Seasons, and the Atmosphere

These boys and a donkey haul water on Fogo Island in the tropical West African country of Cape Verde. Note their shadow is cast almost directly beneath them. The inset photo captures the experience of having the Sun directly overhead—the subsolar point. [Bobbé Christopherson.]

KEY LEARNING CONCEPTS

After reading the chapter, you should be able to:

- ***Distinguish*** among galaxies, stars, and planets, and ***locate*** Earth.
- ***Describe*** the Sun's operation, and ***explain*** the characteristics of the solar wind and the electromagnetic spectrum of radiant energy.
- ***Define*** solar altitude, solar declination, and daylength, and ***describe*** the annual variability of each—Earth's seasonality.
- ***Construct*** a general model of the atmosphere based on composition, temperature, and function, and ***diagram*** this model in a simple sketch.
- ***Describe*** conditions within the stratosphere; specifically, ***review*** the function and status of the ozonosphere, or ozone layer.
- ***Distinguish*** between natural and anthropogenic variable gases and materials in the lower atmosphere, and ***describe*** the sources and effects of air pollution and acid deposition.

Humans Help Define the Atmosphere

The survival of humans in space depends on our knowledge of the upper atmosphere. Astronaut Mark Lee, on a spacewalk in 1994 (*STS-64*), was 241 km (150 mi) above the surface, in orbit (Figure GN 1). Beyond the protective shield of Earth's atmosphere, he was traveling at 28,165 kmph (17,500 mph), which is almost nine times faster than a high-speed rifle bullet. Where the Sun hit his spacesuit, temperatures reached +120°C (+248°F) and in the shadows, temperatures dropped to some −150°C (−238°F). The vacuum of space was around him. Radiation and solar wind impacted his suit's surface. To survive in the upper atmosphere is an obvious challenge, one that relies on the ability of National Aeronautics and Space Administration (NASA) spacesuits to duplicate the Earth's atmosphere.

What features must a spacesuit provide for human survival? The suit must give all the protection provided by the atmosphere, such as blocking radiation and particle impacts. The suit needs to protect the interior from thermal extremes.

FIGURE GN 1 An untethered *STS-64* astronaut as a satellite in Earth orbit on a working spacewalk. [NASA.]

Earth's oxygen–carbon dioxide processing systems must be replicated in the suit, as must fluid delivery and waste management systems. The suit must maintain an internal air pressure against the space vacuum, and for pure oxygen, this is 4.7 psi (32.4 kPa), which roughly equals the pressure of only oxygen, water vapor, and CO_2 gases together at sea level. All 18,000 parts of the spacesuit work to duplicate what the atmosphere does for us on a daily basis.

In an earlier era before orbital flights, scientists didn't know how a human could survive in space or how to design an artificial atmosphere that is the modern spacesuit. In 1960, Air Force Captain Joseph Kittinger, Jr., stood at the opening of a small, unpressurized compartment, floating at 31.3 km (19.5 mi) altitude, dangling from a helium-filled balloon. The air pressure is barely measurable—this altitude is the beginning of space in experimental aircraft testing. He then leaped into the stratospheric void and placed himself at tremendous personal risk for an experimental reentry into the atmosphere (Figure GN 2). He carried an instrument pack on his seat, his main chute, and pure oxygen for his breathing mask.

Initially frightening to him was that he heard nothing, no rushing sound, for there was not enough air to produce any sound. The fabric of his pressure suit did not flutter, for there was not enough air to create friction against the cloth. His speed was remarkable, owing to the lack of air resistance in the stratosphere. Captain Kittinger quickly accelerated to

FIGURE GN 2 A remotely triggered camera captures a stratospheric leap into history. [Volkmar Wentzel/NGS Image Collection, *National Geographic Magazine*, Dec. 1960, p. 855. All rights reserved.]

988 kmph (614 mph), near the speed of sound at sea level.

His free fall took him through the stratosphere and its ozone layer, as the frictional drag of denser layers of atmospheric gases slowed his body. He dropped into the lower atmosphere, finally falling below airplane flying altitudes. His free fall lasted 4 minutes and 25 seconds to the opening of his main chute at 5500 m (18,000 ft). He safely drifted to Earth's surface. This remarkable 13-minute 35-second voyage through 99% of the atmospheric mass remains a record to this day.

The experiences of these two men illustrate the evolution of our understanding of upper atmosphere survival. From Kittinger's dangerous leap of discovery to the now routine spacewalks of astronauts such as Mark Lee, scientists have gained the ability to duplicate the atmosphere. This chapter explores solar energy, the seasons, and Earth's atmosphere. ■

The Universe is populated with at least 125 billion galaxies. One of these is our own Milky Way Galaxy, and it contains about 300 billion stars, according to a new 2010 estimate. Among these stars is an average yellow star, the Sun, although the dramatic *SOHO* satellite image in Figure 2 seems anything but average! Our Sun radiates energy in all directions and upon its family of orbiting planets. Of special interest to us is the solar energy that falls on the third planet, our immediate home.

In this chapter: Incoming solar energy that arrives at the top of Earth's atmosphere establishes the pattern of energy input that drives Earth's physical systems and that daily influences our lives. This solar energy input to the atmosphere, plus Earth's tilt and rotation, produces daily, seasonal, and annual patterns of changing daylength and Sun angle. The Sun is the ultimate energy source for most life processes in our biosphere.

We examine the modern atmosphere using criteria of composition, temperature, and function. Our look at the atmosphere also includes the spatial aspects of both natural and human-produced air pollution. We all participate in the atmosphere with each breath we take, the energy we consume, the traveling we do, and the products we buy. Human activities cause stratospheric ozone losses and the blight of acid deposition on ecosystems. These topics are essential to physical geography, for we are influencing the atmospheric composition for the future.

The Solar System

Our Solar System is located on a remote, trailing edge of the **Milky Way Galaxy**, a flattened, disk-shaped mass of stars with a core in the form of a barred, or elongated, shape. A super-massive black hole some 2 million solar masses in size, named *Sagittarius A** (pronounced "*Sagittarius A Star*"), sits in the galactic center. From our Earth-bound perspective in the Milky Way, the galaxy appears to stretch across the night sky like a narrow band of hazy light. On a clear night, the unaided eye can see only a few thousand of these billions of stars (Figure 1a, b)

According to prevailing theory, our Solar System condensed from a large, slowly rotating and collapsing cloud of dust and gas, a *nebula*. **Gravity**, the mutual attraction exerted by the mass of an object upon all other objects, was the key force in this condensing solar nebula. The beginnings of the formation of the Sun and its Solar System are estimated to have occurred more than 4.6 billion years ago.

The **planetesimal hypothesis**, or *dust-cloud hypothesis*, explains how suns condense from nebular clouds with planetesimals forming in orbits about the central mass. Astronomers study this formation process in other parts of the Galaxy, where planets are observed orbiting distant stars. By 2011, astronomers had discovered more than 1800 planets orbiting other stars. Initial results from the orbiting Kepler Telescope estimate the number of planets in the Milky Way at 50 billion, with some 500 million planets in habitable zones—moderate temperatures and water—a staggering discovery.

Dimensions, Distances, and Earth's Orbit

The **speed of light** is 300,000 kmps (kilometers per second), or 186,000 mps (miles per second)*—in other words, about 9.5 trillion kilometers per year, or nearly 6 trillion miles per year. This tremendous distance that light travels in a year is known as a *light-year*, and it is used as a unit of measurement for the vast Universe.

For spatial comparison, our Moon is an average distance of 384,400 km (238,866 mi) from Earth, or about 1.28 seconds in terms of light speed—for the *Apollo* astronauts this was a 3-day space voyage. Our entire Solar System is approximately 11 hours in diameter, measured by light speed (Figure 1c). In contrast, the Milky Way is about 100,000 light-years from side to side, and the known Universe that is observable from Earth stretches approximately 13 billion light-years in all directions. (See a Solar System simulator at http://space.jpl.nasa.gov/.)

Earth's orbit around the Sun is presently *elliptical*—a closed, oval path (Figure 1d). Earth's average distance from the Sun is approximately 150 million km (93 million mi), which means that light reaches Earth from the Sun in an average of 8 minutes and 20 seconds. Earth is at **perihelion**, its closest position to the Sun, during the Northern Hemisphere winter on January 3 at 147,255,000 km (91,500,000 mi). It is at **aphelion**, its farthest position from the Sun, during the Northern Hemisphere summer on July 4 at 152,083,000 km (94,500,000 mi). This seasonal difference in distance from the Sun causes a slight variation in the solar energy incoming to Earth, but is not an immediate reason for seasonal change.

Solar Energy: From Sun to Earth

Our Sun is unique to us, but is a commonplace star in the Galaxy. It is the ultimate energy source for most life processes in our biosphere. In the entire Solar System, the Sun is the only object having the enormous mass needed to sustain a nuclear reaction in its core and produce radiant energy. The solar mass produces tremendous pressure and high temperatures deep in its dense interior. Under these conditions, the Sun's abundant hydrogen atoms are forced together, and pairs of hydrogen nuclei are joined in the process of **fusion**, liberating enormous quantities of energy.

A sunny day can seem so peaceful, certainly unlike the violence taking place on the Sun. The Sun's principal outputs consist of the *solar wind* and radiant energy in portions of the *electromagnetic spectrum*. Let us trace each of these emissions across space to Earth.

*In more precise numbers, light speed is 299,792 kmps, or 186,282 mps.

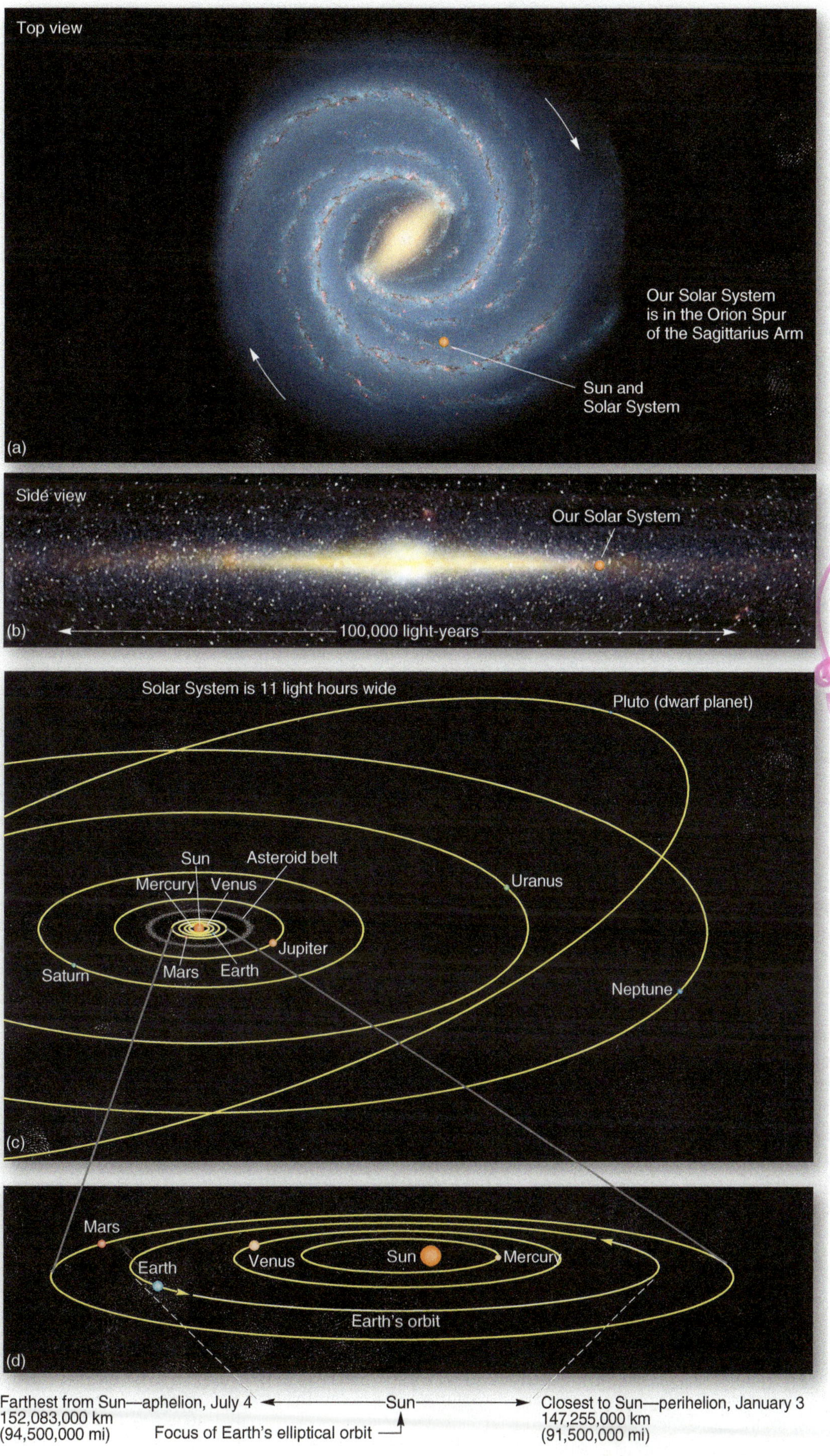

MG Animation Nebular Hypothesis

earth

FIGURE 1 Milky Way Galaxy, Solar System, and Earth's orbit. (a) The Milky Way Galaxy viewed from above in an artist's conception, and (b) an image in cross-section side view. (c) All of the planets except dwarf Pluto have orbits closely aligned to the plane of the ecliptic. In 2006, Pluto was reclassified as part of the Kuiper Asteroid Belt. (d) The four inner terrestrial planets and the structure of Earth's elliptical orbit, illustrating perihelion (closest) and aphelion (farthest) positions during the year, are shown. Have you ever observed the Milky Way Galaxy in the night sky? [(a) and (b) illustration courtesy of NASA/JPL.]

Solar Activity and Solar Wind

The Sun constantly emits clouds of electrically charged particles (principally hydrogen nuclei and free electrons) that surge outward in all directions from the Sun's surface. This stream of energetic material travels more slowly than light—at about 50 million km (31 million mi) a day—taking approximately 3 days to reach Earth. The term **solar wind** was first applied to this phenomenon in 1958.

The Sun's most conspicuous features are large **sunspots**, caused by magnetic storms on the Sun. Individual sunspots may range in diameter from 10,000 to 50,000 km (6200 to 31,000 mi), with some growing as large as 160,000 km (100,000 mi), more than 12 times Earth's diameter. These surface disturbances produce flares and prominences (Figure 2a). In addition, outbursts of charged material, referred to as *coronal mass ejections*, contribute to the solar wind flow of material into space—a large outburst occurred in February 2011.

A regular cycle exists for sunspot occurrences, averaging 11 years from maximum to maximum; however, the cycle may vary from 7 to 17 years (Figure 2b)—with a minimum in 2008 and a forecasted maximum in 2013. (For more on the sunspot cycle, see http://www.solarscience.msfc.nasa.gov/SunspotCycle.shtml; for the latest space weather, see http://www.spaceweather.com/.)

The charged particles of the solar wind first interact with Earth's magnetic field as they approach Earth. The **magnetosphere** is a magnetic field surrounding Earth, generated by dynamo-like motions within our planet. The magnetosphere deflects the solar wind toward both of Earth's poles, so that only a small portion of it enters the upper atmosphere.

Because the solar wind does not reach Earth's surface, research on this phenomenon must be conducted in space. In 1969, the *Apollo XI* astronauts exposed a piece of foil on the lunar surface as a solar wind experiment (Figure 3). When examined back on Earth, the exposed foil exhibited particle impacts that confirmed the character of the solar wind.

This interaction of the solar wind and the upper layers of Earth's atmosphere produces the remarkable **auroras** that occur toward both poles. These lighting effects are the *aurora borealis* (northern lights) and *aurora australis* (southern lights) in the upper atmosphere, 80–500 km (50–300 mi) above Earth's surface. They appear as folded sheets of green, yellow, blue, and red light that undulate across the skies of high latitudes poleward of 65°, as shown in Figure 4. During the 2001 solar maximum, auroras were visible as far south as Jamaica, Texas, and California. (For auroral activity, see http://www.swpc.noaa.gov/pmap/; for forecasts, see http://www.gi.alaska.edu.)

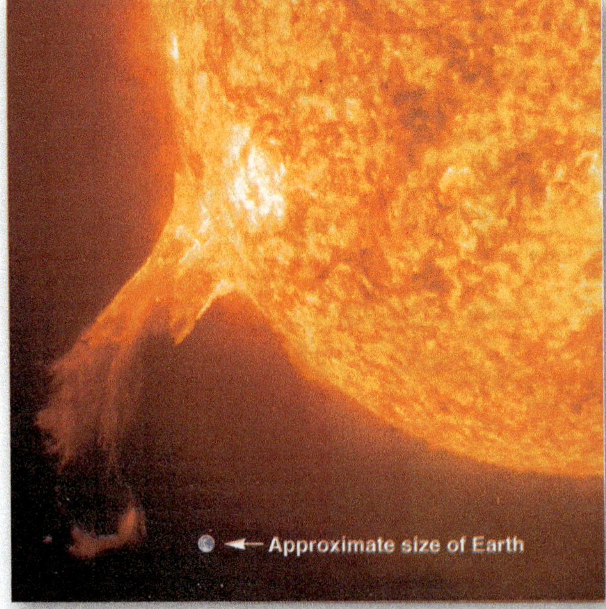

(a)

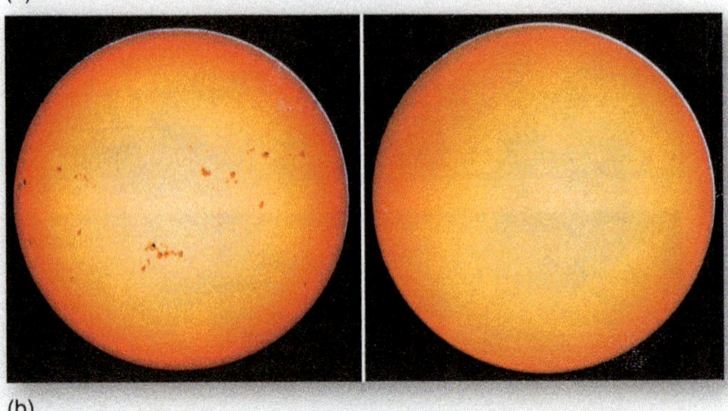

(b)

FIGURE 2 Image of the Sun and sunspots. (a) A dramatic Sun captured by instruments aboard the *SOHO* satellite. A prominence rises into the Sun's corona. Earth is shown for scale and is actually far smaller than the average sunspot. (b) The Sun at solar maximum in July 2000 and minimum in March 2009. Imaged by MDI (Michelson Doppler Imager) aboard satellite *SOHO*. [Images courtesy of SOHO/EIT Consortium (NASA and ESA); see http://sohowww.nascom.nasa.gov/.]

GEO REPORT 1 *Recent solar cycle*

In recent sunspot cycles, a solar minimum occurred in 1976 and a solar maximum in 1979, with more than 100 sunspots visible. Another minimum was reached in 1986, and an extremely active solar maximum followed in 1990–1991, with more than 200 sunspots visible at some time during the year. A sunspot minimum occurred in 1997, followed by an intense maximum of more than 200 in 2000–2001. The forecast for the maximum in 2013 is that it will be less than the 2000 max. The present solar cycle began in 2008 and carries the name *Cycle 24*. The record-tying global temperatures of 2010 took place during a solar minimum. Solar cycles are ruled out by scientists as a cause for increasing temperature trends.

FIGURE 3 Astronaut and solar wind experiment. Without a protective atmosphere, the lunar surface receives solar wind charged particles and all the Sun's electromagnetic radiation. An *Apollo XI* astronaut in 1969 deploys a sheet of foil in the solar wind experiment. Earth-bound scientists analyzed the foil upon the astronauts' return. Why wouldn't this experiment work if we set it up on Earth's surface? [NASA.]

(a)

(b)

FIGURE 4 Auroras from an orbital perspective. (a) Aurora australis and (b) aurora borealis, as seen from orbit. [(a) *Image* spacecraft, GSFC/NASA. (b) ISS astronaut Don Pettit/NASA.]

Electromagnetic Spectrum of Radiant Energy

The essential solar input to life is electromagnetic energy of various wavelengths. Solar radiation occupies a portion of the **electromagnetic spectrum** of radiant energy. This radiant energy travels at the speed of light to Earth. The total spectrum of this radiant energy is made up of different wavelengths. A **wavelength** is the distance between corresponding points on any two successive waves. The number of waves passing a fixed point in 1 second is the *frequency*. Note the wavelength plot below the chart in Figure 5.

The Sun emits radiant energy composed of 8% ultraviolet, X-ray, and gamma-ray wavelengths; 47% visible light wavelengths; and 45% infrared wavelengths. A portion of the electromagnetic spectrum is illustrated in Figure 5, with wavelengths increasing from the left to right side of the illustration. Note the wavelengths at which various phenomena and human applications of energy occur.

An important physical law states that all objects radiate energy in wavelengths related to their individual surface temperatures: The hotter the object, the shorter the wavelengths emitted. This law holds true for the Sun and Earth. Figure 6 shows that the hot Sun radiates shorter wavelength energy, concentrated around 0.5 μm (micrometer).

The Sun's surface temperature is about 6000 K (6273°C, 11,459°F), and its emission curve shown in the figure is similar to that predicted for an idealized 6000 K surface, or *blackbody radiator* (shown in Figure 6). An ideal blackbody absorbs and subsequently emits all the radiant energy that it receives. A hotter object like the Sun emits a much greater amount of energy per unit area of its surface than does a similar area of a cooler object like Earth. Shorter wavelength emissions are dominant at these higher temperatures.

Although cooler than the Sun, Earth radiates nearly all that it absorbs and acts as a blackbody (also shown in Figure 6). Because Earth is a cooler radiating body, longer wavelengths are emitted as radiation mostly in the infrared portion of the spectrum, centered around 10.0 μm. Some of the atmospheric gases vary in their response to radiation received, being transparent to some while absorbing others.

Figure 7 illustrates the flows of energy into and out of Earth systems. To summarize, the Sun's radiated energy is *shortwave radiation* that peaks in the short visible wavelengths, whereas Earth's radiated energy is *longwave radiation* concentrated in infrared wavelengths. Earth, clouds, sky, ground, and things that are terrestrial radiate longer wavelengths, in contrast to the Sun.

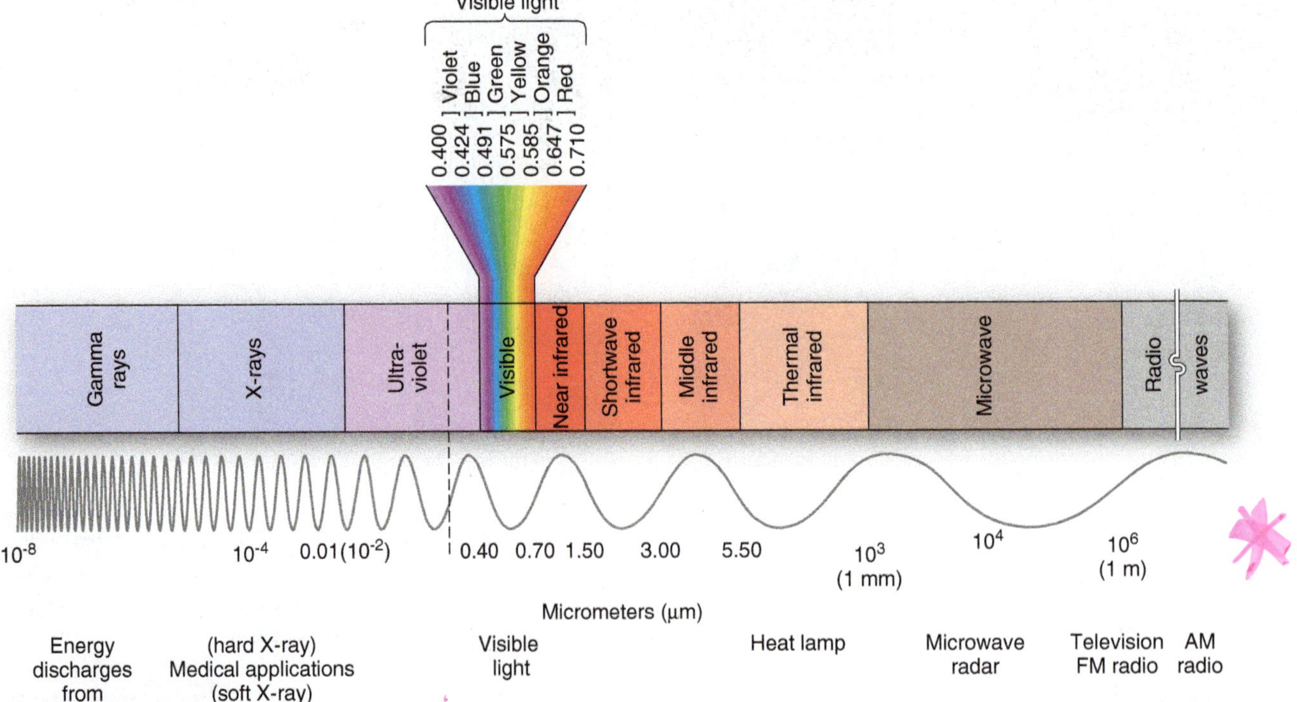

FIGURE 5 A portion of the electromagnetic spectrum of radiant energy.
Wavelength and frequency are two ways of describing electromagnetic wave motion. Short wavelengths (at left) are higher in frequency; long wavelengths (at right) are lower in frequency.

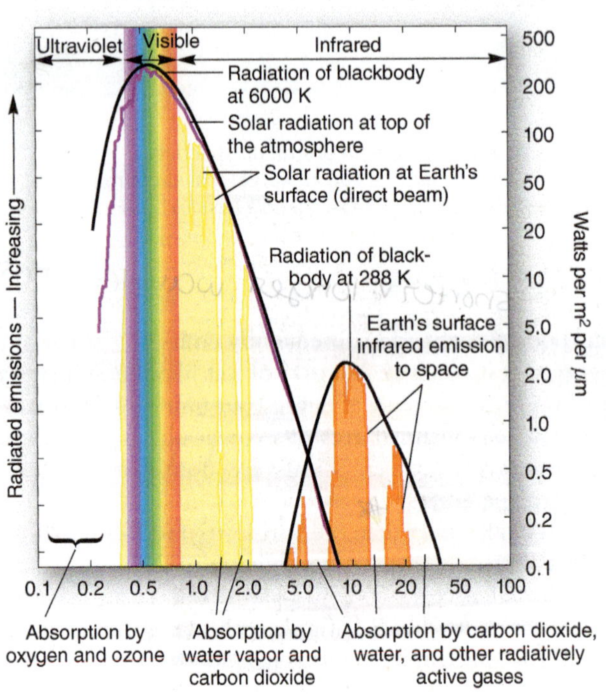

FIGURE 6 Solar and terrestrial energy distribution by wavelength.
A hotter Sun radiates shorter wavelengths, whereas a cooler Earth emits longer wavelengths. Dark lines represent ideal blackbody curves for the Sun and Earth. The dropouts in the plot lines for solar and terrestrial radiation represent absorption bands of water vapor, water, carbon dioxide, oxygen, ozone (O_3), and other gases. [Adapted from W. D. Sellers, *Physical Climatology* (Chicago: University of Chicago Press), p. 20. Used by permission.]

Incoming Energy at the Top of the Atmosphere

thermopause

The region at the top of the atmosphere, approximately 480 km (300 mi) above Earth's surface, is the **thermopause.** It is the outer boundary of Earth's energy system and provides a useful point at which to assess the arriving solar radiation before it is diminished by scattering and absorption in passage through the atmosphere.

Earth's distance from the Sun results in its interception of only one two-billionth of the Sun's total energy output. Nevertheless, this tiny fraction of energy from the Sun is an enormous amount of energy flowing into Earth's systems. Solar radiation that reaches a horizontal plane at Earth is **insolation**, derived from the words *incoming solar radiation*. Insolation specifically applies to radiation arriving at Earth's atmosphere and surface. The amount of insolation at the top of the atmosphere is expressed as the *solar constant*.

Solar Constant Knowing the amount of insolation is important to climatologists and other scientists. The **solar constant** is the average insolation received at the thermopause when Earth is at its average distance from the Sun, a value of 1372 W/m² (watts per square meter).* As

*A *watt* is equal to 1 joule (a unit of energy) per second and is the standard unit of power in the International System of Units (SI). In nonmetric *calorie* heat units, the solar constant is expressed as approximately 2 calories per square centimeter per minute, or 2 *langleys* per minute (a langley being 1 cal/cm²). A calorie is the amount of energy required to raise the temperature of 1 gram of water (at 15°C) 1 degree Celsius and is equal to 4.184 joules.

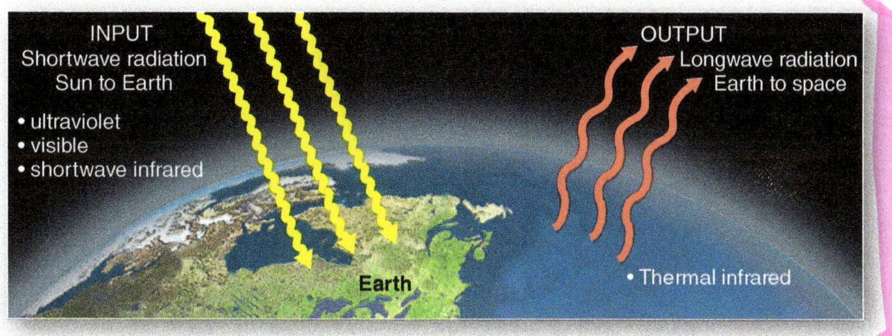

FIGURE 7 Earth's energy budget simplified.

we follow insolation through the atmosphere to Earth's surface, we see that the value of the solar constant is reduced by half or more through reflection, scattering, and absorption of shortwave radiation.

Uneven Distribution of Insolation Earth's curved surface presents a continually varying angle to the incoming parallel rays of insolation (Figure 8). Differences in the angle of solar rays at each latitude result in an uneven distribution of insolation and heating. The only point receiving insolation perpendicular to the surface (from directly overhead) is the **subsolar point**.

During the year, this point occurs at lower latitudes between the tropics (about 23.5° north and 23.5° south latitudes), where the energy received is more concentrated. All other places away from the subsolar point receive insolation at an angle less than 90° and thus experience more diffuse energy; this effect is pronounced at higher latitudes. In the opening photo for this chapter, we were at the subsolar point. Note the shadows are cast not at an angle, but directly below the boys hauling water—this was May 1 at 14.8° N latitude.

The thermopause above the equatorial region receives 2.5 times more insolation annually than the thermopause above the poles. Of lesser importance is the fact that the lower-angle solar rays toward the poles must pass through a greater thickness of atmosphere, resulting in greater losses of energy due to scattering, absorption, and reflection.

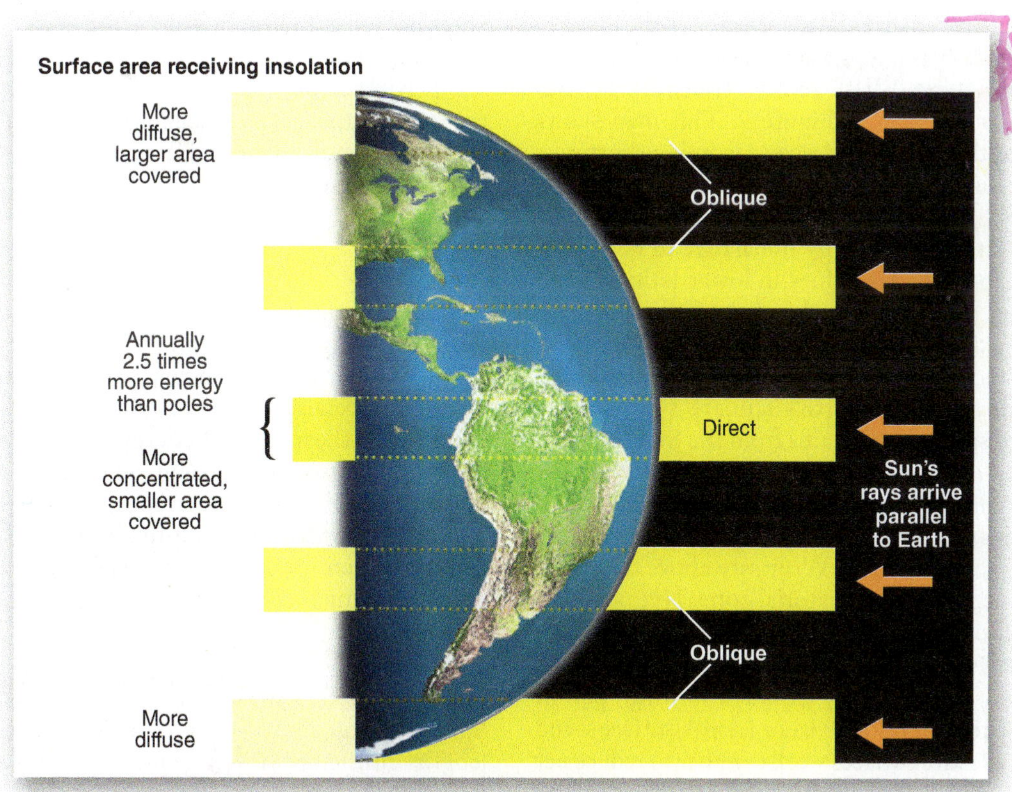

FIGURE 8 **Insolation receipts and Earth's curved surface.**
Solar insolation angles determine the concentration of energy receipts by latitude.

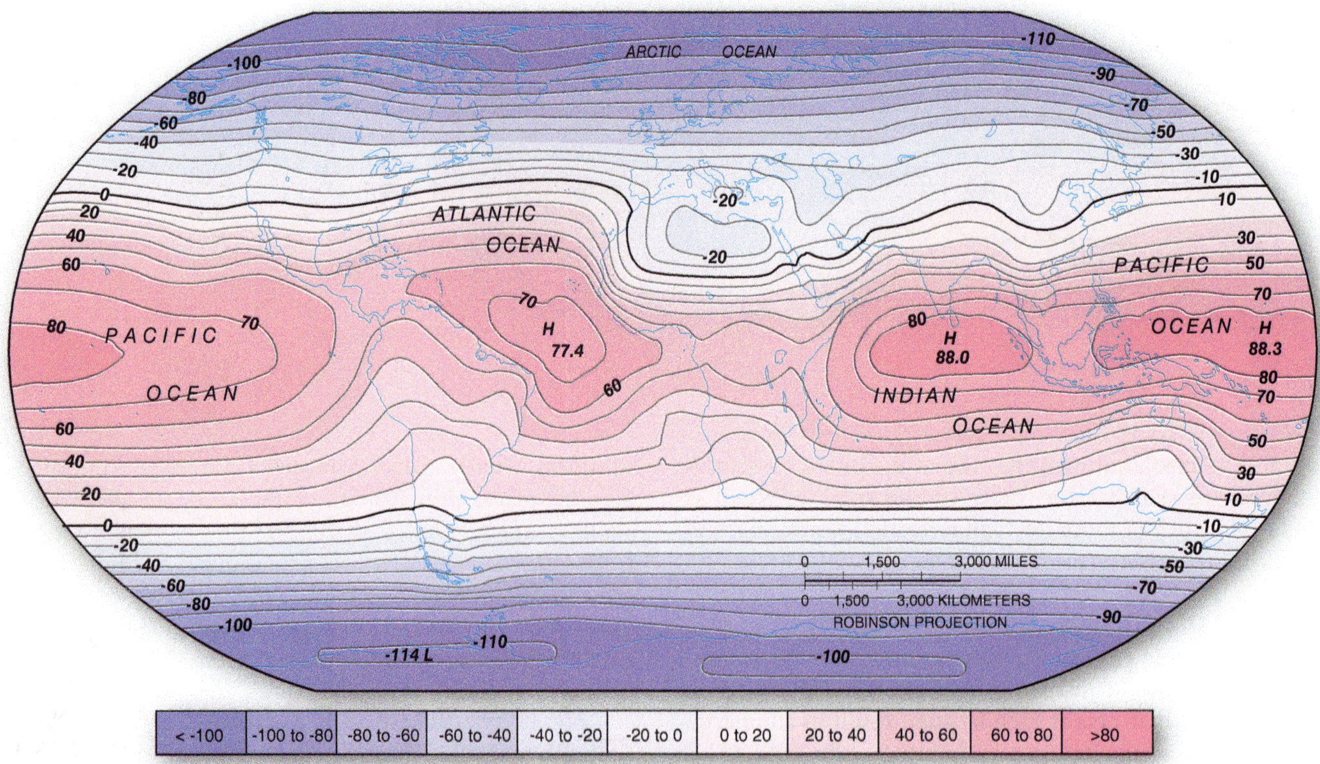

FIGURE 9 Daily net radiation patterns at the top of the atmosphere. Averaged daily net radiation flows measured at the top of the atmosphere by the Earth Radiation Budget Experiment (ERBE). Units are W/m². [Data for map courtesy of GSFC/NASA.]

Global Net Radiation Earth Radiation Budget Experiment (ERBE) instruments aboard several satellites measured shortwave and longwave flows of energy at the top of the atmosphere. ERBE sensors collected the data used to develop the map in Figure 9. This map shows *net radiation*, or the balance between incoming shortwave and outgoing longwave radiation—energy inputs minus energy outputs.

Note the latitudinal energy imbalance in net radiation on the map—positive values in lower latitudes and negative values toward the poles. In middle and high latitudes, approximately poleward of 36° north and south latitudes, net radiation is negative. This occurs in these higher latitudes because Earth's climate system loses more energy to space than it gains from the Sun, as measured at the top of the atmosphere. In the lower atmosphere, these polar energy deficits are offset by flows of energy from tropical energy surpluses. The largest net radiation values, averaging 80 W/m², are above the tropical oceans along a narrow equatorial zone. Net radiation minimums are lowest over Antarctica.

Of interest is the −20 W/m² area over the Sahara region of North Africa. Here typically clear skies—which permit great longwave radiation losses from Earth's surface—and light-colored reflective surfaces work together to reduce net radiation values at the thermopause. In other regions, clouds and atmospheric pollution in the lower atmosphere also affect net radiation patterns at the top of the atmosphere by reflecting more shortwave energy to space.

Having examined the flow of solar energy to Earth and the top of the atmosphere, let us now look at how seasonal changes affect the distribution of insolation as Earth orbits the Sun during the year.

The Seasons

Earth's periodic rhythms of warmth and cold, dawn and daylight, twilight and night, have fascinated humans for centuries. In fact, many ancient societies demonstrated an intense awareness of seasonal change and formally commemorated these natural energy rhythms with festivals, monuments, ground markings, and calendars (Figure 10). Such seasonal monuments and calendar markings are found worldwide, including thousands of sites in North America, demonstrating an ancient awareness of seasons and astronomical relations.

Seasonality

Seasonality refers to both the seasonal variation of the Sun's position above the horizon and the changing daylengths during the year. Seasonal variations are a response to changes in the Sun's **altitude**, or the angle between the horizon and the Sun. At sunrise or sunset, the Sun is

FIGURE 10 Stonehenge on the Salisbury Plain, England.
Neolithic peoples beginning about 5000 years ago constructed this complex of standing rock. The layout indicates important seasonal dates and precise lunar-cycle predictions. [Bobbé Christopherson.]

at the horizon, so its altitude is 0°. If during the day the Sun reaches halfway between the horizon and directly overhead, it is at 45° altitude. If the Sun reaches the point directly overhead, it is at 90° altitude. The Sun is directly overhead (90° altitude, or *zenith*) only at the *subsolar point*, where insolation is at a maximum.

The Sun's **declination** is the latitude of the subsolar point. Declination annually migrates through 47° of latitude, moving between the Tropic of Cancer and Tropic of Capricorn latitudes. Other than Hawai'i, which is between 19° N and 22° N latitude, the subsolar point does not reach the continental United States or Canada; all other states and provinces are too far north.

Also, seasonality means changing **daylength**, or duration of exposure to insolation. Daylength varies during the year, depending on latitude. The equator always receives equal hours of day and night: If you live in Ecuador, Kenya, or Singapore, every day and night is 12 hours long, year-round. People living along 40° N latitude (Philadelphia, Denver, Madrid, Beijing) or 40° S latitude (Buenos Aires, Capetown, Melbourne) experience about 6 hours' difference in daylight between winter (9 hours) and summer (15 hours). At 50° N or S latitude (Winnipeg, Paris, Falkland, Malvinas Islands), people experience almost 8 hours of annual daylength variation.

II CRITICAL THINKING 1

A way to calculate sunrise and sunset

Sunrise is the moment when the disk of the Sun first appears above the horizon in the east; *sunset* is that moment when it totally disappears below the horizon in the west. For a useful sunrise and sunset calculator for any location, go to http://www.srrb.noaa.gov/highlights/sunrise/sunrise.html, select a city near you or select "Enter lat/long" and enter your coordinates, enter your time difference offset from UTC and whether you are on daylight saving time, and enter the date you are checking. Then click "Calculate" to see the solar declination and times for sunrise and sunset. Give this a try.

Reasons for Seasons

Seasons result from variations in the Sun's *altitude* above the horizon, the Sun's *declination* (latitude location of the subsolar point), and *daylength* during the year. These, in turn, are created by several physical factors that operate in concert: Earth's *revolution* in orbit around the Sun, its daily *rotation* on its axis, its *tilted axis*, the unchanging *orientation of its axis*, and its *sphericity* (Table 1). Of course, the essential ingredient is having a single source of radiant energy—the Sun. We now look at each of these factors individually. As we do, please note the distinction between revolution—Earth's travel around the Sun—and rotation—Earth's spinning on its axis (Figure 11).

Revolution Earth's orbital **revolution** about the Sun is shown in Figures 1d and 11. Earth's speed in orbit averages 107,280 kmph (66,660 mph). This speed, together with Earth's distance from the Sun, determines the time required for one revolution around the Sun and therefore the length of the year and duration of the seasons. Earth completes its annual revolution in 365.2422 days. This number is based

TABLE 1 Five Reasons for Seasons

Factor	Description
Revolution	Orbit around the Sun; requires 365.24 days to complete at 107,280 kmph (66,660 mph)
Rotation	Earth turning on its axis; takes approximately 24 hours to complete
Tilt	Axis is aligned at about 23.5° angle from a perpendicular to the plane of the ecliptic (the plane of Earth's orbit)
Axial parallelism	Remains in a fixed alignment, with Polaris directly overhead at the North Pole throughout the year
Sphericity	Appears as an oblate spheroid to the Sun's parallel rays; the geoid

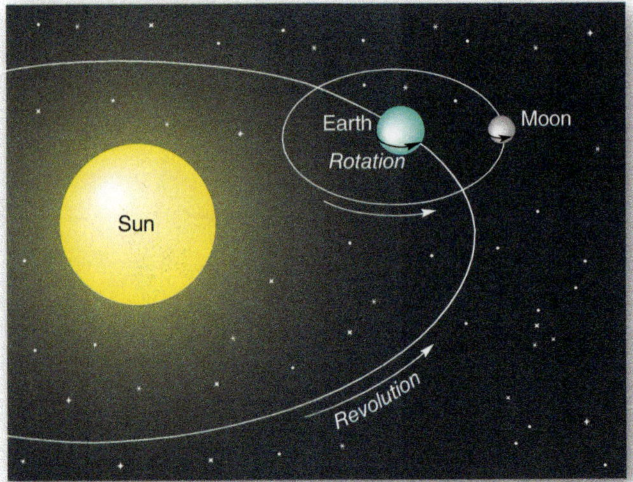

FIGURE 11 Earth's revolution and rotation.
Earth's *revolution* about the Sun and *rotation* on its axis, viewed from above Earth's orbit. Note the Moon's rotation on its axis and revolution are counterclockwise, as well.

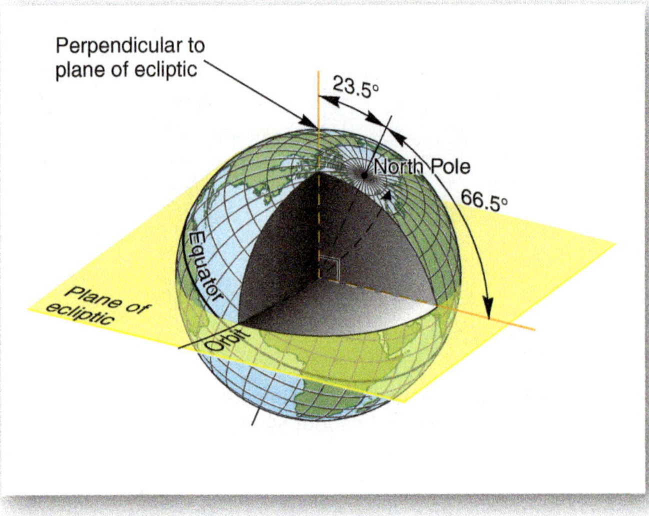

FIGURE 12 The plane of Earth's orbit—the ecliptic—and Earth's axial tilt.
Note on the illustration that the plane of the equator is inclined to the plane of the ecliptic at about 23.5°.

on a *tropical year*, measured from equinox to equinox, or the elapsed time between two crossings of the equator by the Sun.

Rotation Earth's **rotation**, or turning on its axis, is a complex motion that averages slightly less than 24 hours in duration. Rotation determines daylength, creates the apparent deflection of winds and ocean currents, and produces the twice-daily rise and fall of the ocean tides in relation to the gravitational pull of the Sun and the Moon.

Earth rotates about its *axis*, an imaginary line extending through the planet from the geographic North Pole to the South Pole. When viewed from above the North Pole, Earth rotates counterclockwise around this axis. Viewed from above the equator, Earth rotates west to east, or eastward. This eastward rotation creates the Sun's *apparent* westward daily journey from sunrise in the east to sunset in the west. Of course, the Sun actually remains in a fixed position in the center of the Solar System.

Although every point on Earth takes the same 24 hours to complete one rotation, the linear velocity of rotation at any point on Earth's surface varies dramatically with latitude. The equator is 40,075 km (24,902 mi) long; therefore, rotational velocity at the equator must be approximately 1675 kmph (1041 mph) to cover that distance in one day. At 60° latitude, a parallel is only half the length of the equator, or 20,038 km (12,451 mi) long, so the rotational velocity there is 838 kmph (521 mph). At the poles, the velocity is 0. This variation in rotational velocity establishes the effect of the Coriolis force.

Earth's rotation produces the diurnal (daily) pattern of day and night. The dividing line between day and night is the **circle of illumination** (as illustrated in Figure 13). Because this day–night dividing circle of illumination intersects the equator, *daylength at the equator is always evenly divided*—12 hours of day and 12 hours of night. All other latitudes experience uneven daylength through the seasons, except for 2 days a year, on the equinoxes.

Tilt of Earth's Axis To understand Earth's *axial tilt*, imagine a plane (a flat surface) that intersects Earth's elliptical orbit about the Sun, with half of the Sun and Earth above the plane and half below. Such a plane touching all points of Earth's orbit is the **plane of the ecliptic**. Earth's tilted axis remains fixed relative to this plane as Earth revolves around the Sun. The plane of the ecliptic is important to our discussion of Earth's seasons. Now, imagine a perpendicular (at a 90° angle) line passing through the plane. From this perpendicular, Earth's axis is tilted about 23.5°. It forms a 66.5° angle from the plane itself (Figure 12). The axis through

GEO REPORT 2 ***Why do we always see the same side of the Moon?***

Note in Figure 11 that the Moon both revolves around Earth and rotates on its axis in a counterclockwise direction when viewed from above Earth's North Pole. It does both these motions in the same amount of time. The Moon's speed in orbit varies slightly during the month, whereas its rotation speed is constant, so we see about 59% of the lunar surface during the month, or exactly 50% at any one moment—always the same side facing Earth.

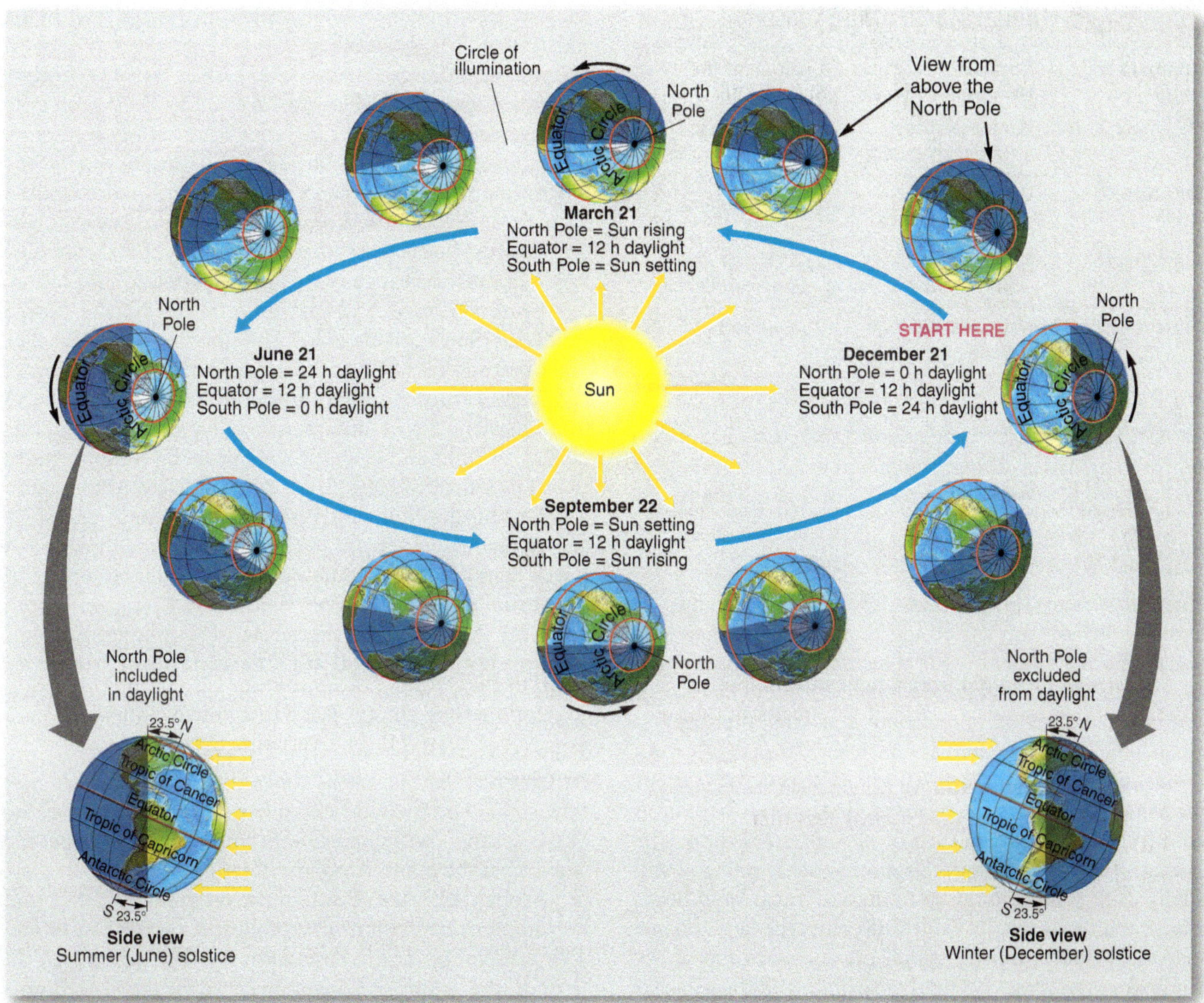

FIGURE 13 Annual march of the seasons.
Annual march of the seasons as Earth revolves about the Sun. Shading indicates the changing position of the circle of illumination. Note the hours of daylight for the equator and the poles. As you read, begin on the right side at December 21 and move counterclockwise. Given this illustration, turn to the back cover of this textbook and see whether you can determine the month during which the *Apollo* astronaut made the Earth photo. (The answer is on this book's copyright page.)

Earth's two poles points just slightly off Polaris, which is named, appropriately, the *North Star*.

This text uses "about" with the tilt angle just described because Earth's axial tilt changes over a complex 41,000-year cycle. The axial tilt ranges roughly between 22° and 24.5° from a perpendicular to the plane of the ecliptic. The present tilt is 23° 27′ (or 66° 33′ from the plane). In decimal numbers, 23° 27′ is approximately 23.45°. For convenience, this is rounded off to a 23.5° tilt (or 66.5° from the plane) in most usage. Scientific evidence shows that the angle of tilt is lessening in its 41,000-year cycle.

Axial Parallelism Throughout our annual journey around the Sun, Earth's axis *maintains the same alignment* relative to the plane of the ecliptic and to Polaris and other stars. You can see this consistent alignment in Figure 13. If we

CRITICAL THINKING 2

Astronomical factors vary over long time frames

Consider the variability of Earth's axial tilt, its orbit about the Sun, and a wobble to the axis. Compare these changing conditions to the information in Table 1 and the related figures in this chapter.

What do you think the effect on Earth's seasons would be if the tilt of the axis was decreased? Or if the tilt was increased? You can take a ball or piece of round fruit and mark the poles and move the sphere around a light bulb, as if revolving it around the Sun. Note the alignment with no tilt and then with a 90° tilt to help complete your analysis. Or what if Earth's orbit was more circular, as opposed to its present elliptical shape? Earth's orbit actually does vary like this in a 100,000-year cycle.

TABLE 2 Annual March of the Seasons

Approximate Date	Northern Hemisphere Name	Location of the Subsolar Point
December 21–22	Winter solstice (December solstice)	23.5° S latitude (Tropic of Capricorn)
March 20–21	Vernal equinox (March equinox)	0° (Equator)
June 20–21	Summer solstice (June solstice)	23.5° N latitude (Tropic of Cancer)
September 22–23	Autumnal equinox (September equinox)	0° (Equator)

compared the axis in different months, it would always appear parallel to itself, a condition known as **axial parallelism**.

Annual March of the Seasons

During the march of the seasons on Earth, daylength is the most obvious way of sensing changes in season at latitudes away from the equator. The extremes of daylength occur in December and June. The times around December 21 and June 21 are *solstices*. Strictly speaking, the solstices are specific points in time at which the Sun's declination is at its position farthest north at the **Tropic of Cancer** or farthest south at the **Tropic of Capricorn**. "Tropic" is from *tropicus*, meaning a turn or change, so a tropic latitude is where the Sun's declination appears to stand still briefly (Sun stance, or *sol stice*); then it "turns" and heads toward the other tropic. Table 2 presents the key seasonal anniversary dates during which the specific time of the equinoxes or solstices occur, their names, and the subsolar point location (declination).

Figure 13 demonstrates the annual march of the seasons and illustrates Earth's relationship to the Sun during the year. Let us begin with December, on the right side of the illustration. On December 21 or 22, at the moment of the **winter solstice** ("winter Sun stance"), or **December solstice**, the circle of illumination excludes the North Pole region from sunlight, but includes the South Pole region. The subsolar point is about 23.5° S latitude, the Tropic of Capricorn parallel. The Northern Hemisphere is tilted away from these more direct rays of sunlight—our northern winter—thereby creating a lower angle for the incoming solar rays and thus a more diffuse pattern of insolation.

From about 66.5° N latitude to 90° N (the North Pole), the Sun remains below the horizon the entire day. This latitude (about 66.5° N) marks the **Arctic Circle**, the southernmost parallel (in the Northern Hemisphere) that experiences a 24-hour period of darkness. During this period, twilight and dawn provide some lighting for more than a month at the beginning and end of the Arctic night.

During the following 3 months, daylength and solar angles gradually increase in the Northern Hemisphere as Earth completes one-fourth of its orbit. The moment of the **vernal equinox**, or **March equinox**, occurs on March 20 or 21. At that time, the circle of illumination passes through both poles so that all locations on Earth experience a 12-hour day and a 12-hour night. People living around 40° N latitude (New York, Denver) have gained 3 hours of daylight since the December solstice. At the North Pole, the Sun peeks above the horizon for the first time since the previous September; at the South Pole, the Sun is setting—a dramatic 3-day "moment" for the people working at the Scott–Amundsen Base.

From March, the seasons move on to June 20 or 21 and the moment of the **summer solstice**, or **June solstice**. The subsolar point migrates from the equator to 23.5° N latitude, the Tropic of Cancer. Because the circle of illumination now includes the North Polar region, everything north of the Arctic Circle receives 24 hours of daylight—the *Midnight Sun* (Figure 14). In contrast, the region

(a)

(b)

FIGURE 14 The Midnight Sun and long days.
(a) Antarctic sunset, 11:30 P.M., approaching the continent of Antarctica at 63° S latitude in December; sunrise was about 2 hours later. The low Sun angle produced incredible sunset colors for hours. Note a large iceberg and ice-covered mountains in the distance. (b) The Midnight Sun seen from a research ship in the Arctic Ocean at 80° N latitude in June. Can you find the December and June perspectives in Figure 13? [Bobbé Christopherson.]

from the **Antarctic Circle** to the South Pole (66.5°–90° S latitude) is in darkness.

September 22 or 23 is the moment in time of the **autumnal equinox**, or **September equinox**, when Earth's orientation is such that the circle of illumination again passes through both poles so that all parts of the globe experience a 12-hour day and a 12-hour night. The subsolar point returns to the equator, with days growing shorter to the north and longer to the south. Researchers stationed at the South Pole see the disk of the Sun just rising, ending their 6 months of darkness. In the Northern Hemisphere, autumn arrives, a time of many colorful changes in the landscape, whereas in the Southern Hemisphere it is spring.

Seasonal Observations In the midlatitudes of the Northern Hemisphere, the position of sunrise on the horizon migrates from day to day, from the southeast in December to the northeast in June. Over the same period, the point of sunset migrates from the southwest to the northwest. The Sun's altitude at local noon at 40° N latitude increases from a 26° angle above the horizon at the winter (December) solstice to a 73° angle above the horizon at the summer (June) solstice—a range of 47° (Figure 15). Seasonal change is quite noticeable across the landscape away from the equator. Think back over the past year. What seasonal changes have you observed in vegetation, temperatures, and weather?

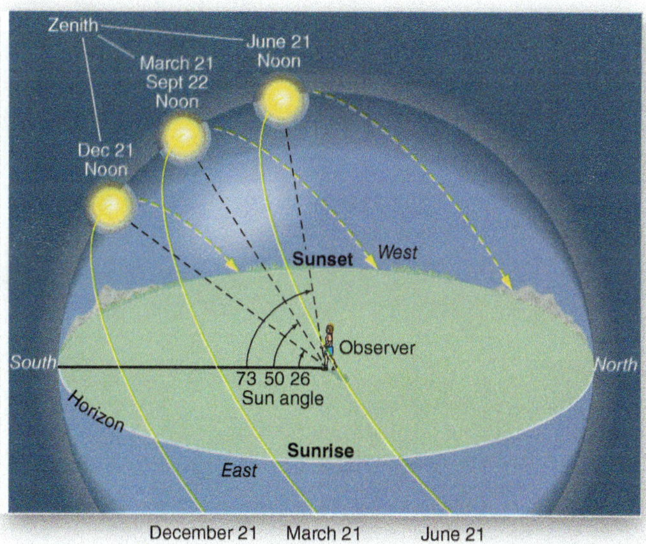

FIGURE 15 Seasonal observations—sunrise, noon, and sunset through the year.
Seasonal observations are at 40° N latitude for the December solstice, March equinox, June solstice, and September equinox. The Sun's altitude increases from 26° above the horizon in December to 73° above the horizon in June—a difference of 47°. Note the changing position of sunrise and sunset along the horizon during the year.

Animation
Earth–Sun Rotations, Seasons

II CRITICAL THINKING 3
Measuring the Sun's changing altitude

Applying the concepts in Figure 15, use a protractor and stick, pencil, or ruler to measure the angle of the Sun's altitude at noon (or 1 P.M., if in daylight saving time). Do not look at the Sun; rather, with your back to the Sun, align the stick so that it casts no shadow as you measure its rays against the protractor. Place this measurement in your notebook and affix a Post-It® in the text to remind you to repeat the measurement near the end of the semester. Compare and analyze seasonal change using your different measurements of the Sun's altitude.

Atmospheric Composition, Temperature, and Function

Earth's atmosphere is a unique reservoir of gases, the product of 4.6 billion years of development. It protects us from hostile radiation and particles from the Sun and beyond. The atmosphere serves as an efficient filter. As shown in *Geosystems Now*, when humans venture away from the lower regions of the atmosphere, they must wear elaborate protective spacesuits that sustain them, providing services the atmosphere performs for us all the time.

The modern atmosphere probably is the fourth general atmosphere in Earth's history, a gaseous mixture of ancient origin, the sum of all the exhalations and inhalations of life interacting on Earth throughout time. The principal substance of this atmosphere is air, the medium of life as well as a major industrial and chemical raw material. *Air* is a simple mixture of gases that is naturally odorless, colorless, tasteless, and formless, blended so thoroughly that it behaves as if it were a single gas.

As a practical matter, we consider the top of our atmosphere to be around 480 km (300 mi) above Earth's surface, the same altitude we used for measuring the solar constant and insolation received. Beyond that altitude is the **exosphere**, which means "outer sphere," where the rarefied, less dense atmosphere is nearly a vacuum. It contains scarce lightweight hydrogen and helium atoms, weakly bound by gravity as far as 32,000 km (20,000 mi) from Earth.

Atmospheric Profile

Think of Earth's modern atmosphere as a thin envelope of imperfectly shaped concentric "shells" or "spheres" that grade into one another, all bound to the planet by gravity. To study the atmosphere, let's view it in layers, each with distinctive properties and purposes. Figure 16 charts the atmosphere in a vertical cross-section profile, or side view, and is a useful reference for the following discussion. To simplify, we use three atmospheric criteria: see *composition*, *temperature*, and *function*, noted along the left side of Figure 16a.

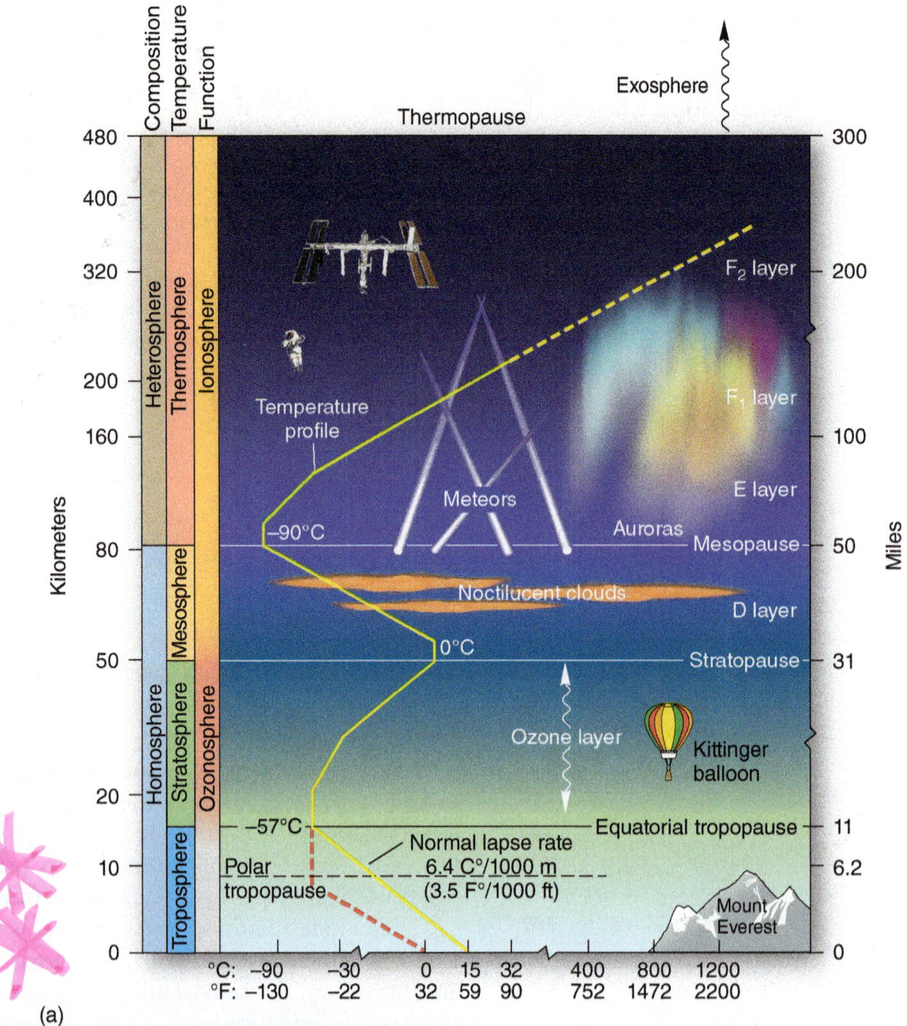

(b)

FIGURE 16 Profile of the modern atmosphere.
(a) The columns along the left side show the division of the atmosphere by composition, temperature, and function. The plot of temperature by altitude refers to the scale along the bottom axis. The small astronaut and balloon show the altitude achieved by astronaut Mark Lee and by Kittinger, discussed in *Geosystems Now*. (b) A sunset from orbit through various atmospheric layers. A silhouetted cumulonimbus thunderhead cloud tops out at the tropopause. [(b) NASA.]

Earth's atmosphere exerts its weight, pressing downward under the pull of gravity. Air molecules create air pressure through their motion, size, and number. Pressure is exerted on all surfaces in contact with the air. The weight (force over a unit area) of the atmosphere, or **air pressure**, pushes in on all of us. Fortunately, that same pressure also exists inside us, pushing outward; otherwise, we would be crushed by the mass of air around us.

The atmosphere exerts an average force of approximately 1kg/cm^2 (14.7 lb/in^2) at sea level. Gravity compresses air, making it denser near Earth's surface; it thins rapidly with increasing altitude (Figure 17a), and with reduced air pressure, less oxygen is carried in each breath a person takes.

Over half the total mass of the atmosphere is compressed below 5500 m (18,000 ft), 75% occurs below

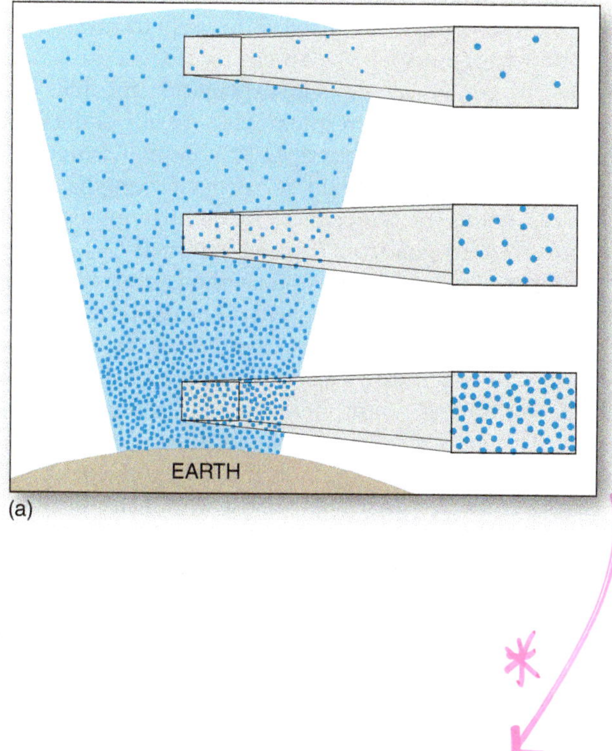

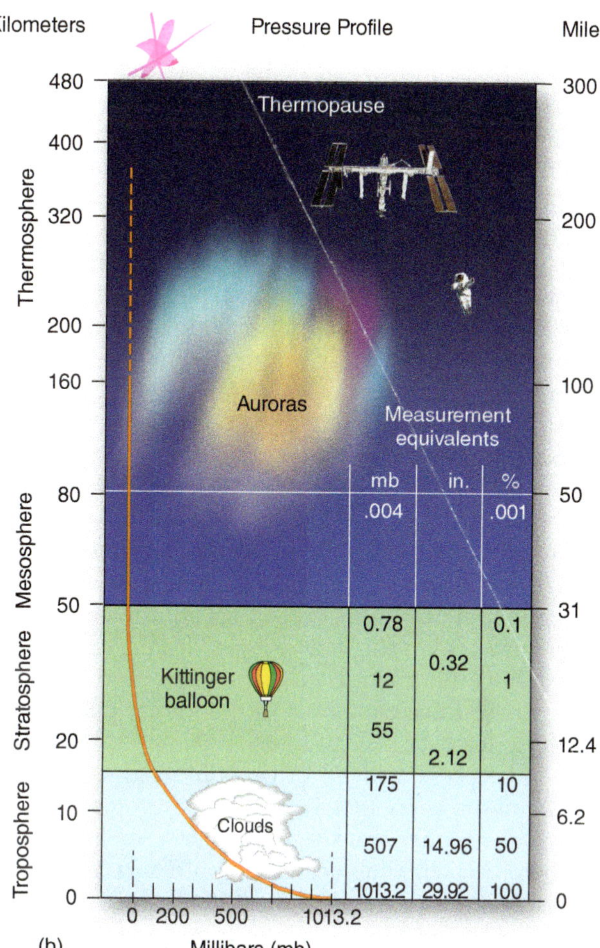

mb	in.	%
.004		.001
0.78		0.1
12	0.32	1
55	2.12	
175		10
507	14.96	50
1013.2	29.92	100

FIGURE 17 Density decreases with altitude.
(a) The atmosphere rapidly decreases in density with altitude. Have you experienced pressure changes that you could feel on your eardrums? How high above sea level were you at the time? (b) In this pressure profile, note the rapid decrease in atmospheric pressure with altitude. The troposphere holds about 90% of the atmospheric mass (far-right % column).

10,700 m (35,100 ft), and 90% is below 16,000 m (52,500 ft). Only 0.1% of the atmosphere remains above an altitude of 50 km (31 mi), as shown in the pressure profile in Figure 17b (percentage column is farthest to the right).

At sea level, the atmosphere exerts a pressure of 1013.2 mb (*millibar*, or *mb*; a measure of force per square meter of surface area), or 29.92 in. of mercury (symbol, Hg), as measured by a barometer. In Canada and other countries, normal air pressure is expressed as 101.32 kPa (*kilopascal*; 1 kPa = 10 mb).

Atmospheric Composition Criterion

Using chemical *composition* as a criterion, the atmosphere divides into two broad regions, the *heterosphere* (80 to 480 km altitude) and the *homosphere* (Earth's surface to 80 km altitude), as shown along the left side of Figure 16a.

Heterosphere The **heterosphere** is the outer atmosphere in terms of composition. It begins at about 80 km (50 mi) altitude and extends outward to the exosphere and interplanetary space (see Figure 16). Less than

GEO REPORT 3 *Outside the airplane*

Next time you fly somewhere consider a couple of things. Few people are aware that in routine air travel they are sitting above 80% of the total atmospheric volume and that the air pressure outside is only about 10% of surface air pressure. This means that only 20% of the atmospheric mass is above you. If your plane is at about 11,000 m (36,090 ft), think of Captain Kittinger's jump described in *Geosystems Now*, for he started another 20 km higher in altitude than your plane!

0.001% of the atmosphere's mass is in this rarefied heterosphere. The International Space Station and most Space Shuttle missions orbit in the middle to upper heterosphere.

As the prefix *hetero-* implies, this region is not uniform—its gases are not evenly mixed. Gases in the heterosphere occur in distinct layers sorted by gravity according to their atomic weight, with the lightest elements (hydrogen and helium) at the margins of outer space and the heavier elements (oxygen and nitrogen) dominant in the lower heterosphere. This distribution is quite different from the blended gases we breathe in the homosphere near Earth's surface.

Homosphere Below the heterosphere is the **homosphere**, extending from an altitude of 80 km (50 mi) to Earth's surface. Even though the atmosphere rapidly changes density in the homosphere—increasing pressure toward Earth's surface—the blend of gases is nearly uniform throughout. The only exceptions are the concentration of ozone (O_3) in the "ozone layer," from 19 to 50 km (12 to 31 mi), and the variations in water vapor, pollutants, and some trace chemicals in the lowest portion of the atmosphere.

The present blend of gases evolved approximately 500 million years ago. Table 3 lists by volume the stable ingredients that constitute dry, clean air in the homosphere. Air sampling occurs at the Mauna Loa Observatory, Hawai'i, operational since 1957. A marine inversion layer keeps volcanic emissions from nearby Kīlauea volcano and dust to a minimum.

The air of the homosphere is a vast reservoir of relatively inert *nitrogen*, originating principally from volcanic sources. Nitrogen is a key element of life, yet we exhale all the nitrogen we inhale. The explanation for this contradiction is that nitrogen integrates into our bodies not from the air we breathe, but through compounds in food. In the soil, nitrogen is tied up by nitrogen-fixing bacteria, and it returns to the atmosphere by denitrifying bacteria that remove nitrogen from organic materials.

Oxygen, a by-product of photosynthesis, also is essential for life processes. Slight spatial variations occur in the percentage of oxygen in the atmosphere because of variations in photosynthetic rates with latitude, seasonal changes, and the lag time as atmospheric circulation slowly mixes the air. Although it forms about one-fifth of the atmosphere, oxygen forms compounds that compose about half of Earth's crust. Oxygen readily reacts with many elements to form these materials. Both nitrogen and oxygen reserves in the atmosphere are so extensive that, at present, they far exceed human capabilities to disrupt or deplete them.

The gas *argon*, constituting less than 1% of the homosphere, is completely inert (an unreactive "noble" gas) and unusable in life processes. Argon is a residue from the radioactive decay of an isotope, or chemical form, of potassium, potassium-40 (symbolized ^{40}K). All the argon present in the modern atmosphere comes from slow accumulation over millions of years. Because industry has found uses for inert argon (in lightbulbs, welding, and some lasers), it is extracted or "mined" from the atmosphere, along with nitrogen and oxygen, for commercial, medical, and industrial uses.

Diechart from slide:

TABLE 3 Stable Components of the Modern Homosphere

Gas (Symbol)	Percentage by Volume	Parts per Million (ppm)
Nitrogen (N_2)	78.084	780,840
Oxygen (O_2)	20.946	209,460
Argon (Ar)	0.934	9,340
Carbon dioxide (CO_2)*	0.0394	394
Neon (Ne)	0.001818	18
Helium (He)	0.000525	5
Methane (CH_4)	0.00014	1.4
Krypton (Kr)	0.00010	1.0
Ozone (O_3)	Variable	
Nitrous oxide (N_2O)	Trace	
Hydrogen (H)	Trace	
Xenon (Xe)	Trace	

*May 2011 average CO_2 measured at Mauna Loa, Hawai'i (see http://www.esrl.noaa.gov/gmd/ccgg/trends/).

Mauna Loa air sampling tower. [Bobbé Christopherson.]

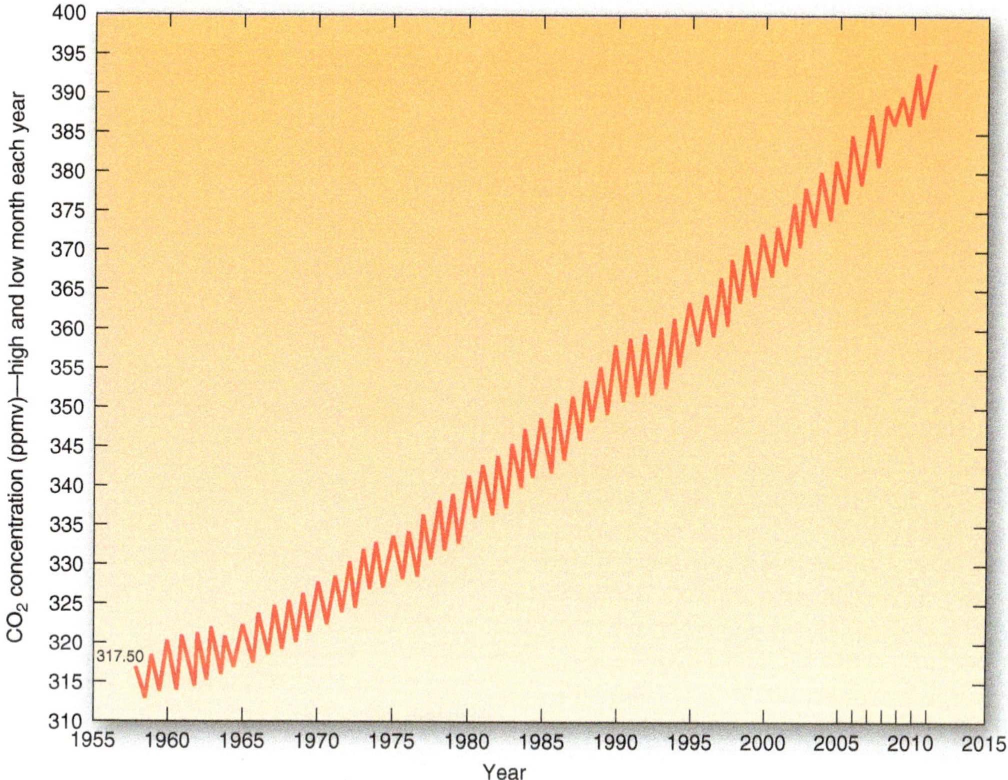

FIGURE 18 Carbon dioxide concentration increase, 1958–2011. Fifty-two years of CO_2 data measured at the Mauna Loa Observatory through May 2011. The highest and lowest average months—usually May and October, respectively—are plotted for each year on the graph in parts per million by volume (ppmv). [Data posted at ftp://ftp.cmdl.noaa.gov/ccg/co2/trends/co2_mm_mlo.txt.]

Carbon dioxide *Carbon dioxide* (CO_2) is a natural by-product of life processes. Although CO_2 is increasing rapidly, it is included with the homosphere's stable components in Table 3. Its present percentage in the atmosphere is small; however, CO_2 is important to global temperatures.

Carbon dioxide concentrations in the atmosphere since 1958 are graphed to 2011 in Figure 18. The annual fluctuation between summer and winter is evidence of seasons and the work of plant photosynthesis. Scientists agree that the increase is human-forced.

Over the past 200 years, the CO_2 percentage increased as a result of human activities, principally the burning of fossil fuels and deforestation. According to ice-core records, CO_2 is higher now than at any time in the past 800,000 years. This increase appears to be accelerating. From 1990 to 1999, CO_2 emissions rose at an average of 1.1% per year; compare this to the average emissions increase since 2000 of 3.1% per year—a 2 to 3 ppm per year increase. A distinct climatic threshold is approaching at 450 ppm, sometime in the decade of the 2020s. Beyond this tipping point, there would be irreversible ice-sheet and species losses.

Atmospheric Temperature Criterion

Shifting to temperature as a criterion, the atmosphere has four distinct temperature zones—the *thermosphere*, *mesosphere*, *stratosphere*, and *troposphere* (labeled in Figure 16). Let's look at each of these, beginning with the highest in altitude.

Thermosphere The **thermosphere** ("heat sphere") roughly corresponds to the heterosphere (80 km out to 480 km, or 50–300 mi). The upper limit of the thermosphere is the *thermopause* (the suffix *-pause* means "to change"). During periods of a less active Sun, with fewer sunspots and coronal bursts, the thermopause may lower in altitude from the average 480 km (300 mi) to only 250 km (155 mi). During periods of a more active Sun, the outer atmosphere swells to an altitude of 550 km (340 mi), where it can create frictional drag on satellites in low orbit.

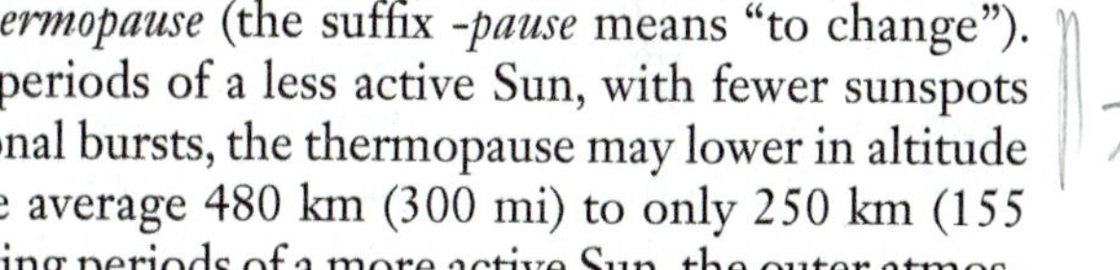

GEO REPORT 4 *Atmospheric carbon dioxide accelerates*

Since 1992, the global concentration of CO_2 in our atmosphere has increased more than 16%, reaching 394 ppm in 2011. For comparison, preindustrial levels of CO_2 were about 280 ppm. CO_2 today far exceeds the natural range of 180 to 300 ppm over the last 800,000 years. If this rate of increase continues the rest of the century, business as usual, then Table 3 could read 1400 ppm CO_2 in A.D. 2100, according to several forecasts.

The temperature profile in Figure 16 (yellow curve) shows that temperatures rise sharply in the thermosphere, to 1200°C (2200°F) and higher. Despite such high temperatures, the thermosphere is not "hot" in the way you might expect. Temperature and heat are different concepts. The intense solar radiation in this portion of the atmosphere excites individual molecules (principally nitrogen and oxygen) to high levels of vibration. This **kinetic energy**, the energy of motion, is the vibrational energy that we measure as *temperature*.

However, the actual heat involved is small. The reason is that the density of molecules is so low. There is little actual *heat* produced, heat being the flow of kinetic energy from one body to another because of a temperature difference between them. Heating in the atmosphere near Earth's surface is different because the greater number of molecules in the denser atmosphere transmits their kinetic energy as **sensible heat**, meaning that we can measure and feel it. (Density, temperature, and heat capacity determine the sensible heat of a substance.)

Mesosphere The **mesosphere** is the area from 50 to 80 km (30 to 50 mi) above Earth and is within the homosphere. As Figure 16 shows, the mesosphere's outer boundary, the *mesopause*, is the coldest portion of the atmosphere, averaging –90°C (–130°F), although that temperature may vary considerably (by 25–30 C°, or 45–54 F°). Note in Figure 17b the extremely low pressures (low density of molecules) in the mesosphere.

Stratosphere The **stratosphere** extends from 18 to 50 km (11 to 31 mi) from Earth's surface. Temperatures increase with altitude throughout the stratosphere, from –57°C (–70°F) at 18 km at the tropopause, warming to 0°C (32°F) at 50 km at the stratosphere's outer boundary, the *stratopause*. This is the location of the ozone layer.

Troposphere The **troposphere** is the final layer encountered by incoming solar radiation as it surges through the atmosphere to the surface. It is the home of the biosphere, the atmospheric layer that supports life, and the region of principal weather activity.

Approximately 90% of the total mass of the atmosphere and the bulk of all water vapor, clouds, and air pollution are within the troposphere. An average temperature of –57°C (–70°F) defines the *tropopause*, the troposphere's upper limit, but its exact altitude varies with the season, latitude, and surface temperatures and pressures. Near the equator, because of intense heating from the surface, the tropopause occurs at 18 km (11 mi); in the middle latitudes, it occurs at an average of 12 km (8 mi); and at the North and South Poles it averages only 8 km (5 mi) or less above Earth's surface. The marked warming with increasing altitude in the stratosphere above the tropopause causes the tropopause to act like a lid, generally preventing whatever is in the cooler (denser) air below from mixing into the warmer (less dense) stratosphere.

CRITICAL THINKING 4

Where is your tropopause?

On your next flight as the plane reaches its highest altitude, ask flight attendants to determine the temperature outside the plane. Some planes have video screens that display the outside air temperature. By definition, the tropopause is wherever the temperature –57°C (–70°F) occurs. Depending on the season of the year, altitude and temperature make an interesting comparison. Is the tropopause at higher altitude in summer or winter?

Figure 19 illustrates the normal temperature profile within the troposphere during daytime. As the graph shows, temperatures decrease rapidly with increasing altitude at an average of 6.4 C° per kilometer (3.5 F° per 1000 ft), a rate known as the **normal lapse rate**. This temperature plot also appears in the troposphere portion of Figure 16.

The normal lapse rate is an average. The actual lapse rate may vary considerably because of local weather conditions and is the *environmental lapse rate*. This variation in temperature gradient between normal and environmental rates in the lower troposphere is central to the study of weather processes.

Atmospheric Function Criterion

Looking at our final atmospheric criterion of function, the atmosphere has two specific zones, the *ionosphere* and the *ozonosphere* (*ozone layer*), which remove most of the harmful wavelengths of incoming solar radiation and charged particles. Figure 20 depicts in a general way the absorption of radiation by the various functional layers of the atmosphere.

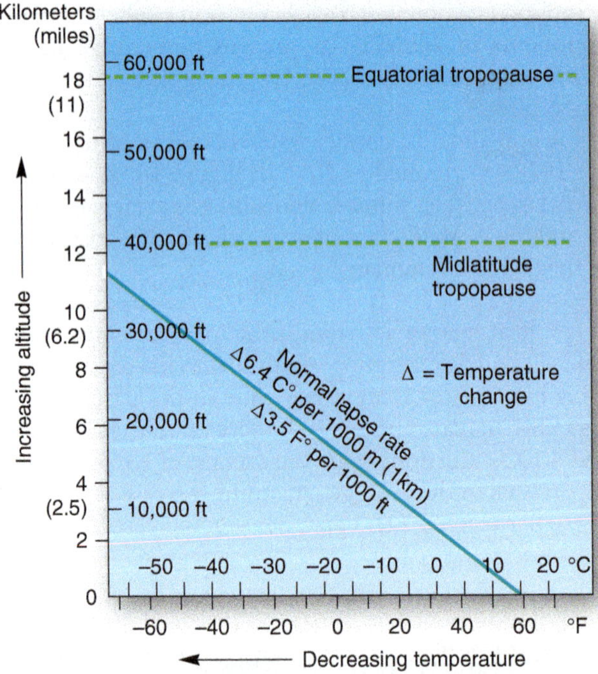

FIGURE 19 The temperature profile of the troposphere. Temperature decreases with increased altitude at a rate known as the *normal lapse rate*. Scientists use the *standard atmosphere* as a description of air temperature and pressure changes with altitude. Note the approximate locations of the equatorial and midlatitude tropopauses.

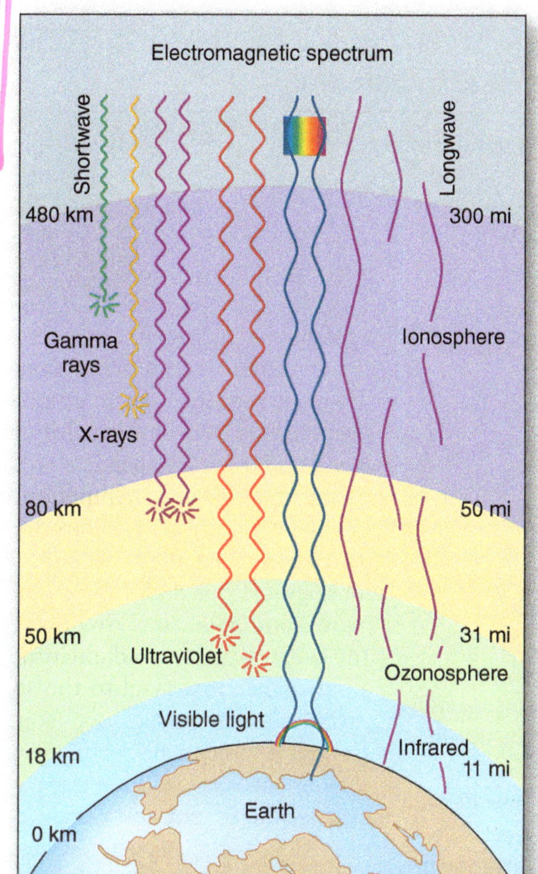

FIGURE 20 The atmosphere protects Earth's surface.
As solar energy passes through the atmosphere, the shortest wavelengths are absorbed. Only a fraction of the ultraviolet radiation, and most of the visible light and infrared, reaches Earth's surface.

Animation Ozone Breakdown, Ozone Hole

Ionosphere The outer functional layer, the **ionosphere**, extends throughout the thermosphere and into the mesosphere below (Figure 16). The ionosphere absorbs cosmic rays, gamma rays, X-rays, and shorter wavelengths of ultraviolet radiation, changing atoms to positively charged ions and giving the ionosphere its name. The glowing auroral lights occur principally within the ionosphere.

CRITICAL THINKING 5

Finding your ozone column

To determine the total ozone column at your present location, go to "What was the total ozone column at your house?" at http://toms.gsfc.nasa.gov/teacher/ozone_overhead.html.

Select a point on the map or enter your latitude and longitude and the date you want to check. The ozone column is measured by the Ozone Monitoring Instrument (OMI) sensor aboard the *Aqua* satellite and is mainly sensitive to stratospheric ozone. (Note also the limitations listed on the extent of data availability.) If you check for several different dates, when do the lowest values occur? The highest values? Briefly explain and interpret the values you found.

Ozonosphere That portion of the stratosphere that contains an increased level of ozone is the **ozonosphere**, or **ozone layer**. Ozone is a highly reactive oxygen molecule made up of three oxygen atoms (O_3) instead of the usual two atoms (O_2) that make up oxygen gas. Ozone absorbs certain wavelengths of ultraviolet (principally, all the UVC, 100–290 nm, and about 90% of the UVB, 290–320 nm).* This absorbed energy subsequently radiates at longer wavelengths as infrared radiation. This process converts most harmful ultraviolet radiation, effectively "filtering" it and safeguarding life at Earth's surface. The UVA, at 320–400 nm, makes up about 98% of all UV radiation that reaches Earth's surface.

The ozone layer is presumed to have been relatively stable over the past several hundred million years (allowing for daily and seasonal fluctuations). Today, however, it is in a state of continuous change. Focus Study 1 presents an analysis of the crisis in this critical portion of our atmosphere.

UV Index Helps Save Your Skin Newspaper and television weather reports regularly include the *UV Index* (UVI) in daily forecasts, as reported by the National Weather Service (NWS) and the Environmental Protection Agency (EPA). Think of this as a status report on stratospheric functions.

The UVI, as shown in Table 4, forecasts the expected risk of overexposure to the Sun, using a scale from 1 to

(text continued after Focus Study 1)

*Nanometer (nm) = one-billionth of a millimeter; 1 nm = 10^{-9} m. For comparison, a micrometer, or micron, (μm) = one-millionth of a meter; 1 μm = 10^{-6} m. A millimeter (mm) = one-thousandth of a meter; 1 mm = 10^{-3}.

TABLE 4 UV Index*

Exposure Risk Category	UVI Range	Comments
Low	less than 2	Low danger for average person. Wear sunglasses on bright days. Watch out for reflection off snow.
Moderate	3–5	Take covering precautions, such as sunglasses, sunscreen, hats, and protective clothing, and stay in shade during midday hours.
High	6–7	Use sunscreens with SPF of 15 or higher. Reduce time in the Sun between 11 A.M. and 4 P.M. Use protections mentioned above.
Very High	8–10	Minimize Sun exposure 10 A.M. to 4 P.M. Use sunscreens with SPF ratings of over 15. Use protections mentioned above.
Extreme	11+	Unprotected skin is at risk of burn. Sunscreen application every two hours if out-of-doors. Avoid direct Sun exposure during midday hours. Use protections listed above.

*The NWS and EPA began reporting UVI in 1991. A revision in 2004 aligned the UVI with guidelines adopted by the World Health Organization (WHO) and World Meteorological Organization (WMO).

FOCUS STUDY 1

Stratospheric Ozone Losses: A Continuing Health Hazard

Consider:

- The area of stratospheric ozone depletion above Antarctica during the months of antarctic spring (September to November) has grown larger since 1979, with the record depletion in 2006 covering about 30 million km²; subsequent years had similar losses, with 2008 recording the 5th largest loss and with 2009 15th on the list by area and 5th on the list of lowest ozone concentration. Recovery is proceeding slower than previously thought, despite the slowing rate of accumulation of offending chemicals.
- As stratospheric ozone flows into the depleted region from lower latitudes in spring, ozone thins over southern South America, southern Africa, Australia, and New Zealand. In Ushuaia, Argentina, surface UVB intensity increases more than 225% compared to normal levels.
- An international scientific consensus confirmed the anthropogenic, or human-caused, disruption of the ozone layer. See *Scientific Assessment of Ozone Depletion* at http://www.esrl.noaa.gov/csd/assessments/ozone/2006/.
- At Earth's opposite pole, a similar ozone depletion over the Arctic and annually exceeds 30%, with a record 45% loss during spring 1997. The Canadian and U.S. governments report an "ultraviolet index" to help the public protect themselves (http://www.ec.gc.ca/ozone/).
- Increased ultraviolet radiation is affecting atmospheric chemistry, biological systems, oceanic phytoplankton (small photosynthetic organisms that form the basis of the ocean's primary food production), fisheries, crop yields, and human skin, eye tissues, and immunity.

More ultraviolet radiation than ever before is breaking through Earth's protective ozone layer. What is going on in the stratosphere everywhere and in the polar regions specifically? Why is this happening, and how are people and their governments responding?

Monitoring Earth's Fragile Safety Screen

A sample from the ozone layer's densest part (at an altitude of 29 km, or 18 mi) contains only 1 part ozone per 4 million parts of air—compressed to surface pressure, the ozone layer would be only 3 mm thick. Yet this rarefied layer was in steady-state equilibrium for several hundred million years, absorbing intense ultraviolet radiation and permitting life to proceed safely on Earth.

Scientists have monitored the ozone layer from ground stations since the 1920s. The *Total Ozone Mapping Spectrometer* (TOMS) began operations in 1978 aboard various satellites. Since 2004, the Ozone Monitoring Instrument (OMI) on board NASA's *Aura* satellite has tracked ozone depletion. Figure 1.1 shows the 2008 "ozone hole." (See http://ozonewatch.gsfc.nasa.gov/.)

Ozone Losses Explained

What is causing the decline in stratospheric ozone? In 1974, two atmospheric chemists, F. Sherwood Rowland and Mario Molina, hypothesized that some synthetic chemicals were releasing chlorine atoms that decompose ozone. These **chlorofluorocarbons**, or **CFCs**, are synthetic molecules of chlorine, fluorine, and carbon.

CFCs are stable, or inert, under conditions at Earth's surface, and they possess remarkable heat properties. Both qualities made them valuable as propellants in aerosol sprays and as refrigerants. Also, some 45% of CFCs were used as solvents in the electronics industry and as foaming agents. Being inert, CFC molecules do not dissolve in water and do not break down in biological processes. (In contrast, chlorine compounds derived from volcanic eruptions and ocean sprays are water soluble and rarely reach the stratosphere.)

Researchers Rowland and Molina hypothesized that stable CFC molecules slowly migrate into the stratosphere, where intense ultraviolet radiation splits them, freeing chlorine (Cl) atoms. This process produces a complex set of reactions that breaks up ozone molecules (O_3) and leaves oxygen gas molecules (O_2) in their place. The effect is severe, for single chlorine atoms decompose more than 100,000 ozone molecules. The long residence time of chlorine atoms in the ozone layer (40 to 100 years) is likely to produce long-term consequences through this century from the chlorine already in place. Tens of millions of tons of CFCs were sold worldwide since 1950 and subsequently released into the atmosphere.

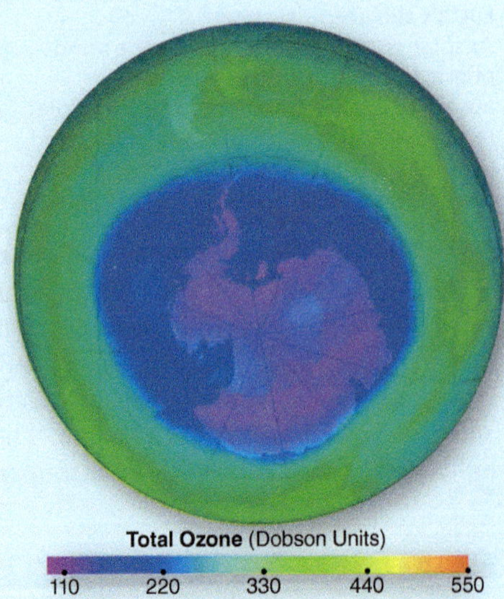

FIGURE 1.1 The Antarctic ozone hole. OMI image for September 12, 2008. The "hole," at nearly 27 million km² (10.4 million mi²), ranks fifth in size in the satellite monitoring era; 2006 was the worst depletion year. Measurements dropped below 100 Dobson units in the region of blues and purples; greens, yellows, and reds denote more ozone. [OMI aboard *Aqua*, GSFC/NASA.]

An International Response

As the science became established, sales and production of CFCs declined until a March 1981 presidential order permitted the export and sales of banned products. Sales increased and hit a new peak in 1987 at 1.2 million metric tons (1.32 million tons), when an international agreement went into effect halting further sales growth.

Chemical manufacturers once claimed that no hard evidence existed to prove the ozone-depletion model, and they successfully delayed remedial action for 15 years. Today, with extensive scientific evidence and verification of losses, even the CFC manufacturers admit that the problem is serious.

The *Montreal Protocol on Substances That Deplete the Ozone Layer* (1987), as amended in 1990, 1992, 1995, 1997, and 1999, aims to reduce and eliminate CFC damage to the ozone layer. With 189 signatory countries, the protocol is regarded as probably the most successful international agreement in history (see http://ozone.unep.org/).

CFC sales continue their decline, and all production of harmful CFCs ceased in 2010, although there is concern over some of the substitute compounds and a robust black market for banned CFCs, rivaling drug trafficking at some ports. If the protocol is fully enforced, scientists estimate that the stratosphere will return to more normal conditions in a century.

The world without this treaty might prove challenging. Imagine possible stratospheric global ozone losses of two-thirds, producing more cases of malignant melanoma (a skin cancer), and by 2100 a nonexistent ozone layer. We owe much to Doctors Rowland and Molina.

For their work, Rowland, Molina, and another colleague, Paul Crutzen, received the 1995 Nobel Prize for Chemistry. In making the award, the Royal Swedish Academy of Sciences said, "By explaining the chemical mechanism that affects the thickness of the ozone layer, the three researchers have contributed to our salvation from a global environmental problem that could have catastrophic consequences."

Ozone Losses over the Poles

How do Northern Hemisphere CFCs become concentrated over the South Pole? Evidently, chlorine freed in the Northern Hemisphere midlatitudes concentrates over Antarctica through the work of atmospheric winds. Persistent cold temperatures over the South Pole and the presence of thin, icy clouds in the stratosphere promote development of the ozone hole, which develops in the Antarctic spring and usually peaks in September ... the North Pole ... changeable, s... although grow... each year.

Polar stratospheric clouds (*PSCs*) are thin clouds that are important catalysts in the release of chlorine for ozone-depleting reactions. During the long, cold winter months, a tight circulation pattern forms over the Antarctic continent—the polar vortex. Chlorine that is freed from droplets in PSCs triggers the breakdown of the otherwise inert molecules and frees the chlorine for catalytic reactions.

Make a note to check some of the Internet data sources listed to see how our stratosphere is doing in years to come. What we learn here will be with us for the rest of this century.

MG Satellite Southern Hemisphere Ozone 2002–2003

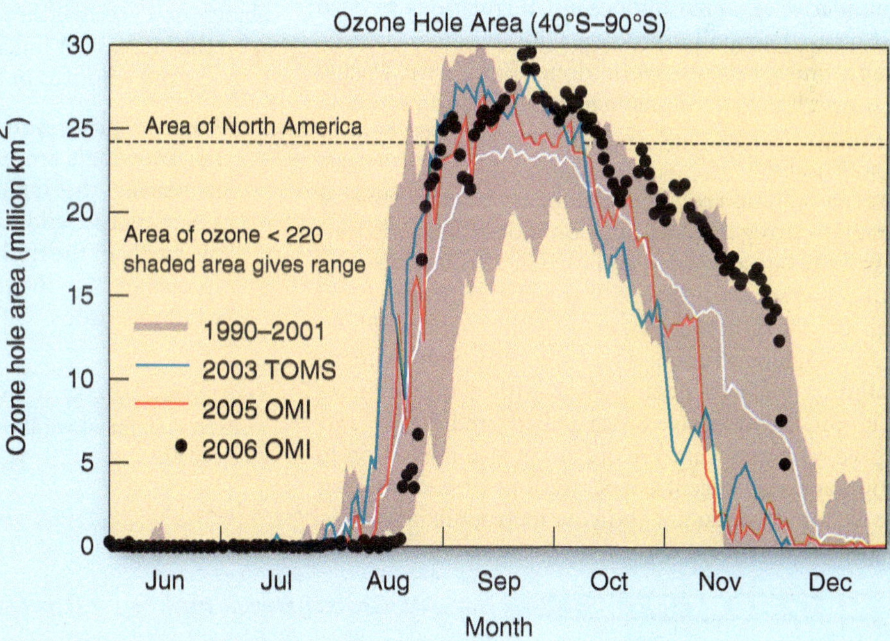

FIGURE 1.2 The timing and extent of ozone damage. The area of ozone depletion generally peaks in late September, reaching a record low size in 2006. [Data from GSFC/NASA.]

stratospheric ozone levels at thinner-than- conditions, surface exposure to cancer-causing on increases. The public, especially babies and chil- n, now is alerted to take extra precautions in the form of sunscreens, hats, protective clothing, and sunglasses. Remember, damage accumulates, and it may be decades before you experience the ill effects triggered by this summer's sunburn. See http://www.epa.gov/sunwise/uvindex.html for a UVI forecast for your location.

Variable Atmospheric Components

The troposphere contains natural and human-caused variable gases, particles, and other chemicals. The spatial aspects of these variables are important applied topics in physical geography and have important human-health implications.

Air pollution is not a new problem. Romans complained more than 2000 years ago about the foul air of their cities. Filling Roman air was the stench of open sewers, smoke from fires, and fumes from ceramic-making kilns and smelters (furnaces) that converted ores into metals. Throughout human civilization, cities have stressed the environment's natural ability to process and recycle waste. Historically, air pollution has occurred around population centers and is closely linked to human production and consumption of energy and resources.

Solutions require regional, national, and international strategies because the pollution sources often are distant from the observed impact—moving across political boundaries and crossing oceans. Regulations to curb human-caused air pollution have achieved great success, although much remains to be done. Before we discuss these topics, let's examine some natural pollution sources.

Natural Sources

Natural air pollution sources produce a greater quantity of pollutants—nitrogen oxides, carbon monoxide, hydrocarbons from plants and trees, and carbon dioxide—than do human-made sources. Table 5 lists some of these natural sources and the substances they contribute to the air. However, any attempt to dismiss the impact of human-made air pollution through a comparison with natural sources is irrelevant, for we evolved with and adapted to the natural ingredients in the air. We did not evolve in relation to the comparatively recent concentrations of *anthropogenic* (human-caused) contaminants in our metropolitan regions.

TABLE 5 Sources of Natural Variable Gases and Materials

Source	Contribution
Volcanoes	Sulfur oxides, particulates
Forest fires	Carbon monoxide and dioxide, nitrogen oxides, particulates
Plants	Hydrocarbons, pollens
Decaying plants	Methane, hydrogen sulfides
Soil	Dust and viruses
Ocean	Salt spray and particulates

A dramatic natural source of pollution was the 1991 eruption of Mount Pinatubo in the Philippines (15° N 120° E), perhaps the 20th century's second largest eruption. This event injected nearly 20 million tons of sulfur dioxide (SO_2) into the stratosphere.

Devastating wildfires on several continents produce natural air pollution as each year's fire season worsens (Figure 21). Soot, ash, and gases darken skies and damage health in affected regions. Wind patterns spread the pollution from the fires to nearby cities, closing airports and forcing evacuations to avoid the health-related dangers. Wildfire smoke contains particulate matter (dust, smoke, soot, ash), nitrogen oxides, carbon monoxide, and volatile organic compounds.

Scientists established the connection between climate change and U.S. wildfire occurrence. This source of smoke is on the increase. A linkage exists between climate-change impacts and wildfires in the western United States:

> Higher spring and summer temperatures and earlier snowmelt are extending the wildfire season and increasing the intensity of wildfires in the western US . . . large wildfire activity increased suddenly and markedly in the mid-1980s, with higher large-wildfire frequency . . . longer wildfire durations, and longer wildfire seasons.*

*A. L. Westerling et al., "Warming and earlier spring increase western U.S. forest wildfire activity," *Science* 313, 5789 (Aug. 18, 2006): 940.

GEO REPORT 5 ***NASA's Global Hawk makes first scientific flight***

Small unpiloted aerial vehicles (UAVs) are lightweight aircraft guided by remote control. These instrumental drones can gather all types of data and carry various remote-sensing devices. In 2010, NASA's unpiloted *Global Hawk* completed its first scientific flight over the Pacific Ocean, flying for 14 hours on a preprogrammed flight path to altitudes above 60,000 ft (18.3 km) and carrying instruments to sample ozone-depleting substances, aerosols, and other components of air quality in the upper troposphere and lower stratosphere. In September, the *Global Hawk* flew over Hurricane Karl, collecting new and unprecedented data for hurricane research.

(a)

(b)

FIGURE 21 California wildfires fill the atmosphere with smoke.
(a) Wildfires in drought- and high-temperature-plagued portions of California, October 2007. More than 117,000 hectares (500,000 acres) burned in fires that continued through November. (b) Sierra Nevada mountain wildfires move along uncontrolled in 2008, consuming millions of acres of drought-damaged forest and chaparral. [(a) *Terra* MODIS, NASA/GSFC. (b) Bobbé Christopherson.]

(a)

(b)

FIGURE 22 Natural variable dust in the atmosphere.
(a) In 2009, dust in eastern Washington state from dryland agricultural fields was moved by winds up to 69 kmph (43 mph), closing some highways at the time. (b) Typical wind-carried dust moves off West Africa, across the Atlantic. The Cape Verde islands are usually in the path of African dust. Beneath such dust on Cape Verde at 15° N latitude, the ocean surface is difficult to distinguish from the sky on the horizon (inset photo). *Terra* MISR is able to gather data obscured by sunglint into the MODIS sensor. [(a) *Terra* MODIS and (b) *Terra* MODIS and MISR sensors; both NASA/GSFC; (inset) Bobbé Christopherson.]

These connections occur across the globe, as in drought-plagued Australia, where thousands of wildfires burned millions of hectares in recent years; or, the 2011 record wildfires in Texas. Each year, worldwide, wildfire acreage breaks the record of the previous year.

Natural Factors That Affect Air Pollution

The problems resulting from both natural and human-made atmospheric contaminants are made worse by several important natural factors. Among these, wind, local and regional landscape characteristics, and temperature inversions in the troposphere dominate.

Winds Winds gather and move pollutants, sometimes reducing the concentration of pollution in one location, while increasing it in another. Wind can produce dramatic episodes of dust movement, tracked by chemical analysis used by scientists to determine source areas. (Dust is defined as particles less than 62 μm, microns, or 0.0025 in.). Traveling on prevailing winds, dust from Africa contributes to the soils of South America and Europe, and Texas dust ends up across the Atlantic (Figure 22).

Winds make the atmosphere's condition an international issue. For example, prevailing winds transport air pollution from the United States to Canada, causing much complaint and negotiation between the two governments. Pollution from North America adds to European air problems. In Europe, the cross-boundary drift of pollution is an issue because of the proximity of countries, a factor in the formation of the European Union (EU).

Arctic haze is a term from the 1950s, when pilots noticed decreased visibility, either horizontally or at a slant angle from their aircraft, across the Arctic region. Haze is a concentration of microscopic particles and air pollution that diminishes air clarity. Since there is no heavy industry at these high latitudes and only sparse population, this seasonal haze is a remarkable attribute of industrialization in the Northern Hemisphere. Also, an increase in wildfires across the Northern Hemisphere and agricultural burning in the midlatitudes contribute to Arctic haze. Simply put, winds of atmospheric circulation transport pollution to sites far distant from points of origin. There is no comparable haze over the Antarctic continent. Based on this analysis, can you think of why Antarctica lacks such a condition?

Local and Regional Landscapes Local and regional landscapes are another important factor in air pollution. Surrounding mountains and hills can form barriers to air movement or can direct pollutants from one area to another. Some of the worst incidents result when local landscapes trap and concentrate air pollution.

Places with volcanic landscapes such as Iceland and Hawai'i have their own natural pollution. During periods of sustained volcanic activity at Kīlauea, some 2000 metric tons (2200 tons) of sulfur dioxide are produced a day. Concentrations are sometimes high enough to merit broadcast warnings about health concerns. The resulting acid rain and volcanic smog, called *vog* by Hawaiians (for *vo*lcanic smog), cause losses to agriculture as well as other economic impacts.

Temperature Inversions Vertical temperature and atmospheric density in the troposphere also can worsen pollution conditions. A **temperature inversion** occurs when the normal temperature that usually decreases with altitude (normal lapse rate) reverses trend and begins to increase at some point. This can happen at any elevation from ground level to several thousand meters.

Figure 23 compares a normal temperature profile with that of a temperature inversion. The normal profile (Figure 23a) permits warmer (less dense) air at the surface to rise, ventilating the valley and moderating surface pollution. But the warm-air inversion (Figure 23b) prevents the rise of cooler (denser) air beneath, halting the vertical mixing of pollutants with other atmospheric gases. Thus, instead of being carried away, pollutants are trapped under the *inversion layer*.

Inversions most often result from certain weather conditions, such as when the air near the ground is radiatively cooled on clear nights, or from topographic situations that produce cold-air drainage into valleys. In addition, the air above snow-covered surfaces or beneath subsiding air in a high-pressure system may cause a temperature inversion.

Anthropogenic Pollution

Anthropogenic, or human-caused, air pollution remains most prevalent in urbanized regions. Approximately 2%

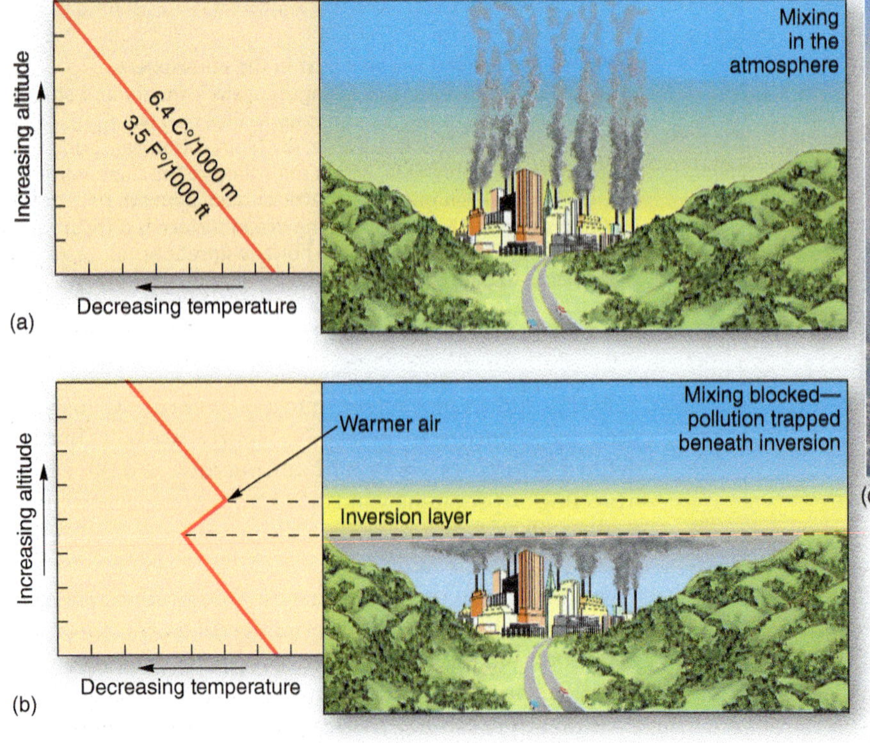

FIGURE 23 Normal and inverted temperature profiles.
(a) A normal temperature profile. (b) A temperature inversion in the lower atmosphere. Note how the warmer air layer prevents mixing of the denser (cooler) air below the inversion, thereby trapping pollution. (c) An inversion layer is visible in the morning hours over a valley. [(c) Bobbé Christopherson.]

TABLE 6 Anthropogenic Gases and Materials in the Lower Atmosphere

Name	Symbol	Sources	Description and Effects of Criteria Pollutants
Carbon monoxide	CO	Incomplete combustion of fuels, mainly vehicle emissions	Odorless, colorless, tasteless gas Toxicity; affinity for hemoglobin Displaces O_2 in bloodstream; 50 to 100 ppm causes headaches and vision and judgment losses
Nitrogen oxides	NO_x (NO, NO_2)	Agricultural activities, fertilizers, and high temperature/pressure combustion, mainly from vehicle emissions	Reddish-brown choking gas Inflames respiratory system, destroys lung tissue Leads to acid deposition
Volatile organic compounds	VOC	Incomplete combustion of fossil fuels such as gasoline; cleaning and paint solvents	Prime agents of surface ozone formation
Ozone	O_3	Photochemical reactions	Highly reactive, unstable gas Irritates human eyes, nose, and throat Damages plants
Peroxyacetyl nitrates	PAN	Photochemical reactions	No human health effects Major damage to plants, forests, crops
Sulfur oxides	SO_x (SO_2, SO_3)	Combustion of sulfur-containing fuels	Colorless, but with irritating smell, Impairs breathing, taste threshold Causes human asthma, bronchitis, emphysema Leads to acid deposition
Particulate matter	PM	Industrial activities, fuel combustion, vehicle emissions, agriculture	Complex mixture of solids and aerosols, including dust, soot, salt, metals, and organics Dust, smoke, and haze affect visibility Various health effects: bronchitis, pulmonary function
Carbon dioxide	CO_2	Complete combustion of fossil fuels	Principal greenhouse gas
Methane	CH_4	Organic processes	Secondary greenhouse gas
Water vapor	H_2O vapor	Combustion processes, steam	Requires its own chapter

of annual deaths in the United States are attributable to air pollution. Comparable risks are identified in Canada, Europe, Mexico, and Asia, especially China and India.

As urban populations grow, human exposure to air pollution increases. By 2012, more than 50% of world population will live in metropolitan regions, some one-third with unhealthful levels of air pollution. This represents a potentially massive public health issue in this century.

Table 6 lists the names, chemical symbols, principal sources, and impacts of variable anthropogenic components in the air. The first seven pollutants in the table result from combustion of fossil fuels in transportation (specifically automobiles, including light trucks). Overall, automobiles contribute more than 60% of U.S. and 50% of Canadian human-caused air pollution. Reducing air pollution from the transportation sector involves known technologies and strategies, monetary savings for the consumer, and significant health benefits. These facts make the continuing delays in the effort to achieve better efficiency all the more confusing.

Stationary sources, such as electric power plants and industrial plants that use fossil fuels, contribute the most sulfur oxides and particulates. For this reason, concentrations are focused in the Northern Hemisphere and the industrial, developed countries. The last three gases shown in Table 6 are not discussed in detial in this chapter: Water vapor would be examined with water and weather; carbon dioxide and methane are discussed in the context of greenhouse gases and climate.

GEO REPORT 6 ***Smoke gets in your eyes***

As your car idles at a downtown intersection or you walk through a parking garage, you may be exposed to between 50 ppm and 100 ppm of carbon monoxide, a colorless, odorless gas. Smoking a cigarette, CO levels reach 42,000 ppm at the burning ash. Secondhand smoke affects CO levels of anyone breathing nearby and produces measurable health affects. What happens physiologically? CO combines with the oxygen-carrying hemoglobin of the blood; thus, the hemoglobin no longer transports adequate oxygen to vital organs such as the heart and brain.

Photochemical Smog Although not generally experienced until the advent of the automobile, photochemical smog is now the major component of anthropogenic air pollution. **Photochemical smog** results from the interaction of sunlight and the combustion products in automobile exhaust (nitrogen oxides and VOCs). Although the term *smog*—a combination of the words *sm*oke and f*og*—is a misnomer, it is generally used to describe this pollution. Smog is responsible for the hazy sky and reduced sunlight in many of our cities.

Figure 24 summarizes how car exhaust is converted into major air pollutants—PAN, ozone, and nitric acid. The high temperatures in automobile engines produce nitrogen dioxide (NO_2). Also, to a lesser extent, nitrogen dioxide is emitted from power plants. Worldwide, the problem with *nitrogen dioxide* production is its concentration in metropolitan regions. North American urban areas may have from 10 to 100 times higher nitrogen dioxide concentrations than nonurban areas. Nitrogen dioxide interacts with water vapor to form nitric acid (HNO_3), a contributor to acid deposition by precipitation, the subject of Focus Study 2.

In the photochemistry reaction in the illustration, ultraviolet radiation liberates atomic oxygen (O) and a nitric oxide (NO) molecule from the NO_2. The free oxygen atom combines with an oxygen molecule, O_2, to form the oxidant ozone, O_3. In addition, the nitric oxide (NO) molecule reacts with VOCs to produce *peroxyacetyl nitrates*. **Peroxyacetyl nitrates (PAN)** produce no known health effect in humans, but they are particularly damaging to plants, including both agricultural crops and forests.

Ozone is the primary ingredient in photochemical smog. (This is the same gas that is beneficial to us in the stratosphere because it absorbs ultraviolet radiation.) The reactivity of ozone is a health threat, for it damages biological tissues. For several reasons, children are at greatest risk from ozone pollution—one in four children in U.S. cities is at risk of developing health problems from ozone pollution. This ratio is significant; it means that more than 12 million children are vulnerable in those metropolitan regions with the most polluted air (Los Angeles, New York City, Atlanta, Houston, and Detroit). For more information and city rankings, see http://www.lungusa.org (enter "city rankings" in the search box on the web site).

Industrial Smog and Sulfur Oxides Over the past 300 years, except in some developing countries, coal slowly replaced wood as the basic fuel used by society. The Industrial Revolution required high-grade energy to run machines. The changes involved conversion from *animate* energy (energy from animal sources, such as animal-powered farm equipment) to *inanimate* energy (energy from nonliving sources, such as coal, steam, and water). Air pollution associated with coal-burning industries is known as **industrial smog** (Figure 25). The term *smog* was coined by a London physician in 1900 to describe the combination of fog and smoke containing sulfur gases (sulfur is an impurity in fossil fuels).

Once in the atmosphere, **sulfur dioxide (SO_2)** reacts with oxygen (O) to form sulfur trioxide (SO_3), which is highly reactive and, in the presence of water or water vapor, forms *sulfate aerosols*, tiny particles about 0.1 to 1 μm in diameter. Sulfuric acid (H_2SO_4) can form even in moderately polluted air at normal temperatures. Coal-burning elec-

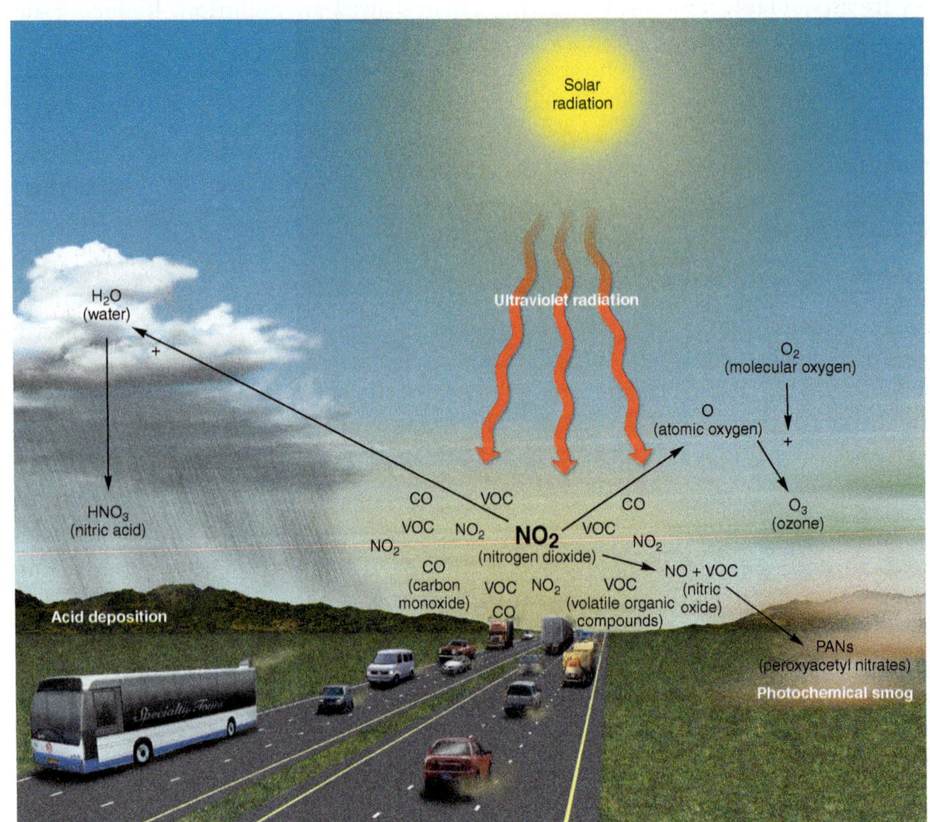

FIGURE 24 Photochemical reactions.
The interaction of automobile exhaust (NO_2, VOCs, CO) and ultraviolet radiation in sunlight causes photochemical reactions. To the left, note the formation of nitric acid and acid deposition.

tric utilities and steel manufacturing are the main sources of sulfur dioxide. Sulfur dioxide–laden air is dangerous to health, corrodes metals, and deteriorates stone building materials at accelerated rates. Sulfuric acid deposition, added to nitric acid deposition, has increased in severity since it was first described in the 1970s. Focus Study 2 discusses this vital atmospheric issue and recent progress.

Particulates A diverse mixture of fine particles, both solid and liquid, that impact human health is **particulate matter (PM)**. Haze, smoke, and dust are visible reminders of particulate material in the air we breathe. Such small particles in the air comprise **aerosols**. Remote sensing now provides a global portrait of such aerosols.

The effects of PM on human health vary with the size of the particle. $PM_{2.5}$, particulates smaller than 2.5 microns (2.5 μm or less) in diameter, pose the greatest health risk. For comparison, a human hair can range from 50 μm to 70 μm in diameter. These fine particles, such as combustion particles, organics, and metallic aerosols, can get into the lungs and bloodstream. Coarse particles (PM_{10}) are of less concern, although they can irritate a person's eyes, nose, and throat. New studies are implicating even smaller particles, known as *ultrafines*, which are $PM_{0.1}$. These are many times more potent than the larger $PM_{2.5}$ and PM_{10} particles because they can get into smaller channels in lung tissue and cause scarring, abnormal thickening, and damage called *fibrosis*. Asthma prevalence has nearly doubled since 1980 in the United States, a major cause being motor vehicle–related air pollution, specifically sulfur dioxide, ozone, and fine particulate matter.

We are now contributing significantly to the creation of the **anthropogenic atmosphere**, a tentative label for Earth's next atmosphere. The urban air we breathe today may be just a preview. What is the air quality like where you live, work, and go to college? Where could you go to find out its status?

Benefits of the Clean Air Act

The concentration of many air pollutants declined over the past several decades because of Clean Air Act (CAA) legislation (1970, 1977, 1990), resulting in the avoidance of trillions of dollars in health, economic, and environmental losses. Despite this reality, air pollution regulations are subject to a continuing political debate.

Since 1970 and the CAA, there have been significant reductions in atmospheric concentrations of carbon monoxide (−45%), nitrogen oxides (−22%), volatile organic compounds (−48%), PM_{10} particulates (−75%), sulfur oxides (−52%; see Focus Study 2, Figure 2.2), and lead (−98%). Prior to the CAA, lead was added to gasoline, emitted in exhaust, and dispersed over great distances, finally settling in living tissues, especially in children. These remarkable reductions show the successful linking of science and public policy.

To be justified, abatement (mitigation and prevention) costs must not exceed the financial benefits derived from reducing pollution damage. Compliance with the CAA affected patterns of industrial production, employment, and capital investment. Although these expenditures were investments that generated benefits, the dislocation and job loss in some regions were difficult—reductions in high-sulfur coal mining and cutbacks in polluting industries such as steel, for example.

FIGURE 25 Typical industrial smog.
Pollution generated by industry and coal-fired electrical generation differs from that produced by transportation. Industrial pollution has high concentrations of sulfur oxides, particulates, and carbon dioxide. This coal-fired power plant at Barentsburg, Svalbard, lacks scrubbers to reduce stack emissions. [Bobbé Christopherson.]

In 1990, Congress requested the Environmental Protection Agency (EPA) to analyze the overall health, ecological, and economic benefits of the CAA compared with the costs of implementing the law. In response, the EPA's Office of Policy, Planning, and Evaluation performed an exhaustive cost–benefit analysis and published a report in 1997: *The Benefits of the Clean Air Act, 1970 to 1990*. The analysis found a 42-to-1 benefit-over-cost ratio and provides a good lesson in cost–benefit analysis, valid to this day. The EPA report calculated that the *total direct cost* to implement all the federal, state, and local CAA rules from 1970 to 1990 was *\$523 billion* (in 1990 dollars). This cost was borne by businesses, consumers, and government entities. The estimate of *direct economic benefits* from the CAA from 1970 to 1990 had a central mean of *\$22.2 trillion*, making the estimated *net financial benefit* of the CAA *\$21.7 trillion!*

Econometric studies by the EPA are ongoing that measure these continuing benefits. In 2010, the CAA saved society \$110 billion and some 23,000 lives, whereas related costs of implementation in 2010 were \$27 billion. More than 4 million lost workdays were avoided.

The benefits to society, directly and indirectly, are widespread across the entire population, including improved health and environment, less lead to harm children, lowered cancer rates, and less acid deposition. These CAA benefits took place during a period in which the U.S. population grew by 22% and the economy expanded by 70%. Political efforts to weaken CAA regulations seem counterproductive to the progress made.

(text continued after Focus Study 2)

FOCUS STUDY 2

Acid Deposition: Damaging to Ecosystems

Acid deposition is a major environmental problem in some areas of the United States, Canada, Europe, and Asia. Such deposition is most familiar as "acid rain," but it also occurs as "acid snow" and in dry form as dust or aerosols—tiny liquid droplets or solid particles.

Acid deposition is causally linked to serious environmental problems: declining fish populations and fish kills, widespread forest damage, changes in soil chemistry, and damage to buildings, sculptures, and historic artifacts. Regions that have suffered most are the northeastern United States, southeastern Canada, Sweden, Norway, Germany, much of eastern Europe, and China.

Acid Formation

The problem begins as sulfur dioxide and nitrogen oxides are emitted as by-products of fertilizers and fossil fuel combustion. Winds may carry these gases many kilometers from their sources. Once in the atmosphere, the chemicals are converted to nitric acid (HNO_3) and sulfuric acid (H_2SO_4). These acids are removed from the atmosphere by wet and dry deposition processes, falling as rain or snow, or attached to other particulate matter. The acid then settles on the landscape and eventually enters streams and lakes, carried by runoff and groundwater flows.

The acidity of precipitation is measured on the pH scale, which expresses the relative abundance of free hydrogen ions ($H+$) in a solution. Free hydrogen ions in a solution are what make an acid corrosive, for they easily combine with other ions. The pH scale is logarithmic: Each whole number represents a tenfold change. A pH of 7.0 is neutral (neither acidic nor basic). Values less than 7.0 are increasingly *acidic*, and values greater than 7.0 are increasingly *basic*, or *alkaline*.

Natural precipitation dissolves carbon dioxide from the atmosphere to form carbonic acid. This process releases hydrogen ions and produces an average pH reading for precipitation of 5.65. The normal range for precipitation is 5.3–6.0. Thus, normal precipitation is always slightly acidic. Scientists have measured precipitation as acidic as pH 2.0 in the eastern United States, Scandinavia, and Europe. By comparison, vinegar and lemon juice register slightly less than 3.0. In lakes, aquatic plant and animal life perishes when pH drops below 4.8.

Effects on Natural Systems

More than 50,000 lakes and some 100,000 km (62,000 mi) of streams in the United States and Canada are at a pH level below normal (that is, below pH 5.3), with several hundred lakes incapable of supporting any aquatic life. Acid deposition causes the release of aluminum and magnesium from clay minerals in the soil, and both of these are harmful to fish and plant communities.

Also relatively harmless mercury deposits in lake-bottom sediments convert in acidified lake waters into highly toxic *methylmercury*, which is deadly to aquatic life. Local health advisories are regularly issued in two Canadian provinces and 22 U.S. states to warn those who fish of the methylmercury problem. Mercury atoms rapidly bond with carbon and move throughout biological systems.

Acid deposition affects soils by killing microorganisms and causing a decline in soil nutrients. In New Hampshire's Hubbard Brook Experimental Forest (http://www.hubbardbrook.org/), an ongoing study from 1960 to the present found that half the nutrient calcium and magnesium base cations were leached from the soil; excess acids are the cause of the decline.

Damage to forests results from deficiencies in soil nutrients. The most advanced impact is seen in forests in eastern Europe, principally because of its long history of burning coal and the density of industrial activity. In Germany and Poland, up to 50% of the forests are dead or damaged.

In the eastern United States, some of the worst forest decline has occurred in the spruce and fir forests of North Carolina and Tennessee (Figure 2.1). In the Adirondacks, red spruce and sugar maples have been especially hard hit. Affected trees are susceptible to winter cold, insects, and droughts. In red spruce, decline is evidenced by poor crown condition, reduced growth shown in tree ring analyses, and unusually high levels of tree mortality. For sugar maples, an indicator of forest damage is the reduction by almost half of the annual production of U.S. and Canadian maple sugar.

Nitrogen Oxides: A Worsening Cause

In the United States, the problem of acid deposition appeared to be solved with

FIGURE 2.1 Acid deposition blight.
Stressed forests on Mount Mitchell in the Appalachians. [Will and Deni McIntyre/Photo Researchers.]

the passage of the 1990 CAA amendments, which targeted emissions of sulfur dioxide and nitrogen oxides. From 1990 to 2008, sulfur emissions from power plants decreased almost 70%, and wet sulfate deposition rates dropped across the eastern United States (Figure 2.2). However, nitrogen emissions declined little and in some areas have increased. Nitric oxide (NO) emissions come from three main sources: agricultural operations (specifically, fertilizers and animal-feeding operations, which produce nitrogen and ammonia), motor vehicles, and coal combustion power plants.

Europe shows similar trends: Several studies have recently found areas with high levels of atmospheric nitrogen oxides in Switzerland and northern Italy, presumably associated with intensive agriculture and fossil-fuel burning, as well as in Norway, where acid deposition in streams could have impacts on the economically important salmon industry. However, 49 European countries began regulating nitrogen emissions in 1999, resulting in a regional decrease in nitrogen emissions of about one-third.

In China, overuse of nitrogen fertilizers (an increase of 191% from 1991 to 2007) has led to acid deposition in soils, lessening crop production by 30% to 50% in some regions. If this trend continues, scientists fear that soil pH could drop as low as 3.0, far below the optimal level of 6.0 to 7.0 required for cereals such as rice.

Government estimates of damage from acid deposition in the United States, Canada, and Europe exceed $50 billion annually. Acid deposition is an issue of global spatial significance. Because wind and weather patterns are international, efforts at addressing the problem also must be international in scope. Reductions in acid-causing emissions are closely tied to energy conservation and therefore directly related to production of greenhouse gases and global climate change concerns—thus linking these environmental issues. With recent research pinpointing nitrogen as the leading cause of acid deposition, this issue also is linked to food production and global sustainability issues.

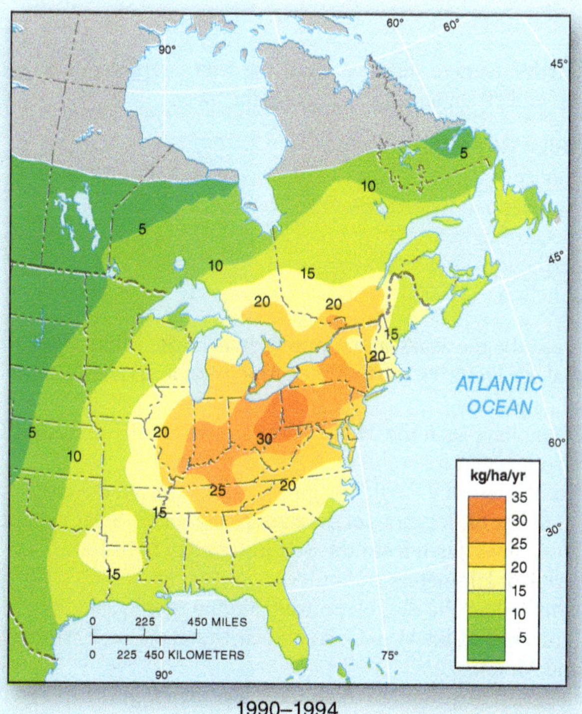

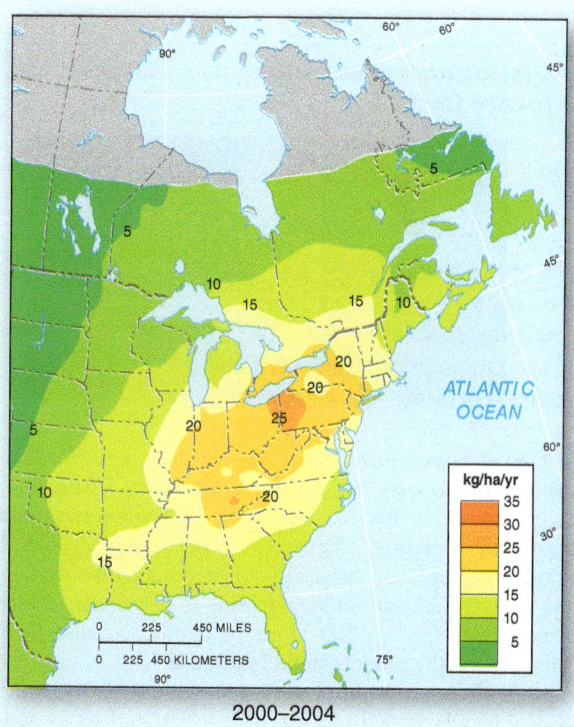

FIGURE 2.2 Improvement in sulfate wet deposition rate.
Spatial portrayal of annual sulfate (principally SO_4) wet deposition on the landscape, between two 5-year periods, in kilograms per hectare per year. The Canadian Environmental Protection Act, the Canada–United States Border Air Quality Strategy, and the U.S. Clean Air Act regulations together lowered levels of emissions that add acid to the environment. Research shows that power plants and other sources must cut sulfur dioxide emissions 80% beyond the Clean Air Act mandate to truly reverse damage trends. [Maps from Environment Canada, 2004. Reproduced with the permission of the Minister of Public Works and Government Services Canada.]

As you reflect on this chapter, the path of insolation to Earth's surface, our modern atmosphere, the treaties to protect stratospheric ozone, and the benefits from the CAA, you should feel encouraged. Scientists did the research and society knew what to do, took action, and reaped enormous economic and health benefits. Decades ago scientists learned to sustain and protect Astronaut Mark Lee by providing him an "atmosphere" with a spacesuit. Today, we must, in turn, learn to sustain and protect Earth's atmosphere so that it continues to ensure our own survival.

CRITICAL THINKING 6

Evaluating costs and benefits

In the scientific study *The Benefits of the Clean Air Act, 1970 to 1990* and in ongoing analyses, the EPA determined that the Clean Air Act provided health, welfare, ecological, and economic benefits 42 times greater than its costs. In 2010 alone, estimated benefits over costs were at a ratio of 4-to1. Do you think this is significant? Should this be part of the debate about future weakening or strengthening of the Clean Air Act? In your opinion, why is the public generally unaware of these details? What are the difficulties in informing the public?

GEOSYSTEMS CONNECTION

Consider our place in the Universe and the relations among the Milky Way Galaxy, Sun, planets, and satellites. From the Sun, the solar wind and electromagnetic spectrum of radiate energy flow across space to Earth, where we see its distribution along the top of the atmosphere and how this changes in a seasonal rhythm. We constructed Earth's atmosphere and examined its composition, temperature, and functions. Electromagnetic energy cascades toward Earth's surface, through the layers of the atmosphere where harmful wavelengths are filtered out. Also we examined human impacts on the atmosphere: the depletion of the ozone layer, acid deposition, and variable atmospheric ingredients, including human-made air pollution.

KEY LEARNING CONCEPTS REVIEW

■ ***Distinguish*** among galaxies, stars, and planets, and ***locate*** Earth.

Our Solar System—the Sun and eight planets—is located on a remote, trailing edge of the **Milky Way Galaxy**, a flattened, disk-shaped mass estimated to contain up to 300 billion stars. **Gravity**, the mutual attracting force exerted by the mass of an object upon all other objects, is an organizing force in the Universe. The process of stars (like our Sun) condensing from nebular clouds with planetesimals (protoplanets) forming in orbits around their central masses is the **planetesimal hypothesis**.

The Solar System, planets, and Earth began to condense from a nebular cloud of dust, gas, debris, and icy comets approximately 4.6 billion years ago. Distances in space are so vast that the **speed of light** (300,000 kmps, or 186,000 mps, which is about 9.5 trillion km, or nearly 6 trillion mi, per year) is used to express distance. In its orbit, Earth is at **perihelion** (its closest position to the Sun) during our Northern Hemisphere winter (January 3 at 147,255,000 km, or 91,500,000 mi). It is at **aphelion** (its farthest position from the Sun) during our Northern Hemisphere summer (July 4 at 152,083,000 km, or 94,500,000 mi). Earth's average distance from the Sun is approximately 8 minutes and 20 seconds in terms of light speed.

Milky Way Galaxy
gravity
planetesimal hypothesis
speed of light
perihelion
aphelion

1. Describe the Sun's status among stars in the Milky Way Galaxy. Describe the Sun's location, size, and relationship to its planets.
2. If you have seen the Milky Way at night, briefly describe it. Use specifics from the text in your description.
3. Briefly describe Earth's origin as part of the Solar System.
4. Compare the locations of the eight planets of the Solar System.
5. How far is Earth from the Sun in terms of light speed? In terms of kilometers and miles?
6. Briefly describe the relationship among these concepts: Universe, Milky Way Galaxy, Solar System, Sun, Earth, and Moon.
7. Diagram in a simple sketch Earth's orbit about the Sun. How much does it vary during the course of a year?

■ ***Describe*** the Sun's operation, and ***explain*** the characteristics of the solar wind and the electromagnetic spectrum of radiant energy.

The **fusion** process—hydrogen nuclei forced together under tremendous temperature and pressure in the Sun's interior—generates incredible quantities of energy. Solar energy in the

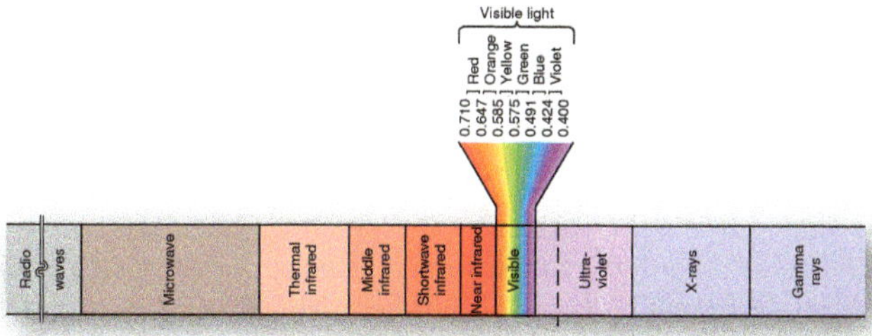

form of charged particles of **solar wind** travels outward in all directions from magnetic disturbances on the Sun, such as from large **sunspots**. Solar wind is deflected by Earth's **magnetosphere**, producing various effects in the upper atmosphere, including spectacular **auroras**, the northern and southern lights, which surge across the skies at higher latitudes. Another effect of the solar wind in the atmosphere is its possible influence on weather.

The **electromagnetic spectrum** of radiant energy travels outward in all directions from the Sun. The total spectrum of this radiant energy is made up of different **wavelengths**—the distance between corresponding points on any two successive waves of radiant energy. Eventually, some of this radiant energy reaches Earth's surface.

Electromagnetic radiation from the Sun passes through Earth's magnetic field to the top of the atmosphere—the **thermopause,** at an altitude of approximately 500 km (300 mi). Incoming solar radiation that reaches a horizontal plane at Earth is **insolation**, a term specifically applied to radiation arriving at Earth's surface and atmosphere. The term **solar constant** describes insolation at the top of the atmosphere: the average insolation received at the thermopause when Earth is at its average distance from the Sun. The solar constant is measured as an average of 1372 W/m^2 (2.0 $cal/cm^2/min$, 2 langleys/min). The place receiving maximum insolation is the **subsolar point**, where solar rays are perpendicular to the surface (radiating from directly overhead). All other locations away from the subsolar point receive slanting rays and more diffuse energy.

fusion
solar wind
sunspot
magnetosphere
aurora
electromagnetic spectrum
wavelength
thermopause
insolation
solar constant
subsolar point

8. How does the Sun produce such tremendous quantities of energy?
9. What is the sunspot cycle? At what stage is the cycle in the year 2013?
10. Describe Earth's magnetosphere and its effects on the solar wind and the electromagnetic spectrum.
11. Summarize the presently known effects of the solar wind relative to Earth's environment.
12. Describe the various segments of the electromagnetic spectrum, from shortest to longest wavelength. What are the main wavelengths produced by the Sun? Which wavelengths does Earth radiate to space?
13. What is the solar constant? Why is it important to know?
14. If Earth were *flat* and oriented at right angles to incoming solar radiation (insolation), what would be the latitudinal distribution of solar energy at the top of the atmosphere?

■ ***Define*** solar altitude, solar declination, and daylength, and ***describe*** the annual variability of each—Earth's seasonality.

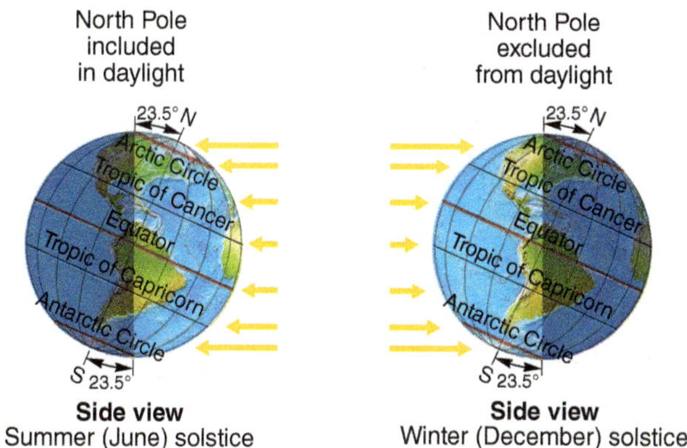

The angle between the Sun and the horizon is the Sun's **altitude.** The Sun's **declination** is the latitude of the subsolar point. Declination annually migrates through 47° of latitude, moving between the *Tropic of Cancer* at about 23.5° N latitude (June) and the *Tropic of Capricorn* at about 23.5° S latitude (December). Seasonality means an annual change in the Sun's altitude and changing **daylength**, or duration of exposure.

Earth's distinct seasons are produced by interactions of **revolution** (annual orbit about the Sun) and **rotation** (Earth's turning on its *axis*). As Earth rotates, the boundary that divides daylight and darkness is the **circle of illumination.** Other reasons for seasons include *axial tilt* (at about 23.5° from a perpendicular to the **plane of the ecliptic**), **axial parallelism** (the parallel alignment of the axis throughout the year), and *sphericity*.

Earth rotates about its axis, an imaginary line extending through the planet from the geographic North Pole to the South Pole. In the Solar System, an imaginary plane touching all points of Earth's orbit is the *plane of the ecliptic*. The **Tropic of Cancer** parallel marks the farthest north the subsolar point migrates during the year, about 23.5° N latitude. The **Tropic of Capricorn** parallel marks the farthest south the subsolar point migrates during the year, about 23.5° S latitude.

On December 21 or 22, at the moment of the **winter solstice** ("winter Sun stance"), or **December solstice**, the circle of illumination excludes the North Pole, but includes the South Pole. The subsolar point is at about 23.5° S latitude, the parallel called the Tropic of Capricorn. The Sun remains below the horizon the entire day. This latitude (about 66.5° N latitude) marks the **Arctic Circle**, the southernmost parallel (in the Northern Hemisphere) that experiences a 24-hour period of darkness or, on June 21 or 22, a 24-hour period of daylight. The moment of the **vernal equinox**, or **March equinox**, occurs on March 20 or 21. At that time, the circle of illumination passes through both poles so that all locations on Earth experience a 12-hour day and a 12-hour night.

June 20 or 21 is the moment of the **summer solstice**, or **June solstice**. The subsolar point migrates from the equator to about 23.5° N latitude, the Tropic of Cancer. Because the circle of illumination now includes the North Polar region, everything north of the Arctic Circle receives 24 hours of daylight—the "Midnight Sun." In contrast, the area from the **Antarctic Circle** to the South Pole (66.5°–90° S latitude) is in darkness the entire 24 hours or, on December 21 or 22, in constant daylight. September 22 or 23 is the time of the **autumnal equinox**, or **September equinox**, when Earth's orientation is such that the circle of illumination again passes through both poles so that all parts of the globe experience a 12-hour day and a 12-hour night.

altitude
declination
daylength
revolution
rotation
circle of illumination
plane of the ecliptic
axial parallelism
Tropic of Cancer
Tropic of Capricorn
winter solstice, December solstice
Arctic Circle
vernal equinox, March equinox
summer solstice, June solstice
Antarctic Circle
autumnal equinox, September equinox

15. The concept of seasonality refers to what specific phenomena? How do these two aspects of seasonality change during a year at 0° latitude? At 40°? At 90°?
16. Differentiate between the Sun's altitude and its declination at Earth's surface.
17. For the latitude at which you live, how does daylength vary during the year? How does the Sun's altitude vary? Does your local newspaper publish a weather calendar containing such information?
18. List the five physical factors that operate together to produce seasons.
19. Describe Earth's revolution and rotation and differentiate between them.
20. Define Earth's present tilt relative to its orbit about the Sun.
21. Describe seasonal conditions at each of the four key seasonal anniversary dates during the year. What are the solstices and equinoxes, and what is the Sun's declination at these times?

■ ***Construct*** a general model of the atmosphere based on composition, temperature, and function, and ***diagram*** this model in a simple sketch.

Our modern atmosphere is a gaseous mixture so evenly mixed it behaves as if it were a single gas. The principal substance of this atmosphere is air—the medium of life. *Air* is naturally odorless, colorless, tasteless, and formless.

Above an altitude of 480 km (300 mi), the atmosphere is rarefied (nearly a vacuum) and is the **exosphere**, which means "outer sphere." The weight (force over a unit area) of the atmosphere, exerted on all surfaces, is **air pressure**. It decreases rapidly with altitude.

By *composition*, we divide the atmosphere into the **heterosphere**, extending from 480 km (300 mi) to 80 km (50 mi), and the **homosphere**, extending from 80 km to Earth's surface. Within the heterosphere and using *temperature* as a criterion, we identify the **thermosphere**. Its upper limit, called the *thermopause*, is at an altitude of approximately 480 km (300 mi). **Kinetic energy**, the energy of motion, is the vibrational energy that we measure and call temperature. The actual heat produced in the thermosphere is very small. The density of the molecules is so low that little actual *heat*, the flow of kinetic energy from one body to another because of a temperature difference between them, is produced. Nearer Earth's surface, the greater number of molecules in the denser atmosphere transmits their kinetic energy as **sensible heat**, meaning that we can feel it.

The homosphere includes the **mesosphere, stratosphere**, and **troposphere**, as defined by temperature criteria. The top of the troposphere is wherever a temperature of –57°C (–70°F) is recorded, a transition known as the *tropopause*. The normal temperature profile within the troposphere during the daytime decreases rapidly with increasing altitude at an average of 6.4 C° per kilometer (3.5 F° per 1000 ft), a rate known as the **normal lapse rate**. The actual lapse rate at any particular time and place may deviate considerably because of local weather conditions and is called the *environmental lapse rate*.

We distinguish a region in the heterosphere by its *function*. The **ionosphere** absorbs cosmic rays, gamma rays, X-rays, and shorter wavelengths of ultraviolet radiation and converts them into kinetic energy. A functional region within the stratosphere is the **ozonosphere**, or **ozone layer**, which absorbs life-threatening ultraviolet radiation, subsequently raising the temperature of the stratosphere.

exosphere
air pressure
heterosphere
homosphere
thermosphere
kinetic energy
sensible heat
mesosphere
stratosphere
troposphere
normal lapse rate
ionosphere
ozonosphere, ozone layer

22. What is air? Where did the components in Earth's present atmosphere originate?
23. What three distinct criteria are employed in dividing the atmosphere for study?
24. Describe the overall temperature profile of the atmosphere and list the four layers defined by temperature.
25. Describe the two divisions of the atmosphere on the basis of composition.
26. What are the two overall primary functional layers of the atmosphere and what does each do?
27. Name the four most prevalent stable gases in the homosphere. Where did each originate? Is the amount of any of these changing at this time?

■ ***Describe*** conditions within the stratosphere; specifically, ***review*** the function and status of the ozonosphere, or ozone layer.

The overall reduction of the stratospheric ozonosphere, or ozone layer, during the past several decades represents a hazard for society

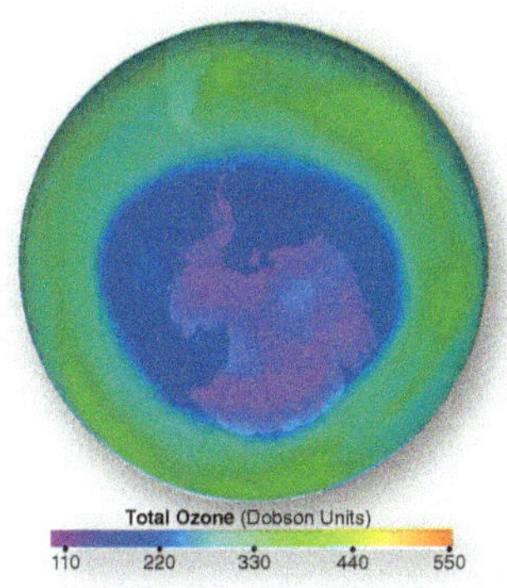

and many natural systems and is caused by chemicals introduced into the atmosphere by humans. Since World War II, quantities of human-made **chlorofluorocarbons (CFCs)** and bromine-containing compounds have made their way into the stratosphere. The increased ultraviolet light at those altitudes breaks down these stable chemical compounds, thus freeing chlorine and bromine atoms. These atoms act as catalysts in reactions that destroy ozone molecules.

chlorofluorocarbon (CFC)

28. Why is stratospheric ozone so important? Describe the effects created by increases in ultraviolet light reaching Earth's surface.
29. Summarize the ozone predicament, and describe trends and any treaties to protect the ozone layer.
30. Evaluate Crutzen, Rowland, and Molina's use of the scientific method in investigating stratospheric ozone depletion and the public reaction to their findings.

■ ***Distinguish*** between natural and anthropogenic variable gases and materials in the lower atmosphere, and ***describe*** the sources and effects of air pollution and acid deposition.

Within the troposphere, both natural and human-caused variable gases, particles, and other chemicals are part of the atmosphere. We coevolved with natural "pollution" and thus are adapted to it. But we are not adapted to cope with our own anthropogenic pollution. It constitutes a major health threat, particularly where people are concentrated in cities.

Vertical temperature and atmospheric density distribution in the troposphere can worsen pollution conditions. A **temperature inversion** occurs when the normal temperature decrease with altitude (normal lapse rate) reverses. In other words, temperature begins to increase at some altitude.

Photochemical smog results from the interaction of sunlight and the products of automobile exhaust, the single largest contributor of pollution that produces smog. Car exhaust, containing *nitrogen dioxide* and *volatile organic compounds* (*VOCs*), in the presence of ultraviolet light in sunlight converts into the principal photochemical by-products—*ozone*, *peroxyacetyl nitrates* (*PAN*), and *nitric acid.*

Ozone (O_3) causes negative health effects, oxidizes surfaces, and kills or damages plants. **Peroxyacetyl nitrates (PAN)** produce no known health effects in humans, but are particularly damaging to plants, including both agricultural crops and forests. *Nitrogen dioxide* (*NO_2*) damages and inflames human respiratory systems, destroys lung tissue, and damages plants. Nitric oxides participate in reactions that form nitric acid (HNO_3) in the atmosphere, forming both wet and dry acidic deposition. The *volatile organic compounds* (*VOCs*), including hydrocarbons from gasoline, surface coatings, and electric utility combustion, are important factors in ozone formation.

The distribution of human-produced **industrial smog** over North America, Europe, and Asia is related to transportation and electrical production. Such characteristic pollution contains **sulfur dioxide (SO_2)**. Sulfur dioxide in the atmosphere reacts to produce *sulfate aerosols*, which produce sulfuric acid (H_2SO_4) deposition, which can be dangerous to health and affect Earth's energy budget by scattering and reflecting solar energy. **Particulate matter (PM)** consists of dirt, dust, soot, and ash from industrial and natural sources. Small particles of dust, soot, and pollution suspended in the air are **aerosols**.

Conserving energy, making energy use more efficient, and reducing emissions are key to reducing air pollution. Earth's next atmosphere most accurately may be described as the **anthropogenic atmosphere** (human-influenced atmosphere).

temperature inversion
photochemical smog
peroxyacetyl nitrate (PAN)
industrial smog
sulfur dioxide
particulate matter (PM)
aerosol
anthropogenic atmosphere

31. Why are anthropogenic gases more significant to human health than those produced from natural sources?
32. In what ways does a temperature inversion worsen an air pollution episode? Why?
33. What is the difference between industrial smog and photochemical smog?
34. Describe the relationship between automobiles and the production of ozone and PAN in city air. What are the principal negative impacts of these gases?
35. How are sulfur impurities in fossil fuels related to the formation of acid in the atmosphere and acid deposition on the land?
36. In summary, what are the cost–benefit results from the first 20 years under Clean Air Act regulations?

Visit **http://www.masteringgeography.com/** for several figure animations, satellite loops, self-study quizzes, flashcards, visual glossary, case studies, career links, text reference maps, RSS Feeds, and an ebook version of *Elemental Geosystems.* Included are many geography web links to interesting Internet sources that support this chapter.

Atmospheric Energy and Global Temperatures

Atmospheric Energy and Global Temperatures

The phenomenal growth of the Phoenix metropolitan area between 1989 and 2009 is highlighted in these two *Landsat-5* images of southeastern Phoenix. The suburbs of Chandler to the lower right and Mesa just to the north represent urban sprawl with no central business core. South Mountain is to the lower left. This urban growth enhances the urban heat island effect on surface energy budgets. Because of the darker surfaces, impervious to water, Phoenix is about 7 C° to 11 C° warmer than surrounding rural regions. [*Landsat-5* TM images, NASA/GSFC.]

KEY LEARNING CONCEPTS

After reading the chapter, you should be able to:

- ***Identify*** the pathways of solar energy through the troposphere to Earth's surface: transmission, scattering, diffuse radiation, refraction, albedo (reflectivity), conduction, convection, and advection.
- ***Describe*** the greenhouse effect and the patterns of global net radiation and surface energy balances.
- ***Review*** the temperature concepts and temperature controls that produce global temperature patterns.
- ***Interpret*** the pattern of Earth's temperatures from their portrayal on January and July temperature maps and on a map of annual temperature ranges.
- ***Contrast*** wind chill and heat index, and ***determine*** human response to these apparent temperature effects.
- ***Portray*** typical urban heat island conditions, and ***contrast*** the microclimatology of urban areas with that of surrounding rural environments.

Albedo Impacts, a Limit on Future Arctic Shipping?

For hundreds of years, explorers searched for the fabled "Northwest Passage"—a sea route connecting the Atlantic and Pacific Oceans through the inland waterways of the Canadian Archipelago. The "Northeast Passage," or Northern Sea Route, is another Arctic shipping lane traversing the Russian coast and linking Europe and Asia. These northern routes eliminate the need to go through the Panama and Suez Canals, respectively.

Arctic Ocean sea ice blocked these routes, making them unavailable for shipping—that is, until recently. In 2009, the first commercial navigation of the Northeast Passage by a pair of German container ships was successful, owing to losses of Arctic ice associated with climate change.

The prospect of an ice-free Arctic Ocean is triggering commercial excitement for freighter and oil tanker traffic across these northern passages. With record losses of Arctic sea ice in 2007, the Northwest Passage achieved ice-free status and the Northeast Passage continued its ice-free summer status (Figure GN 1). The three years following had comparable ice losses caused by higher ocean and air temperatures across the region.

Given significant losses to multi-year ice, the National Snow and Ice Data Center (NSIDC) forecasted that summer ice-free conditions could happen for the Arctic Ocean before 2015. As the multi-year core ice fails, only the seasonal ice remains. This younger, thinner ice takes less energy to melt. Also, scientists report that strong Arctic winds blow ice southward, where it melts in warmer ocean waters, accounting for nearly a third of sea-ice loss.

FIGURE GN 1 2007 Arctic sea-ice extent. Trace possible new shipping routes across the Northeast and Northwest passages on the satellite image. [NASA/GSFC Image.]

The impacts of surface albedo also play a key role in sea-ice melting. Day-to-day observations tell us that lighter surfaces tend to reflect sunlight and remain cooler, whereas darker surfaces tend to absorb sunlight and heat up. Snow- and ice-covered surfaces are great natural reflectors; in fact, sea ice reflects about 80%–95% of the solar energy it receives. The ocean surface is darker, reflecting only an average of about 10% of insolation. This percentage is albedo, or the reflective value of a surface. As the ice-covered area in the Arctic retreats, darker water or land receives direct sunlight and absorbs more heat, which adds to warming—a positive feedback.

Particulates in the atmosphere appear to enhance this albedo impact. Scientists now have evidence that soot and particulate aerosol fallout are significant causes of glacial snow and ice losses across the Himalayas. On the Greenland Ice Sheet, black soot, dust, and particulates accumulate with snow and harden into the ice, darkening the surface. As surface albedo decreases, ice absorbs more insolation, and increased melting causes soot to become even more concentrated and darker. The stack emissions from Arctic shipping produce similar impacts.

The 2009 *Arctic Marine Shipping Assessment* (Arctic Council, p. 140) stated that "ship stack emissions in and near the Arctic will increase." Shipping has already expanded by more than three weeks in the Arctic and two months in Hudson Bay and Manitoba since 2000 (Figure GN 2). The stack emissions from new freighter and tanker traffic will add soot and particulate material into the Arctic atmosphere. Fallout from these ship emissions could prove to be an albedo disaster, darkening remaining ice shelves and glaciers.

Whether to open the Northwest and Northeast Passages to ship traffic is a question of surface albedo values and the principles we cover in this chapter. So far, these surface-energy budget considerations and spatial analysis have not entered political or economic discussions. ■

FIGURE GN 2 Ship traffic and shipments in the Arctic Ocean. [Left–Canadian Coast Guard; right–German Shipowners Association.]

Earth's biosphere pulses with flows of solar energy that sustain our lives and empower natural systems. Changing seasons, daily weather conditions, and the variety of Earth's climates remind us of this constant flow of energy cascading through the atmosphere. Energy and moisture exchanges between Earth's surface and the atmosphere are essential elements of weather and climate.

In this chapter: We follow solar energy through the troposphere to Earth's surface. The *outputs* of reflected light and emitted longwave energy from the atmosphere and surface environment counter the *input* of insolation. Together, this input and output determine the net energy available to perform work. We examine surface energy budgets and analyze how net radiation is spent. Focus Study 1 discusses solar energy, an applied aspect of surface energy and a renewable energy resource of great potential.

We also look at temperature, which affects societies, decision making, and resources consumed across the globe. Understanding temperature concepts helps us begin our study of these Earth systems. We look at the principal temperature controls of latitude, altitude and elevation, cloud cover, and land–water heating differences as they interact to produce Earth's temperature patterns. We examine the effect of temperature on the human body and discuss current temperature trends associated with global warming. The chapter concludes with a look at the unique energy and moisture environment in our cities. The view across a hot parking lot of cars and pavement in summer is all too familiar—the air shimmers as heat energy radiates skyward. The climate of our urban areas differs measurably from that of surrounding rural areas.

Energy Essentials

When you look at a picture of Earth taken from space, you clearly see the surface receipts of incoming insolation. Land and water surfaces, clouds, and atmospheric gases and dust intercept solar energy. The flows of energy are in swirling weather patterns, powerful oceanic currents, and varied land-cover vegetation. Specific energy patterns differ for deserts, oceans, mountaintops, plains, rain forests, and ice-covered landscapes. In addition, the presence or absence of clouds may make a 75% difference in the amount of energy that reaches the surface because clouds reflect incoming energy.

Energy Pathways and Principles

Solar energy that heats Earth's atmosphere and surface is unevenly distributed by latitude and fluctuates seasonally. Figure 1 is a simplified flow diagram of shortwave and longwave radiation in the Earth–atmosphere system, discussed in the pages that follow. You will find it helpful to refer to this figure, and the more detailed energy-balance illustration in Figure 9, as you read through the following section. We first look at some important pathways and principles for insolation as it passes through the atmosphere to Earth's surface.

Transmission refers to the passage of shortwave and longwave energy through either the atmosphere or water. Our budget of atmospheric energy comprises shortwave radiation *inputs* (ultraviolet light, visible light, and near-infrared wavelengths) and longwave radiation *outputs* (thermal infrared) that pass through the atmosphere by transmission.

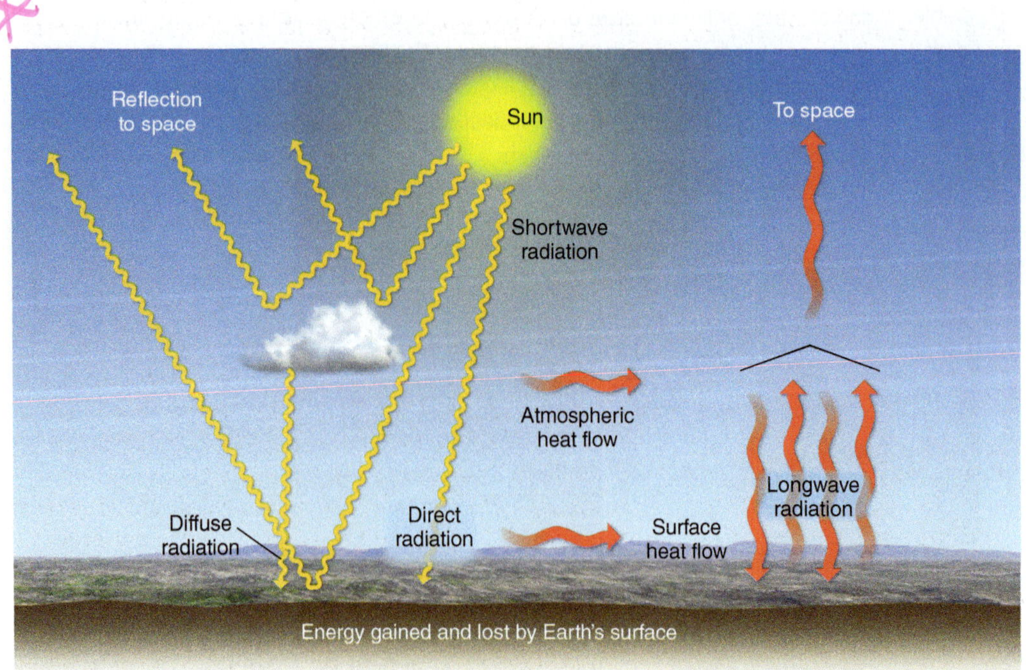

FIGURE 1 Simplified view of the Earth–atmosphere energy system. Energy gained and lost by Earth's surface and atmosphere. Circuits include incoming shortwave radiation, reflected shortwave radiation, and outgoing longwave radiation.

Animation
Global Warming, Climate Change

Animation
Earth–Atmosphere Energy Balance

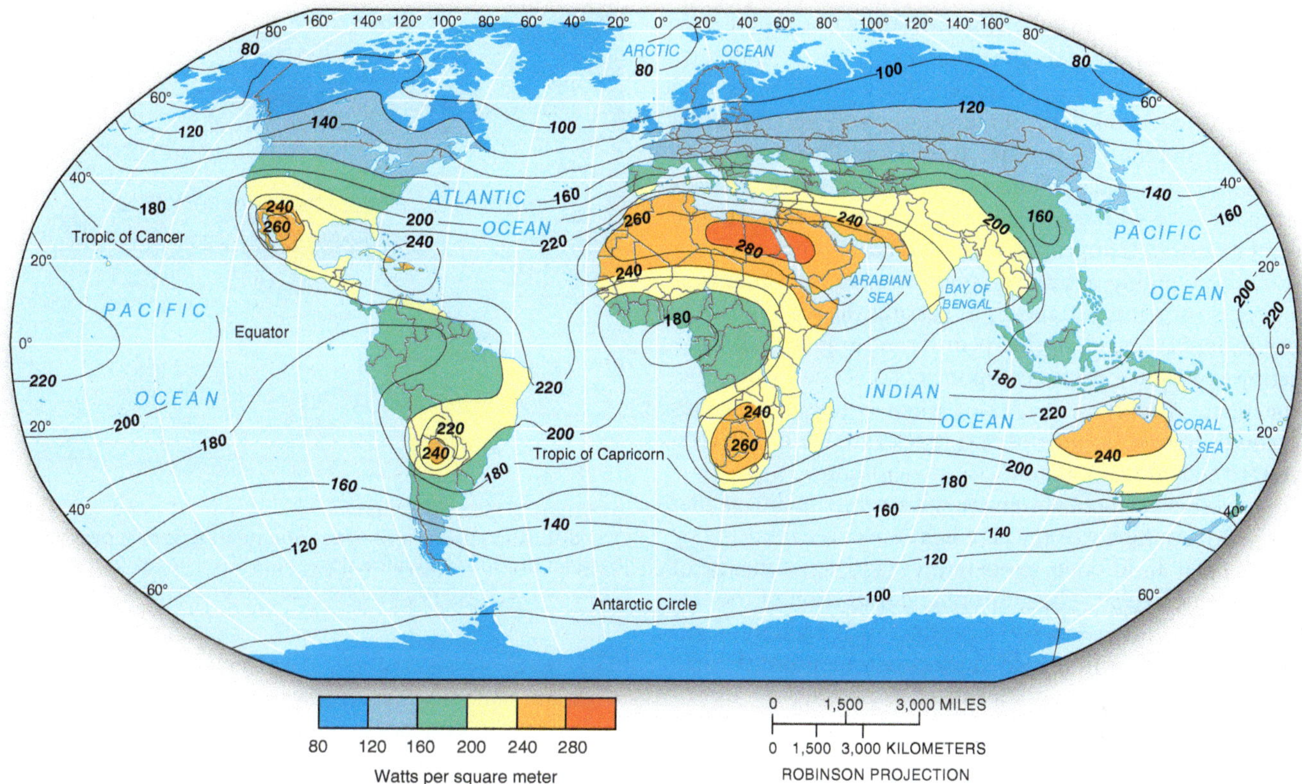

FIGURE 2 Insolation at Earth's surface.
Average annual solar radiation received on a horizontal surface at ground level in watts per square meter (100 W/m^2 = 75 kcal/cm^2/year). [After M. I. Budyko, *The Heat Balance of the Earth's Surface* (Washington, DC: U.S. Department of Commerce, 1958), p. 99.]

Insolation Input

Insolation is the single energy input driving the Earth–atmosphere system. The world map in Figure 2 shows the distribution of average annual solar energy received at Earth's surface. It includes all the radiation that arrives at Earth's surface, both direct and diffuse (scattered by the atmosphere).

Several patterns are notable on the map. Insolation decreases poleward from about 25° latitude in both the Northern and the Southern Hemispheres. Consistent daylength and high Sun altitude produce average annual values of 180–220 watts per square meter (W/m^2) throughout the equatorial and tropical latitudes. In general, greater insolation of 240–280 W/m^2 occurs in low-latitude deserts worldwide because of frequently cloudless skies. Note this energy pattern in the cloudless subtropical deserts in both hemispheres (for example, the Sonoran, Saharan, Arabian, Atacama, Namib, Kalahari, and Australian Deserts).

Scattering (Diffuse Radiation) Insolation encounters an increasing density of atmospheric gases as it travels toward the surface. Atmospheric gases, dust, cloud droplets, water vapor, and pollutants physically interact with insolation. The gas molecules redirect radiation, changing the direction of the light's movement without altering its wavelengths. **Scattering** describes this phenomenon and represents 7% of Earth's reflectivity, or albedo (see Figure 9).

Have you wondered why Earth's sky is blue? And why sunsets and sunrises are often red? These simple questions have an interesting explanation, based upon a principle known as Rayleigh scattering (named for English physicist Lord Rayleigh, 1881). This principle relates wavelength to the size of molecules or particles that cause the scattering.

The general rule is this: *The shorter the wavelength, the greater the scattering; the longer the wavelength, the lesser the scattering.* Small gas molecules in the air scatter shorter wavelengths of light. Thus, the shorter wavelengths of visible light—the blues and violets—scatter the most and dominate the lower atmosphere. And because there are more blue than violet wavelengths in sunlight, a blue sky prevails. A sky filled with smog and haze appears almost white because the larger particles associated with air pollution act to scatter all wavelengths of visible light.

The angle of the Sun's rays determines the thickness of the atmosphere through which they must pass to reach the surface. Therefore, direct rays (from overhead) experience less scattering and absorption than do low, oblique-angle rays, which must travel farther through the atmosphere. Insolation from the low-altitude Sun undergoes more scattering of shorter wavelengths, leaving only the residual oranges and reds to reach the observer at sunset or sunrise.

Some incoming insolation is diffused by clouds and atmosphere and transmits to Earth as **diffuse radiation**, the downward component of scattered light (labeled in

Figure 9). Such diffuse light is multidirectional and thus casts shadowless light on the ground.

Refraction As insolation enters the atmosphere, it passes from one medium to another, from virtually empty space into atmospheric gases. This occurs when insolation passes from air into water, as well. The transition subjects the insolation to a change of speed, which also shifts its direction, the bending action of **refraction**. In the same way, a crystal or prism refracts light passing through it, bending different wavelengths to different angles and separating the light into its component colors to display the spectrum. A rainbow is created when visible light passes through myriad raindrops and is refracted and reflected toward the observer at a precise angle (Figure 3).

Another example of refraction is a *mirage*, an image that appears near the horizon where light waves are refracted by layers of air at different temperatures (and consequently of different densities). The atmospheric distortion of the setting Sun in Figure 4 is also a product of refraction—light from the Sun low in the sky must penetrate more air than when the Sun is high; it is refracted through air layers of different densities on its way to the observer.

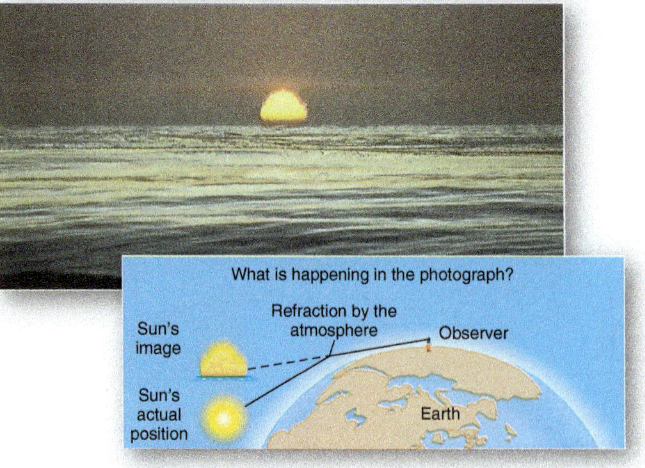

FIGURE 4 Sun refraction.
The distorted appearance of the Sun nearing sunset over the ocean is produced by refraction of the Sun's image in the atmosphere. Have you ever noticed this effect? [Author.]

FIGURE 3 A rainbow.
Raindrops—and in this photo moisture droplets from the Niagara River—refract and reflect light to produce a primary rainbow. Note that in the primary rainbow the colors with the shortest wavelengths are on the inside and those with the longest wavelengths are on the outside. In the secondary bow, note that the color sequence is reversed because of an extra angle of reflection within each moisture droplet. [Bobbé Christopherson.]

An interesting function of refraction is that it adds approximately 8 minutes of daylight that we would lack if Earth had no atmosphere. We see the Sun's image about 4 minutes before the Sun actually peeks over the horizon. Similarly, as the Sun sets, its refracted image is visible from over the horizon for about 4 minutes afterward. These extra minutes vary with atmospheric temperature, moisture, and pollutants.

Albedo and Reflection A portion of arriving energy bounces directly back into space without being absorbed or performing any work—this is the **reflection** process. **Albedo** is the reflective quality, or intrinsic brightness, of a surface. It is an important control over the amount of insolation that is available for absorption by a surface. We state albedo as the percentage of insolation that is reflected (0% is total absorption; 100% is total reflectance). Examine the different surfaces and their albedo values in Figure 5.

In the visible wavelengths, darker colors have lower albedos, and lighter colors have higher albedos. On water surfaces, the angle of the solar rays also affects albedo values: lower angles produce a greater reflection than do higher angles. In addition, smooth surfaces increase albedo, whereas rougher surfaces reduce it.

GEO REPORT 1 Earthshine

Some of Earth's reflection of light to space shines on the Moon. We have all seen the effect of *earthshine* as a faint illumination of the dark portion of the Moon, especially in crescent phase, when the dark area of the lunar disk is barely visible. In contrast, the Moon reflects only 6% to 8% of the sunlight that hits its surface, producing the "moonlight" familiar to us all. Scientists from the New Jersey Institute of Technology and California Institute of Technology now measure earthshine at the Big Bear Solar Observatory (see http://www.bbso.njit.edu/). Earthshine studies began in 1925. Think about earthshine on the Moon the next time you take a moonlit walk.

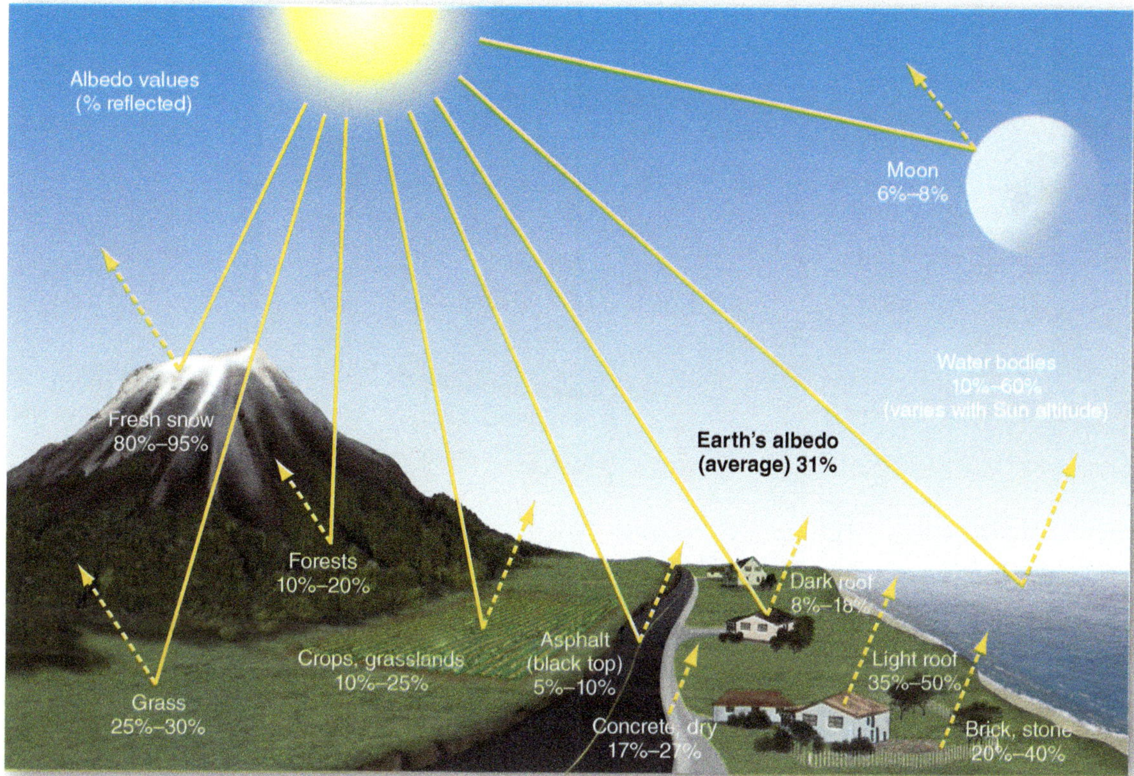

Satellite
Global Albedo Values, Global Shortwave Radiation

FIGURE 5 Various albedo values.
In general, light surfaces are more reflective than dark surfaces and thus have higher albedo values.

Specific locations experience highly variable albedo values during the year in response to changes in cloud and ground cover. Earth Radiation Budget (ERB) sensors aboard the *Nimbus*-7 satellite measured average albedos of 19%–38% for all surfaces between the tropics (23.5° N to 23.5° S), whereas albedos for the polar regions measured as high as 80% as a result of ice and snow. Tropical forests are characteristically low in albedo (15%), whereas generally cloudless deserts have higher albedos (35%).

Earth and its atmosphere reflect 31% of all insolation when averaged over a year. By comparison, a full Moon, which is bright enough to read by under clear skies, has only a 6%–8% albedo value. Thus, with *earthshine* being four times brighter than moonlight (four times the albedo) and with Earth four times greater in diameter than the Moon, it is no surprise that astronauts report how startling our planet looks from space.

Clouds, Aerosols, and the Atmosphere's Albedo

Clouds are an unpredictable factor in the tropospheric energy budget and therefore in the refining of climatic models. They reflect insolation and thus cool Earth's surface. The term **cloud-albedo forcing** refers to an increase in albedo caused by clouds. Yet clouds act as insulation, trapping longwave radiation from Earth and raising minimum temperatures. **Cloud-greenhouse forcing** is an increase in greenhouse warming caused by clouds. Figure 6 illustrates the general effects of clouds on shortwave radiation and longwave radiation.

The eruption of Mount Pinatubo in the Philippines, which began explosively during June 1991, illustrates how Earth's internal processes affect the atmosphere. Approximately 15–20 megatons of sulfur dioxide droplets were injected into the stratosphere; winds rapidly spread these aerosols worldwide. As a result, atmospheric albedo increased worldwide and produced a temporary average cooling of 0.5 C° (0.9 F°).

Other mechanisms affect atmospheric albedo and therefore atmospheric and surface energy budgets. Industrialization is producing a haze of pollution, including sulfate aerosols, soot and fly ash, and black carbon, that is increasing the reflectivity of the atmosphere. These aerosols act as an insolation-reflecting haze in clear-sky conditions.

Pollution causes both an atmospheric warming through absorption by the pollutants and a surface cooling through reduction in insolation reaching the surface. An overall term describes this decline in insolation making it to Earth's surface—**global dimming**. In determining present temperature increases associated with climate change, the dimming of sunlight is causing an underestimation of the actual amount of warming.

Absorption The *assimilation* of radiation by molecules of matter and its conversion from one form of energy to another is **absorption**. Insolation, both direct and diffuse, that is not part of the 31% reflected from Earth's surface and atmosphere is absorbed. It is converted into either longwave radiation or chemical energy by plants in photosynthesis.

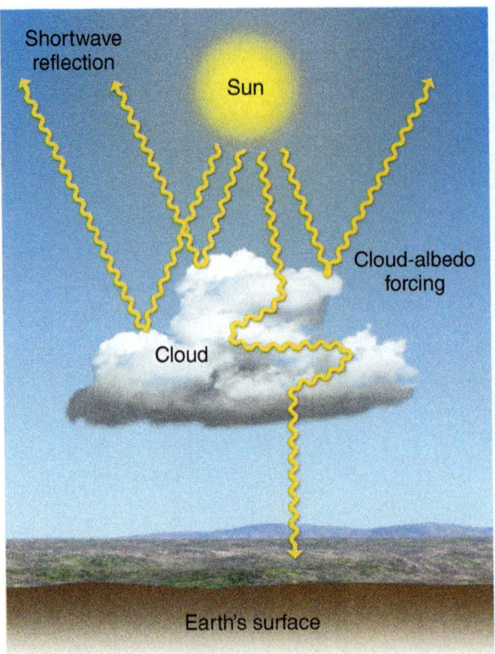

(a) Shortwave radiation

(b) Longwave radiation

FIGURE 6 The effects of clouds on shortwave and longwave radiation. (a) Clouds reflect and scatter shortwave radiation; a high percentage is returned to space. (b) Clouds absorb and radiate longwave radiation emitted by Earth; some longwave energy returns to space and some toward the surface.

The temperature of the absorbing surface is raised in the process, and warmer surfaces radiate more total energy at shorter wavelengths—thus, *the hotter the surface, the shorter the wavelengths that are emitted.* Examples are an electric burner beginning to glow as it heats and molten metal glowing at high temperatures. In addition to absorption by land and water surfaces (about 45% of incoming insolation), absorption occurs in atmospheric gases, dust, clouds, and stratospheric ozone (together about 24% of incoming insolation). Figure 9 summarizes the pathways of insolation and the flow of heat in the atmosphere and at the surface.

Conduction, Convection, and Advection Heat energy can be transferred in a system in several ways. **Conduction** is the molecule-to-molecule transfer of heat energy as it diffuses through a substance. As molecules warm, their vibration increases, causing collisions that produce motion in neighboring molecules, thus transferring heat from warmer to cooler materials.

Different materials (gases, liquids, and solids) conduct sensible heat directionally from areas of higher temperature to those of lower temperature. This heat flow transfers energy through matter at varying rates, depending on the conductivity of the material—Earth's land surface is a better conductor than air; moist air is a slightly better conductor than dry air.

Gases and liquids also transfer energy by movements of **convection** when the physical mixing involves a strong vertical motion. When horizontal motion dominates, the term **advection** applies. In the atmosphere or in bodies of water, warmer (less dense) masses tend to rise and cooler (more dense) masses tend to sink, establishing patterns of convection. Sensible heat transports physically through the medium in this way.

You experience such energy flows in the kitchen: Energy is conducted through the handle of a pan, and boiling water bubbles in the saucepan in convective motions (Figure 7). Also in the kitchen, you may use a convection oven that has a fan to circulate heated air to uniformly cook food.

In physical geography, we find many examples of each physical transfer mechanism:

- *Conduction* includes surface energy budgets, temperature differences between land and water bodies and between darker and lighter surfaces, the heating of surfaces and overlying air, and soil temperatures;
- *Convection* is in atmospheric and oceanic circulation, air mass movements and weather systems, internal motions deep within Earth that produce a magnetic field, and movements in the crust; and
- *Advection* involves horizontal movement of winds from land to sea and back, fog that forms and moves to another area, and air mass movements from source regions.

GEO REPORT 2 *Monitoring Earth's radiant energy systems*

To better understand the role of natural clouds, as well as jet contrails and aerosols, National Aeronautics and Space Administration (NASA) began operating sensors aboard satellites in 1997 with the Tropical Rainfall Measuring Mission (TRMM), followed by *Terra* and *Aqua* in 1999 and 2002, respectively. See CERES (Clouds and Earth's Radiant Energy System) at http://science.larc.nasa.gov/; click on "Site Map" and then "Clouds and Aerosols" to review the various programs and spacecraft involved in this science.

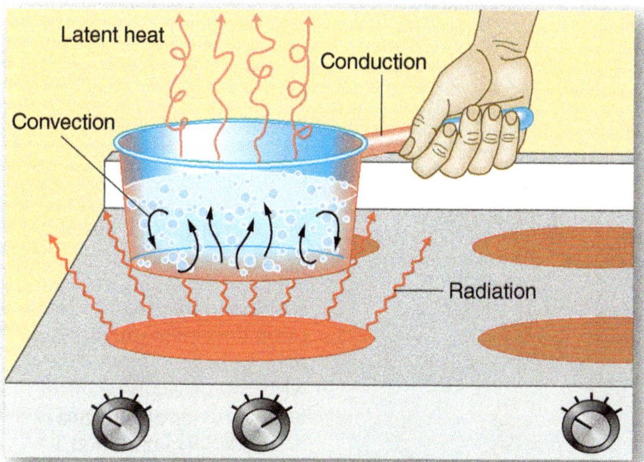

FIGURE 7 A pan of water on the stove illustrates heat transfer processes.
Infrared energy *radiates* from the burner to the saucepan and the air. Energy *conducts* through the molecules of the pan and the handle. The water physically mixes, carrying heat energy by *convection*.

Now, with these pathways and principles in mind, we put it all together to describe the energy budget of the lower atmosphere.

CRITICAL THINKING 1

A kelp indicator of surface energy dynamics

Examine Figure CT 1. In Antarctica, on Petermann Island off the Graham Land Coast, a piece of kelp (a seaweed) was dropped by a passing bird. The kelp was resting about 10 cm (4 in.) deep in the snow, in a hole about the shape of the kelp. In your opinion, what energy factors operated to make this scene?

Now, expand your conclusion to the issue of mining in Antarctica. There are coal deposits and other minerals in Antarctica. The international Antarctic Treaty blocks mining exploitation, although reconsideration is possible after 2048. Given your energy budget analysis of the kelp in the snow, information on surface energy budgets in this chapter, the dust and particulate output of mining, and the importance of a stable sea level, construct a case opposed to such mining activities based on these factors. Further, what factors can you think of that would favor such mining?

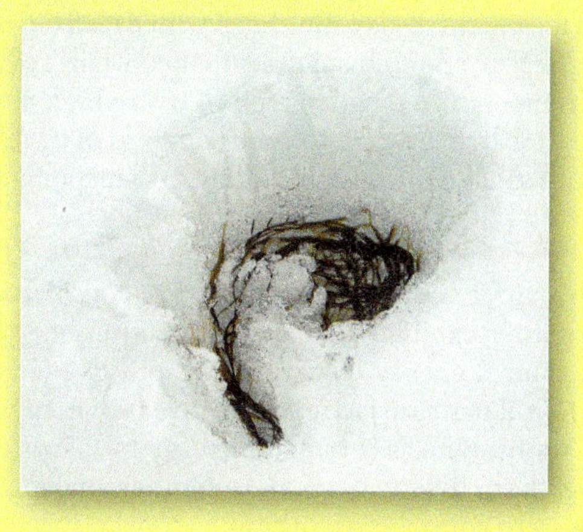

[Bobbé Christopherson]

The Greenhouse Effect and Atmospheric Warming

Previously, we characterized Earth as a cool-body radiator, emitting energy in longer wavelengths from its surface and atmosphere toward space. However, some of this longwave radiation is absorbed by carbon dioxide, water vapor, methane, nitrous oxide, chlorofluorocarbons (CFCs), and other gases in the lower atmosphere and then emitted back toward Earth. This absorption and emission of energy are an important factor in warming the troposphere. The rough similarity between this process and the way a greenhouse operates gives the process its name—the **greenhouse effect**.

In a greenhouse, the glass is transparent to shortwave insolation, allowing light to pass through to the soil, plants, and materials inside, where absorption and conduction take place. The absorbed energy is then radiated as longwave radiation toward the glass, but the glass physically traps both the longer wavelengths and the warmed air inside the greenhouse. Thus, the glass acts as a one-way filter, allowing the shortwave energy in, but not allowing the longwave energy out except through conduction. You experience the same process in a car parked in direct sunlight.

Opening the greenhouse roof vent, or the car windows, allows the air inside to mix with the outside environment, thereby removing heated air physically from one place to another by convection. The interior of a car gets surprisingly hot, even on a day with mild temperatures outside. Many people place a removable sunscreen across the windshield to prevent shortwave energy from entering the car to begin the greenhouse process. Have you taken steps to reduce the insolation input into your car's interior or through windows at home?

Overall, the atmosphere behaves a bit differently. In the atmosphere, the greenhouse analogy does not fully apply because longwave radiation is not trapped as in a greenhouse. Rather, its passage to space is delayed as the longwave radiation is absorbed by certain gases, clouds, and dust in the atmosphere and is emitted to Earth's surface. According to scientific consensus, today's increasing carbon dioxide concentration is forcing more longwave radiation absorption in the lower atmosphere, thus producing a warming trend and changes in the Earth–atmosphere energy system.

Clouds and Earth's "Greenhouse"

Clouds affect the heating of the lower atmosphere in several ways, depending on cloud type. Not only is the percentage of cloud cover important, but also the cloud type, height, and thickness (water content and density) have an effect. High-altitude, ice-crystal clouds reflect insolation with albedos of about 50%, whereas thick, lower cloud cover reflects about 90% of incoming insolation.

To understand the actual effects on the atmosphere's energy budget, we must consider both transmission of shortwave and longwave radiation and cloud type. Figure 8a portrays the *cloud-greenhouse forcing* caused by high

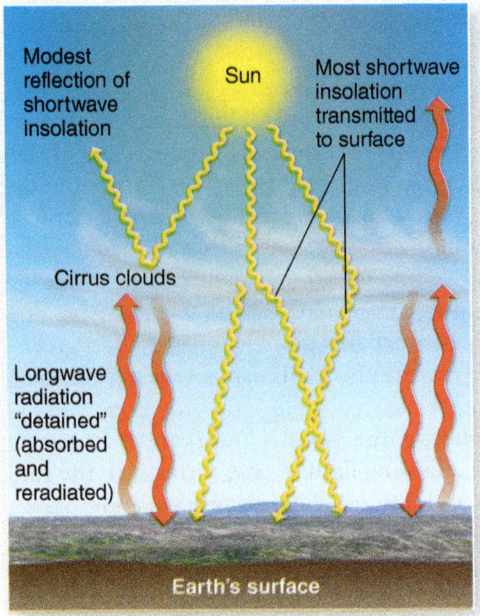

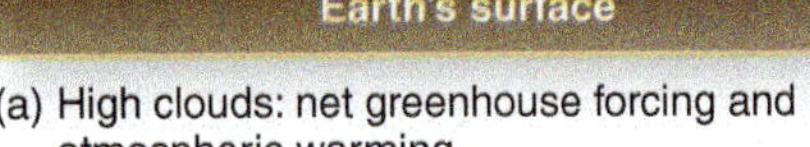
(a) High clouds: net greenhouse forcing and atmospheric warming

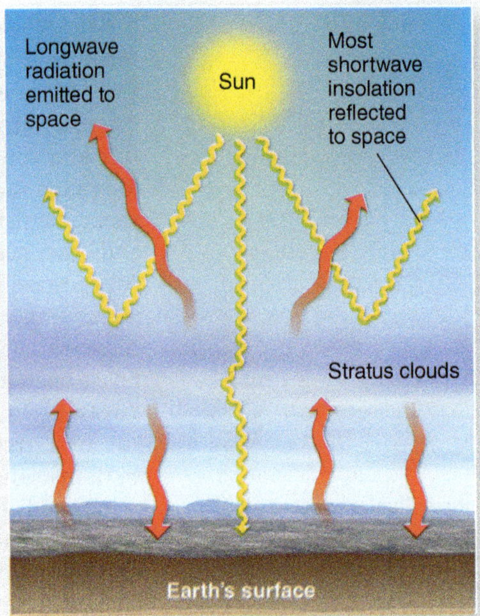

(b) Low clouds: net albedo forcing and atmospheric cooling

FIGURE 8 Energy effects of cloud types and contrails. (a) High, ice-crystal clouds (*cirrus*) produce a greater greenhouse forcing and a net warming of Earth. (b) Low, thick clouds (*stratus*) reflect most of the incoming insolation and produce a greater albedo forcing and a net cooling of Earth. (c) Jet aircraft exhaust triggers denser cirrus-cloud development. (d) Compare a newer, thinner contrail with one spreading to form false-cirrus clouds. [(c) NASA/JSC. (d) Bobbé Christopherson.]

(c)

(d)

clouds (warming because their greenhouse effects exceed their albedo effects), and Figure 8b portrays the *cloud-albedo forcing* produced by lower, thicker clouds (cooling because albedo effects exceed greenhouse effects).

Jet contrails (condensation trails) produce high cirrus clouds stimulated by aircraft exhaust (Figure 8c and d)—sometimes called *false cirrus clouds*. As shown in Figure 8a, high-altitude ice-crystal clouds are efficient at reducing outgoing longwave radiation and therefore contribute to global heating. However, these contrail-seeded false cirrus clouds have a higher density and higher albedo than normal cirrus clouds, thus reducing some surface insolation.

The three-day grounding of commercial air traffic following the September 11, 2001, terrorist attacks on the World Trade Center provided an opportunity to assess contrail effects on daytime maximum and nighttime minimum temperatures. Scientists compared weather data from 4000 stations for the three-day shutdown with data from the past 30 years. Their research suggests that contrails reduce the diurnal temperature range in regions with a high density of aircraft. Research is active to refine analysis of contrail signatures on satellite images, including GIS mapping tools.

Earth–Atmosphere Energy Balance

If Earth's surface and its atmosphere are considered separately, neither exhibits a balanced radiation budget. The average annual energy distribution is positive (an energy surplus) for Earth's surface and negative (an energy deficit) for the atmosphere as it radiates energy to space. Considered together, these two equal each other, making it possible for us to construct an overall energy balance.

Figure 9 summarizes the Earth–atmosphere radiation balance. It brings together all the elements discussed to this point in the chapter by following 100% of arriving insolation through the troposphere. The shortwave portion of the budget is on the left in the illustration; the longwave part of the budget is on the right.

Out of 100% of the solar energy arriving, Earth's average albedo is 31%. Absorption by atmospheric clouds, dust, and gases involves another 21% and accounts for the atmospheric heat input. Stratospheric ozone absorption and radiation account for another 3% of the atmospheric budget. About 45% of the incoming insolation transmits through to Earth's surface as direct and diffuse shortwave radiation. Earth eventually emits the longwave radiation part of the budget into space: 21% (atmosphere heating) +45% (surface heating) +3% (ozone emission) =69% .

Figure 10 shows global monthly values in W/m^2 flux (meaning energy "flow") of both reflected and emitted radiation in Figure 9. In Figure 10a, lighter regions indicate where more sunlight is reflected into space than is absorbed—for example, by lighter-colored land surfaces such as deserts or by cloud cover such as that over tropical lands. Green and blue areas illustrate where less light is reflected.

In Figure 10b, orange and red pixels indicate regions where more longwave radiation was absorbed and emitted to space; less longwave energy is escaping in the blue and purple regions. Those blue regions of lower longwave emissions over tropical lands are due to tall, thick clouds along the equatorial region (the Amazon, equatorial Africa, and Indonesia); these clouds also cause higher shortwave reflection. Subtropical desert regions exhibit greater longwave radiation emissions, owing to the presence of little cloud cover and greater radiative energy losses from surfaces that absorb a lot of energy.

Figure 11 summarizes the Earth–atmosphere energy balance for all shortwave and longwave energy by latitude. Between the tropics, the angle of incoming insolation is high and daylength is consistent, with little seasonal variation, so more energy is gained than lost—*energy surpluses dominate.* In the polar regions, the Sun is low in the sky, surfaces are light (ice and snow) and reflective, and for up to 6 months during the year no insolation is received, so more energy is lost than gained—*energy deficits prevail.* At around 36° latitude, a balance exists between energy gains and losses for the Earth–atmosphere system.

The imbalance of net radiation from the *tropical surpluses* and the *polar deficits* drives global circulation

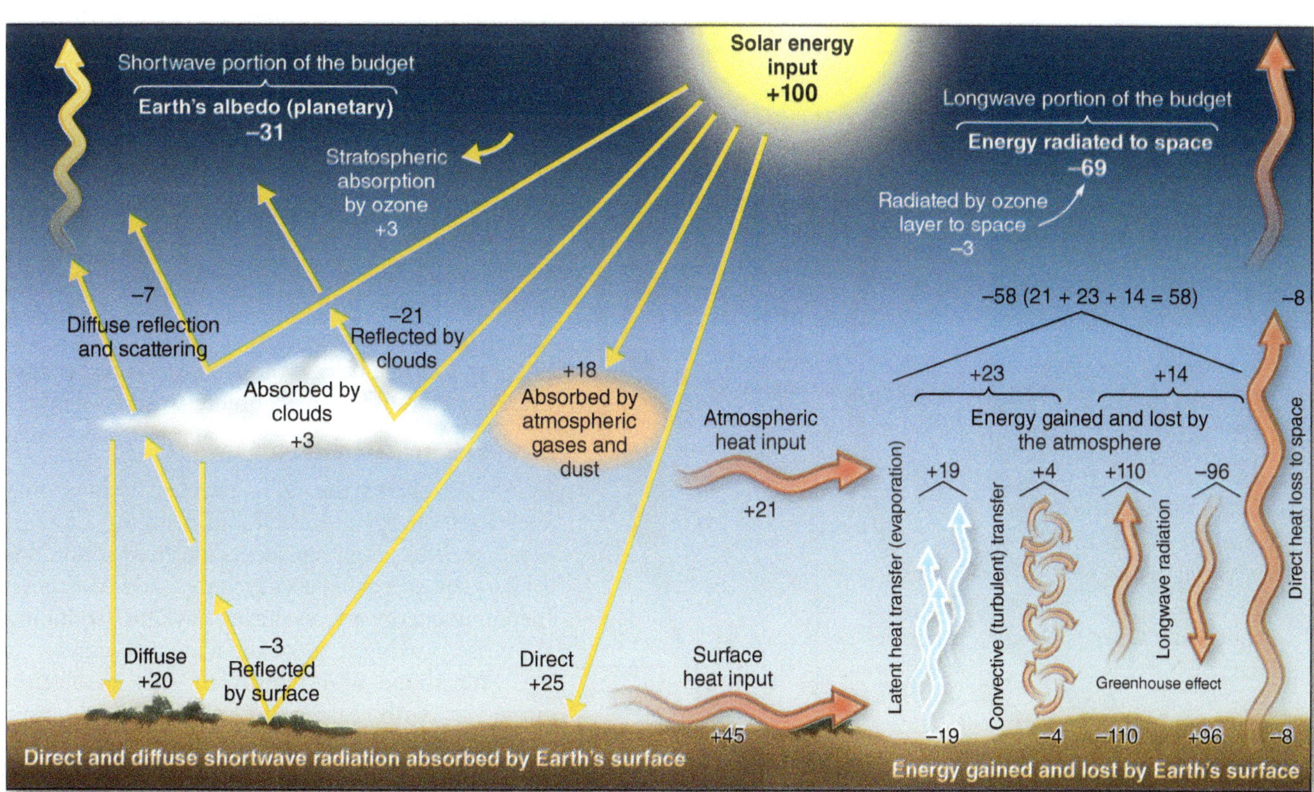

FIGURE 9 Detail of the Earth–atmosphere energy balance. Solar energy cascades through the lower atmosphere (left-hand portion of the illustration), where it is absorbed, reflected, and scattered. Clouds, atmosphere, and the surface reflect 31% of this insolation back to space. Atmospheric gases and dust and Earth's surface absorb energy and radiate longwave radiation (right-hand portion of the illustration). Over time, Earth emits, on average, 69% of incoming energy to space. When added to Earth's average albedo (31%, reflected energy), this equals the total energy input from the Sun (100%).

MG Animation Global Warming, Climate Change

MG Animation Earth–Atmosphere Energy Balance

(a) Outgoing shortwave – Earth's albedo.

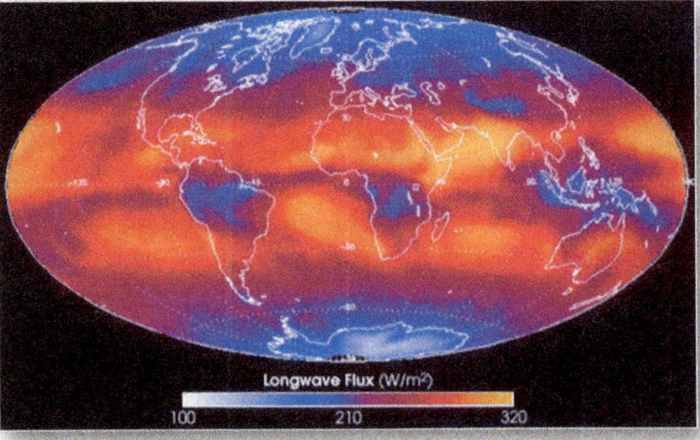

(b) Longwave energy flux to space.

FIGURE 10 Shortwave and longwave images show Earth's radiation budget components.
The CERES sensors aboard *Terra* made these portraits, capturing (a) outgoing shortwave energy flux reflected from clouds, land, and water—Earth's albedo—and (b) longwave energy flux emitted by these surfaces back to space. The scale beneath each image displays values in W/m². [CERES, Langley Research Center, NASA.]

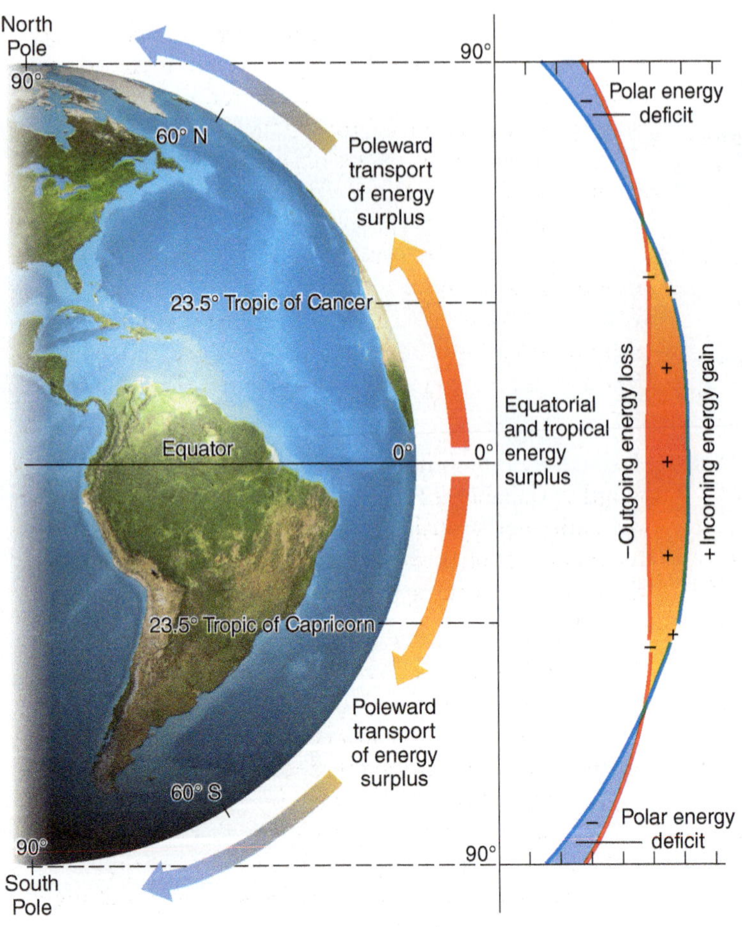

FIGURE 11 Energy budget by latitude.
Earth's energy surpluses and deficits produce poleward transport of energy and mass in each hemisphere—atmospheric circulation and ocean currents. Outside of the tropics, atmospheric winds dominate the transport of energy toward each pole.

patterns. The meridional (north–south) transfer agents are winds, ocean currents, dynamic weather systems, and related phenomena. Dramatic examples of such energy and mass transfers are tropical cyclones—hurricanes and typhoons. Forming in the tropics, these powerful storms mature and migrate to higher latitudes, carrying with them energy, water, and water vapor.

Energy Balance at Earth's Surface

Solar energy is the principal heat source at Earth's surface. Figure 9 illustrates the direct and diffuse shortwave radiation and longwave radiation arriving at the ground surface. These radiation patterns at Earth's surface are of great interest to geographers and should be of interest to everyone because these are the surface environments where we live.

Daily Radiation Patterns

Figure 12 shows the daily pattern of incoming shortwave energy absorbed and resulting air temperature. This graph represents idealized conditions for bare soil on a cloudless day in the middle latitudes. Incoming energy arrives during daylight, beginning at sunrise, peaking at noon, and ending at sunset.

The shape and height of this insolation curve vary with season and latitude. The highest trend for such a curve occurs at the time of the summer solstice (around June 21 in the Northern Hemisphere and December 21 in the Southern Hemisphere). The air temperature plot also responds to seasons and variations in insolation input. Within a 24-hour day, air temperature generally peaks between 3:00 and 4:00 P.M. and dips to its lowest point right at or slightly after sunrise.

The relationship between the insolation curve and the air temperature curve on the graph is

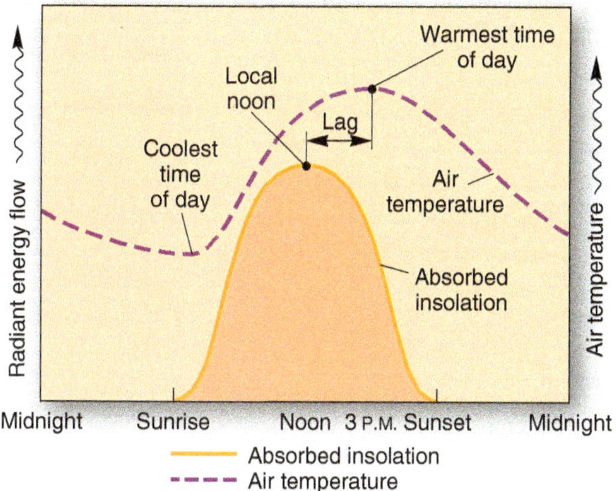

FIGURE 12 Daily radiation curves.
Sample radiation plot for a typical day shows the changes in insolation (orange line) and air temperature (dashed line). Comparing the curves demonstrates a lag between local noon (the insolation peak for the day) and the warmest time of day.

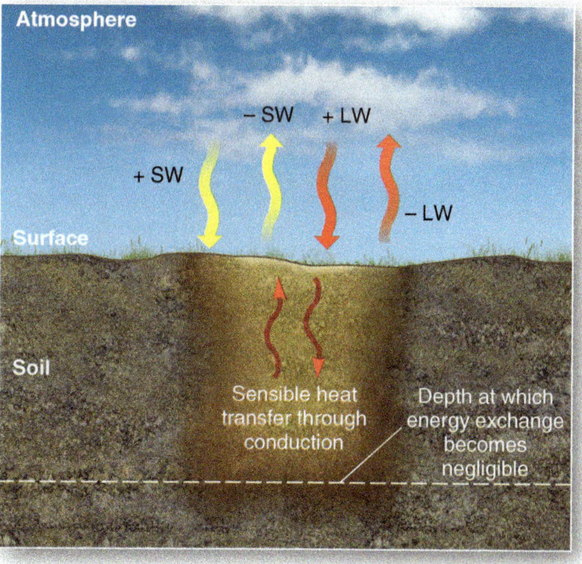

FIGURE 13 Surface energy budget.
Idealized input and output energy budget components for surface and a soil column. Sensible heat transfer in the soil is downward during the day or in summer and toward the surface at night or in winter (SW = shortwave, LW = longwave).

interesting—they do not align; a *lag* occurs. The warmest time of day occurs not at the moment of maximum insolation, but at the moment when a maximum of insolation is absorbed and emitted to the atmosphere from the ground. As long as the incoming energy exceeds the outgoing energy, air temperature continues to increase, not peaking until the incoming energy begins to diminish as the afternoon Sun's altitude decreases. In contrast, if you have ever gone camping in the mountains, you no doubt experienced the coldest time of day with a wake-up chill at sunrise!

The annual pattern of insolation and air temperature exhibits a similar lag. For the Northern Hemisphere, January is usually the coldest month, occurring after the December solstice and the shortest days. Similarly, the warmest months of July and August occur after the June solstice and the longest days.

Simplified Surface Energy Balance

Energy and moisture are continually exchanged at the surface, creating worldwide "boundary-layer climates" of great variety. **Microclimatology** is the science of physical conditions at or near Earth's surface. The following discussion is more meaningful if you visualize an actual surface—perhaps a park, a front yard, or a place on campus.

The surface receives visible light and longwave radiation and it reflects light and longwave radiation according to the following simple scheme:

$$\underset{\text{(Insolation)}}{+\text{SW}\downarrow}\ \underset{\text{(Reflection)}}{-\text{SW}\uparrow}\ \underset{\text{(Infrared)}}{+\text{LW}\downarrow}\ \underset{\text{(Infrared)}}{-\text{LW}\uparrow} = \underset{\text{(Net Radiation)}}{\text{NET R}}$$

We use SW for shortwave and LW for longwave for simplicity. You may come across other symbols in the microclimatology literature, such as K for shortwave, L for longwave, and Q* for NET R (net radiation).

Figure 13 shows these components of a surface energy balance. The soil column shown continues to a depth at which energy exchange with surrounding materials or with the surface becomes negligible, usually less than a meter. Sensible heat transfer in the soil is through conduction, predominantly downward during the day or in summer and toward the surface at night or in winter. Energy from the atmosphere that is moving toward the surface is a positive (a gain) to the surface account, and energy that is moving away from the surface, through sensible and latent heat transfers, is a negative (a loss) to the surface account.

Adding and subtracting the energy flow at the surface completes the calculation of **net radiation (NET R)**, or the balance of all radiation at Earth's surface. As the components of this simple equation vary with daylength through the seasons, cloudiness, and latitude, NET R varies.

Net Radiation The net radiation (NET R of all wavelengths) available at Earth's surface is the final outcome of the entire energy-balance process discussed in this chapter. Net radiation is expended from a nonvegetated surface through three pathways:

- *Sensible heat* is the back-and-forth transfer between air and surface in turbulent eddies through convection and conduction within materials.
- *Latent heat of evaporation* is the energy that is stored in water vapor as water evaporates. Water absorbs large quantities of this *latent heat* as it changes state to water vapor, thereby removing this heat energy from the surface. Conversely, this heat energy releases to the environment when water vapor changes state back to a liquid.
- *Ground heating and cooling,* is the energy that flows into and out of the ground surface (land or water) by conduction.

Understanding net radiation is essential to solar energy technologies that concentrate shortwave energy

(text continued after Focus Study 1)

FOCUS STUDY 1

Solar Energy Applications

Consider the following:

- Earth receives 100,000 terawatts (TW) of solar energy per hour, enough to meet world power needs for a year.* In the United States, the energy produced by fossil fuels in a year arrives in equivalent insolation every 35 minutes.
- An average commercial building in the United States receives 6 to 10 times more energy from the Sun hitting its exterior than is required to heat the inside.
- Photographs from the early 1900s show solar (flat-plate) water heaters used on rooftops. Today, installed solar water heating is making a comeback, serving 50 million households worldwide, more than 300,000 of these in the United States.
- Photovoltaic capacity is more than doubling every 2 years. Solar-electric power passed 20,000 megawatts installed in 2010.

*Terawatt (10^{12} watts) = 1 trillion W; gigawatt (10^{9} watts) = 1 billion W; megawatt (10^{6} watts) = 1 million W; kilowatt (10^{3} watts) = 1 thousand W.

Not only does insolation warm Earth's surface, but also it provides an inexhaustible supply of energy for humanity. Sunlight is direct and widely available, and solar power installations are decentralized, labor-intensive, and renewable. Although collected for centuries using various technologies, sunlight remains underutilized. The utility energy industry appears to prefer indirect, centralized, power-plant-specific, capital-intensive, and nonrenewable sources.

Rural villages in developing countries could benefit greatly from the simplest, most cost-effective solar application—the *solar cooker*. For example, people in Latin America and Africa walk many kilometers collecting fuel wood for cooking fires, stripping nearby areas bare. With access to solar cookers, villagers are able to cook meals and sanitize their drinking water without scavenging for wood (Figure 1.1a). These solar devices in Figure 1.1b and (c) are simple, yet efficient, reaching temperatures between 107°C and 127°C (225°F and 260°F). See http://solarcookers.org/ for more information.

In less-developed countries, the pressing need is for *decentralized* energy sources, appropriate in scale to everyday needs, such as cooking, heating and boiling water, and pasteurizing other liquids and food. Net per capita (per person) cost for solar cookers is far less than for centralized electrical production, regardless of fuel source.

Collecting Solar Energy

Any surface that receives light from the Sun is a *solar collector*. But the diffuse nature of solar energy received at the surface requires that it be collected, concentrated, transformed, and stored to

(a)

(b)

(c)

FIGURE 1.1 The solar-cooking solution. (a) Women in East Africa carry home solar-box cookers that they made at a workshop. Construction is easy, using cardboard components. (b) Kenyan women in training to use solar-panel cookers. (c) These simple cookers collect insolation through transparent glass or plastic and trap longwave radiation in an enclosed box or cooking bag. [(a) and (b) Solar Cookers International, Sacramento, California. (c) Bobbé Christopherson.]

be useful. Space heating is the simplest application. Windows that are carefully designed and placed allow sunlight to shine into a building, where it is absorbed and converted into sensible heat—an everyday application of the greenhouse effect.

A *passive solar system* captures heat energy and stores it in a "thermal mass," such as water-filled tanks, adobe, tile, or concrete. An *active solar system* involves heating water or air in a collector and then pumping it through a plumbing system to a tank, where it can provide hot water for direct use or for space heating.

Solar energy systems can generate heat energy of an appropriate scale for approximately half the present domestic applications in the United States, which includes space heating and water heating. In marginal climates, solar-assisted water and space heating is feasible as a backup; even in New England and the Northern Plains states, solar collection systems prove effective.

Kramer Junction, California, in the Mojave Desert near Barstow, California, has the world's largest operating solar-electric generating system, with a capacity of 150 MW (megawatts), or 150 million watts (W). Long troughs of computer-guided curved mirrors concentrate sunlight to create temperatures of 390°C (735°F) in vacuum-sealed tubes filled with synthetic oil. The heated oil heats water; the heated water produces steam that rotates turbines to generate cost-effective electricity. The facility converts 23% of the sunlight it receives into electricity during peak hours (Figure 1.2a), and operation and maintenance costs continue to decrease.

Electricity Directly from Sunlight

Photovoltaic cells (PVs) were first used to produce electricity in spacecraft in 1958. Familiar to us all are the solar cells in pocket calculators (hundreds of millions are now in use). When light shines upon a semiconductor material in these cells, it stimulates a flow of electrons (an electrical current) in the cell.

The efficiency of these cells, often assembled in large arrays, has improved to the level that they are cost-competitive, especially if government policies and subsidies were to be balanced evenly among all energy sources. The residential installation in Figure 1.2b features 36 panels, generating 205 W each, or 7380 W total, at a 21.5% conversion efficiency. People are able to run their electric meters in reverse and supply electricity to the power grid.

The National Renewable Energy Laboratory (NREL; http://www.nrel.gov) and the National Center for Photovoltaics were established in 1974 to coordinate solar energy research, development, and testing in partnership with private industry. At NREL's Outdoor Test Facility in Golden, Colorado, testing is ongoing and includes development of solar cells that broke the 40% conversion efficiency barrier!

Rooftop photovoltaic electrical generation is now cheaper than power line construction to rural sites. PV roof systems provide power to hundreds of thousands of homes in Mexico, Indonesia, Philippines, South Africa, India, and Norway. (See the "Photovoltaic Home Page," at http://www.eere.energy.gov/solar/.)

Obvious drawbacks of both solar heating and solar electric systems are periods of cloudiness and night, which inhibit operations. Research is under way to enhance energy storage and to improve battery technology.

The Promise of Solar Energy

Solar energy is a wise choice for the future. Solar is economically preferable to further development of our decreasing fossil-fuel reserves, further increases in oil imports and tanker and offshore oil-drilling spills, investment in foreign military incursions, or the addition of more troubled nuclear power, especially in a world with security issues.

Whether or not we follow the alternative path of solar energy is a matter of political control and not technological innovation. Much of the technology is ready for installation and is cost-effective when all direct and indirect costs are considered for the alternatives.

(a)

(b)

FIGURE 1.2 Solar thermal and photovoltaic energy production. (a) Kramer Junction solar-electric generating system in southern California. (b) A residence with a 7380-W rooftop solar photovoltaic array generates electricity. Excess electricity is fed to the grid for credits that offset 100% of the home's electric bill. [Bobbé Christopherson.]

for use. Solar energy offers great potential worldwide and is presently the fastest-growing form of energy conversion by humans. Focus Study 1 briefly reviews such direct application of surface energy budgets.

CRITICAL THINKING 2

Know more about applied solar technologies

On the *MasteringGeography* web site for Chapter 3, as well as in this chapter, you can find URLs relating to solar energy applications. Take some time and explore the Internet for information about these necessary technologies (solar thermal, solar electric photovoltaic cells, solar-box cookers, and the like). Which developing countries have benefited from using solar cookers, and why? As we near the climatic limitations of the fossil-fuel era and the depletion of fossil-fuel resources, renewable energy technologies are essential to the fabric of our lives. Is solar technology available in your area?

Variation in the expenditure of NET R among sensible heat (energy we can feel), latent heat (energy for evaporation), and ground heating and cooling produces the variety of environments we experience in nature. On the *Mastering-Geography* web site, you can find a comparison of daily radiation budgets for a station in the southern California desert and one in an agricultural valley in British Columbia. Photos and graphs illustrate the contrasting radiation expenditures in these two different environments.

Temperature Concepts and Measurement

Global temperatures rose at an average of 0.17 C° per decade since 1970, and this rate is accelerating. Surface temperature anomalies by decade are in Figure 14, as compared to the standard 1951–1980 base period in the record. Ice-core data and other proxy measures indicate that present temperatures are higher than at any time during the past 125,000 years. This warming trend in air temperature is the subject of much scientific, geographic, and political action.

Heat and temperature are not the same. *Heat* is a form of energy that flows from one system or object to another because the two are at different temperatures. **Temperature** is a measure of the average kinetic energy (motion) of individual molecules in matter. We feel the effect of temperature as the *sensible heat* transfer from warmer objects to cooler objects. For instance, when you jump into a cool lake, you can sense the heat transfer from your skin to the water as kinetic energy leaves your body and flows to the water.

Temperature and heat are related because changes in temperature are caused by the absorption or emission (gain or loss) of heat energy. The term *heat energy* is frequently used to describe energy that is added to or removed from a system or substance.

Temperature Scales

The temperature at which atomic and molecular motion in matter completely stops is *absolute zero*, or *0° absolute temperature*. Its value on the different temperature-measuring scales is −273° Celsius (C), −459.4° Fahrenheit (F), and 0 Kelvin (K). Figure 15 compares these three scales. Consult formulas for converting among Celsius, SI (Système International), and English units.

The Fahrenheit scale places the melting point of ice at 32°F, with 180 subdivisions to the boiling point of water at 212°F. The scale is named for its developer, Daniel G. Fahrenheit, a German physicist (1686–1736). Note that there is only one melting point for ice, but there are many freezing points for water, ranging from 32°F down to −40°F , depending on its purity, its volume, and certain conditions in the atmosphere.

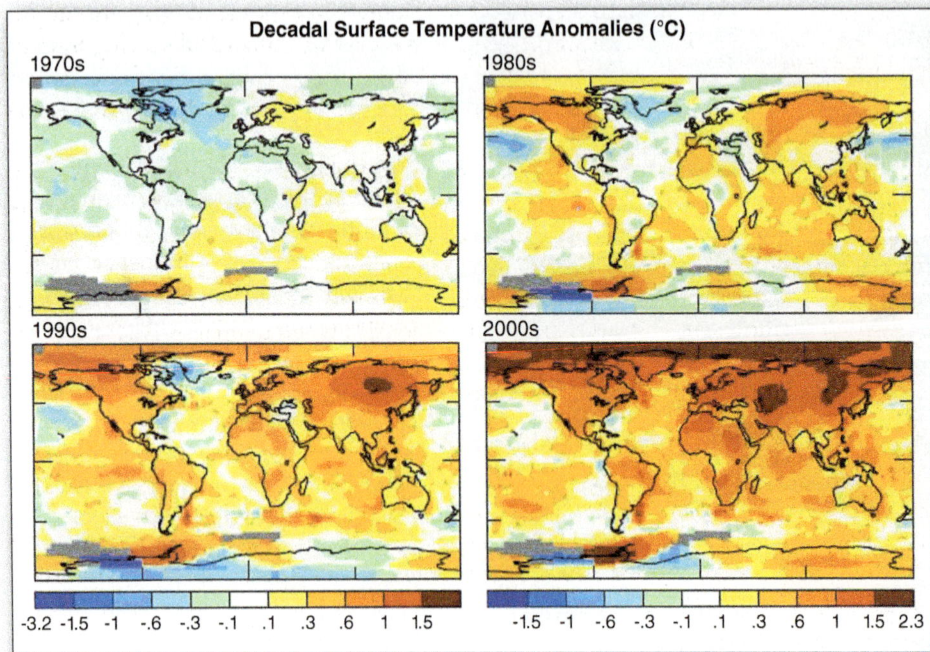

FIGURE 14 Surface temperature anomalies by decade. Increasing temperature patterns are apparent in this decadal look at temperature anomalies for four decades, as compared to the 1951–1980 baseline. [GISS/NASA.]

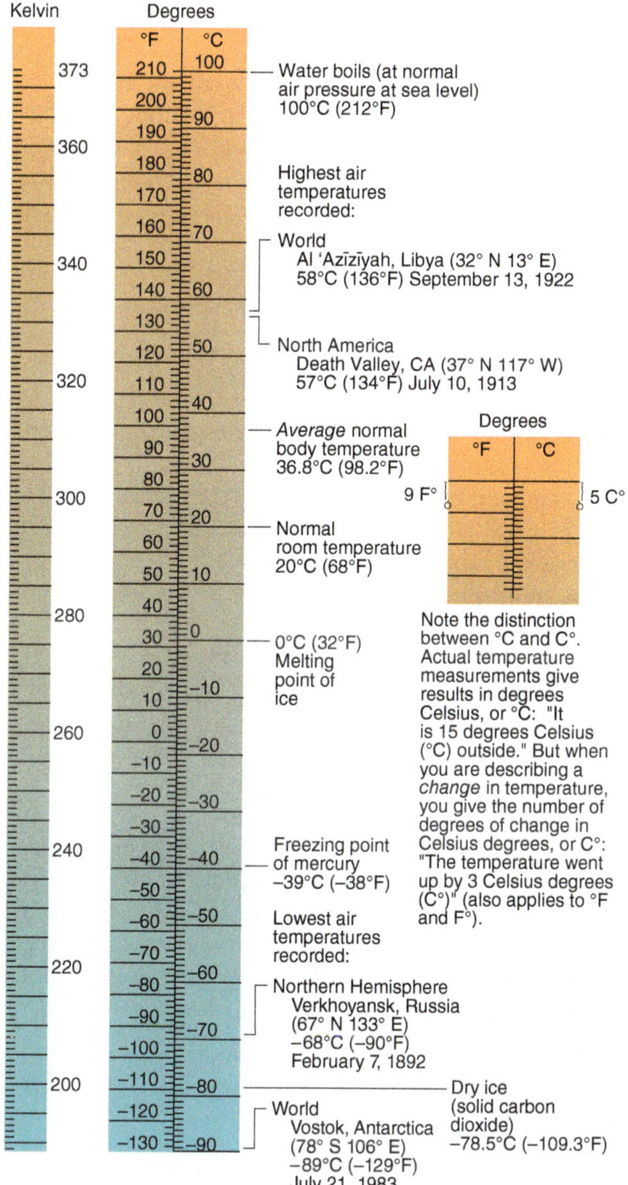

FIGURE 15 Temperature scales.
Scales for expressing temperature in Kelvin (K) and degrees Celsius (°C) and Fahrenheit (°F), with details of what we experience. Note the distinction between temperature and units of temperature expression, and the placement of the degree symbol.

About a year after the adoption of the Fahrenheit scale, Swedish astronomer Anders Celsius (1701–1744) developed the Celsius scale (formerly centigrade). He placed the melting point of ice at 0°C and the boiling temperature of water at sea level at 100°C, dividing his scale into 100 degrees using a decimal system.

British physicist Lord Kelvin (born William Thomson, 1824–1907) proposed the Kelvin scale in 1848. Science uses this scale because it starts at absolute zero temperature and thus readings are proportional to the actual kinetic energy in a material. The Kelvin scale's melting point for ice is 273 K, and its boiling point of water is 373 K.

Most countries use the Celsius scale to express temperature. The United States remains the only major country still using the Fahrenheit scale. The continuing pressure from the scientific community, not to mention the rest of the world, makes adoption of Celsius and SI units inevitable in the United States. This text presents Celsius (with Fahrenheit equivalents in parentheses) throughout.

Measuring Temperature

A *mercury thermometer* or *alcohol thermometer* is a sealed glass tube that measures outdoor temperatures. Fahrenheit invented both the alcohol and the mercury thermometers. Cold climates demand alcohol thermometers because alcohol freezes at −112°C (−170°F), whereas mercury freezes at −39°C (−38.2°F). The principle of these thermometers is simple: When fluids are heated, they expand; upon cooling, they contract. A thermometer stores fluid in a small reservoir at one end and is marked with calibrations to measure the expansion or contraction of the fluid, which reflects the temperature of the thermometer's environment.

Thermometers for standardized official readings are placed outdoors in small shelters that are white (for high albedo) and louvered (for ventilation) to avoid overheating of the instruments. They are placed at least 1.2–1.8 m (4–6 ft) above a surface, usually on turf; in the United States, 1.2 m (4 ft) is standard. Official temperature measurements are made in the shade to prevent the effect of direct insolation.

Temperature readings are taken daily, sometimes hourly, at more than 16,000 weather stations worldwide. Some stations with recording equipment also report the duration of temperatures, rates of rise or fall, and temperature variation over time throughout the day and night. One of the goals of the Global Climate Observing System (GCOS) is to establish a reference network of one station per 250,000 km^2 (95,800 mi^2). (See the World Meteorological Organization at http://www.wmo.ch/.)

The *daily mean temperature* is an average of daily minimum–maximum readings. The *monthly mean temperature* is the total of daily mean temperatures for the month divided by the number of days in the month. An *annual temperature range* expresses the difference between the lowest and highest monthly mean temperatures for a given year.

GEO REPORT 3 *Getting the measurement right*

The Goddard Institute for Space Studies, NASA, constantly refines the methodology of gathering global temperature readings. The temperature data used for the maps in Figure 14 were gathered from 6300 stations. Corrections are calibrated for city settings where the urban heat island affects temperatures. Population data and the pattern of nightlights captured by satellites further refine the database. For more discussion, see http://data.giss.nasa.gov/.

Principal Temperature Controls

The interaction of several physical controls produces Earth's temperature patterns. These principal influences upon temperatures include latitude, altitude and elevation, cloud cover, and land–water heating differences.

Latitude

Insolation is the single most important influence on temperature variations. Insolation intensity decreases as one moves away from the sub-solar point—a point that migrates annually between the Tropic of Cancer and Tropic of Capricorn (between 23.5° N and 23.5° S). In addition, daylength and Sun angle change throughout the year, increasing seasonal effect with increasing latitude. The five cities graphed in Figure 16 demonstrate the effects of latitudinal position on temperature. From equator to poles, Earth ranges from continually warm, to seasonally variable, to continually cold.

Altitude/Elevation

Within the troposphere, temperatures decrease with increasing altitude above Earth's surface. Recall that the *normal lapse rate* of temperature change with altitude is 6.4 C°/1000 m, or 3.5 F°/1000 ft. The density of the atmosphere also diminishes with increasing altitude. In fact, the density of the atmosphere at an elevation of 5500 m (18,000 ft) is about half that at sea level. As the atmosphere thins, there is a loss in its ability to absorb and radiate sensible heat. Thus, worldwide, mountainous areas experience lower temperatures than do regions nearer sea level, even at similar latitudes.

The consequences are that, at high elevations, average air temperatures are lower, nighttime cooling is greater, and the temperature range between day and night is greater than at low elevations. The temperature difference between areas of sunlight and shadow is greater at elevation than at sea level. You may have felt temperatures decrease noticeably in the shadows and shortly after sunset when you were in the mountains. Surfaces both gain energy rapidly from and lose energy rapidly to the thinner atmosphere.

The snow line seen in mountain areas indicates where winter snowfall exceeds the amount of snow lost through summer melting and evaporation. The snow line's location is a function both of elevation and latitude and of local microclimatic conditions of exposure. Permanent ice fields and glaciers exist on equatorial mountain summits in the Andes and East Africa. In equatorial mountains, the snow line occurs at approximately 5000 m (16,400 ft). With increasing latitude, snow lines gradually lower in elevation from 2700 m (8850 ft) in the midlatitudes to less than 900 m (2950 ft) in southern Greenland.

In the Andes Mountains of South America, the city of La Paz is 4103 m (13,461 ft) above sea level at about 16° S latitude. This region has nearly consistent daylength and moderate temperatures, allowing the growth of crops such as wheat, barley, and potatoes despite the high elevation (Figure 17). For comparison, this elevation is near the summit of Pike's Peak in Colorado (4301 m, or 14,111 ft) at about 38° N latitude and Mount Rainier in Washington (4392 m, or 14,410 ft) at about 47° N latitude.

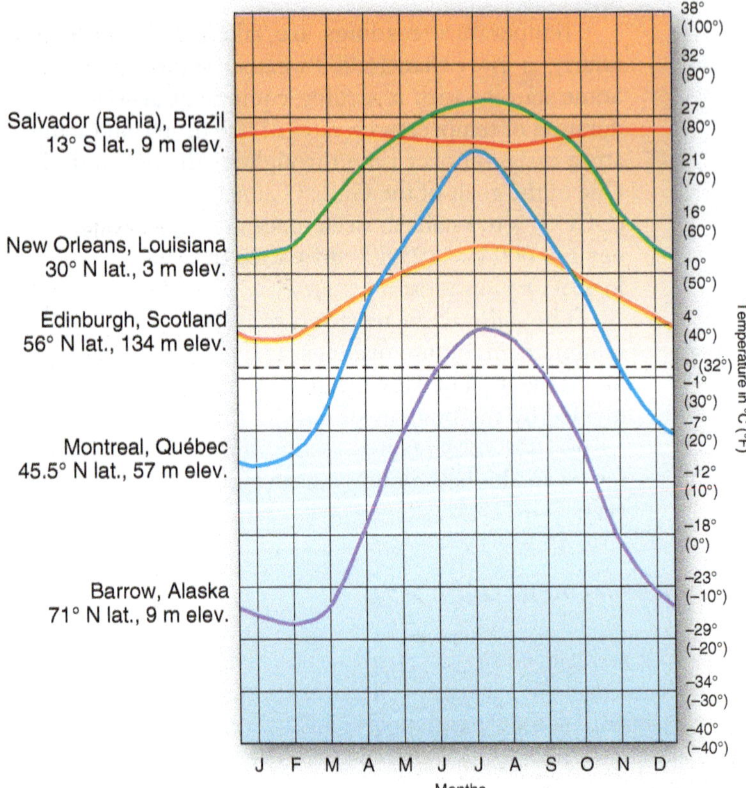

FIGURE 16 Latitude affects temperatures. A comparison of five cities from near the equator to north of the Arctic Circle demonstrates changing seasonality and increasing differences between average minimum and maximum temperatures as one moves to higher latitudes.

FIGURE 17 High-elevation farming in Bolivia.
People in these high-elevation villages grow potatoes and wheat in view of the permanent ice-covered peaks of the Bolivian Cordillera Real in the Andes Mountains. The combination of low latitude and high elevation creates consistent, moderate temperatures throughout the year, averaging about 11°C (52°F). [Seux Paule/AGE Fotostock America, Inc.]

Cloud Cover

Orbiting satellites reveal that approximately 50% of Earth is cloud-covered at any given moment. Clouds moderate temperature, and their effect varies with cloud type, height, and density. Cloud moisture reflects, absorbs, and liberates large amounts of energy released upon condensation and cloud formation.

At night, clouds act as insulation and radiate longwave energy, preventing rapid energy loss. During the day, clouds reflect insolation as a result of their high albedo values. In general, they lower daily maximum temperatures and raise nighttime minimum temperatures (review Figures 6 and 8). They also reduce latitudinal and seasonal temperature differences. Clouds are the most variable factor influencing Earth's radiation budget and are the subject of extensive research (see http://isccp.giss.nasa.gov/ and http://science.larc.nasa.gov/ceres/ for a sampling of projects).

Land–Water Heating Differences

Another major control over temperature is the different ways in which land and water respond to insolation. Water bodies tend to produce moderate temperature patterns, whereas inland in continental interiors more extreme temperatures occur. The physical nature of land (rock and soil) and water (oceans, seas, and lakes) is the reason for **land–water heating differences**—land heats and cools faster than water, producing continental and marine temperature contrasts. Figure 18 visually summarizes the following discussion of the land–water temperature controls: evaporation, transparency, specific heat, movement, ocean currents, and sea-surface temperatures.

Evaporation Evaporation consumes more of the energy arriving at the ocean's surface than is expended over a comparable area of land simply because water is available. An estimated 84% of all evaporation on Earth is from the oceans. When water evaporates and thus changes to water vapor, heat energy is absorbed in the process and is stored in the water vapor as latent heat.

You experience this evaporative heat loss (cooling) by wetting the back of your hand and then blowing on the moist skin. Sensible heat energy is drawn from your skin to supply some of the energy for evaporation, and you feel the cooling. Similarly, as surface water evaporates, it absorbs energy from the immediate environment, resulting in a lowering of temperatures. Temperatures over land, with far less water, experience less evaporative cooling than do marine locations.

Transparency The transmission of light obviously differs between soil and water: Solid ground is opaque; water is transparent. Consequently, light striking a soil surface does not penetrate, but is absorbed, heating the ground surface.

FIGURE 18 Land–water heating differences.
The differential heating of land and water produces contrasting marine (more moderate) and continental (more extreme) temperature regimes.

FIGURE 19 The ocean is transparent.
The transparency of the ocean permits insolation to penetrate to greater depths than does land, increasing the volume of water that absorbs energy. Sunlight empowers myriad forms of life covering the substrate, including a sea urchin at a depth of 3.0 m (9.8 ft). [Bobbé Christopherson.]

That energy is accumulated during times of exposure and is rapidly lost at night or in shadows. Maximum and minimum temperatures generally are experienced right at ground level. Below the surface, even at shallow depths, temperatures remain about the same throughout the day.

In contrast, when light reaches a body of water, it penetrates the surface because of water's **transparency**—water is clear and light passes through it to an average depth of 60 m (200 ft) in the ocean (Figure 19). This illuminated zone is the *photic layer* and occurs in some ocean waters to depths of 300 m (1000 ft). This characteristic of water results in the distribution of available heat energy over a much greater depth and volume, forming a larger energy reservoir than that of land surfaces.

Specific Heat When comparing equal volumes of water and land, water requires far more energy to increase its temperature than does land. In other words, *water can hold more heat than can soil or rock*, and therefore water is said to have a higher **specific heat**, the heat capacity of a substance. On average, the specific heat of water is about four times that of soil. A given volume of water represents a more substantial energy reservoir than does an equal volume of soil or rock and therefore heats and cools more slowly. For this reason, day-to-day temperatures near a substantial body of water tend to be moderated.

Movement Land is a rigid, solid material, whereas water is a fluid and is capable of movement. Differing temperatures and currents result in a mixing of cooler and warmer waters, and that mixing spreads the available energy over an even greater volume than if the water were still. Surface water and deeper waters mix, redistributing energy. Both ocean and land surfaces radiate longwave radiation at night, but land loses its energy more rapidly than does the moving oceanic energy reservoir.

Ocean Currents and Sea-Surface Temperatures The **Gulf Stream** moves northward off the east coast of North America, carrying warm water far into the North Atlantic (Figure 20). As a result, the southern third of Iceland experiences much milder temperatures than would be expected for a latitude of 65° N, just south of the Arctic Circle (66.5°). In Reykjavík, on the southwestern coast of Iceland, monthly temperatures average above

FIGURE 20 The Gulf Stream.
Satellite instruments sensitive to thermal infrared wavelengths imaged the Gulf Stream. Temperature differences are noted by computer-enhanced false colors: reds/oranges = 25°–29°C (76°–84°F); yellows/greens = 17°–24°C (63°–75°F); blues = 10°–16°C (50°–62°F); and purples = 2°–9°C (36°–49°F). [Imagery by RSMAS, University of Miami.]

GEO REPORT 4 ***Referring to heights above sea level***

Altitude and elevation are different. Note that *altitude* refers to airborne objects or heights above Earth's surface, whereas *elevation* usually refers to the height of a point on Earth's surface above some plane of reference. For example, we ask, "At what altitude did the jet fly?" and, "The ski resort is at what elevation?"

freezing during all months of the year. Similarly, the Gulf Stream moderates temperatures in coastal Scandinavia and northwestern Europe. In the western Pacific Ocean, the Kuroshio, or Japan Current, functions much the same as the Gulf Stream, having a warming effect on Japan, the Aleutians, and the northwestern margin of North America.

Higher ocean temperatures produce higher evaporation rates, and more energy is lost from the ocean as latent heat. As the water vapor content of the overlying air mass increases, the ability of the air to absorb longwave radiation also increases. Therefore, the air mass becomes warmer. The warmer the air and the ocean become, the more evaporation that occurs, increasing the amount of water vapor entering the air mass. More water vapor leads to cloud formation, which reflects insolation and produces lower temperatures. Lower temperatures of air and ocean reduce evaporation rates and the ability of the air mass to absorb water vapor—an interesting *negative feedback* mechanism.

Sea-surface temperature (SST) satellite data correlate well with actual sea-surface measurements. Figure 21 displays SST satellite data for January 2010 and July 2009. The Western Pacific Warm Pool is the deep red color in the southwestern Pacific Ocean with temperatures above 30°C (86°F). This region has the highest average ocean temperatures in the world. Note the seasonal change in ocean temperatures and the cool currents off the west coasts of North and South America, Europe, and Africa.

Mean annual SSTs increased steadily from 1982 through 2010 to record-high levels—2010 broke records for both ocean and land temperatures. Increasing warmth is measured at depths to 1000 m (3200 ft), and even slight increases in the temperature of deep bottom water were first reported in 2004. Scientists suggest that the ocean's ability to absorb excess heat energy from the atmosphere may be nearing its capacity. See http://podaac.jpl.nasa.gov/ for more on SSTs and the physical state of the ocean.

Summary of Marine Effects Versus Continental Effects As noted, Figure 18 summarizes the operation of the land–water temperature controls presented: evaporation, transparency, specific heat, movement, ocean currents, and sea-surface temperatures. The term **marine effect**, or *maritime*, describes locations that exhibit the moderating influences of the ocean, usually along coastlines or on islands. **Continental effect**, a condition of *continentality*, refers to areas less affected by the sea and therefore having a greater range between maximum and minimum temperatures on both a daily and a yearly basis.

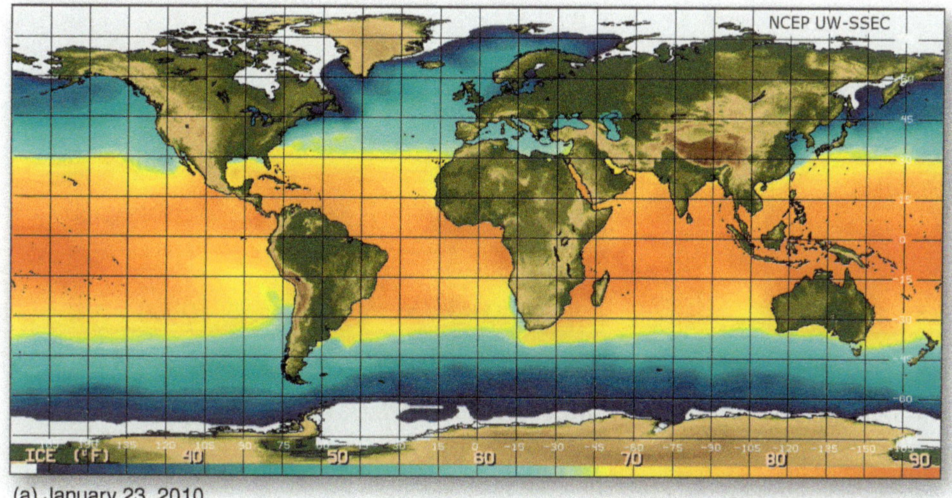

(a) January 23, 2010

MG™ Satellite Global Sea-surface Temperatures

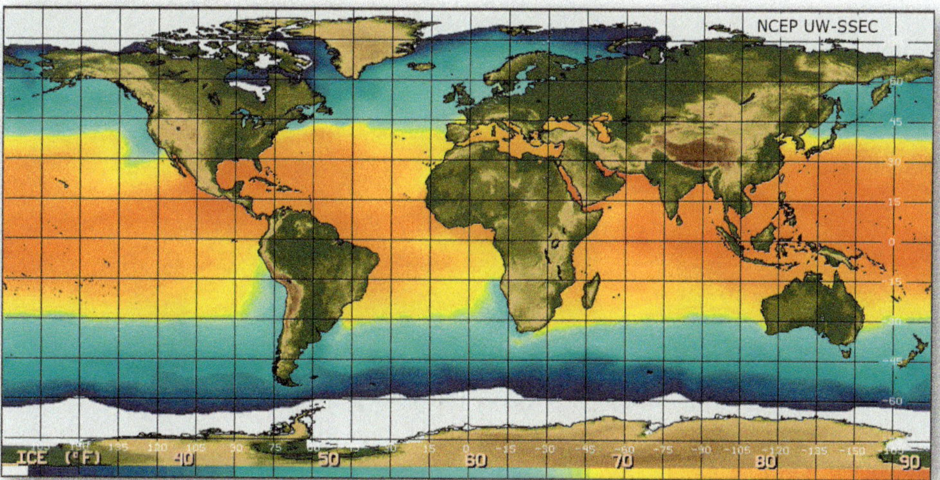

(b) July 23, 2009

FIGURE 21 Sea-surface temperatures. Average annual sea-surface temperatures for (a) January 23, 2010, and (b) July 23, 2009. [Satellite data courtesy of Space Science and Engineering Center, University of Wisconsin, Madison.]

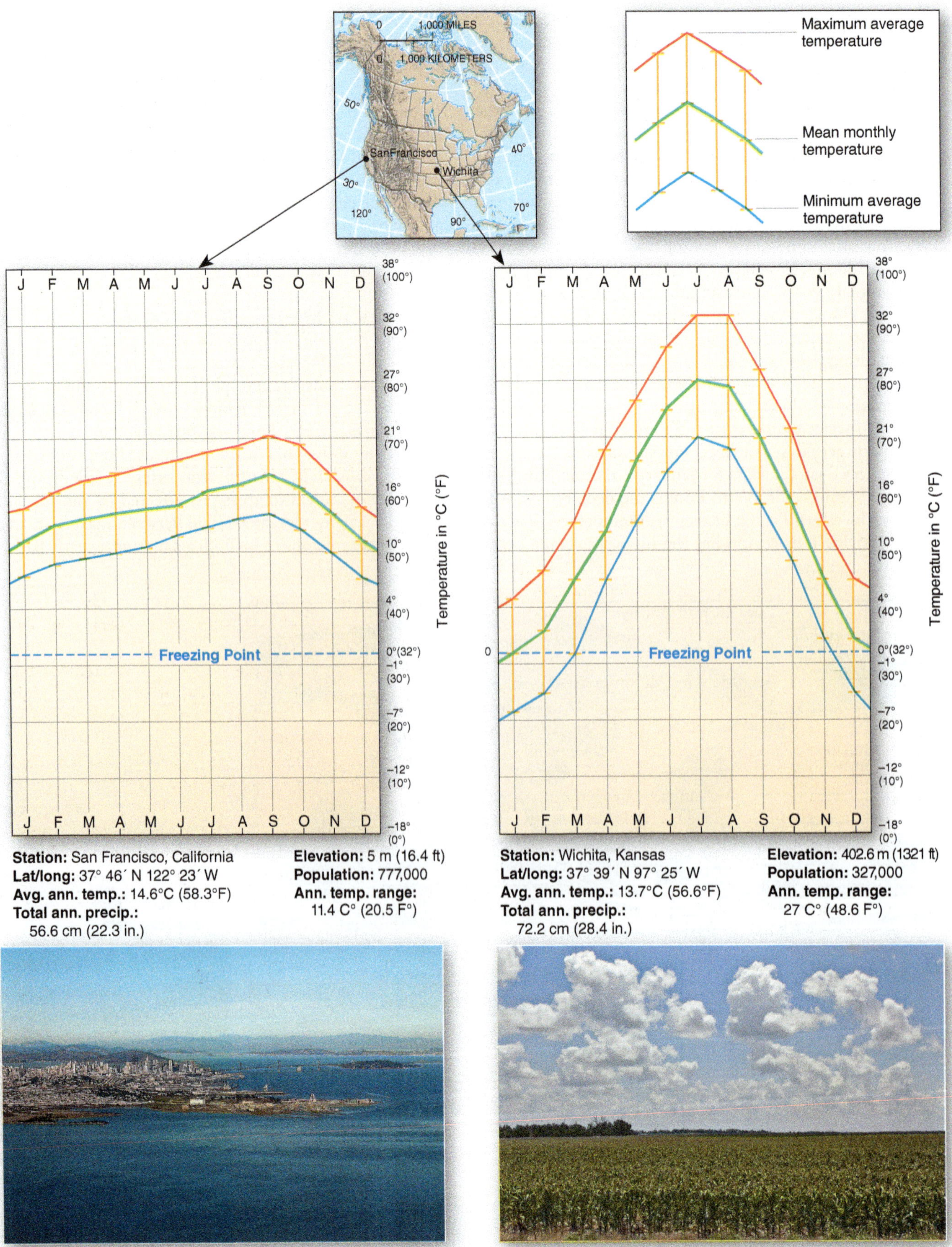

FIGURE 22 Marine and continental cities—United States.
Compare temperatures in coastal San Francisco, California, with those of the continental region near Wichita, Kansas. [Bobbé Christopherson.]

San Francisco, California, and Wichita, Kansas, provide us an example of marine and continental conditions (Figure 22). Both cities are at approximately 37° 40' N latitude. The cooling waters of the Pacific Ocean and San Francisco Bay surround San Francisco on three sides. Summer fog helps delay the warmest summer month in San Francisco until September. In 100 years of weather records, marine effects moderated temperatures, so that only a few days a year have summer maximums that exceed 32.2°C (90°F). Winter minimums rarely drop below freezing.

In contrast, the continental location of Wichita is susceptible to freezes from late October to mid-April, with daily variations slightly increased by its elevation, and has experienced −30°C (−22°F) as a record low. West of Wichita, winters increase in severity with increasing distance from the moderating influences of invading air masses from the Gulf of Mexico. Wichita's temperature reaches 32.2°C (90°F) or higher more than 65 days each year, with 46°C (114°F) as a record high. Temperatures exceeded 38°C (100°F) for 23 nonconsecutive days in 2003.

Earth's Temperature Patterns

Earth's temperature patterns result from the combined effect of the controlling factors in our discussion. Let us now look at maps for January and July of mean air temperatures worldwide (Figures 23 and 24) and for the polar regions (Figures 25 and 26). To complete the analysis, Figure 28 presents the temperature range differences between the January and July maps, or the differences between the averages of the coolest and warmest months. Maps are for January and July instead of the solstice months of December and June because a lag occurs between insolation received and maximum or minimum temperatures experienced.

The lines on temperature maps are known as isotherms. An **isotherm** is an isoline—a line along which there is a constant value—that connects points of equal temperature and portrays the temperature pattern, just as a contour line on a topographic map illustrates points of equal elevation. Isotherms help with the spatial analysis of temperatures.

CRITICAL THINKING 3

Begin a record and physical geography profile

With each temperature map (Figures 23, 24, and 28), begin by finding your own city or town and noting the temperatures indicated by the isotherms for January and July and the annual temperature range. Record the information from these maps in your notebook. Remember that the small scale of these maps permits only generalizations about actual temperatures at specific sites, allowing you to make only a rough approximation for your location.

As you work through the different maps throughout this text, note atmospheric pressure and winds, annual precipitation, climate type, landforms, soil orders, vegetation, and terrestrial biomes. Add this information to your profile in your notebook. By the end of the course, you will have a complete physical geography profile for your regional environment.

January and July Temperature Maps

Figure 23 maps January's mean temperatures for the world. In the Southern Hemisphere, the higher Sun altitude causes longer days and summer weather conditions; in the Northern Hemisphere, the lower Sun angle causes the short days of winter. Isotherms generally are zonal, trending east–west, parallel to the equator, and they appear to be interrupted by the presence of landmasses. Isotherms mark the general decrease in insolation and net radiation with distance from the equator.

The **thermal equator** is an isotherm connecting all points of highest mean temperature, roughly 27°C (80°F); it trends southward into the interior of South America and Africa, indicating higher temperatures over landmasses. In the Northern Hemisphere, isotherms shift equatorward as cold air chills the continental interiors.  The oceans, in contrast, are more moderate, with warmer conditions extending farther north than over land at comparable latitudes.

As an example, in Figure 23, follow along 50° N latitude (the 50th parallel) and compare isotherms: 3°C to 6°C in the North Pacific and 3°C to 9°C in the North Atlantic, as contrasted to −18°C in the interior of North America and −24°C to −30°C in central Asia. Also, note the orientation of isotherms over areas with mountain ranges and how they illustrate the cooling effects of elevation. Check the South American Andes as an example of these elevation effects.

Figure 24 maps average July worldwide temperatures for comparison. The longer days of summer and higher Sun altitude are in the Northern Hemisphere. Winter dominates the Southern Hemisphere, although it is milder than winters north of the equator because continental landmasses are smaller and the dominant oceans and seas store and release more energy. The *thermal equator* shifts northward with the high summer Sun and reaches the Persian Gulf–Pakistan–Iran area. The Persian Gulf is the site of the highest recorded sea-surface temperature of 36°C (96°F), difficult to imagine for a large water body.

During July in the Northern Hemisphere, isotherms shift poleward over land as higher temperatures dominate continental interiors. July temperatures in Verkhoyansk average more than 13°C (56°F), which represents a 63 C° (113 F°) seasonal range between January and July averages. The Verkhoyansk region of Siberia is probably Earth's most dramatic example of temperature continentality.

The hottest places on Earth occur in Northern Hemisphere deserts during July. The reasons are simple: clear skies, strong surface heating, virtually no surface water, and few plants. Prime examples are portions of the Sonoran Desert of North America and the Sahara of Africa. The most extreme shade temperature ever recorded, higher than 58°C (136°F), occurred on September 13, 1922, at Al 'Azīzīyah, Libya.

The highest maximum and annual average temperatures in North America occurred in Death Valley, California,

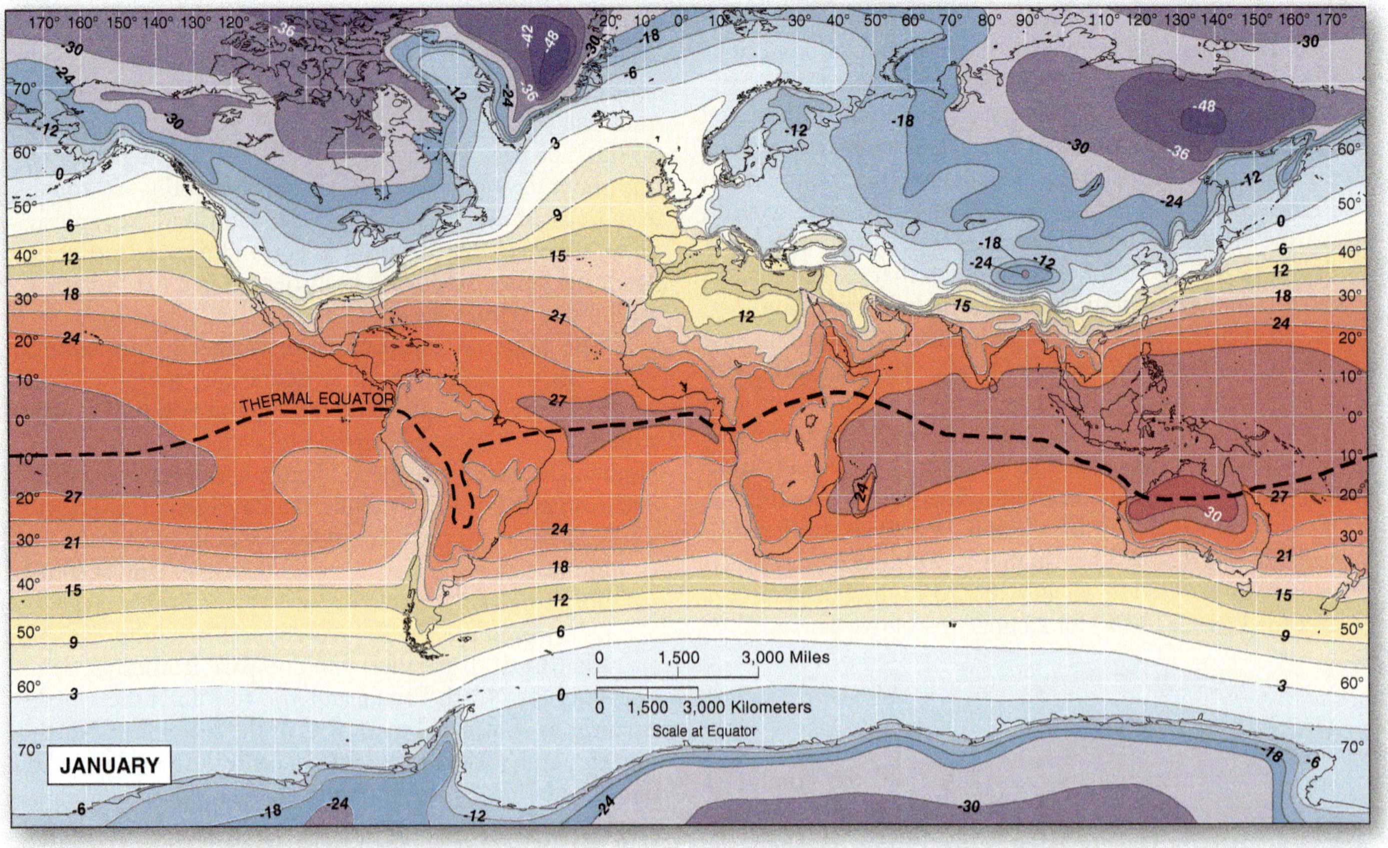

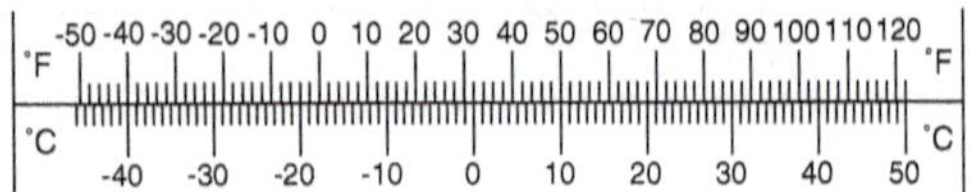

Satellite
Global Surface Temperatures, Land and Ocean

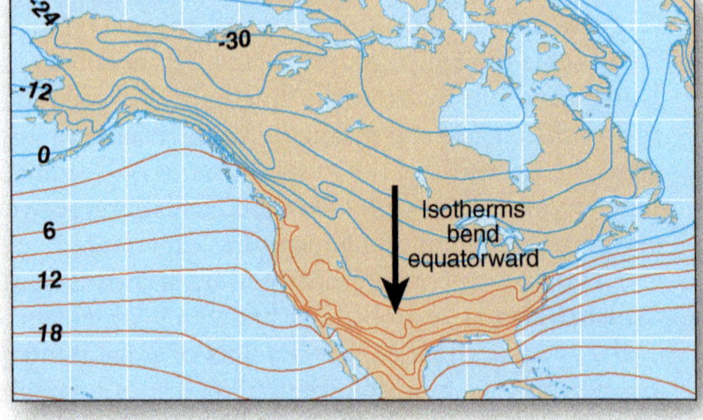

FIGURE 23 Global mean temperatures for January.
Temperatures are in Celsius (convertible to Fahrenheit by means of the scale) as taken from separate air-temperature databases for ocean and land. Note the inset map of North America and the equatorward-trending isotherms in the interior. Compare with Figure 24. [Adapted by author and redrawn from National Climatic Data Center, *Monthly Climatic Data for the World*, 47 (January 1994), and WMO and NOAA.]

GEO REPORT 5 *Polar regions show greatest warming*

Climate change is affecting the higher latitudes at a pace exceeding the middle and lower latitudes. Since 1978, warming has increased in the Arctic region to a rate of 1.2 C° (2.2 F°) per decade, which means the last 20 years warmed at nearly seven times the rate of the last 100 years. Since 1970, nearly 60% of the Arctic sea ice has disappeared in response to increasing air and ocean temperatures, with record low levels of ice from 2007 through 2010. Similar warming trends are impacting the Antarctic Peninsula and the West Antarctic Ice Sheet, as ice shelves collapse and retreat along the coast.

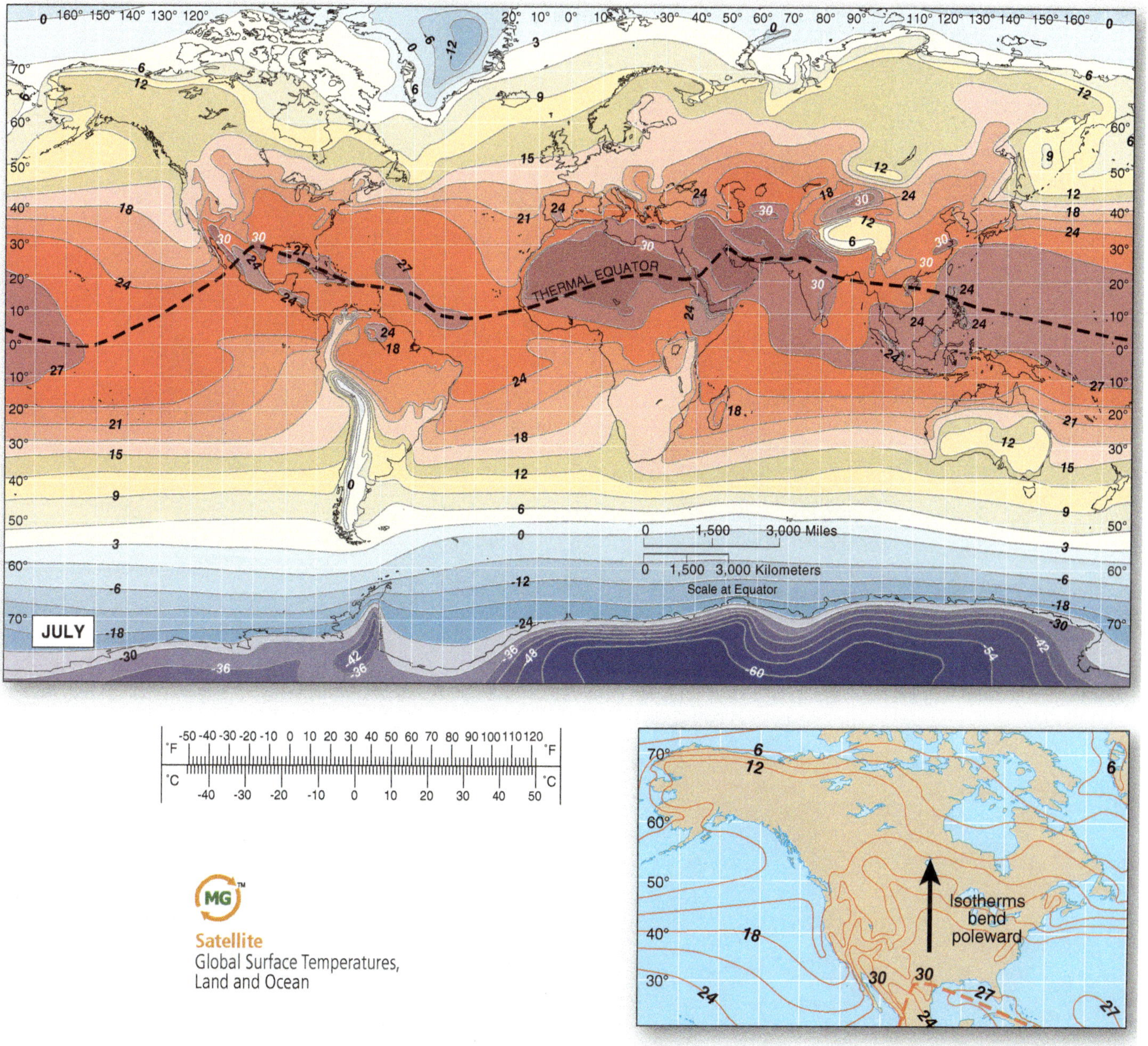

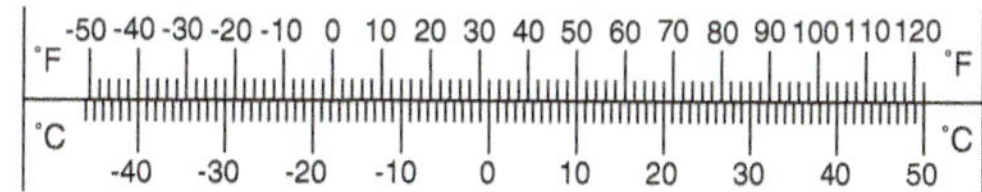

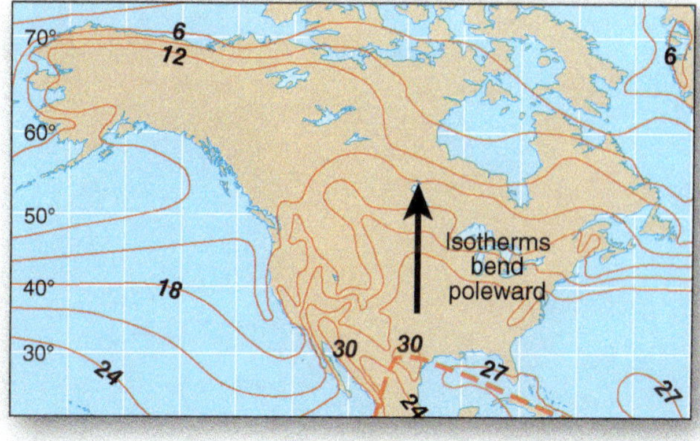

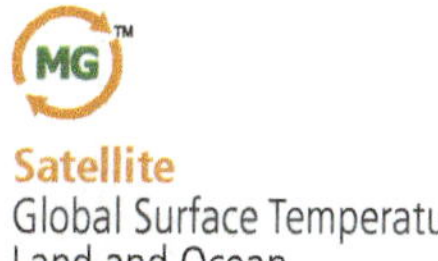

Satellite
Global Surface Temperatures, Land and Ocean

FIGURE 24 Global mean temperatures for July.
Temperatures are in Celsius (convertible to Fahrenheit by means of the scale) as taken from separate air-temperature data bases for ocean and land. Note the inset map of North America and the poleward-trending isotherms in the interior. Compare with Figure 23. [Adapted by author and redrawn from National Climatic Data Center, *Monthly Climatic Data for the World,* 47 (July 1994), and WMO and NOAA.]

where the Greenland Ranch Station reached a high of 57°C (134°F) in 1913. The station is at 37° N and is −54.3 m, or −178 ft (the minus indicates meters or feet below sea level.

Polar Region Temperature Maps

Figures 25 and 26 show January and July temperatures in the north polar and south polar regions. Remember, the north polar region is an ocean surrounded by land, in contrast to the south polar region, which is the Antarctic continent surrounded by ocean. The island of Greenland has a summit elevation of 3240 m (10,630 ft) on Earth's second largest ice sheet, the highest elevation north of the Arctic Circle. This combination of high latitude and interior high elevation on the ice sheet produces cold midwinter temperatures in January (Figure 25a).

In Antarctica (Figure 25b), it is "summer" in December and January. This is Earth's coldest and highest

January
North Pole
South Pole
Vostok
McMurdo
(a)
0 250 1000 Miles
0 1000 Kilometers
(b)
0 250 500 Miles
0 500 Kilometers

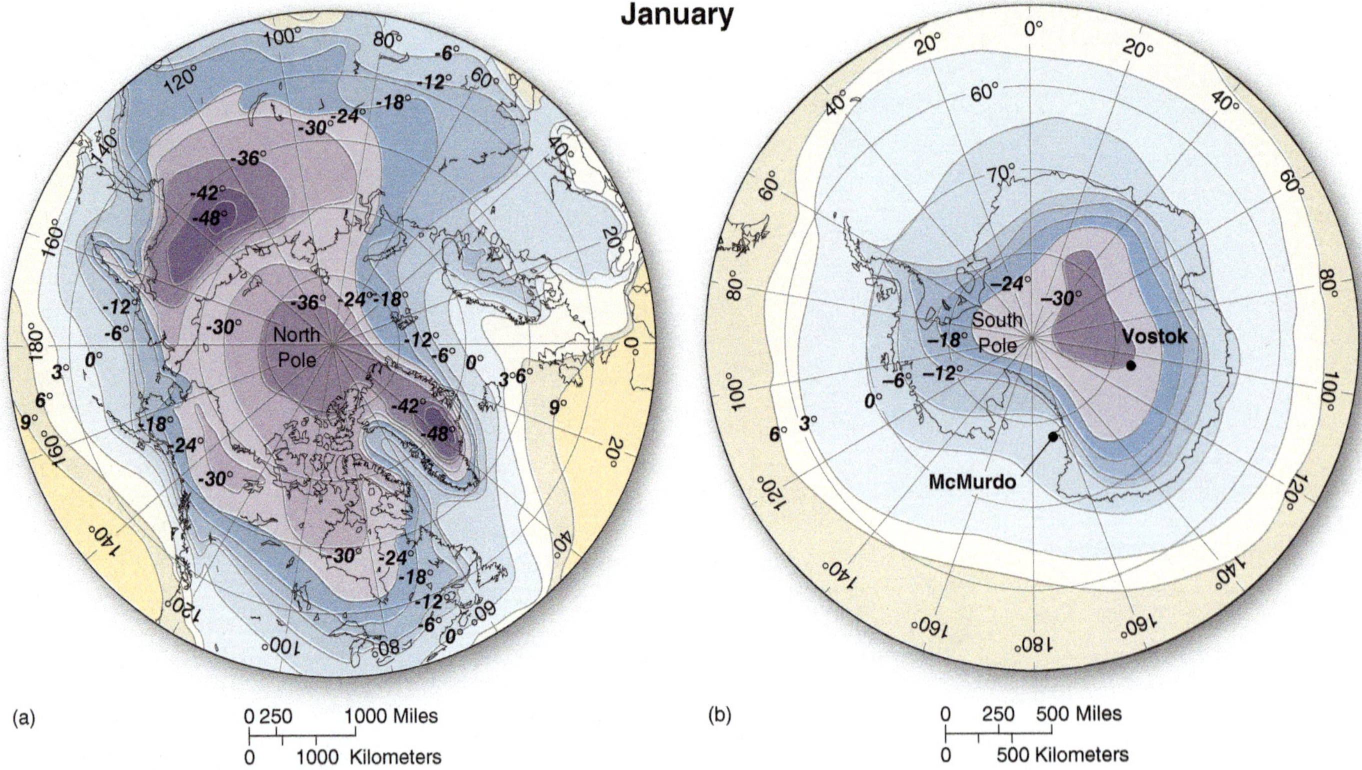

FIGURE 25 January mean temperatures for polar regions.
January temperatures in (a) north polar region and (b) south polar region. Use temperature conversions in Figures 23 and 24. Note that each map is at a different scale. [Author-prepared maps using same sources as Figures 23 and 24.]

July
North Pole
South Pole
Vostok
McMurdo
(a)
0 250 1000 Miles
0 1000 Kilometers
(b)
0 250 500 Miles
0 500 Kilometers

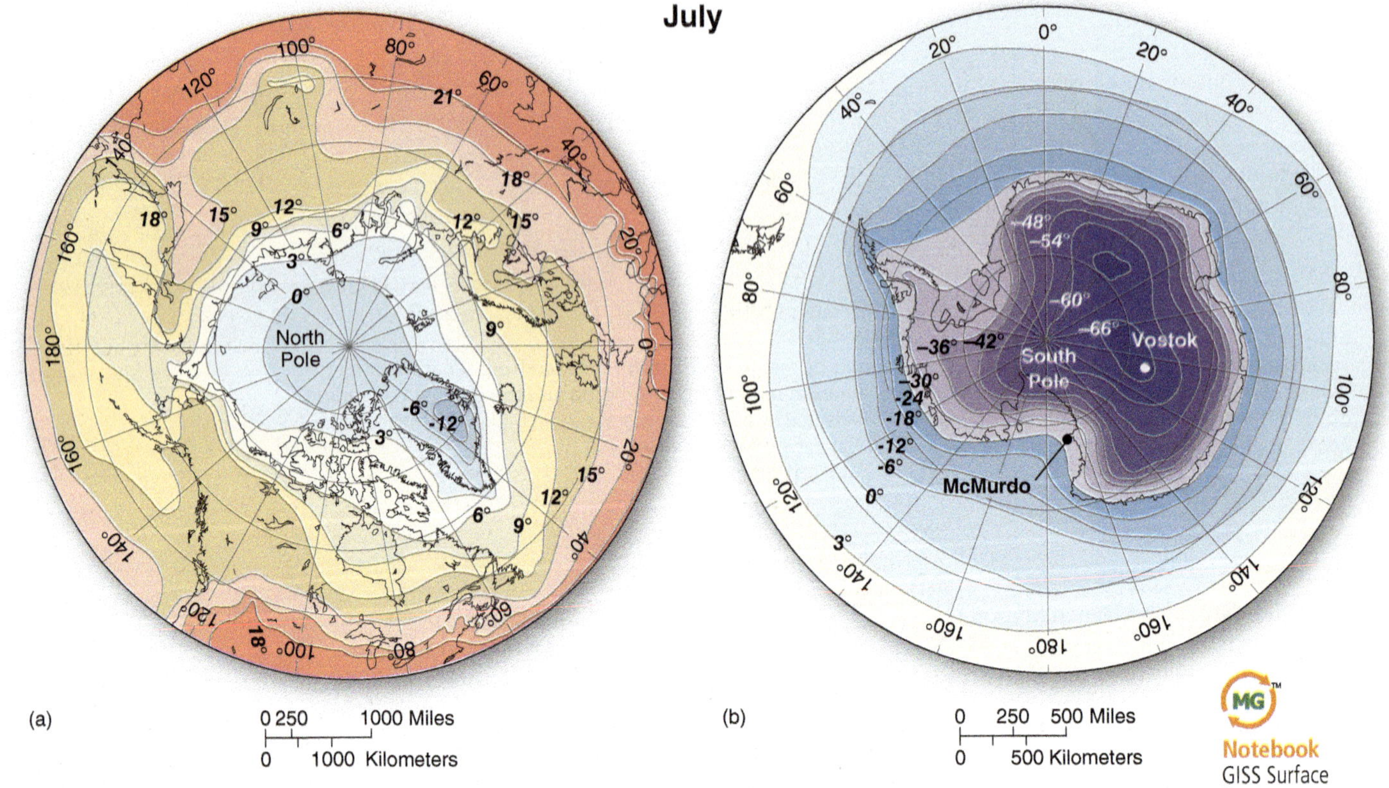

FIGURE 26 July mean temperatures for polar regions.
July temperatures in (a) north polar region and (b) south polar region. Use temperature conversions in Figures 23 and 24. Note that each map is at a different scale. [Author-prepared maps using same sources as Figures 23 and 24.]

MG Notebook
GISS Surface Temperature Analysis, 1891–2006

average elevation landmass. January average temperatures for the three scientific bases noted on the map are McMurdo Station, on the coast, −3°C ; the Amundsen–Scott Station at the South Pole (elevation 2835 m, 9301 ft), −28°C ; and the Russian Vostok Station at a more continental location (elevation 3420 m, 11,220 ft), −32°C ; respectively, 26.6°F, −18.4°F , and −25.6°F.

Figure 26 maps July temperatures in the north and south polar regions. July is "summer" in the Arctic Ocean (Figure 26a) and brings a thinning of multi-year and seasonal pack ice. Open cracks and leads stretched all the way to the North Pole over the past several years.

In July, nights in Antarctica are 24 hours long. This lack of insolation results in the lowest natural temperature reported on Earth, a frigid −89.2°C (−128.6°F) recorded on July 21, 1983, at the Russian Vostok Station, Antarctica. Such a temperature is 11 C° (19.8 F°) colder than the freezing point of dry ice (solid carbon dioxide). If the concentration of carbon dioxide were large enough, such a cold temperature would theoretically freeze tiny carbon dioxide dry-ice particles out of the sky.

The average July temperature around Vostok is −68°C (−90.4°F). For average temperature comparisons, the Amundsen–Scott Station at the South Pole experiences −60°C (−76°F), and McMurdo Station has a −26°C (−14.8°F) reading. Note that the coldest temperatures in Antarctica are usually in August, not July, just before the equinox sunrise in September at the end of the long polar night.

For a continental region other than Antarctica, Russia—and specifically, northeastern Siberia—is the coldest area (Figure 25a). The intense cold results from winter conditions of consistently clear, dry, calm air; small insolation input; and an inland location far from moderating maritime effects. Prevailing global winds prevent moderating effects from the Pacific Ocean to the east. Verkhoyansk, Russia (located within the −48°C isotherm on the map), actually recorded a minimum temperature of −68°C (−90°F) and experiences a daily average of −50.5°C (−58.9°F) for January. Verkhoyansk (see Figure 27) has 7 months of temperatures below freezing, including at least 4 months below −34°C (−30°F) .

In contrast, Verkhoyansk was hit with a maximum temperature of +37°C (+98°F) in July—an incredible 105 C° (189 F°) minimum–maximum range! People do live and work in Verkhoyansk, which has a population of 1400; the town has been occupied continuously since 1638 and is today a secondary mining district.

Trondheim, Norway, is near the latitude of Verkhoyansk and at a similar elevation. But Trondheim's coastal location moderates its annual temperature regime (Figure 27). January minimum and maximum temperatures range between −17°C and +8°C (+1.4°F and +46°F), and July minimum and maximum temperatures range between +5°C and +27°C (+41°F and +81°F). The lowest minimum and highest maximum temperatures ever recorded in Trondheim are −30°C and +35°C (−22°F and +95°F)—quite a difference from the extremes at Verkhoyansk.

Annual Temperature Range Map

The temperature range map helps identify regions that experience the greatest annual extremes and, in contrast, the most moderate temperature regimes, as demonstrated in Figure 28. As you might expect from our discussion of Verkhoyansk, the largest temperature ranges occur at subpolar locations within the continental interiors of North America and Asia, where average ranges of 64 C° (115 F°) are recorded (dark brown area on the map). The Southern Hemisphere, in contrast, has little seasonal variation in mean temperatures, owing to the lack of large landmasses and the vast expanses of water to moderate temperature extremes.

Southern Hemisphere temperature patterns are generally maritime, and Northern Hemisphere patterns feature continentality, although interior regions in the Southern Hemisphere experience some continentality effects. For example, in January (Figure 23), Australia is dominated by isotherms of 20°–30°C (68°–86°F), whereas in July (Figure 24), Australia is crossed by the 12°C (54°F) isotherm. The Northern Hemisphere, with greater land area overall, registers a slightly higher average surface temperature than does the Southern Hemisphere.

Imagine living in some of these regions and the degree to which you would need to adjust your personal wardrobe and make other comfort adaptations. See Focus Study 2 for more on air temperature and the human body. Summer heat-wave deaths remain a powerful reminder of the role of temperatures in our lives.

The Urban Environment

Because almost 50% of the world's population lives in cities, urban microclimatology and other specific environmental effects related to cities are important topics for physical geographers. Urban microclimates generally differ from those of nearby nonurban areas. In fact, the surface energy characteristics of urban areas are similar to those of desert locations, mainly because vegetation is lacking in both environments.

The physical characteristics of urbanized regions produce an **urban heat island** (UHI) that has, on average, both maximum and minimum temperatures higher than nearby rural settings. For an average city in North America, the sources of heating are modified urban surfaces such as asphalt and glass, building geometry, pollution, and human activity such as industry and transportation. For example, an average car (25 mpg or 10 km/l) produces enough heat to melt a 14-lb bag of ice for every mile driven (4.5 kg ice per km driven).

Figure 29 illustrates a generalized cross section of a typical UHI, showing increasing temperatures toward the downtown central business district. Note that temperatures drop over areas of trees and parks. Sensible heat is lessened because of plant effects such as transpiration and shade. Urban forests are important factors in cooling cities. NASA measurements in an outdoor mall parking lot found temperatures of 48°C (118°F), but a small planter with trees in the same lot was significantly cooler at 32°C (90°F)—16 C° (29 F°) lower in temperature! In Central

(text continued after figures and Focus Study 2)

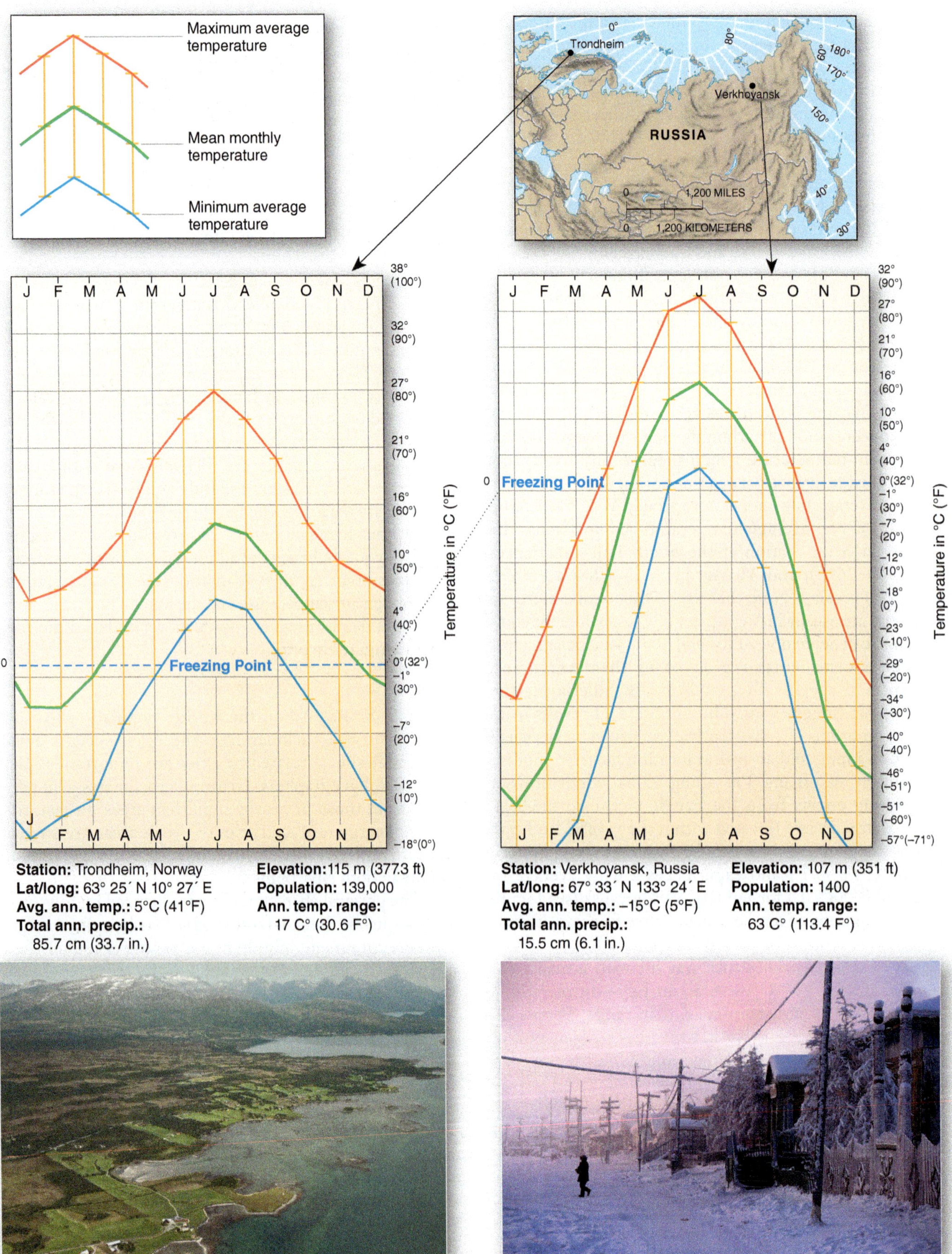

FIGURE 27 Marine and continental cities—Eurasia.
Compare temperatures in coastal Trondheim, Norway, and continental Siberian Russia. Note that the freezing levels on the two graphs are positioned differently to accommodate the contrasting data. [Coastal Norway by Bobbé Christopherson; Verkhoyansk by Bryan and Cherry Alexander/Arcticphoto.]

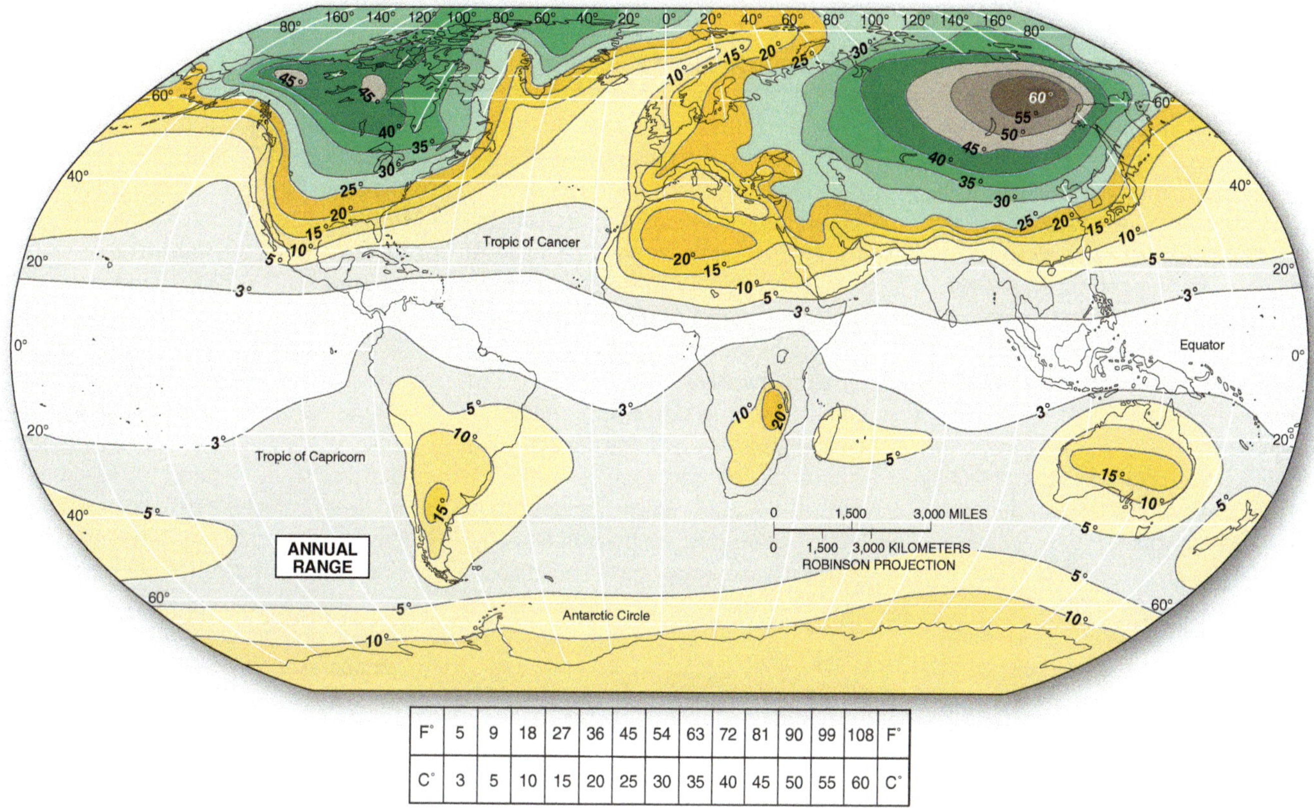

F°	5	9	18	27	36	45	54	63	72	81	90	99	108	F°
C°	3	5	10	15	20	25	30	35	40	45	50	55	60	C°

FIGURE 28 Global annual temperature ranges.
The annual range of global temperatures in Celsius degrees, C°, with conversions to Fahrenheit degrees, F°, shown on the scale. The mapped data show the difference between average January and July temperature maps.

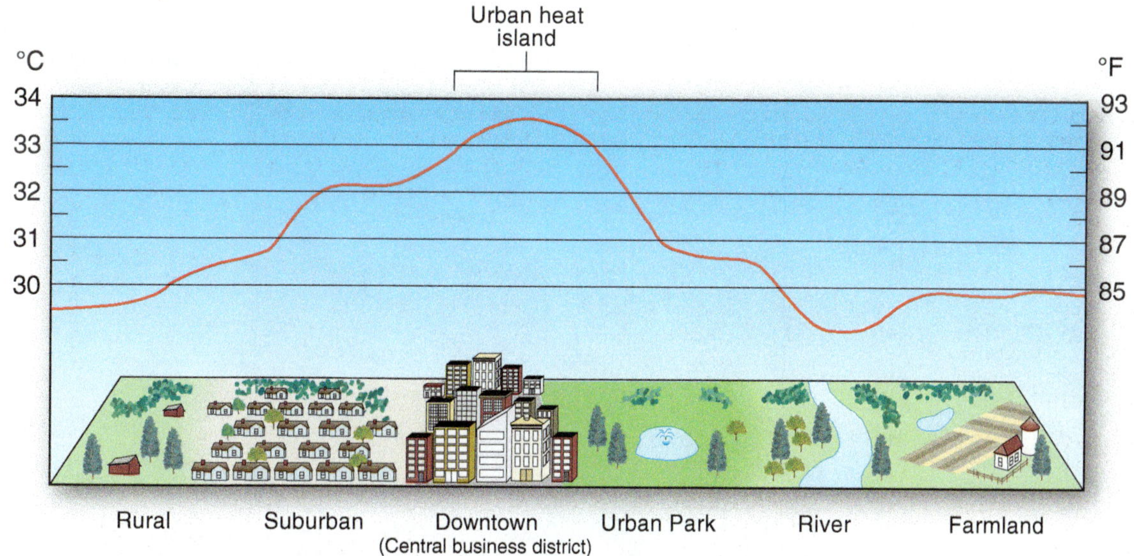

FIGURE 29 Typical urban heat island profile.
Cross section of a typical urban heat island from rural to downtown. Temperatures steeply rise in urban settings, plateau over the suburban built-up area, and peak where temperature is highest at the urban core. Note the cooling over the park area and river.

FOCUS STUDY 2

Air Temperature and the Human Body

We humans are capable of sensing small changes in temperature in the environment around us. Our perception of temperature is described by the terms *apparent temperature* and *sensible temperature*. This perception of temperature varies among individuals and cultures. Through complex mechanisms, our bodies maintain an average internal temperature ranging within a degree of 36.8°C (98.2°F), slightly lower in the morning or in cold weather and slightly higher at emotional times or during exercise and work.*

*The traditional value for "normal" body temperature, 37°C (98.6°F), was set in 1868 using old methods of measurement. According to Dr. Philip Mackowiak of the University of Maryland School of Medicine, a more accurate modern assessment places normal at 36.8°C (98.2°F), with a range of 2.7 C° (4.8 F°) for the human population ("A Critical Appraisal of 98.6°F, the Upper Limit of the Normal Body Temperature," *Journal of the American Medical Association* 268,September 23, 1992: 1581–87).

Taken together, the water vapor content of air, wind speed, and air temperature affect each individual's sense of comfort. High temperatures, high humidity, and low winds produce the most heat discomfort, whereas low humidity and strong winds enhance cooling rates. Although modern heating and cooling systems, if available and affordable, can reduce the impact of uncomfortable temperatures indoors, the danger to human life from excessive heat or cold persists outdoors. When changes occur in the surrounding air, the human body reacts in various ways to maintain its core temperature and to protect the brain at all cost.

Wind-Chill and Heat Indexes

The *wind-chill index* is important to those who experience winters with freezing temperatures. The wind-chill factor indicates the enhanced rate at which body heat is lost to the air. As wind speeds increase, heat loss from the skin increases. The National Weather Service (NWS; http://www.nws.noaa.gov/om/windchill/) and the Meteorological Services of Canada (MSC) developed the Wind Chill Temperature (WCT) Index in Figure 2.1.

Using the chart, if the air temperature is −7°C (20°F) and the wind is blowing at 32 kmph (20 mph), skin temperatures will be at −16°C (4°F). The lower wind-chill values present a serious freezing hazard to exposed flesh. Imagine the wind chill experienced by a downhill ski racer going 130 kmph (80 mph)—frostbite is a definite possibility during a 2-minute run. The wind chill does omit consideration of sunlight intensity, a person's physical activity, and the use of protective clothing, such as a windbreaker, that prevents wind access to your skin.

The *heat index* (HI) indicates the human body's reaction to air temperature and water vapor. The water vapor in air is expressed as relative humidity. For now, we simply can assume that the amount of water vapor in the air affects the evaporation rate of perspiration from the skin because the more water vapor

Actual Air Temperature in °C (°F)

Wind speed, kmph (mph)									
Calm	4° (40°)	−1° (30°)	−7° (20°)	−12° (10°)	−18° (0°)	−23° (−10°)	−29° (−20°)	−34° (−30°)	−40° (−40°)
8 (5)	2° (36°)	−4° (25°)	−11° (13°)	−17° (1°)	−24° (−11°)	−30° (−22°)	−37° (−34°)	−43° (−46°)	−49° (−57°)
16 (10)	1° (34°)	−6° (21°)	−13° (9°)	−20° (−4°)	−27° (−16°)	−33° (−28°)	−41° (−41°)	−47° (−53°)	−54° (−66°)
24 (15)	0° (32°)	−7° (19°)	−14° (6°)	−22° (−7°)	−28° (−19°)	−36° (−32°)	−43° (−45°)	−50° (−58°)	−57° (−71°)
32 (20)	−1° (30°)	−8° (17°)	−16° (4°)	−23° (−9°)	−30° (−22°)	−37° (−35°)	−44° (−48°)	−52° (−61°)	−59° (−74°)
40 (25)	−2° (29°)	−9° (16°)	−16° (3°)	−24° (−11°)	−31° (−24°)	−38° (−37°)	−46° (−51°)	−53° (−64°)	−61° (−78°)
48 (30)	−2° (28°)	−9° (15°)	−17° (−1°)	−24° (−12°)	−32° (−26°)	−39° (−39°)	−47° (−53°)	−55° (−67°)	−62° (−80°)
56 (35)	−2° (28°)	−10° (14°)	−18° (0°)	−26° (−14°)	−33° (−27°)	−41° (−41°)	−48° (−55°)	−56° (−69°)	−63° (−82°)
64 (40)	−3° (27°)	−11° (13°)	−18° (−1°)	−26° (−15°)	−34° (−29°)	−42° (−43°)	−49° (−57°)	−57° (−71°)	−64° (−84°)
72 (45)	−3° (26°)	−11° (12°)	−19° (−2°)	−27° (−16°)	−34° (−30°)	−42° (−44°)	−50° (−58°)	−58° (−72°)	−66° (−86°)
80 (50)	−3° (26°)	−11° (12°)	−19° (−3°)	−27° (−17°)	−35° (−31°)	−43° (−45°)	−51° (−60°)	−59° (−74°)	−67° (−88°)

Frostbite times: 30 min. 10 min. 5 min.

FIGURE 2.1 Wind Chill Temperature Index for various temperatures and wind speeds.

in the air (the higher the humidity), the less water from perspiration the air can absorb through evaporation, thus reducing natural evaporative cooling. The heat index indicates how the air feels to an average person—in other words, its apparent temperature.

Figure 2.2 is an abbreviated version of the heat index used by the NWS and now included in its daily weather summaries during appropriate months. The table beneath the graph describes the effects of heat-index categories on higher-risk groups. A combination of high temperature and high humidity can severely reduce the body's natural ability to regulate internal temperature. The NWS provides a heat-index forecast warning map at http://www.nws.noaa.gov/om/heat/index.shtml; a heat-index calculator is at http://www.crh.noaa.gov/jkl/?n=heat_index_calculator.

Summer Heat-Wave Deaths

Heat waves are a major cause of weather-related deaths, causing the loss of more than 8000 lives in the United States between 1979 and 1999. In an NRC/NAS report the National Academy of Sciences stated, "Hot days, hot nights, and heat waves have become more frequent in recent decades, and their frequency, intensity, and duration are projected to increase. . . ."

Europe was paralyzed in the summer of 2003 with high heat-index conditions when temperatures topped 40°C (104°F) in June, July, and August. Official estimates across the continent placed the death count at more than 20,000.

For nearly a week during July 1995, Chicago's heat-index values went to category I in dwellings that lacked air conditioning. Chicago had never experienced a 48-hour period during which temperatures did not go below 31.5°C (89°F)! With high pressure (hot, stable air) dominating from the Midwest to the Atlantic and moist air from the Gulf of Mexico, all the ingredients for disaster were present.

This combination of high temperatures and water vapor produced stifling conditions, particularly affecting the sick and elderly. As record temperatures occurred at Midway Airport (41°C;106°F), some apartments without air conditioning exceeded indoor heat-index temperatures of 54°C (130°F). In Chicago, 700 people died. Nearly 1000 people died overall in the Midwest and East from these conditions.

Climate change is forcing more heat index days because of higher temperatures and increased humidity levels from enhanced air masses.

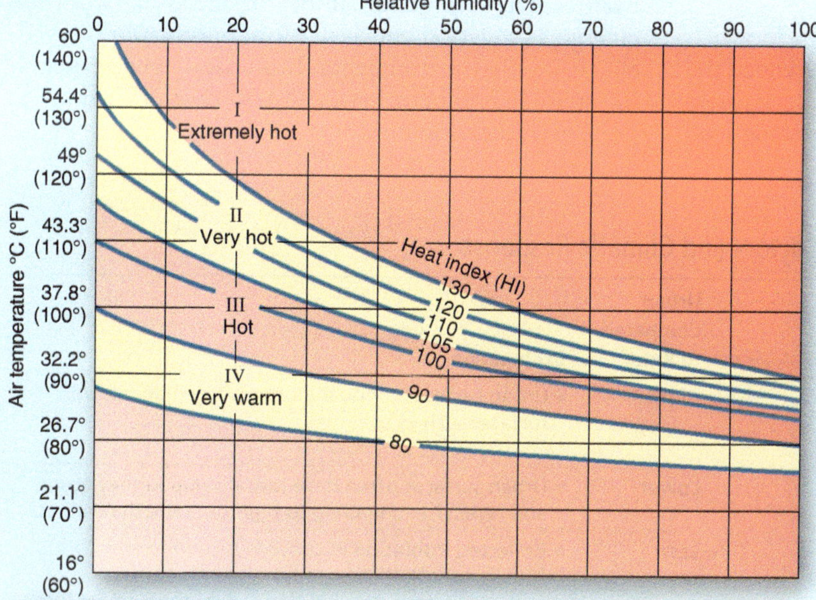

Level of concern	Category	Heat Index Apparent Temperature	General Effect of Heat Index on People in High-Risk Groups
Extreme danger	I	54°C (130°F) or higher	Heat/sunstroke highly likely with continued exposure
Danger	II	41° – 54°C (105° – 130°F)	Sunstroke, heat cramps, or heat exhaustion likely and heatstroke possible with prolonged exposure and/or physical activity
Extreme caution	III	32° – 41°C (90° – 105°F)	Sunstroke, heat cramps, and heat exhaustion possible with prolonged exposure and/or physical activity
Caution	IV	27° – 32°C (80° – 90°F)	Fatigue possible with prolonged exposure and/or physical activity

FIGURE 2.2 Heat index for various temperatures and relative humidity levels.

Park in New York City, daytime temperatures average 5–10 C° (9–18 F°) cooler than in urban areas outside the park.

Figure 30 illustrates some of the processes that cause UHI effects, which increase as the size of a city grows. Most major cities produce a **dust dome** of airborne pollution, which can be blown from the city in elongated plumes; such domes affect urban energy budgets. Table 1 lists some of the factors that cause UHIs and compares selected climatic elements of rural and urban environments.

Many known methods to make cities cooler await application. In addition to lowering urban temperatures, such strategies could reduce energy consumption and fossil-fuel use, thus reducing greenhouse gas emissions. An experiment in Phoenix, Arizona, shown in the chapter-opening image, lightened the color of rooftops on commercial buildings. The albedo of original roof gravel was 31%, whereas whitish gravel has an albedo of 72%. The resulting roof temperature difference was from 10 C° to 14 C° cooler, thus reducing energy costs. For structures with solar panel arrays, temperatures dropped dramatically with the roof under the shade of the panels.

When you look across the urban landscape in which you live, what strategies do you think would reduce the urban heat island effect? Possibilities include lighter-colored surfaces for buildings, streets, and parking lots; more reflective roofs; and more trees, parks, and open space. With 60% of the global population living in cities by the year 2030 and with rising air and water temperatures from climate change, urban heat island issues will soon emerge as a critical concern. More information is available from the Environmental Protection Agency, including strategies, publications, and hot topic discussions, at http://www.epa.gov/hiri/.

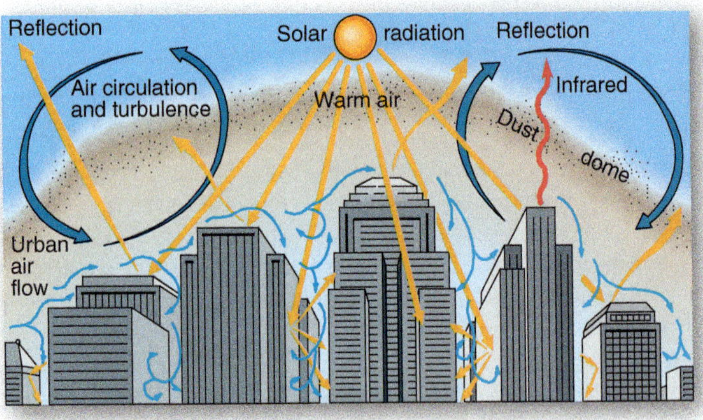

FIGURE 30 The urban environment.
Insolation, wind movements, and dust dome in city environments.

TABLE 1 Urban Heat Islands: Driving Factors and Climatic Response

Driving Factor	Climatic Element	Urban Compared to Rural	Explanation
Thermal properties of urban surfaces: metal, glass, asphalt, concrete, or brick	Net radiation	Higher	▪ Urban surfaces conduct more energy than natural surfaces such as soil.
Reflective properties of urban surfaces	Albedo	Lower	▪ Urban surfaces often have low albedo, so they absorb and retain heat, leading to high net radiation values.
Urban canyon effect	Wind speed ▪ annual mean ▪ extreme gusts Calm periods	Less More	▪ Reflected insolation in canyons is conducted into surface materials, thus increasing temperatures. ▪ Buildings interrupt wind flows, diminishing heat loss through advection (horizontal movement), and block nighttime radiation to space. ▪ Maximum UHI effects occur on calm, clear days and nights.
Anthropogenic heating	Temperature ▪ annual mean ▪ winter minima ▪ summer maxima	Higher	▪ Heat is generated by homes, vehicles, and factories. Heat output may surge in winter with power for heating or in summer with power for air conditioning.
Pollution	Air pollution ▪ condensation nuclei ▪ particulates Cloudiness, including fog Precipitation Snowfall, inner city Snowfall, downwind	More More More Less More	▪ Airborne pollutants (dust, particulates, aerosols) in urban dust dome raise temperatures by absorbing insolation and reradiating heat to surface. ▪ Increased particulates are condensation nuclei for water vapor, increasing cloud formation and precipitation; heating enhances convection processes.
Urban desert effect: less plant cover and more sealed surfaces	Relative humidity ▪ annual mean Infiltration Runoff Evaporation	Less Less More Less	▪ Cooling effect of evaporation and plant transpiration is reduced or absent. ▪ Water cannot infiltrate through sealed surfaces to soil; more water flows as runoff. ▪ Urban surfaces respond as desert landscapes—storms may cause "flash floods."

3. List several types of surfaces and their albedo values. Explain the differences among these surfaces. What determines the reflectivity of a surface?
4. Define the concepts transmission, absorption, diffuse radiation, conduction, and convection.

■ *Describe* the greenhouse effect and the patterns of global net radiation and surface energy balances.

Longwave energy flux to space.

The Earth–atmosphere energy system naturally balances itself in a steady-state equilibrium. It does so through energy transfers that are *nonradiative* (convection, conduction, and the latent heat of evaporation) and *radiative* (longwave radiation among the surface, the atmosphere, and space).

Carbon dioxide, water vapor, methane, CFCs (chlorofluorocarbons), and other gases in the lower atmosphere absorb infrared radiation that is then emitted to Earth, thus delaying energy loss to space. This process is the **greenhouse effect**. In the atmosphere, longwave radiation is not actually trapped, as it would be in a greenhouse, but its passage to space is delayed (heat energy is detained in the atmosphere) through absorption and counterradiation. **Jet contrails**, or *condensation trails*, are produced by aircraft exhaust, particulates, and water vapor and can form high cirrus clouds, sometimes called *false cirrus clouds*.

In the tropical latitudes, high insolation angle and consistent daylength cause more energy to be gained than lost, forming energy surpluses. In the polar regions, an extremely low insolation angle, highly reflective surfaces, and up to 6 months of no insolation annually cause more energy to be lost, forming energy deficits. This imbalance of net radiation from tropical surpluses to polar deficits drives a vast global circulation of both energy and mass.

Surface energy balances are used to summarize the energy expenditure for any location. Surface energy measurements are used as an analytical tool of **microclimatology**. Adding and subtracting the energy flow at the surface lets us calculate **net radiation (NET R)**, or the balance of all radiation at Earth's surface available to do work—shortwave (SW) and longwave (LW).

The greatest insolation input occurs at the time of the summer solstice in each hemisphere. Air temperature responds to seasons and variations in insolation input. Within a 24-hour day, air temperature peaks between 3:00 and 4:00 P.M. and dips to its lowest point right at or slightly after sunrise. Air temperature lags behind each day's peak insolation. The warmest time of day occurs not at the moment of maximum insolation, but at that moment when a maximum of insolation is absorbed.

greenhouse effect
jet contrail
microclimatology
net radiation (NET R)

5. What are the similarities and differences between an actual greenhouse and the gaseous atmospheric greenhouse? Why is Earth's greenhouse effect changing?
6. Generalize the pattern of global net radiation. How might this pattern drive the atmospheric weather machine? (See Figure 11.)
7. In terms of surface energy balance, explain the term *net radiation* (NET R).
8. What are the expenditure pathways for surface net radiation? What kind of work is accomplished?
9. What is the role played by latent heat in surface energy budgets?
10. Compare the daily surface energy balances of El Mirage, California, and Pitt Meadows, British Columbia. Explain the differences.
11. Why is there a temperature lag between the highest Sun altitude and the warmest time of day? Relate your answer to the insolation and temperature patterns during the day.

■ *Review* the temperature concepts and temperature controls that produce global temperature patterns.

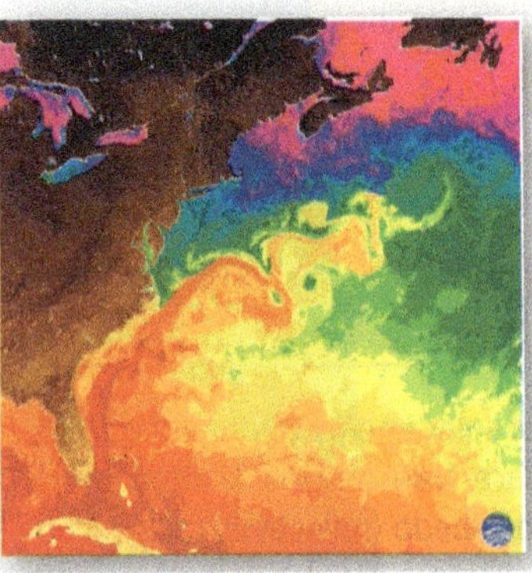

Temperature is a measure of the average kinetic energy (motion) of individual molecules in matter. We feel the effect of temperature as the sensible heat transfer from warmer objects to cooler objects when these objects are touching. Principal controls and influences upon temperature patterns include *latitude* (the distance north or south of the equator), *altitude* and *elevation*, *cloud cover* (reflection, absorption, and radiation of energy), and *land–water heating differences* (the nature of evaporation, transparency, specific heat, movement, ocean currents, and sea-surface temperatures).

The physical nature of land (rock and soil) and water (oceans, seas, and lakes) is the reason for **land–water heating differences**, the fact that land heats and cools faster than water. Moderate temperature patterns are associated with water bodies, and extreme temperatures occur inland. The controls that cause differences between land and water surfaces are *evaporation, transparency, specific heat, movement, ocean currents, and sea-surface temperatures*.

Light penetrates water because of its **transparency**. Water is clear and light transmits to an average depth of 60 m (200 ft) in the ocean. This penetration distributes available heat energy over a much greater volume than could occur on opaque land; thus, a larger energy reservoir is formed. When equal volumes of water and land are compared, water requires far more energy to increase its temperature than does land. In other words, water can hold more energy than can soil or rock, so water has a higher **specific heat**, the heat capacity of a substance, averaging about four times that of soil.

Ocean currents affect temperature. An example of the effect of ocean currents is the **Gulf Stream**, which moves northward off the east coast of North America, carrying warm water far into the North Atlantic. As a result, the southern third of Iceland experiences much milder temperatures than would be expected for a latitude of 65° N, just below the Arctic Circle (66.5°).

Marine effect, or maritime, describes locations that exhibit the moderating influences of the ocean, usually along coastlines or on islands. **Continental effect** refers to the condition of areas that are less affected by the sea and therefore have a greater range between maximum and minimum temperatures diurnally and yearly.

temperature
land–water heating differences
transparency

specific heat
Gulf Stream
marine effect
continental effect

12. Explain the effect of altitude/elevation on air temperature. Why is air at higher altitude/elevation lower in temperature? Why does it feel cooler standing in shadows at higher elevation than at lower elevation?
13. What noticeable effect does air density have on the absorption and radiation of energy? What role does elevation play in that process?
14. How is it possible to grow moderate-climate-type crops such as wheat, barley, and potatoes at an elevation of 4103 m (13,460 ft) near La Paz, Bolivia, so near the equator?
15. Describe the effect of cloud cover with regard to Earth's temperature patterns. Review cloud-albedo forcing and cloud-greenhouse forcing, and relate the concepts with a simple sketch.
16. Differentiate between marine and continental temperatures. Referring back to the chapter text, give geographic examples of each from the United States, Norway, and Russia.

- ***Interpret*** the pattern of Earth's temperatures from their portrayal on January and July temperature maps and on a map of annual temperature ranges.

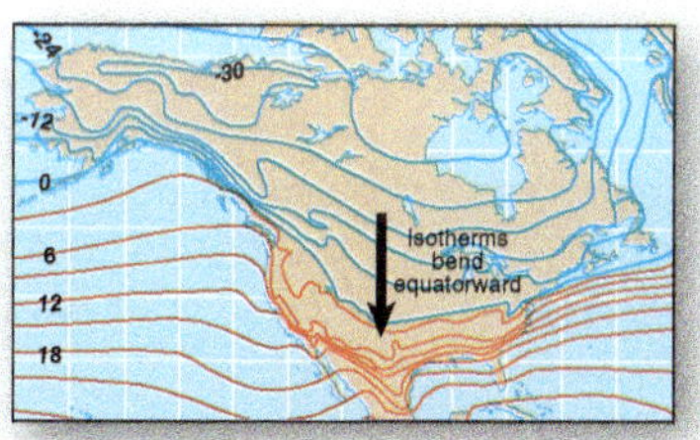

Maps for January and July instead of the solstice months of December and June are used for temperature comparison because of the natural lag that occurs between insolation received and maximum or minimum temperatures experienced. Each line on these temperature maps is an **isotherm**, an isoline that connects points of equal temperature. Isotherms portray temperature patterns.

Isotherms generally are zonal, trending east–west, parallel to the equator. They mark the general decrease in insolation and net radiation with distance from the equator. The **thermal equator** (the isoline connecting all points of highest mean temperature) trends southward in January and shifts northward with the high summer Sun in July.

isotherm
thermal equator

17. What is the thermal equator? Describe its location in January and in July. Explain why it shifts position annually.
18. Observe trends in the pattern of isolines over North America and compare the January average temperature map with the July map. Why do the patterns shift locations?
19. Describe and explain the extreme temperature range experienced in north-central Siberia between January and July.
20. Where are the hottest places on Earth? Are they near the equator or elsewhere? Explain. Where is the coldest place on Earth?

- ***Contrast*** wind chill and heat index, and ***determine*** human response to these apparent temperature effects.

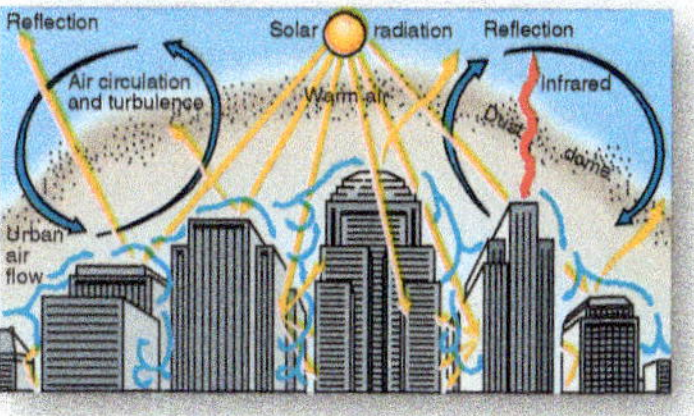

The *wind-chill factor* indicates the enhanced rate at which body heat is lost to the air. As wind speeds increase, heat loss from the skin increases. The *heat index* (HI) indicates the human body's reaction to air temperature and water vapor. The level of humidity in the air affects our natural ability to cool through evaporation from skin.

21. What is the wind-chill temperature on a day with an air temperature of −12°C (10°F) and a wind speed of 32 kmph (20 mph)?
22. On a day when the temperature reaches 37.8°C (100°F), how does a relative humidity reading of 50% affect apparent temperature?

- ***Portray*** typical urban heat island conditions, and ***contrast*** the microclimatology of urban areas with that of surrounding rural environments.

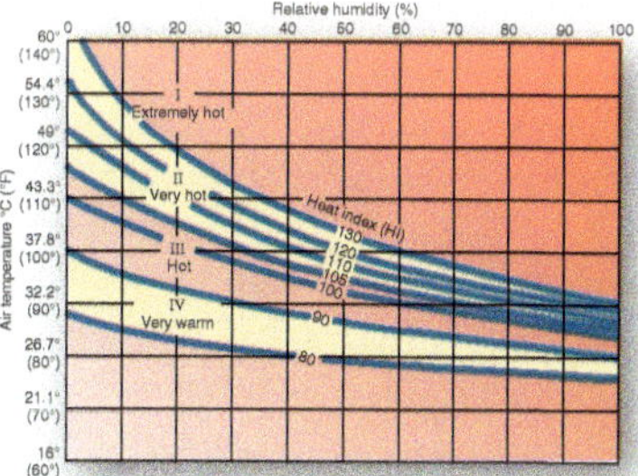

A growing percentage of Earth's people live in cities and experience a unique set of altered microclimatic effects: increased conduction, lower albedos, higher NET R values, increased water runoff, complex radiation and reflection patterns, anthropogenic heating, and the gases, dusts, and aerosols of urban pollution. These effects combine to raise temperatures, producing an **urban heat island**. Air pollution, including gases and aerosols, is greater in urban areas than in rural ones. Every major city produces its own **dust dome** of airborne pollution.

urban heat island
dust dome

23. What is the basis for the urban heat island concept? Describe the climatic effects attributable to urban as compared with nonurban environments.
24. Which of the items in Table 1 have you yourself experienced? Explain.
25. Assess the potential for solar energy applications in our society. What are some negatives? What are some positives?

Visit **http://www.masteringgeography.com/** for several figure animations, satellite loops, self-study quizzes, flashcards, visual glossary, case studies, career links, text reference maps, RSS Feeds, and an ebook version of *Elemental Geosystems.* Included are many geography web links to interesting Internet sources that support this chapter.

Atmospheric and Oceanic Circulations

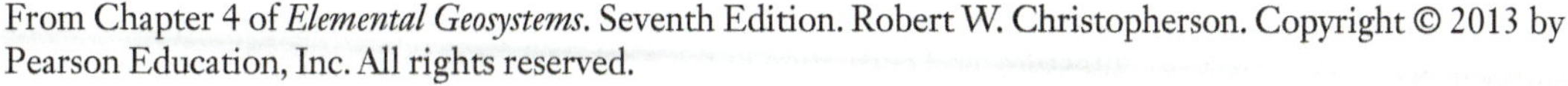

Atmospheric and Oceanic Circulations

Wind turbines in corn fields near Spearville, Ford County, Kansas, in the Spearville Wind Energy Facility. This is a 100.5 MW wind farm—67 1.5-MW turbines. [Bobbé Christopherson.]

KEY LEARNING CONCEPTS

After reading the chapter, you should be able to:

- ***Define*** the concept of air pressure, and ***describe*** instruments used to measure air pressure.
- ***Define*** wind, and ***explain*** how wind is measured, how wind direction is determined, and how winds are named.
- ***Explain*** the four driving forces within the atmosphere—gravity, pressure gradient force, Coriolis force, and friction force—and ***locate*** the primary high- and low-pressure areas and principal winds.
- ***Describe*** upper-air circulation, and ***define*** the jet streams.
- ***Explain*** several types of local winds and the regional monsoons.
- ***Discern*** the basic pattern of Earth's major surface ocean currents and deep thermohaline circulation.
- ***Summarize*** several multi-year oscillations of air temperature, air pressure, and circulation in the Arctic, Atlantic, and Pacific Oceans.

Ocean Currents Bring Invasive Species

As human civilization pumps and throws more refuse and chemicals into the oceans, the garbage travels in currents that sweep across the globe. A dramatic episode of such ocean-current transport happened in the South Atlantic in 2006. Let us begin this story here in this chapter. Although not covered here, the ecological impacts continue.

High-pressure systems guide the winds and ocean currents in the major oceanic basins. These systems flow clockwise in the Northern Hemisphere and counterclockwise in the Southern Hemisphere. In the South Atlantic, this counterclockwise flow drives the South Equatorial Current westward and the West Wind Drift eastward (Figure GN 1). Along the African coast, the cool Benguela Current flows northward, while the warm Brazil Current moves south along the coast of South America. This is the circulation gyre of the South Atlantic.

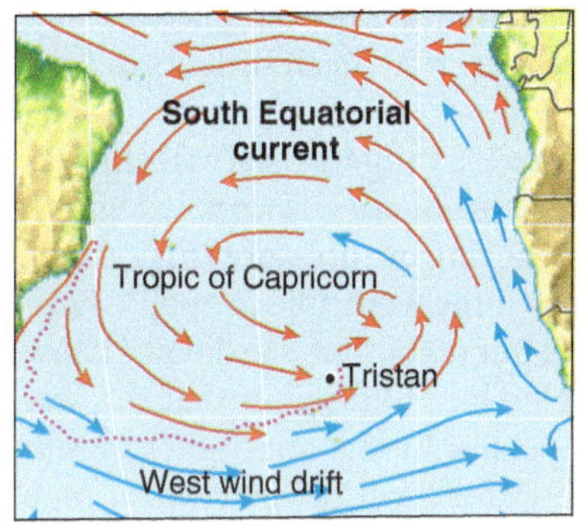

FIGURE GN 1 Principal ocean currents of the South Atlantic. Tristan da Cunha is at approximately 37° 4′ S and 12° 19′ W. Note the probable route of the oil-drilling platform.

Along the southeastern portion of this gyre is a remote island group, the Tristan da Cunha Archipelago comprising four islands, some 2775 km (1725 mi) from Africa and 3355 km (2085 mi) from South America (see location in Figure GN 1). Only 298 people live on Tristan in the village of Edinburgh (Figure GN 2).

FIGURE GN 2 Village of Edinburgh, Tristan da Cunha. [Bobbé Christopherson.]

The people in this unique small society do subsistence farming, collectively grow and export potatoes, and depend on rich marine life that they carefully manage. The Tristan rock lobster (a crawfish) is harvested and quick frozen at a community factory and exported around the world. Although Tristan lacks an airport and has no pier or port, several ships a year transport these commodities. In 2006, ocean currents brought to this island a grim reminder of the outside world.

Oil-drilling platforms are like small ships that can be towed to a desired site for drilling undersea wells. Petrobras, Brazil's state-controlled oil company, had such a platform, the *Petrobras XXI*. The oil company towed the 80-m × 67-m × 34-m high (264-ft × 220-ft × 113-ft high) platform from Macae, Brazil, on March 5, 2006—destination Singapore.

The company chartered a tug, the *Mighty Deliverer*, to do the job. This tug was actually built for inland work as a "pusher" tug, like ones you might see on the Mississippi River or in the Great Lakes. Yet it was contracted to haul this drilling rig across the Southern Ocean, easily the most treacherous seas on Earth. The *Deliverer* headed south, encountering rough seas after a few weeks. Conditions forced the tug's crew to cut the platform loose on April 30, and after a few days, the rig was lost at sea.

The *Petrobras XXI* was missing in rough seas, caught in the currents of the West Wind Drift and westerlies. Sometime in late May, after almost a month adrift, the oil-drilling platform ran aground on Tristan in Trypot Bay, where it was discovered by Tristanian fishermen on June 7 (Figure GN 3).

FIGURE GN 3 *Petrobras XXI* aground in Trypot Bay, Tristan. [Photo by biologist Sue Scott. All rights reserved.]

The owners of the drilling platform had not cleaned it prior to towing, which is the usual practice. Clean rigs move through the water with less friction, require less fuel, and result in lower labor costs. Consequently, *Petrobras XXI* carried some 62 non-native species of marine life, including free-swimming silver porgy and blenny fish that tagged along with the rig as it drifted in the currents.

While surveying the rig, marine scientists found an unprecedented potential species invasion of Tristan. Here in this chapter, we learn about wind and ocean circulation, the forces that brought the *Petrobras XXI* to Tristan. ■

After 635 years of dormancy, Mount Pinatubo in the Philippines erupted in 1991 (Figure 1a). This event had tremendous impact, lofting 15–20 million tons of ash, dust, and sulfur dioxide (SO_2) into the atmosphere. As the sulfur dioxide rose into the stratosphere, it quickly formed sulfuric acid (H_2SO_4) aerosols, which concentrated at an altitude of 16–25 km (10–15.5 mi). This debris increased atmospheric albedo about 1.5%, giving scientists an estimate of the aerosol volume generated by the eruption (see Figure 1).

The advanced very high resolution radiometer (AVHRR) instrument aboard *NOAA-11* monitored the reflected solar radiation from Mount Pinatubo's aerosols as global winds swept them around Earth. Figure 1b–e shows images made at 3-week intervals that clearly track the spread of the debris worldwide. Some 60 days after the eruption (the last satellite image in the sequence), the aerosol cloud spanned about 42% of the globe, from 20° S to 30° N. For almost 2 years, colorful sunrises and sunsets and a small temporary lowering of average temperatures followed. The eruption provided a unique insight into the dynamics of atmospheric circulation.

Today, technology permits a depth of analysis unknown in the past—satellites now track the atmospheric effects from dust storms, forest fires, industrial haze, warfare, and the dispersal of volcanic explosions. As an example, millions of tons of dust from African soils cross the Atlantic each year, borne by the winds of atmospheric circulation, visible in Figure 1b. International concerns about transboundary air pollution and the banning of nuclear weapon testing illustrate how the fluid movement of the atmosphere links humanity more than perhaps any other natural or cultural factor. The global spread of low-level radioactive debris from Japan's nuclear disaster and meltdowns in 2011 brought back memories of these previous issues. Our atmosphere makes the world a spatially bound society—one person's or country's exhalation is another's inhalation.

In this chapter: We begin with a discussion of wind essentials, consisting of air pressure and its measurement and a description of wind. The driving forces that produce surface winds are pressure gradient, Coriolis, and friction. We examine the circulation of Earth's atmosphere and the patterns of global winds, including principal pressure systems. We consider Earth's wind-driven oceanic currents and explain multi-year oscillations in atmospheric flows, local winds, and the powerful monsoons. The energy driving all this movement comes from one source: the Sun.

Wind Essentials

The primary circulation of winds across Earth has fascinated travelers, sailors, and scientists for centuries, although only in the modern era is a true picture emerging of global winds. Driven by the imbalance between equatorial energy surpluses and polar energy deficits, Earth's atmospheric circulation transfers both energy and mass on a grand scale, determining Earth's weather patterns and the flow of ocean currents. Scientists at the National Center for Atmospheric Research determined that the atmosphere is the dominant medium for redistributing energy from about 35° latitude to the poles in each hemisphere, whereas ocean currents redistribute more heat in a zone straddling the equator between the 17th parallels in each hemisphere. Atmospheric circulation also spreads air pollutants, whether natural or human-caused, worldwide, far from their point of origin.

Atmospheric circulation is categorized at three levels: primary circulation, consisting of general worldwide circulation; secondary circulation of migratory high-pressure and low-pressure systems; and tertiary circulation, which includes local winds and temporal weather patterns. Winds that move principally north or south along meridians of longitude are meridional flows. Winds moving east or west along parallels of latitude are zonal flows.

Air Pressure and Its Measurement

Air pressure, including its measurement and expression, is key to understanding wind. The molecules that constitute air create **air pressure** through their motion, size, and number—the factors that determine the temperature and density of the air. Pressure is exerted on all surfaces in contact with air.

In 1643, Galileo's pupil Evangelista Torricelli was working on a mine-drainage problem. His work led him to discover a method for measuring air pressure (Figure 2a). He knew that pumps in the mine were able to "pull" water upward about 10 m (33 ft), but no higher. He did not know why. Careful observation led him to discover that this was caused not by weak pumps, but by the atmosphere itself. Torricelli noted that the water level in the vertical pipe fluctuated from day to day. He figured out that air pressure, the weight of the air, varies with weather conditions.

To simulate the problem at the mine, Torricelli devised an instrument, at Galileo's suggestion, using a much denser fluid than water—mercury (Hg)—in a glass tube 1 m high. Torricelli sealed the glass tube at one end, filled it with mercury, and inverted it into a dish of mercury

Blowing in the wind

Dust originating in Africa sometimes increases the iron content of the waters off Florida, promoting the toxic algal blooms (*Karenia brevis*) known as "Red Tides." In the Amazon, soil samples bear the dust print of these former African soils that crossed the Atlantic. Active research on such dust is part of the U.S. Navy's Aerosol Analysis and Prediction System (NAAPS); see links at http://www.nrlmry.navy.mil/aerosol/.

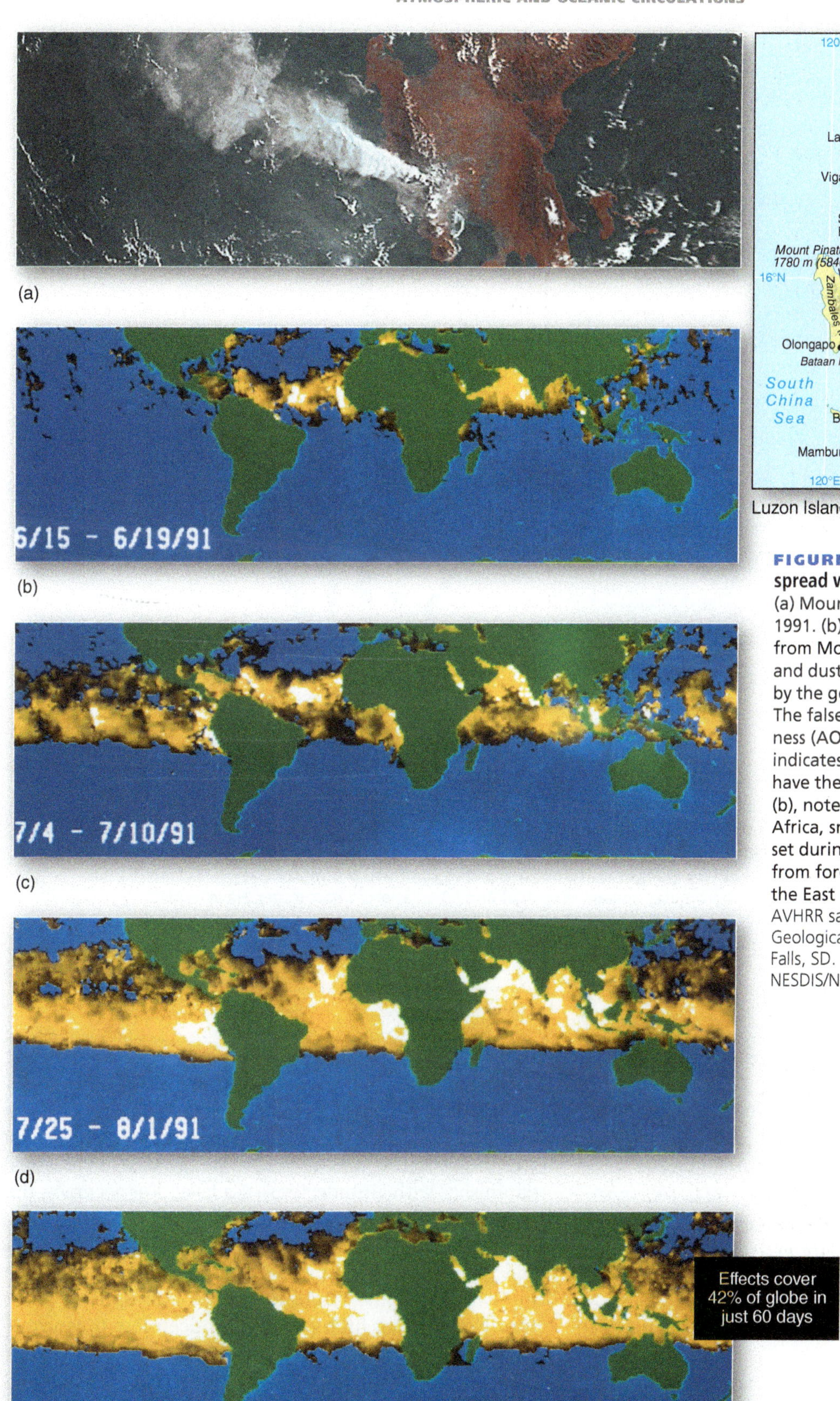

FIGURE 1 Volcanic eruption effects spread worldwide by winds. (a) Mount Pinatubo eruption, June 15, 1991. (b)–(e) False-color images of aerosols from Mount Pinatubo, smoke from fires, and dust storms, all swept about the globe by the general atmospheric circulation. The false color shows aerosol optical thickness (AOT): White is densest, dull yellow indicates medium values, and brown areas have the lowest aerosol concentration. In (b), note the dust moving westward from Africa, smoke from Kuwaiti oil well fires set during the first Persian Gulf War, smoke from forest fires in Siberia, and haze off the East Coast of the United States. [(a) AVHRR satellite image, data available from U.S. Geological Survey, EROS Data Center, Sioux Falls, SD. (b–e) AVHRR satellite AOT images NESDIS/NOAA.]

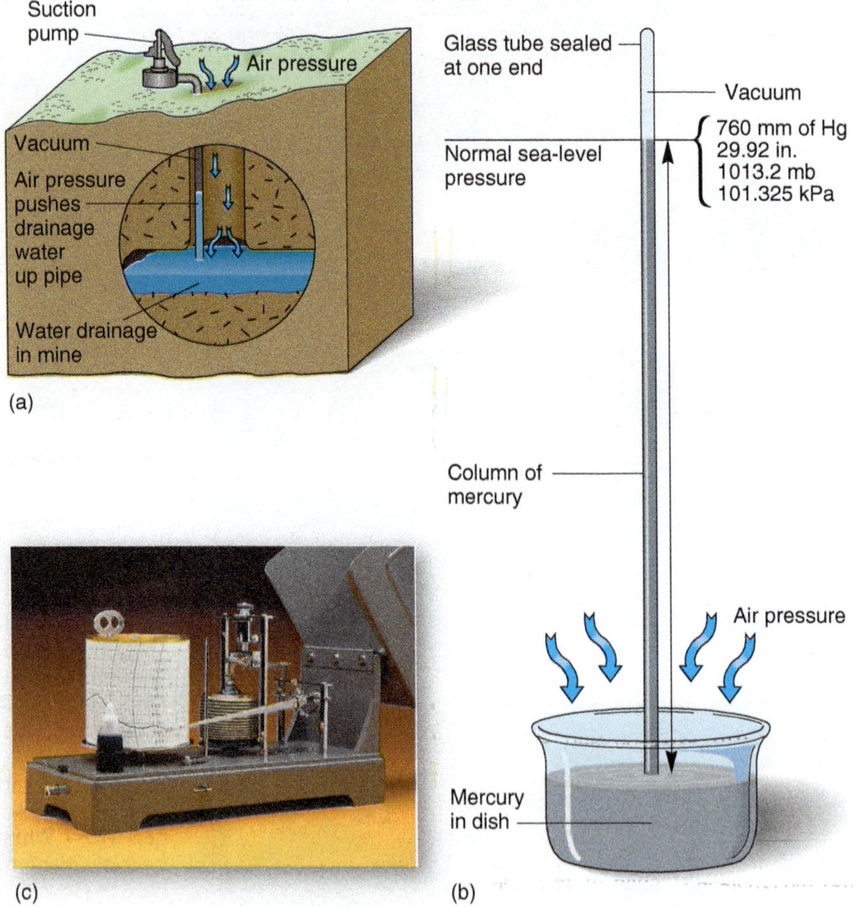

FIGURE 2 Developing the barometer.
(a) Torricelli developed the barometer to measure air pressure while trying to solve a mine-drainage problem. Two types of instruments are used to measure atmospheric pressure: (b) a mercury barometer (idealized sketch) and (c) an aneroid barometer. Have you used a barometer? If so, what type is it? Have you tried to reset it using a local weather information source? [(c) Qualimetrics, Inc.]

(Figure 2b). He determined that the average height of the column of mercury in the tube was 760 mm (29.92 in.) and that it did vary day to day as the weather changed. He concluded that the mass of surrounding air was exerting pressure on the mercury in the dish that counterbalanced the column of mercury.

Using similar instruments, scientists set a standard of normal sea-level pressure at 1013.2 mb (millibar, which expresses force per square meter of surface area) or 29.92 in. of mercury (Hg). In Canada and other countries, normal air pressure is expressed as 101.32 kPa (kilopascal; 1 kPa = 10 mb).

Any instrument that measures air pressure is a barometer (from the Greek *baros*, meaning "weight"). Torricelli developed a **mercury barometer.** A more compact barometer design, which works without a meter-long tube of mercury, is the **aneroid barometer**, shown in Figure 2c. Aneroid means "using no liquid." The aneroid barometer principle is simple: Imagine a small chamber, partially emptied of air, that is sealed and connected to a mechanism attached to a needle on a dial. As air pressure increases, it presses on the chamber; as air pressure decreases, it relieves pressure on the chamber—changes in air pressure move the needle. An aircraft altimeter is a type of aneroid barometer. It accurately measures altitude because air pressure diminishes with altitude above sea level. For accuracy, the altimeter must be adjusted for temperature changes.

Figure 3 illustrates comparative scales in millibars and inches used to express air pressure and its relative force. The normal range of Earth's atmospheric pressure from strong high pressure to deep low pressure is about 1050 to 980 mb (31.00 to 29.00 in.). The figure also indicates the extreme highest and lowest pressures ever recorded in the United States and on Earth.

Wind: Description and Measurement

Simply stated, **wind** is generally the horizontal motion of air across Earth's surface. Turbulence adds wind updrafts and downdrafts and a vertical component to this definition. Differences in air pressure (density) between one

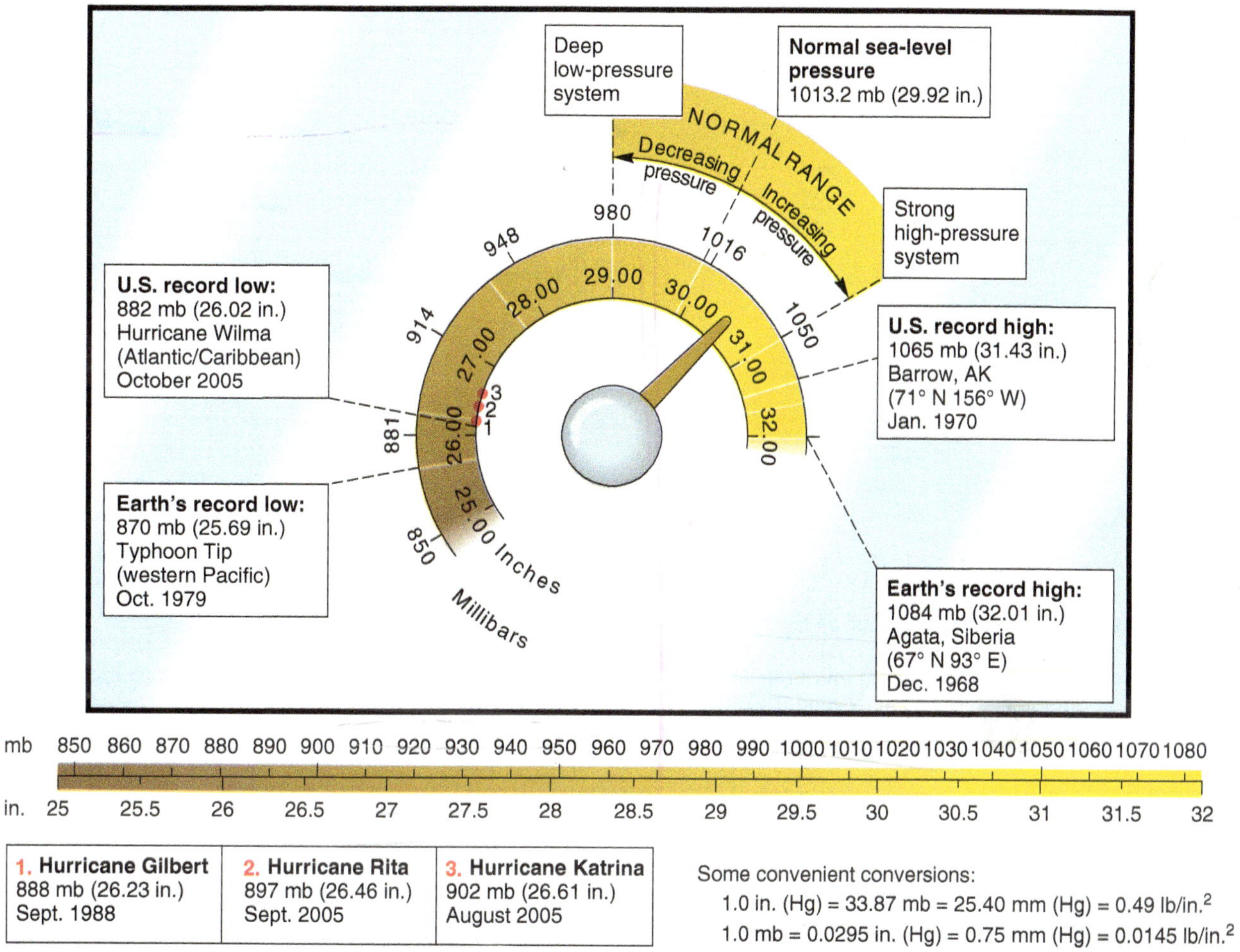

Deep low-pressure system

Normal sea-level pressure 1013.2 mb (29.92 in.)

NORMAL RANGE

Decreasing pressure

Increasing pressure

Strong high-pressure system

U.S. record low: 882 mb (26.02 in.) Hurricane Wilma (Atlantic/Caribbean) October 2005

U.S. record high: 1065 mb (31.43 in.) Barrow, AK (71° N 156° W) Jan. 1970

Earth's record low: 870 mb (25.69 in.) Typhoon Tip (western Pacific) Oct. 1979

Earth's record high: 1084 mb (32.01 in.) Agata, Siberia (67° N 93° E) Dec. 1968

Inches: 25.00, 26.00, 27.00, 28.00, 29.00, 30.00, 31.00, 32.00

Millibars: 850, 881, 914, 948, 980, 1016, 1050

mb	850	860	870	880	890	900	910	920	930	940	950	960	970	980	990	1000	1010	1020	1030	1040	1050	1060	1070	1080

in.	25	25.5	26	26.5	27	27.5	28	28.5	29	29.5	30	30.5	31	31.5	32

1. Hurricane Gilbert	2. Hurricane Rita	3. Hurricane Katrina
888 mb (26.23 in.) Sept. 1988	897 mb (26.46 in.) Sept. 2005	902 mb (26.61 in.) August 2005

Some convenient conversions:

1.0 in. (Hg) = 33.87 mb = 25.40 mm (Hg) = 0.49 lb/in.^{2}

1.0 mb = 0.0295 in. (Hg) = 0.75 mm (Hg) = 0.0145 lb/in.^{2}

FIGURE 3 Air pressure readings and conversions.
Scales express barometric air pressure in millibars and inches, with average air pressure values and recorded pressure extremes. Canadian values include kilopascal equivalents (10 mb = 1 kPa). The intensity of the 2005 hurricane season is evident; note the positions of Katrina, Rita, and Wilma on the pressure dial.

location and another produce wind. Wind's two principal properties are speed and direction, and instruments measure each. An **anemometer** measures wind speed in kilometers per hour (kmph), miles per hour (mph), meters per second (mps), or knots. (A knot is a nautical mile per hour, covering 1 minute of Earth's arc in an hour, equivalent to 1.85 kmph, or 1.15 mph.) A **wind vane** determines wind direction; the standard measurement is taken 10 m (33 ft) above the ground to reduce the effects of local topography on wind direction (Figure 4).

Winds are named for the direction from which they originate. For example, a wind from the west is a westerly wind (it blows eastward); a wind out of the south is a southerly wind (it blows northward). Figure 5 illustrates a simple wind compass, naming 16 principal wind directions used by meteorologists.

The traditional Beaufort wind scale, introduced by Admiral Beaufort of the British Navy in 1806, is a descriptive scale useful in visually estimating wind speed by observing the ocean surface or elements of the landscape.

FIGURE 4 Wind vane and anemometer.
Instruments used to measure wind direction (wind vane, left) and wind speed (anemometer, right) at a weather station installation. [NOAA Photo Library.]

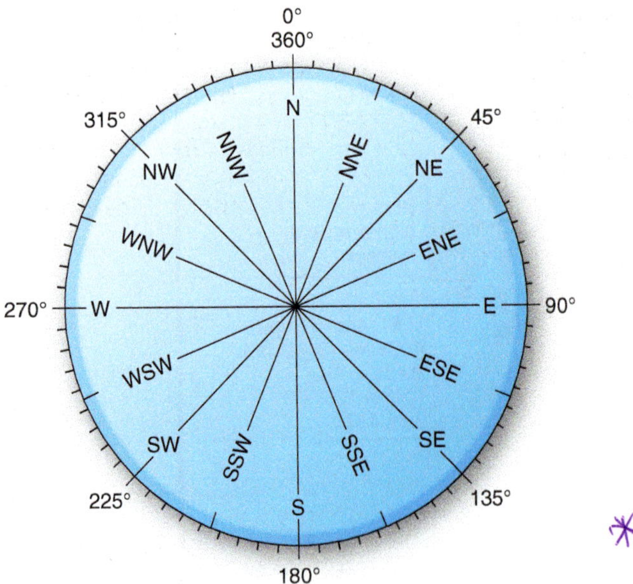

FIGURE 5 Sixteen wind directions identified on a wind compass.
Winds are named for the direction from which they originate. For example, a wind from the west is a westerly wind.

The National Weather Service (old Weather Bureau) standardized the scale in 1955 (see http://www.hpc.ncep.noaa.gov/html/beaufort.shtml). The scale is still referenced on ocean charts, enabling estimation of wind speed without instruments. Although most ships use sophisticated equipment to perform such measurements, you find the Beaufort scale posted on the bridge of many ships and on our *MasteringGeography* web site.

CRITICAL THINKING 1

Measure the wind

Estimate wind speed and direction as you walk across campus on a day with wind. You might access the URL given above or go to *MasteringGeography* to view the Beaufort scale to assist you. Record your estimates at least twice during the day, more often if you note changing wind patterns. For wind direction, moisten your finger, hold it in the air, and sense evaporative cooling on one side of your finger to indicate from which direction the wind is blowing. Check the Internet to find a weather station on your campus or in a nearby location, and compare your measurements to actual data. What changes in wind speed and direction do you notice over several days? How did these changes relate to the weather you experienced?

Driving Forces Within the Atmosphere

Four forces determine both speed and direction of winds:

- The pressure that Earth's *gravitational force* exerts on the atmosphere is virtually uniform. Gravity equally compresses the atmosphere worldwide, with the density decreasing as altitude increases. The gravitational force counteracts the outward centrifugal force acting on Earth's spinning surface and atmosphere. Without gravity, there would be no atmospheric pressure—or atmosphere, for that matter.
- **Pressure gradient force** drives air from areas of higher barometric pressure (more dense air) to areas of lower barometric pressure (less dense air), thereby causing winds. Without a pressure gradient force, there would be no wind.
- **Coriolis force**, a deflective force, makes wind that travels in a straight path appear to be deflected in relation to Earth's rotating surface. The Coriolis force deflects wind to the right in the Northern Hemisphere and to the left in the Southern Hemisphere. Without Coriolis force, winds would move along straight paths between high- and low-pressure areas.
- **Friction force** drags on the wind as it moves across surfaces; it decreases with height above the surface. Without friction, winds would simply move in paths parallel to isobars and at high rates of speed.

All four of these forces operate on moving air and ocean currents at Earth's surface and influence global wind circulation patterns. The following sections describe the actions of the pressure gradient, Coriolis, and friction forces. (The gravitational force operates uniformly worldwide.)

Pressure Gradient Force

High- and low-pressure areas exist in the atmosphere principally because Earth's surface is unequally heated. For example, cold, dense air at the poles exerts greater pressure than warm, less dense air along the equator. These pressure differences establish a pressure gradient force.

An **isobar** is an isoline (a line along which there is a constant value) plotted on a weather map to connect points of equal pressure. A pattern of isobars on a weather map provides a portrait of the pressure gradient between an area of higher pressure and one of lower pressure. The spacing between isobars indicates the intensity of the pressure difference, or pressure gradient.

GEO REPORT 2 *A force is with us*

Note that we call Coriolis a *force*. This label is appropriate because, as physicist Sir Isaac Newton (1643–1727) stated, when something is accelerating over a space, a force is in operation (mass times acceleration). This apparent force (in classical mechanics, an inertial force) acts as an effect on moving objects. It is named for Gaspard Coriolis (1792–1843), a French mathematician and researcher of applied mechanics, who first described the force in 1831.

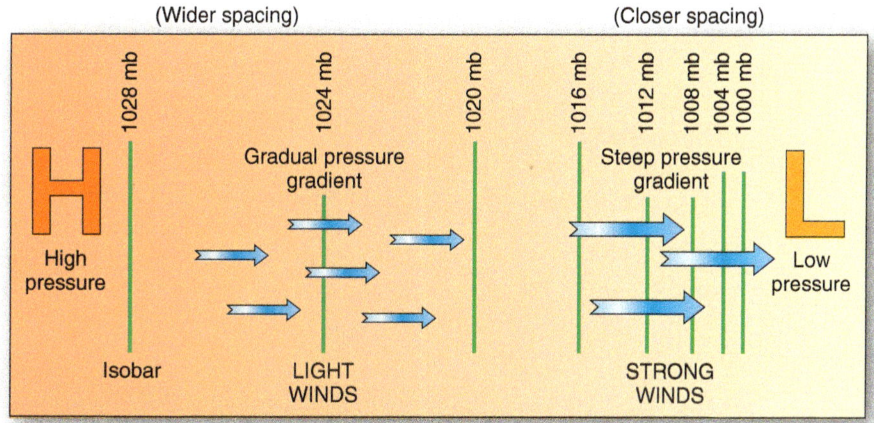

(a)

FIGURE 6 Pressure gradient determines wind speed. Pressure gradient (a) portrayed on a weather map (b). See the relationship between pressure gradient and wind strength. Here we see surface winds spiraling clockwise out of a high-pressure system and spiraling counterclockwise into a low-pressure system.

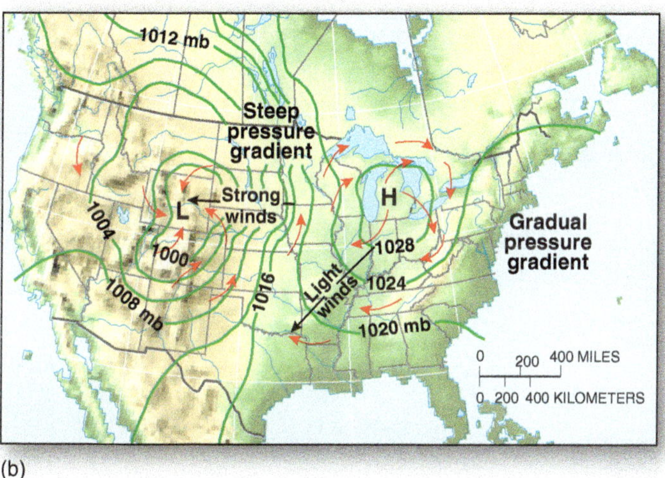

(b)

Just as closer contour lines on a topographic map indicate a steeper slope on land, so closer isobars denote steepness in the pressure gradient. In Figure 6a, note the spacing of the isobars (green lines). A steep gradient causes faster air movement from a high-pressure area to a low-pressure area. Isobars spaced wider apart from one another mark a more gradual pressure gradient, one that creates a slower airflow. Along a horizontal surface, the pressure gradient force alone acts at right angles to the isobars, so wind blows across isobars at right angles. Note the location of steep ("strong winds") and gradual ("light winds") pressure gradients and their relationship to wind intensity on the map in Figure 6b.

Figure 7 illustrates the forces that direct winds. Figure 7a shows the pressure gradient force acting alone. A field of subsiding, or sinking, air develops in a high-pressure area. Air descends in a high-pressure area and diverges outward at the surface in all directions. In contrast, in a low-pressure area, as air rises, it pulls air from all directions, converging into the area of lower pressure at the surface.

Coriolis Force

You might expect surface winds to move in a straight line from areas of higher pressure to areas of lower pressure. On a nonrotating Earth, they would. But on our rotating planet, the Coriolis force deflects anything that flies or flows across Earth's surface—wind, an airplane, or ocean currents—from a straight path. In simplest terms, this force is an effect of Earth's rotation. Earth's rotational speed varies with latitude, increasing from 0 kmph at the poles (surface is at Earth's axis) to 1675 kmph (1041 mph) at the equator (surface is farthest from Earth's axis).

The deflection occurs regardless of the direction in which the object is moving. Because Earth rotates eastward, objects appear to curve to the right in the Northern Hemisphere and to the left in the Southern Hemisphere (Figure 8a). The Coriolis force is zero along the equator, increases to half the maximum deflection at 30° N and 30° S latitude, and reaches maximum deflection flowing away from the poles. The effect of the Coriolis force increases as the speed of the moving object increases; thus, the faster the wind speed, the greater its apparent deflection. The Coriolis force does not normally affect small-scale motions that cover insignificant distance and time.

With this in mind, we observe the Coriolis force from different viewpoints. From the viewpoint of an airplane that is passing over Earth's surface, the surface is

GEO REPORT 3 *Coriolis: Not a force on sinks or toilets*

A common misconception about the Coriolis force is that it affects water draining out of a sink, tub, or toilet. Moving water or air must cover some distance across space and time before the Coriolis force noticeably deflects it. Long-range artillery shells and guided missiles do exhibit small amounts of deflection that must be corrected for accuracy. But water movements down a drain are too small in spatial extent to be noticeably affected by this force.

(a) Pressure gradient

Top view and side view of air movement in an idealized high-pressure area and low-pressure area on a nonrotating Earth.

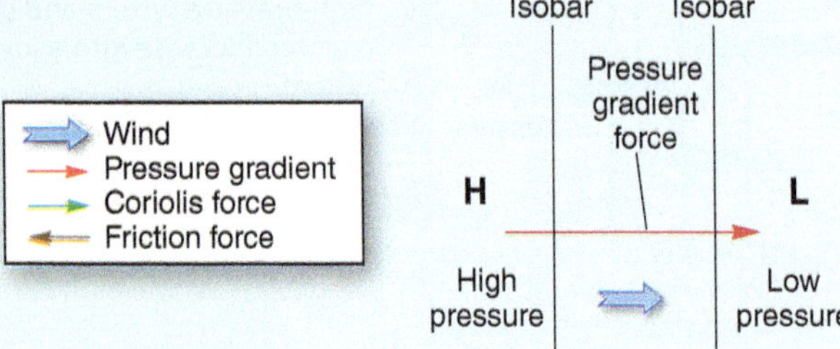

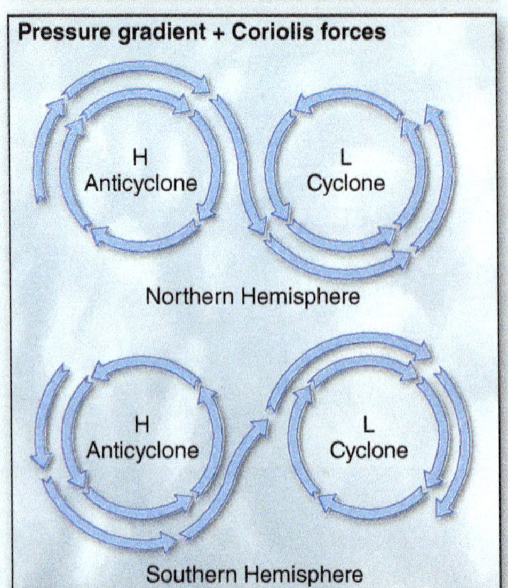

(b) Pressure gradient + Coriolis forces (upper level winds)

Earth's rotation adds the Coriolis force and a "twist" to air movements. High-pressure and low-pressure areas develop a rotary motion, and wind flowing between highs and lows flows parallel to isobars.

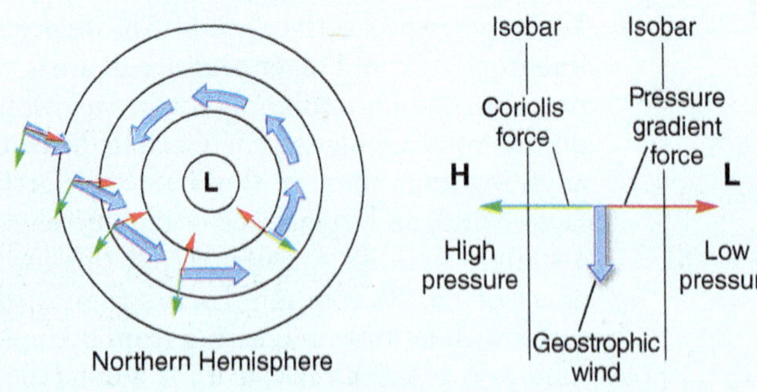

(c) Pressure gradient + Coriolis + friction forces (surface winds)

Surface friction adds a countering force to Coriolis, producing winds that spiral out of a high-pressure area and into a low-pressure area. Surface winds cross isobars at an angle. Air flows into low-pressure cyclones and turns to the left, because of deflection to the right.

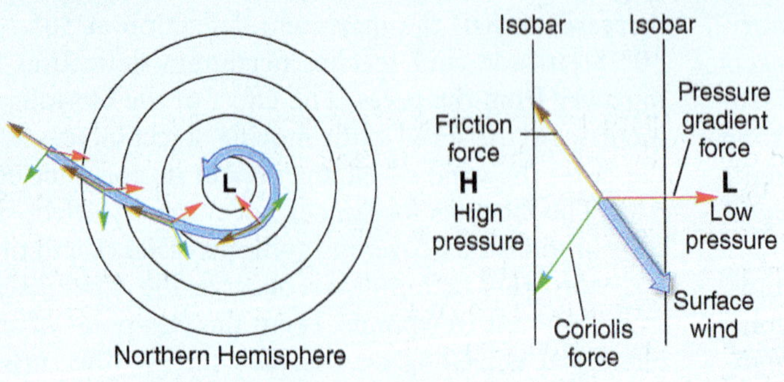

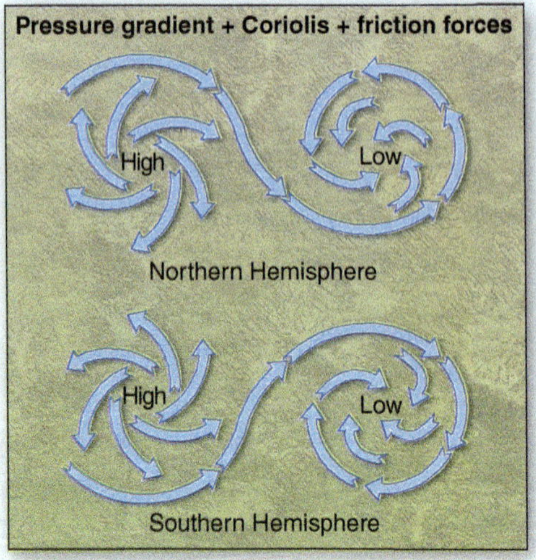

FIGURE 7 Three physical forces that produce winds.
Three physical forces interact to produce wind patterns at the surface and aloft: (a) pressure gradient force; (b) Coriolis force, which counters the pressure gradient force, producing a geostrophic wind flow in the upper atmosphere; and (c) friction force, which, combined with the other two forces, produces characteristic surface winds.

Animation
Wind Pattern Development

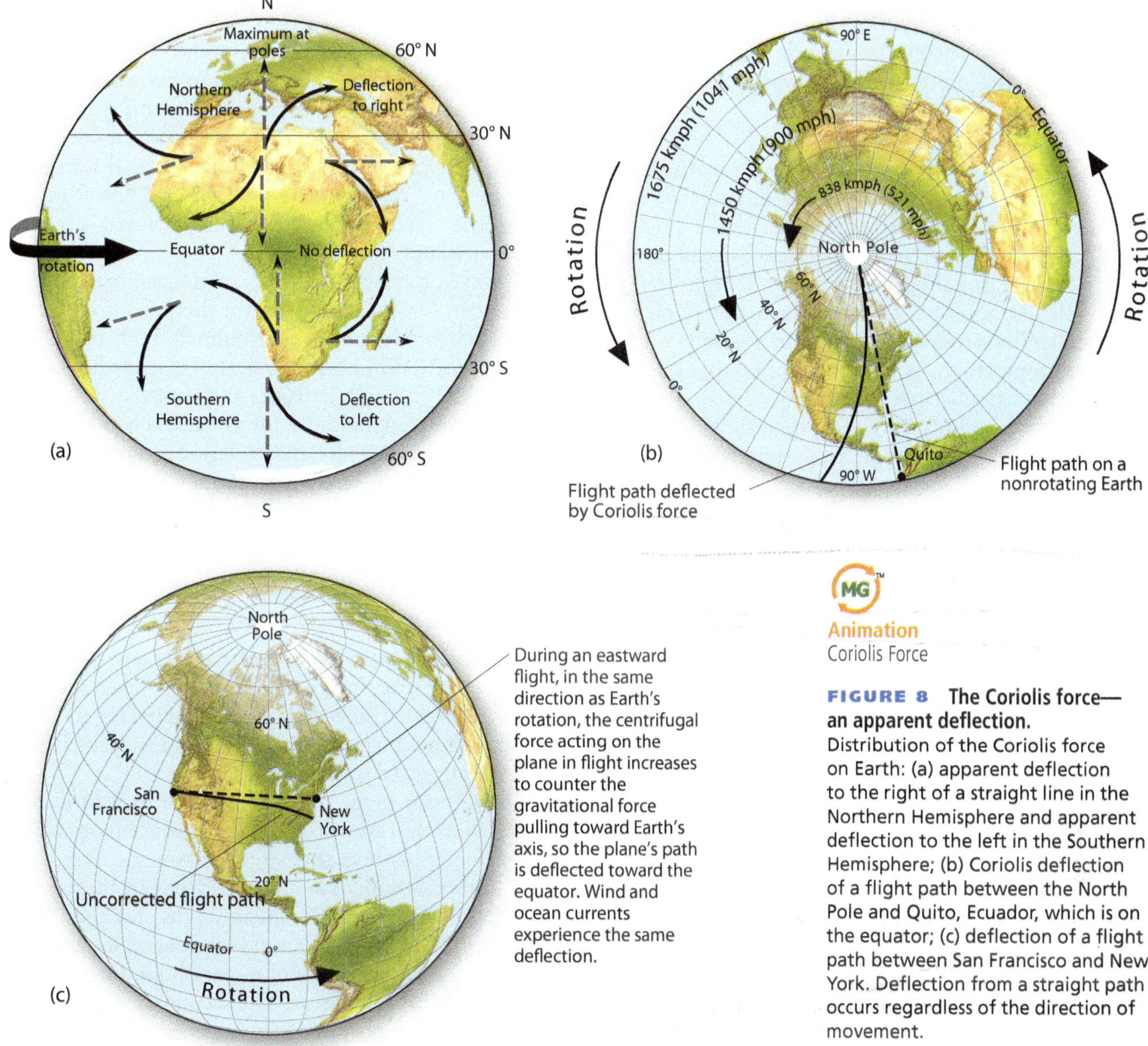

FIGURE 8 The Coriolis force—an apparent deflection. Distribution of the Coriolis force on Earth: (a) apparent deflection to the right of a straight line in the Northern Hemisphere and apparent deflection to the left in the Southern Hemisphere; (b) Coriolis deflection of a flight path between the North Pole and Quito, Ecuador, which is on the equator; (c) deflection of a flight path between San Francisco and New York. Deflection from a straight path occurs regardless of the direction of movement.

seen to rotate slowly below. But, looking from the surface at the airplane, the surface seems stationary, and the airplane appears to curve off course. The airplane does not actually deviate from a straight path, but it appears to do so because we are standing on Earth's rotating surface beneath the airplane. Because of this apparent deflection, the airplane must make constant corrections in flight path to maintain its "straight" heading relative to a rotating Earth.

As an example of the effect of this force, see Figure 8b. A pilot leaves the North Pole and flies due south toward Quito, Ecuador. If Earth were not rotating, the aircraft would simply travel along a meridian of longitude and arrive at Quito. But Earth is rotating eastward beneath the aircraft's flight path. If the pilot does not allow for this increase in rotational speed, the plane will reach the equator over the ocean along an apparently curved path, far to the west of the intended destination. Likewise, flying northward on a return flight, the plane maintains its eastward speed as it makes its way northward over slower rotational speeds of Earth. Without correction, the plane ends up to the east of the pole, in a right-hand deflection. Pilots must correct for this Coriolis deflection in their navigational calculations.

This effect occurs regardless of the direction of the moving object. A flight from California to New York provides an example in Figure 8c. The Coriolis deflection occurs as the airplane flies to New York because Earth continues to rotate eastward; this increases the centrifugal force acting on the plane (Earth rotation speed + plane speed), so the plane moves toward the equator in a right-hand deflection (moving farther from Earth's axis at a lower latitude). Unless the pilot corrects for this deflective force, the flight would end up somewhere in North

Carolina. Likewise, flying westward on a return flight opposite Earth's rotation direction, which decreases the centrifugal force (Earth rotation speed − plane speed), the plane moves away from the equator, in a right-hand deflection (moving closer to Earth's axis at a higher latitude).

Coriolis Force and Winds How does the Coriolis force affect wind? As air rises from the surface through the lowest levels of the atmosphere, it leaves the drag of surface friction behind and increases speed. This increases the Coriolis force, spiraling the winds to the right in the Northern Hemisphere or to the left in the Southern Hemisphere, generally producing upper-air westerly winds from the subtropics to the poles. In the upper troposphere, the Coriolis force just balances the pressure gradient force. Consequently, the winds between higher-pressure and lower-pressure areas in the upper troposphere flow parallel to the isobars.

Figure 7b illustrates the combined effect of the pressure gradient force and the Coriolis force on air currents aloft. Together, they produce winds that do not flow directly from high to low, but that flow around the pressure areas, remaining parallel to the isobars. Such winds are **geostrophic winds** and are characteristic of upper tropospheric circulation. (The suffix *-strophic* means "to turn.") Note the inset illustration showing the effect of the pressure gradient and Coriolis forces, which produce a geostrophic flow of air. Geostrophic winds produce the characteristic pattern shown on the upper-air weather map just ahead in Figure 13.

Friction Force

Figure 7c adds the effect of friction to the Coriolis and pressure gradient forces on wind movements; combining all three forces produces the wind patterns we see along Earth's surface. The effect of surface friction extends to a height of about 500 m (around 1600 ft) and varies with surface texture, wind speed, time of day and year, and atmospheric conditions. In general, rougher surfaces produce more friction.

Near the surface, friction disrupts the equilibrium established in geostrophic wind flows between the pressure gradient and Coriolis forces—note the inset illustration in Figure 7c. Because surface friction decreases wind speed, it reduces the effect of the Coriolis force and causes winds to move across isobars at an angle. The reason the balance of forces causes the winds to curve to the left into low-pressure cyclones as they are deflected to the right is shown.

In Figure 7c, you can see that the Northern Hemisphere winds spiral out from a high-pressure area *clockwise* to form an **anticyclone** and spiral into a low-pressure area *counterclockwise* to form a **cyclone**. (In the Southern Hemisphere, these circulation patterns are reversed, with winds flowing counterclockwise out of anticyclonic high-pressure cells and clockwise into cyclonic low-pressure cells.)

Atmospheric Patterns of Motion

With these forces and motions in mind, we are ready to build a general model of total atmospheric circulation. The warmer, less-dense air along the equator rises, creating low pressure at the surface, and the colder, more-dense air at the poles sinks, creating high pressure. If Earth did not rotate, the result would be a simple wind flow from the poles to the equator, a meridional flow caused solely by pressure gradient.

However, Earth does rotate, creating a more complex flow system. On a rotating Earth, the poles-to-equator flow is predominantly zonal (latitudinal), both at the surface and aloft. Winds are westerly (eastward-moving) in the middle and high latitudes and easterly (westward-moving) in the low latitudes toward the equator in both hemispheres. Earth's global circulation system transfers thermal energy, air, and water masses from equatorial energy surpluses to polar energy deficits, using waves, streams, and eddies on a planetary scale.

Primary High-Pressure and Low-Pressure Areas

The following discussion of Earth's pressure and wind patterns refers often to Figure 9, isobaric maps showing average surface barometric pressure in January and July. Indirectly, these maps indicate prevailing surface winds, which are suggested by the isobars.

The primary high- and low-pressure areas of Earth's general circulation appear on these maps as cells or uneven belts of similar pressure that stretch across the face of the planet, interrupted by landmasses. Between these areas flow the primary winds. Secondary highs and lows, from a few hundred to a few thousand kilometers in diameter and hundreds to thousands of meters high, form within these primary pressure areas. The secondary systems seasonally migrate to produce changing weather patterns in the regions over which they pass.

Four broad pressure areas cover the Northern Hemisphere, and a similar set exists in the Southern Hemisphere. In each hemisphere, two of the pressure areas are stimulated by thermal (temperature) factors. These are the **equatorial low-pressure trough** (marked by the intertropical convergence zone, or ITCZ, line on the maps) and the weak **polar high-pressure cells** at the North and South Poles (not shown, as the maps are cut off at 80° N and 80° S). The other two pressure areas—the **subtropical high-pressure cells** (H) and **subpolar low-pressure cells** (L)—are formed by dynamic (mechanical) factors. Table 1 summarizes the characteristics of these pressure areas.

Equatorial Low-Pressure Trough: Warm and Rainy Constant high Sun altitude and consistent daylength (12 hours a day, year-round) make large amounts of energy available in this region throughout the year. The warming creates lighter, less-dense, ascending air, with surface winds converging along the entire

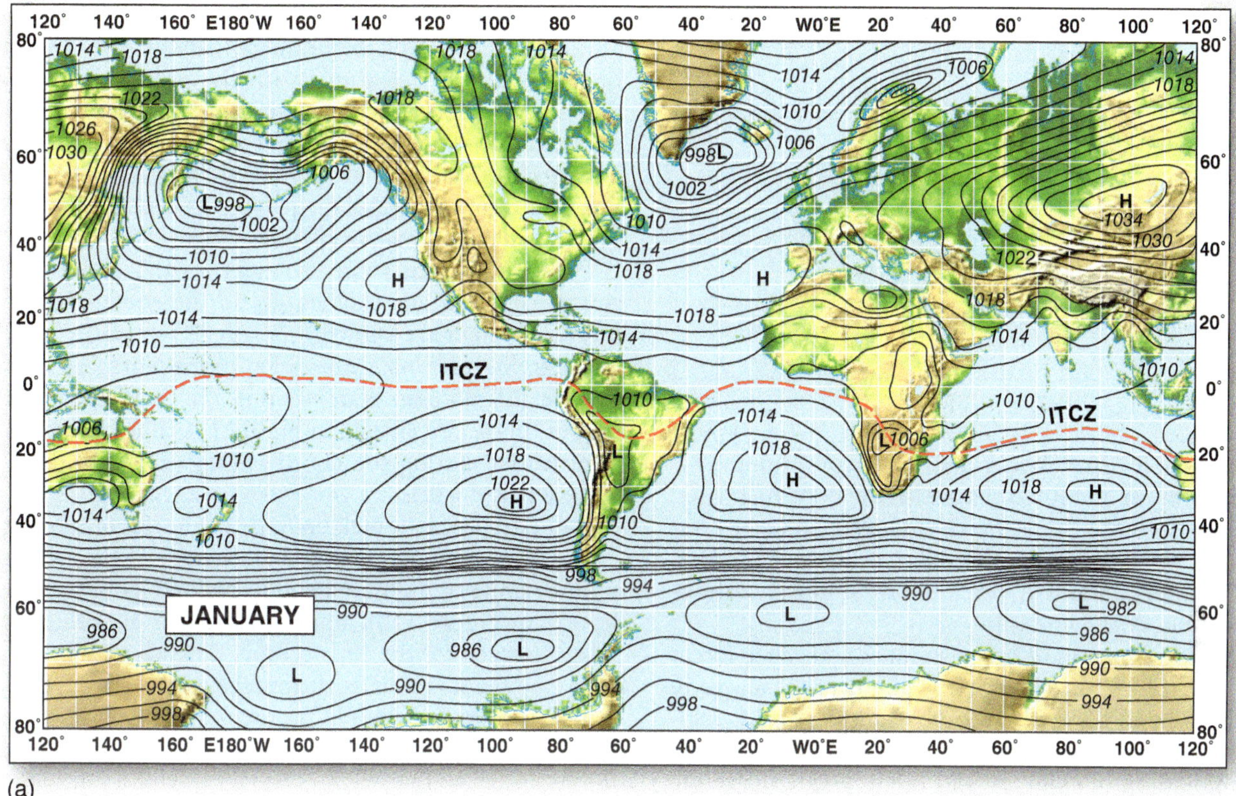

(a)

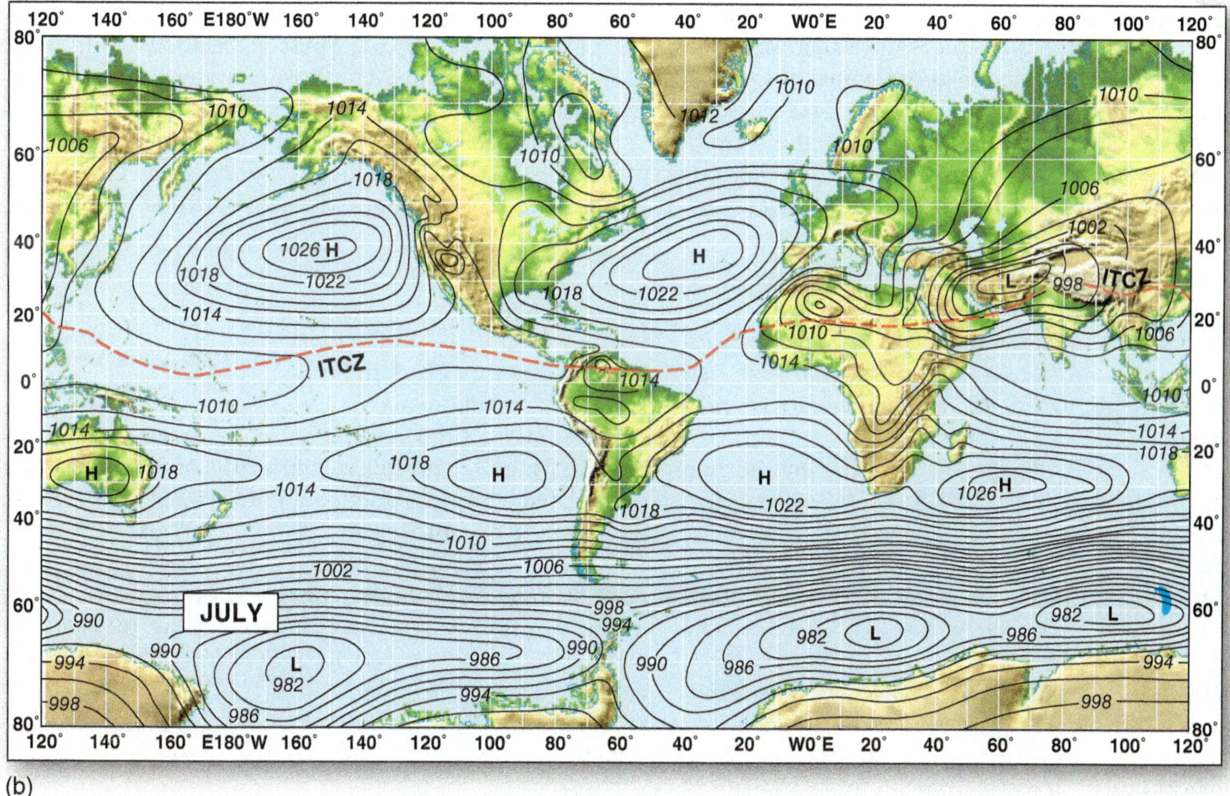

(b)

FIGURE 9 Global barometric pressures for January and July.
Maps portray average surface barometric pressure (millibars) for (a) January and (b) July. The dashed line marks the general location of the intertropical convergence zone (ITCZ). Compare specific regions for January and July—for instance, the North Pacific, the North Atlantic, and the central Asian landmass. [Adapted by author and redrawn from National Climatic Data Center, *Monthly Climatic Data for the World*, 46 (January and July 1993), and WMO and NOAA.]

Animation Global Patterns of Pressure

Satellite Global Sea-Level Pressure

TABLE 1 Four Hemispheric Pressure Areas

Name	Cause	Location	Air Temperature/ Moisture
Polar high-pressure cells	Thermal	90° N, 90° S	Cold/dry
Subpolar low-pressure cells	Dynamic	60° N, 60° S	Cool/wet
Subtropical high-pressure cells	Dynamic	20°–35° N 20°–35° S	Hot/dry
Equatorial low-pressure trough	Thermal	10° N to 10° S	Warm/wet

extent of the low-pressure trough. This converging air is extremely moist and full of latent heat energy. As it rises, the air expands and cools, producing condensation; consequently, rainfall is heavy throughout this zone. Vertical cloud columns frequently reach the tropopause, in thunderous strength and intensity.

The combination of heating and convergence forces air aloft and forms the **intertropical convergence zone (ITCZ).** The ITCZ is identified by bands of clouds associated with the convergence of winds along the equator and is noted on the January and July pressure maps (see Figure 9; the maps show the ITCZ as a dashed line). In January, the zone crosses northern Australia and dips southward in eastern Africa and South America. During summer, a marked wet season accompanies the shifting ITCZ over various regions.

Figure 10 features satellite images showing the equatorial low-pressure trough of the ITCZ using associated precipitation for January and July. A broken band of precipitation accumulation (monthly averages) reveals this low-pressure system and its position slightly north of the equator in July. Note the position of the ITCZ in Figure 9 and compare this with the precipitation pattern in Figure 10. The equatorial low-pressure trough is an elongated, undulating narrow band of low pressure (converging, ascending airflow), cloudiness, and precipitation that nearly encircles the planet, consistently over the oceans and interrupted over land surfaces.

Figure 11 shows two views of Earth's general circulation. The winds converging on the equatorial low-pressure trough are known generally as the **trade winds**, or *trades*. *Northeast trade winds* blow in the Northern Hemisphere and *southeast trade winds* in the Southern Hemisphere. These are labeled in Figure 11a. The trade winds were named during the era of sailing ships that carried trade across the seas.

The trade winds pick up large quantities of moisture as they return through the Hadley circulation cells for another cycle of uplift and condensation (shown in cross section in Figure 11b). These *Hadley cells* in each hemisphere, named for the 18th-century English scientist who described the trade winds, denote the circuit completed by winds rising along the ITCZ. Air moves northward and southward into the subtropics, descending to the surface and returning to the ITCZ as the trade winds. During the year in each hemisphere, this circulation pattern appears most vertically symmetrical near the equinoxes.

Within the ITCZ, winds are calm or mildly variable because of the even pressure gradient and the vertical ascent of air. These equatorial calms are the doldrums, a name formed from an older English word meaning "foolish," because of the difficulty sailing ships encountered when attempting to move through this zone. The rising air

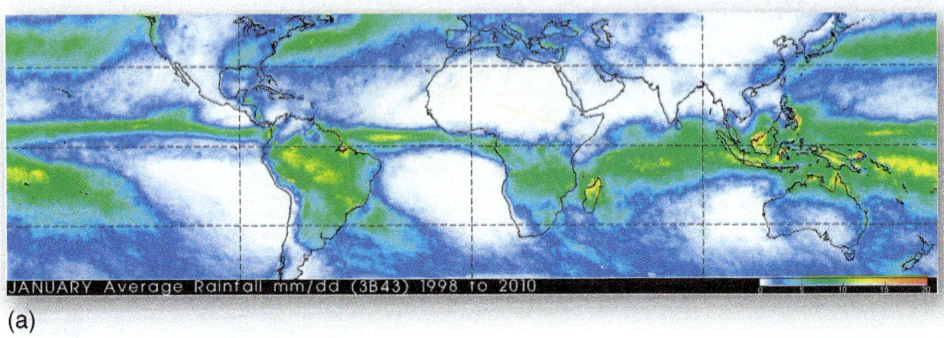

(a)

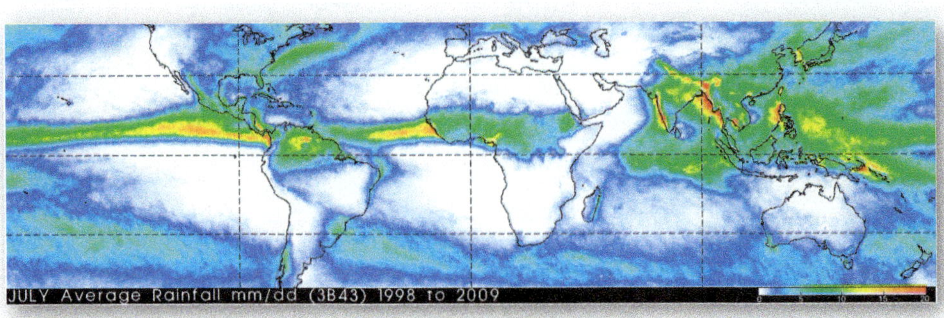

(b)

FIGURE 10 Precipitation accumulation portrays equatorial and subtropical circulation patterns.
(a) January average rainfall 1998–2010. An interrupted band of average precipitation in millimeters per day for 31 days along the intertropical convergence zone (ITCZ). (b) July average rainfall 1998–2010. Note to the north and south of the ITCZ in the subtropics several high-pressure systems and clear skies (lacking coloration). [TRMM Microwave Imager on several geosynchronous satellites, courtesy of GSFC/NASA.]

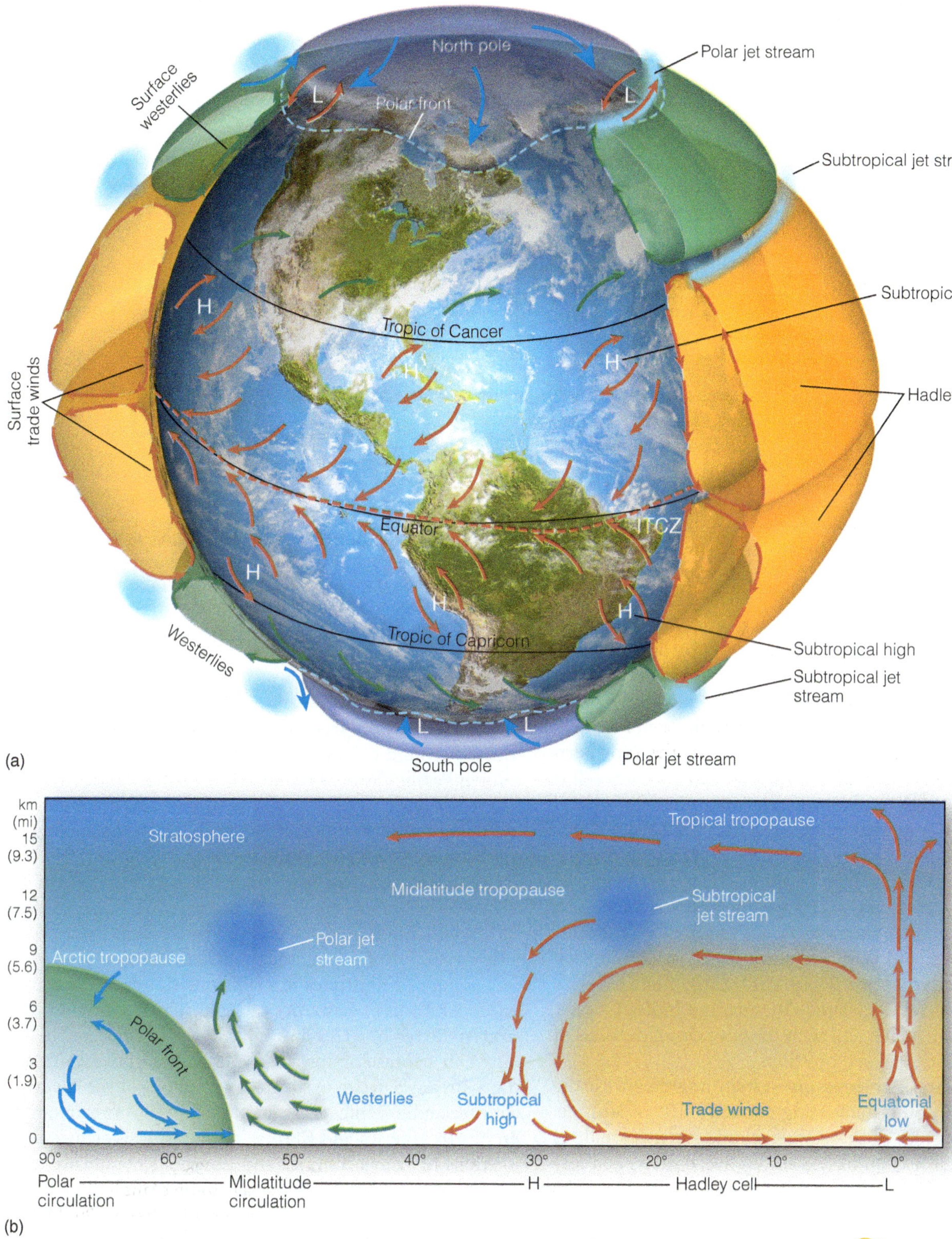

FIGURE 11 General atmospheric circulation model.
Two views of the general atmospheric circulation: (a) general circulation schematic; (b) equator-to-pole cross section of the Northern Hemisphere. Both views show Hadley cells, subtropical highs, the polar front, subpolar low-pressure cells, and approximate locations of the subtropical and polar jet streams.

Satellite
Global Infrared

Animation
Global Wind Circulation, Hadley Cells

from the equatorial low-pressure area spirals upward into a geostrophic flow to the north and south. These upper-air winds turn eastward, flowing from west to east, beginning at about 20° N and 20° S, and form descending masses of air and high-pressure systems in the subtropical latitudes.

Subtropical High-Pressure Cells: Hot and Dry Between 20° and 35° latitude in both hemispheres, a broad high-pressure zone of hot, dry air is evident across the globe (see Figures 9 and 10). Clear, frequently cloudless skies over the Sahara and the Arabian Deserts and portions of the Indian Ocean dominate these regions.

The dynamic cause of these subtropical anticyclones is too complex to detail here, but they generally form as air above the subtropics is mechanically pushed downward and heats by compression on its descent to the surface (shown in Figure 11). Warmer air has a greater capacity to absorb water vapor than does cooler air, making this descending warm air relatively dry (large water-vapor capacity, low water-vapor content). The air is also dry because heavy precipitation along the equatorial portion of the circulation removes moisture.

Surface air diverging from the subtropical high-pressure cells generates Earth's principal surface winds: the westerlies and the trade winds. The **westerlies** are the dominant surface winds from the subtropics to high latitudes. They diminish somewhat in summer and are stronger in winter in both hemispheres.

As you examine the global pressure maps in Figure 9, you find several high-pressure areas. In the Northern Hemisphere, the Atlantic subtropical high-pressure cell is the *Bermuda high* (in the western Atlantic) or the *Azores high* (when it migrates to the eastern Atlantic in winter). The area in the Atlantic under subtropical high pressure features clear, warm waters and large quantities of Sargassum (a seaweed) that gives the area its name—the Sargasso Sea. The *Pacific high*, or *Hawaiian high*, dominates the Pacific in July, retreating southward in January. In the Southern Hemisphere, three large high-pressure centers dominate the Pacific, Atlantic, and Indian Oceans, especially in January, and tend to move along parallels of latitude in shifting zonal positions.

The entire high-pressure system migrates with the summer high Sun, fluctuating about 5°–10° in latitude. The eastern sides of these anticyclonic systems are drier and more stable (exhibit less convective activity) and feature cooler ocean currents than do the western sides. The drier eastern sides of these systems and dry-summer conditions influence climate along subtropical and midlatitude west coasts (Figure 12). In fact, Earth's major deserts generally occur within the subtropical belt and extend to the west coast of each continent except Antarctica.

These zones of windless, hot, dry desert air, so deadly in the era of sailing ships, earned the name *horse latitudes*. Although the term's true origin is uncertain, it is popularly attributed to becalmed and stranded sailing crews of past centuries who destroyed the horses on board, not wanting to share food or water with the livestock.

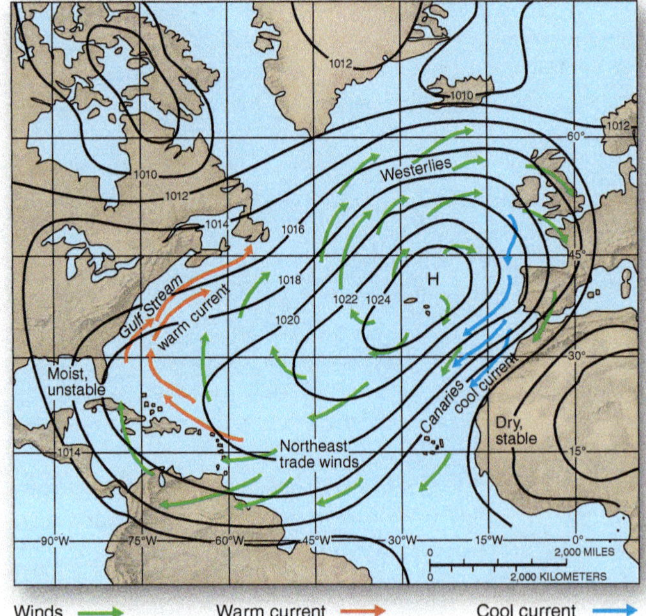

FIGURE 12 Subtropical high-pressure system in the Atlantic. Characteristic circulation in the Northern Hemisphere. Note deserts extending to the shores of Africa with offshore cool currents, whereas the southeastern United States is moist and humid, with offshore warm currents.

Subpolar Low-Pressure Cells: Cool and Moist In January, two low-pressure cyclonic cells exist over the oceans around 60° N latitude, near their namesakes: the North Pacific *Aleutian low* and the North Atlantic *Icelandic low* (see Figure 9a). Both cells are dominant in winter and weaken or disappear in summer with the strengthening of high-pressure systems in the subtropics. The area of contrast between cold air from higher latitudes and warm air from lower latitudes forms the **polar front**, where masses of air with different characteristics battle. This front encircles Earth, focused in these low-pressure areas.

Figure 11 illustrates this confrontation between warm, moist air from the westerlies and cold, dry air from the polar and Arctic regions. Cooling and condensation occurs in the lifted air because of upward displacement of the warm air. Low-pressure cyclonic storms migrate out of the Aleutian and Icelandic frontal areas and may produce precipitation in North America and Europe, respectively. Northwestern sections of North America and Europe generally are cool and moist as a result of the passage of these cyclonic systems onshore—consider the weather in British Columbia, Washington, Oregon, Ireland, and the United Kingdom.

Polar High-Pressure Cells: Frigid and Dry Polar high-pressure cells are weak. The polar atmospheric mass is small, receiving little energy from the Sun to put it into motion. Variable winds, cold and dry, move away from the polar region in an anticyclonic direction. They descend and diverge clockwise in the Northern Hemisphere and counterclockwise in the Southern Hemisphere and form the weak, variable winds of the **polar easterlies**.

Of the two polar regions, the **Antarctic high** is stronger and more persistent, forming over the Antarctic landmass. Less pronounced is a polar high-pressure cell over the Arctic Ocean. When it does form, it tends to locate over the colder northern continental areas in winter (Canadian and Siberian highs) rather than directly over the relatively warmer Arctic Ocean.

Upper Atmospheric Circulation

Circulation in the middle and upper troposphere is an important component of the atmosphere's general circulation. Just as sea level is a reference datum for evaluating air pressure at the surface, we use a pressure level such as 500 mb as a **constant isobaric surface** for a pressure-reference datum in the upper atmosphere.

On upper-air pressure maps, we plot the height above sea level at which an air pressure of 500 mb occurs. The isobaric chart and illustration for an April day in Figure 13a and Figure 13b illustrates such an undulating isobaric surface, upon which all points have the same pressure. In contrast, on surface weather maps we plot different pressures at the fixed elevation of sea level—a *constant-height surface*.

We use this 500-mb level to analyze upper-air winds and the possible support they provide for surface weather conditions. Similar to surface maps, closer spacing of the isobars indicates faster winds; wider spacing indicates slower winds. On this constant-isobaric-pressure surface, altitude variations from the reference datum are ridges for high pressure (with isobars on the map bending poleward) and troughs for low pressure (with isobars on the map bending equatorward). Looking at the figure, can you identify such ridges and troughs in the isobaric surface?

The pattern of ridges and troughs in the upper-air wind flow is important in sustaining surface cyclonic (low-pressure) and anticylonic (high-pressure) circulation. Winds near the ridges in the isobaric surface slow and converge (pile up), whereas winds near the area of maximum wind speeds along the troughs in the isobaric surface accelerate and diverge (spread out). Note the wind-speed indicators and labels in Figure 13a near the ridge (over Alberta, Saskatchewan, Montana, and Wyoming); now compare these with the wind-speed indicators around the trough (over Kentucky, West Virginia, the New England states, and the Maritimes). Also note the wind relationships off the Pacific Coast.

Now look at Figure 13c. Divergence in the upper-air flow is important to cyclonic circulation at the surface because it creates an outflow of air aloft that stimulates an inflow of air into low-pressure cyclones (like what happens when you open a chimney damper to create an upward draft). Convergence aloft, in contrast, drives descending airflows and divergent winds at the surface, moving out from high-pressure anticyclones.

Rossby Waves Within the westerly flow of geostrophic winds are great waving undulations, the **Rossby waves,** named for meteorologist Carl G. Rossby, who first described them mathematically in 1938. The polar front is the line of conflict between colder air to the north and warmer air to the south (Figure 14). Rossby waves bring tongues of cold air southward, with warmer tropical air moving northward. The development of Rossby waves in the upper-air circulation is shown in the three-part figure. As these disturbances mature, distinct cyclonic circulation forms, with warmer air and colder air mixing along distinct fronts. These wave-and-eddy formations and upper-air divergences support cyclonic storm systems at the surface. Rossby waves develop along the flow axis of a jet stream.

Jet Streams The most prominent movements in these upper-level westerly wind flows are the **jet streams**, irregular, concentrated bands of wind occurring at several different locations that influence surface weather systems. (Figure 11a shows the location of four jet streams.) Rather flattened in vertical cross section, the jet streams normally are 160–480 km (100–300 mi) wide by 900–2150 m (3000–7000 ft) thick, with core speeds that can exceed 300 kmph (190 mph). Jet streams in each hemisphere tend to weaken during the hemisphere's summer and strengthen during its winter as the streams shift closer to the equator. The pattern of ridges and troughs causes variation in jet-stream speeds (convergence and divergence).

The *polar jet stream* meanders between 30° and 70° N latitude, at the tropopause along the polar front, at altitudes between 7600 and 10,700 m (24,900 and 35,100 ft). The polar jet stream can migrate as far south as Texas, steering colder air masses into North America and influencing surface storm paths traveling eastward. In the summer, the polar jet stream exerts less influence on storms by staying over higher latitudes. Figure 15 shows a stylized view of a polar jet stream and two jet streams over North America.

GEO REPORT 4 *Icelandic ash caught in the jet stream*

Although smaller than either the Mount St. Helens 1980 eruption or the Mount Pinatubo 1991 eruption, the 2010 eruption of Eyjafjallajökull volcano in Iceland injected about a tenth of a cubic kilometer of volcanic debris into the jet-stream flow. The ash cloud from Iceland was swept toward the European mainland and the United Kingdom. Aircraft cannot risk ingesting volcanic ash into jet engines; therefore, airports were shut down, and thousands of flights canceled. People's attention was focused on the guiding jet stream as it impacted their flight schedules and lives.

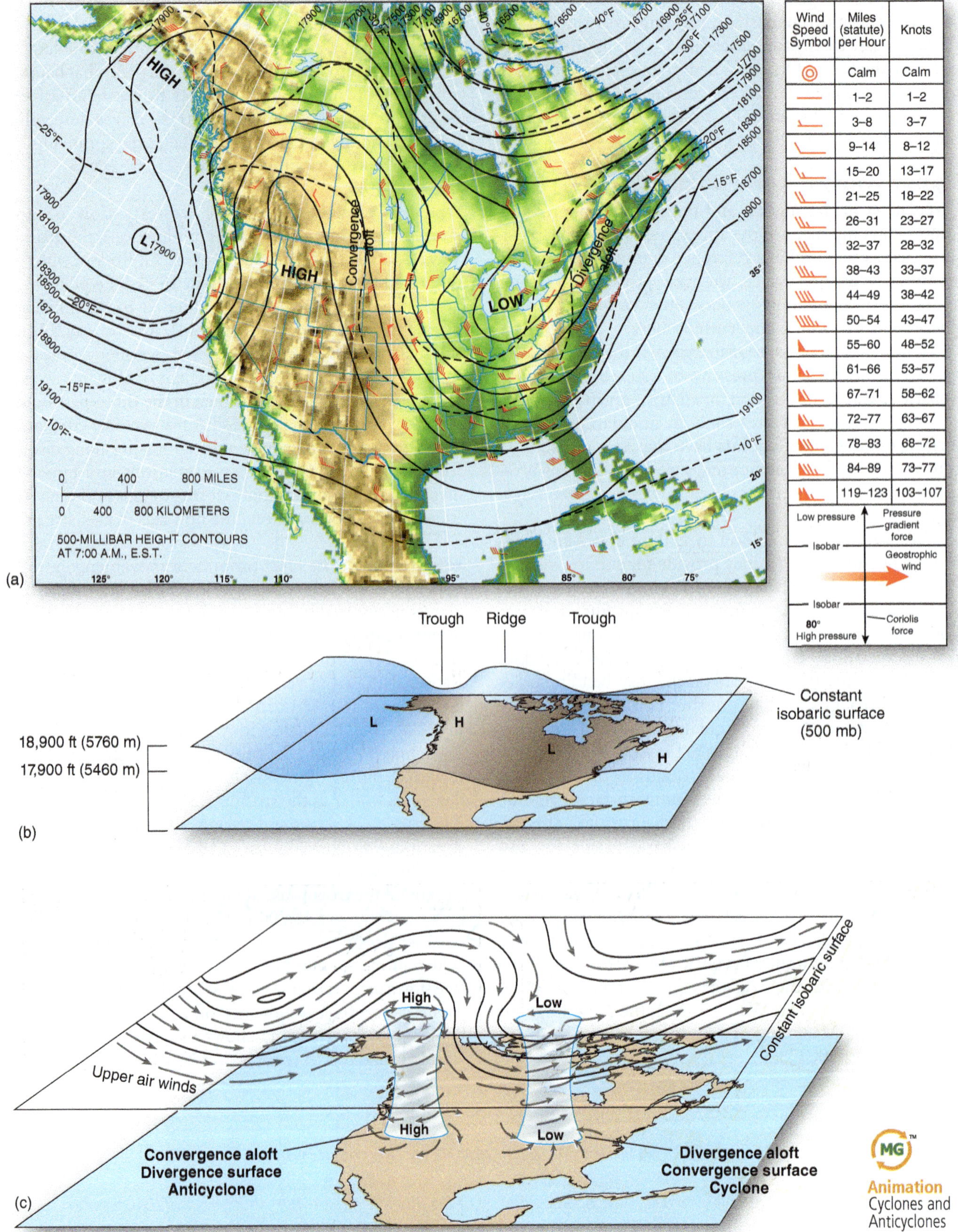

Wind Speed Symbol	Miles (statute) per Hour	Knots
	Calm	Calm
	1–2	1–2
	3–8	3–7
	9–14	8–12
	15–20	13–17
	21–25	18–22
	26–31	23–27
	32–37	28–32
	38–43	33–37
	44–49	38–42
	50–54	43–47
	55–60	48–52
	61–66	53–57
	67–71	58–62
	72–77	63–67
	78–83	68–72
	84–89	73–77
	119–123	103–107

MG™ Animation Cyclones and Anticyclones

FIGURE 13 Analysis of a constant isobaric surface for an April day.
(a) Contours show elevation (in feet) at which 500 mb of pressure occurs—a constant isobaric surface. The pattern of contours reveals a 500-mb isobaric surface and geostrophic wind patterns in the troposphere ranging from 16,500 to 19,100 ft in elevation. (b) Note on the map and in the sketch beneath the chart the "ridge" of high pressure over the Intermountain West, at an altitude of 5760 m, and the "trough" of low pressure over the Great Lakes region and off the Pacific Coast, at an altitude of 5460 m. (c) Note areas of convergence aloft (corresponding to surface divergence) and divergence aloft (corresponding to surface convergence).

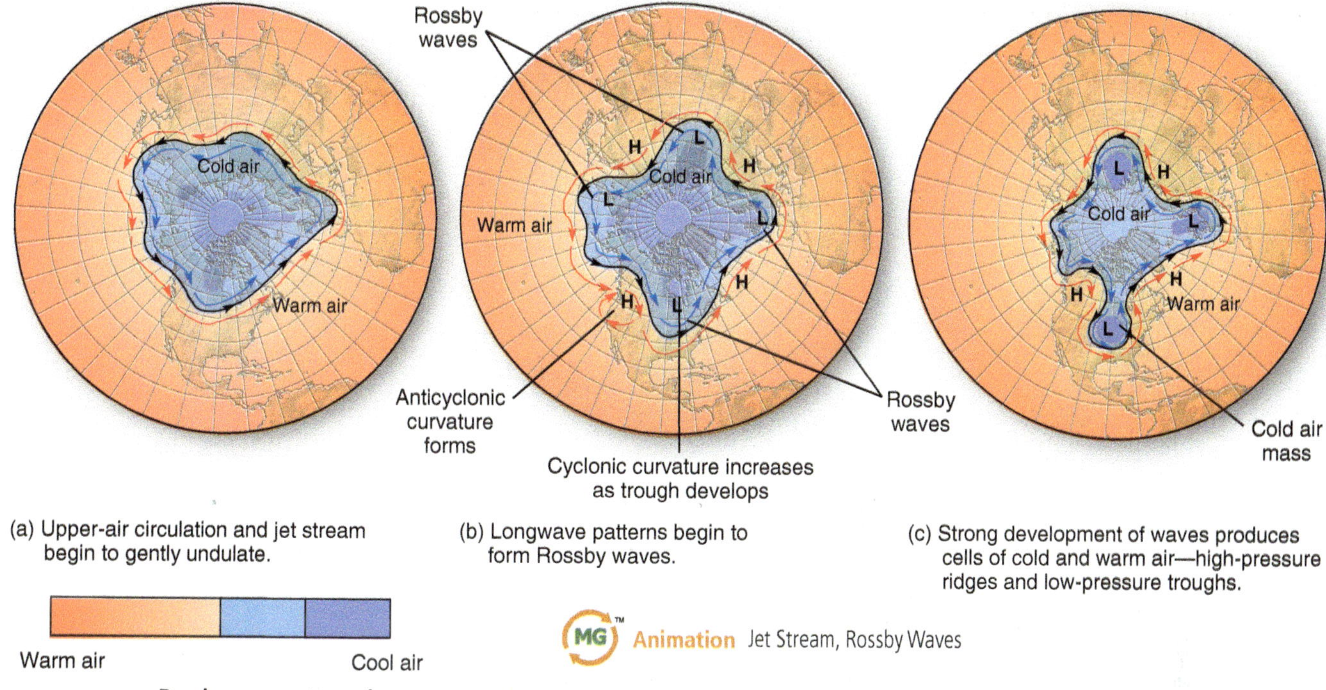

FIGURE 14 Rossby upper-atmosphere waves.
Development of waves in the upper-air circulation. Note undulations in Rossby waves, labeled "L" for troughs and "H" for ridges.

In subtropical latitudes, near the boundary between tropical and midlatitude air, the *subtropical jet stream* flows near the tropopause (see Figure 11). The subtropical jet stream meanders from 20° to 50° north latitude and may occur over North America simultaneously with the polar jet stream—sometimes the two will actually merge for brief episodes.

Local Winds

Land and sea breezes occur on most coastlines (Figure 16). Different heating characteristics of land and water surfaces create these breezes. Land gains heat energy and warms faster than the water offshore during the day. Because warm air is less dense, it rises and triggers an onshore flow of cooler marine air to

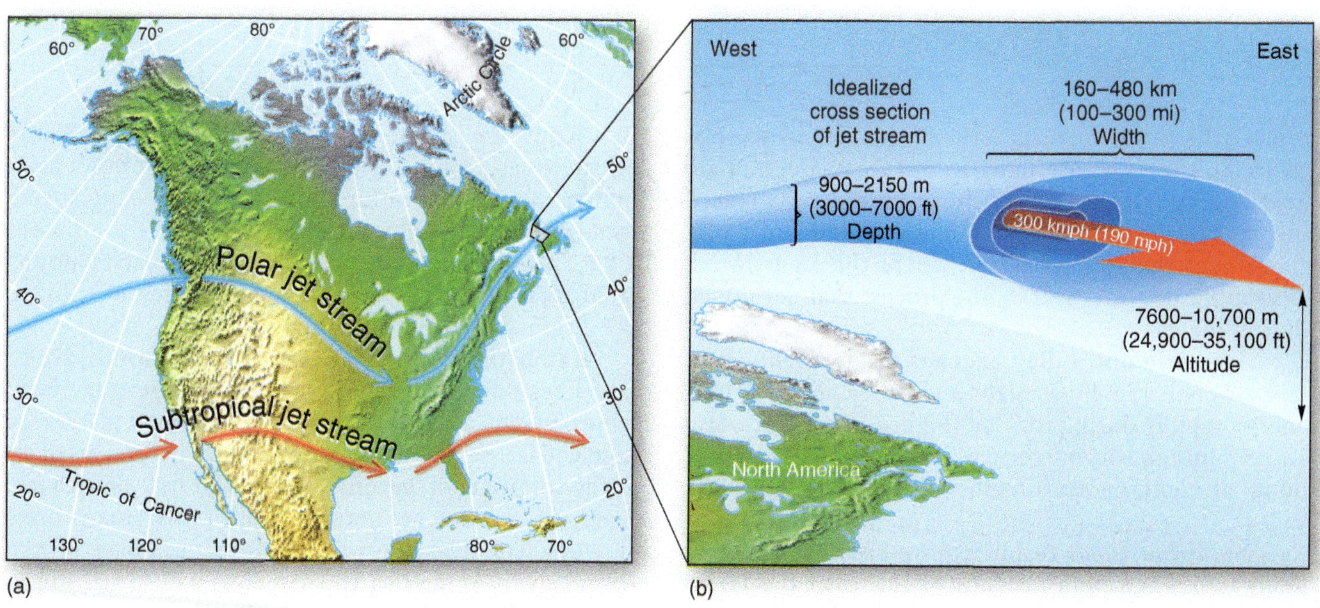

FIGURE 15 Jet streams.
(a) Average locations of the two jet streams over North America. (b) Stylized portrait of a polar jet stream.

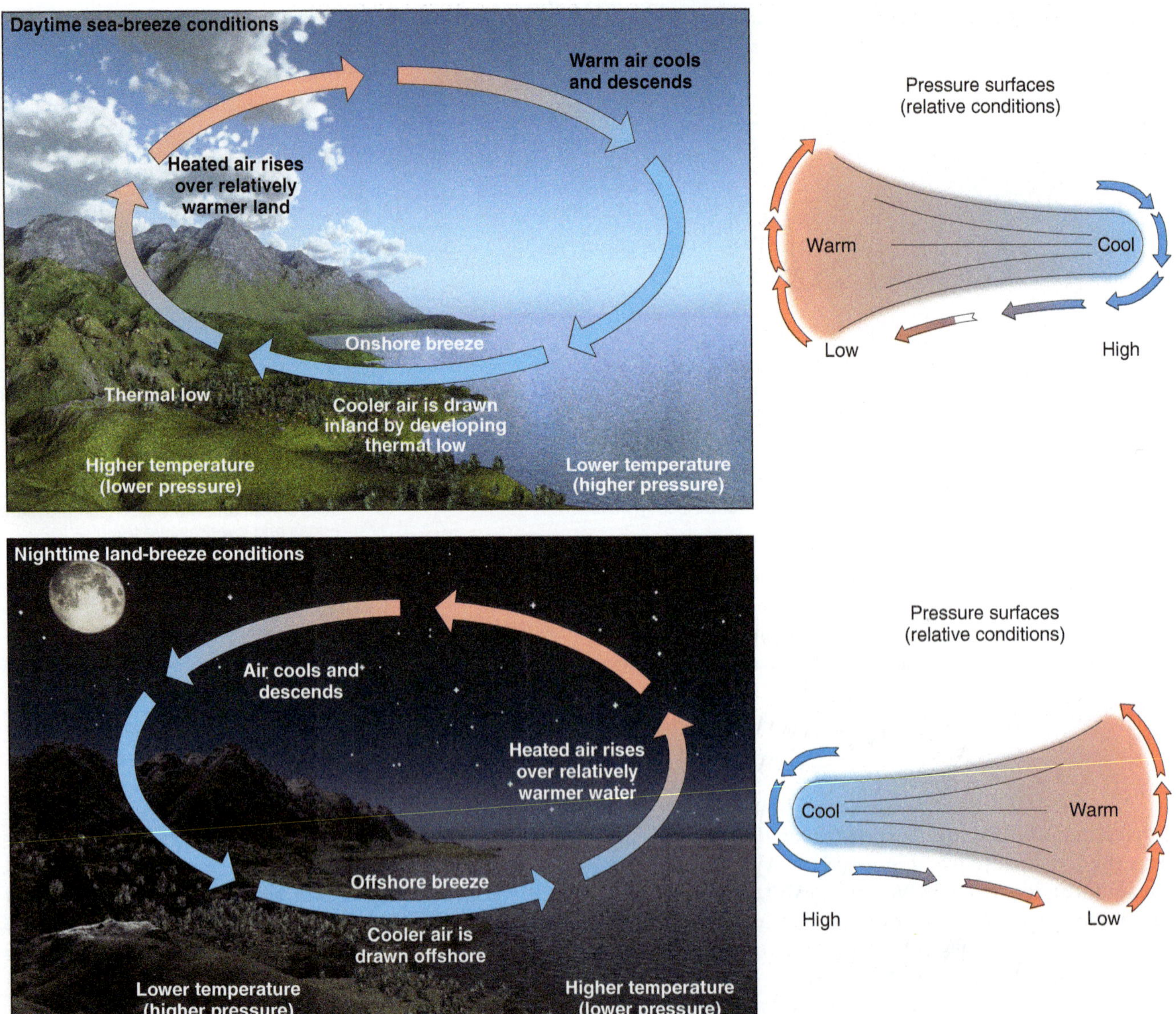

FIGURE 16 Land and sea breezes characteristic of day and night.

replace the rising warm air—the flow is usually strongest in the afternoon. At night, inland areas cool (radiate heat energy) faster than offshore waters. As a result, the cooler air over the land subsides and flows offshore over the warmer water, where the air is lifted. This night pattern reverses the process that developed during the day.

Mountain and valley breezes result when mountain air cools rapidly at night and valley air gains heat energy rapidly during the day (Figure 17). Thus, warm air rises upslope during the day, particularly in the afternoon; at night, cooler air subsides downslope into the valleys.

Santa Ana winds result from a pressure gradient generated when high pressure builds over the Great Basin of the western United States. A strong, dry wind flows out across the desert to southern California coastal areas. Compression heats the air as it flows from higher to lower elevations, and with increasing speed, it moves through constricting valleys to the southwest. These winds bring dust, dryness, and heat to populated areas near the coast and create dangerous wildfire conditions.

Katabatic winds, or gravity drainage winds, are of larger regional scale and are usually stronger than local winds, under certain conditions. An elevated plateau or highland is essential to their formation, where layers of air at the surface cool, become denser, and flow downslope. Such gravity winds are not specifically related to the pressure gradient. The ferocious winds that can blow off the ice sheets of Antarctica and Greenland are katabatic in nature.

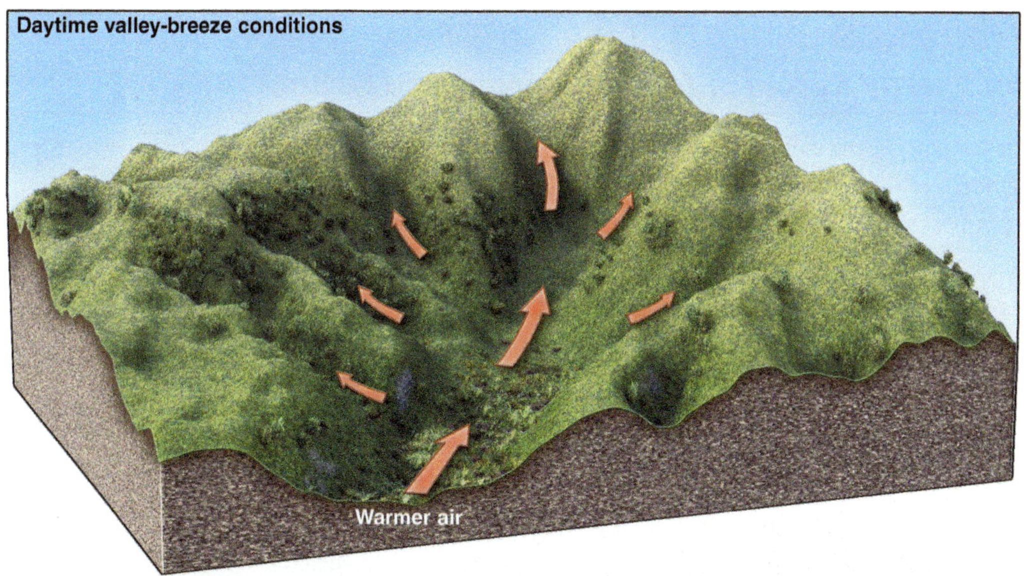

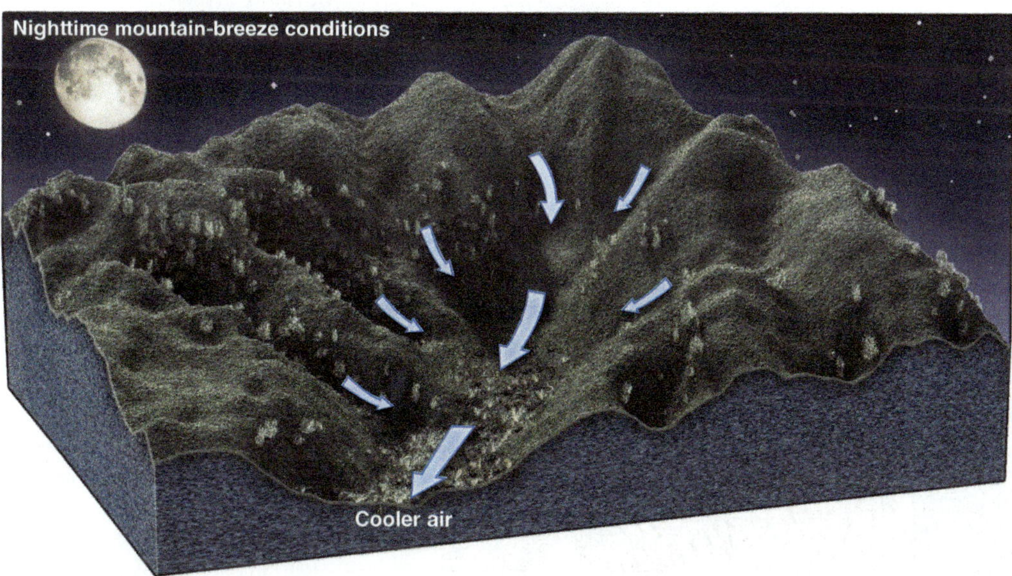

FIGURE 17 Pattern of mountain and valley breezes day and night.

Regionally, wind represents a significant source of renewable energy of increasing importance. Focus Study 1 briefly explores the wind-power resource.

II CRITICAL THINKING 2

Construct your own wind-power assessment report

Go to http://www.awea.org/ and http://www.ewea.org/, the web sites of the American Wind Energy Association and the European Wind Energy Association, respectively. Sample the materials presented as you assess the potential for wind-generated electricity. What are your thoughts concerning this resource—its potential, the reasons for delays, and the competitive economics presented? Propose a brief action plan for the future of this resource.

Monsoonal Winds

Some regional wind systems seasonally change direction. Intense, seasonally shifting wind systems occur in the tropics over Southeast Asia, Indonesia, India, northern Australia, and equatorial Africa. A mild version of such a monsoonal-type flow affects the extreme southwestern United States. These winds involve an annual cycle of returning precipitation with the summer Sun.

The Arabic word for season, *mausim*, or **monsoon**, is the source of the name. The location and size of the Asian landmass and its proximity to the Indian Ocean drive the monsoons of southern and eastern Asia (Figure 18). Also important to the generation of monsoonal flows are wind and pressure patterns in the upper-air circulation.

(text continued after Focus Study 1)

FOCUS STUDY 1

Wind Power: An Energy Resource for the Present and Future

The principles of wind power are ancient, but the technology is modern and the benefits are substantial. Scientists estimate that wind as a resource could potentially produce many times more energy than is currently in demand on a global scale. Yet, despite the available technology, wind-power development continues to be slowed mainly by the changing politics of renewable energy.

The Nature of Wind Energy

Power generation from wind depends on site-specific characteristics of the wind resource. Favorable settings for consistent wind are areas (1) along coastlines influenced by trade winds and westerly winds; (2) where mountain passes constrict air flow and interior valleys develop thermal low-pressure areas, thus drawing air across the landscape; and (3) where localized winds occur, such as an expanse of relatively flat prairies, or in areas with katabatic or monsoonal winds. Many developing countries are generally located in areas blessed by such steady winds, such as the trade winds across the tropics.

Where winds are sufficient, electricity is generated by groups of wind turbines, in wind farms, or by individual installations (Figure 1.1). If winds are reliable less than 25%–30% of the time, only small-scale use of wind power is economically feasible.

(a)

(b)

FIGURE 1.1 Kansas wind farm.
(a) The Gray County Wind Farm, 40 km (25 mi) west of Dodge City, Kansas, generates 112 MW of electricity. All the towers and roads combined occupy only 6 acres of land, allowing 12,000 acres to stay in agricultural production. (b) Wind turbines on Ascension Island, 8° S latitude. Only four of the turbines in the right-hand photo offset the importation of 300,000 barrels of oil. [Bobbé Christopherson.]

The potential of wind power in the United States is enormous (Figure 1.2). In the Midwest, power from the winds of North and South Dakota and Texas alone could meet all U.S. electrical needs. In the California Coast Ranges, land–sea breezes blow between the Pacific and Central Valley, peaking in intensity from April to October, which happens to match peak electrical demands for air conditioning during the hot summer months.

On the eastern shore of Lake Erie sits a closed Bethlehem Steel mill, contaminated with industrial waste until the site was redeveloped with eight 2.5-MW wind-power turbines in 2007 (Figure 1.3). This former "brownfield" site now supplies the equivalent of 75% of the electricity for Lackawanna, New York. Twelve turbines will soon be added, making this a 50-MW electrical generation facility, the largest urban installation in the country. An additional proposal for 500 MW of wind power from some 167 turbines is in the works for an installation offshore in Lake Erie. This former steel town is using wind power to lift itself out of an economic depression with the slogan "Turning the Rust Belt into the Wind Belt."

While most U.S. wind power is land-based, offshore wind development has high potential. The proposed Cape Wind Farm near Cape Cod, Massachusetts, was recently approved as the nation's first offshore project. Proponents hope that despite the additional expense, offshore production will increase, especially along the eastern seaboard, where population centers are close together. At least 12 offshore projects are currently under consideration, most of them on the East Coast.

Land-based wind-power development is enhanced by the income it brings. Farmers in Iowa and Minnesota receive about $2000 in annual income from electrical production by a leased turbine and about $20,000 a year from electrical production by an owned turbine—requiring only one-quarter acre to site the wind machine. The Midwest is on the brink of an economic boom if this wind-energy

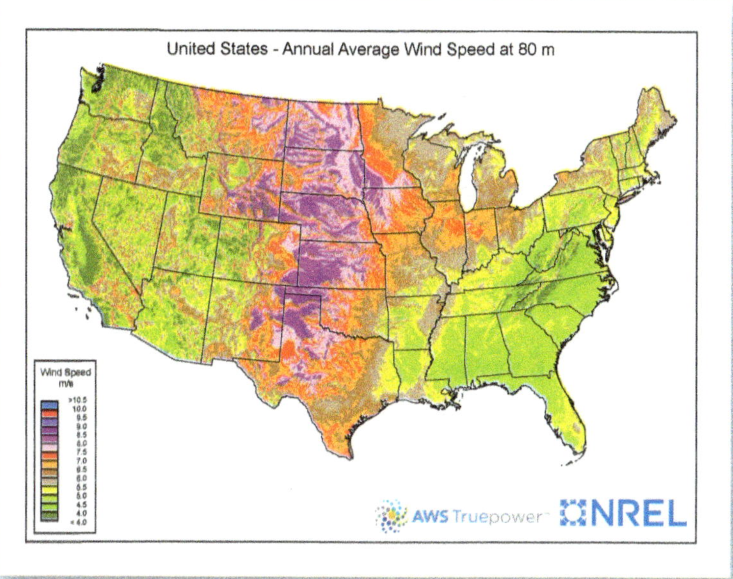

FIGURE 1.2 Annual average wind speed map of the United States. Wind speeds measured at 50 m (164 ft) indicate the potential for wind-power generation at a spatial resolution of 2.5 km. [NREL and AWS Truepower.]

FIGURE 1.3 Wind turbines at a former industrial site on Lake Erie. Known as "The Steel Wind," eight turbines deliver 20 MW of wind power in Lackawanna, New York, on the eastern shore of Lake Erie, south of Buffalo. [Bobbé Christopherson.]

potential is developed and transmission line capacity installed. In fact, Iowa now ranks second for installed wind-power capacity in the United States.

Wind-Power Status and Benefits

Wind-generated energy resources are the fastest-growing energy technology—capacity has risen worldwide in a continuing trend of doubling every 3 years. Total world capacity approached 190,000 MW (megawatts), or 190 GW (gigawatts), by the end of 2010 from installations in 81 countries. Globally, the wind-power industry employs more than 550,000 people, with global investments passing the U.S.$63 billion mark in 2009. Forecasts state that employment will top the million-worker mark in 2012. Average-size wind farms produce more than 100 MW.

In the United States, installed wind capacity exceeded 40,180 MW through 2011, an increase of 300% in 4 years. Installations are operating in 37 states, with the most capacity in Texas, Iowa, California, Minnesota, Washington, Oregon, and Illinois. This puts U.S. installed wind capacity second highest on a global level behind China's 41,800 MW, with Germany third.

The European Wind Energy Association announced installed capacity exceeding 84,000 MW at the end of 2010. Germany has the most, followed by Spain, Italy, France, and the United Kingdom. The European Union has a goal of 20% of all energy from renewable sources by 2020.

The economic and social benefits from using wind resources are numerous. With all costs considered, wind energy is cost-competitive and actually cheaper than oil, coal, natural gas, and nuclear power. Wind power is renewable and does not cause adverse human health effects or environmental degradation. The main challenges of wind-generated power are the high initial financial investment required to build the turbines and the cost of building transmission lines to bring electricity from rural wind farms to urban locations.

To put numbers in meaningful perspective, every 10,000 MW of wind-generation capacity reduces carbon dioxide emissions by 33 million metric tons if it replaces coal or by 21 million metric tons if it replaces mixed fossil fuels. As an example, if countries rally and create a proposed $600 billion industry by installing 1,250,000 MW of wind capacity by 2020, that would supply 12% of global electrical needs.

Whether or not governments and transnational energy corporations support full-scale implementation of renewable resources such as wind, the energy realities of the near future leave no alternative, and global political realities affirm this urgency. By the middle of this century, wind-generated electricity could be routine, along with other renewable energy sources, conservation, and energy efficiency.

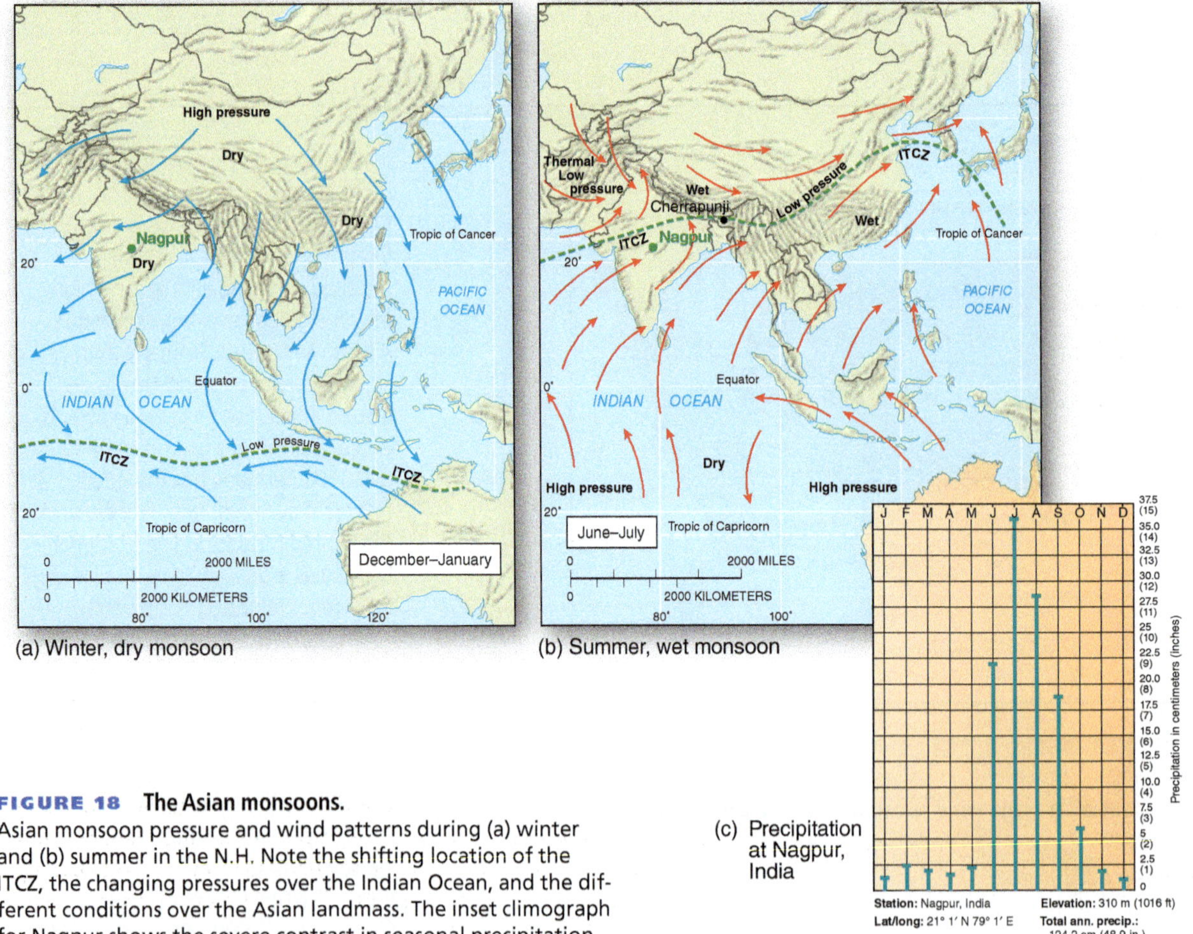

FIGURE 18 The Asian monsoons.
Asian monsoon pressure and wind patterns during (a) winter and (b) summer in the N.H. Note the shifting location of the ITCZ, the changing pressures over the Indian Ocean, and the different conditions over the Asian landmass. The inset climograph for Nagpur shows the severe contrast in seasonal precipitation.

The extreme temperature range from summer to winter over the Asian landmass is due to its continentality (isolation from the modifying effects of the ocean). An intense high-pressure anticyclone dominates this continental landmass in winter (see Figures 9a and 18a), whereas the equatorial low-pressure trough (ITCZ) dominates the central area of the Indian Ocean. This pressure gradient produces cold, dry winds from the Asian interior over the Himalayas and across India. Average temperatures range between 15°C and 20°C (between 60°F and 68°F) at lower elevations. These winds desiccate, or dry out, the landscape, giving way to hot weather from March through May.

During the June–September wet period, the subsolar point (direct overhead rays of sunlight) shifts northward to the Tropic of Cancer, near the mouths of the Indus and Ganges Rivers. The ITCZ shifts northward over southern Asia, and the Asian continental interior develops a thermal low pressure, associated with high average temperatures (consider the summer warmth in Verkhoyansk, Siberia). Meanwhile, subtropical high pressure dominates the Indian Ocean, with a surface temperature of 30°C (86°F). As a result of this reversed pressure gradient, hot subtropical air sweeps over the warm ocean, producing extremely high evaporation rates (Figure 18b).

By the time this air mass and the convergence zone reach India, the air is laden with moisture in thunderous, dark clouds. When the monsoonal rains arrive from June to September, they are welcome relief from the dust, heat, and parched land of Asia's springtime. World-record rainfalls of the wet monsoon drench India. Cherrapunji, India, noted on map, received both the second highest average annual rainfall (1143 cm, or 450 in.) and the highest single-year rainfall (2647 cm, or 1042 in.) on Earth.

The fact that the monsoons of southern Asia involve vast global pressure systems leads us to ask whether future climate change might affect present monsoonal patterns. Concern increases following events such as the monsoonal deluge on July 27, 2005, that drowned Mumbai (Bombay)—in only a few hours, 94.2 cm (37.1 in.) of rain fell, causing widespread flooding. Again in August 2007, extensive flooding from an intense monsoon occurred across India, and in 2010, Pakistan was devastated by record-breaking monsoon rains.

Oceanic Currents

The driving force for ocean currents is the frictional drag of the winds, thus linking the atmospheric and oceanic systems. Also important in shaping these currents is the interplay of the Coriolis force, density differences caused by temperature and salinity, the configuration of the continents and ocean floor, and astronomical forces (the tides).

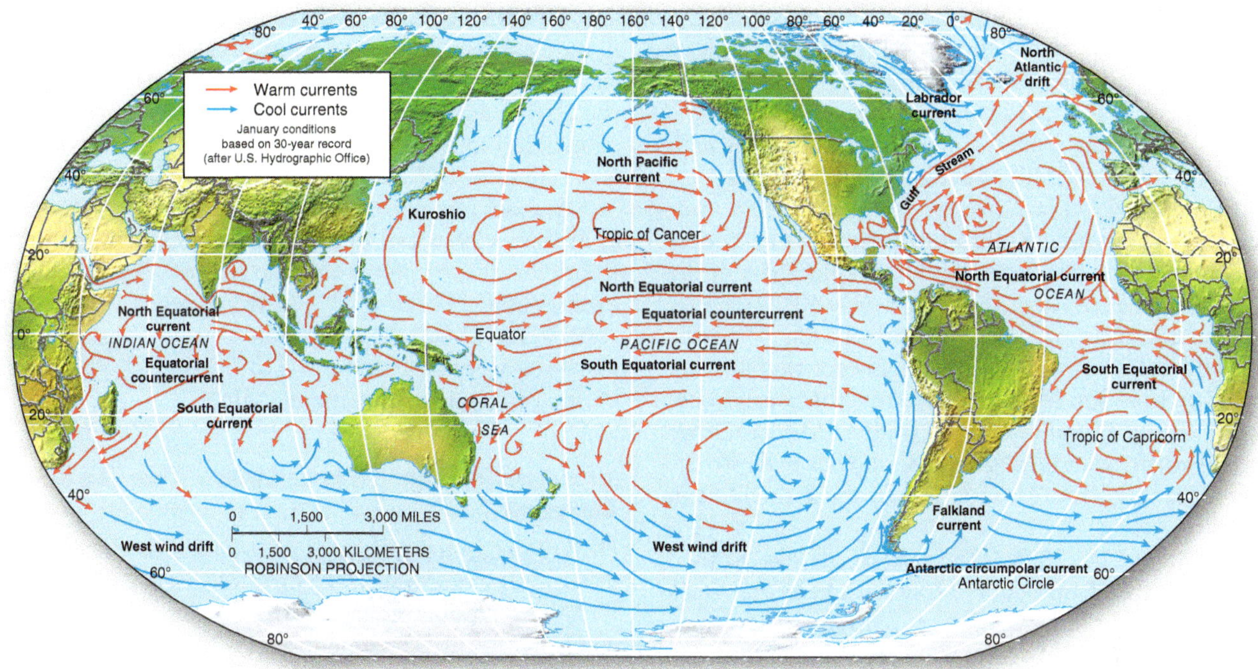

FIGURE 19 **Major ocean currents.** [After the U.S. Naval Oceanographic Office.]

Animation Ocean Circulation

Surface Currents

Figure 19 portrays the general patterns of major ocean currents. Because ocean currents flow over distance and through time, the Coriolis force deflects them. However, their pattern of deflection is not as tightly circular as that of the atmosphere. Compare this ocean-current map with the map showing Earth's pressure systems (see Figure 9), and you can see that ocean currents are driven by the circulation around subtropical high-pressure cells in both hemispheres. These circulation systems are known as *gyres* and generally appear to be offset toward the western side of each ocean basin. Remember, in the Northern Hemisphere, winds and ocean currents move clockwise about high-pressure cells; in the Southern Hemisphere, circulation is counterclockwise, as is evident on the map. You saw in *Geosystems Now* how these currents guided an oil-drilling platform to Tristan da Cunha, where it ran aground.

Examples of Gyre Circulation In 1992, a child at Dana Point, California (33.5° N), a small seaside community south of Los Angeles, placed a letter in a glass juice bottle and tossed it into the waves. Thoughts of distant lands and fabled characters filled the child's imagination as the bottle disappeared. The vast circulation around the Pacific high, clockwise-circulating gyre now took command (Figure 20).

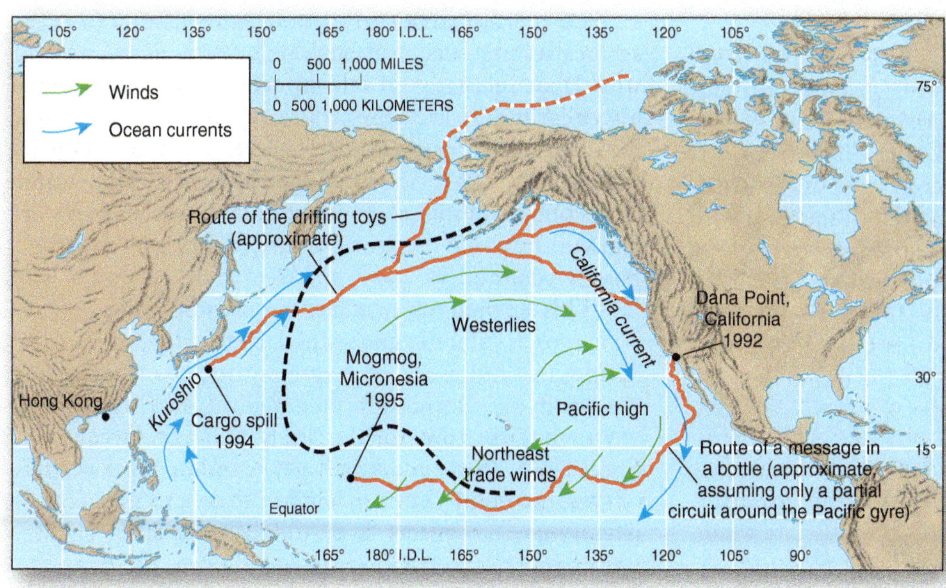

FIGURE 20 **Pacific Ocean currents transport human artifacts.** The travels of a message in a bottle and toy rubber duckies, and the path of Typhoon Ioke (dashed black line), in currents moving clockwise around the Pacific gyre.

Three years passed before ocean currents carried the message in a bottle to the coral reefs and white sands of Mogmog, a small island in Micronesia (7° N). A 7-year-old child there had found a pen pal from afar. Imagine the journey of that note from California—traveling through storms and calms, clear moonlit nights and typhoons.

In January 1994, a powerful storm ravaged a container ship from Hong Kong loaded with toys and other goods. One of the containers on board split apart in the wind off the coast of Japan, dumping nearly 30,000 rubber ducks, turtles, and frogs into the North Pacific. Westerly winds and the North Pacific current swept this floating cargo at up to 29 km (18 mi) a day across the ocean to the coast of Alaska, Canada, Oregon, and California. Other toys, still adrift, went through the Bering Sea and into the Arctic Ocean (this route is indicated by the dashed line in Figure 20).

On August 19, 2006, Tropical Storm Ioke formed about 1285 km (800 mi) south of Hawai'i. The storm's track (dashed black line in Figure 20) moved across the Pacific Ocean, becoming the strongest Super Typhoon in recorded history—a category 5. Turning northward east of Japan and the Kamchatka Peninsula of Russia, the storm moved into higher latitudes. Typhoon Ioke remnants eventually crossed over the Aleutian Islands, reaching 55° N as an extratropical depression. The storm roughly followed the path around the Pacific gyre and along the track of the rubber duckies. Scientists are using such incidents as the message in a bottle and rubber duckies and such remarkable storm tracks to learn more about wind systems and ocean currents.

Equatorial Currents In Figure 19, you can see that trade winds drive the ocean surface waters westward in a concentrated channel along the equator. These equatorial currents are kept near the equator by the Coriolis force, which diminishes to zero at the equator. As these surface currents approach the western margins of the oceans, the water actually piles up against the eastern shores of the continents. The average height of this pileup is 15 cm (6 in.). This phenomenon is the **western intensification**.

The piled-up ocean water then spills northward and southward in strong currents, flowing in tight channels along the eastern shorelines. In the Northern Hemisphere, the *Gulf Stream* and the *Kuroshio* (a current east of Japan) move forcefully northward as a result of western intensification. Their speed and depth increase with the constriction of the area they occupy. The warm, deep, clear water of the ribbon-like Gulf Stream usually is 50–80 km (30–50 mi) wide and 1.5–2.0 km (0.9–1.2 mi) deep, moving at 3–10 kmph (1.8–6.2 mph). In 24 hours, ocean water can move 70–240 km (40–150 mi) in the Gulf Stream.

Upwelling and Downwelling Flows Where surface water is swept away from a coast, either by surface divergence (induced by the Coriolis force) or by offshore winds, an **upwelling current** occurs. This cool water generally is nutrient-rich and rises from great depths to replace the vacating water. Such cold upwelling currents exist off the Pacific coasts of North and South America and the subtropical and midlatitude west coast of Africa. These areas are some of Earth's prime fishing regions.

In other regions with an accumulation of water—such as at the western end of an equatorial current, or in the Labrador Sea, or along the margins of Antarctica—the excess water gravitates downward in a **downwelling current**. These are the deep currents that flow vertically and along the ocean floor and travel the full extent of the ocean basins, carrying heat energy and salinity.

Thermohaline Circulation—The Deep Currents

Differences in temperatures and salinity produce density differences important to the flow of deep currents. This is Earth's **thermohaline circulation**, and it is different from wind-driven surface currents. Traveling at slower speeds than surface currents, the thermohaline circulation hauls larger volumes of water. Compare the ocean's physical structure with profiles of temperature, salinity, and dissolved gases; note the temperature and salinity differences with depth.

To picture such a deep, salty current, imagine a continuous channel of water beginning with cold water downwelling in the North Atlantic and along Antarctica and upwelling in the Indian Ocean and North Pacific (Figure 21). Here it warms and then is carried in surface currents back to the North Atlantic. A complete circuit of the current may require 1000 years from downwelling, to deep cold current covering thousands of kilometers, to its reemergence at the surface elsewhere. Even deeper Antarctic bottom water flows northward in the Atlantic Basin beneath these currents.

These current systems appear to play a profound role in global climate; in turn, global warming has the potential to disrupt the downwelling in the North Atlantic and the thermohaline circulation. A freshening of ocean surface waters occurs in both polar regions, contrasted with large increases in salinity in the surface waters at lower latitudes. Increased rates of glacial, sea-ice, and ice-sheet melting produce these fresh, lower-density surface waters that ride on top of the denser saline water. The concern is that such changes in ocean temperature and salinity could dampen the rate of downwelling in the North Atlantic.

This is a vital research frontier because Earth's hydrologic cycle is still little understood. Research groups such as Scripps Institution of Oceanography (http://sio.ucsd.edu/), Woods Hole Oceanographic Institution (http://www.whoi.edu/), Institute for the Study of Earth, Oceans, and Space (http://www.eos.sr.unh.edu/), and Bedford Institute of Oceanography (http://www.bio.gc.ca/), to name only a few of many, are places to periodically check for updated information.

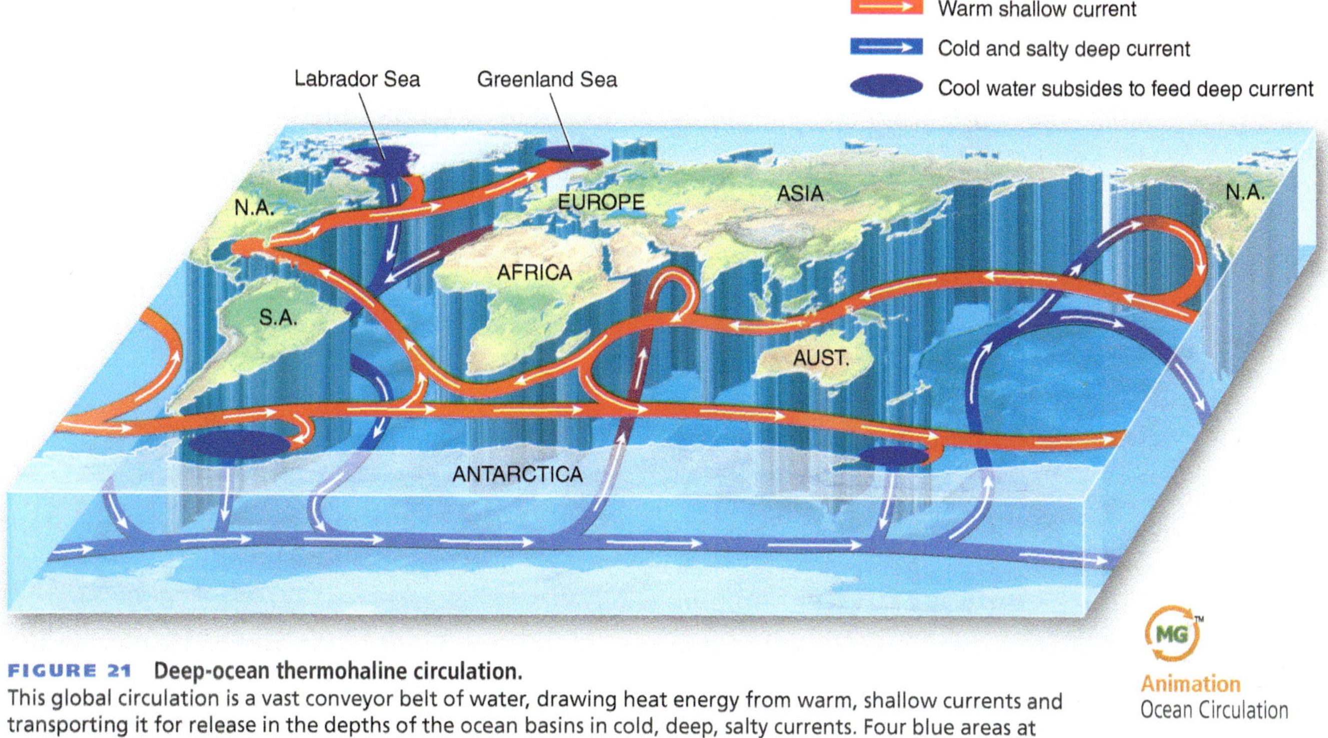

FIGURE 21 Deep-ocean thermohaline circulation.
This global circulation is a vast conveyor belt of water, drawing heat energy from warm, shallow currents and transporting it for release in the depths of the ocean basins in cold, deep, salty currents. Four blue areas at high latitudes are where surface water cools, sinks, and feeds the deep circulation.

Natural Oscillations in Global Circulation

Several system fluctuations that occur in multi-year or shorter periods are important in the global circulation picture. Multi-year oscillations affect temperatures, air masses, and air pressure patterns and thus affect global winds and climates. The most famous of these is the El Niño–Southern Oscillation (ENSO) phenomenon, which affects temperature and precipitation on a global scale. Here we describe ENSO and briefly introduce three other hemisphere-scale oscillations.

El Niño–Southern Oscillation

Climate is the consistent behavior of weather over time, but average weather conditions also include extremes that depart from the normal. The **El Niño–Southern Oscillation (ENSO)** in the Pacific Ocean forces the greatest interannual variability of temperature and precipitation on a global scale. Peruvians coined the name El Niño ("the boy child") because these episodes seem to occur around the time of the traditional December celebration of Christ's birth. Actually, El Niños can occur as early as spring and summer and persist through the year.

In Figure 19, you can see that the northward-flowing Peru Current dominates the region off South America's west coast. These cold waters move toward the equator and join the westward movement of the South Equatorial Current. The Peru Current is part of the normal counterclockwise circulation of winds and surface ocean currents around the subtropical high-pressure cell dominating the eastern Pacific in the Southern Hemisphere. As a result, a location such as Guayaquil, Ecuador, normally receives 91.4 cm (36 in.) of precipitation each year under dominant high pressure, whereas islands in the Indonesian archipelago receive more than 254 cm (100 in.) under dominant low pressure. This normal alignment of pressure is shown in Figure 22a.

El Niño–ENSO's Warm Phase Occasionally, for unexplained reasons, pressure patterns and surface ocean temperatures shift from their usual locations. Higher pressure than normal develops over the western Pacific and lower pressure develops over the eastern Pacific. Trade winds normally moving from east to west weaken and can be reduced or even replaced by an eastward (west-to-east) flow. The shifting of atmospheric pressure and wind patterns across the Pacific is the *Southern Oscillation*.

Sea-surface temperatures increase, sometimes more than 8 C° (14 F°) above normal in the central and eastern Pacific during an ENSO, replacing the normally cold, nutrient-rich water along Peru's coastline. Such ocean-surface warming, the "warm pool," may extend to the International Date Line. This surface pool of warm water is known as El Niño. Thus, the designation ENSO—El Niño–Southern Oscillation—is derived. This condition is shown in Figure 22b in illustration and satellite image. Note that the thermocline (boundary of colder, deep-ocean water) lowers in depth in the eastern Pacific Ocean. The change in wind direction and warmer surface water

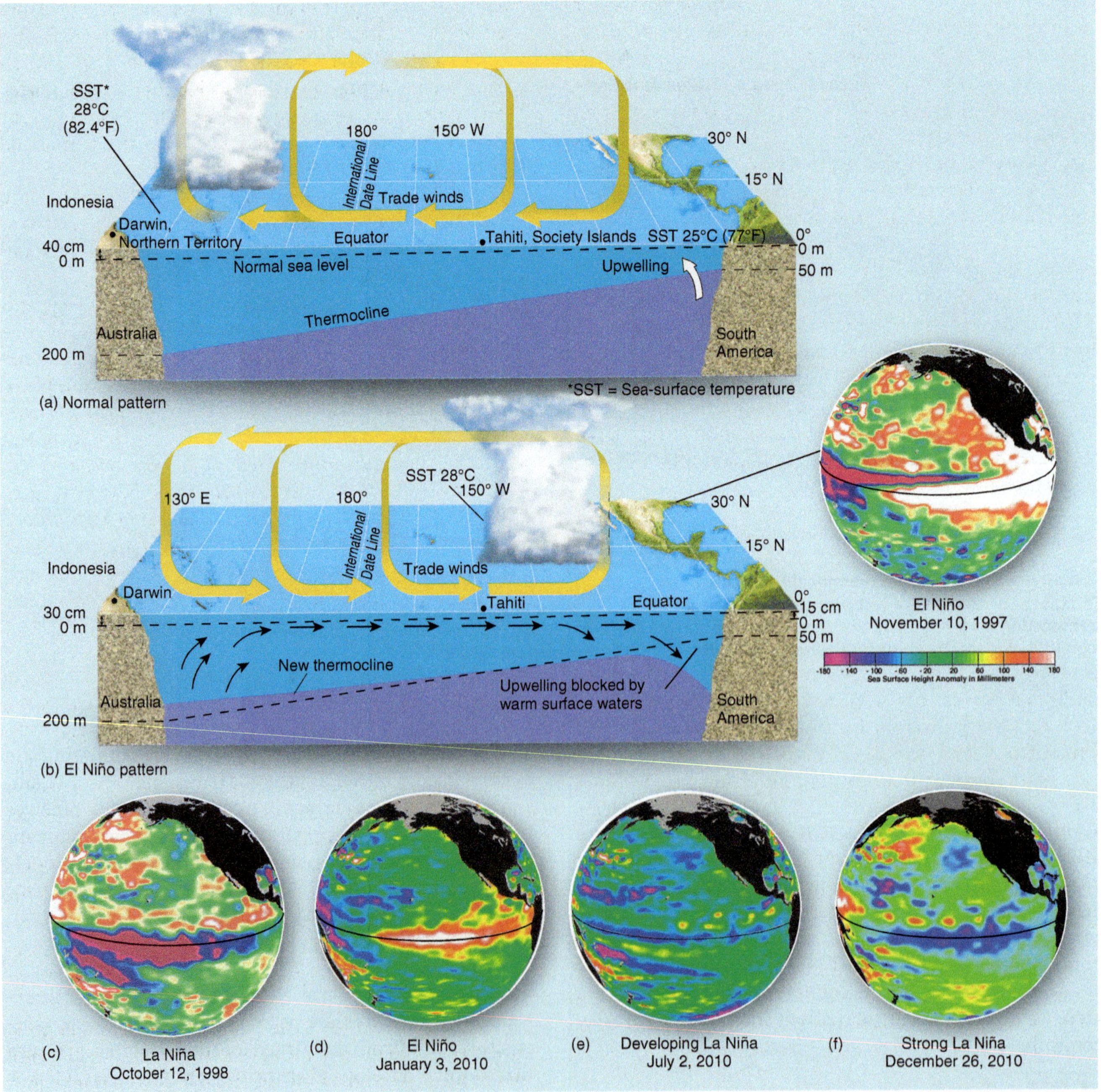

FIGURE 22 Normal, El Niño, and La Niña changes in the Pacific.
(a) Normal patterns in the Pacific. (b) El Niño wind and weather patterns across the Pacific Ocean and satellite image for November 1997 (white and red colors indicate warmer surface water—a warm pool). (c) Image of La Niña conditions in transition in the Pacific in October 12, 1998 (purple and blue colors indicate cooler surface water—a cool pool). (d) through (f) track La Niña and El Niño conditions during 2010. [(a) and (b) adapted and author corrected from C. S. Ramage, "El Niño." © 1986 by *Scientific American, Inc.* (b image)–(c) *TOPEX/Poseidon,* (d)–(e) *Jason–1,* (f) *OSTM-Jason–2* images courtesy of Jet Propulsion Laboratory, NASA.]

slow the normal upwelling currents that control nutrient availability. This loss of nutrients affects the phytoplankton and food chain, depriving fish, marine mammals, and predatory birds of nourishment.

The expected interval for ENSO recurrence is 3 to 5 years, but the interval may range from 2 to 12 years. The frequency and intensity of ENSO events increased through the 20th century, a topic of extensive scientific research looking for a link to global climate change. Recent studies suggest that this phenomenon might be more responsive to global change than previously thought.

The two strongest ENSO events in 120 years hit in 1982–1983 and 1997–1998. The latest El Niño subsided in May 2010, followed by a brief neutral period and the start of La Niña conditions in July 2010, intensifying through December 2010. See the satellite images in Figure 22d–f.

La Niña—ENSO's Cool Phase When surface waters in the central and eastern Pacific cool to below normal by 0.4 C° (0.7 F°) or more, the condition is dubbed *La Niña*, Spanish for "the girl." This condition is weaker and less consistent than El Niño. There is no correlation in the strength or weakness of each. For instance, following the record 1997–1998 ENSO event, the subsequent La Niña was not as strong as predicted and shared the Pacific with lingering warm water (Figure 22c, 22e, and 22f).

In contrast, the 2010–2011 La Niña was one of the strongest on record, according to atmospheric indicators. This event corresponded with the wettest December in history and widespread flooding in Queensland and across eastern Australia, where heavy rainfall led to the country's worst flooding in 50 years. Weeks of precipitation caused the Fitzroy River to overflow its banks, inundating an area the size of France and Germany combined and causing the evacuation of thousands of people.

Global Effects Related to ENSO Weather and short-term climate effects related to ENSO occur worldwide. El Niño is tied to droughts in South Africa, southern India, Australia, and the Philippines; strong hurricanes in the Pacific, including Tahiti and French Polynesia; and flooding in the United States (in the southwestern and mountain states), Bolivia, Cuba, Ecuador, and Peru. In India, every drought for more than 400 years seems linked to this warm phase of ENSO. La Niña often brings wetter conditons throughout Indonesia, the South Pacific, and northern Brazil. The Atlantic hurricane season weakens during El Niño years and strengthens during La Niña years. The study of the spatial impacts of ENSO is at the heart of physical geography. (For ENSO monitoring and forecasts, see the National Climate Prediction Center at http://www.cpc.ncep.noaa.gov/, the Jet Propulsion Laboratory at http://sealevel.jpl.nasa.gov/science/el-nino.html, or the National Oceanic and Atmospheric Administration's (NOAA's) El Niño Theme Page at http://www.pmel.noaa.gov/toga-tao/el-nino/nino-home.html.)

Pacific Decadal Oscillation

The *Pacific Decadal Oscillation (PDO)* is a pattern of sea-surface temperatures, air pressure, and winds that shifts between the northern and tropical western Pacific (off the coast of Asia) and the eastern tropical Pacific (along the U.S. West Coast). The PDO, lasting 20 to 30 years, is longer-lived than the 2- to 12-year variation in the ENSO. The PDO is strongest in the North Pacific, rather than in the tropical Pacific, another distinction from the ENSO.

The PDO negative phase, or cool phase, occurs when higher-than-normal temperatures dominate in the northern/tropical western Pacific and lower temperatures occur in the eastern tropical region; such conditions occurred between 1947 and 1977.

A switch to a positive phase, or warm phase, in the PDO ran from 1977 to the 1990s, when lower-than-normal temperatures were found in the northern and western Pacific and higher-than-normal temperatures dominated the eastern tropical region. This coincided with a time of more intense ENSO events. In 1999, a negative phase began for 4 years, a mild positive phase continued for 3 years, and now the PDO has been in a negative phase since 2008. This PDO negative phase can mean a decade or more of drier conditions in the U.S. Southwest, as well as cooler and wetter winters in the U.S. Northwest.

The PDO affects fisheries along the U.S. Pacific coast, with more productive regions shifting northward toward Alaska during PDO warm phases and southward along the California coast during cool phases. Causes of the PDO and its cyclic variability over time are unknown. For more information, see http://jisao.washington.edu/pdo/.

North Atlantic and Arctic Oscillations

A north–south fluctuation of atmospheric variability marks the *North Atlantic Oscillation (NAO)*, as pressure differences between the Icelandic low and the Azores high in the Atlantic alternate from a weak to a strong pressure gradient. The NAO is in its positive phase when the Icelandic low-pressure system is lower than normal and the Azores (west of Portugal) high-pressure cell is higher than normal. Strong westerly winds and jet streams cross the eastern Atlantic. In the eastern United States, winters tend to be less severe in contrast to the strong, warm, wet storms hitting northern Europe; however, the Mediterranean region is dry.

In its negative phase, the NAO features a weaker pressure gradient than normal between the Azores and Iceland and reduced westerlies and jet streams. Storm tracks shift southward in Europe, bringing moist conditions to the Mediterranean and cold, dry winters to northern Europe. The eastern United States experiences cold, snowy winters as Arctic air masses plunge to lower latitudes.

While the NAO flips unpredictably between positive and negative phases, sometimes changing from week to week, a trend toward more positive than negative phases has emerged since 1960. From 1980 to 2008, the NAO

GEO REPORT 5 ***2010–2011 La Niña breaks records***

The Southern Oscillation Index (SOI) measures the difference in air pressure between Tahiti and Darwin, Australia, and is one of several atmospheric indexes used to monitor ENSO. In general, the SOI is negative during an El Niño and positive during a La Niña. This index corresponds with sea-surface temperature (SST) changes across the Pacific: Negative SOI values coincide with warm SSTs (El Niño), and positive SOI values correlate with cold SSTs (La Niña). During the 2010–2011 La Niña, the SOI reached record levels, coinciding with dramatic weather events in Australia.

was averaging a more positive phase condition; however, through 2009 and into early 2010, the NAO was in a more negative phase through the winter (see http://www.ldeo.columbia.edu/NAO/).

Variable fluctuations between middle- and high-latitude air mass conditions over the Northern Hemisphere produce the *Arctic Oscillation (AO)*. The AO is associated with the NAO, especially in winter, and their phases correlate. In the AO positive, or warm, phase (positive NAO), the pressure gradient is affected by lower pressure than normal over the North Pole region and relatively higher pressures at lower latitudes. This sets up stronger westerly winds and a consistently strong jet stream as well as the flow of warmer Atlantic water currents into the Arctic Ocean. Cold air masses do not migrate as far south in winter, whereas winters are colder than normal in Greenland.

In the AO negative, or cold, phase (negative NAO), the pattern reverses. Higher-than-normal pressure is over the polar region, and relatively lower pressure is over the central Atlantic. The weaker zonal wind flow during the winter allows cold air masses into the eastern United States, northern Europe, and Asia, and sea ice in the Arctic Ocean becomes a bit thicker. Greenland, Siberia, northern Alaska, and the Canadian Archipelago are all warmer than normal. The Northern Hemisphere winter of 2009–2010 featured unusual flows of cold air into the midlatitudes. As temperatures dropped in the U.S. Northeast and Midwest, the circumpolar region was experiencing conditions 15 to 20 C° (27 to 36 F°) above average. In December 2009, the AO was in its most negative phase since 1970; it was even more negative in February 2010 (see http://nsidc.org/arcticmet/patterns/arctic_oscillation.html).

GEOSYSTEMS CONNECTION

In this chapter, we have examined ways Earth systems impact our lives and the many ways human society is impacting these same systems.

KEY LEARNING CONCEPTS REVIEW

■ ***Define*** the concept of air pressure, and ***describe*** instruments used to measure air pressure.

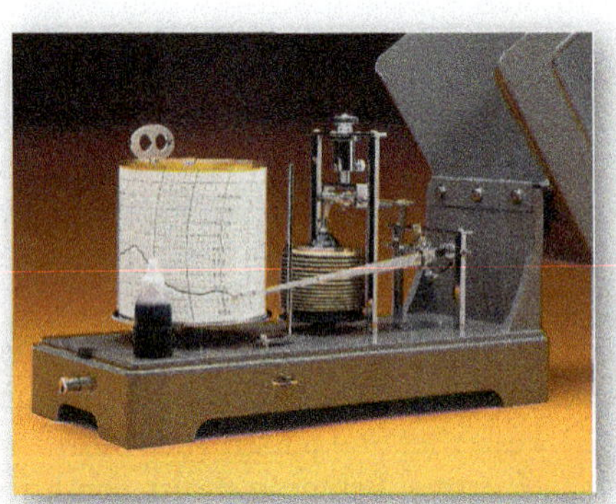

The weight (created by motion, size, and number of molecules) of the atmosphere is **air pressure,** which exerts an average force of approximately 1 kg/cm² (14.7 lb/in.²). A **mercury barometer** (mercury in a tube—closed at one end and open at the other, with the open end placed in a vessel of mercury—that changes level in response to pressure changes) measures air pressure at the surface, as does an **aneroid barometer** (a closed cell, partially evacuated of air, that detects changes in pressure).

air pressure
mercury barometer
aneroid barometer

1. How does air exert pressure? Describe the basic instrument used to measure air pressure. Compare the operation of two different types of instruments discussed.
2. What is normal sea-level pressure in millimeters? Millibars? Inches? Kilopascals?

■ ***Define*** wind, and ***explain*** how wind is measured, how wind direction is determined, and how winds are named.

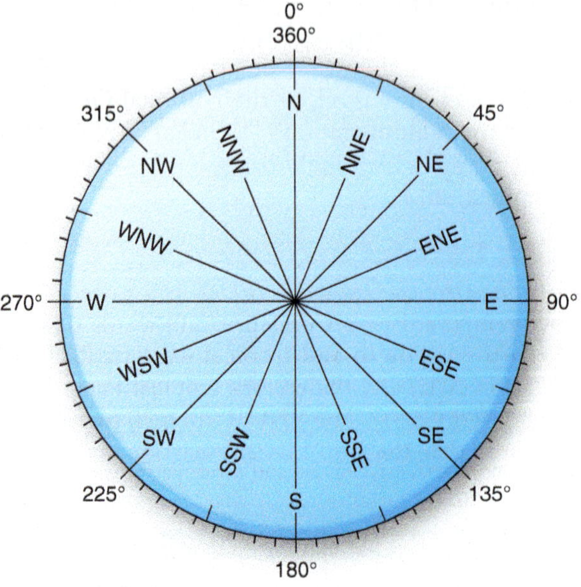

Wind is the horizontal movement of air across Earth's surface; turbulence adds wind updrafts and downdrafts, and thus a vertical component to the definition. Its speed is measured with an **anemometer** (a device with cups that are pushed by the wind)

and its direction with a **wind vane** (a flat blade or surface that is directed by the wind).

wind
anemometer
wind vane

3. What is a possible explanation for the beautiful sunrises and sunsets during the summer of 1992 in North America? Relate your answer to global circulation.
4. Explain this statement: "The atmosphere socializes humanity, making the world a spatially linked society." Illustrate your answer with some examples.
5. Define wind. How is it measured? How is its direction determined?

■ ***Explain*** the four driving forces within the atmosphere—gravity, pressure gradient force, Coriolis force, and friction force—and ***locate*** the primary high- and low-pressure areas and principal winds.

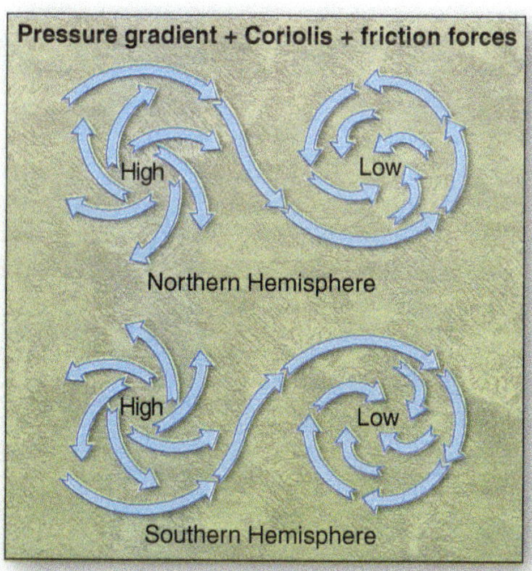

The pressure that Earth's gravitational force exerts on the atmosphere is virtually uniform worldwide. Winds are driven by the **pressure gradient force,** as air moves from areas of high pressure to areas of low pressure. Winds are deflected by the **Coriolis force,** an apparent deflection in the path of winds or ocean currents caused by the rotation of Earth and surface distance from Earth's axis as the gravitational force and centrifugal force work in opposition, deflecting objects to the right in the Northern Hemisphere and to the left in the Southern Hemisphere. Finally, winds are dragged by the **friction force,** in which Earth's varied surfaces exert a drag on wind movements in opposition to the pressure gradient. Maps portray air pressure patterns using the **isobar**—an isoline that connects points of equal pressure. A combination of the pressure gradient and Coriolis forces produces **geostrophic winds,** which move parallel to isobars, characteristic of winds above the surface frictional layer.

Winds descend and diverge, spiraling outward to form an **anticyclone** (clockwise in the Northern Hemisphere), and they converge and ascend, spiraling upward to form a **cyclone** (counterclockwise in the Northern Hemisphere). The pattern of high and low pressures on Earth in generalized belts in each hemisphere produces the distribution of specific wind systems. These primary pressure regions are the **equatorial low-pressure trough,** the weak **polar high-pressure cells** (at both the North and the South Poles), the **subtropical high-pressure cells,** and the **subpolar low-pressure cells.**

Along the equator, winds converge into the equatorial low, creating the **intertropical convergence zone (ITCZ).** Air rises along the equator and descends in the subtropics in each hemisphere. The winds returning to the ITCZ from the northeast in the Northern Hemisphere and from the southeast in the Southern Hemisphere produce the **trade winds.**

Winds flowing out of the subtropics to higher latitudes produce the **westerlies** in each hemisphere. The subtropical high-pressure cells on Earth, generally between 20° and 35° latitude in each hemisphere, are variously named the *Bermuda high*, *Azores high*, and *Pacific high*.

Along the polar front and the series of low-pressure cells, the *Aleutian low* and *Icelandic low* dominate the North Pacific and Atlantic, respectively. This region of contrast between colder air toward the poles and warmer air toward the equator is the **polar front.** The weak and variable **polar easterlies** diverge from the polar high-pressure cells, particularly the **Antarctic high.**

pressure gradient force
Coriolis force
friction force
isobar
geostrophic wind
anticyclone
cyclone
equatorial low-pressure trough
polar high-pressure cell
subtropical high-pressure cell
subpolar low-pressure cell
intertropical convergence zone (ITCZ)
trade winds
westerlies
polar front
polar easterlies
Antarctic high

6. What does an isobaric map of surface air pressure portray? Contrast pressures over North America for January and July.
7. Describe the effect of the Coriolis force. Explain how it apparently deflects atmospheric and oceanic circulations.
8. What are geostrophic winds, and where are they encountered in the atmosphere?
9. Describe the horizontal and vertical air motions in a high-pressure anticyclone and in a low-pressure cyclone.
10. Construct a simple diagram of Earth's general circulation; begin by labeling the four principal pressure belts or zones, and then add arrows between these pressure systems to denote the three principal wind systems.
11. How is the intertropical convergence zone (ITCZ) related to the equatorial low-pressure trough? How does it appear on satellite images of accumulated precipitation for January and July in Figure 10?
12. Characterize the belt of subtropical high pressure on Earth: Name the specific cells. Describe the generation of westerlies and trade winds. Discuss sailing conditions.

■ ***Describe*** upper-air circulation and ***define*** the jet streams.

A **constant isobaric surface**, or surface along which the same pressure, such as 500 mb, occurs regardless of altitude, describes

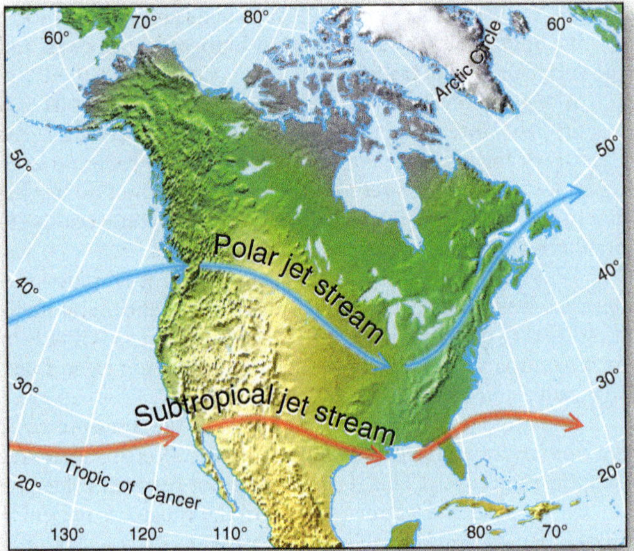

air pressure in the middle and upper troposphere. The height of this surface above the ground forms ridges and troughs that support the development of and help sustain surface pressure systems; surface lows are sustained by divergence aloft, and surface highs are sustained by convergence aloft.

Vast, flowing, longwave undulations in these upper-air westerlies form wave motions, the **Rossby waves**. Prominent streams of high-speed westerly winds in the upper-level troposphere are the **jet streams**. Depending on their latitudinal position in either hemisphere, they are termed the *polar jet stream* or the *subtropical jet stream*.

constant isobaric surface
Rossby wave
jet stream

13. What is the relation between wind speed and the spacing of isobars?
14. How is the constant isobaric surface (ridges and troughs) related to surface pressure systems? To divergence aloft and surface lows? To convergence aloft and surface highs?
15. Relate the jet-stream phenomenon to general upper-air circulation. Describe the average locations of the jet streams over North America.

Explain several types of local winds and the regional monsoons.

Different heating characteristics of land and water surfaces create **land and sea breezes**. Temperature differences during the day and evening between valleys and mountain summits cause **mountain and valley breezes**. **Katabatic winds**, or gravity drainage winds, are of larger regional scale and are usually stronger than mountain–valley breezes, under certain conditions. An elevated plateau or highland is essential, where layers of air at the surface cool, become denser, and flow downslope.

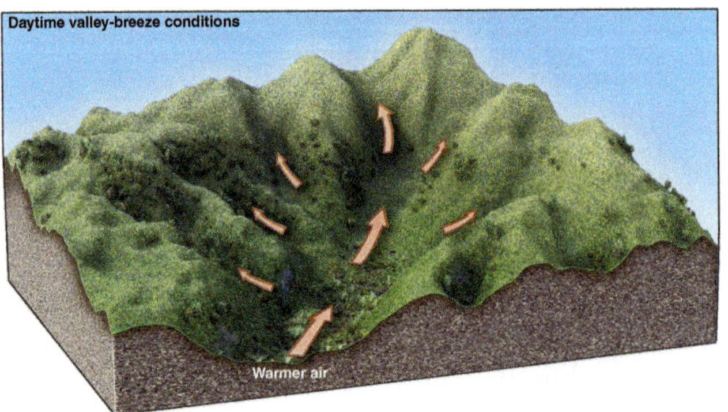

Intense, seasonally shifting wind systems occur in the tropics over Southeast Asia, Indonesia, India, northern Australia, equatorial Africa, and southern Arizona. These winds involve an annual cycle of returning precipitation with the summer Sun and carry the Arabic word for season, *mausim*, or **monsoon**. The location and size of the Asian landmass and its proximity to the Indian Ocean and the seasonally shifting ITCZ drive the monsoons of southern and eastern Asia.

land and sea breezes
Mountain and valley breezes
katabatic winds
monsoon

16. People living along coastlines generally experience variations in winds from day to night. Explain the factors that produce these changing wind patterns.
17. The arrangement of mountains and nearby valleys produces local wind patterns. Explain the day and night winds that might develop.
18. Describe the seasonal pressure patterns that produce the Asian monsoonal wind and precipitation patterns. Contrast January and July conditions.
19. This chapter presents wind power as well developed and cost-effective. Given the information presented and your additional critical thinking work, what conclusions or observations have you made?

Discern the basic pattern of Earth's major surface ocean currents and deep thermohaline circulation.

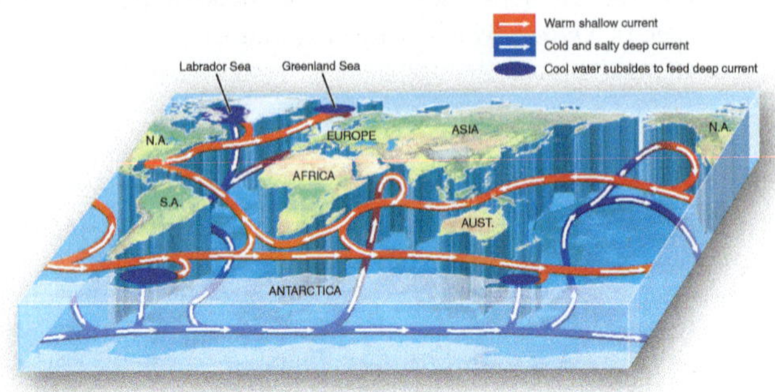

Ocean currents are primarily caused by the frictional drag of wind and occur worldwide at varying intensities, temperatures, and speeds, both along the surface and at great depths in the oceanic basins. The circulation around subtropical high-pressure cells in both hemispheres is notable on the ocean circulation map—these gyres are usually offset toward the western side of each ocean basin.

The trade winds converge along the ITCZ and push enormous quantities of water that pile up along the eastern shore of continents in a process known as the **western intensification**. Where surface water is swept away from a coast, either by surface divergence (induced by the Coriolis force) or by offshore winds, an **upwelling current** occurs. This cool water generally is nutrient-rich and rises from great depths to replace the vacating water. In other portions of the sea where there is an accumulation of water, the excess water gravitates downward in a **down-**

welling c
currents t
of the oce

Diff
differenc
currents
slower s
line circ
concerr
atmosp
alter th

w
u
d
t

20. e

21. at
of

22 At
la-
ic

2 ing
ts?

■ ***Summarize*** sever...
temperature, air pressure, and circulation in the A...
Atlantic, and Pacific Oceans.

Several system fluctuations that occur in multi-year or shorter periods are important in the global circulation picture. The most famous of these is the **El Niño–Southern Oscillation (ENSO)** in the Pacific Ocean, which affects interannual variability in climate on a global scale.

El Niño
November 10, 1997

Across the Pacific Ocean, the *Pacific Decadal Oscillation (PDO)* involves variability between two regions of sea-surface temperatures and related air pressure: the northern and tropical western Pacific and the area of the eastern tropical Pacific, along the U.S. West Coast. The PDO switches between positive and negative phases in 20- to 30-year cycles.

A north–south fluctuation of atmospheric variability marks the *North Atlantic Oscillation (NAO)* as pressure differences between the Icelandic low and the Azores high in the Atlantic alternate between weaker and stronger pressure gradients. The *Arctic Oscillation (AO)* is the variable fluctuation between middle- and high-latitude air mass conditions over the Northern Hemisphere. The AO is associated with the NAO, especially in winter. During the winter of 2009–2010, the AO was at the lowest negative phase since 1970.

El Niño–Southern Oscillation (ENSO)

24. Describe the changes in sea surface temperatures and atmospheric pressure that occur during El Niño and La Niña, the warm and cool phases of the ENSO. What are some of the climatic effects that occur worldwide?

25. What is the apparent relation between the PDO and the strength of El Niño events? Between PDO phases and climate in the western United States?

26. What phases are identified for the NAO and AO? What winter weather conditions generally affect the eastern United States during each phase? What happened during the 2009–2010 winter season in the Northern Hemisphere?

Mastering**GEOGRAPHY**™

Visit **http://www.masteringgeography.com/** for several figure animations, satellite loops, self-study quizzes, flashcards, visual glossary, case studies, career links, text reference maps, RSS Feeds, and an ebook version of *Elemental Geosystems.* Included are many geography web links to interesting Internet sources that support this chapter.

Atmospheric Water and Weather

Atmospheric Water and Weather

An EF-05 tornado tore across the entire state of Alabama in 2011, destroying several small towns and crushing a path through Tuscaloosa pictured here, passing near the University of Alabama. At its base, this tornado was almost 2 km wide (see inset photo). This was part of a historic 3-day April outbreak of more than 300 tornadoes killing 320 people. On April 27 alone, 188 tornadoes hit the Southeast US, with 15 of these rated EF-04 or -05 on the Enhanced Fujita Scale. [x77/Press/Newscom; inset: David Mabe/Alamy.]

KEY LEARNING CONCEPTS

After reading the chapter, you should be able to:

- ***Describe*** the heat properties of water, and ***identify*** the traits of its three phases: solid, liquid, and gas.
- ***Define*** humidity, relative humidity, and dew-point temperature, and ***illustrate*** stable and unstable atmospheric conditions
- ***Explain*** cloud formation, and ***identify*** major cloud classes and types, including fog.
- ***Describe*** air masses that affect North America, and ***identify*** four types of atmospheric lifting mechanisms.
- ***Describe*** the life cycle of a midlatitude cyclonic storm system, and ***list*** the measurable elements that contribute to weather forecasting.
- ***Analyze*** various types of violent weather—thunderstorms, tornadoes, and tropical cyclones, including recent trends.

On the Front Lines of Intense Weather

As we follow violent weather events in the news, images of tornadoes, hurricanes, floods, and their aftermath are everywhere. Although the intensity is apparent, how often do we imagine what people face on the front lines of these events? What happens after the media leave and survivors return to their day-to-day lives? Improved warnings have reduced loss of life, yet higher storm intensities and frequencies have caused huge increases in property damage.

Think of Greensburg, Kansas, southeast of Dodge City, with its 1600 residents. For tourists, the town features the world's largest hand-dug water well. Nearby stood the old water tower with the town's name inscribed before the tornado hit—here is small town, Midwest, USA.

On the evening of May 4, 2007, a frontal system moved through. As tornado warning sirens and National Oceanic and Atmospheric Administration (NOAA) weather radio signaled the alert, people went to their basements and storm shelters. Just before 10 P.M., an EF-5-intensity tornado roared in from the southwest. This was the first designated "5" since the Fujita Scale revision in February 2007, described in this chapter.

The monster was 2.7 km (1.7 mi) wide, and it attacked Greensburg. It shredded all that was familiar into a chaotic mess in less than 10 minutes. People emerged into the now-silent evening; lights were out as some called for help. Flashlights came on, as did headlights when an owner could find keys and a surviving car. Sunrise brought shock; all the tree-lined streets were barren, trees pruned and broken by the winds. Eleven people died that night (Figure GN 1).

FIGURE GN 1 Most of Greensburg, Kansas, was erased by an EF-5 tornado in 2007. A new water tower stands a year later where the old one fell. [Bobbé Christopherson.]

Heroism was all about as the National Guard mobilized and a federal disaster area was declared. The media arrived, and in a few days politicians began their tours. Residents appeared on TV, interviewed for their anecdotes. Disaster assistance programs required forms and processing, and weeks of delays began. In the void of factual information, rumors spread quickly.

In a couple of weeks, the outsiders left, and streets and lots were cleared of debris, piled into a hastily prepared dump. All that was familiar was in the pile north of town. The months rolled by with no media coverage, just the daily task of dealing with shattered reality. A year later, when we asked people about that night, they readily told their stories. How do people on disaster front lines physically and mentally deal with such changes in their lives?

We drive along the Bolivar Peninsula on the Gulf Coast of Texas, one year after the September 13, 2008, 2 A.M. landfall of Hurricane Ike. We pass 35 km (21 mi) of leveled coastal neighborhoods. Ike's winds were hurricane force for more than 177 km (110 mi) along the coast (Figure GN 52). Debris protrudes from the barrier island sand, power is still out in spots, and few trees are left standing. Near the western end of the island, toward the Galveston ferry dock, large piles of former homes and businesses stand above the sand. Several piles are burning, filling the air with foul smoke—and this is a year after the hurricane.

Bolivar, like Hatteras and many other barrier islands, uses septic sewage systems, which become disrupted by storm surge. In 2009, residents in Bolivar were wrestling with whether to attach to a sewer line for the first time. One developer is constructing small houses on 8.5-m (28-ft) stilts, perched in ominous preparation for the next hurricane.

We can easily expand this narrative to New Orleans years after Katrina, Rita, Gustav, and Cindy, and now the BP oil-spill disaster; or the floods in Missouri, North Dakota, Oklahoma City, parts of Texas, Milwaukee, Chicago, and elsewhere; or the Alabama, tornado in the chapter-opening photo; or the Joplin, Missouri, tornado disaster of May 2011. Again the question, How do people on the front lines cope with such disaster? Contemplate the human dimension as you work through this chapter. ■

FIGURE GN 2 Hurricane Ike swept away all the homes and the pavement in this neighborhood. Many kilometers of coastline were destroyed on Bolivar Peninsula, Texas. [Bobbé Christopherson.]

Water is critical to our daily lives and is an extraordinary compound in nature. It is the only common substance that naturally occurs in all three states of matter: liquid, solid, and vapor. Pure water is colorless, odorless, and tasteless. Known as "the universal solvent," water is able to dissolve many solid substances; yet, because it is a solvent, pure water rarely occurs in nature. Water weighs 1 g/cm^3 (gram per cubic centimeter), or 1 kg/L (kilogram per liter), or 62.3 lb/ft^3, or 8.337 lb/gal.

Because water changes from one state of matter to another (gas, liquid, and solid), water in the atmosphere is the primary driver of weather. As water changes phase, the heat energy absorbed or liberated helps power the general circulation of the atmosphere, which drives daily weather patterns.

Weather is the short-term, day-to-day condition of the atmosphere, contrasted with *climate*, which is the long-term average (over decades) of weather conditions and extremes in a region. Weather is, at the same time, both a "snapshot" of atmospheric conditions and a technical status report of the Earth–atmosphere heat-energy budget. Important elements that contribute to weather are temperature, air pressure, relative humidity, wind speed and direction, and seasonal factors such as insolation receipt related to daylength and Sun angle.

Meteorology is the scientific study of the atmosphere—*meteor* means "heavenly" or "of the atmosphere." Meteorologists study the atmosphere's physical characteristics and motions; related chemical, physical, and geologic processes; the complex linkages of atmospheric systems; and weather forecasting. Understanding atmospheric water—how it affects air masses, frontal systems, and violent weather—is an essential part of meteorology and weather prediction.

In this chapter: We examine the properties of water and the dynamics of atmospheric moisture and stability—the essentials of weather. Water's unique heat properties and existence in all three states in nature are critical to powering Earth's weather systems. We discuss humidity, saturation, and dew point—all related to water vapor. Condensation of water vapor and atmospheric conditions of stability and instability are key to cloud formation. We follow huge air masses across North America, observe powerful lifting mechanisms in the atmosphere, and examine migrating cyclonic systems with attendant cold and warm fronts. We conclude with a portrait of violent and dramatic weather so often in the news in recent years. The spatial implications of these weather phenomena and their relationship to human activities strongly link meteorology and weather forecasting to physical geography and this chapter.

Water's Unique Properties

Earth's distance from the Sun places it within a most remarkable temperate zone when compared with the locations of the other planets. This temperate location allows all three states of water—ice, liquid, and vapor—to occur naturally on Earth. Two atoms of hydrogen and one of oxygen, which readily bond, comprise each water molecule. The resulting molecule exhibits a unique stability, is a versatile solvent, and possesses extraordinary heat characteristics. As the most common compound on the surface of Earth, water exhibits uncommon properties.

The nature of the hydrogen–oxygen bond gives the hydrogen side of a water molecule a positive charge and the oxygen side a negative charge (see Figure 1, upper right). This *polarity* of water molecules explains why water "acts wet," dissolving many substances. Because of this solvent ability, pure water is rare in nature because something is usually dissolved in it.

Water molecules are attracted to each other because of their polarity; the positive, hydrogen, side of one water molecule is attracted to the negative, oxygen, side of another. Note this bonding pattern in the molecular illustrations in Figure 1b and c. The bonding between water molecules is *hydrogen bonding*. The effects of hydrogen bonding in water are observable in everyday life. Hydrogen bonding creates the *surface tension* and is the cause of capillarity, which you observe when you "dry" something with a paper towel. The towel draws water through its fibers because hydrogen bonds make each molecule pull on its neighbor. Capillary action is an important component of soil-moisture processes. Without hydrogen bonding to hold molecules together in water and ice, water would be a gas at normal surface temperatures.

Heat Properties

For water to change from one state to another (solid, liquid, or vapor), *heat energy must be added to it or released from it.* To cause a change of state, the amount of heat energy must be sufficient to affect the hydrogen bonds between molecules. This relation between water and heat energy is an important driving force in producing weather. In fact, the heat exchanged between physical states of water provides more than 30% of the energy that powers the general circulation of the atmosphere.

Figure 1 presents the three states of water and the terms describing a change from one state to another, a **phase change**. Along the bottom of the illustration, *melting* and *freezing* describe the familiar phase change between solid and liquid. At the right, the terms *condensation* and *evaporation* (or *vaporization* at boiling temperature) apply to the change between liquid and vapor. At the left, the term **sublimation** refers to the direct change of ice to water vapor or water vapor to ice—although when water vapor attaches directly to an ice crystal, it is referred to as *deposition*. The deposition of water vapor to ice may form *frost* on surfaces.

Ice, the Solid Phase As water cools, it behaves like most compounds and contracts in volume. However, it reaches its greatest density not as ice, but as water at 4°C (39°F). Below that temperature, water behaves differently from

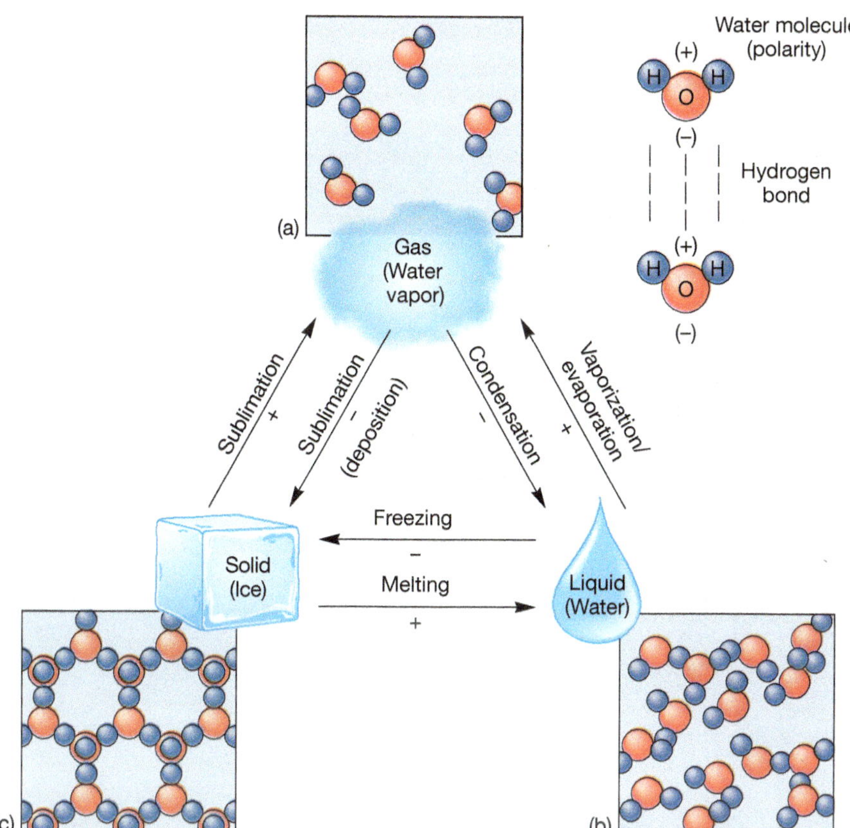

FIGURE 1 Water and water's phase changes.
The three physical states of water: (a) gas, or water vapor; (b) water; and (c) ice. Note the molecular arrangement in each state and the terms that describe the changes from one phase to another. The plus and minus symbols in the phase changes denote whether heat energy is absorbed (+) or liberated (released) (–).

Animation
Water Phase Changes

other compounds. It begins to expand as more hydrogen bonds form among the slower-moving molecules, creating the hexagonal (six-sided) structures shown in Figure 1c and Figure 2a. This six-sided preference applies to ice crystals of all shapes: plates, columns, needles, and dendrites (branching or treelike forms). Ice crystals demonstrate a unique interaction of chaos (all ice crystals are different) and the determinism of physical principles (all have a six-sided structure).

This expansion of water and ice that begins at 4°C continues to a temperature of –29°C (–20°F)—up to a 9% increase in volume is possible. This expansion is important in the weathering of rocks, highway and pavement damage, and burst water pipes. For more on ice crystals and snowflakes, see http://www.its.caltech.edu/~atomic/snowcrystals/ or http://emu.arsusda.gov/snowsite/default.html.

The expansion in volume that accompanies the freezing process results in a decrease in density (the same number of molecules occupies a larger space). Specifically, pure ice has 0.91 times the density of water, so it floats. Without this change in density, much of Earth's freshwater would be bound in masses of ice on the ocean floor.

In nature, this density varies slightly, given the age of the ice and air content. Therefore, icebergs float with slightly varying displacements that average about 1/7 (14%) of their mass exposed and about 6/7 (86%) submerged beneath the ocean's surface (Figure 2d). With underwater portions melting faster than those above water, icebergs are inherently unstable and will overturn. You see in Figure 2b the notch at the water line, which was previously underwater.

GEO REPORT 1 ***Breaking roads and pipes***

Road crews are busy in the summer repairing winter damage to streets and freeways in regions where winters are cold. Rainwater seeps into roadway cracks and then expands as it freezes, thus breaking up the pavement. Perhaps you have noticed that bridges suffer the greatest damage, where cold air can circulate beneath a bridge and produce more freeze–thaw cycles. The expansion of freezing water is powerful enough to crack plumbing or an automobile radiator or engine block. Wrapping water pipes with insulation to avoid damage is a common winter task in many places. Historically, this physical property of water was put to useful work in quarrying rock for building materials. Holes were drilled and filled with water before winter so that, when cold weather arrived, the water would freeze and expand, cracking the rock into manageable shapes.

FIGURE 2 The uniqueness of ice forms.
(a) Computer-enhanced photo reveals ice-crystal patterns, dictated by the internal structure between water molecules. (b) Iceberg arch in the Antarctic Sound near 63.5° S latitude. (c) Ice needles form in the freezing process of a meltwater stream. (d) A bergy bit (small iceberg) off the coast of Antarctica illustrates the density–buoyancy state of floating ice. [(a) Photo enhancement © Scott Camazine/Photo Researchers, Inc., after W. A. Bentley. (b), (c), and (d) Bobbé Christopherson.]

II CRITICAL THINKING 1

Iceberg analysis

Examine the iceberg photographs in Figure 2b and Figure 2d. These photos show iceberg formations in Antarctic waters. Determine what caused the thermal notch above the ocean surface around the iceberg. Why do you think the iceberg appears to be riding higher in the water as it melts? In a clear glass almost filled with water, place an ice cube. Then approximate the amount of ice above the water's surface compared to the amount below water. Pure ice is 0.91 the density of water, whereas ice actually contains air bubbles, so icebergs are about 0.86 the density of water. How do your measurements compare with this range of density?

Water, the Liquid Phase As a liquid, water assumes the shape of its container and is a noncompressible fluid. For ice to change to water, heat energy must increase the motion of the water molecules to break some of the hydrogen bonds. Despite the fact that no change occurs in sensible temperature between ice at 0°C (32°F) and water at 0°C, 80 calories* of heat energy must be absorbed for the phase change of 1 g of ice to melt to 1 g of water (Figure 3, upper left). Heat energy involved in the phase change is **latent heat** and is hidden within the structure of water. It becomes liberated whenever the phase reverses and a gram of water freezes. The *latent heat of freezing* and the *latent heat of melting* each involve 80 calories.

To raise the temperature of 1 g of water at 0°C (32°F) to boiling at 100°C (212°F), we must add 100 cal, gaining an increase of 1 C° (1.8 F°) for each calorie added. No phase change is involved in this temperature gain.

*Remember that a calorie is the amount of energy required to raise the temperature of 1 g of water (at 15°C) 1 degree Celsius and is equal to 4.184 joules.

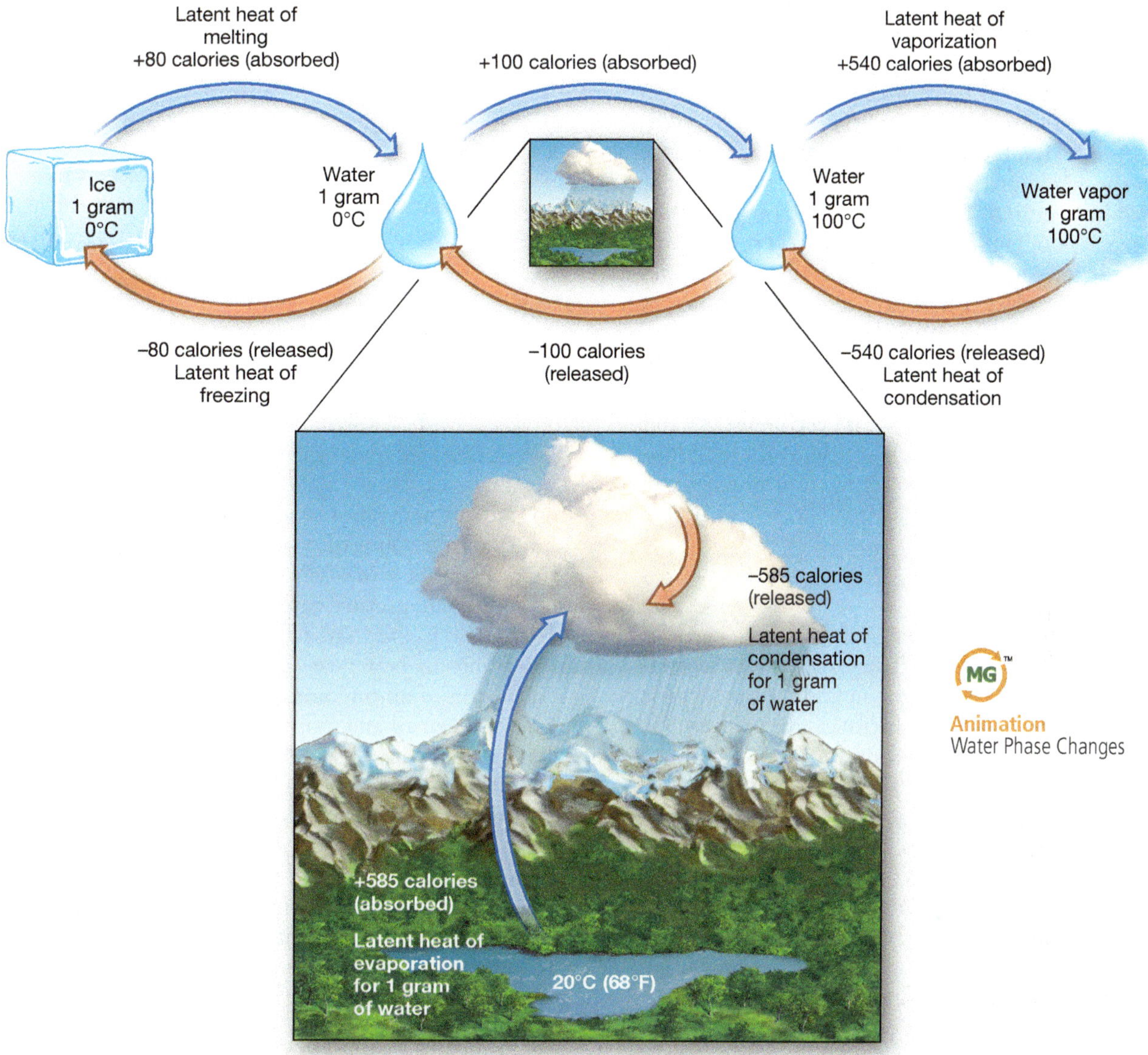

MG Animation Water Phase Changes

FIGURE 3 Water's heat-energy characteristics.
The phase changes of water absorb or release a lot of latent heat energy. To transform 1 g of ice at 0°C to 1 g of water vapor at 100°C requires 720 cal: 80 + 100 + 540. The landscape illustrates phase changes between water (lake at 20°C) and water vapor under typical conditions.

Water Vapor, the Gas Phase Water vapor is an invisible and compressible gas in which each molecule moves independently of the others (Figure 1a). The phase change from liquid to vapor at boiling temperature, under normal sea-level pressure, requires the addition of 540 cal for each gram, the **latent heat of vaporization** (Figure 3). When water vapor condenses to a liquid, each gram gives up its hidden 540 cal as the **latent heat of condensation.**

In summary, changing the phase of 1 g of ice at 0°C to water and then to water vapor at 100°C—from a solid, to a liquid, to a gas—*absorbs* 720 cal (80 cal + 100 cal + 540 cal). Reversing the process, or changing the phase of 1 g of water vapor at 100°C to water and then to ice at 0°C, *liberates* 720 cal into the surrounding environment. On the *MasteringGeography* web site is an excellent animation illustrating these concepts.

GEO REPORT 2 *Katrina had the power*

Meteorologists estimated that the moisture in Hurricane Katrina (2005) weighed more than 30 trillion tons at its maximum power and mass. With 585 cal released for every gram as the latent heat of condensation, a weather event such as a hurricane involves a staggering amount of energy. Do the quick math in English units (585 cal times 28 g to an ounce, 16 ounces to the pound, 2000 pounds to the ton, times 30 trillion tons).

Heat Properties of Water in Nature

In a lake or stream or in soil water, at 20°C (68°F), every gram of water that breaks away from the surface through evaporation must absorb from the environment approximately 585 cal as the **latent heat of evaporation** (see the natural scene in Figure 3). This is slightly more energy than would be required if the water was at a higher temperature such as boiling (540 cal). You can feel this absorption of latent heat as evaporative cooling on your skin when it is wet. This latent heat exchange is the dominant cooling process in Earth's energy budget.

The process reverses when air cools and water vapor condenses back into the liquid state, forming moisture droplets and thus liberating 585 cal for every gram of water as the *latent heat of condensation*. Because of these unique heat properties, water is a major contributor of energy to the atmosphere.

Humidity

Humidity refers to water vapor in the air. The capacity of air for water vapor is primarily a function of temperature—the temperatures of both the air and the water vapor, which are usually the same. Humidity can be expressed in several ways, discussed in this section.

We are all aware of humidity in the air, for its relationship to air temperature determines our sense of comfort. North Americans spend billions of dollars a year to adjust humidity, either with air-conditioning (extracting water vapor and cooling) or with air-humidifying (adding water vapor). To determine the energy available for powering weather, one has to know the water vapor content of air and relate this in a ratio to the air's *saturation equilibrium* at a given temperature.

Relative Humidity

After air temperature and barometric pressure, relative humidity is the most common piece of information given in local weather broadcasts. **Relative humidity** is a ratio (expressed as a percentage) of the amount of water vapor that is actually in the air compared to the maximum water vapor possible in the air at a given temperature.

Relative humidity varies because of water vapor or temperature changes in the air. The formula to calculate the relative humidity ratio and express it as a percentage places the actual moisture as the numerator and the water vapor possible in the air as the denominator:

$$\text{Relative humidity} = \frac{\text{Actual water vapor in the air}}{\text{Maximum water vapor possible in the air at that temperature}} \times 100$$

Warmer air increases the evaporation rate from water surfaces, whereas cooler air tends to increase the condensation rate of water vapor to water surfaces. Because there is a maximum amount of water vapor that can exist in a volume of air at a given temperature, the rates of evaporation and condensation can reach equilibrium at some point; the air is then saturated with humidity. Relative humidity tells us how near the air is to saturation and is an expression of an ongoing process of water molecules moving between air and moist surfaces.

In Figure 4 at 5 P.M., the evaporation rate exceeds condensation at the higher temperatures of this time of day and relative humidity is at 20%. Earlier in the day at 11 A.M., the evaporation rate still exceeds condensation, though not by as much, since daytime temperatures are not as high, so the same volume of water vapor now occupies 50% of the maximum possible capacity. At 5 A.M., in the cooler morning air, saturation equilibrium exists, and any further cooling or addition of water vapor produces net condensation. When the air is saturated with maximum water vapor for its temperature, the relative humidity percentage is 100%.

As stated, air is at **saturation**, at 100% relative humidity, when the rate of evaporation and the rate of condensation—the net transfer of water molecules—reach

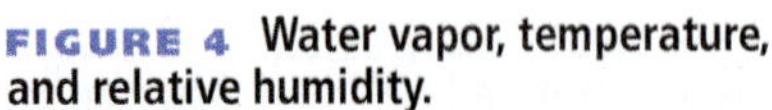
FIGURE 4 Water vapor, temperature, and relative humidity.
The maximum water vapor possible in warm air is greater (net evaporation) than that possible in cold air (net condensation), so relative humidity changes with temperature, even though in this example the actual water vapor present in the air stays the same during the day.

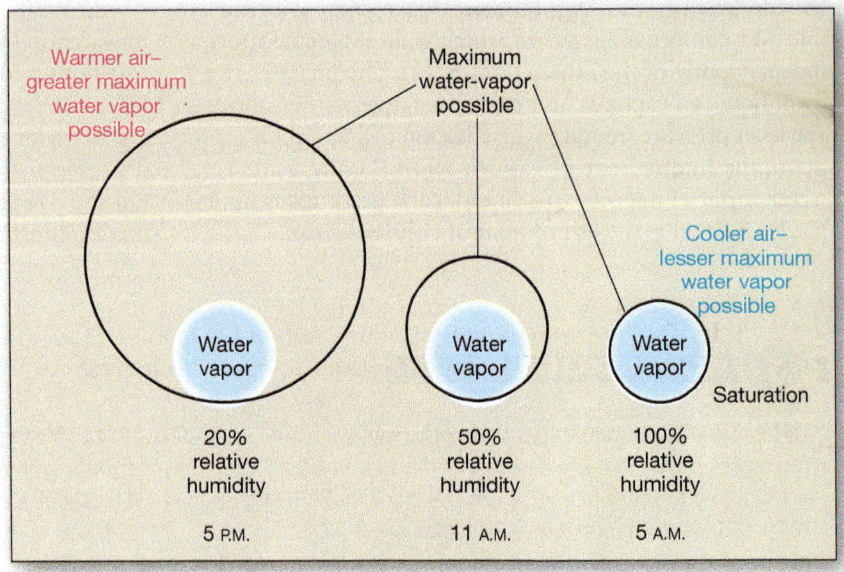

FIGURE 5 Dew-point temperature examples.
(a) The low temperature of the glass chills the surrounding air layer to the dew-point temperature and saturation. Thus, water vapor condenses out of the air and onto the glass as dew. (b) Cold air above the rain-soaked rocks is at the dew point and is saturated. Water evaporates from the rock into the air and condenses in a changing veil of clouds. [Author.]

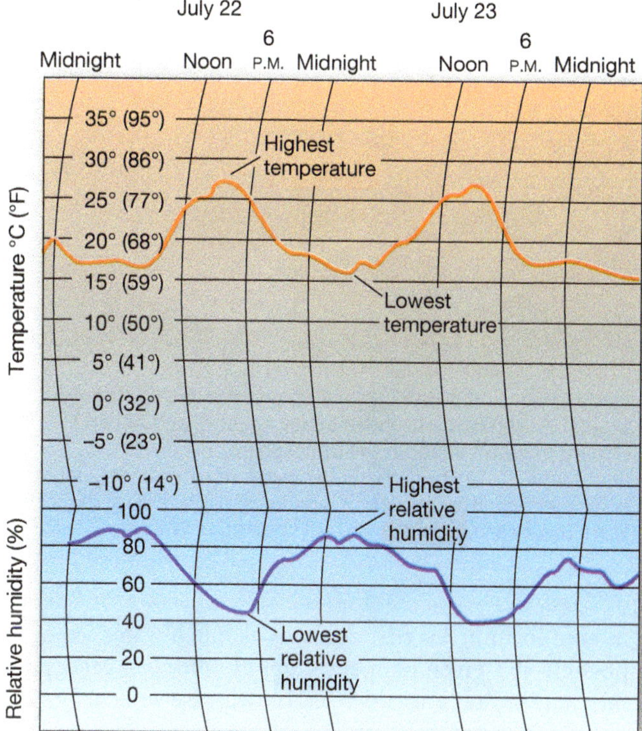

FIGURE 6 Daily relative humidity patterns.
Typical daily variations demonstrate temperature and relative humidity relations.

equilibrium. Saturation indicates that any further addition of water vapor or any decrease in temperature that reduces the evaporation rate results in active condensation (clouds, fog, or precipitation).

The temperature at which a given mass of air becomes saturated and net condensation begins to form water droplets is the **dew-point temperature**. *The air is saturated when the dew-point temperature and the air temperature are the same.* When temperatures are below freezing, the term *frost point* is sometimes used.

A cold drink in a glass provides a common example of these conditions (Figure 5a). The water droplets that form on the outside of the glass condense from the air because the air layer next to the glass is chilled to below its dew-point temperature and thus becomes saturated.

An inverse relation occurs during a typical day between air temperature and relative humidity—as temperature rises, relative humidity falls (Figure 6). Relative humidity is highest at dawn, when air temperature is lowest. If you park outdoors, you know about the wetness of the dew that condenses on your car or bicycle overnight. Relative humidity is lowest in the late afternoon, when higher temperatures increase the rate of evaporation. As shown in Figure 4, the actual water vapor present in the air may remain the same throughout the day, as relative humidity varies.

Satellites using infrared sensors now routinely sense water vapor in the lower atmosphere. Water vapor absorbs long wavelengths (infrared), making it possible to distinguish areas of relatively high water vapor from areas of low water vapor. Figure 7 includes a global image composite by satellite sensors of the "water-vapor channel." This ability is important to forecasting because it shows the moisture available to weather systems and therefore the available latent heat energy and precipitation potential.

Expressions of Humidity

Scientists express humidity and relative humidity in several ways, each with its own utility and application. Two measures involve vapor pressure and specific humidity.

Vapor Pressure As free water molecules evaporate from surfaces into the atmosphere, they become water vapor. Now part of the air, water-vapor molecules exert a portion of the air pressure. The share of air pressure that is made up of water-vapor molecules is **vapor pressure**, expressed in millibars (mb).

As explained earlier, *saturation* is reached when the movement of water molecules between surface and air is

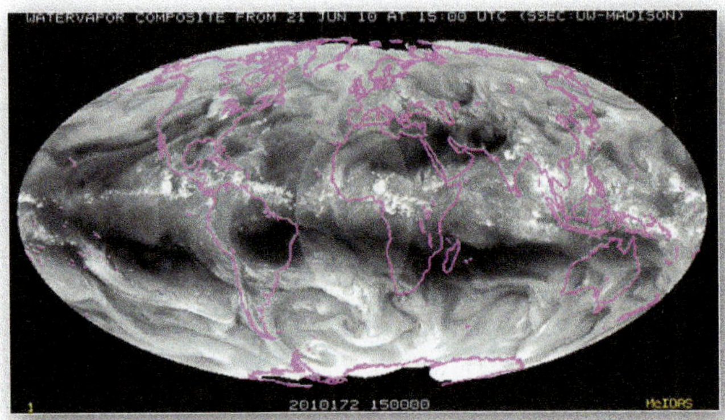

FIGURE 7 Composite infrared image from *GOES* (United States), *Meteosat* (European Space Agency), and *MTSAT* (Japan) of water vapor in the atmosphere.
In this June 21, 2010, image, higher water-vapor content is lighter and lower water-vapor content is darker. [Satellite data courtesy of Space Science and Engineering Center, University of Wisconsin, Madison.]

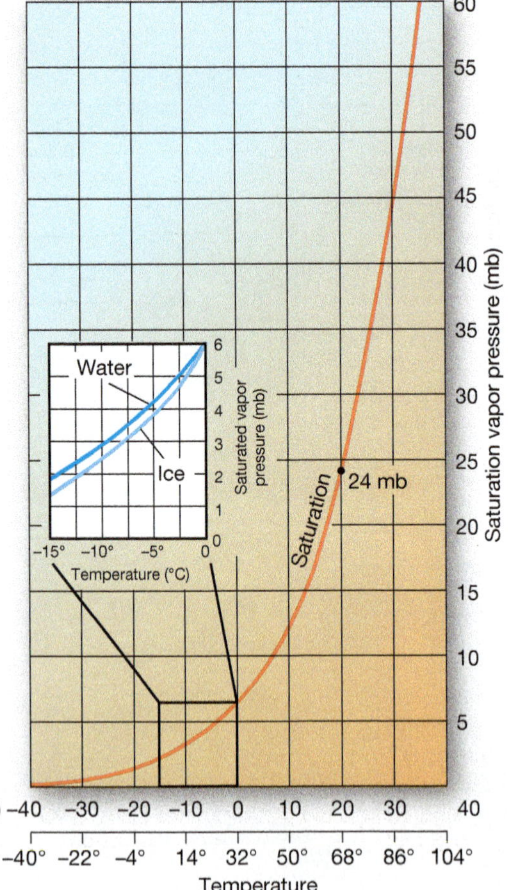

FIGURE 8 Saturation vapor pressure at various temperatures.
Saturation vapor pressure is the maximum possible water vapor, as measured by the pressure it exerts (mb). Inset compares saturation vapor pressures over water surfaces with those over surfaces at subfreezing temperatures. Note the 24-mb label for the text discussion.

in equilibrium. Air that contains as much water vapor as possible at a given temperature is at *saturation vapor pressure*. Any temperature increase or decrease will change the saturation vapor pressure.

Figure 8 graphs the saturation vapor pressure at various air temperatures. The graph illustrates that, for every temperature increase of 10 C° (18 F°), the saturation water vapor pressure in air nearly doubles. This relation explains why warm tropical air over the ocean can contain so much water vapor, thus providing latent heat to power tropical storms. It also explains why cold air is "dry" and why cold air toward the poles does not produce a lot of precipitation—the air contains too little water vapor, even though it is near the dew-point temperature.

As marked on the graph, air at 20°C (68°F) has a saturation vapor pressure of 24 mb; that is, the air is saturated if the water-vapor portion of the air pressure also is at 24 mb. Thus, if the water vapor actually present is exerting a vapor pressure of only 12 mb in 20°C air, the relative humidity is 50% (12 mb ÷ 24 mb = 0.50 × 100 = 50%). The inset in Figure 8 compares saturation vapor pressure over water and over ice surfaces at subfreezing temperatures. You can see that saturation vapor pressure is greater above a water surface than over an ice surface—that is, it takes more water-vapor molecules to saturate air above water than it does air above ice.

Specific Humidity A useful humidity measure is one that remains constant as temperature and pressure change. **Specific humidity** is the mass of water vapor (in grams) per mass of air (in kilograms) at any specified temperature. Because it is measured in mass, specific humidity is not affected by changes in temperature or pressure, such as when an air parcel rises to higher elevations. Specific humidity stays constant despite volume changes.*

*Another similar measure used in relative humidity that approximates specific humidity is the *mixing ratio*, that is, the ratio of the mass of water vapor (grams) to mass of dry air (kilograms), as in g/kg.

The maximum mass of water vapor possible in a kilogram of air at any specified temperature is the *maximum specific humidity*, plotted in Figure 9. Noted on the graph is that a kilogram of air can hold a maximum specific humidity of 47 g of water vapor at 40°C (104°F), 15 g at 20°C (68°F), and about 4 g at 0°C (32°F). Therefore, if a kilogram of air at 40°C has a specific humidity of 12 g, its relative humidity is 25.5% (12 g ÷ 47 g = 0.255 × 100 = 25.5%). Specific humidity is useful in describing the moisture content of large air masses that are interacting in a weather system and provides information necessary for weather forecasting.

Instruments for Measuring Humidity Various instruments measure relative humidity. The *hair hygrometer* uses the principle that human hair changes as much as 4% in length between 0% and 100% relative humidity. The instrument connects a standardized bundle of human hair through a mechanism to a gauge. As the hair absorbs or loses water in the air, it changes length, indicating relative humidity.

Another instrument used to measure relative humidity is a *sling psychrometer*, which consists of two thermometers

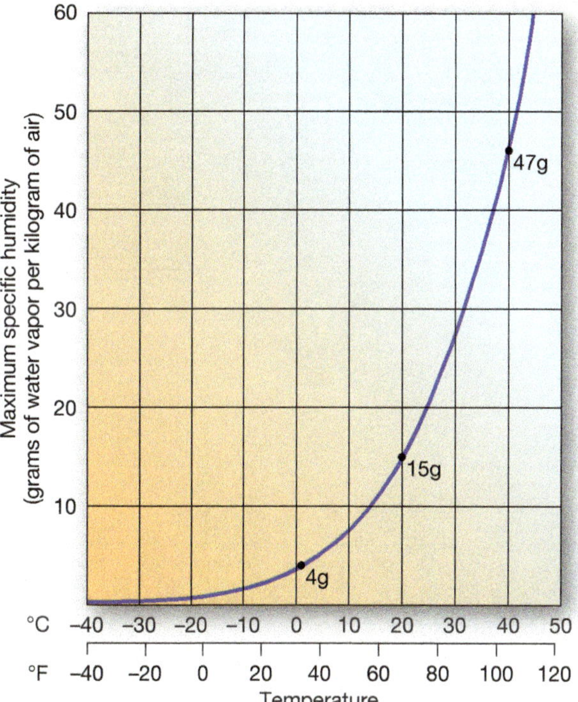

FIGURE 9 Maximum specific humidity at various temperatures.
Maximum specific humidity is the maximum possible water vapor in a mass of water vapor per unit mass of air (g/kg). Note the 47-g, 15-g, and 4-g labels for the text discussion.

mounted side by side on a holder. One is the *dry-bulb thermometer*; it simply records the ambient (surrounding) air temperature. The other thermometer is the *wet-bulb thermometer*; it is set lower in the holder, and its bulb is covered by a moistened cloth wick. The psychrometer is then spun, or "slung," by its handle or placed where a fan forces air over the wet-bulb wick.

The rate at which water evaporates from the wick depends on the relative saturation of the surrounding air. If the air is dry, water evaporates quickly; the air *absorbs specific heat as the latent heat of evaporation from the wet-bulb thermometer and its wick*, cooling the thermometer and causing its temperature to lower (the *wet-bulb depression*). On the other hand, in conditions of high humidity, little water evaporates from the wick.

CRITICAL THINKING 2

Using relative humidity and dew-point maps

Please refer to our discussion of relative humidity, air temperature, dew-point temperature, and saturation on the *Mastering-Geography* web site. View the dew-point temperature map in relation to the map of air temperatures. As you compare and contrast the maps, describe in general terms what relative humidity conditions you find in the Northwest. How about along the Gulf Coast? How does this contrast to the Southeast and to the Southwest? Remember the closer the air temperature is to the dew-point temperature, the closer the air is to saturation and the possibility of condensation.

Atmospheric Stability

Meteorologists use the term *parcel* to describe a body of air that has specific temperature and humidity characteristics. Think of an air parcel as a volume of air, perhaps 300 m (1000 ft) in diameter or more. The temperature of the volume of air determines the density of the air parcel. Warm air produces a lower density in a given volume of air; cold air produces a higher density.

Two opposing forces work on a parcel of air: an upward *buoyant force* and a downward *gravitational force*. A parcel of lower density than the surrounding air rises (is more buoyant); a rising parcel expands as external pressure decreases. In contrast, a parcel of higher density descends (is less buoyant); a falling parcel compresses as external pressure increases. Figure 10 illustrates these relationships.

An indication of weather conditions is the relative stability of air parcels in the atmosphere. **Stability** refers to the tendency of an air parcel, with its water-vapor cargo, either to remain in place or to change vertical position by ascending (rising) or descending (falling). An air parcel is *stable* if it resists displacement upward or, when disturbed, tends to return to its starting place. An air parcel is *unstable* if it continues to rise until it reaches an altitude where the surrounding air has a density and temperature similar to its own.

To visualize this, imagine a hot-air balloon launch. The air-filled balloon sits on the ground with the same air temperature inside as in the surrounding environment, like a stable air parcel. As the burner ignites, the balloon fills with hot (less-dense) air and rises buoyantly (Figure 11), like an unstable parcel of air. In the photo, why do you think these launches are taking place in the early morning? The concepts of stable and unstable air lead us to the specific temperature characteristics that produce these conditions.

Adiabatic Processes

The **normal lapse rate** is the average decrease in temperature with increasing altitude, a value of 6.4 C°/1000 m (3.5 F°/1000 ft). This rate of

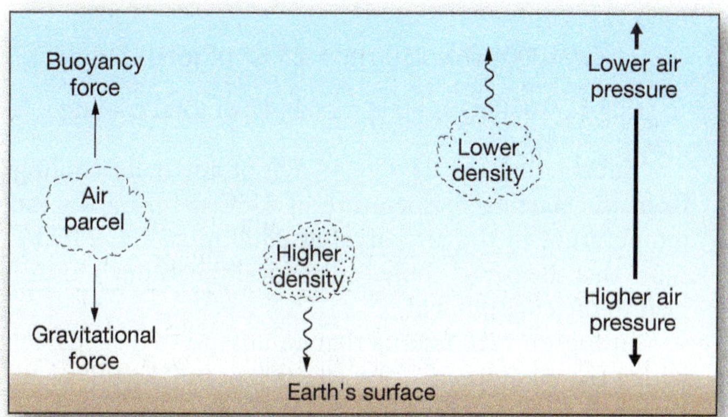

FIGURE 10 The forces acting on an air parcel.
Buoyancy and gravitational forces work on an air parcel. Different densities produce rising or falling parcels in response to imbalance in these forces.

Animation
Atmospheric Stability

FIGURE 11 Principles of air stability and balloon launches. Hot-air balloons being launched in southern Utah illustrate the principles of stability. As the temperature inside a balloon increases, the air in the balloon becomes less dense than the surrounding air, and the buoyancy force causes the balloon to rise, acting like a warm-air parcel. [Steven K. Huhtala.]

temperature change is for still, calm air, and it can vary greatly under different weather conditions. Consequently, the **environmental lapse rate** is the actual lapse rate at a particular place and time. It can vary by several degrees per thousand meters.

Adiabatic describes the warming and cooling rates for a parcel of expanding or compressing air. *An ascending parcel of air tends to cool by expansion*, responding to the reduced pressure at higher altitudes. In contrast, *descending air tends to heat by compression*. *Diabatic* means occurring with an exchange of heat; *adiabatic* means occurring without a loss or gain of heat—in this case, without any heat exchange between the surrounding environment and the vertically moving parcel of air. Adiabatic temperatures are measured with one of two specific rates, depending on moisture conditions in the parcel: dry adiabatic rate (DAR) and moist adiabatic rate (MAR).

Dry Adiabatic Rate The **dry adiabatic rate (DAR)** is the rate at which "dry" air cools by expansion (if ascending) or heats by compression (if descending). "Dry" refers to air that is less than saturated (relative humidity is less than 100%). The average DAR is 10 C°/1000 m (5.5 F°/1000 ft).

The rising parcel at the left in Figure 12a illustrates the principle. To see how a specific sample of dry air behaves, consider an unsaturated parcel of air at the surface with a temperature of 27°C (81°F). It rises, expands, and cools adiabatically at the DAR as it rises to 2500 m (approximately 8000 ft). Calculate the temperature change in the parcel, using the dry adiabatic rate:

$$(10\ \text{C°}/1000\ \text{m}) \times 2500\ \text{m} = 25\ \text{C° of total cooling}$$

$$(5.5\ \text{F°}/1000\ \text{ft}) \times 8000\ \text{ft} = 44\ \text{F° of total cooling}$$

Subtracting the 25 C° (44 F°) of adiabatic cooling from the starting temperature of 27°C (81°F) gives the temperature in the air parcel at 2500 m as 2°C (36°F). Note that the parcel cooled adiabatically, without a loss of heat to the environment.

In Figure 12b, assume that an unsaturated air parcel with a temperature of –20°C at 3000 m (–4°F at 9800 ft) descends to the surface, heating adiabatically. Using the dry adiabatic lapse rate, we determine the temperature of the air parcel when it arrives at the surface:

$$(10\ \text{C°}/1000\ \text{m}) \times 3000\ \text{m} = 30\ \text{C° of total warming}$$

$$(5.5\ \text{F°}/1000\ \text{ft}) \times 9800\ \text{ft} = 54\ \text{F° of total warming}$$

Adding the 30 C° (54 F°) of adiabatic warming to the starting temperature of −20°C (−4°F) gives the temperature in the air parcel at the surface as 10°C (50°F).

Moist Adiabatic Rate The **moist adiabatic rate (MAR)** is the rate at which an ascending air parcel that is moist, or saturated, cools by expansion. The average MAR is 6 C°/1000 m (3.3 F°/1000 ft). This is roughly 4 C° (2 F°) less than the dry adiabatic rate. From this average, the MAR varies with moisture content and temperature and can range from 4 C° to 10 C° per 1000 m (2 F° to 5.5 F° per 1000 ft).

The cause of this variability, and the reason that the MAR is lower than the DAR, is the latent heat of condensation. As water vapor condenses in the saturated air, latent heat is liberated, becoming sensible heat, thus decreasing the adiabatic rate. The release of latent heat may vary with temperature and water-vapor content. The MAR is much lower than the DAR in warm air, whereas the two rates are more similar in cold air.

Stable and Unstable Atmospheric Conditions

Now we bring this discussion together to determine atmospheric stability. The relation among the DAR, the MAR, and the environmental lapse rate at a given time and place determines the stability of the atmosphere over an area. You see the range of possible stability relationships in Figure 13—from unstable to stable.

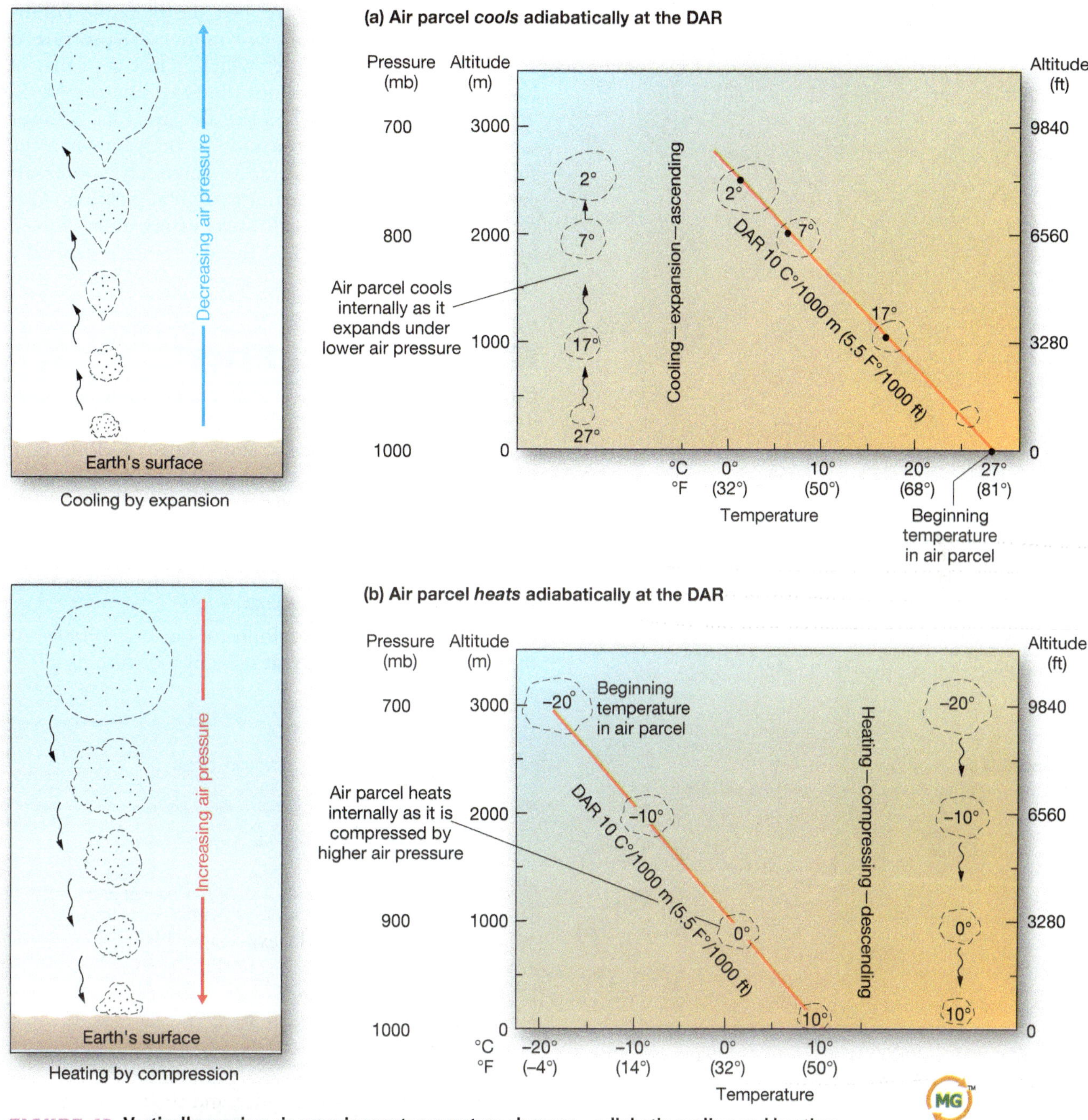

FIGURE 12 Vertically moving air experiences temperature changes—adiabatic cooling and heating. (a) A rising air parcel that is less than saturated cools adiabatically at the dry adiabatic rate (DAR). (b) A descending air parcel that is less than saturated heats adiabatically by compression at the DAR.

In Figure 14, we see temperature relationships in the atmosphere that produce two different conditions: unstable and stable. For the sake of illustration, both conditions begin with an air parcel at the surface at 25°C (77°F). In each example, compare the temperatures of the air parcel and the surrounding environment. Assume that a lifting mechanism is present—such as surface heating, a mountain range, or weather fronts—to get the parcel started (we examine lifting mechanisms later in this chapter).

Given unstable conditions in Figure 14a, the air parcel continues to rise through the atmosphere because it is warmer (less dense and more buoyant) than the surrounding environment. Note the air surrounding the lifting parcel is cooler by an environmental lapse rate of 12 C°/1000 m (6.6 F°/1000 ft). By 1000 m (about 3300 ft), the rising air parcel has adiabatically cooled by expansion at the DAR from 25° to 15°C, while the surrounding air has cooled from 25°C at the surface to 13°C. By comparing the temperatures in the air parcel and the surrounding environment, you see that the temperature in the parcel is 2 C° (3.6 F°) warmer than the surrounding air at 1000 m. *Unstable* describes this condition because the less-dense air parcel will continue to lift. As it lifts, cools, and becomes saturated, clouds may form.

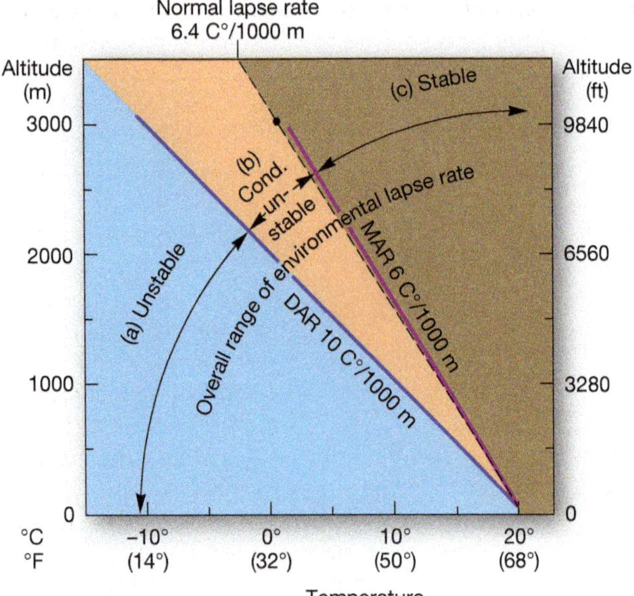

FIGURE 13 Temperature relationships and atmospheric stability.
The relationship among the dry adiabatic rate, moist adiabatic rate, and environmental lapse rate (ELR) produces three atmospheric conditions: (a) unstable (ELR exceeds the DAR), (b) conditionally unstable (ELR is between the DAR and MAR), and (c) stable (ELR is less than the MAR).

The example in Figure 14b shows stable conditions resulting when the environmental lapse rate is 5 C°/1000 m (3 F°/1000 ft), which is less than that in Figure 14a and less than both the DAR and the MAR. This condition occurs when the air parcel has a lower temperature (is more dense and less buoyant) than the surrounding environment. The relatively cooler air parcel tends to settle back to its original position—it is *stable*. The denser air parcel resists lifting unless forced by updrafts or a barrier, and the sky remains generally cloud-free.

Clouds and Fog

Clouds and fog are the most visible expressions of stability in the atmosphere. Clouds are fundamental indicators of stability, moisture content, and weather. A **cloud** is an aggregation, or grouping, of moisture droplets and ice crystals suspended in air that is great enough in volume and density to be visible. Fog is simply a cloud in contact with the ground. Cloud types are too numerous to fully describe here, so we present the most common examples in a simple classification scheme.

Clouds may contain raindrops, but not initially. At the outset, clouds are a great mass of moisture droplets,

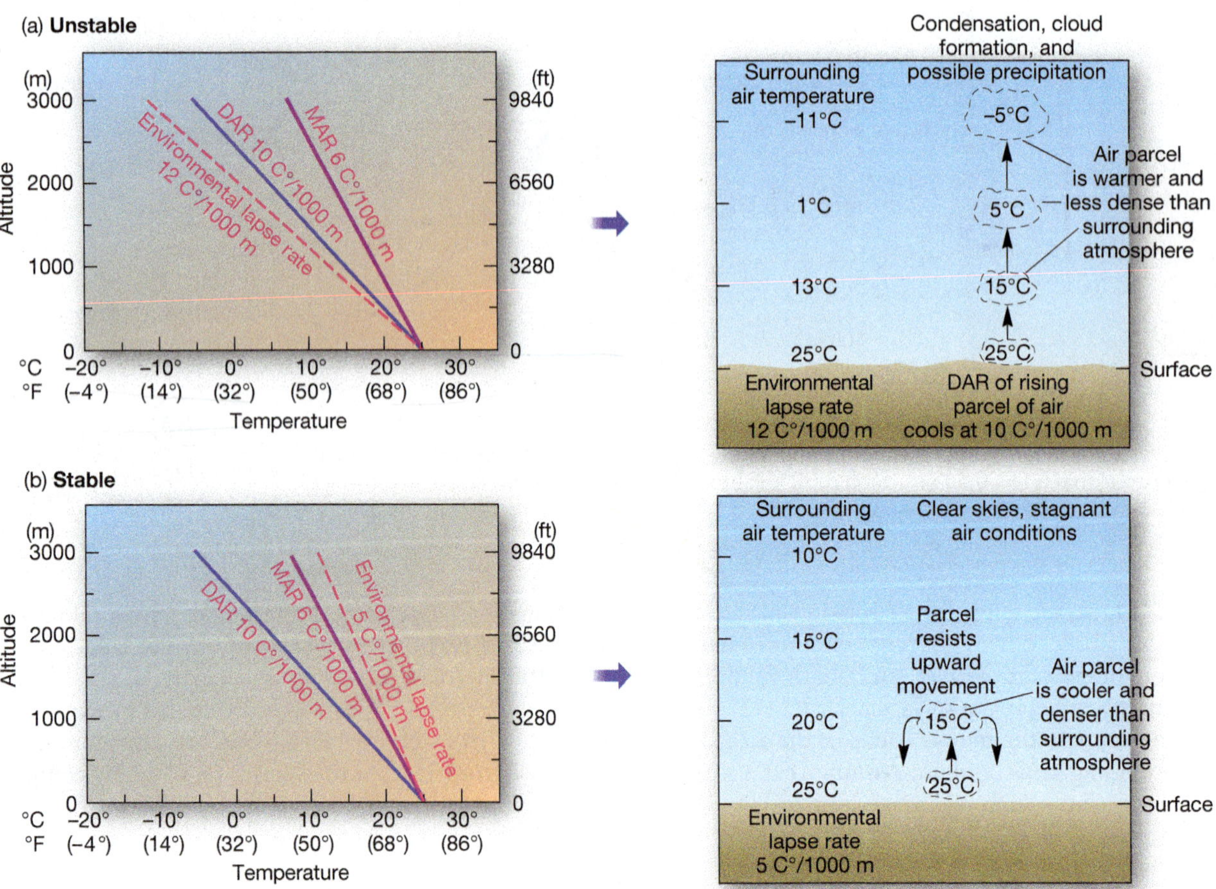

FIGURE 14 Unstable and stable conditions.
Specific examples of (a) unstable and (b) stable conditions in the lower atmosphere. Note the environmental lapse rate in each graph and the conditions in the air parcel on the right side of each diagram.

each invisible without magnification. A **moisture droplet** is approximately 20 μm (micrometers) in diameter (0.002 cm, or 0.0008 in.). It takes a million or more such droplets to form an average raindrop.

As an air parcel rises, it may cool to the dew-point temperature and 100% relative humidity. More lifting of the air parcel cools it further, producing condensation of water vapor into water. Water does not just condense among the air molecules. Condensation requires **condensation nuclei**, microscopic particles that always are present in the atmosphere.

Continental air masses average 10 billion cloud-condensation nuclei per cubic meter. Ordinary dust, soot, and ash from volcanoes and forest fires and particles from burned fuel, such as sulfate aerosols, typically provide these nuclei. The air over cities contains great concentrations of such nuclei. In maritime air masses, nuclei average 1 billion per cubic meter, including sea salts derived from ocean sprays. Given the presence of saturated air, the availability of condensation nuclei, and the presence of cooling (lifting) mechanisms in the atmosphere, condensation occurs. Clouds are the result of these processes.

Cloud Types and Identification

In 1803, English biologist and amateur meteorologist Luke Howard, in his article "On the Modification of Clouds," established a classification system for clouds and coined Latin names for them that we still use. *Altitude* and *shape* are key classification factors. Clouds occur in three basic forms—flat, puffy, and wispy—and in four primary altitude classes and ten basic cloud types. Horizontally developed clouds—flat and layered—are *stratiform* clouds. Vertically developed clouds—puffy and globular—are *cumuliform* clouds. Wispy clouds usually are quite high in altitude and are made of ice crystals; these are *cirroform* clouds.

These three basic forms occur in four altitudinal classes: low, middle, high, and those vertically developed through the troposphere. Figure 15 illustrates

FIGURE 15 Principal cloud types.
Principal cloud types, classified by form (cirroform, stratiform, and cumuliform) and altitude (low, middle, high, and vertically developed across altitude): (a) altocumulus (aerial), (b) altostratus, (c) cirrus, (d) cirrostratus, (e) nimbostratus, (f) stratus, (g) cumulus, and (h) cumulonimbus. [(a), (b), (c), (g), and (h) Bobbé Christopherson. (d), (e), and (f) author.]

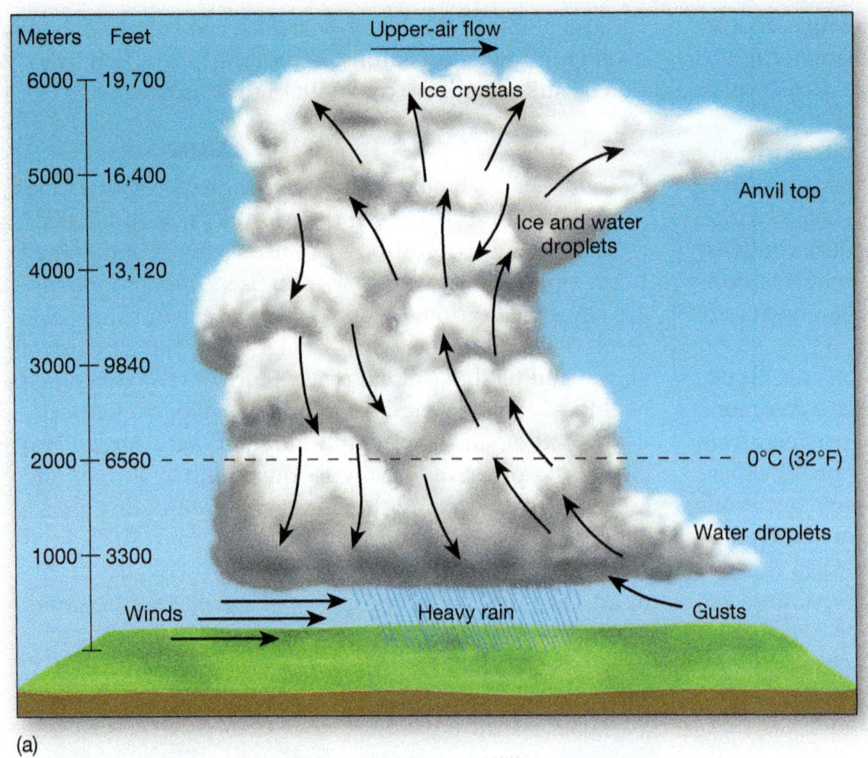

(a)

(b)

FIGURE 16 Cumulonimbus thunderhead.
Structure and form of a cumulonimbus cloud. Violent updrafts and downdrafts mark the circulation within the cloud. Blustery wind gusts occur along the ground. (b) Space Shuttle astronauts capture a dramatic cumulonimbus thunderhead as it moves over Galveston Bay, Texas. [NASA.]

the general appearance of each type and includes representative photographs.

Low clouds, ranging from the surface up to 2000 m (6500 ft) in the middle latitudes, are simply *stratus* or *cumulus* (Latin for "layer" and "heap," respectively). **Stratus** clouds appear dull, gray, and featureless. When they yield precipitation, they become **nimbostratus** (*nimbo-* denotes "stormy" or "rainy"), and their showers typically fall as drizzling rain (Figure 15e).

Cumulus clouds appear bright and puffy, like cotton balls. When they do not cover the sky, they float by in infinitely varied shapes. Vertically developed cumulus clouds extend beyond low altitudes into middle and high altitudes (Figure 15g).

Sometimes near the end of the day, **stratocumulus** may fill the sky in patches of lumpy, grayish, low-level clouds. Near sunset, these spreading puffy stratiform remnants may catch and filter the Sun's rays, sometimes indicating clearing weather.

The prefix *alto-* (meaning "high") denotes middle-level clouds. They are made of water droplets and, when cold enough, can be mixed with ice crystals. **Altocumulus** clouds, in particular, represent a broad category that occurs in many different styles: patchy rows, wave patterns, a "mackerel sky," and lens-shaped (lenticular) clouds.

Ice crystals in thin concentrations compose clouds occurring above 6000 m (20,000 ft). These wispy filaments, usually white except when colored by sunrise or sunset, are **cirrus** clouds (Latin for "curl of hair"), sometimes dubbed mares' tails. Cirrus clouds look as though an artist took a brush and added delicate feathery strokes high in the sky. Cirrus clouds can indicate an oncoming storm, especially if they thicken and lower in elevation. The prefix *cirro-*, as in *cirrostratus* and *cirrocumulus*, indicates other high clouds that form a thin veil or puffy appearance, respectively.

A cumulus cloud can develop into a towering giant called **cumulonimbus** (again, *-nimbus* in Latin denotes "rain storm" or "thundercloud"; Figure 16). Such clouds are called thunderheads because of their shape and associated lightning and thunder. Note the surface wind gusts, updrafts and downdrafts, heavy rain, and ice crystals at the

GEO REPORT 3 Lenticular clouds signal mountain weather

Along the mountains of the world, lenticular clouds provide spectacular beauty and photo opportunities. Yet these altostratus clouds may warn of high-speed winds at altitude, sometimes signaling the onset of severe weather. Lenticular, or lens-shaped, clouds form on the lee side of mountain ranges, where winds passing over the terrain develop a wave pattern. These clouds often appear stationary, but they are not. The flow of moist air continuously resupplies the cloud on the windward side as air evaporates from the cloud on the leeward side.

top of the rising cloud column. High-altitude winds may then shear the top of the cloud into the characteristic anvil shape of the mature thunderhead.

Fog

By international definition, **fog** is a cloud layer on the ground, with visibility restricted to less than 1 km (3300 ft). The presence of fog tells us that the air temperature and the dew-point temperature at ground level are nearly identical, indicating saturated conditions. A temperature-inversion layer generally caps a fog layer (warmer temperatures above and cooler temperatures below the inversion altitude), with as much as 22 C° (40 F°) of difference in air temperature between the cool ground under the fog and the warmer, sunny skies above.

Advection Fog When surface air in one place *migrates* to another place where conditions are right for saturation, an **advection fog** forms. For example, when warm, moist air overlays cooler ocean currents, lake surfaces, or snow masses, the layer of migrating air directly above the surface becomes chilled to the dew point, and fog develops. Off all subtropical west coasts in the world, summer fog forms in the manner just described (Figure 17).

Another type of advection fog forms when cold air lies over the warm water of a lake, an ocean surface, or even a swimming pool. This wispy **evaporation fog**, or *steam fog*, may form as water molecules evaporate from the water surface into the cold overlying air, effectively humidifying the air to saturation followed by condensation to form fog (Figure 18). When evaporation fog happens at sea, it is a shipping hazard called *sea smoke*.

FIGURE 18 Evaporation fog.
Evaporation fog, or sea smoke, highlights dawn on a cold morning at Donner Lake, California. Later that morning as air temperatures rose, what do you think happened to the evaporation fog? [Bobbé Christopherson.]

FIGURE 17 Advection fog.
San Francisco's Golden Gate Bridge shrouded by an invading advection fog characteristic of summer conditions along a western coast. [Author.]

Advection fog also forms when moist air flows to higher elevations along a hill or mountain. This upslope lifting leads to adiabatic cooling by expansion as the air rises. The resulting **upslope fog** forms a stratus cloud at the condensation level of saturation. Along the Appalachians and the eastern slopes of the Rockies, such fog is common in winter and spring. Another advection fog associated with topography is **valley fog**. Because cool air is denser than warm air, it settles in low-lying areas, producing a fog in the chilled, saturated layer near the ground in the valley (Figure 19).

Radiation Fog When radiative cooling of a surface chills the air layer directly above that surface to the dew-point temperature, creating saturated conditions, a **radiation fog**

FIGURE 19 Valley fog.
Cold air settles in the valleys of the Appalachian Mountains, chilling the air to the dew point and forming a valley fog. [Author.]

FIGURE 20 Winter radiation fog.
Radiation fog in the southern Great Valley of California. Note the snow-capped peaks of the Sierra Nevada to the east. This fog is locally known as a ***tule fog*** (pronounced "toolee") because of its association with the tule (bulrush) plants that line the low-elevation islands and marshes of the Sacramento River and San Joaquin River delta regions. [*Terra* MODIS image, GSFC/NASA.]

forms. This fog occurs over moist ground, especially on clear nights; it does not occur over water because water does not cool appreciably overnight. Slight movements of air deliver even more moisture to the cooled area for more fog formation of greater depth (Figure 20).

II CRITICAL THINKING 3

Identify two kinds of fog

In Figure 1.1, can you tell which two kinds of fog are pictured? These questions may help: How does the temperature of the river water compare to that of the overlying air, especially beyond the bend in the river? Could the temperature of the moist farmlands have changed overnight, and if so, how? Might that contribute to fog formation? Can you see any evidence of air movement, such as a light breeze? How might this affect the presence of fog?

FIGURE 1.1 Two kinds of fog. [Bobbé Christopherson.]

Air Masses

Each area of Earth's surface imparts its temperature and moisture characteristics to overlying air. The effect of the surface on the air creates regional air masses with a homogenous mix of temperature, humidity, and stability. These masses of air interact to produce weather patterns. Such a distinctive body of air is an **air mass**, and it initially reflects the characteristics of its *source region* and sometimes extends through the lower half of the troposphere. For example, weather forecasters speak of a "cold Canadian air mass" and "moist tropical air mass."

We classify air masses generally according to the moisture and temperature characteristics of their source regions:

- *Moisture*—designated **m** for maritime (wet) and **c** for continental (dry).
- *Temperature* (latitude factor)—designated **A** for arctic, **P** for polar, **T** for tropical, **E** for equatorial, and **AA** for antarctic.

The principle air masses that affect North America in winter and summer are mapped in Figure 21.

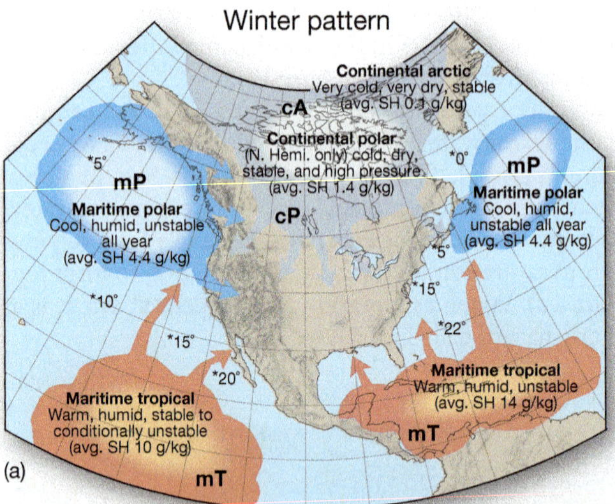

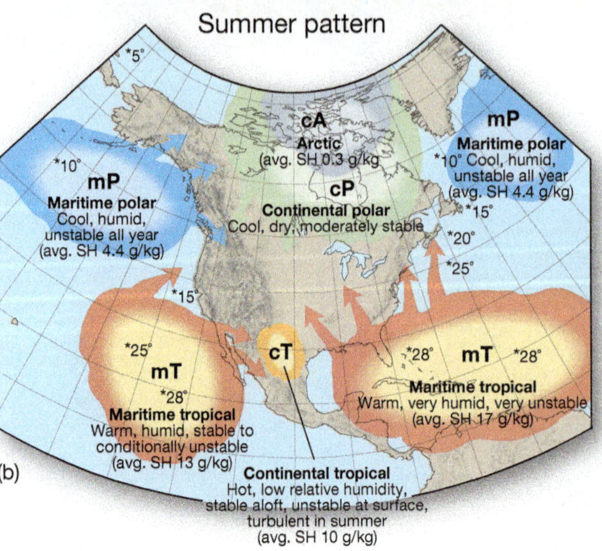

FIGURE 21 Principal air masses.
Air masses and their source regions influence North America during (a) winter and (b) summer. (*Sea-surface temperature in °C; SH = specific humidity.)

Continental polar (cP) air masses form only in the Northern Hemisphere and are most developed in winter and cold-weather conditions. An area covered by cP air in winter experiences cold, stable air; clear skies; high pressure; and anticyclonic wind flow. The Southern Hemisphere lacks the necessary continental landmasses at high latitudes to create such a cP air mass.

Maritime polar (mP) air masses in the Northern Hemisphere exist over the northern oceans. Within them, cool, moist, unstable conditions prevail throughout the year. The Aleutian and Icelandic subpolar low-pressure cells reside within these mP air masses, especially in their well-developed winter pattern.

Two *maritime tropical* (mT) air masses—the mT Gulf/Atlantic and the mT Pacific—influence North America. The humidity experienced in the East and Midwest is created by the mT Gulf/Atlantic air mass, which is particularly unstable and active from late spring to early fall. In contrast, the mT Pacific air mass is stable to conditionally unstable and generally lower in moisture content and available energy. As a result, the western United States, influenced by this weaker Pacific air mass, receives lower average precipitation than the rest of the country. Please review subtropical high-pressure cells.

Air Mass Modification

As air masses migrate from source regions, their temperature and moisture characteristics modify and slowly take on the characteristics of the land over which they pass. For example, an mT Gulf/Atlantic air mass may carry humidity to Chicago and on to Winnipeg, but may gradually lose its initial characteristics of high humidity and warmth with each day's passage northward.

Similarly, below-freezing temperatures occasionally reach into southern Texas and Florida, brought by an invading winter cP air mass from the north. However, that air mass warms from the −50°C (−58°F) of its winter source region in central Canada, especially after it leaves areas covered by snow.

Modification of cP air as it moves south and east produces snowbelts that lie to the east of each of the Great Lakes. As below-freezing cP air passes over the warmer Great Lakes, it absorbs heat energy and moisture from the lake surfaces and becomes *humidified*. This enhancement produces heavy lake-effect snowfall downwind into Ontario, Québec, Michigan, Pennsylvania, and New York—with some areas receiving annual average snowfalls in excess of 250 cm (100 in.) (Figure 22).

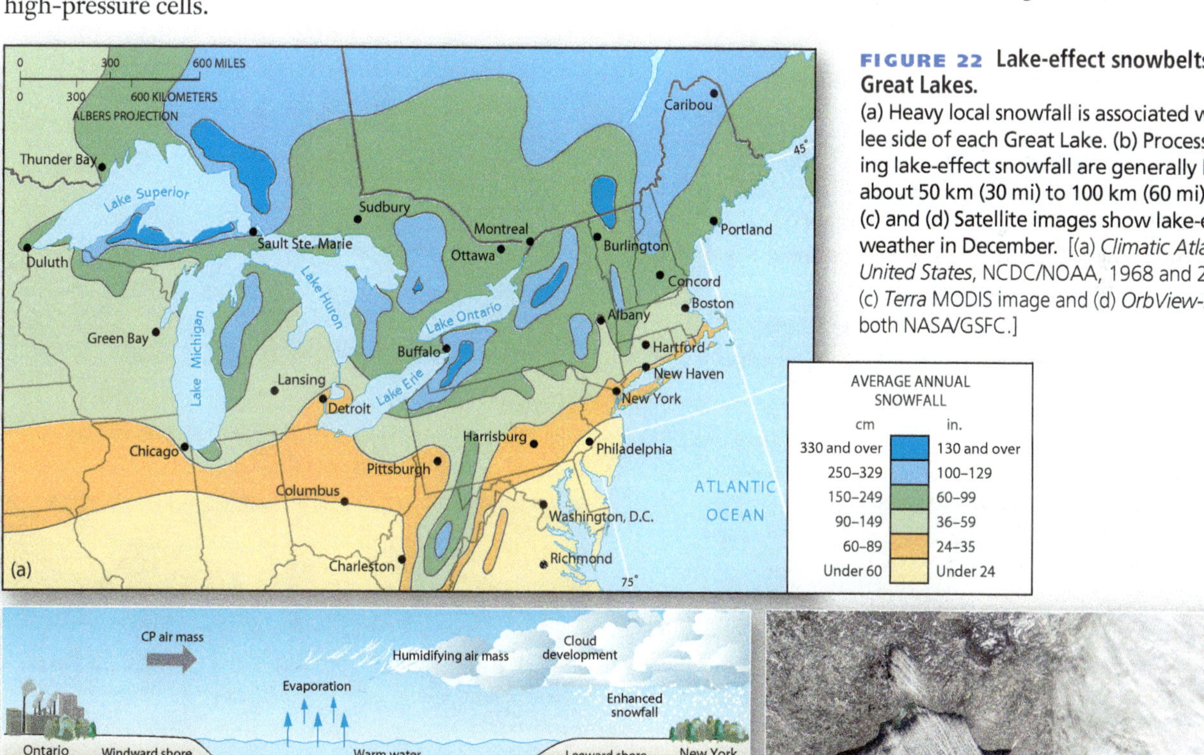

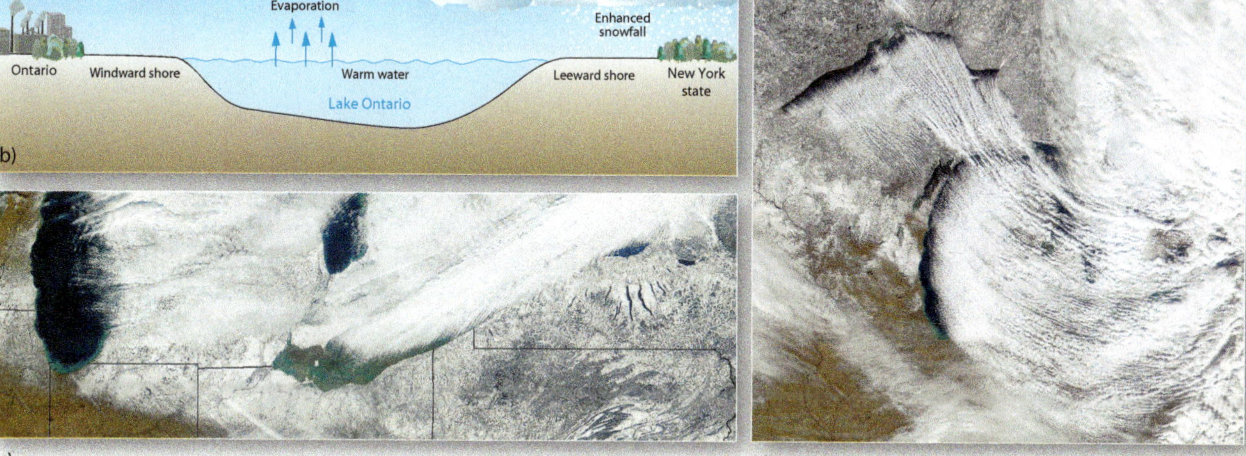

FIGURE 22 Lake-effect snowbelts of the Great Lakes.
(a) Heavy local snowfall is associated with the lee side of each Great Lake. (b) Processes causing lake-effect snowfall are generally limited to about 50 km (30 mi) to 100 km (60 mi) inland. (c) and (d) Satellite images show lake-effect weather in December. [(a) *Climatic Atlas of the United States*, NCDC/NOAA, 1968 and 2000, p. 53. (c) *Terra* MODIS image and (d) *OrbView-2* image; both NASA/GSFC.]

Snowfall produced from the lake effect depends on the passage of cold air over warmer waters. When lakes freeze over, usually in January, this turns off the lake effect by effectively shutting off the moisture supply and drying out the air. If air and lake temperatures continue to rise, lakes may freeze over later in the season, or not at all. Thus, lake-effect snows may increase with climate change.

Atmospheric Lifting Mechanisms

Lifting air masses cool adiabatically (by expansion) to reach the dew-point temperature. Moisture in the saturated air then can condense and form clouds, and perhaps precipitation. Four principal lifting mechanisms operate in the atmosphere:

- Convergent lifting—air flows toward an area of low pressure
- Convectional lifting—air is stimulated by local surface heating
- Orographic lifting—air is forced over a barrier such as a mountain range
- Frontal lifting—air is displaced upward along the leading edges of contrasting air masses

Descriptions of all four mechanisms follow and are included in Figure 23.

Convergent Lifting

Air flowing from different directions into the same low-pressure area is converging, displacing air upward in **convergent lifting**. All along the equatorial region, the southeast and northeast trade winds converge, forming the intertropical convergence zone (ITCZ) and areas of

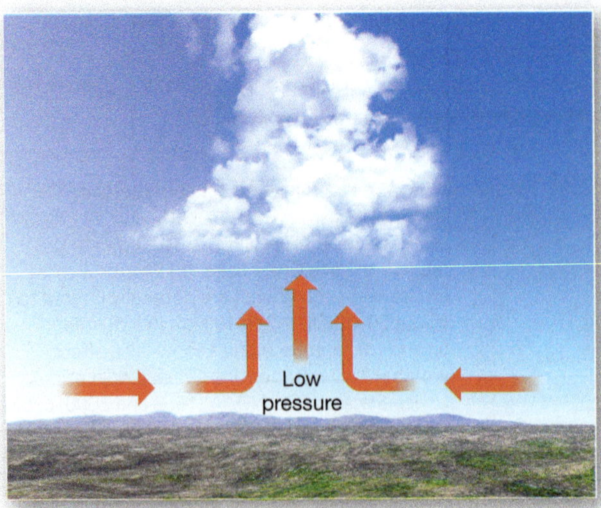

(a) Convergent lifting

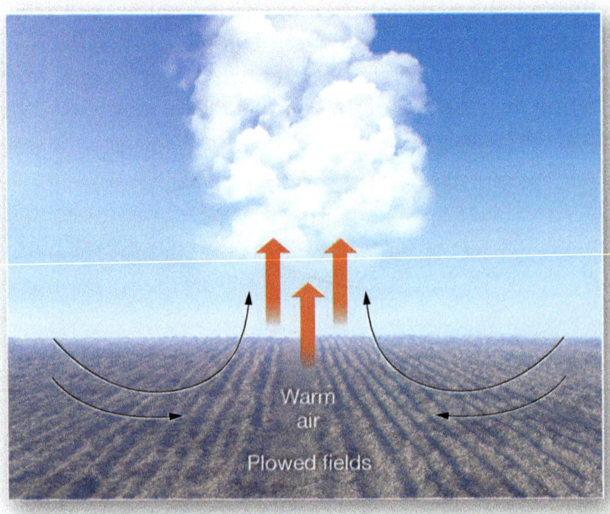

(b) Convectional lifting

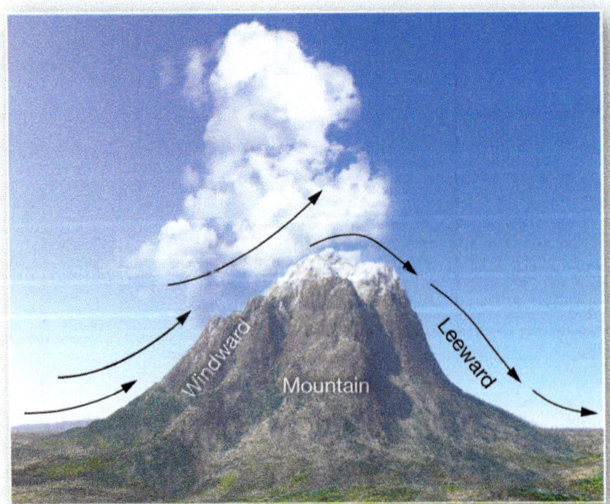

(c) Orographic lifting

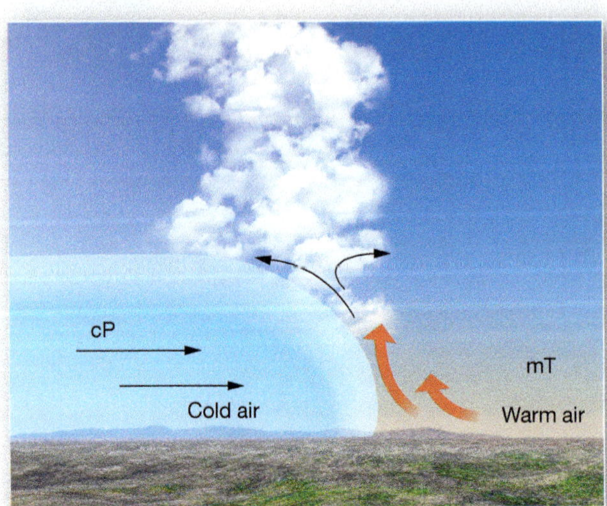

(d) Frontal lifting, cold front example

FIGURE 23 Four atmospheric lifting mechanisms.

Animation Atmospheric Stability

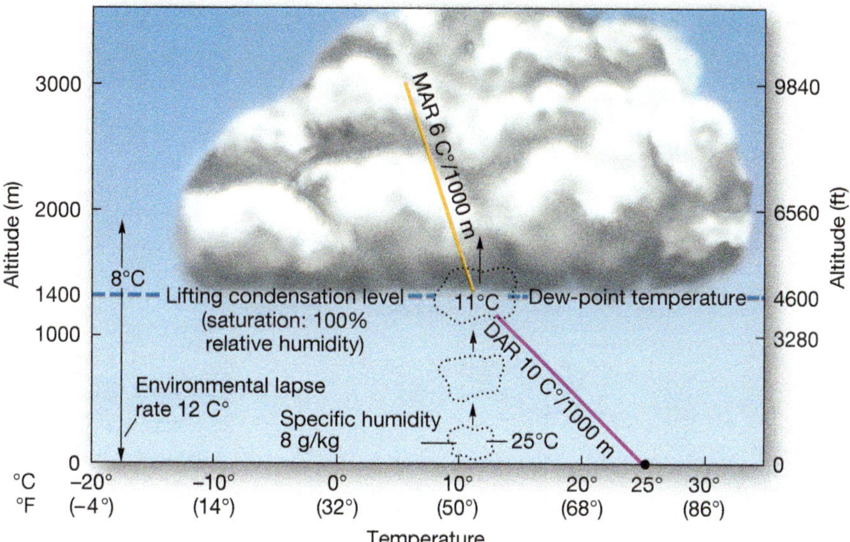

FIGURE 24 Convectional activity in unstable conditions.
Work through these unstable atmospheric conditions, with an environmental lapse rate of 12 C°/1000 m. Look at the initial conditions: The specific humidity of the air parcel is 8 g/kg, and the beginning temperature is 25°C. Here the dew point is reached after 14 C° of adiabatic cooling at 1400 m (4600 ft). Note that the DAR is used when the air parcel is less than saturated, changing to the MAR above the lifting-condensation level at 1400 m.

extensive uplift, towering cumulonimbus cloud development, and high average annual precipitation.

Convectional Lifting

When an air mass passes from a maritime source region to a warmer continental region, heating from the warmer land causes lifting and convection in the air mass. Other sources of surface heating might include an urban heat island or an area of dark soil in a plowed field—the warmer surfaces produce **convectional lifting**. If conditions are unstable, initial lifting continues and clouds develop. Figure 23 illustrates convectional action stimulated by local heating, with unstable conditions present in the atmosphere. The rising parcel of air continues its ascent because it is warmer and therefore less dense than the surrounding environment (Figure 24).

Florida's precipitation generally illustrates both these lifting mechanisms: convergence and convection. Heating of the land produces convergence of onshore winds from the Atlantic Ocean and the Gulf of Mexico. As an example of local heating and convectional lifting, Figure 25 depicts a day on which the landmass of Florida is warmer than the surrounding Gulf of Mexico and Atlantic Ocean. Because the Sun's radiation gradually heats the land throughout the day and warms the air above it, convectional showers tend to form in the afternoon and early evening. Thus, Florida has the highest frequency of days with thunderstorms in the United States.

Orographic Lifting

The physical presence of a mountain acts as a topographic barrier to migrating air masses. **Orographic lifting** occurs when air is forcibly lifted upslope as it is pushed against a mountain. The lifting air cools adiabatically. Stable air forced upward in this manner may produce stratiform clouds, whereas unstable or conditionally unstable air usually forms a line of cumulus and cumulonimbus clouds. An orographic barrier enhances convectional activity and causes additional lifting during the passage of weather fronts and cyclonic systems, thereby extracting more moisture from passing air masses.

Figure 26a illustrates the operation of orographic lifting. The wetter intercepting slope is the *windward slope*, as opposed to the drier far-side slope, known as the *leeward slope*. Moisture condenses from the lifting air mass on the windward side of the mountain; on the leeward side, the descending air mass heats by compression, and any remaining water in the air evaporates. Thus, air beginning its ascent up a mountain can be warm and moist, but finishing its descent on the leeward slope, it becomes hot and dry.

In North America, *chinook winds* (called *föhn* or *foehn* winds in Europe) are the warm, downslope air flows characteristic of the leeward side of mountains. Such winds can bring a 20 C° (36 F°) jump in temperature and greatly reduced relative humidity.

The term **rain shadow** is applied to dry regions leeward of mountains. East of the Cascade Range, Sierra

Lake-effect snow makes an avalanche of a storm

In October 2006, a lake-effect storm dubbed the "surprise storm" dropped 0.6 m (2 ft) of wet snow in the Buffalo, New York, area. This was the earliest date for such a storm in 137 years of records and remarkable because the ratio of snow to water content was 6:1. An "avalanche of a storm," as the media described it, hit upstate New York in February 2007 when 2 m (6.5 ft) of snow fell in 1 day and over 3.7 m (12 ft) fell over 7 days.

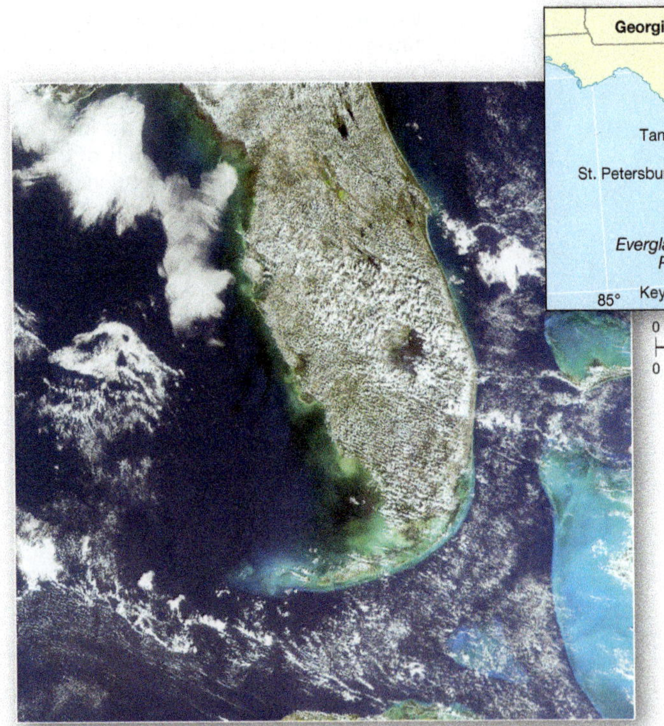

Satellite
Convectional Activity over the Florida Peninsula

FIGURE 25 Convectional activity over the Florida peninsula. Cumulus clouds cover the land, with several cells developing into cumulonimbus thunderheads. [*Terra* MODIS image, NASA/GSFC.]

Nevada, and Rocky Mountains, such rain-shadow patterns predominate. In fact, the precipitation pattern of windward and leeward slopes persists worldwide, as confirmed by the precipitation maps for North America and the world.

Frontal Lifting: Cold and Warm Fronts

The leading edge of an advancing air mass is its *front*. Vilhelm Bjerknes (1862–1951) first applied the term while working with a team of meteorologists in Norway during World War I. Weather systems seemed to them to be migrating air mass "armies" doing battle along fronts. A front is a place of atmospheric discontinuity, a narrow zone forming a line of conflict between two air masses of different temperature, pressure, humidity, wind direction and speed, and cloud development. The leading edge of a cold air mass is a **cold front**, whereas the leading edge of a warm air mass is a **warm front**.

Cold Front On weather maps, such as in Figure 29, a cold front is a line with triangular spikes that point in the direction of frontal movement along an advancing cP or mP air mass. The steep face of the cold air mass suggests its ground-hugging nature, caused by its greater density and uniform physical character compared to the warmer air mass it displaces (Figure 27a).

Warm, moist air in advance of the cold front lifts upward abruptly and experiences the same adiabatic rates of cooling and factors of stability or instability that pertain to all lifting air parcels. A day or two ahead of the cold

GEO REPORT 5 *Mountains cause record rains*

Mount Waialeale, on the island of Kaua'i, Hawai'i, rises 1569 m (5147 ft) above sea level. On its windward slope, rainfall averaged 1234 cm (486 in., or 40.5 ft) a year for the years 1941–1992. In contrast, the rain-shadow side of Kaua'i receives only 50 cm (20 in.) of rain annually. If no islands existed at this location, this portion of the Pacific Ocean would receive only an average 63.5 cm (25 in.) of precipitation a year. (These statistics are from established weather stations with a consistent record of weather data; several stations claim higher rainfall values, but do not have dependable measurement records.)

Cherrapunji, India, is 1313 m (4309 ft) above sea level at 25° N latitude, in the Assam Hills south of the Himalayas. Summer monsoons pour in from the Indian Ocean and the Bay of Bengal, producing 930 cm (366 in., or 30.5 ft) of rainfall in 1 month. Not surprisingly, Cherrapunji is the all-time precipitation record holder for a single year, 2647 cm (1042 in., or 86.8 ft), and for every other time interval from 15 days to 2 years. The average annual precipitation there is 1143 cm (450 in., or 37.5 ft), placing it second only to Mount Waialeale.

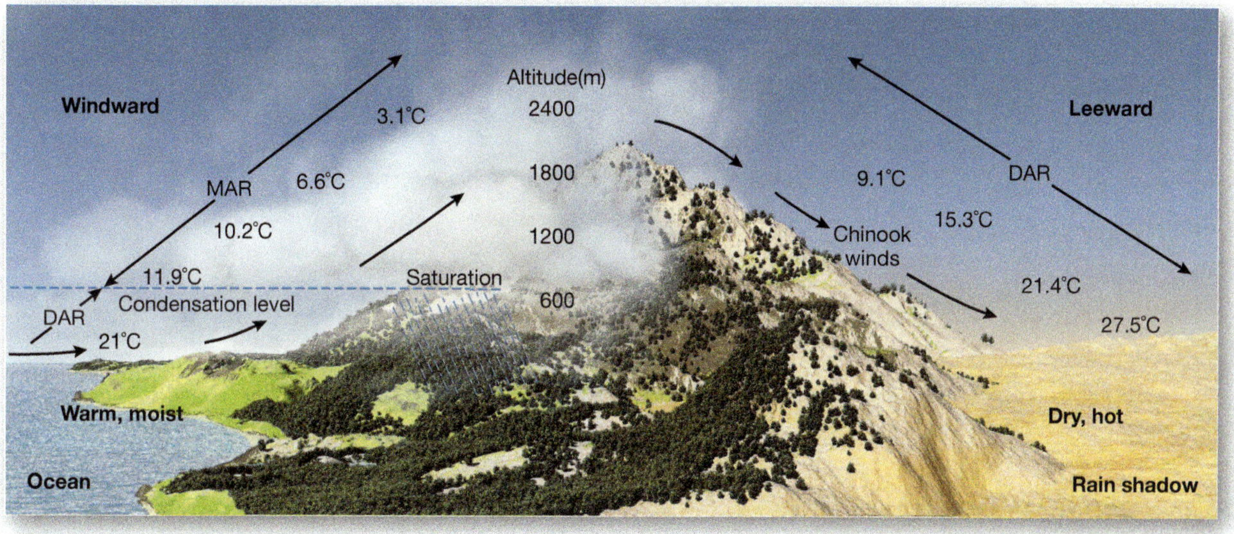

(a)

(b) (c)

FIGURE 26 Orographic precipitation, unstable conditions assumed.
(a) Prevailing winds force warm, moist air upward against a mountain range, producing adiabatic cooling, eventual saturation and net condensation, cloud formation, and precipitation. On the leeward slope, as the "dried" air descends, compressional heating warms it and net evaporation dominates, creating the hot, relatively dry rain shadow. (b) Rain shadow produced by descending, warming air contrasts with the clouds of the windward side. Dust is stirred up by leeward downslope winds. (c) The wetter windward slopes (to the left) are in contrast to the drier leeward landscapes (to the right) in Washington state. [(b) Author. (c) *Terra* MODIS image, NASA/GSFC.]

front's passage, high cirrus clouds appear, telling observers that a lifting mechanism is on the way.

A wind shift, temperature drop, and lowering barometric pressure mark a cold front's advance due to lifting along the front. As the line of most intense lifting passes, usually just ahead of the front itself, air pressure drops to a local low. Clouds may build along the cold front into characteristic cumulonimbus form and may appear as an advancing wall of clouds. Precipitation usually is heavy, containing large droplets, and can be accompanied by hail, lightning, and thunder.

The aftermath of a cold-front passage usually brings northerly winds in the Northern Hemisphere and southerly winds in the Southern Hemisphere as anticyclonic

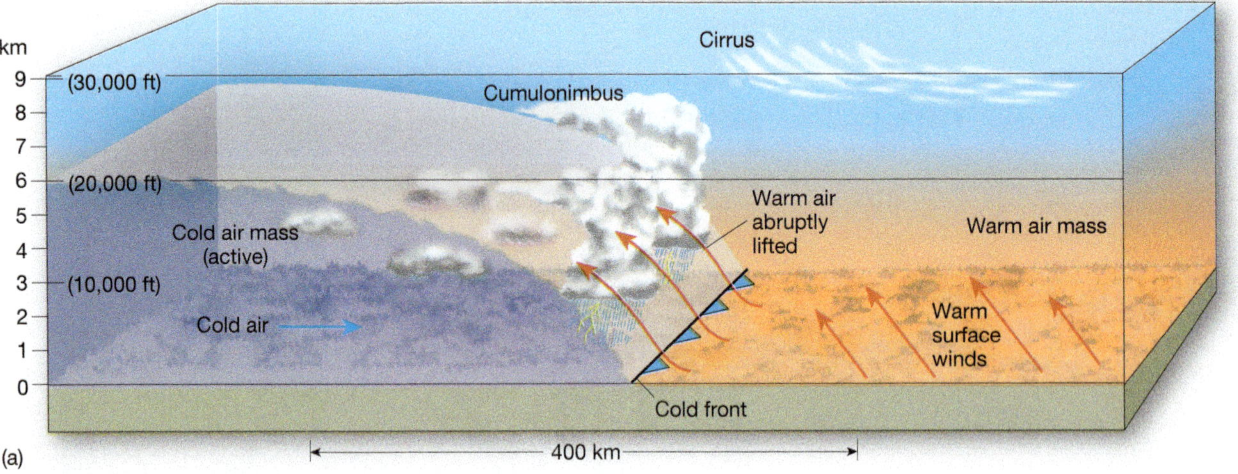

FIGURE 27 A typical cold front.
(a) Denser, advancing cold air forces warm, moist air to lift abruptly. As the air is lifted, it cools by expansion at the DAR, cooling to the dew-point temperature as it rises to a level of condensation and cloud formation. (b) A sharp line of cumulonimbus clouds near the Texas coast and Gulf of Mexico marks a cold front and squall line. This cloud formation rises to 17,000 m (56,000 ft). The passage of such a frontal system over land often produces strong winds, cumulonimbus clouds, large raindrops, heavy showers, lightning and thunder, hail, and the possibility of tornadoes. [NASA.]

high-pressure advances. Temperatures are lower and air pressure higher in response to the cooler, more dense air. Cloud cover breaks and clears.

A fast-advancing cold front can cause violent lifting and create a zone right along or slightly ahead of the front called a **squall line**. Along a squall line, such as the one in the Gulf of Mexico shown in Figure 27b, wind patterns are turbulent and wildly changing, and precipitation is intense. The well-defined frontal clouds in the photograph rise abruptly, with new thunderstorms forming along the front. Tornadoes also may develop along such a squall line.

Warm Front A line with semicircles facing in the direction of frontal movement denotes a warm front on weather maps (see the map in Figure 29). The leading edge of an advancing warm air mass is unable to displace cooler, passive air, which is denser along the surface. Instead, the warm air tends to push the cooler, underlying air into a characteristic wedge shape, with the warmer air sliding up over the cooler air. Thus, in the cooler-air region a temperature inversion is present, sometimes causing poor air drainage and stagnation.

Figure 28 illustrates a typical warm front in which mT air is gently lifted, leading to stratiform cloud development and characteristic nimbostratus clouds and to drizzly precipitation. A warm front presents a progression of cloud development to an observer: High cirrus and cirrostratus clouds announce the advancing frontal system; then clouds lower and thicken to altostratus; finally, the clouds lower and thicken to stratus within several hundred kilometers of the front.

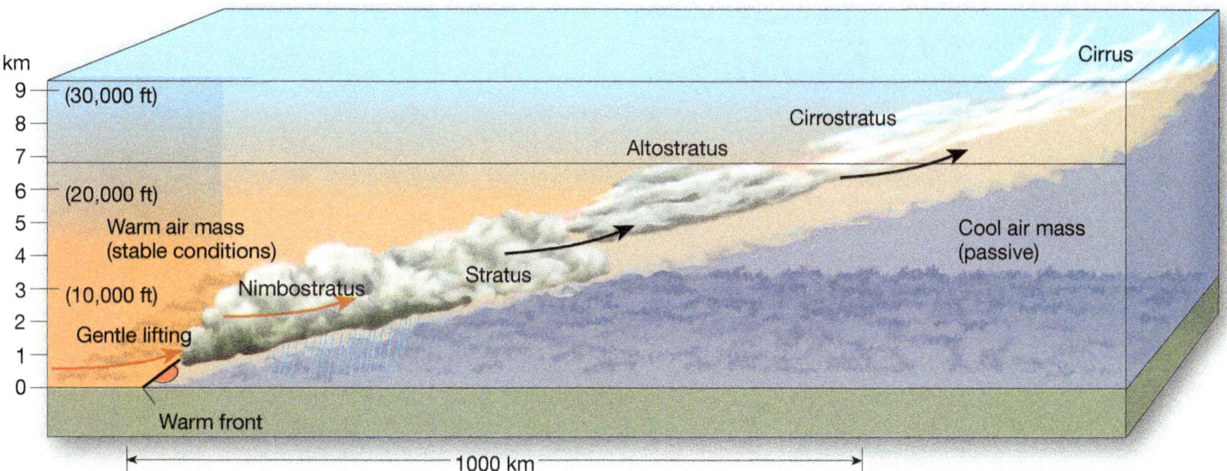

FIGURE 28 A typical warm front.
Note the sequence of cloud development as the warm front approaches. Warm air slides upward over a wedge of cooler, passive air near the ground. Gentle lifting of the warm, moist air produces nimbostratus and stratus clouds and drizzly rain showers, in contrast to the more dramatic cold-front precipitation.

Animation
Cold and Warm Fronts

Midlatitude Cyclonic Systems

The conflict between contrasting air masses can develop a **midlatitude cyclone**, or **wave cyclone**. This migrating low-pressure center with converging, ascending air spirals inward counterclockwise in the Northern Hemisphere and inward clockwise in the Southern Hemisphere. Because of the undulating nature of frontal boundaries and the steering flow of the jet streams, the term *wave* is appropriate. The combination of the *pressure gradient force*, *Coriolis force*, and *surface friction* generates this cyclonic motion.

Wave cyclones, which can be 1600 km (1000 mi) wide, dominate weather patterns in the middle and higher latitudes of both the Northern and the Southern Hemispheres. A midlatitude cyclone can initiate along the polar front, particularly in the region of the Icelandic and Aleutian subpolar low-pressure cells in the Northern Hemisphere. Certain other areas are associated with cyclone development and intensification: the eastern slope of the Rocky Mountains, home of the Colorado Low in the United States and the Alberta Clipper in Canada; the Gulf Coast, home of the Gulf Low; and the eastern seaboard, home of the Nor'easter and Hatteras Low.

The intense high-speed winds of the jet streams guide cyclonic systems, with their attendant air masses, across the continent along *storm tracks*. These tracks shift in latitude with the Sun and the seasons. Typical storm tracks that cross North America are farther northward in summer and farther southward in winter. As the storm tracks begin to shift northward in the spring, cP and mT air masses are in their clearest conflict. This is the time of strongest frontal activity, featuring thunderstorms and tornadoes.

Life Cycle of a Midlatitude Cyclone

Figure 29 shows the birth, maturity, and death of a typical midlatitude cyclone in several stages, along with an idealized weather map. On the average, a midlatitude cyclonic system takes 3–10 days to progress through this life cycle from the area where it develops to the area where it finally dissolves.

- The first stage is *cyclogenesis*, the atmospheric process in which low-pressure wave cyclones develop and strengthen. This process usually begins along the polar front, where cold and warm air masses converge and are drawn into conflict, creating potentially unstable conditions. For a wave cyclone to form along the polar front, a compensating area of divergence aloft must match a surface point of air convergence. Even a slight disturbance along the polar front, perhaps a small change in the path of the jet stream, can initiate the converging, ascending flow of air and thus a surface low-pressure system (Figure 29a).
- In the *open stage*, to the east of the developing low-pressure center, warm air begins to move northward along an advancing front, while cold air advances southward to the west of the center. See this organization in Figure 29b and around the center of low pressure, located over western Nebraska. As the midlatitude cyclone matures, the counterclockwise flow draws the cold air mass from the north and west and the warm air mass from the south. In the cross section, you can see the profiles of both a cold front and a warm front and each air mass segment.
- Next is the *occluded stage* (Figure 29c). Remember the relation between air temperature and the density of an air mass. The colder cP air mass is denser than the warmer mT air mass. This cooler, more unified air mass acts like a bulldozer blade and therefore moves faster than the warm front. Cold fronts can travel at an average 40 kmph (25 mph), whereas warm fronts average roughly half that at 16–24 kmph (10–15 mph). Thus, a cold front often overtakes the cyclonic warm front, wedging beneath it, producing an **occluded front**.

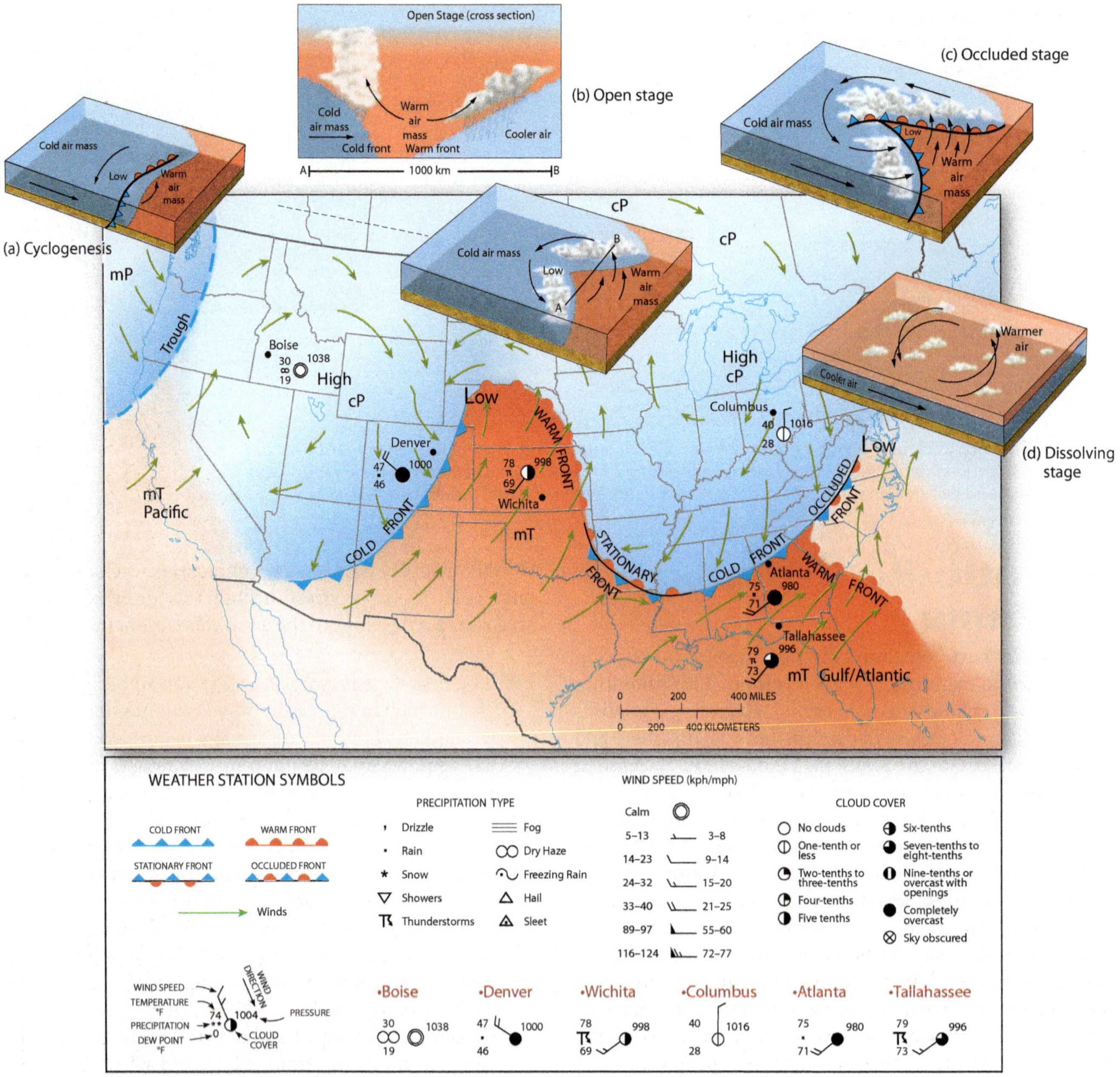

FIGURE 29 Idealized stages of a midlatitude wave cyclone.
Standard weather station symbols and current conditions for six cities appear below the map. The block diagrams show (a) cyclogenesis where surface convergence and lifting begin, (b) the open stage, (c) the occluded stage, and (d) the dissolving stage, reached at the end of the storm track as the cyclone spins down, no longer energized by the latent heat from condensing moisture.

Animation
Midlatitude Cyclones

- Finally, the *dissolving stage* of the midlatitude cyclone occurs when its lifting mechanism is completely cut off from the warm air mass, which was its source of energy and moisture. Remnants of the cyclonic system then dissipate in the atmosphere, perhaps after passage across the country (Figure 29d).

Weather Maps and Forecasting

Synoptic analysis is the evaluation of weather data collected at a specific time. Building a database of wind, pressure, temperature, and moisture conditions is key to numerical weather prediction and the development of weather-forecasting models. The accuracy of forecasts continues to improve with technological advancements in instruments and software and with our increasing knowledge of the atmospheric interactions that produce weather.

Weather data necessary for the preparation of a synoptic map and forecast include:

- Barometric pressure (sea level and altimeter setting)
- Pressure tendency (steady, rising, falling)
- Surface air temperature
- Dew-point temperature
- Wind speed, direction, and character (gusts, squalls)
- Type and movement of clouds
- Current weather

- State of the sky (current sky conditions)
- Visibility; vision obstruction (fog, haze)
- Precipitation since last observation

Environmental satellites are one of the key tools in forecasting weather and analyzing climate. Massive computers handle volumes of data from surface, aircraft, and orbital platforms for accurate forecasting of near-term weather. These data are also used for assessing climatic change. In the United States, the National Weather Service (NWS) provides weather forecasts and current satellite images (see http://www.nws.noaa.gov/). Internationally, the World Meteorological Organization coordinates weather information (see http://www.wmo.ch/).

An essential element of weather forecasting is Doppler radar. Using backscatter from two radar pulses, it detects the direction of moisture droplets toward or away from the radar, indicating wind direction and speed. This information is critical to making accurate severe-storm warnings. As part of the Next Generation Weather Radar (NEXRAD) program, the NWS operates 159 Doppler radar systems, mainly in the United States; installations also exist in Japan, Guam, South Korea, and the Azores (Figure 30). For links to weather maps, current forecasts, satellite images, and the latest radar, please go to the *MasteringGeography* web site.

Weather information in the United States comes mainly from the Automated Surface Observing System (ASOS), which is installed at over 900 airports across the country. An ASOS instrument array is made up of numerous sensors that supply continuous data for weather elements, helping the NWS increase the timeliness and accuracy of its forecasts using on-the-ground information. Because weather data come from a large number of sources, NOAA developed the Advanced Weather Interactive Processing System (AWIPS), which consists of high-tech computer workstations that assemble information, thereby improving forecast accuracy and severe-weather warnings. AWIPS is able to display and integrate a variety of data—for example, air pressure, water vapor, humidity, Doppler radar, lightning strikes in real time, and wind profiles.

Examples of the standard weather symbols used on maps are shown in Figure 29. Although the actual patterns of cyclonic passage over North America are widely varied in shape and duration, you can apply this general model, along with your understanding of warm and cold fronts, to reading the daily weather map.

CRITICAL THINKING 4

Analyzing a weather map

After studying the text, test your knowledge by determining the conditions in Boise, Denver, Wichita, Columbus, Atlanta, and Tallahassee as depicted on the weather map in Figure 29. On the map, Denver has just experienced the passage of a cold front. Look at the conditions ahead of the cold front, and compare them to the current Denver weather. What changes occurred in wind direction, temperature, and humidity as the front passed? How did the influence of air masses change? What changes occurred in Wichita with the passing of the warm front?

(a)

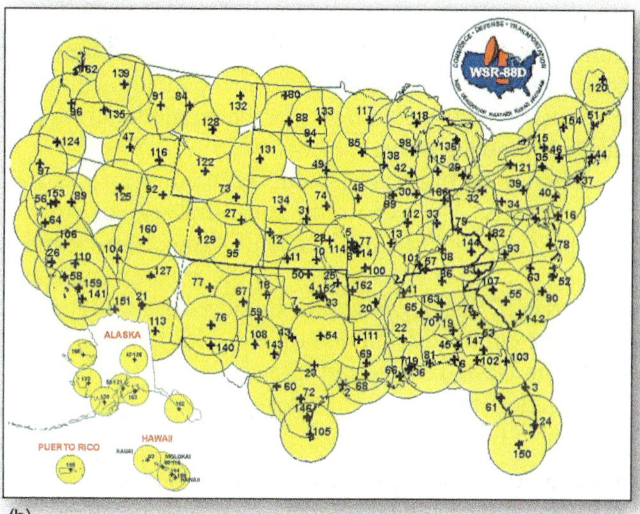

(b)

FIGURE 30 NWS weather installation.
(a) A radar antenna is within the dome structure at the Indianapolis International Airport. (b) WSR-88D (Weather Surveillance Radar) Doppler radar coverage in the United States.
[(a) Bobbé Christopherson. (b) NWS Radar Operations Center, Norman, Oklahoma.]

Violent Weather

Weather provides a continuous reminder of the flow of energy across the latitudes that at times can set into motion destructive, violent weather conditions. Although we discuss a number of severe weather phenomena, we focus mainly on thunderstorms, tornadoes, and hurricanes in this chapter.

The cost of weather-related destruction—from droughts, floods, hail, tornadoes, derechos, tropical systems, storm surges, blizzards and ice storms, and wildfires—has risen more than 500% since 1975 as population has increased in areas prone to violent weather and as climate change intensifies weather anomalies. NOAA's National Climate Data Center publication *Billion Dollar Climate and Weather Disasters, 1980–2009* (http://www.ncdc.noaa.gov/img/reports/billion/billionz-2009.pdf) summarizes 96 events surpassing $1 billion in cost. Hurricane Katrina and the 2005 season alone caused $130 billion in damages, and Hurricanes Gustav and Ike (2008) caused more than $32 billion in damages! Government research on and monitoring of violent weather is centered at NOAA's National Severe Storms Laboratory and Storm Prediction Center—see http://www.nssl.noaa.gov/ and http://www.spc.noaa.gov/; consult these sites for the discussion that follows.

Thunderstorms

Tremendous energy is liberated by the condensation of large quantities of water vapor. This process locally heats the air, causing violent updrafts and downdrafts as rising parcels of air pull surrounding air into the column and as the frictional drag of raindrops pulls air toward the ground. Giant cumulonimbus clouds can create dramatic weather moments—squall lines of heavy precipitation, lightning, thunder, hail, blustery winds, and tornadoes. Thunderstorms may develop within an air mass, in a line along a front (particularly a cold front), or where mountain slopes cause orographic lifting.

Thousands of thunderstorms occur on Earth at any given moment. Many are in the equatorial regions around the ITCZ, exemplified by the city of Kampala in Uganda, East Africa, which sits virtually on the equator and averages a record 242 days a year of thunderstorms. Figure 31 shows the annual distribution of days with thunderstorms across the United States and Canada. You can see that, in North America, most thunderstorms occur in areas dominated by mT air masses.

Atmospheric Turbulence Most airplane flights experience at least some turbulence—the encountering of air of different densities or air layers moving at different speeds and directions. This is a natural state of the atmosphere, and passengers are asked to keep seat belts fastened when in their seats to avoid injury, even if the seat-belt light is turned off.

Thunderstorms can produce severe turbulence in the form of downbursts, which are exceptionally strong downdrafts. Downbursts are classified by size: A *macroburst* is at least 4.0 km (2.5 mi) wide and with winds in excess of 210 kmph (130 mph); a *microburst* is smaller in size and speed. A microburst causes rapid changes in wind speed and direction, and it causes the dreaded *wind shear* that can bring down aircraft. Such turbulence events are short-lived and hard to detect, although NOAA's laboratories are making progress in developing forecasting methods.

Lightning and Thunder An estimated 8 million lightning strikes occur each day on Earth. **Lightning** refers to flashes of light caused by enormous electrical discharges—tens of millions to hundreds of millions of volts—that briefly superheat the air to temperatures of 15,000°–30,000°C (27,000°–54,000°F). A buildup of electrical energy polarity between areas within a cumulonimbus cloud or between the cloud and the ground creates lightning. The violent expansion of this abruptly heated air sends shock waves through the atmosphere as the sonic bang of **thunder**.

Lightning poses a hazard to aircraft, people, animals, trees, and structures. Certain precautions are mandatory when a lightning discharge threatens because lightning causes nearly 200 deaths and thousands of injuries each year in the United States and Canada. When lightning is imminent, the NWS issues *severe storm warnings* and cautions people to remain indoors.

The National Aeronautics and Space Administration's (NASA's) Lightning Imaging Sensor (LIS) aboard the *Tropical Rainfall Measuring Mission* (*TRMM*) satellite monitors lightning and other phenomena. The LIS can image lightning strikes day or night, within clouds or between cloud and ground. The sensor's data show that about 90% of all strikes occur over land in response to increased convection over relatively warmer continental surfaces. Strikes shift with expected seasonal shifts of the high Sun, as shown in Figure 32a and b (see http://thunder.msfc.nasa.gov/lis/).

Hail Ice pellets of **hail** generally form within a cumulonimbus cloud. Raindrops circulate repeatedly above and below the freezing level in the cloud, adding layers of ice until the circulation in the cloud can no longer support

GEO REPORT 6 *Kentucky ice storm causes record power losses*

In late January 2009, an ice storm hit southern Indiana and central Kentucky. Over a 3-day period, precipitation began as freezing rain, later changing to sleet (consisting of freezing rain, ice glaze, and ice pellets) and finally to snow. Across Kentucky, power lines collapsed and trees fell under the weight of the ice, resulting in 609,000 homes and businesses without power; outages continued for up to 10 days, and area schools were closed for a week. Ice storms of similar intensity blanketed the Midwest, upper South, and Northeast in February 2011.

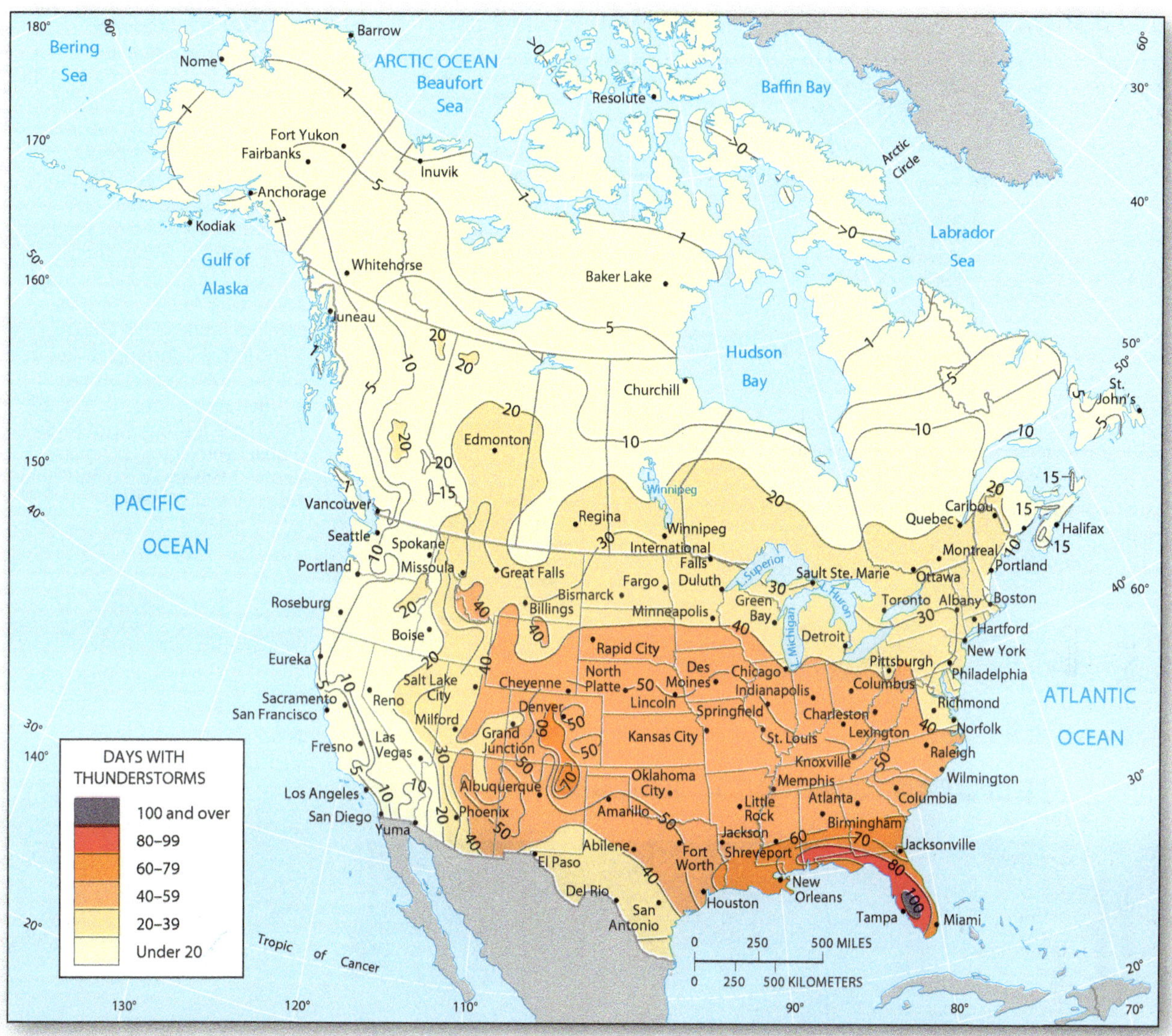

FIGURE 31 Thunderstorm occurrence.
Average annual number of days experiencing thunderstorms. [Data courtesy of NWS; Map Series 3; *Climatic Atlas of Canada*, Atmospheric Environment Service, Canada.]

their weight. Hail may also grow from the addition of moisture on a snow pellet.

Pea-sized (0.25 in.) hail is common, although hail the size of quarters (1.00 in.), golf balls (1.75 in.), hen's eggs (2.00 in.), baseballs (2.75 in.), and softballs (4.50 in.) is known to happen. Baseball-sized hail fell a half dozen times in 2010 in the United States alone. For larger hail to form, the frozen pellets must stay aloft for longer periods. The largest authenticated hailstone in the world fell from a thunderstorm supercell in Aurora, Nebraska, on June 22, 2003; it measured 17.8 cm (7.0 in.) in diameter and 47.6 cm (18.75 in.) in circumference.

Hail is common in the United States and Canada, although somewhat infrequent at any given place. Hail occurs perhaps every 1 or 2 years in the highest-frequency areas. Annual hail damage in the United States tops $800 million. The pattern of hail occurrence across the United States and Canada is similar to that of thunderstorms shown in Figure 31. Days with hail have been increasing each year since 2000.

Derechos

Straight-line winds in excess of 26 m/s (58 mph) associated with rapidly moving thunderstorms and bands of showers

GEO REPORT 7 *You can feel the warning*

If the hair on your head or neck begins to stand on end, get indoors, or if you are in the open, get low to the ground, crouched on both feet and not laying down, in a low spot, if possible. Your hair is telling you that a lightning charge is building in that area. The place *not* to seek shelter is beneath a tree, for trees are good conductors of electricity and often are hit by lightning.

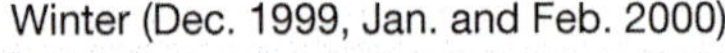

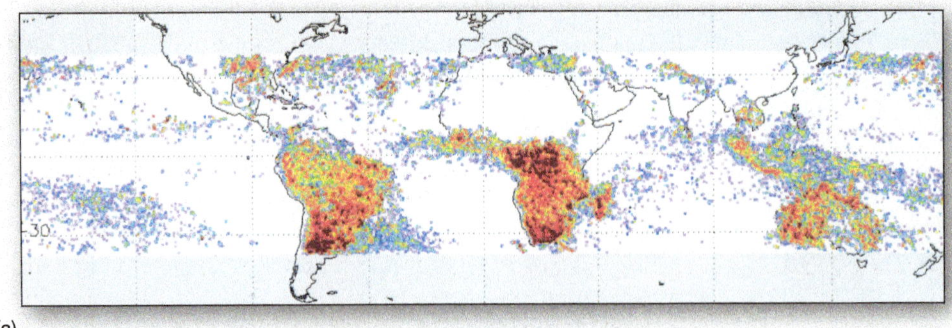

(a)

Summer (June, July, August 2000)

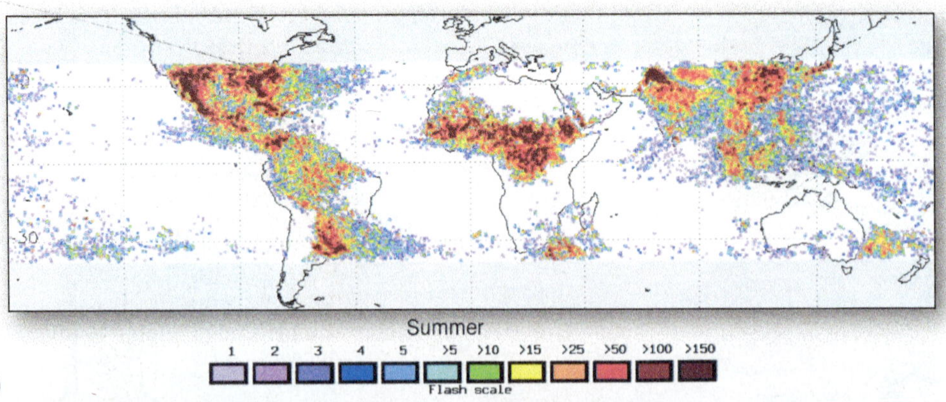

Summer

1 2 3 4 5 >5 >10 >15 >25 >50 >100 >150

Flash scale

(b)

(c)

FIGURE 32 Seasonal images show global lightning. A composite of 3 months' data derived from NASA's Lightning Imaging Sensor (LIS) records of all lightning strikes between 35° N and 35° S latitude during (a) winter (December 1999–February 2000) and (b) summer (June–August 2000). The LIS is aboard the *Tropical Rainfall Measuring Mission* (*TRMM*) satellite launched in 1997. (c) Multiple lightning strikes in southern Arizona captured in a time-lapse photo. [(a) and (b) *TRMM* images courtesy of NASA's Global Hydrology and Climate Center, MSC. (c) Keith Kent/Photo Researchers.]

are known as **derechos.** These strong winds can cause significant damage and crop losses. Wind outbursts from convective storms can produce groups of downburst clusters from a thunderstorm system. These derechos tend to blast in linear paths fanning out along curved-wind fronts over a wide swath of land. The name, coined by physicist Gustavus Hinrichs in 1888, derives from a Spanish word meaning "direct" or "straight ahead."

A derecho in 1998 in eastern Wisconsin exceeded 57 m/s (128 mph). In August 2007, a series of derechos across northern Illinois reached this same intensity. Researchers identified 377 events between 1986 and 2003, an average of about 21 per year. Derechos pose distinct hazards to summer outdoor activities by overturning boats, hurling flying objects, and causing broken trees and limbs. Their highest frequency (about 70%) is from May to August in the region stretching from Iowa, across Illinois, and into the Ohio River Valley. By September and on through to April, areas of activity migrate southward to eastern Texas through Alabama. Reported wind events are on the increase. For more information and a description of numerous derechos, see http://www.spc.noaa.gov/misc/AbtDerechos/derechofacts.htm.

In May 2009, a fierce windstorm crossed Kansas, Missouri, and Illinois, reaching wind speeds of 100 mph and creating a path of destruction 100 miles wide. Scientists coined the term "super derecho" to describe this new phenomenon: a derecho with an eyelike structure similar to a hurricane

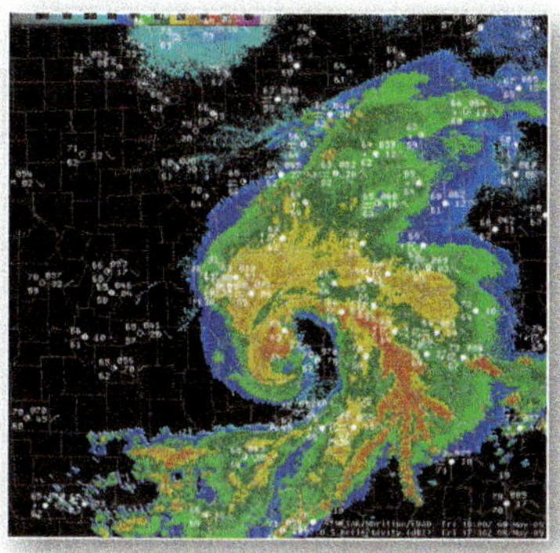

FIGURE 33 Super derecho conditions displayed by radar image.
A super derecho emerged from this weather system across Kansas, Missouri, and Illinois on May 8, 2009. Rainbands form an "eye" structure visible in this image. [Radar image from NOAA/NWS, courtesy of M. Weisman.]

that spun off 18 tornadoes as it moved across Kansas (Figure 33). Scientists were able to forecast this wind event 24 hours in advance and are using their forecasting models to investigate the development of this weather event.

Tornadoes

The updrafts associated with a cold-front squall line and cumulonimbus cloud development appear on satellite images as pulsing bubbles of clouds. According to one hypothesis, a spinning, cyclonic, rising column of mid-troposphere-level air forms a mesocyclone. Ranging up to 10 km (6 mi) in diameter, a **mesocyclone** rotates vertically within a *supercell cloud* (the parent cloud) to a height of thousands of meters (Figure 34a). A well-developed mesocyclone will produce heavy rain, large hail, blustery winds, and lightning; some mature mesocyclones will generate tornado activity.

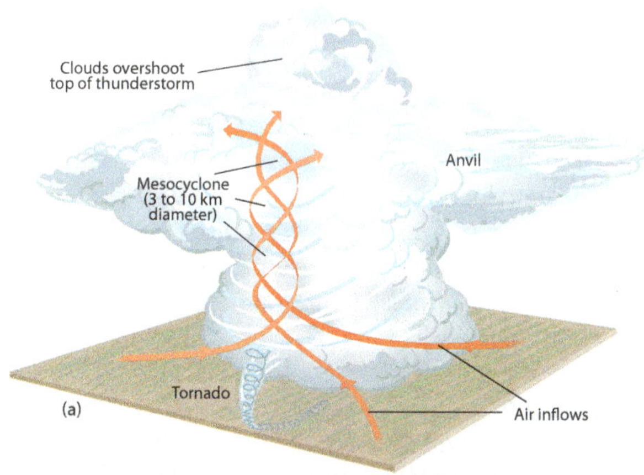

MG Animation Tornado Wind Patterns

FIGURE 34 Mesocyclone and tornado formation.
(a) Strong wind aloft establishes spinning; as updraft from thunderstorm development tilts the rotating air, a mesocyclone forms as a rotating updraft within the thunderstorm. If one forms, a tornado will descend from the lower portion of the mesocyclone. (b) A supercell tornado descends from the cloud base near Spearman, Texas. Strong hail is falling to the left of the tornado. (c) The power of 322-kmph (200-mph) tornadic wind bends steel poles in Wadena, Minnesota. (d) 2007 EF-5 tornado leveled whole neighborhoods in Greensburg, Kansas; photograph taken in 2008. [(b) Photo by Howard Bluestein, all rights reserved. (c) and (d) Bobbé Christopherson.]

As more moisture-laden air is drawn up into the circulation of a mesocyclone, more energy is liberated, and the rotation of air increases speed. The narrower the mesocyclone, the faster the spin of converging parcels of air being sucked into the rotation. The swirl of the mesocyclone itself is visible, as are smaller, dark gray **funnel clouds** that pulse from the bottom side of the parent cloud. The potential of this stage of development is the lowering of a funnel cloud to Earth—a **tornado** (Figure 34b).

A tornado can range from a few meters to a few hundred meters in diameter and can last anywhere from a few moments to tens of minutes. Tornadoes have been increasing in average speed and duration over the last two decades. Greensburg, Kansas, was essentially erased from the map by an EF-5 tornado in May 2007. The statistics are unprecedented: Winds exceeded 330 kmph (205 mph) in the 2.7-km-wide (1.7-mi-wide) funnel that was on the ground along a 35-km (22-mi) track. A photo taken 1 year later that appears in *Geosystems Now* for this chapter shows block after block of empty lots in what was a residential district; also shown in Figure 34d.

The power of these tornadoes seems abstract until you see the impacts firsthand, as described in this chapter's *Geosystems Now*. We visited Wadena, Minnesota, 4 days after the EF-4 destroyed 260 homes and many community buildings, a swimming pool, and the high school (Figure 34c). The destruction is especially sobering when one considers the increasing average yearly tornado occurrences and an increase in EF-4 and -5 events in the United States.

A tornado's scoured path is visible on the ground in a series of semicircular "suction" prints and, of course, in the trail of damage; the 2.7-km-wide (1.7-mi-wide) swath cut through Greensburg in 2007 (Figure 34d) and across Alabama in 2011 (see chapter-opening photo) were remarkable. When tornado circulation occurs over water, a **waterspout** forms, and surface water is drawn some 3–5 m (10–16 ft) up into the funnel. The rest of the waterspout funnel is made visible by the rapid condensation of water vapor.

Tornado Measurement and Frequency Pressures inside a tornado usually are about 10% less than those in the surrounding air. The inrushing convergence created by such a horizontal pressure gradient causes high wind speeds. The late Theodore Fujita, a noted meteorologist from the University of Chicago, designed the Fujita Scale, which classifies tornadoes according to wind speed as indicated by related property damage. A refinement in this 1971 scale, adopted in February 2007, is the *Enhanced Fujita Scale*, or *EF Scale* (Table 1). The revision filled the need to better assess damage, correlate wind speed to damage caused, and account for structural construction quality. To assist with wind estimates, the EF Scale contains Damage Indicators relating to types of structures and vegetation affected, along with Degrees of Damage ratings, both of which you can view at the URL listed below the table.

North America experiences more tornadoes than anywhere on Earth because its latitudinal position and topography permit contrasting air masses to confront one another. Tornadoes have struck all 50 states and all the Canadian provinces and territories. May and June are the peak months, as you see in Figure 35, based on 51 years of records. Note the comparison with statistics for the 7-year period from 2003–2009. This suggests climate change is affecting air-mass strength and forcing this trend. Other potential causes of the annual increase in tornado frequency range from more intense thunderstorm activity to better reporting through Doppler radar and a larger population with video recorders.

In the United States, 54,030 tornadoes were recorded in the years from 1950 through 2010; this includes

TABLE 1 The Enhanced Fujita Scale

EF-Number	3-Second-Gust Wind Speed; Damage
EF-0 Gale	105–137 kmph, 65–85 mph; *light damage*: branches broken, chimneys damaged.
EF-1 Weak	138–177 kmph, 86–110 mph; *moderate damage*: beginning of hurricane wind-speed designation, roof coverings peeled off, mobile homes pushed off foundations.
EF-2 Strong	178–217 kmph, 111–135 mph; *considerable damage*: roofs torn off frame houses, large trees uprooted or snapped, boxcars pushed over, small missiles generated.
EF-3 Severe	218–266 kmph, 136–165 mph; *severe damage*: roofs torn off well-constructed houses, trains overturned, trees uprooted, cars thrown.
EF-4 Devastating	267–322 kmph, 166–200 mph; *devastating damage*: well-built houses leveled, cars thrown, large missiles generated (see Figure 34c).
EF-5 Incredible	More than 322 kmph, >200 mph; *incredible damage*: houses lifted and carried distance to disintegration, car-sized missiles fly farther than 100 m, bark removed from trees.

Note: See http://www.depts.ttu.edu/weweb/Pubs/fscale/EFScale.pdf for details.

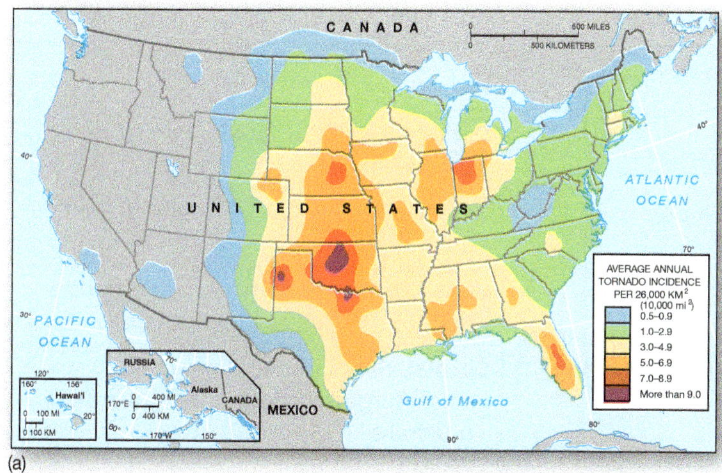

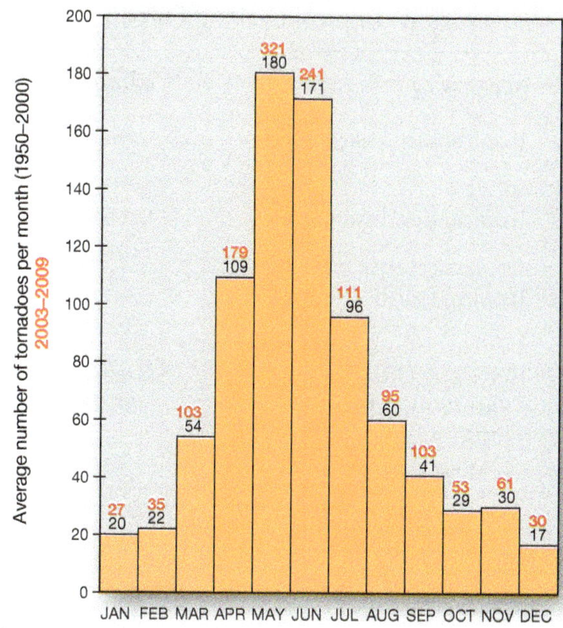

FIGURE 35 Trends in tornado occurrence in the United States. (a) Average number of tornadoes per 26,000 km^2 (10,000 mi^2). (b) Average number of tornadoes per month from 1950 to 2000. Remarkably, the 7 years from 2003 to 2009 show a significant increase in the average number of tornadoes per month. [Data courtesy of the Storm Prediction Center, NWS, and NOAA sources.]

29 tornadoes in December 2010. In these 60 years, tornadoes caused over 5000 deaths, or about 85 deaths per year. Of note is the fact that these tornadoes resulted in more than 80,000 injuries and property damage of over $28 billion for this period of record. The yearly average of $500 million in damage is rising each year. Record-setting tornado outbreaks continued through 2011.

The Storm Prediction Center in Kansas City, Missouri, provides short-term forecasting for thunderstorms and tornadoes to the public and to NWS field offices. Warning times of 12 to 30 minutes are possible with current technology.

Canada experiences an average of 80 observed tornadoes per year, although unpopulated rural areas go unreported. University of Leeds researchers report that in the United Kingdom observers report 60 to 80 a year. Other continents experience a small number of tornadoes each year.

The long-term annual average number of tornadoes before 1990 was 787. Interestingly, after 1990 the average per year rose to over 1000. In 1998, the annual average reached 1270 tornadoes; the peak year was 2004, with 1820 tornadoes; 1156 tornadoes were reported in 2009 and 1180 tornadoes in 2010, although 2011 broke these records..

Tropical Cyclones

A powerful manifestation of the Earth–atmosphere energy budget is the **tropical cyclone**, which originates entirely within tropical air masses. The tropics extend from the Tropic of Cancer at 23.5° N latitude to the Tropic of Capricorn at 23.5° S latitude, containing the equatorial zone between 10° N and 10° S latitude. Approximately 80 tropical cyclones occur annually worldwide. Some 45 per year are powerful enough to be classified as hurricanes, typhoons, or cyclones—different regional names for the same type of tropical storm—with 30% of these occurring in the western North Pacific. The classification depends on wind speed: A full-fledged **hurricane**, **typhoon**, or *cyclone* has wind speeds greater than 119 kmph (74 mph, or 65 knots). The three names are based on location: Hurricanes occur around North America, typhoons in the western Pacific (mainly in Japan and the Philippines), and cyclones in Indonesia, Bangladesh, and India.

Worldwide, about 10% of all tropical disturbances have the right ingredients to become hurricanes or typhoons. For coverage and reporting, see the National Hurricane Center at http://www.nhc.noaa.gov/ or the Joint Typhoon Warning Center at http://www.usno.navy.mil/JTWC. Table 2 presents the criteria for classification of tropical cyclones based on wind speed.

Cyclonic systems that form in the tropics are quite different from midlatitude cyclones because the air of the tropics is essentially homogenous, with no fronts or conflicting air masses of differing temperatures. In addition, the warm air and warm seas ensure abundant water vapor and thus the necessary latent heat to fuel these storms. Tropical cyclones convert heat energy from the ocean into mechanical energy in the wind—the warmer the ocean and atmosphere, the more intense the conversion and the more powerful the storm.

What mechanism triggers the start of a tropical cyclone? Meteorologists now think that cyclonic motion begins with slow-moving easterly waves of low pressure in the trade-wind belt of the tropics. For these processes, sea-surface temperatures must exceed approximately

TABLE 2 Tropical Cyclone Classification

Designation	Winds	Features
Tropical disturbance	Variable, low	Definite area of surface low pressure; patches of clouds
Tropical depression	Up to 63 kmph (38 mph); up to 34 knots	Gale force, organizing circulation; light to moderate rain
Tropical storm	63–118 kmph (39–73 mph); 35–63 knots	Closed isobars; definite circular organization; heavy rain; assigned a name
Hurricane (Atlantic and East Pacific) Typhoon (West Pacific) Cyclone (Indian Ocean, Australia)	Greater than 119 kmph (74 mph); 65 knots	Circular, closed isobars; heavy rain, storm surges; tornadoes in right-front quadrant

26°C (79°F). Tropical cyclones form along the eastern (leeward) side of these migrating troughs of low pressure, a place of convergence and rainfall. Surface air flow then converges into the low-pressure area, ascends, and flows outward aloft. This important divergence aloft acts as a chimney, pulling more moisture-laden air into the developing system.

Storm Tracks The map in Figure 36a shows areas in which tropical cyclones form and some of their characteristic storm tracks. This map also indicates the range of months during which tropical cyclones are most likely to appear. For example, storms that strike the southeastern United States do so mostly between August and October. Officially, tropical cyclone season for the Atlantic is from June 1 to November 30 each year. Figure 36d shows the pattern of actual tracks and intensities for tropical cyclones between 1856 and 2006.

Relative to North and Central America, the low pressure areas that form tropical depressions intensify into tropical storms as they cross the Atlantic. A rule of thumb has emerged: If tropical storms mature early along their track, they tend to curve northward toward the North Atlantic and miss the United States. The critical position is approximately 40° W longitude. If a tropical storm matures after it reaches the longitude of the Dominican Republic (70° W), then it has a higher probability of hitting the United States.

In contradiction to these average conditions, in October 2005, the remnants of Tropical Storm Vince became the first-ever Atlantic tropical cyclone to strike Spain (Figure 36b). In the Southern Hemisphere, no hurricane was ever observed turning from the equator into the South Atlantic (note on the storm track map). Yet, in March 2004, Hurricane Catarina made landfall in Brazil near the resorts at Laguna, in the state of Santa Catarina. NASA's *Terra* satellite in Figure 37a clearly shows an organized hurricane, with characteristic central eye and rainbands. Compare the circulation patterns of Hurricane Gilbert (see Figure 37a) to this satellite image of Catarina. What do you see? Note the Coriolis force in action, counterclockwise in the Northern Hemisphere and clockwise in the Southern Hemisphere.

Then in 2006, the first tropical storm to become a category 5 super typhoon developed in the Central Pacific, some 1285 km (800 mi) south of Hawai'i. Super Typhoon Ioke continued for almost 3 weeks, with final remnants causing large-scale erosion along Alaskan shores (see Ioke's track). And in 2007, Super Cyclone Gonu became the strongest tropical cyclone on record occurring in the Arabian Sea, eventually hitting Oman and the Arabian Peninsula. Another tropical cyclone, Phet, took an unusual path into the Arabian Peninsula during June 2010. In January 2011, an unusually strong category 5 tropical cycle hit northeastern Australia in the same area that had gone through severe floods. These storms apparently are signaling changes under way in tropical meteorology relative to the increased occurrence and intensity of cyclonic systems, which are related to higher oceanic and atmospheric temperatures.

Damage Potential When you hear meteorologists speak of a "category 4" hurricane, they are using the *Saffir–Simpson Hurricane Damage Potential Scale* to estimate possible damage from hurricane-force winds. Table 3 presents this scale, which uses sustained wind speed to rank hurricanes and typhoons in five categories, from smaller, category 1 storms to extremely dangerous, category 5 storms. This scale does not address other potential hurricane impacts, such as storm surge, flooding, and tornadoes. Damage depends on the degree of property development at a storm's landfall site, how prepared citizens are for the blow, and the local building codes in effect. Newer building codes, such as those that have taken effect since 2000 in North Carolina, South Carolina, and Florida, will likely reduce the structural damage to newer buildings from that predicted by this scale.

FIGURE 36 Worldwide pattern of the most intense tropical cyclones. (a) Typical tropical storm tracks with principal months of occurrence and regional names. Super Typhoon Ioke (2006) and Super Cyclone Gonu (2007) are noted. (b) The remnants of Tropical Storm Vince hit Spain in October 2005, the first storm to take such a track from the tropics. (c) Hurricane Catarina approaches Brazil's southeastern coast, March 27, 2004—a unique occurrence in recorded history. (d) Global tropical cyclone tracks from 1856 to 2006. Can you find Hurricane Catarina on the map? [(b) October 11, 2005, *Meteosat*-7 image University of Ulm. (c) *Terra* MODIS image, NASA/GSFC. (d) R. Rohde/NASA/GSFC.]

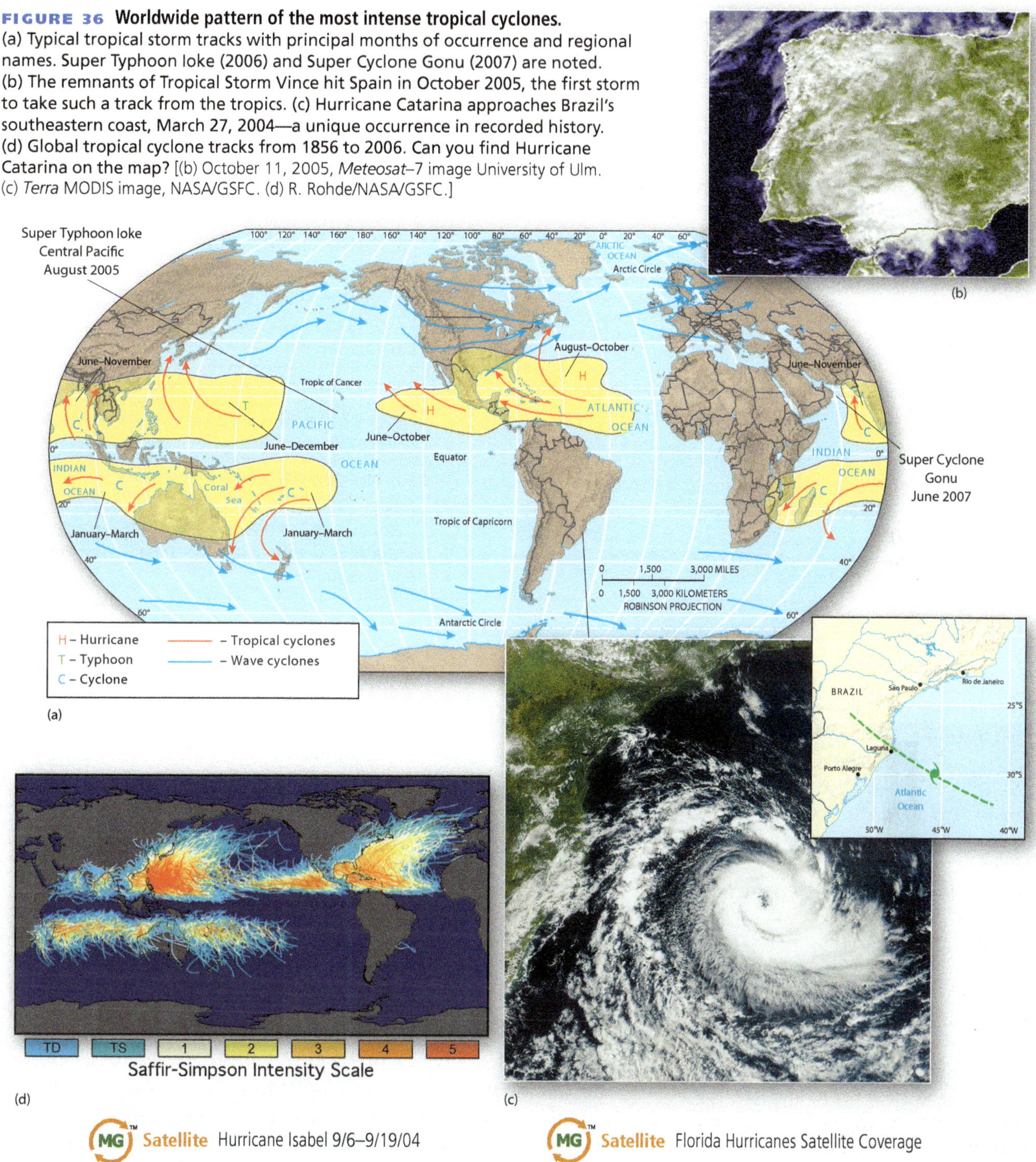

MG Satellite Hurricane Isabel 9/6–9/19/04

MG Satellite Florida Hurricanes Satellite Coverage

Physical Structure Fully organized tropical cyclones have an intriguing physical appearance (Figure 37). They range in diameter from a compact 160 km (100 mi), to 1000 km (600 mi), to some western Pacific super typhoons that attain 1300–1600 km (800–1000 mi). Vertically, these storms dominate the full height of the troposphere.

The inward-spiraling clouds form dense rainbands, with a central area designated the *eye*. Around the eye swirls a thunderstorm cloud called the *eyewall*, which is the area of most intense precipitation. The eye remains an enigma, for in the midst of devastating winds and torrential rains the eye is quiet and warm with even a glimpse of blue sky or stars possible. The structure of the rainbands, central eye, and eyewall is clearly visible for Hurricane Gilbert in Figure 37a (top view), 37b (oblique view from an artist's perspective), and 37c (side-radar view).

The strongest winds of a tropical cyclone are usually recorded in its right-front quadrant (relative to the storm's directional path), where dozens of fully developed tornadoes

TABLE 3 Saffir–Simpson Hurricane Wind Scale

Category	Wind Speed	Notable Atlantic Examples (landfall rating)
1	119–154 kmph (74–95 mph) 65–82 knots [Dangerous, some damage]	
2	155–178 kmph (96–110 mph) 83–95 knots [Dangerous, extensive damage]	1954 Hazel; 1999 Floyd; 2003 Isabel (was a cat. 5), Juan; 2004 Francis; 2008 Dolly; 2010 Alex
3	179–210 kmph (111–130 mph) 96–113 knots [Devastating damage]	1985 Elena; 1991 Bob; 1995 Roxanne, Marilyn; 1998 Bonnie; 2003 Kate; 2004 Ivan (was a cat. 5), Jeanne; 2005 Dennis, Katrina, Rita, and Wilma (were cat. 5); 2007 Henrietta; 2008 Gustav and Ike (were cat. 4)
4	211–250 kmph (131–155 mph) 114–135 knots [Catastrophic damage]	1979 Frederic; 1985 Gloria; 1995 Felix, Luis, Opal; 1998 Georges; 2004 Charley; and 2005 Emily (was a cat. 5).
5	> 250 kmph (> 155 mph) > 135 knots [Catastrophic damage]	1935 No. 2; 1938 No. 4; 1960 Donna; 1961 Carla; 1969 Camille; 1971 Edith; 1977 Anita; 1979 David; 1980 Allen; 1988 Gilbert, Mitch; 1989 Hugo; 1992 Andrew; 2004 Ivan; 2007 Dean, Felix

(a)

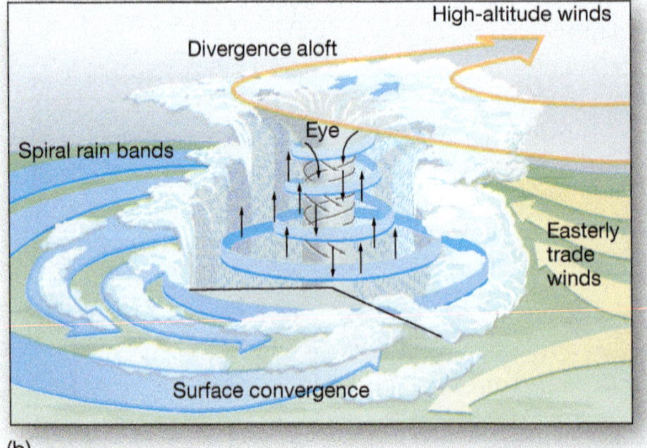

(b)

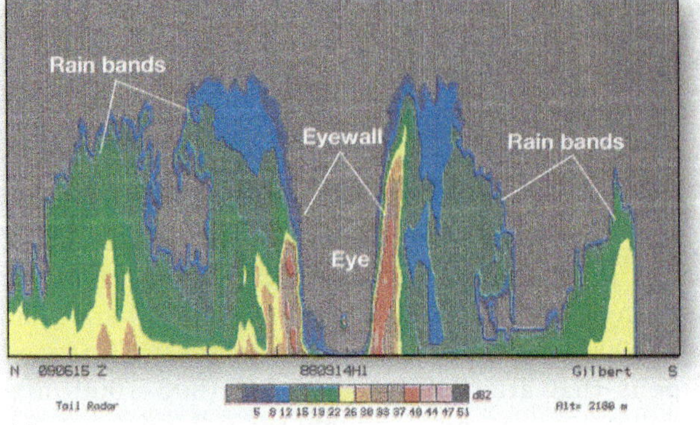

(c)

FIGURE 37 Profile of a hurricane.
For the Western Hemisphere, Hurricane Gilbert attained the record size (1600 km, or 1000 mi, in diameter) and second lowest barometric pressure (888 mb, or 26.22 in.). Gilbert's sustained winds reached 298 kmph (185 mph), with peaks exceeding 320 kmph (200 mph). Hurricane Gilbert, September 13, 1988: (a) *GOES-7* satellite image; (b) a stylized portrait of a mature hurricane, drawn from an oblique perspective (cutaway view shows the eye, rainbands, and wind-flow patterns). (c) *SLAR* (side-looking airborne radar) image from an aircraft flying through the center of the storm. Rainbands of greater cloud density are false-colored in yellows and reds. The clear sky in the central eye is dramatically portrayed. [(a) and (c) NOAA/NHC.]

Animation
Hurricane Wind Patterns

Satellite
Hurricane Georges

may be embedded at the time of landfall. For example, Hurricane Camille in 1969 had up to 100 tornadoes embedded in that quadrant.

A tropical cyclone moves along at 16–40 kmph (10–25 mph). When it makes *landfall*, or moves ashore, the storm pushes seawater inland, causing dangerous *storm surges* often several meters in depth. Storm surges frequently catch people by surprise and cause the majority of hurricane drownings. In 1998, Hurricanes Bonnie, Georges, and Mitch moved slowly onshore, producing damaging storm surges along North Carolina, Mississippi, and Central America, respectively. The slow progress of these storms produced extensive flooding from the sustained rains.

The storm surge from Hurricane Katrina in 2005 (see Focus Study 1, Figure 1.1) caused failure in numerous poorly conceived and constructed levees and canals. The flood disaster that befell New Orleans after Katrina resulted more from human engineering and construction errors than from the storm itself, which was actually downgraded to a category 3 hurricane when it made landfall.

Tropical Cyclone Devastation Tropical cyclones are potentially the most destructive storms experienced by humans, claiming thousands of lives each year worldwide. The tropical cyclone that struck Bangladesh in 1970 killed an estimated 300,000 people, and the one in 1991 claimed over 200,000. In the United States, death tolls are much lower, but still significant. The Galveston, Texas, hurricane of 1900 killed 6000; Hurricane Katrina and engineering failures killed more than 1830 in Louisiana, Mississippi, and Alabama in 2005; Hurricane Audry (1957), 400; Hurricane Gilbert (1988), 318; Hurricane Camille (1969), 256; Hurricane Agnes (1972), 117. Hurricane Mitch (October 26–November 4, 1998) was the deadliest Atlantic hurricane in two centuries, killing more than 12,000 people in Central America. In 2007, for the first time in history in a single Atlantic season, two hurricanes made landfall at category 5 status, Hurricane Dean (Yucatán) and Hurricane Felix (Honduras), resulting in 162 deaths.

As discussed, the costs of destruction from tropical cyclones can be substantial. In 2008, Hurricanes Gustav and Ike caused over $5 billion and $27 billion in damages, respectively; Gustav hit Louisiana, while Ike struck the southeast Texas and southern Louisiana coasts. Ike made landfall as a category 2 on Galveston Island, with the worst storm surge and damage striking to the east on the Bolivar Peninsula, destroying 80% to 95% of the homes; see the photo and discussion in *Geosystems Now* for this chapter.

The tragedy of Hurricane Andrew, which struck Florida in 1992, is that the storm destroyed or seriously damaged 70,000 homes and left 200,000 people homeless between Miami and the Florida Keys. The Everglades, the coral reefs north of Key Largo, some 10,000 acres of mangrove wetlands, and coastal southern pine forests all had significant damage from Andrew. Scientific assessments judge the Everglades to be quite resilient because the region's ecosystems evolved naturally with periodic hurricanes over the millennia. In fact, urbanization, agriculture, pollution, and water diversion pose a greater ongoing threat to the Everglades than do hurricanes.

Thus, tropical cyclones usually damage human structures more than they damage natural systems. This recurrent, yet avoidable, cycle—construction, devastation, reconstruction, devastation—was reinforced ironically in *Fortune* magazine more than 40 years ago after the destruction caused by Hurricane Camille:

> Before long the beachfront is expected to bristle with new motels, apartments, houses, condominiums, and office buildings. Gulf Coast businessmen, incurably optimistic, doubt there will ever be another hurricane like Camille, and even if there is, they vow, the Gulf Coast will rebuild bigger and better after that.*

Sadly, Hurricane Katrina obliterated the same Gulf Coast towns in 2005—Waveland, Bay Saint Louis, Pass Christian, Long Beach, and Gulfport, among others—that Camille washed away in 1969. The below-sea-level sections of New Orleans may never recover their former status; however, we are told that "the Gulf Coast will rebuild bigger and better after that."

**Fortune*, October 1969, p. 62.

GEO REPORT 8 *Research aircraft dissect Hurricane Karl*

During the summer of 2010, NASA and NOAA scientists launched the Genesis and Rapid Intensification Processes (GRIP) mission to study hurricane development using satellites, aircraft, and unmanned aerial vehicles. On September 17, an aircraft flew into category 3 Hurricane Karl as it made landfall along the Mexican coast. At 37,000 feet, the plane collected data using nine instruments and launched dropsondes, which record measurements as they fall through the atmosphere to the ocean surface. Another aircraft flew at 56,000 feet, using specialized radiometers to measure rain-cloud systems and surface winds. Meanwhile, the remotely piloted *Global Hawk* flew over the storm for more than 15 hours, sampling the upper reaches of a hurricane for the first time ever. From space, satellite *Aqua* added a wider view as it collected additional data. More information is at http://www.nasa.gov/mission_pages/hurricanes/missions/grip/main/index.html.

FOCUS STUDY 1

Atlantic Hurricanes and the Future

Forecasters at the National Hurricane Center (NHC) in Miami were busy throughout the 1995–2010 hurricane seasons. This was the most active 16-year period in the history of the NHC, with 226 named tropical storms, including 123 hurricanes (53 of which were intense, meaning category 3 or higher). This was a record level of activity and individual storm intensity despite the reduced number of tropical cyclones during the 1997 El Niño season.

Statistically, the damage caused by tropical cyclones is increasing substantially as more and more development occurs along susceptible coastlines, whereas loss of life is decreasing in most parts of the world, owing to better forecasting of these storms. The journal *Science* offered this "Perspective":

> The risk of human losses is likely to remain low, however, because of a well-established warning and rescue system and ongoing improvements in hurricane prediction. A main concern is the risks of high damage costs (up to $100 billion in a single event) because of ongoing population increases in coastal areas and increasing investment in buildings and extensive infrastructure in general.*

As an example, the 2005 Atlantic hurricane season broke several records, including the most named tropical storms in a single year, totaling 27 (the average is 10); the most hurricanes, totaling 15 (the average is 5); and the highest number of intense hurricanes, greater than category 3, totaling 7 (the average is 2). The 2005 season was the only time three category 5 storms occurred in the Gulf of Mexico (Katrina, Rita, and Wilma) and the first time three category 3 or greater hurricanes made U.S. landfall in subsequent years (2004 and 2005). The 2005 season also recorded the greatest damage total in one year, at more than $130 billion. Hurricane Wilma is now the most intense storm (lowest central pressure) in recorded history for the Atlantic. On our *MasteringGeography* web site a map and table detail all the storms in this remarkable season of tropical cyclones and hurricanes.

* L. Bengtsson, "Hurricane threats," *Science* 293 (July 20, 2001): 441.

The Gulf Coast and Atlantic Seaboard sustained hits and near misses in 2005 from Hurricanes Cindy, Dennis, Katrina, Ophelia, Rita, Wilma, and Gamma; and, when added to Charley, Francis, Ivan, and Jeanne in 2004 and Dolly, Fay, Gustav, and Ike in 2008, the United States sustained more than $250 billion in damages and more than 2500 lives lost.

In the aftermath of Hurricane Ike in 2008, government delays held up water, ice, and food supplies for the 2 million evacuees until 4 or 5 days after landfall, thus repeating mistakes made after Katrina. As we learn through investigations of the post-storm failure to respond and assist these regions and as we see continuing mistakes in planning and engineering, the case for an integrated scientific approach to natural hazard management is clearly made.

Notebook
Record-breaking 2005 Atlantic hurricane season

Prediction and the Future

The Tropical Prediction Center, at the NHC in Miami, Florida, posts tropical cyclone forecasts on its web site. Its analysis of weather records for the period 1900–2006 disclosed a significant causal relationship between Atlantic tropical storms, including hurricanes that make landfall along the U.S. Gulf and East Coasts, and several meteorological variables, one of which was sea-surface temperatures. Subsequent research published in 2008 is more specific, correlating longer storm lifetimes and greater storm intensity with rising sea-surface temperatures:

> Atlantic tropical cyclones are getting stronger on average, with a 30-year trend that has been related to an increase in ocean temperatures. . . . The results presented here are conclusive in showing significant increasing trends in the satellite-derived lifetime-maximum wind speeds of the strongest tropical cyclones globally, and are quantitatively consistent with the heat-engine theory of cyclone intensity. Thus, as seas warm, the ocean has more energy that can be converted to tropical cyclone wind.*

Hurricanes Katrina, Rita, and Wilma in 2005 and Dean and Felix in 2007 all recorded remarkable central pressure drops as they passed over record sea-surface temperatures (see the satellite image of Katrina in Figure 1.1a). Wilma experienced a 100-mb central pressure drop in a little over 24 hours on October 19, 2005. The record sea-surface temperatures being recorded across the globe produce warmer water to depth, and the natural mixing that such storms trigger only brings up more heat to fuel the circulation. Many scientists now suggest that future warming with climate change, when considered alongside increased coastal population settlement, will produce unwanted, yet substantial, hurricane-related damage losses (Figure 1.1b and c).

Ironically, the relatively mild hurricane seasons from 1971 to 1994 encouraged weak zoning and rapid development of vulnerable coastal lowlands. New buildings, apartments, and government offices are opening right next to still visible rubble and bare foundation pads. The consequence of poor hazard planning is that our entire society bears the financial cost, not to mention those victims who directly shoulder the physical, emotional, and economic hardship of the event.

* J. B. Elsner, J. P. Kossin, and T. H. Jagger, "The increasing intensity of the strongest tropical cyclones," *Nature* 455 (September 4, 2008): 92–95.

No matter how accurate storm forecasts become, coastal and lowland property damage will continue to increase until better hazard zoning and development restrictions are in place. The property insurance industry appears to be taking action to promote these improvements. It is requiring tougher building standards to obtain coverage—and, in some cases, it is refusing to insure property along vulnerable coastal lowlands. Given the increased intensity and "power dissipation" of these storms and a rise in sea level, the public, their politicians, and business interests must respond to somehow mitigate this hazardous predicament. Given what we have experienced and what we know of Earth systems, did society learn anything? The Atlantic hurricane season begins each June 1.

(a)

FIGURE 1.1 Katrina surge clears neighborhoods and destroys highway bridge. (a) Hurricane Katrina, August 28, 2005, 11 A.M. CDT, category 5 strength. (b) NOAA aerial photo shows the power of wind and storm surge as entire Mississippi Gulf Coast neighborhoods are obliterated, such as here in Long Beach, with the debris carried by storm surge a kilometer from shore. (c) Remnants of the U.S. 90 bridge and causeway out of Bay St. Louis, Mississippi. [(a) *Terra* image, NASA/GSFC. (b) NOAA. (c) Randall Christopherson.]

Satellite
2005: 27 Storms, Arlene to Zeta

(b)

(c)

CRITICAL THINKING 5

Hazard perception and planning: What seems to be missing?

Relative to coastal devastation from tropical weather, the following statement appears in the text: "This recurrent, yet avoidable, cycle—construction, devastation, reconstruction, devastation." This describes the ever-increasing cost of property losses from tropical storms and hurricanes at a time when improved forecasts have resulted in a significant reduction in loss of life. Given the rising sea levels along coastlines and the doubling of total power dissipation in these tropical storms since 1970, in your opinion, what is the solution to halting this cycle of destruction and increasing losses? How would you implement your ideas?

GEOSYSTEMS CONNECTION

We explored the remarkable physical properties of water. The role of water in the atmosphere and humidity concepts formed the basis for examining stability and instability conditions, which lead to clouds and fog formation. We identified air masses and the conditions that force these to lift, cool, condense, and produce weather phenomena, including violent weather events such as tornadoes and tropical cyclones. The patterns of precipitation produced across the globe form the input to water resource analysis. We use the water balance model to examine inputs and outputs of the water budget. Water quality and quantity and the availability of potable water loom as major issues for the global society.

KEY LEARNING CONCEPTS REVIEW

Weather is the short-term condition of the atmosphere; **meteorology** is the scientific study of the atmosphere. The spatial implications of atmospheric phenomena and their relationship to human activities strongly link meteorology to physical geography.

weather
meteorology

■ ***Describe*** the heat properties of water, and ***identify*** the traits of its three phases: solid, liquid, and gas.

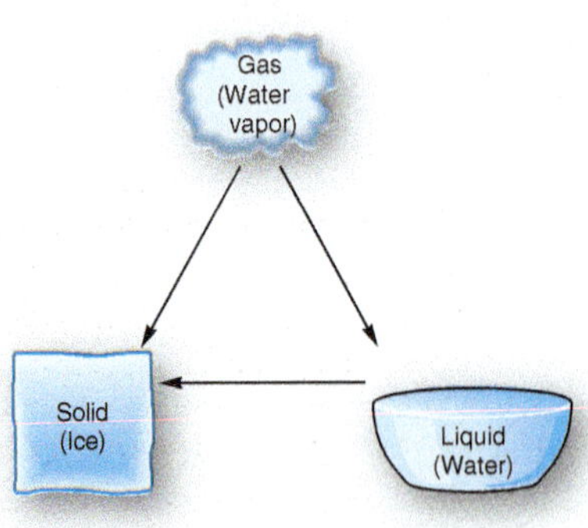

Part of Earth's uniqueness is that its water exists naturally in all three states—solid, liquid, and gas—owing to Earth's temperate position relative to the Sun. A change from one state to another is a **phase change**. The change from solid to vapor is **sublimation**; from liquid to solid, freezing; from solid to liquid, melting; from vapor to liquid, condensation; and from liquid to vapor, vaporization or evaporation.

The heat energy required for water to change phase is **latent heat** because, once absorbed, it is hidden within the structure of the water, ice, or water vapor. For 1 g of water to become 1 g of water vapor at boiling requires the addition of 540 cal, or the **latent heat of vaporization.** When this 1 g of water vapor condenses, the same amount of heat energy, 540 cal, is liberated as the **latent heat of condensation.** The *latent heat of sublimation* is the energy exchanged in the phase change from ice to vapor and vapor to ice. At less than boiling, such as in a natural setting, the **latent heat of evaporation** describes the energy absorbed during phase change. Weather is powered by the tremendous amount of latent heat energy involved in the phase changes among the three states of water.

phase change
sublimation
latent heat
latent heat of vaporization
latent heat of condensation
latent heat of evaporation

1. Describe the three states of matter as they apply to ice, water, and water vapor.
2. What happens to the physical structure of water as it cools below 4°C (39°F)? What are some visible indications of these physical changes?
3. What is latent heat? How is it involved in the phase changes of water?
4. Take 1 g of water at 0°C and follow it through to 1 g of water vapor at 100°C, describing what happens along the way. What amounts of energy are involved in the changes that take place?

■ ***Define*** humidity, relative humidity, and dew-point temperature, and ***illustrate*** stable and unstable atmospheric conditions.

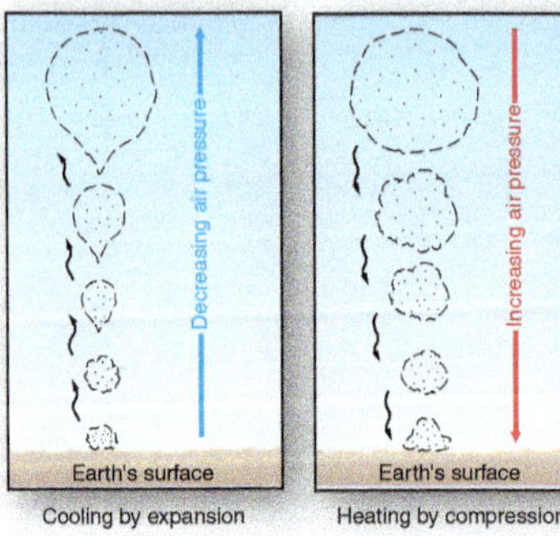

The amount of water vapor in the atmosphere is **humidity.** The maximum water vapor possible in air is principally a function of the temperature of the air and of the water vapor (usually these temperatures are the same). **Relative humidity** is a ratio of the amount of water vapor actually in the air to the maximum possible at a given temperature. Relative humidity tells us how near the air is to saturation. Relatively dry air has a lower relative humidity value; relatively moist air has a higher relative humidity percentage. Air is said to be at **saturation** when the rate of evaporation and the rate of condensation reach equilibrium, and any further addition of water vapor or temperature lowering will result in active condensation (100% relative humidity). The temperature at which air achieves saturation is the **dew-point temperature.**

Among the various ways to express humidity and relative humidity are vapor pressure and specific humidity. **Vapor pressure** is that portion of the atmospheric pressure produced by the presence of water vapor. A comparison of vapor pressure with the saturation vapor pressure at any moment yields a relative humidity percentage. **Specific humidity** is the mass of water vapor (in grams) per mass of air (in kilograms) at any specified temperature. A comparison of specific humidity with the maximum specific humidity at any moment produces a relative humidity percentage.

Meteorologists use the term *parcel* to describe a body of air that has specific temperature and humidity characteristics. Warm air has a lower density in a given volume of air; cold air has a higher density.

Stability refers to the tendency of an air parcel, with its water-vapor cargo, either to remain in place or to change vertical position by ascending (rising) or descending (falling). An air parcel is *stable* if it resists displacement upward or, when disturbed, it tends to return to its starting place. An air parcel is *unstable* if it continues to rise until it reaches an altitude where the surrounding air has a density (air temperature) similar to its own.

An ascending (rising) parcel of air cools by expansion, responding to the reduced air pressure at higher altitudes. A descending (falling) parcel heats by compression. The **normal lapse rate** is the average decrease in temperature with increasing altitude, a value of 6.4 C°/1000 m (3.5 F°/1000 ft). This rate of temperature change is for still, calm air and can vary greatly with weather conditions. Thus, the actual lapse rate at a particular place and time is labeled the **environmental lapse rate.**

The warming and cooling rates for a parcel of expanding or compressing air are termed **adiabatic.** The **dry adiabatic rate (DAR)** is the rate at which "dry" air cools by expansion (if ascending) or heats by compression (if descending). The term *dry* is used when air is less than saturated (relative humidity less than 100%). The DAR is 10 C°/1000 m (5.5 F°/1000 ft). The **moist adiabatic rate (MAR)** is the average rate at which moist (saturated) air cools by expansion (if ascending) or warms by compression (if descending). The average MAR is 6 C°/1000 m (3.3 F°/1000 ft). This is roughly 4 C° (2 F°) less than the dry rate. The MAR, however, varies with moisture content and temperature and can range from 4 to 10 C° per 1000 m (2 to 5.5 F° per 1000 ft).

A simple comparison of the DAR and MAR in a vertically moving parcel of air with the environmental lapse rate in the surrounding air determines the atmosphere's stability—whether it is unstable (lifting of air parcel continues) or stable (air parcel resists vertical displacement).

humidity
relative humidity
saturation
dew-point temperature
vapor pressure
specific humidity
stability
normal lapse rate
environmental lapse rate
adiabatic
dry adiabatic rate (DAR)
moist adiabatic rate (MAR)

5. What is humidity? How is it related to the energy present in the atmosphere? To our personal comfort and how we perceive apparent temperatures?
6. Define relative humidity. What does the concept represent? What is meant by the terms *saturation* and *dew-point temperature*?
7. Using different measures of humidity in the air than those used in the chapter, derive relative humidity values (vapor pressure/saturation vapor pressure; specific humidity/maximum specific humidity) in Figures 8 and 9.
8. How does a sling psychrometer measure relative humidity? Does your Geography Department have one?
9. Differentiate between stability and instability relative to a parcel of air rising vertically in the atmosphere.
10. What are the forces acting on a vertically moving parcel of air? How are they affected by the density of the air parcel?
11. How do the adiabatic rates of heating and cooling in vertically displaced air parcels differ from the normal lapse rate and environmental lapse rate?
12. What atmospheric temperature and moisture conditions would you expect on a day when the weather is unstable? When it is stable? Relate in your answer what you would experience if you were outside watching.
13. Use the "Atmospheric Stability" animation on the *MasteringGeography* web site. Try different temperature settings on the sliders to produce stable and unstable conditions.

■ ***Explain*** cloud formation, and ***identify*** major cloud classes and types, including fog.

A **cloud** is an aggregation of tiny moisture droplets and ice crystals suspended in the air. Clouds are a constant reminder of the powerful heat-exchange system in the environment. **Moisture droplets** form in a cloud when saturated air and the presence of **condensation nuclei** lead to *condensation*.

Low clouds, ranging from the surface up to 2000 m (6500 ft) in the middle latitudes, are **stratus** (flat clouds, in layers) or **cumulus** (puffy clouds, in heaps). When stratus clouds yield precipitation, they are **nimbostratus**. Sometimes near the end of the day, lumpy, grayish, low-level clouds called **stratocumulus** may fill the sky in patches. Middle-level clouds are denoted by the prefix *alto-*. **Altocumulus** clouds, in particular, represent a broad category that occurs in many different styles. Clouds at high altitude, principally composed of ice crystals, are called **cirrus.** A cumulus cloud can develop into a towering giant **cumulonimbus** cloud (*-nimbus* in Latin denotes "rain storm" or "thundercloud"). Such clouds are called *thunderheads* because of their shape and their associated lightning, thunder, surface wind gusts, updrafts and downdrafts, heavy rain, and hail.

Fog is a cloud that occurs at ground level. **Advection fog** forms when air in one place migrates to another place where conditions exist that can cause saturation—for example, when warm, moist air moves over cooler ocean currents. Another type of advection fog forms when cold air flows over the warm water of a lake, ocean surface, or swimming pool. This **evaporation fog**, or steam fog, may form as the water molecules evaporate from the water surface into the cold overlying air. **Upslope fog** is produced when moist air is forced to higher elevations along a hill or mountain. Another fog caused by topography is **valley fog**, formed because cool, denser air settles in low-lying areas, producing fog in the chilled, saturated layer near the ground.

Radiative cooling of a surface that chills the air layer directly above the surface to the dew-point temperature creates saturated conditions and a **radiation fog**.

cloud
moisture droplet
condensation nuclei
stratus
nimbostratus
cumulus
stratocumulus
altocumulus
cirrus
cumulonimbus
fog
advection fog
evaporation fog
upslope fog
valley fog
radiation fog

14. Specifically, what is a cloud? Describe the droplets that form a cloud.
15. Explain the condensation process: What are the requirements? What two principal processes are discussed in this chapter?
16. What are the basic forms of clouds? Using Figure 15, describe how the basic cloud forms vary with altitude.
17. Explain how clouds might be used as indicators of the conditions of the atmosphere and of expected weather.
18. What type of cloud is fog? List and define the principal types of fog.

■ ***Describe*** air masses that affect North America, and ***identify*** four types of atmospheric lifting mechanisms.

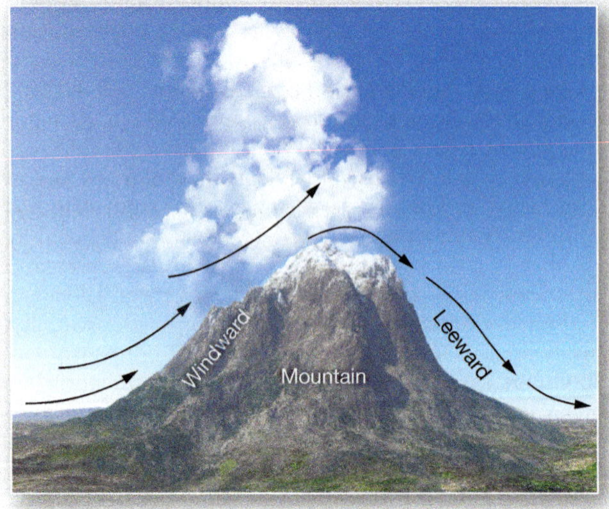

Specific conditions of humidity, stability, and cloud coverage occur in a regional, homogenous **air mass**. The longer an air mass remains stationary over a region, the more definite its physical attributes become. Air masses are categorized by their moisture content—**m** for maritime (wetter) and **c** for continental (drier)—and their temperature, a function of latitude—designated **A** (arctic), **P** (polar), **T** (tropical), **E** (equatorial), and **AA** (antarctic).

Air masses can rise through **convergent lifting** (converging air flows conflict, forcing some of the air to lift), **convectional lifting** (air passing over warm surfaces gains buoyancy), **orographic lifting** (passage over a topographic barrier), and *frontal lifting*. In North America, *chinook winds* (called *föhn* or *foehn* winds in Europe) are the warm, downslope air flows characteristic of the leeward side of mountains. Orographic lifting creates wetter windward slopes and drier leeward slopes situated in the **rain shadow** of the mountain. Conflicting air masses at a front produce a **cold front** (and sometimes a zone of strong wind and rain) or a **warm front**. A zone right along or slightly ahead of the front, called a **squall line**, is characterized by turbulent and wildly changing wind patterns and intense precipitation.

air mass
convergent lifting
convectional lifting
orographic lifting
rain shadow
cold front
warm front
squall line

19. How does a source region influence the type of air mass that forms over it? Give specific examples of each basic classification.
20. Of all the air masses, which are of greatest significance to the United States and Canada? What happens to them as they migrate to locations different from their source regions? Give an example of air mass modification.
21. Explain why it is necessary for an air mass to be lifted if there is to be saturation, condensation, and precipitation.
22. What are the four principal lifting mechanisms that cause air masses to ascend, cool, condense, form clouds, and perhaps produce precipitation? Briefly describe each.
23. Differentiate between the structures of a cold front and a warm front.

■ ***Describe*** the life cycle of a midlatitude cyclonic storm system, and ***list*** the measurable elements that contribute to weather forecasting.

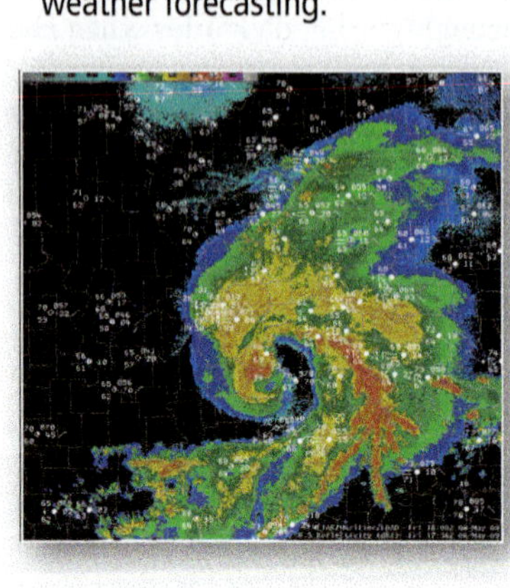

A **midlatitude cyclone**, or **wave cyclone**, is a vast low-pressure system that migrates across the continent, pulling air masses into conflict along fronts. These systems are guided by the jet streams of the upper troposphere along seasonally shifting *storm tracks*. *Cyclogenesis*, the birth of the low-pressure circulation, can occur off the west coast of North America, along the polar front, along the lee slopes of the Rockies, in the Gulf of Mexico, and along the East Coast. A midlatitude cyclone can be thought of as having a life cycle of birth, maturity, old age, and dissolution. An **occluded front** is produced when a cold front overtakes a warm front in the maturing cyclone.

Synoptic analysis involves the collection of weather data at a specific time. Computer-based weather prediction and the development of weather forecasting models rely on data such as barometric pressure, surface air temperatures, dew-point temperatures, wind speed and direction, clouds, sky conditions, and visibility. On weather maps, these elements appear as specific weather station symbols.

midlatitude cyclone
wave cyclone
occluded front

24. Differentiate between a cold front and a warm front as to types of frontal lifting and describe what you would experience with each one.
25. How does a midlatitude cyclone act as a catalyst for conflict between air masses?
26. Diagram a midlatitude cyclonic storm during its open stage. Label each of the components in your illustration and add arrows to indicate wind patterns in the system.
27. What is your principal source of weather data, information, and forecasts? Where does your source obtain its data? Have you used the Internet and World Wide Web to obtain weather information? What benefits do you see?

■ ***Analyze*** various types of violent weather—thunderstorms, tornadoes, and tropical cyclones, including recent trends.

The violent power of some weather phenomena poses a hazard to society. Thunderstorms produce **lightning** (electrical discharges in the atmosphere), **thunder** (sonic bangs produced by the rapid expansion of air after intense heating by lightning), and **hail** (ice pellets formed within cumulonimbus clouds).

Strong linear winds in excess of 26 m/s (58 mph) are known as **derechos** and are associated with thunderstorms and bands of showers crossing a region. Straight-line winds can cause significant damage and crop losses. A spinning, cyclonic column rising to mid-troposphere level—a **mesocyclone**—is sometimes visible as the swirling mass of a cumulonimbus cloud, especially in a *supercell* system. Dark gray **funnel clouds** pulse from the bottom side of the parent cloud. A **tornado** is formed when the funnel connects with Earth's surface. A **waterspout** forms when a tornado circulation occurs over water.

Within tropical air masses, large low-pressure centers can form along easterly wave troughs. Under the right conditions, a tropical cyclone is produced. Depending on wind speeds and central pressure, a **tropical cyclone** can become a **hurricane, typhoon,** or *cyclone* when winds exceed 65 knots (74 mph, or 119 kmph). As forecasting of weather-related hazards improves, loss of life decreases, although property damage continues to increase.

lightning
thunder
hail
derecho
mesocyclone
funnel cloud
tornado
waterspout
tropical cyclone
hurricane
typhoon

28. What constitutes a thunderstorm? What type of cloud is involved? What type of air mass would you expect in an area of thunderstorms in North America?
29. Lightning and thunder are powerful phenomena in nature. Briefly describe how they develop.
30. Describe the formation process of a mesocyclone. How is this development associated with that of a tornado?
31. Evaluate the pattern of tornado activity in the United States. What generalizations can you make about the distribution and timing of tornadoes? Do you perceive a trend in tornado occurrences in the United States? Explain.
32. What are the different classifications for tropical cyclones? List the various names used worldwide for hurricanes. Have any hurricanes ever occurred in the South Atlantic?
33. What have scientists said to explain the intensity of tropical cyclones since 1970? Put into your own words the quotations in this chapter from scientific journals related to changes in storm intensity.
34. Relative to improving weather forecasting, what are some of the technological innovations discussed in this chapter?

Visit **http://www.masteringgeography.com/** for several figure animations, satellite loops, self-study quizzes, flashcards, visual glossary, case studies, career links, text reference maps, RSS Feeds, and an ebook version of *Elemental Geosystems.* Included are many geography web links to interesting Internet sources that support this chapter.

Water Resources

Water Resources

The western United States, particularly the Southwest, is experiencing a prolonged drought. Hoover Dam on the Arizona–Nevada border backs up Lake Mead on the Colorado River. The maximum reservoir elevation of 374.6 m (1229 ft) is shown in the July 1983 photo of Lake Mead. Twenty-seven years later, in 2010, Lake Mead was at 330 m (1083 ft), or about 44.6 m (146 ft) lower than 1983. More on this in Focus Study 1 in this chapter. The roadway over the dam closed in late 2010 as a new bypass bridge opened. [(1983) Author. (2010) Bobbé Christopherson.]

KEY LEARNING CONCEPTS

After reading the chapter, you should be able to:

- ***Describe*** the origin of Earth's waters, ***define*** the quantity of water that exists today, and ***list*** the locations of Earth's freshwater supply.
- ***Illustrate*** the hydrologic cycle with a simple sketch, and ***label*** it with definitions for each water pathway.
- ***Relate*** the importance of the water-budget concept to your understanding of the hydrologic cycle, water resources, and soil moisture for a specific location.
- ***Construct*** the water-balance equation as a way of accounting for the expenditures of the water supply, and ***define*** each of the components in the equation and its specific operation.
- ***Describe*** the nature of groundwater, and ***define*** the elements of the groundwater environment.
- ***Evaluate*** the U.S. water budget, and ***identify*** critical aspects of present and future freshwater supplies.

GEOSYSTEMS NOW

Lake Baikal: Earth's Oldest Lake Provides a Warming Signal

Lake Baikal, located between 52° and 56° north latitude in south-central Siberia, is the world's largest (by volume), deepest, oldest, and most biologically diverse lake. Holding 23,600 km^3 (5,662 mi^3) of water, more than all five of the U.S. Great Lakes combined, the lake contains 20% of the world's liquid freshwater, earning it the well-deserved label "well of the planet." At its deepest point, the lake descends 1642 m (5387 ft) and is deeper than the Grand Canyon. At nearly 644 km (400 mi) long with a surface area of 31,500 km^2 (12,200 mi^2), this enormous crescent-shaped lake is easily seen in satellite images or on a world map (Figure GN 1).

The region around Lake Baikal is currently experiencing some of the most rapid climate change on Earth. During the past century, annual air temperatures increased 1.2 C° (2.1 F°), twice the global average, with a greater temperature increase occurring in winter than summer. Water temperatures warmed rapidly to a depth of 25 m (82 ft) during the past 60 years. By the end of this century, scientists predict Baikal's winters will be warmer by 4.3 C° (7.7 F°) and much wetter, with 26% more winter precipitation than present averages. As air temperatures warm and winter snow increases, several changes occur in the lake environment: The timing of ice cover is altered and duration is reduced, the ice becomes thinner, wind patterns change, and the transparency of the ice is reduced as more snow accumulates and less wind clears the snow away. These changes are already affecting Lake Baikal's ecosystems.

Warmer water interrupts vertical mixing of the lake water and nutrient cycling. Normally, stratification occurs in the summer in most lakes, with warmer water at the surface and cooler water at depth. This leads to a depletion of nutrients in the shallows by late summer. In the fall, as the surface cools, water sinks, creating a turnover that replenishes surface nutrients throughout the lake. In Lake Baikal, wind assists such mixing. As regional temperatures warm, the summerlike stratification appears earlier in the year and persists later in the fall, and mixing slows or stops. Scientists suggest that prolonged stratification could adversely affect Baikal's phytoplankton, microscopic algae that form the basis of the lake's food web (Figure GN 2).

Since the lake freezes for 4 to 5 months every year, ice is an important variable at Baikal. It is the only lake in the world in which both the dominant primary producers (phytoplankton) and the top predator (the Baikal seal, locally known as the Nerpa) require ice for reproduction. Thickness and transparency determine the amount of light penetrating through the ice and are critical for phytoplankton. For centuries, these organisms adapted to life under the ice; present changes affect spring algal blooms and decrease growth rates.

FIGURE GN 2 Unique lake ecosystem. [Debra Sharkey.]

The effects of decreasing algae populations then move up the food chain, which includes tiny crustaceans that occur in enormous quantities and are a major food source for fish, as well as Baikal's many fish species, the main food source for seals. The Baikal seal (*Phoca sibirica*), smallest of the world's seals and the only species exclusively living in freshwater, mates and gives birth on the lake ice. Changes to ice cover and thickness are critical for these seals, which require ice in early spring. If ice melt occurs early, the seals are forced into the water, and the extra energy expended affects female fertility.

From a systems perspective, the timing and thickness of Lake Baikal's ice cover, and related changes to its water temperature, exemplify how changes in the atmosphere link to changes in the hydrosphere and biosphere. The lake's unique living ecosystem is already feeling the effects of changing climate, as are Earth's other major lakes that are experiencing similar warming trends. ■

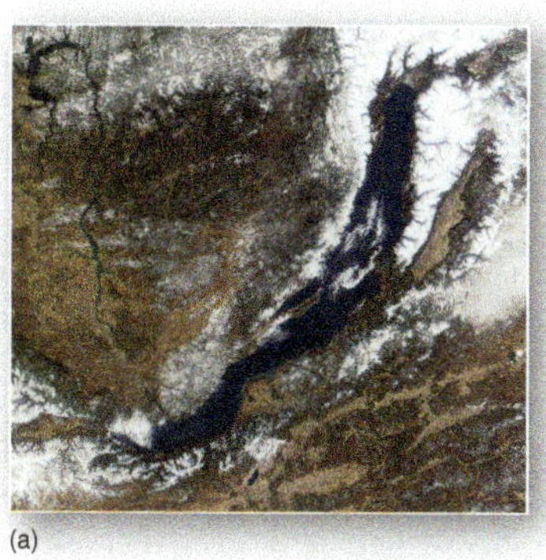

(a)

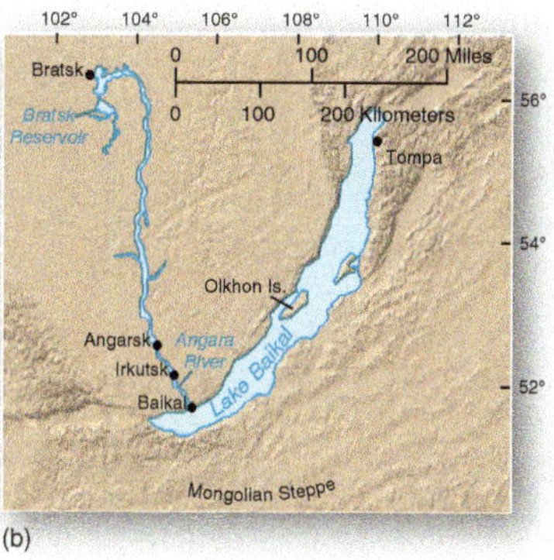

(b)

FIGURE GN 1 Lake Baikal.
(a) An October view of the lake as snowpack accumulates in the mountains. (b) Some 300 rivers flow in but only the Angara River flows out. [(a) Terra MODIS, NASA/GSFC.]

The physical reality of life is defined by water. Our lives are infused with water. Our own bodies are about 70% water, as are plants and animals. We use water to cook, bathe, wash clothing, and dilute our wastes. We water small gardens and vast agricultural tracts. Most industrial processes would be impossible without water. It is the essence of our existence and is therefore the most critical resource supplied by Earth systems—the essential resource for life.

In the Solar System, water occurs in significant quantities only on our planet—water covers 71% of Earth by area. Yet water is not always naturally available where and when we want it. Consequently, we rearrange surface water resources to suit our needs. We drill wells, build cisterns and reservoirs, and dam and divert streams to redirect water either spatially (geographically, from one area to another) or temporally (over time, from one part of the calendar to another). All of this activity constitutes water-resource management.

Fortunately, water is a renewable resource, constantly cycling through the environment. Even so, some 1.1 billion people lack safe drinking water. People in 80 countries face impending water shortages, either in quantity or in quality, or both. Approximately 2.4 billion people lack adequate sanitary facilities—80% of these in Africa and 13% in Asia. This translates to approximately 2 million deaths a year due to lack of water and 5 million deaths a year from waterborne infections and disease. An investment in safe drinking water, sanitation, and hygiene could decrease these numbers.

During the first half of this century, water availability per person will drop by 74% as population increases and adequate water decreases. Author Peter Gleick summarized:

> The overall economic and social benefits of meeting basic water requirements far outweigh any reasonable assessment of the costs of providing those needs. . . . Water-related diseases cost society on the order of $125 billion per year. . . . Yet the cost of providing new infrastructure needs for all major urban water sectors has been estimated at around $25 to $50 billion per year.*

Thus, one role for geographic science with its integrative, spatial approach is to analyze water resources with a comprehensive global portrait in mind, striving toward a world water economy that would more effectively allocate investment to better mitigate the coming crisis (see the World Water Assessment Program, UNESCO, http://www.unesco.org/water/wwap/).

In this chapter: We begin with water on Earth, including its origin and distribution on the planet. We examine the hydrologic cycle, which gives us a model for understanding the global water balance. We look at water resources using a water-budget approach—similar in many ways to a money budget—in which we examine water "receipts" and "expenses" at specific locations. This budget approach can be applied at any scale, from a small garden, to a farm, to a regional landscape such as the High Plains aquifer or Lake Baikal in Asia, discussed in *Geosystems Now*.

About half the U.S. population draws freshwater from groundwater resources, yet groundwater is tied to surface-water supplies for recharge. This chapter concludes by considering the quantity and quality of the water we withdraw and consume for irrigation, industrial, and municipal uses—our specific water supply. Water supplies of adequate quantity and quality loom as the most important resource issue for many parts of the world in this century.

*P. Gleick, *The World's Water*, a biennial report (Washington, DC: Island Press, 2008; http://www.worldwater.org/).

Water on Earth

Earth's hydrosphere contains about 1.36 billion cubic kilometers of water (specifically, 1,359,208,000 km^3, or 326,074,000 mi^3). According to scientific evidence, much of Earth's water originated from icy comets and hydrogen- and oxygen-laden debris that were part of the planetesimals that coalesced to form the planet. In 2007, the orbiting Spitzer Space Telescope observed for the first time the presence of water vapor and ice as planets form in a system 1000 light-years from Earth. Such discoveries prove water to be abundant throughout the Universe. As a planet forms, water from within migrates to its surface and outgasses.

Outgassing is a continuing process by which water and water vapor emerge from layers deep within and below the crust, 25 km (15.5 mi) or more below Earth's surface. Figure 1 presents two such areas, among many sites worldwide, in Iceland and Wyoming.

In the early atmosphere, massive quantities of outgassed water vapor condensed and then fell to Earth in torrential rains. For water to remain on Earth's surface, land temperatures had to drop below the boiling point of 100°C (212°F), something that occurred about 3.8 billion years ago. The lowest places across the face of Earth then began to fill with water—first ponds, then lakes and seas, and eventually ocean-sized bodies of water. Massive flows of water washed over the landscape, carrying both dissolved and solid materials to these early seas and oceans. Outgassing of water has continued ever since and is visible in volcanic eruptions, geysers, and seepage to the surface.

Worldwide Equilibrium

Today, water is the most common compound on the surface of Earth, having attained the present volume approximately 2 billion years ago. This quantity has remained relatively constant, even though water is continuously being lost from the system. Water is lost when it dissociates into hydrogen and oxygen and the hydrogen escapes

(a)

(b)

FIGURE 1 Water outgassing from the crust.
Outgassing of water from Earth's crust in geothermal areas: (a) in southern Iceland west of where the Eyjafjallajökull volcano erupted in 2010 and (b) thermal features, travertine deposits, and hot mineral pools visible from the trail in Yellowstone National Park, Wyoming. [(a) Bobbé Christopherson. (b) Author.]

Earth's gravity to space or when it breaks down and forms new compounds with other elements. As pristine water not previously at the surface emerges from within Earth's crust, it replaces lost water in the system. The net result of these water inputs and outputs is that Earth's hydrosphere is in a steady-state equilibrium in terms of quantity.

Despite this overall net balance in water quantity, worldwide changes in sea level do occur. The concept **eustasy** describes the global sea-level condition. Eustatic changes relate to the water volume in the oceans and not changes in the overall quantity of planetary water. Some of these changes result when the amount of water stored in glaciers and ice sheets varies; these are *glacio-eustatic* factors. In cooler times, as more water is bound up in glaciers (on mountains worldwide and in high latitudes) and in ice sheets (on Greenland and Antarctica), sea level lowers. In warmer times, less water is stored as ice, so sea level rises.

Some 18,000 years ago, during the most recent ice age, sea level was more than 100 m (330 ft) lower than it is today; 40,000 years ago it was 150 m (about 500 ft) lower. Over the past 100 years, mean sea level has risen by 20–40 cm (8–16 in.) and is still rising worldwide at an accelerating pace as higher temperatures melt more ice and cause ocean water to thermally expand.

Distribution of Earth's Water Today

From a geographic point of view, ocean and land surfaces are distributed unevenly. If you examine a globe, it is obvious that most of Earth's continental land is in the Northern Hemisphere, whereas water dominates the Southern Hemisphere. In fact, when you look at Earth from certain angles, it appears to have an *oceanic hemisphere* and a *land hemisphere* (Figure 2).

The present location of all of Earth's liquid and frozen water—whether fresh or saline, surface or underground—is indicated in Figure 3. The oceans contain 97.22% of all water (Figure 3a). Only 2.78% of all of Earth's water is freshwater (nonoceanic). The middle pie chart details this freshwater portion—surface water and subsurface water (Figure 3b). Ice sheets and glaciers are the greatest single repository of surface freshwater; they contain 77.14% of all of Earth's freshwater. Adding subsurface groundwater to frozen surface water accounts for 99.36% of all freshwater. The remaining freshwater, which resides in lakes, rivers, and streams, actually represents less than 1% of all water (Figure 3c).

GEO REPORT 1 *Earth's lakes respond to climate change*

Increasing air temperatures are affecting lakes throughout the world, as some lake levels rise in response to the melting of glacial ice, and some lake levels fall as a result of drought and high evaporation rates. Longer, warmer summers change the thermal structure of a lake, blocking the normal mixing between deep and surface waters. Lake Tahoe in the Sierra Nevada mountain range along the California–Nevada border is warming at about 1.3 C° (2.3 F°) per decade. The rate of warming is highest in the upper 10 m (33 ft), and mixing has slowed. Invasive large-mouth bass, carp, and Asian clam are on the rise, while cold-water species decline. Lake Tanganyika in East Africa is surrounded by an estimated 10 million people, with most depending on its fish stocks, especially freshwater sardines, for food. Present water temperatures are unprecedented, reaching 26°C (79°F), the highest in a 1500-year climate record exposed by lake sediment cores. The mixing of surface and deep waters is necessary to replenish nutrients in the upper 200 m (656 ft) of the lake, where the sardines reside. Scientists fear that fish stocks will continue to decline.

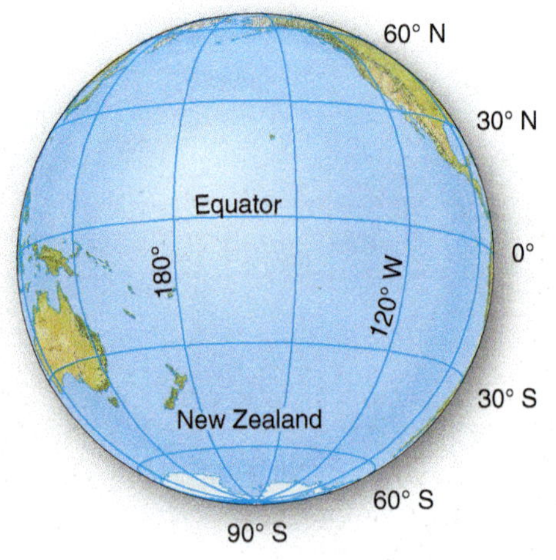

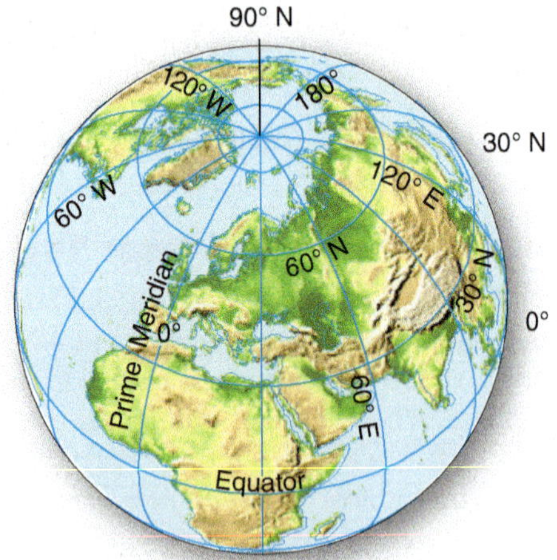

FIGURE 2 Land and water hemispheres. Two perspectives that roughly illustrate Earth's ocean hemisphere and land hemisphere.

The Hydrologic Cycle

Vast currents of water, water vapor, ice, and energy are flowing about us continuously in an elaborate, open, global plumbing system. Together, they form the **hydrologic cycle**, which has operated for billions of years, from the lower atmosphere to several kilometers beneath Earth's surface. The cycle involves the circulation and transformation of water throughout Earth's atmosphere, hydrosphere, lithosphere, and biosphere.

A Hydrologic Cycle Model

Figure 4 is a simplified model of this complex system. Let us use the ocean as a starting point for our discussion, although we could jump into the model at any point. More than 97% of Earth's water is in the ocean, and here most evaporation and precipitation occur. We can trace 86% of all evaporation to the ocean. The other 14% is from the land, including water moving from the soil into plant roots and passing through their leaves (the process of *transpiration*, described later in this chapter). Estimates of the volume of water involved in these pathways are given in thousands of km^3.

In the figure, you can see that of the 86% of evaporation rising from the ocean, 66% combines with 12% advected (moving horizontally) from the land to produce the 78% of all precipitation that falls back into the ocean. The remaining 20% of moisture evaporated from the ocean, plus 2% of land-derived moisture, produces the 22% of all precipitation that falls over land. Clearly, the bulk of continental precipitation comes from the oceanic portion of the cycle. Regionally, the different parts of the cycle will vary, creating imbalances and, depending on climate, surpluses in one region and shortages in another.

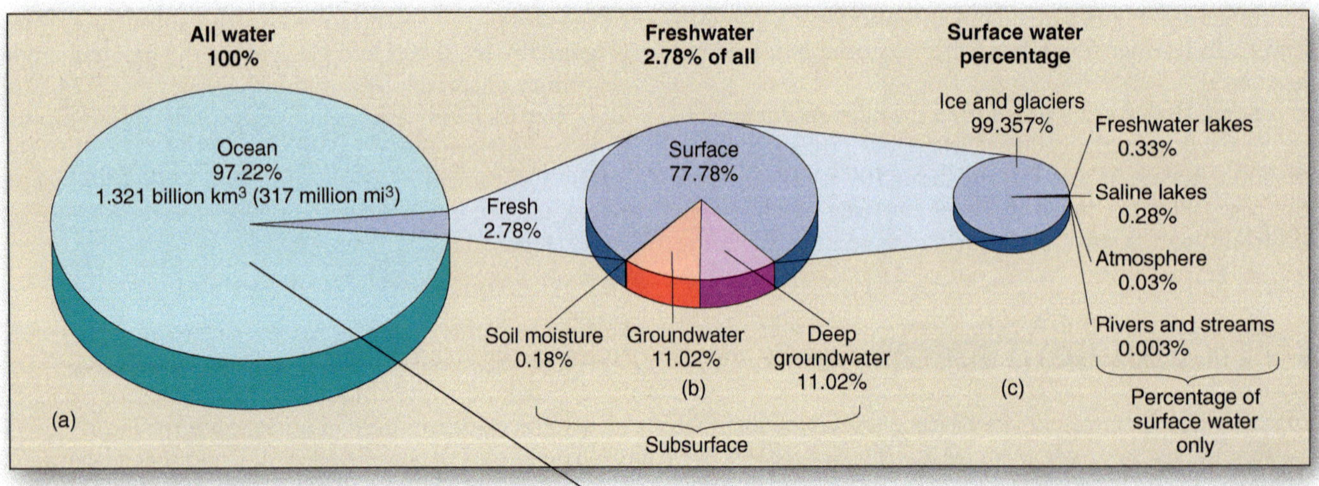

Ocean	Earth's Ocean Area (%)	*Area (km^2 [mi^2])	*Volume (km^3 [mi^3])	Mean Depth of Main Basin (m [ft])
Pacific	48	179,670 (69,370)	724,330 (173,700)	4280 (14,040)
Atlantic	28	106,450 (41,100)	355,280 (85,200)	3930 (12,890)
Indian	20	74,930 (28,930)	292,310 (70,100)	3960 (12,900)
Arctic	4	14,090 (5440)	17,100 (4100)	1205 (3950)

*Data in thousands (000): includes all marginal seas.

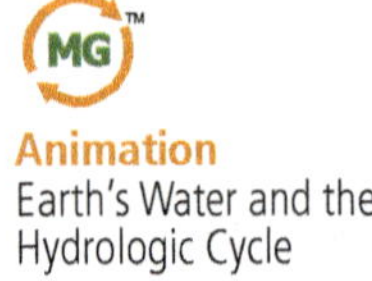

Animation
Earth's Water and the Hydrologic Cycle

FIGURE 3 Ocean and freshwater distribution on Earth. The location and percentages of (a) all water, (b) freshwater including subsurface water, and (c) surface water only.

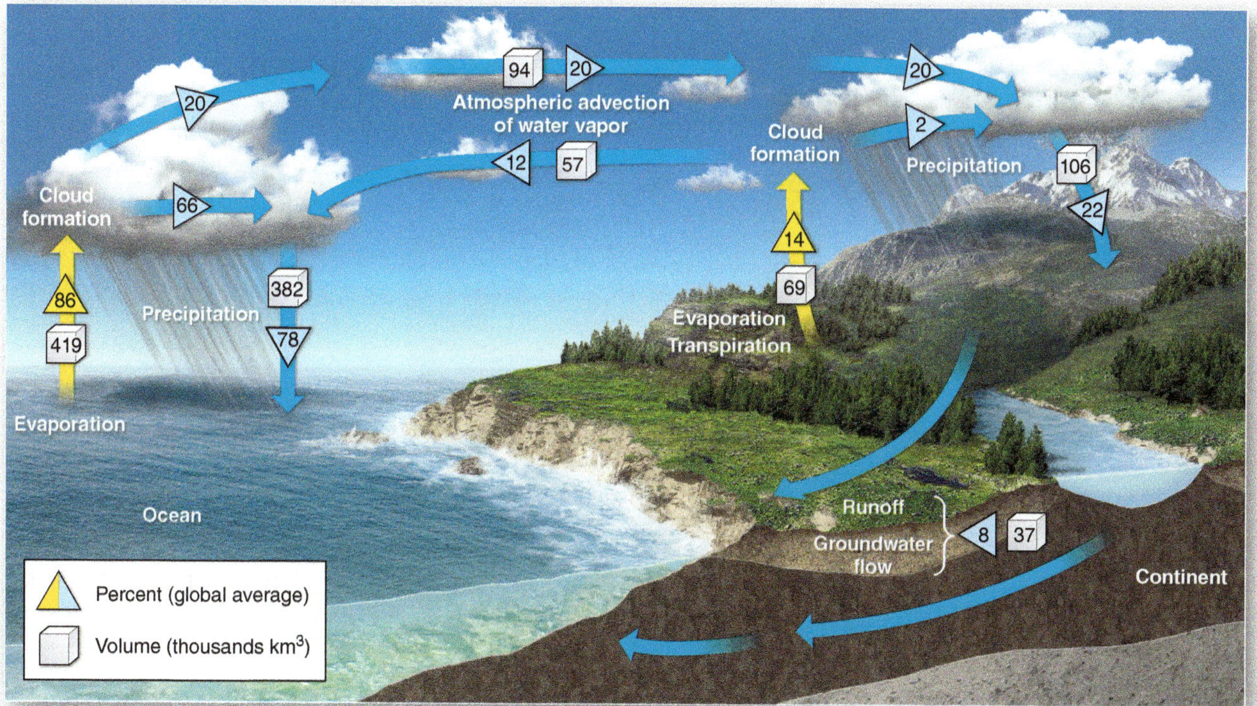

FIGURE 4 The hydrologic cycle model.
Water travels endlessly through the hydrosphere, atmosphere, lithosphere, and biosphere. The triangles show global average values as percentages. Note that all evaporation (86% + 14% = 100%) equals all precipitation (78% + 22% = 100%), and advection in the atmosphere is balanced by surface and subsurface water runoff when all of Earth is considered (1 $km^3 \times 0.24 = 1\ mi^3$).

Animation
Earth's Water and the Hydrologic Cycle

Surface Water

Precipitation that reaches Earth's surface follows two basic pathways: It either flows overland or soaks into the soil. Water soaks into the subsurface through **infiltration**, or penetration of the soil surface. It further permeates soil or rock through the downward movement of **percolation**. These concepts are shown in Figure 5.

The atmospheric advection of water vapor from sea to land and land to sea at the top of Figure 4 appears to be unbalanced, with 20% (94,000 km^3) moving inland, but only 12% (57,000 km^3) moving out to sea. However, this exchange is balanced by the 8% (37,000 km^3) that is land runoff, which flows to the sea. Most of this runoff—about 95%—comes from surface waters that wash across land as overland flow and streamflow. Only 5% of runoff is slow-moving subsurface groundwater. These percentages indicate that the small amount of water in rivers and streams is dynamic; in contrast, the large quantity of subsurface water is sluggish and represents only a small portion of total runoff.

The residence time for a water molecule in any part of the hydrologic cycle determines its relative importance in affecting Earth's climates. The short time spent by water in transit through the atmosphere (an average of 10 days) plays a role in temporary fluctuations in regional weather patterns. Long residence times, such as the 3000–10,000 years in deep-ocean circulation, groundwater aquifers, and glacial ice, act to moderate temperature and climatic changes. These slower parts of the cycle work as a "system memory"; the long periods over which heat energy is stored and released can buffer the effects of system changes.

Soil-Water-Budget Concept

An effective method for assessing water resources is to establish a **soil-water budget** for any area of Earth's surface—a continent, country, region, field, or front yard. Key is measuring the precipitation "supply" input and its distribution to satisfy the "demand" outputs of plants,

The water we use

On an individual level in the United States, urban dwellers directly use an average of 680 L (180 gal) of water per person per day, whereas rural populations average only 265 L (70 gal) or less per person per day. Take a moment and speculate why there is a difference. However, overall individual water use is actually much higher than these figures because of indirect use, such as consuming food and beverages made using water-intensive practices. See *World's Water 2008–2009,* Table 19, at http://www.worldwater.org/data.html, for more on these indirect uses of water.

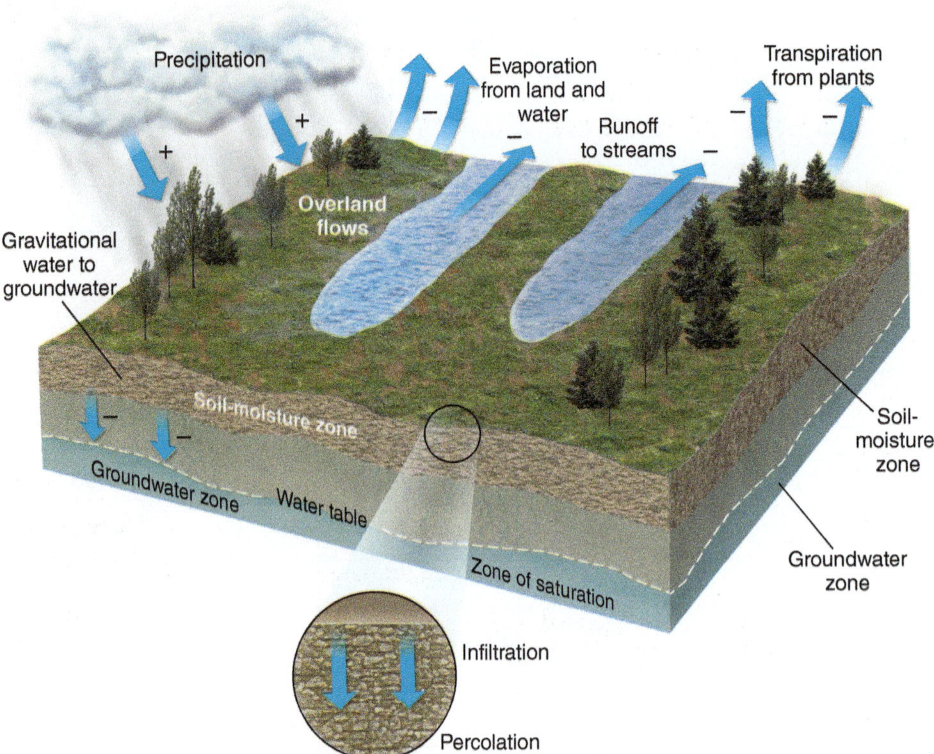

FIGURE 5 The soil-moisture environment.
The principal pathways for precipitation include interception by plants; throughfall to the ground; collection on the surface, forming overland flow to streams; transpiration and evaporation from plants; evaporation from land and water; and gravitational water moving to subsurface groundwater.

evaporation, and soil-moisture storage in the area considered. Geographer Charles W. Thornthwaite (1899–1963) pioneered applied water-resource analysis and worked with others to develop a water-balance methodology. They applied water-balance concepts to solving problems, especially related to irrigation, which requires accurate quantity and timing of water application to maximize crop yields.

The Soil-Water-Balance Equation

To understand Thornthwaite's water-balance methodology and "accounting" or "bookkeeping" procedures, we must first understand some terms and concepts. Figure 5 illustrates the essential aspects of a soil-water budget. Precipitation (mostly rain and snow) provides the moisture input. The object, as with a money budget, is to account for the ways in which this supply is distributed: actual water taken by evaporation and plant transpiration, extra water that exits in streams and subsurface groundwater, and recharge or utilization of soil-moisture storage.

Figure 6 organizes the water-balance components into an equation. As in all equations, the two sides must balance; that is, the precipitation receipt (left side) must be fully accounted for by expenditures (right side). Follow this water-balance equation as you read the following paragraphs. To help you learn these concepts, we use letter abbreviations (such as PRECIP) for the components.

Precipitation (PRECIP) Input The moisture supply to Earth's surface is **precipitation** (PRECIP, or P). It arrives in several different forms depending on temperature and moisture supply. On the *MasteringGeography* web site, Table 1 summarizes the different types of precipitation. As you read through this table, recall which types of precipitation you have experienced—rain, sleet, snow, and hail being most common.

Precipitation is measured with the **rain gauge**, essentially a large measuring cup that collects rainfall and snowfall so the water can be measured by depth, weight,

GEO REPORT 3 *How is water measured?*

In most of the United States, hydrologists measure streamflow in cubic feet per second (ft^3/s); Canadians use cubic meters per second (m^3/s). In the eastern United States, and for large-scale assessments, water managers use millions of gallons a day (MGD), billions of gallons a day (BGD), or billions of liters per day (BLD).

In the western United States, where irrigated agriculture is so important, the measure frequently used is acre-feet per year. One acre-foot is an acre of water, 1 ft deep, equivalent to 325,872 gal (43,560 ft^3, or 1234 m^3, or 1,233,429 L). An acre is an area that is about 208 ft on a side and is 0.4047 hectares. For global measurements, 1 km^3 = 1 billion m^3 = 810 million acre-feet; 1000 m^3 = 264,200 gal = 0.81 acre-feet. For smaller measures, 1 m^3 = 1000 L = 264.2 gal.

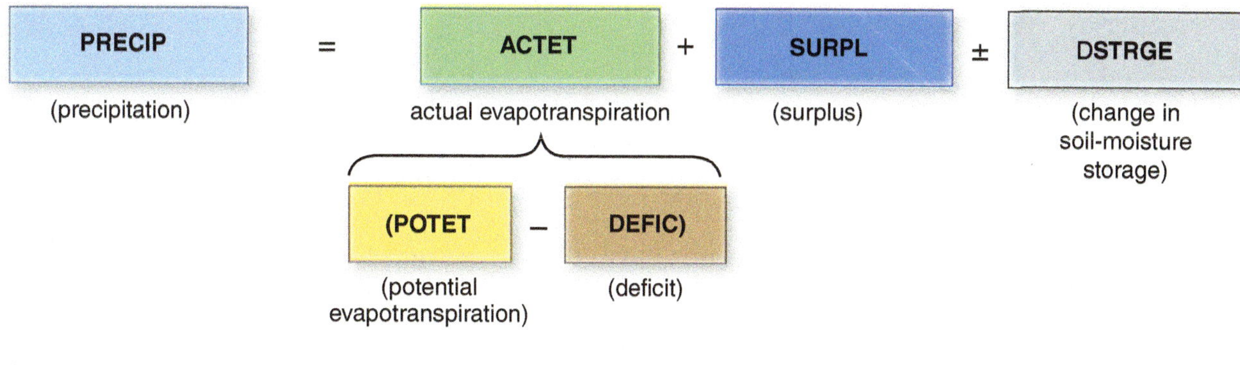

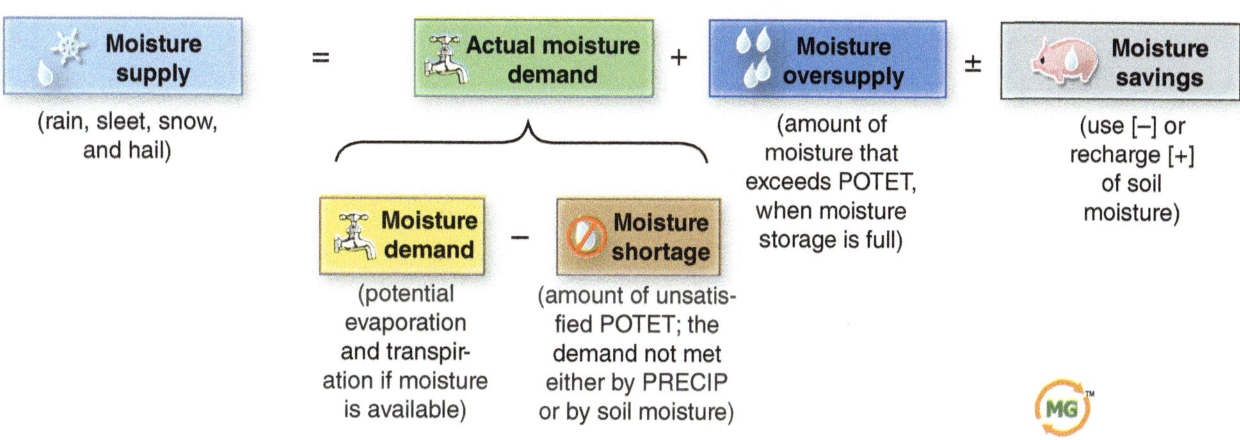

FIGURE 6 The water-balance equation explained.
The outputs (components to the right of the equal sign) are an accounting of expenditures from the precipitation moisture-supply input (to the left).

MG™ Satellite Global Water Balance Components

or volume (Figure 7). Wind can cause an undercatch because the drops or snowflakes are not falling vertically. For example, a wind of 37 kmph (23 mph) produces an undercatch as great as 40%, meaning that an actual 1-in. rainfall might gauge at only 0.6 in. The *wind shield* you see above the gauge's opening reduces this error by catching raindrops that arrive at an angle. According to the World Meteorological Organization (http://www.wmo.ch/), more than 40,000 weather-monitoring stations are operating worldwide, with more than 100,000 places measuring precipitation.

Figure 8 maps precipitation patterns for the United States and Canada. Note the patterns of wetness and dryness as you remember air masses and lifting mechanisms. PRECIP is the principal input to the water-balance equation in Figure 6. All the components discussed next are outputs or expenditures of this water.

Actual Evapotranspiration (ACTET) **Evaporation** is the net movement of free water molecules away from a wet surface into air that is less than saturated. **Transpiration** is a flow and cooling mechanism in plants. When a plant transpires, it moves water through small openings called stomata in the

FIGURE 7 A rain gauge.
A funnel guides water into a bucket that is sitting on an electronic weighing device. The gauge minimizes evaporation, which would cause low readings. The wind shield around the top of the gauge minimizes the undercatch produced by wind. [Bobbé Christopherson.]

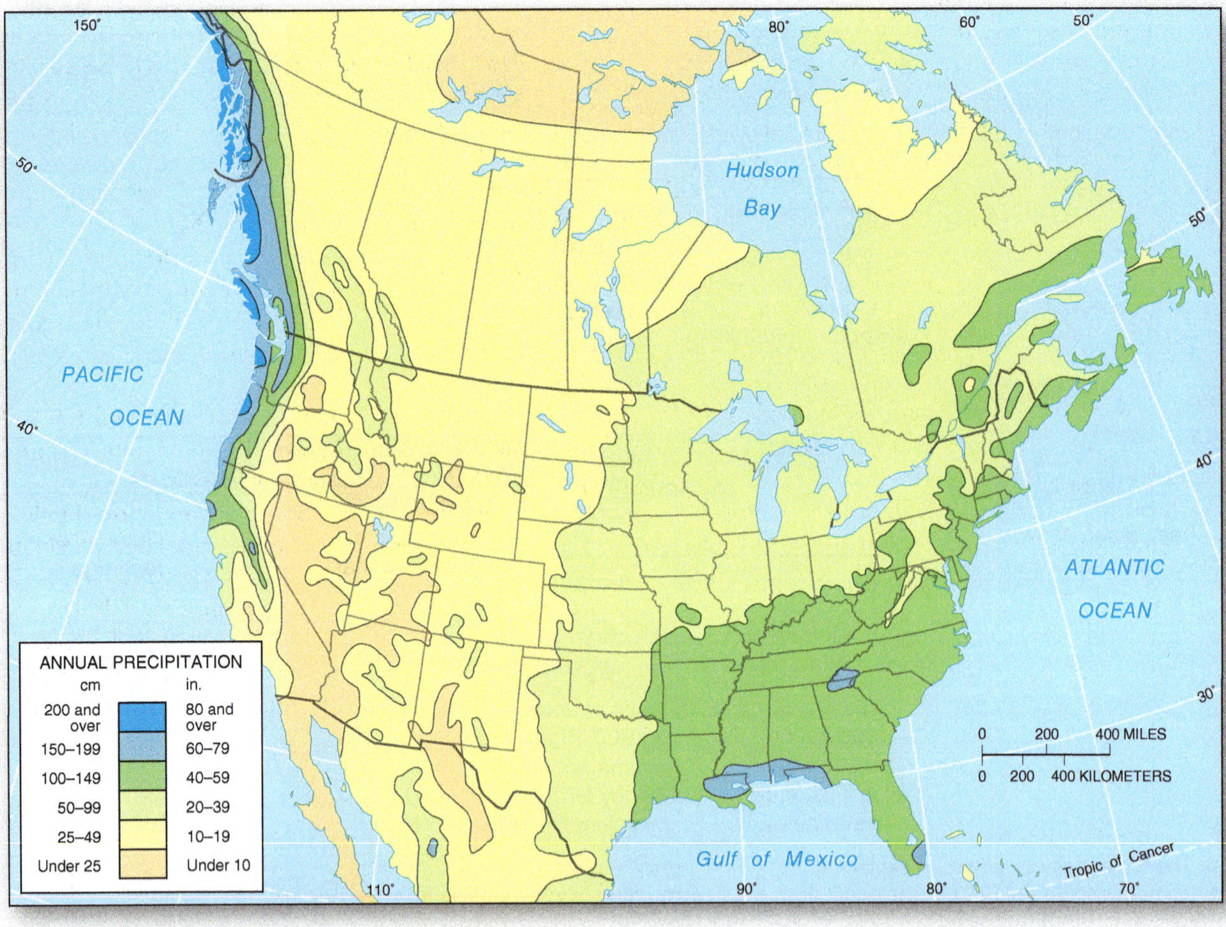

FIGURE 8 Precipitation (PRECIP) in North America—the water supply. [Adapted from NWS, U.S. Department of Agriculture, and Environment Canada.]

underside of its leaves. The water evaporates, cooling the plant, much as perspiration cools humans. Transpiration is partially regulated by the plants themselves. Control cells around the stomata conserve or release water. Transpired quantities can be significant: On a hot day, a single tree can transpire hundreds of liters of water and a forest, millions of liters. Evaporation and transpiration are combined into one term—**evapotranspiration**—and 14% of evapotranspiration occurs from land and plants.

Potential Evapotranspiration (POTET) Evapotranspiration is an actual expenditure of water. In contrast, **potential evapotranspiration** (POTET, or PET, or PE) is the amount of water that would evaporate and transpire under optimum moisture conditions when adequate precipitation and adequate soil-moisture supply are present.

Filling a bowl with water and letting the water evaporate illustrates this concept: When the bowl becomes dry, is there still an evaporation demand? The demand remains, of course, regardless of whether the bowl is dry. If you always kept water in the bowl, the amount of water that would evaporate or transpire is the POTET, or the optimum demand, given a constant supply of water. If you let the bowl dry out, the amount of POTET demand that went unmet is the shortage, or deficit (DEFIC). Note that in the water-balance equation, when we subtract the deficit from the potential evapotranspiration, we derive what actually happened—ACTET.

Figure 9 presents POTET values derived using Thornthwaite's approach for the United States and Canada. Compare this POTET (demand) map with the PRECIP (supply) map in Figure 8. The relation between the two determines the remaining components of the water-balance equation in Figure 6. From the two maps, can you identify regions where PRECIP is greater than POTET (for example, the eastern United States)? Or where POTET is greater than PRECIP (for example, the southwestern United States)? Does your area experience a natural water shortage? How might you find out?

Determining POTET Although exact measurement is difficult, one method of measuring POTET employs an **evaporation pan**, or *evaporimeter*. As evaporation occurs, water in measured amounts is automatically replaced in the pan, equaling the amount that evaporated. Mesh screens over the pan protect against overmeasurement due to wind, which accelerates evaporation.

A more elaborate measurement device is a **lysimeter**. A tank, approximately a cubic meter or larger in size, is buried in a field with its upper surface left open. The lysimeter isolates a representative volume of soil, subsoil, and plant cover, thus allowing measurement of the moisture moving through the sampled area. A weighing lysimeter has this embedded tank resting on a weighing scale (Figure 10). A rain gauge next to the lysimeter measures the precipitation input.

The number of lysimeters and evaporation pans is somewhat limited across North America, but they still provide a database from which to develop ways of estimating POTET. Several methods of estimating POTET on the basis of meteorological data are used widely and are easily implemented for regional applications. Thornthwaite developed one of these methods.

Thornthwaite discovered that, if you know monthly mean air temperature and daylength, you can approximate POTET. These data are readily available, so calculating POTET is easy and fairly accurate for most midlatitude locations. (Recall that daylength is a function of a station's latitude.) His method can work with data from hourly, daily, or annual time frames or with historical data to re-create water conditions in past environments.

Deficit (DEFIC) The POTET demand can be satisfied in three ways: by PRECIP, by moisture stored in the soil, or through artificial irrigation. If these three sources are inadequate to meet moisture demands, the location experiences a moisture shortage. This unsatisfied POTET is **deficit** (DEFIC).

By subtracting DEFIC from POTET, we determine the **actual evapotranspiration**, or ACTET, that takes place (see Figure 6). Under ideal conditions for plants, potential and actual amounts of evapotranspiration are about the same, so plants do not experience a water shortage; droughts result from deficit conditions.

Surplus (SURPL) If POTET is satisfied and the soil is full of moisture, then additional water input becomes **surplus** (SURPL). This excess water might sit on the surface in puddles, ponds, and lakes, or it might flow across the surface toward stream channels or percolate through the soil underground. The *overland flow* combines with precipitation and groundwater flows into river channels to make up the **total runoff**. Because surplus water generates most streamflow, or runoff, the water-balance approach is useful for indirectly estimating streamflow.

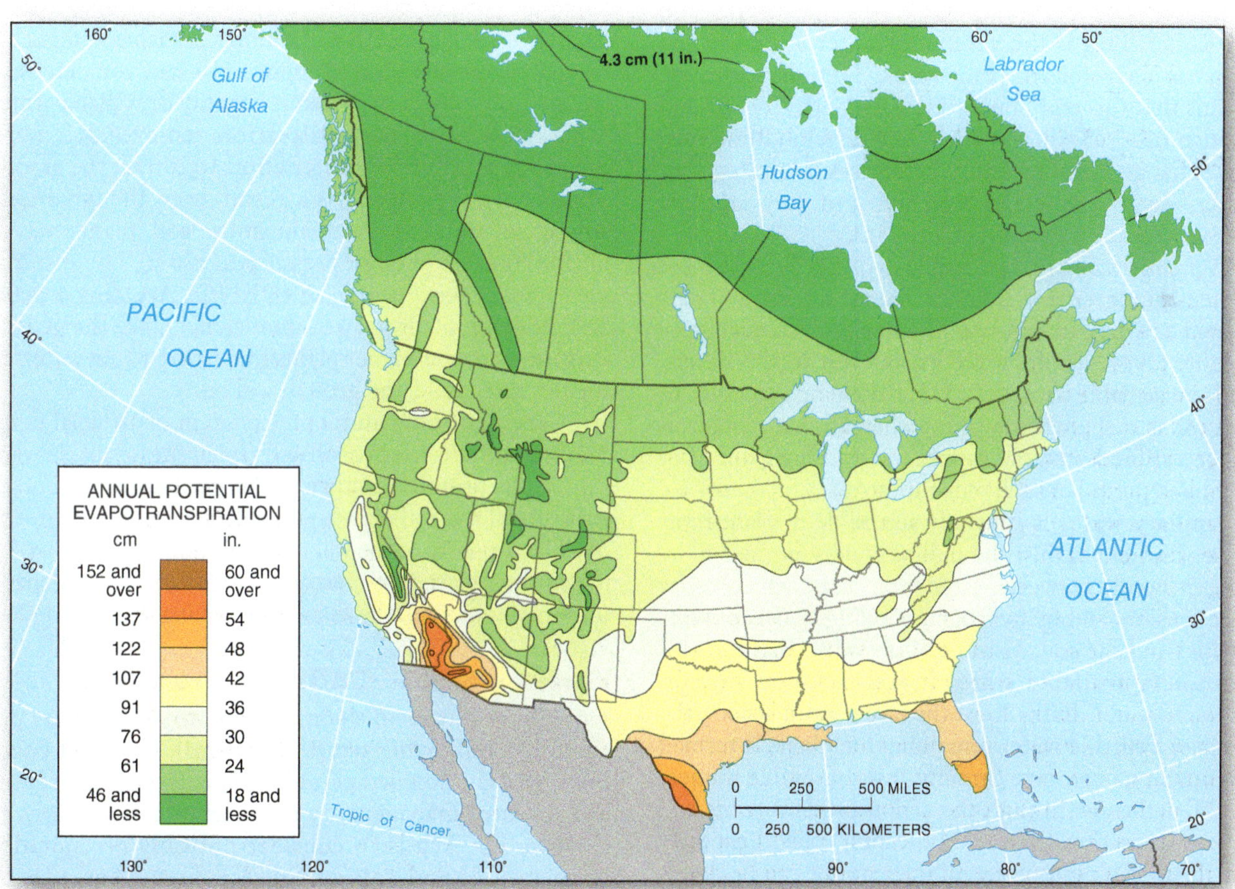

FIGURE 9 Potential evapotranspiration (POTET) for the United States and Canada—the water demand.

[From C. W. Thornthwaite, "An approach toward a rational classification of climate," *Geographical Review* 38 (1948): 64, © American Geographical Society. Canadian data adapted from M. Sanderson, "The climates of Canada according to the new Thornthwaite classification," *Scientific Agriculture* 28 (1948): 501–517.]

Satellite
Global Water Balance Components

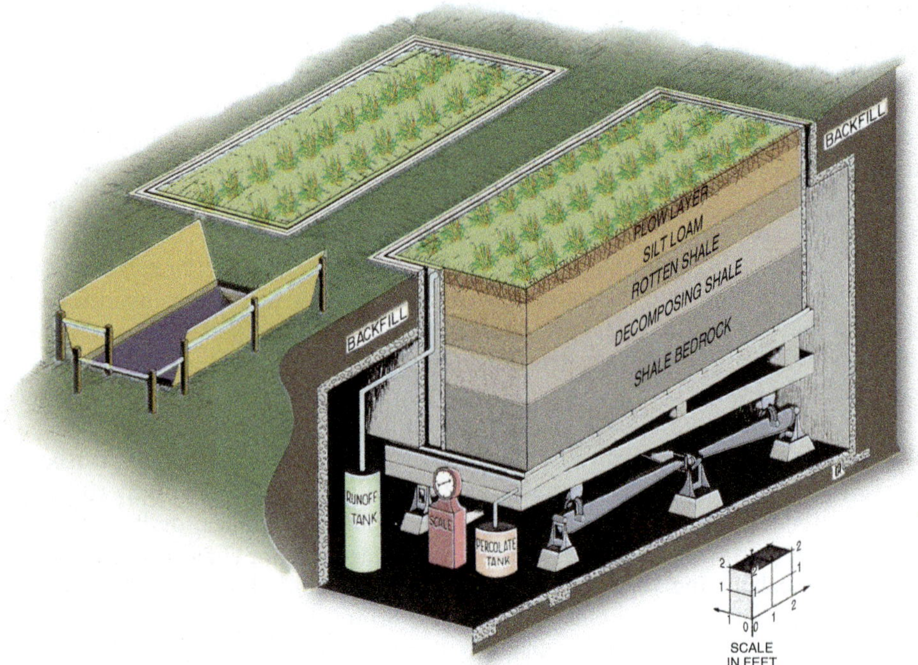

FIGURE 10 A weighing lysimeter for measuring evaporation and transpiration. The various pathways of water are tracked: Some water remains as soil moisture, some is incorporated into plant tissues, some drains from the bottom of the lysimeter, and the remainder is credited to evapotranspiration. Given natural conditions, the lysimeter measures actual evapotranspiration. [Adapted from illustration courtesy of Lloyd Owens, Agricultural Research Service, USDA, Coshocton, Ohio.]

Soil-Moisture Storage (Δ STRGE) A "savings account" of water that receives recharge "deposits" and provides for utilization "withdrawals" is **soil-moisture storage** (Δ STRGE). This is the volume of water stored in the soil that is accessible to plant roots. The delta symbol, Δ, means that this component includes both *recharge* and *utilization* (use) of soil moisture; the Δ symbol in math means "change." Soil moisture comprises two categories of water—hygroscopic and capillary—but only capillary water is accessible to plants (Figure 11a).

Hygroscopic water is inaccessible to plants because it is a molecule-thin layer that is tightly bound to each soil particle by the hydrogen bonding of water molecules (Figure 11a, left). Hygroscopic water exists even in the desert, but it is unavailable to meet POTET demands. Relative to plants, soil is at the **wilting point** when all that remains is this inaccessible water; plants wilt and eventually die after a prolonged period of such moisture stress.

Capillary water is generally accessible to plant roots because it is held against the pull of gravity in the soil by hydrogen bonds between water molecules, which cause surface tension, and by hydrogen bonding between water molecules and the soil. Most capillary water that remains in the soil is **available water** in soil-moisture storage. After some water drains from the larger pore spaces, the amount of available water remaining for plants is termed **field capacity**, or storage capacity. It is removable to meet POTET demands through the action of plant roots and surface evaporation (Figure 11a, center). Field capacity is specific to each soil type, and the amount can be determined by soil surveys.

When soil becomes saturated after a precipitation event, any water surplus in the soil body becomes **gravitational water**. It percolates from the shallower capillary zone to the deeper groundwater zone (Figure 11a, right).

Figure 11b shows the relation of soil texture to soil-moisture content. Different plant species send roots to different depths and therefore reach different amounts of soil moisture. A soil blend that maximizes available water is best for plants. On the basis of Figure 11b, can you determine the soil texture with the greatest quantity of available water?

As **soil-moisture utilization** removes soil water, the plants must exert greater effort to extract the amount of moisture they need. As a result, even though a small amount of water may remain in the soil, plants may be unable to exert enough pressure to use it. The resulting *unsatisfied demand* is a *deficit* (DEFIC). Avoiding a deficit and reducing plant growth inefficiencies are the goals of irrigation, for the harder plants must work to get water, the smaller their yield and growth will be.

Whether from natural precipitation or artificial irrigation, water infiltrates the soil and replenishes available water, the process of **soil-moisture recharge**. The texture and the structure of the soil dictate available pore spaces, or **porosity**. The property of the soil that determines the rate of soil-moisture recharge is its **permeability**. Permeability depends on particle sizes and the shape and packing of soil particles.

Water Deficit—Defining Drought

Drought might seem a simple thing to define: Less precipitation and higher temperatures make for drier conditions over an extended period of time. However, scientists and resource managers use four technical definitions for *drought*. The key is to consider not only precipitation, temperature, and soil-moisture content, but also the water-resource demand as it relates to the lack of water.

- *Meteorological drought* is defined by the degree of dryness, as compared to a regional average, and the duration of dry conditions. This definition is region-

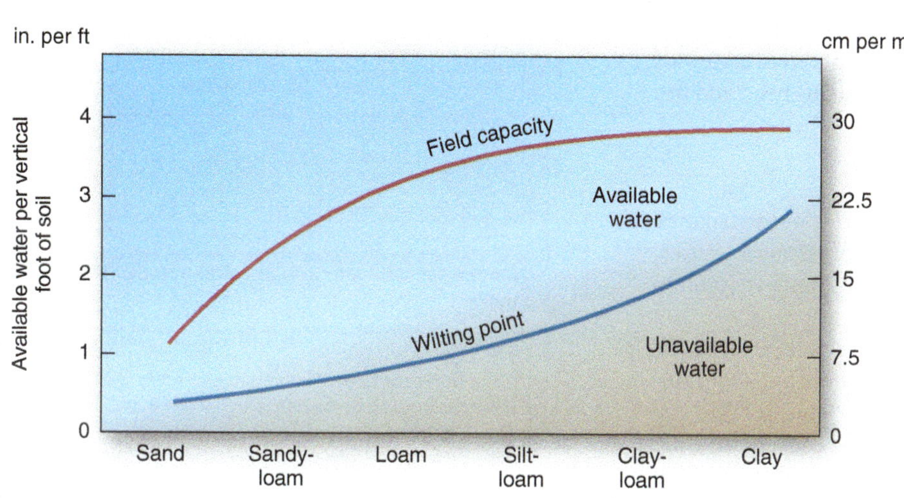

* Note: Some capillary water is bound to hygroscopic water on soil particles and is also unavailable

Satellite Global Water Balance Components

FIGURE 11 Types of soil moisture and its availability. (a) Hygroscopic and gravitational water is unavailable to plants; only capillary water that is not bound hygroscopically to soil is available. (b) The relation between soil-moisture availability and soil texture determines the distance between the two curves that show field capacity and wilting point. A loam soil (one-third each of sand, silt, and clay) has roughly the most available water per vertical foot of soil exposed to plant roots. [(a) After D. Steila, *The Geography of Soils*, © 1976, p. 45, © Pearson Prentice Hall, Inc. (b) After U.S. Department of Agriculture, *1955 Yearbook of Agriculture—Water*, p. 120.]

specific, since it relates to atmospheric conditions that change from area to area.

- *Agricultural drought* occurs when shortages of precipitation and soil moisture affect crop yields. Losses can be significant and are running in the tens of billions of dollars each year in the United States, although agricultural drought evolves slowly and gets little media coverage.
- *Hydrological drought* relates to the effects of precipitation shortages (both rain and snow) on water supply, such as when streamflow decreases, reservoir levels drop, mountain snowpack declines, and groundwater mining increases.
- *Socioeconomic drought* results when reduced water supply causes the demand for goods to exceed the supply, such as when hydroelectric power production declines with reservoir depletion. This is a more comprehensive measure that considers loss of life, water rationing, wildfire events, and other widespread impacts of water shortfalls.

The National Drought Mitigation Center, University of Nebraska–Lincoln (NDMC; http://www.drought.unl.edu/), publishes a weekly Drought Monitor map and includes a variety of resources for assessing and mitigating drought.

Drought is a natural and recurrent feature of climate. Droughts of various intensities were occurring on every continent through 2010. Australia is in a decade-long drought, its worst in 110 years. The first half of 2010 was the driest in that time span for western Australia. The region of western Oklahoma and Texas is in an intense drought, with Texas experiencing nearly 1000 related wildfires through mid-2011. Towns in the Oklahoma Panhandle and the region endured more than a year with little or no precipitation (no day over 6 mm, 0.25 in., of rain). Regarding the U.S. Southwest drought, under way since early 2000, scientists are finding mounting evidence that this remarkable situation links directly to global climate change:

> The projected future climate of intensified aridity in the Southwest is caused by . . . a poleward expansion of the subtropical dry zones. The drying of subtropical land areas . . . imminent or already underway is unlike any climate state we have seen in the instrumental record. It is also distinct from the multi-decadal mega-droughts that afflicted the American Southwest during Medieval times.*

*Richard Seager et al., "Model projections of an imminent transition to a more arid climate in southwestern North America," *Science* 316, no. 5828 (May 25, 2007): 1184.

Many scientists think that natural climate variability is combining with anthropogenic warming to cause severe and lasting drought in the U.S. Southwest. A 2011 climate-model study affirms this concern,

> Climate model analysis shows that the dust-bowl like conditions predicted for the southwestern U.S. over the next century in response to anthropogenic warming arise from a poleward shift of the midlatitude westerlies and the poleward branch of the Hadley cell . . . and would result in a more arid southwestern US. . . . The risk of prolonged aridity is likely to be heightened by anthropogenic forcing.**

The spatial implications of such shifting of Earth's primary circulation systems and semi-permanent drought in a region of explosive population growth and urbanization are serious and suggest the immediate need for water-resource planning and assessment. Focus Study 1 presents an overview of the Colorado River system that illustrates this need and the value of water-budget concepts.

Sample Water Budgets

Using all of these concepts, we graph the water-balance components for stations near several representative cities. Let's begin by looking at Kingsport, Tennessee, at 36.6° N 82.5° W, elevation 390 m (1280 ft).

Figure 12 graphs the water-balance components for long-term supply and demand, using monthly averages. On the graph, a comparison of PRECIP and POTET by month determines whether there is a *net supply* or a *net demand* for water. The cooler time from October to May shows a net supply (blue line), but the warm days from June to September create a net water demand. If we assume a soil-moisture storage capacity of 100 mm (4.0 in.), typical of shallow-rooted plants, the net water-demand months are satisfied through soil-moisture utilization (green area), with a small summer soil-moisture deficit.

Obviously, not all stations experience the surplus moisture patterns of this humid continental region. Different climatic regimes experience different relations among water-balance components. Figure 13 presents water-balance graphs for the moist, cool climate of Ottawa, Ontario, Canada, and the dry, warm climate of Phoenix, Arizona.

CRITICAL THINKING 1

Your local water budget

Select your campus, yard, or perhaps a house plant and apply the water-balance concepts. Where does the water supply originate—what is its source? Estimate the ultimate water supply and demand for the area you selected. For a general idea of PRECIP and POTET, find your locale on Figures 8 and 9. Consider the seasonal timing of this supply and demand, and estimate water needs and how they vary as components of the water-budget change.

**Peter Fawcett et al., "Extended megadroughts in the southwestern U.S. during Pleistocene interglacials," *Nature* 470, no. 7335 (February 24, 2011): 473, 518–521.

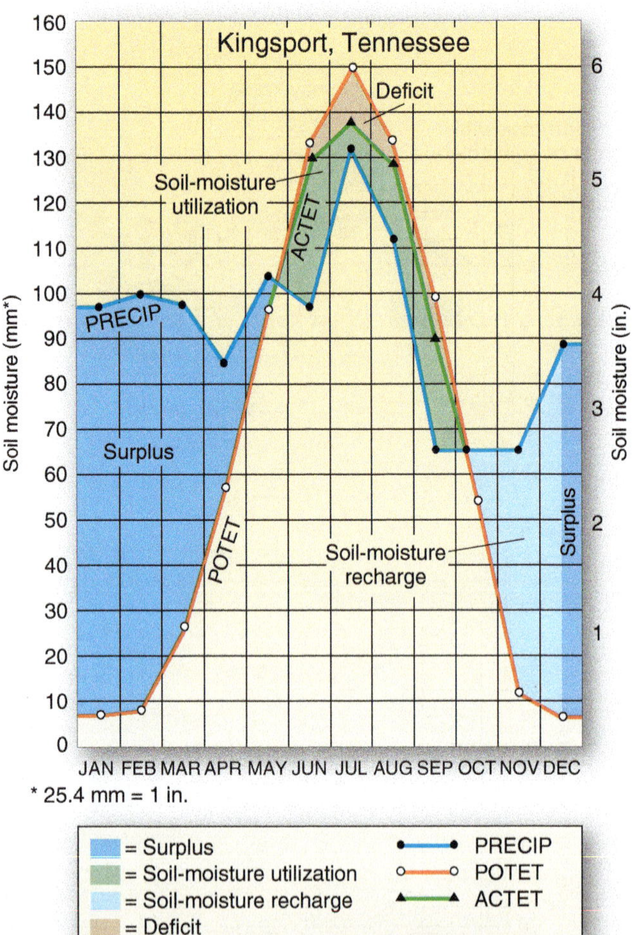

FIGURE 12 Sample water budget for Kingsport, Tennessee. Compare the average plots for precipitation inputs and potential evapotranspiration outputs to determine the condition of the soil-moisture environment. A typical pattern of spring surplus, summer soil-moisture utilization, a small summer deficit, autumn soil-moisture recharge, and ending surplus highlights the year.

Water-Budget Application: Hurricane Camille

An interesting application of the water-balance approach to water resources is analyzing an event such as Hurricane Camille (1969), which generally had positive effects on regional water resources, but caused severe coastal damage. Hurricane Camille was one of the most devastating hurricanes of the 20th century. Hurricanes Ivan in 2004; Rita, Katrina, and Wilma in 2005; Humberto in 2007; and Gustav in 2008 brought back memories of Camille to Gulf Coast residents. Ironically, Camille was significant not only for the disaster it brought (256 dead, $1.5 billion in damage), but also for the drought it ended.

Figure 14 shows Camille inland from the Gulf Coast north of Biloxi, Mississippi. Hurricane-force winds sharply diminished after the hurricane made landfall, leaving a vast rainstorm that traveled from the Gulf Coast through Mississippi, western Tennessee, and Kentucky and into central Virginia. Severe flooding drowned the Gulf Coast near

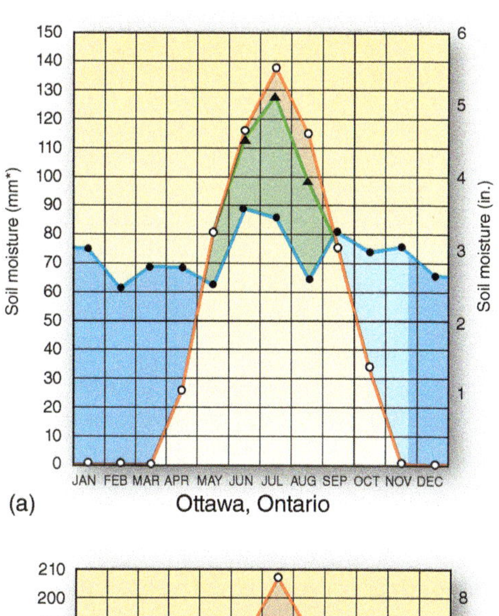

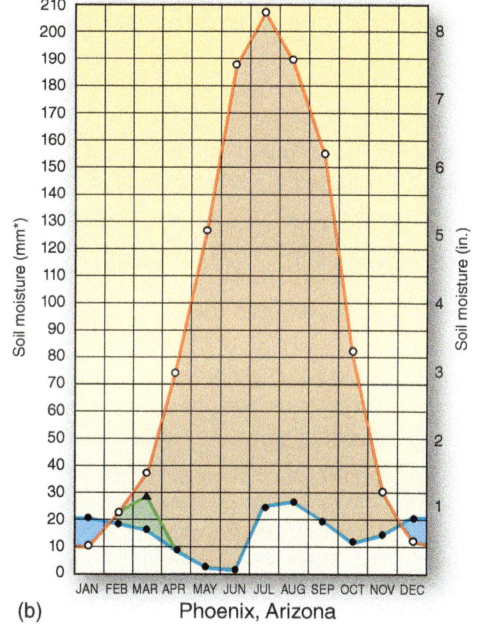

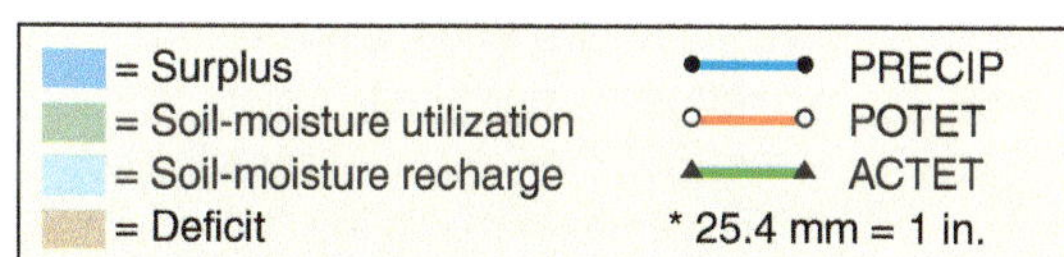

FIGURE 13 Sample water budgets for stations near two cities.

landfall and the James River Basin of Virginia, where torrential rains produced record floods. But Camille actually had a beneficial aspect: It ended a year-long drought along major portions of its storm track.

Figure 15a maps the precipitation from Camille and portrays the storm's track from landfall in Mississippi to the coast of Virginia and Delaware. By comparing actual water budgets along Camille's track with water budgets for the same 3 days with Camille's rainfall totals removed artificially, the moisture impact of the storm on the region's water budget was analyzed. Figure 15b maps the moisture shortages that were avoided because of Camille's rains—termed *deficit abatement*. Think of this as drought that did not continue because Camille's rains occurred. Over vast portions of the affected area, Camille reduced dry-soil conditions, restored pastures, and filled low reservoirs.

(text continued after Focus Study 1)

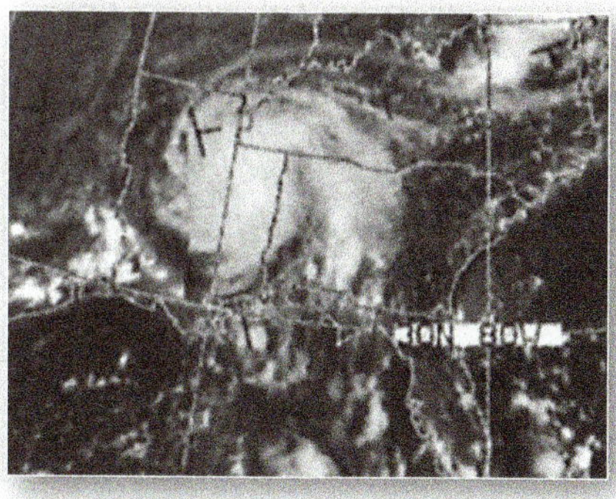

FIGURE 14 *ESSA-9* satellite image of Hurricane Camille. Hurricane Camille made landfall on the night of August 17, 1969, and continued inland on August 18. The storm was progressing northward through Mississippi in the image. [NOAA.]

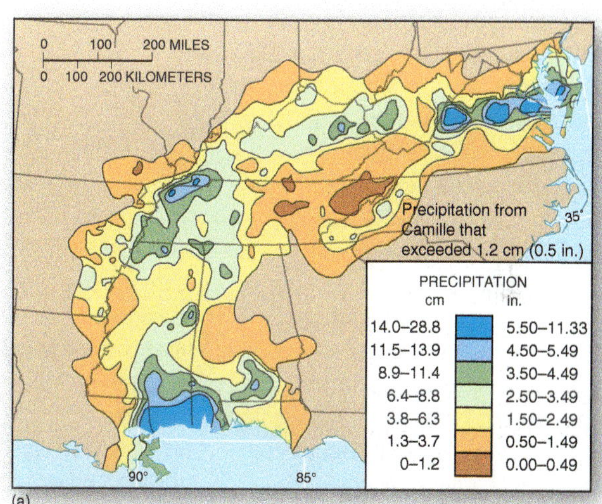

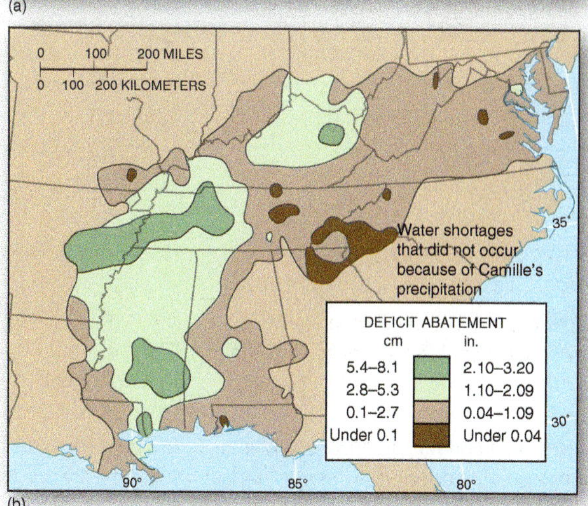

FIGURE 15 Camille affects water budgets in a beneficial way. A water-resource view of Hurricane Camille's impact on local water budgets: (a) Precipitation attributable to the storm (moisture supply). (b) Resulting deficit abatement (avoided moisture shortages) attributable to Camille. [Data and maps by Robert Christopherson.]

FOCUS STUDY 1

The Colorado River: A System Out of Balance

Water resources in the Southwest are linked to the Colorado River system. The Colorado flows almost 2317 km (1440 mi) from Colorado and Wyoming through the southwestern United States. This *exotic stream* is so-called because its headwaters are in a region of water surpluses, but the river and its tributaries flow mostly through arid lands to the sea. Orographic precipitation totaling 102 cm (40 in.) per year falls mostly as snow in the Rockies, feeding the Colorado River headwaters in Rocky Mountain National Park. But at Yuma, Arizona, near the river's end, annual precipitation is a scant 8.9 cm (3.5 in.), an extremely small amount when compared with the high annual potential evapotranspiration demand in the Yuma region of 140 cm (55 in.).

From its source region, the Colorado River quickly leaves the relatively wet Rockies and spills out into the dry climates of western Colorado and eastern Utah. At Grand Junction, Colorado, near the Utah border, annual precipitation is only 20 cm (8 in.) (upstream from Figure 1.1b, on the map). After carving its way through the Utah canyonlands, the river enters Lake Powell, the reservoir behind Glen Canyon Dam (Figure 1.1c), and then flows on through the Grand Canyon. The river then turns southward, marking its final 644 km (400 mi) as the Arizona–California border. Along this stretch sits Hoover Dam, just east of Las Vegas (Figure 1.1d; see the chapter opener); Davis Dam, built to control the releases from Hoover (Figure 1.1e); Parker Dam, for the water needs of Los Angeles; three more dams for irrigation water (Palo Verde, Imperial, and Laguna, Figure 1.1f); and finally, Morelos Dam at the Mexican border. Mexico owns the end of the river and whatever water is left. Hydrologically exhausted, the river rarely carries discharge into Mexico, instead ending as a trickle kilometers short of its former mouth in the Gulf of California (Figure 1.1g).

Figure 1.1h shows the annual water discharge and suspended sediment load for the Colorado River at Yuma, Arizona, from 1905 to 1964. The completion of Hoover Dam in the 1930s dramatically reduced suspended sediment. Subsequent dams upstream from Yuma reduced both discharge and sediment to nearly zero by the mid-1960s.

Overall, the drainage basin encompasses 641,025 km^2 (247,500 mi^2) of mountain, plateau, canyon, basin-and-range, and hot desert landscapes in parts of seven states and two countries. This region includes the four fastest-growing states in terms of population: Nevada, Arizona, Colorado, and Utah. The rapidly expanding urban areas of Las Vegas, Phoenix, Tucson, Denver, San Diego, and Albuquerque all depend on Colorado River water, which supplies approximately 30 million people in seven states. The Colorado River has played a crucial part in the history of the Southwest and will have a defining role in the future of this drought-plagued region.

Dividing Up the Colorado's Dammed Water

John Wesley Powell (1834–1902) was the first Euro-American of record to successfully navigate the Colorado River through the Grand Canyon. Lake Powell is named after him. Powell perceived that the challenge of settling the West was too great for individual efforts and believed that solutions to problems such as water availability could be met only through private cooperative efforts. His 1878 study (reprinted in 1962), *Report of the Lands of the Arid Region of the United States*, is a conservation landmark.

Today, Powell probably would be skeptical of the intervention by government agencies in building large-scale reclamation projects. An anecdote in Wallace Stegner's book *Beyond the Hundredth Meridian* tells of an 1893 international irrigation conference held in Los Angeles, where development-minded delegates bragged that the entire West could be conquered and reclaimed from nature and that "rain will certainly follow the plow." Powell spoke against that sentiment: "I tell you, gentlemen, you are piling up a heritage of conflict and litigation over water rights, for there is not sufficient water to supply the land."* He was booed from the hall, but history has shown Powell to be correct.

The Colorado River Compact was signed by six of the seven basin states in 1923. (The seventh, Arizona, signed in 1944, the same year that the United States signed the Mexican Water Treaty.) With this compact, the Colorado River basin was divided into an upper basin and a lower basin, arbitrarily separated for administrative purposes at Lees Ferry near the Utah–Arizona border (noted on the map in Figure 1.1. Congress adopted the Boulder Canyon Act in 1928, authorizing Hoover Dam as the first major reclamation project on the river. Also authorized was the All-American Canal into the Imperial Valley, which required an additional dam. Los Angeles then began its project to bring Colorado River water 390 km (240 mi) from still another dam and reservoir on the river to the city.

Shortly after Hoover Dam was finished and downstream enterprises were thus offered flood protection, the other projects were quickly completed. There are now eight major dams on the river and many irrigation works. The last effort to redistribute Colorado River water was the Central Arizona Project, which carries water to the Phoenix area.

Highly Variable River Flows

The flaw in all this planning and water distribution is that exotic streams have highly variable flows, and the Colorado is no exception. In 1917, the discharge measured at Lees Ferry totaled 24 million acre-feet (maf), whereas in 1934 it dropped by nearly 80%, to only 5.03 maf. In 1977, the discharge dropped again to 5.02 maf, but in 1984, it rose to an all-time high of 24.5 maf. Yet, in contrast, between 2000 and 2007

*W. Stegner, *Beyond the Hundredth Meridian* (Boston, MA: Houghton Mifflin, 1954), p. 343.

FIGURE 1.1 The Colorado River drainage basin.
The Colorado River basin is divided into upper and lower basins at Lees Ferry in northern Arizona. (a) Headwaters near Mount Richthofen. (b) Near Moab, Utah. (c) Glen Canyon Dam. (d) Hoover Dam and Lake Mead with declining water levels. (e) Davis Dam in full release during the 1983 flood. (f) Irrigated fresh-cut flowers in the Imperial Valley, refrigerated trucks in the field, and a cargo jet at a local airport await shipments to distant markets. (g) The Colorado River (far lower left) stops short of its former delta. (h) Dam construction affects river discharge and sediment yields. [(a), (c), (d), (f) Bobbé Christopherson. (b), (e) Author. (g) *Terra* image, NASA/GSFC. (h) Data from USGS, *National Water Summary 1984*, Water Supply Paper 2275, p. 55.]

river discharge fell to exceptionally low levels, with 2002 dropping to a record low of 3.1 maf and 2003 to 6.4 maf. The 2003–2010 water years marked the lowest 8-year average flow in the total record. The chapter-opening pair of photos compares Lake Mead water levels at Hoover Dam in July 1983 and October 2010 as evidence of this variability. By the end of 2010, lake levels dropped to 330 m (1083 ft), far below the 375-m (1229-ft) capacity reached in 1983.

As a planning basis for the Colorado River Compact, the government used average annual river discharges from 1914 up to the compact signing in 1923, an exceptionally high average of 18.8 maf. That amount was perceived as more than enough for the upper and lower basins, each to receive 7.5 maf, and, later, for Mexico to receive 1.5 maf in the 1944 Mexican Water Treaty.

Should long-range planning be based on such a short time period on a river with highly variable flows? Tree-ring analyses of past climates have disclosed that the only other time Colorado River discharges were at the high 1914–1923 level was between A.D. 1606 and 1625. Planners have consistently overestimated the dependable flows of the river, a situation that has created shortfalls as demand exceeds supply in the water budget (Table 1.1).

Presently, the seven states *ideally* want rights that total as much as 25.0 maf per year. When added to the guarantee for Mexico, this comes up to 26.5 maf of yearly demand (more than in the river by far). And six states share one common opinion: California's right to the water must be limited to a court-ordered 4.4 maf, which it exceeded every year until California's access to surplus Colorado River water was stopped in 2002. At present, no surplus exists in the river's water budget during the ongoing western drought.

Colorado River Water Losses

Several natural processes associated with reservoirs and river flow regulation cause water losses and increase overall water demand, as observed in Table 1.1. Glen Canyon Dam, located 27.4 km (17 mi) north of Lees Ferry, the division point between the upper and lower basins, serves as an example.

Glen Canyon Dam was completed in 1963 and began impounding water in Lake Powell. Glen Canyon Dam's primary purpose, according to the Bureau of Reclamation, was to regulate flows between the upper and lower basins. Additional benefits are the production of hydroelectric power and a new recreation and tourism industry around Lake Powell, as previously inaccessible desert scenery now can be reached by boat.

Lake Powell inundated 299 km (186 mi) of former river channel, which cuts through porous Navajo sandstone for much of its length. This sandstone absorbs an estimated 0.5 maf of the river's overall annual discharge as bank storage when the reservoir is full—the higher the lake level, the greater the loss into the sandstone. The reservoir also experiences evaporative losses as hot, dry winds flow across an open water body in an arid region. Evaporation accounts for another 0.5 maf of discharge lost annually from the reservoir, equaling about a third of all Colorado River reservoir

TABLE 1.1 Estimated Colorado River Budget Through 2010

Water Demand	Quantity (maf)[a]
Upper basin, 7.5; lower basin, 7.5[b]	15.0
Central Arizona Project (rising to 2.8 maf)	1.0
Mexican allotment (1944 treaty)	1.5
Evaporation from reservoirs (when full)	1.5
Bank storage at Lake Powell (when full)	0.5
Phreatophytic losses (water-demanding plants)	0.5
Budgeted total demand	**20.0 maf**
Average Annual Flows at Lees Ferry	
1906–1930 (average flow)	17.70 maf
1930–2003 (average flow)	14.10 maf
1990–2006 (average flow)	11.34 maf
2002	3.10 maf
2003–2010 (average flow)	7.34 maf

Source: Bureau of Reclamation and states of Arizona, California, and Nevada. A water year runs from October 1 to September 30.
[a]1 million acre-feet = 325,872 gallons, or 1.24 million liters, or 43,560 ft^3.
[b]In-basin consumptive uses are 75% agricultural.

evaporation losses—again, higher lake levels mean more losses.

In the upper reaches of large reservoirs where water levels fluctuate, as well as along reaches of regulated river flow below dams throughout the basin, sand bars and banks have become near-permanent features. Riparian vegetation has colonized those surfaces, including dense thickets of water-demanding plants called phreatophytes. These species extract and transpire an additional 0.5 maf per year of the river flow. The three water losses discussed here—bank storage, evaporation, and water use by vegetation—are an increasingly large percentage of the overall streamflow as drought conditions persist.

Ongoing Drought and the Water Budget

Drought conditions affecting the Colorado River system began in 2000 and are ongoing. Reservoirs store water to offset variable Colorado River flows, especially during periods of drought. The largest reservoirs—Lake Mead, formed by Hoover Dam, and Lake Powell, formed by Glen Canyon Dam—together account for over 80% of total system storage. However, Lake Mead and Lake Powell are in water-budget trouble, since water allocations already exceed the long-term average flows in the system and have for years. Thus, an impending water supply crisis is emerging. A convergence of factors in the American Southwest is reducing water inflows to the Colorado River and increasing outflow demands, revealing that current water-management practices are not sustainable.

The current drought is caused by higher temperatures and evaporation rates as well as reduced mountain snowpack and earlier spring melt. According to regional tree-ring records, nine droughts have affected the American Southwest since A.D. 1226. However, the present drought is the first to occur with increasing human demand for water as population growth continues throughout the region.

Whether this drought is part of natural climate variability or a sign of climate change is currently being investigated. Evidence and computer models suggest that the decade-long drought is directly linked to the shifting of subtropical high-pressure systems with climate change. This expansion of subtropical dry zones has given scientists a new approach to understanding drought. In regions such as the American Southwest, application of the term *drought* is changing to consideration of a change in *permanent average climate*. When future droughts occur—for example, during a Pacific Ocean La Niña condition—they will be in addition to this new base state of a drier climate. This is unprecedented in the climate record for this region.

Effects of prolonged drought are evident throughout the Colorado River system. Water inflow to Lake Powell is running at less than one-third of long-term averages—with the low year of 2002 at just 25%. System reservoirs were at record low levels by mid-2010, when system storage dropped to 58% of capacity and the production of hydroelectric power fell to 50% of capacity.

In contrast, basin streamflow increased in 2011 as the La Niña weather pattern shifted, causing high snowpack and producing a late spring melt across the Colorado River headwaters and Rockies. By July 2011, Lake Powell was up to 72% of capacity, its highest level since October 2001. Lake Mead was 46% of capacity, up from a low of 41% in 2010. However, scientists agree that the overall trend of declining snowfall and ongoing drought appears set and will continue to cause declining reservoir levels, despite this La Niña anomaly. Climate change is in fact increasing such natural system variability.

Engineers estimate that it could take 13 normal winters of snowpack in the Rockies and basinwide precipitation to "reset" the system. Such a recovery is much slower than previous drought recoveries because of increasing evaporation associated with increasing temperatures across the Southwest as well as increasing human water use. Present probabilities for the period after 2016 put the chances of surplus streamflow occurring in the Colorado River system in any given year at only 20%.

Government stopgap measures to address water shortages came to a head in December 2007 when the Department of the Interior signed a historic Record of Decision, an agreement representing a consensus among the stakeholders. This agreement sets the rules for dealing with water shortages during the drought and determining where water deliveries will be cut; establishes the drought as a basis for planning in times of water shortages; guides the operation rules for Lake Mead and Lake Powell for better coordination during the risk of drought; sets rules for distributing any surpluses, should they ever again arise; and encourages implementation of water conservation initiatives (see http://www.usbr.gov/lc/region/programs/strategires/RecordofDecisions.pdf).

Conservation (using less water) and efficiency (using water more effectively) are not yet being stressed as ways to reduce the tremendous demand for water across the Southwest; perhaps this Record of Decision will lead to serious conservation and efficiency strategies. For instance, southern Nevada has launched a campaign to replace lawns with drought-tolerant xeroscaping—desert landscaping—but with 150,000 hotel rooms, we might question planning efforts. Las Vegas receives 90% of its water from the Colorado River and could save 30% of its usage by simply requiring water-efficient fixtures and appliances in hotels and residences.

Limiting or halting further metropolitan construction and population growth in the Colorado River Basin is not part of present strategies to lower demand. The focus remains on water supply. We might wonder what John Wesley Powell would think if he were alive today to witness such errant attempts to control the mighty and variable Colorado River. He foretold such a "heritage of conflict and litigation."

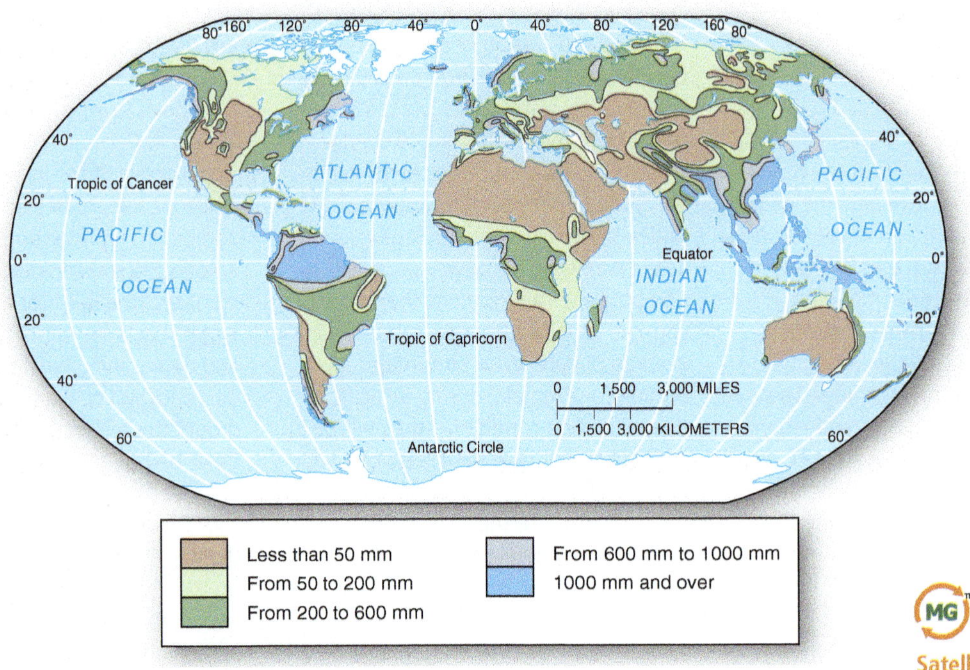

FIGURE 16 Annual global river runoff.
Distribution of runoff that feeds streamflow is closely correlated with climatic region, as expected. But it is poorly correlated with human population distribution and density.

MG Satellite
Global Water Balance Components

Thus, Camille's monetary benefits inland outweighed its damage by an estimated 2-to-1 ratio. (Of course, the tragic loss of life does not fit into a financial equation.) In 2007, Hurricane Humberto, a category 1 storm, brought some needed relief across the Southeast once it moved inland. Hurricanes should be viewed as normal and natural meteorological events that not only have terrible destructive potential, mainly to coastal lowlands, but also contribute to the precipitation regimes of the southern and eastern United States. According to weather records, about one-third of all hurricanes making landfall in the United States provide beneficial precipitation to local water budgets.

Water Surplus—Managing Streamflow

Water distribution is uneven over space and time. Because we require a steady supply, we build large-scale management projects intended to redistribute the water resource either geographically, by moving water from one place to another, or over time, by storing water from time of receipt until it is needed. In this way, deficits are reduced, surpluses are held for later release, and water availability is improved to satisfy evapotranspiration and society's demands. The water balance permits analysis of the contribution that streams make to water resources.

Streams may be *perennial* (constantly flowing; *perennial* is Latin for "through the year") or *intermittent*. In either case, the total streamflow comes from surplus surface water runoff, subsurface throughflow, and groundwater. Figure 16 maps global runoff in terms of average annual streamflow. The highest streamflows occur along the equator within the tropics, reflecting the continual rainfall along the Intertropical Conver-

GEO REPORT 4 *Harvesting fog as a water resource*

Throughout history, people harvested water from fog, perhaps taking a cue from the remarkable adaptations of insects. For example, sand beetles in the Namib Desert in extreme southwestern Africa harvest water from fog by holding up their wings so condensation collects and runs down to their mouths. As the day's heat arrives, they burrow into the sand, only to emerge the next night or morning when the advection fog brings in more water for harvesting. For centuries, coastal villages in the deserts of Oman collected water drips deposited on trees by coastal fogs. In the Atacama Desert of Chile and Peru, residents stretch large nets to intercept advection fog; moisture condenses on the netting and drips into trays, flowing through pipes to a 100,000-L (26,000-gal.) reservoir. At least 30 countries across the globe experience conditions suitable for this water resource technology. (See http://www.oas.org/dsd/publications/unit/oea59e/ch33.htm.)

gence Zone (ITCZ). Southeast Asia also experiences high streamflows, as do northwest coastal mountains in the Northern Hemisphere. In countries having great seasonal fluctuations in runoff, groundwater becomes an important reserve water supply. Regions of lower streamflow coincide with Earth's subtropical deserts, rain-shadow areas, and continental interiors, particularly in Asia.

The Three Gorges Dam on the Yangtze River in China is 2.3 km (1.5 mi) long and 185 m (607 ft) high, making it the largest dam and related construction in the world in overall size (Figure 17). Forced relocation of entire cities and more than 1.2 million people made room for the 600-km-long (370-mi-long) reservoir. Controversies surrounded the immense scale of environmental, historical, and cultural losses. Gained is flood control, water resources for redistribution, and power production. Electrical production capacity is 22,000 MW. In October 2010, the reservoir was filled to its design capacity; however, water pollution and landslides along the reservoir banks may force the relocation of an additional 300,000 people.

In the United States, several large water-management projects already operate: the Bonneville Power Administration (BPA) in Washington State, the Tennessee Valley Authority in the Southeast, the California Water Project, and the Central Arizona Project. BPA comprises 31 hydroelectric dams and a transmission grid and began operation in 1937 (Figure 18a).

Using the California Aqueduct, the California Water Project physically rearranges the water budget in the state by holding back winter runoff for release in summer and

FIGURE 17 Major dam in China.
Satellite views in 2000 (construction) and 2006 (completion) of the $25 billion Three Gorges Dam on the Yangtze River, flowing from upper left to right. For scale, the main portion of the dam is 2.3 km in length. This is the world's largest individual construction project. The channel to the north of the dam is a system of locks for shipping. [*Terra* ASTER images, NASA/GSFC/MITI/ERSDAC/JAROS.]

(a) Grand Coulee Dam, BPA, Washington

(b) California Aqueduct

FIGURE 18 Two major water projects in the United States.
(a) Grand Coulee Dam holds back the Columbia River, as part of the federal Bonneville Power Administration, in Washington State. (b) The California Aqueduct transports water as part of the California Water Project. The Palmdate Reservoir beyond the aqueduct is in a depression of the San Andreas fault zone. [(a) Author. (b) Bobbé Christopherson.]

pumping water from the north to the south. Completed in 1971, this 1207-km-long (750-mi-long) "river" flows from the Sacramento River delta to the Los Angeles region, servicing irrigated agriculture in the San Joaquin Valley along the way (Figure 18b).

The best sites for multipurpose hydroelectric projects are already taken, so battles among conflicting interests and analysis of negative environmental impacts invariably accompany new project proposals. Focus Study 1 examines the impacts of such projects on the Colorado River, a critical water resource for the western United States that is being stressed by climate change and increasing water demands.

Groundwater Resources

Groundwater is an important part of the hydrologic cycle, although it lies beneath the surface, beyond the soil-moisture root zone. It is tied to surface supplies through pores in soil and rock. Groundwater is the largest potential freshwater source in the hydrologic cycle—larger than all surface lakes and streams combined. Between Earth's land surface and a depth of 4 km (13,000 ft) worldwide, some 8,340,000 km³ (2,000,000 mi³) of water reside, a volume comparable to 70 times all the freshwater lakes in the world. Pollution threatens groundwater quality, and overconsumption depletes groundwater volume in quantities beyond natural replenishment rates.

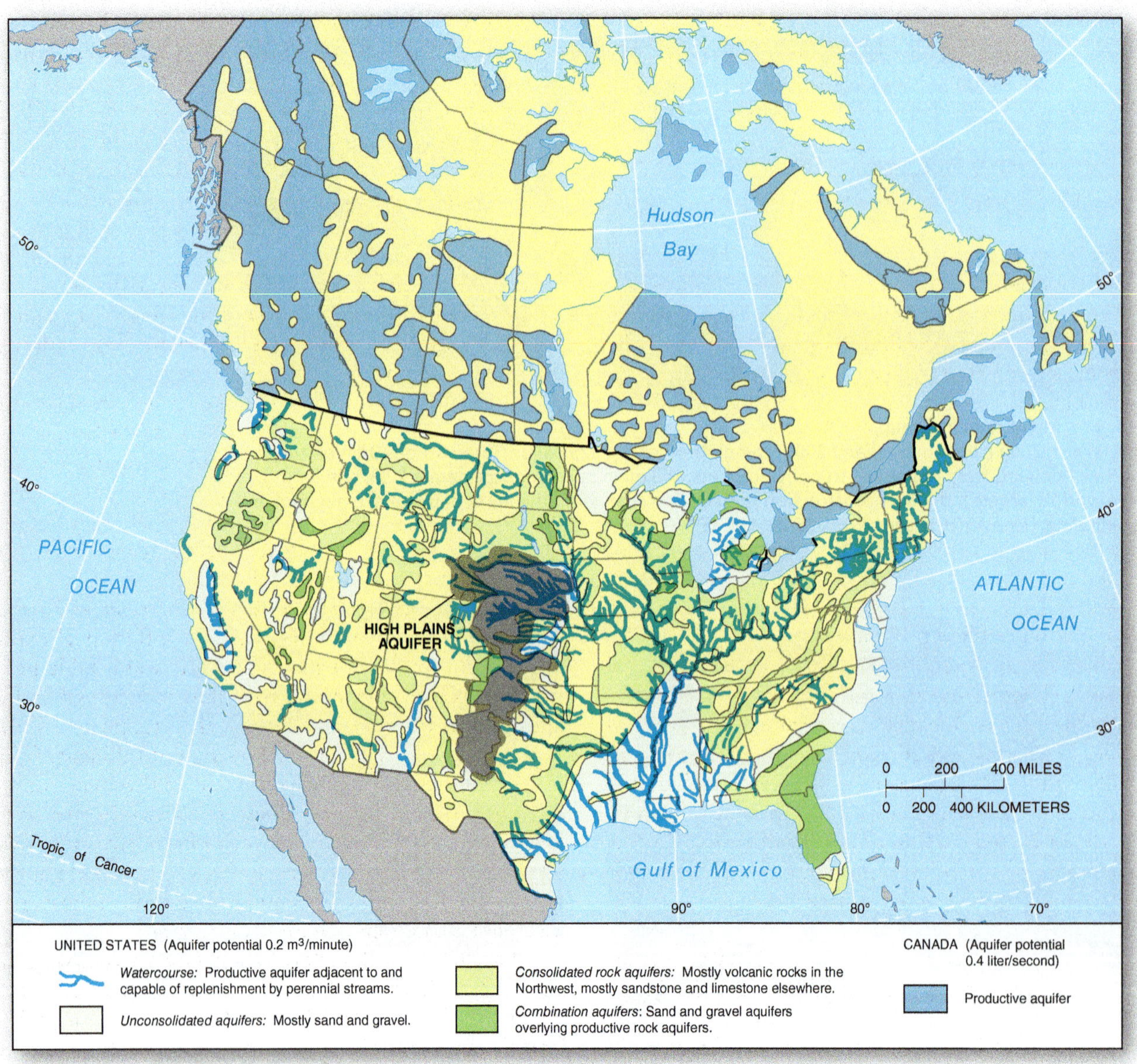

FIGURE 19 Groundwater resource potential for the United States and Canada. Highlighted areas of the United States are underlain by productive aquifers capable of yielding freshwater to wells at 0.2 m³/min or more (for Canada, 0.4 L/s). [Courtesy of Water Resources Council for the United States and the *Inquiry on Federal Water Policy* for Canada.]

Remember: *Groundwater is not an independent source of water, for it is tied to surface supplies for recharge.* An important consideration in many regions is that groundwater accumulation occurred over millions of years, so care must be taken not to exceed this long-term buildup with excessive short-term demands.

About 50% of the U.S. population derives a portion of its freshwater from groundwater sources. In some states, such as Nebraska, groundwater supplies 85% of water needs, with that figure as high as 100% in rural areas. Between 1950 and 2000, annual groundwater withdrawal in the United States and Canada increased more than 150%. Figure 19 shows potential groundwater resources in both countries.

Groundwater Profile and Movement

Figure 20 brings together many groundwater elements in a single illustration and is the basis for the following discussion. Groundwater begins as surplus water, which percolates downward as gravitational water from the zone of capillary water. This excess surface water moves through the **zone of aeration**, where soil and rock are less than saturated (some pore spaces contain air).

The *porosity* of any rock layer depends on the arrangement, size, and shape of its individual particles; the nature of any cementing elements between them; and their degree of compaction. Subsurface rocks are either *permeable* or *impermeable* depending on whether they conduct water readily (higher permeability) or tend to obstruct its flow (lower permeability).

Eventually, the water reaches an area where subsurface water accumulates, the **zone of saturation**. Here the pores are completely filled with water. Like a hard sponge made of sand, gravel, and rock, the saturation zone stores water in its countless pores and voids. The upper limit of the water that collects in the zone of saturation is the **water table**. It is the surface where the zone of saturation, a narrow capillary fringe layer, and the zone of aeration are in transition (all across Figure 20). The slope of the water table, which generally follows the contours of the land surface, controls groundwater movement.

An **aquifer** is a rock layer that is permeable to groundwater flow adequate for wells and springs. An **aquiclude** (also called an *aquitard*) is a body of rock that does not conduct water in usable amounts. The saturated zone may include the saturated portion of the aquifer and a part of the underlying *aquiclude*, even though the latter has such low permeability that its water is inaccessible.

Confined and Unconfined Aquifers

Whether an aquifer is confined or unconfined affects its behavior. A **confined aquifer** is bounded above and below by impermeable layers of rock or sediment. An **unconfined aquifer** has a permeable layer on top and an impermeable one beneath (see Figure 20).

Confined and unconfined aquifers differ in the size of their recharge area, which is the ground surface where water enters an aquifer to recharge it. For an unconfined aquifer, the **aquifer recharge area** generally extends above the entire aquifer; the water simply percolates down to the water table. But in a confined aquifer, the recharge area is far more restricted, as you can see in Figure 20. Pollution of this limited recharge area causes groundwater contamination; note in the illustration the improperly located disposal pond on the aquifer recharge area, contaminating wells to the right.

Confined and unconfined aquifers also differ in their water pressure. A well drilled into an unconfined aquifer (see Figure 20) must be pumped to make the water level rise above the water table. In contrast, the water in a confined aquifer is under the pressure of its own weight, creating a pressure level to which the water can rise on its own, the *potentiometric surface*.

The potentiometric surface actually can be above ground level (right side in figure). Under this condition, **artesian water**, or groundwater confined under pressure, may rise in a well and even flow at the surface without pumping if the top of the well is lower than the potentiometric surface. (These wells are called *artesian* for the Artois area in France, where they are common.) In other wells, however, pressure may be inadequate, and the artesian water must be pumped the remaining distance to the surface.

Wells, Springs, and Streamflows

The slope of the water table, which broadly follows the contour of the land surface, controls groundwater movement (see Figure 20). Groundwater tends to move toward areas of lower pressure and elevation.

Water wells can work only if they penetrate the water table. Where the water table intersects the surface, it creates springs (Figure 21). Such an intersection also occurs in lakes and riverbeds. Ultimately, groundwater may enter stream channels to flow as surface water (stream near center in Figure 20). In fact, during dry periods, the water table may sustain river flows.

Figure 22 illustrates the relation between the water table and surface streamflow in two different climatic settings. In humid climates, where the water table generally supplies a continuous base flow to a stream and is higher than the stream channel, the stream is *effluent* because it receives the water flowing out (effluent) from the surrounding ground. The Mississippi River and countless other streams are examples. In drier climates, with lower water tables, water from *influent* streams flows into the adjacent ground, sustaining vegetation along the stream. The Colorado River and Rio Grande of the American West are examples of influent streams.

The Arkansas River no longer flows across western and central Kansas. As you see in Focus Study 2, "High Plains Aquifer Overdraft," groundwater mining is prevalent throughout this region. When the bottom of the stream bed is no longer in contact with the declining water table, streamflow seeps into the aquifer (Figure 22 b and c). These influent conditions produce dry river, stream, and creek beds across the region.

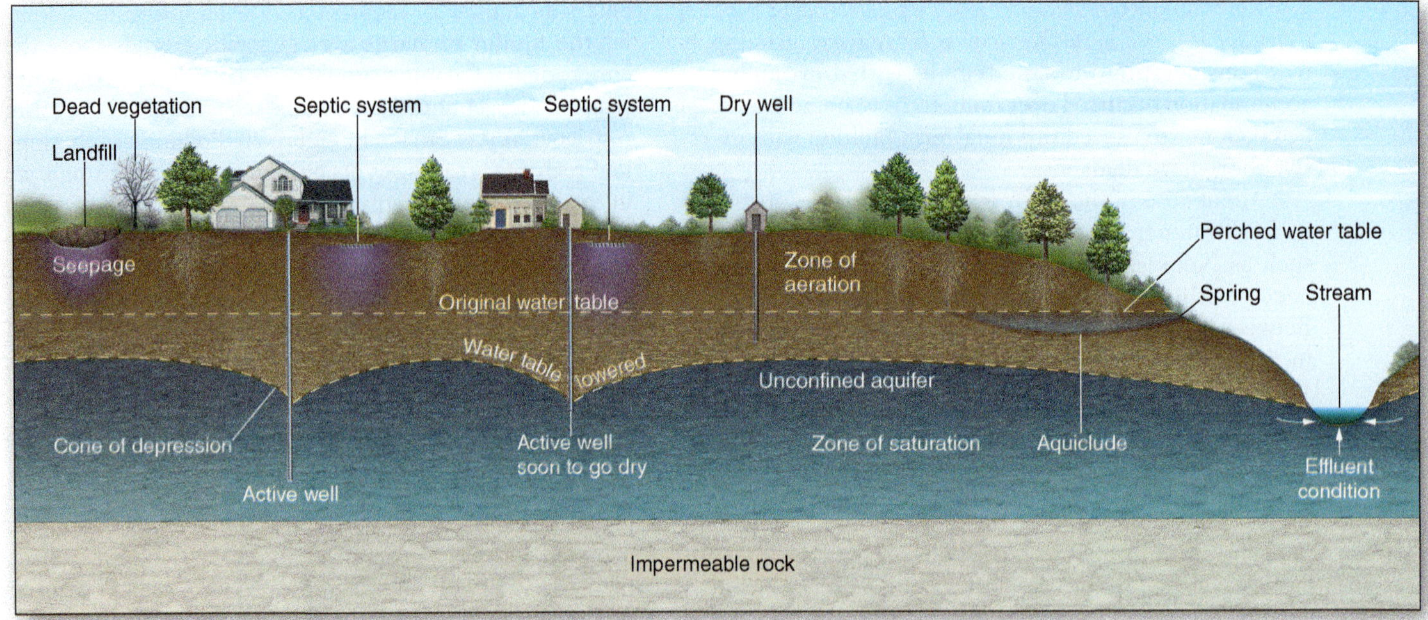

FIGURE 20 Groundwater characteristics.
Subsurface groundwater characteristics, processes, water flows, and human interactions. Follow the concepts across the illustration from left to right as you read along in the text.

Overuse of Groundwater

As water is pumped from a well, the surrounding water table within an unconfined aquifer may experience **drawdown**, or become lowered. Drawdown occurs if the pumping rate exceeds the replenishment flow of water into the aquifer or the horizontal flow around the well. The resultant lowering of the water table around the well is a **cone of depression** (see Figure 20, left).

FIGURE 21 An active spring.
Springs provide evidence of groundwater emerging at the surface. [Author.]

Overpumping Aquifers frequently are pumped beyond their flow and recharge capacities, a condition known as **groundwater mining**. In the United States today, large tracts experience chronic groundwater overdrafts in the Midwest, West, lower Mississippi Valley, and Florida, and in the intensely farmed Palouse region of eastern Washington State. In many places, the water table or artesian water level has declined more than 12 m (40 ft). Groundwater mining is of special concern in the massive High Plains aquifer, which has declined over 30 m (100 ft) in some areas.

About half of India's irrigation water needs and half of its industrial and urban water needs are met by the groundwater reserve. In rural areas, groundwater supplies 80% of domestic water from some 3 million hand-pumped bore holes. And in approximately 20% of India's agricultural districts, groundwater mining through more than 17 million wells (motorized dug wells and tube wells) is beyond recharge rates.

In the Middle East, groundwater overuse is even more severe. The groundwater resource beneath Saudi Arabia accumulated over tens of thousands of years, forming "fossil aquifers," but today's increasing withdrawals are not being naturally recharged due to the desert climate—in essence, groundwater has become a *nonrenewable* resource. Some researchers suggest that groundwater in the region will be depleted in a decade, although worsening water-quality problems will no doubt arise before then. Imagine having the hottest issue in the Middle East become water, not oil!

(text continued after Focus Study 2)

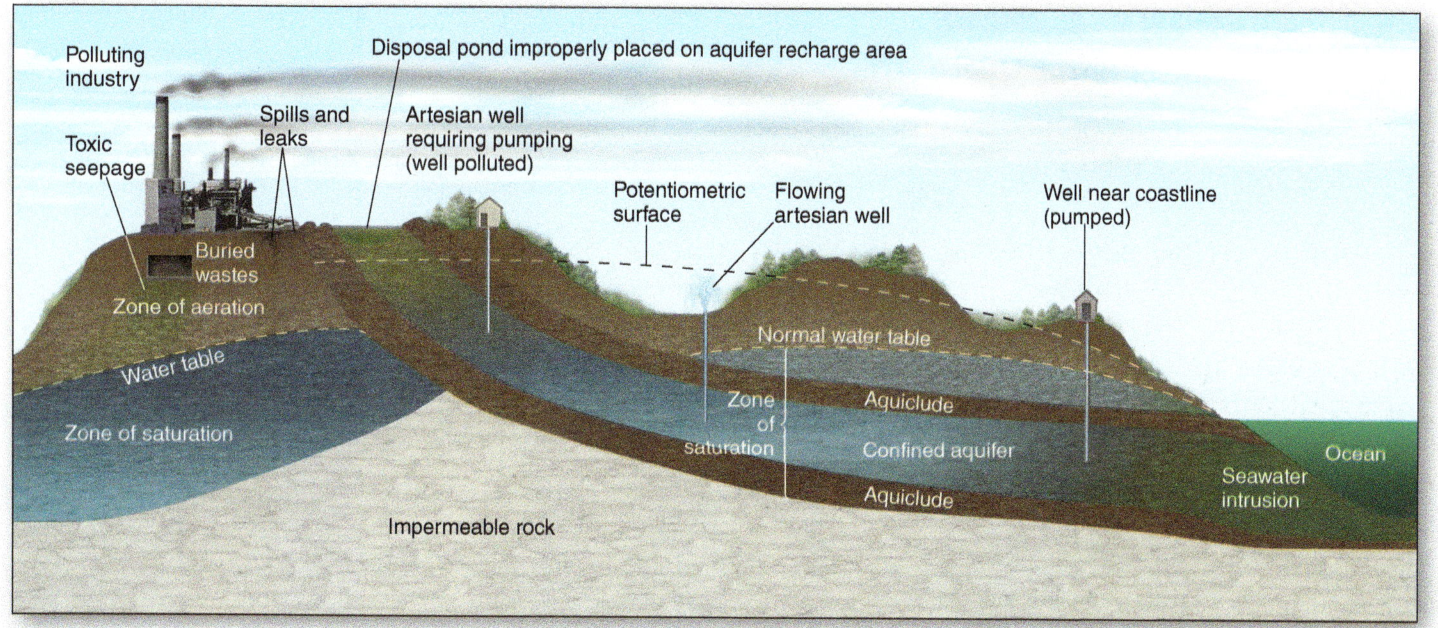

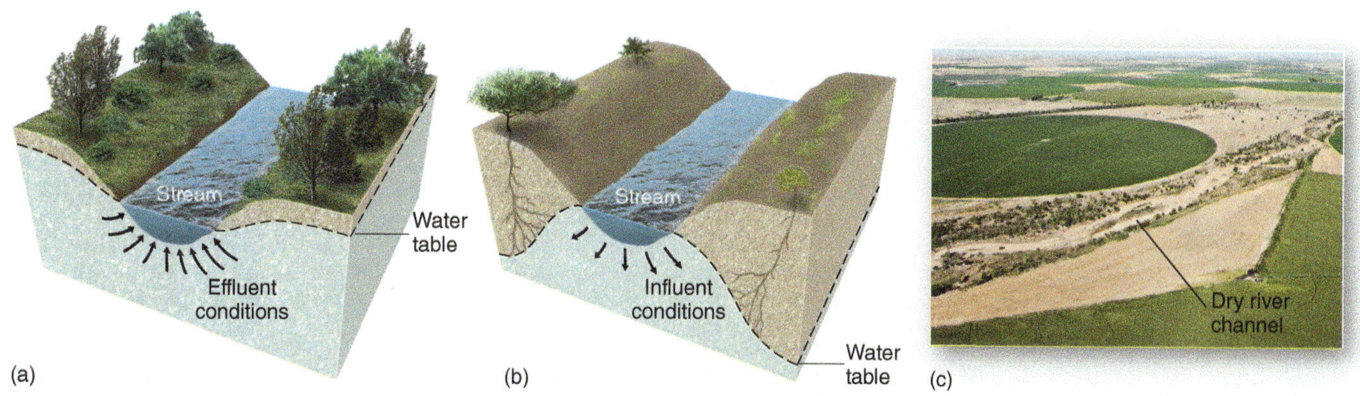

FIGURE 22 Groundwater interaction with streamflow.
(a) Effluent stream base flow is partially supplied by a high water table, characteristic of humid regions. (b) An influent stream supplies a lower water table, characteristic of drier regions. The water table may drop below the stream channel, effectively drying it out. (c) The Arkansas River is dry as water flows into subsurface groundwater aquifers. The channel appears to be used as an off-road course in the photo. [Bobbé Christopherson.]

GEO REPORT 5 *Water pipelines in the Middle East*

One water pipeline proposal brings water overland from Turkey to the Middle East through two branches. The Gulf water line would run southeast through Jordan and Saudi Arabia, with extensions into Kuwait, Abu Dhabi, and Oman. The other branch would run south through Syria, Jordan, and Saudi Arabia to the cities of Makkah (Mecca) and Jeddah. This pipeline would cover some 1500 km (930 mi), the distance from New York City to St. Louis. (See the links listed in Middle East Water Information Network at http://www.columbia.edu/cu/lweb/indiv/mideast/cuvlm/water.html.)

High Plains Aquifer Overdraft

North America's largest known aquifer is the High Plains aquifer, also locally known as the Ogallala aquifer. It lies beneath the American High Plains, an eight-state, 450,600-km^2 (174,000-mi^2) area from southern South Dakota to Texas (Figure 2.1a). Precipitation over the region varies from 30 cm in the southwest to 60 cm in the northeast (12 to 24 in.).

For several hundred thousand years, the aquifer's sand and gravel were charged with meltwaters from retreating glaciers. However, heavy mining of High Plains groundwater began 100 years ago, intensifying after World War II with the introduction of center-pivot irrigation (Figure 2.2). These large, circular devices provide vital water to wheat, sorghums, cotton, corn, and about 40% of the grain fed to cattle in

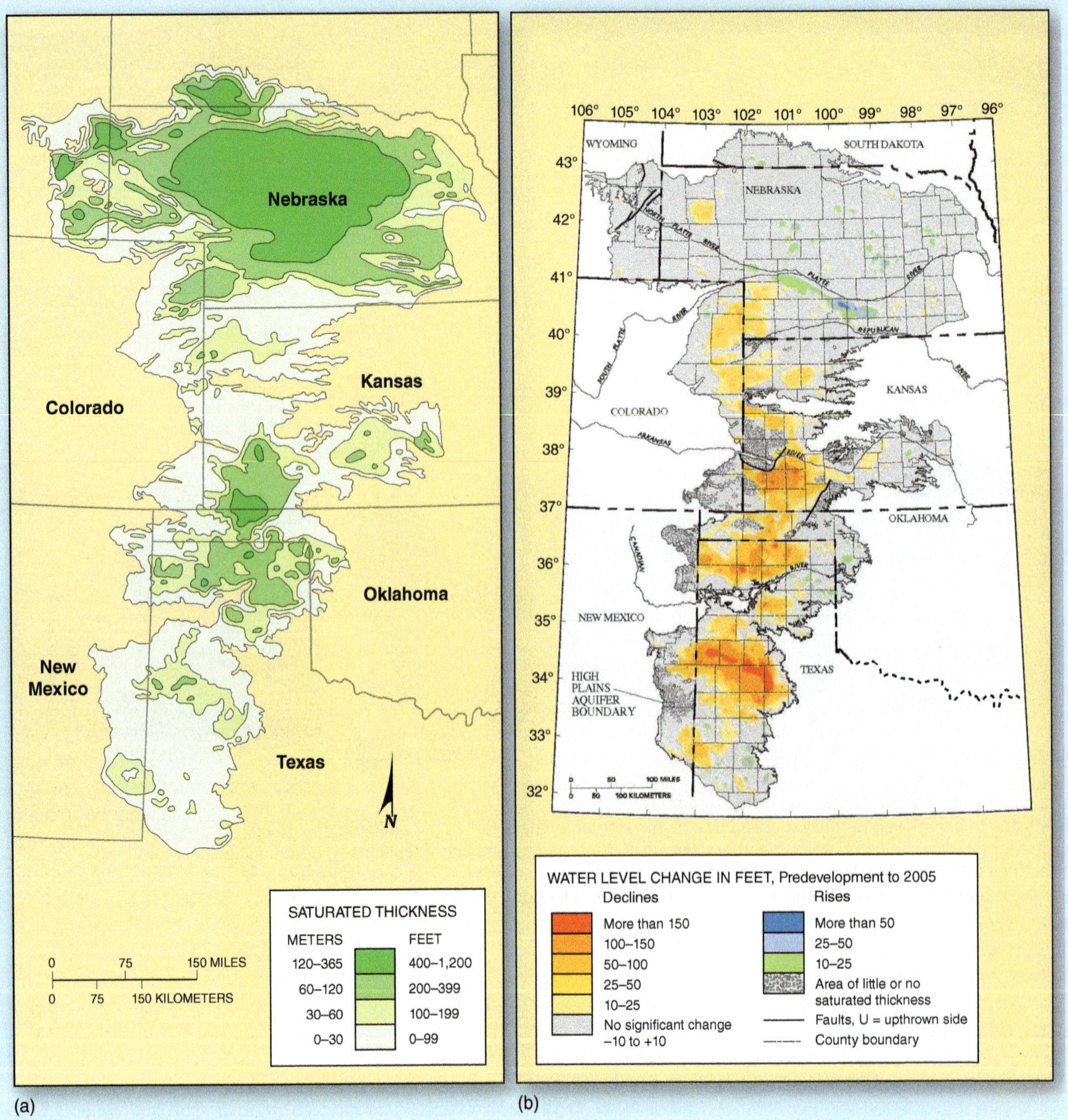

(a)

(b)

FIGURE 2.1 High Plains aquifer.
(a) Average saturated thickness. (b) Water level changes, using 1950 to represent "predevelopment." The color scale in the legend indicates widespread declines and a few areas of water-level rise. [Maps: (a) After D. E. Kromm and S. E. White, "Interstate groundwater management preference differences: The High Plains region," *Journal of Geography* 86, no. 1 (January–February 1987): 5. (b) Adapted from "Water Level changes in the High Plains Aquifer, Predevelopment to 2005," by V. L. McGuire, USGS Fact Sheet 2007-3029, Fig. 1.]

FIGURE 2.2 Center-pivot irrigation.
Myriad center-pivot irrigation systems water crops in the western Great Plains. A growing season for corn requires from 10 to 20 revolutions of the sprinkler arm, depending on the weather. The arm delivers about 3 cm (1.18 in.) of water per revolution (rainfall equivalent). [Bobbé Christopherson.]

the United States. The U.S. Geological Survey (USGS) began monitoring this groundwater mining from a sample of more than 7000 wells in 1988.

A USGS map of the water-level changes from predevelopment (about 1950) to 2005 appears in Figure 2.1b. Wells were measured in the winter or early spring when water levels were recovered from the previous irrigation season. Declining water levels are most severe in northern Texas, where the saturated thickness of the aquifer is least, through the Oklahoma panhandle and into western Kansas. Rising water levels are noted in portions of south-central Nebraska and a portion of Texas due to recharge from surface irrigation, a period of above-normal precipitation years, and downward percolation from canals and reservoirs. (See http://co.water.usgs.gov/nawqa/hpgw/HPGW_home.html.)

The High Plains aquifer irrigates about one-fifth of all U.S. cropland: 120,000 wells provide water for 5.7 million hectares (14 million acres). This is down from the peak of 170,000 wells in 1978. In 1980, water was pumped from the aquifer at the rate of 26 billion cubic meters (21 million acre-feet) a year, an increase of more than 300% since 1950. By the turn of this century, withdrawals had decreased 10% due to declining well yields and increasing pumping costs.

During the past five decades, the water table in the aquifer dropped more than 30 m (100 ft), and throughout the 1980s, it averaged a 2-m (6-ft) drop each year. The USGS estimates that recovery of the High Plains aquifer (those portions that have not collapsed) would take at least 1000 years if groundwater mining stopped today!

Obviously, billions of dollars of agricultural activity cannot be abruptly halted, but neither can profligate water mining continue. This issue raises tough questions: How do we best manage cropland? Can extensive irrigation continue? Can the region continue to meet the demand to produce commodities for export? Should we continue high-volume farming of certain crops that are in chronic over-supply? Should we rethink federal policy on crop subsidies and price supports? What changes will biofuels production force? What would be the impact on farmers and rural communities of any changes to the existing system?

Present irrigation practices, if continued, will deplete about half of the High Plains aquifer resource (and two-thirds of the Texas portion) by 2020. Add to this the approximate 10% loss of soil moisture due to increased evapotranspiration demand caused by climatic warming for this region by 2050, as forecast by computer models, and we have a portrait of a major regional water problem and a challenge for society.

Like any renewable resource, groundwater can be tapped indefinitely as long as the rate of extraction does not exceed the rate of replenishment. But just like a bank account, a groundwater reserve will dwindle if withdrawals exceed deposits. Few governments have established and enforced rules and regulations to insure that groundwater sources are exploited at a sustainable rate. . . . No government has yet adequately tackled the issue of groundwater depletion, but it is at least getting more attention.*

Collapsing Aquifers A possible effect of water removal from an aquifer is that the aquifer, which is a layer of rock or sediment, will lose its internal support. Water in the pore spaces between rock grains is not compressible, so it adds structural strength to the rock. If the water is removed through overpumping, air infiltrates the pores. Air is readily compressible, and the tremendous weight of overlying rock may crush the aquifer. On the surface, the visible result may be land subsidence, cracked house foundations, and changes in drainage.

Houston, Texas, provides an example. The removal of groundwater and crude oil caused land within an 80-km (50-mi) radius of Houston to subside more than 3 m (10 ft) over the years. Yet another example is the Fresno area of California's San Joaquin Valley. After years of intensive pumping of groundwater for irrigation, land levels have dropped almost 10 m (33 ft) because of a combination of water removal and soil compaction from agricultural activity.

Surface mining (also called strip mining) for coal in eastern Texas, northeastern Louisiana, Wyoming, Arizona, and other locales also destroys aquifers. Aquifer collapse is an increasing problem in West Virginia, Kentucky, and Virginia, where low-sulfur coal is mined to meet current air pollution requirements for coal-burning electric power plants.

Unfortunately, collapsed aquifers may not be rechargeable, even if surplus gravitational water becomes available, because pore spaces may be permanently collapsed. The water-well fields that serve the Tampa Bay–St. Petersburg, Florida, area are a case in point. Pond and lake levels, swamps, and wetlands in the area are declining and land surfaces are subsiding as the groundwater drawdown for export to the cities increases.

An additional problem arises when aquifers are overpumped near the ocean or coastal seas. Along a coastline, fresh groundwater and salty seawater establish a natural interface, or *contact surface*, with the less-dense freshwater flowing on top. But excessive withdrawal of freshwater can cause this interface to migrate inland. As a result, wells near the shore may become contaminated with saltwater, and the aquifer may become useless as a freshwater source. Figure 20 illustrates this seawater intrusion (far-right side). Pumping freshwater back into the aquifer may halt contamination by seawater, but once contaminated, the aquifer is difficult to reclaim.

*L. Brown et al. and the Worldwatch Institute, *Vital Signs: The Environmental Trends That Are Shaping Our Future* (New York: W. W. Norton & Co., 2000), pp. 122, 123.

Pollution of Groundwater

When surface water is polluted, groundwater inevitably becomes contaminated because it is recharged from surface water supplies. Surface water flows rapidly and flushes pollution downstream, but slow-moving groundwater, once contaminated, remains polluted virtually forever.

Pollution can enter groundwater from many sources: industrial injection wells (wastes pumped into the ground), septic tank outflows, seepage from hazardous-waste disposal sites, industrial toxic waste, agricultural residues (pesticides, herbicides, fertilizers), urban solid-waste landfills, and natural gas mining through the method of hydraulic fracturing, or hydrofracking. As an example, leakage from some 10,000 underground gasoline storage tanks at U.S. gasoline stations is suspected. Some cancer-causing additives to gasoline, such as the oxygenate MTBE (methyl tertiary butyl ether), are contaminating thousands of local water supplies.

Where *hydrofracking* (hydraulic fracturing) is used, large quantities of water are pumped under high pressure into subsurface rock, fracturing them, and releasing natural gas. The wastewater produced is contaminated with chemicals used in the process, with naturally occurring radioactivity, and often groundwater is polluted. There are more than 500,000 such wells in the United States, more than 50,000 in Pennsylvania alone. In five states, natural gas flowed into groundwater systems contaminating drinking water—imagine turning on a water faucet and being able to light a flame from the natural gas pollution.

For management purposes, about 35% of pollution is *point source*, such as a gasoline tank or septic tank; 65% is *nonpoint source*, coming from a broad area, such as an agricultural field or urban runoff. Regardless of the spatial nature of the source, pollution can spread over a great distance, as illustrated in Figure 20. Since the nature of aquifers makes them inaccessible, the extent of groundwater pollution is underestimated.

Our Water Supply

Human thirst for adequate water supplies, both in quantity and in quality, will be a major issue in this century. Internationally, increases in per capita water use are double the rate of population growth. Since we are so dependent on water, it seems that humans should cluster where good water is plentiful. But accessible water supplies are not well correlated with population distribution or the regions where population growth is greatest.

Table 1 provides statistics that, taken together, indicate the unevenness of Earth's water supply. These data include population, land area, annual streamflow, and projected population change for six world regions. Also note 2006 data on carbon dioxide emissions per person for each region. Earth's water supply is tied, first, to climatic variability and, second, to water demand, which is, in turn, tied to level of development, affluence, and per capita consumption.

For example, North America's mean annual discharge is 4310 BGD and Asia's is 9540 BGD. However, North America has only 6.6% of the world's population, whereas Asia has

TABLE 1 Regional Comparison of Factors Influencing Global Water Supply

Region	2010 Population (in millions)	Share of Global Population	Land Area in Thousands of km² (mi²)	Share of Global Land Area	Mean Annual Streamflow (BGD)	Share of Annual Streamflow	2050 population as a multiple of 2010	Metric Tons of CO_2 Emissions per Person (2006)
Africa	1030	15%	30,600 (11,800)	23%	3060	11%	2.0	0.9
Asia	4157	60%	44,600 (17,200)	33%	9540	34%	103	3.0
Australia–Oceania	37	0.5%	8,420 (3,250)	6%	1420	5%	1.6	19.0 (Australia) 8.9 (New Zealand)
Europe	739	10.8%	9,770 (3,770)	7%	2280	8%	1.0	8.4
North America[a]	455	6.7%	22,100 (8,510)	16%	4310	15%	1.4	18.4 (U.S. and Canada) 4.0 (Mexico)
Central and South America	474	7%	17,800 (6,880)	13%	7510	27%	1.3	3.1
Global (excluding Antarctica)	6892		134,000 (51,600)		28,100		1.4	More developed: 11.5 Less developed: 2.4

[a]Includes Canada, Mexico, and the United States.
Note: BGD, billion gallons per day. Population data from *2010 World Population Data Sheet* (Washington, DC: Population Reference Bureau, 2010). Population change forecast is at present growth rates. Numbers are rounded. Metric tons × 1.1 for short (U.S.) tons.

60%, with a population doubling time less than half that of North America. In northern China, 550 million people living in approximately 500 cities lack adequate water supplies. For comparison, note that the 1990 floods cost China $10 billion, whereas water shortages are running at more than $35 billion a year in costs to the Chinese economy. An analyst for the World Bank stated that China's water shortages pose a more serious threat than floods during this century, yet in news coverage, we hear only of floods when they happen.

CRITICAL THINKING 2

Water on your campus

How much do you know about the water on your campus? If the campus has its own wells, how is the quality tested? Who on campus is in charge of supervising these wells? Lastly, what is your subjective assessment of the water you use: taste, smell, hardness, clarity? Write a brief critique following a taste test. Compare these perceptions with those of others in your class. In your region, find out if hydrofracking mining is being used for natural gas recovery and if any effects on groundwater are reported.

In Africa, 56 countries draw from a varied water-resource base; these countries share more than 50 river and lake watersheds. Increasing population growth and percentage of urban dwellers cause water demands to rise and lead to an overexploitation of the resource. Twelve African countries experience water stress (less than 1700 m^3 per person/year), and 14 have water scarcity (less than 1000 m^3 per person/year).

Water resources are different from other resources in that there is *no alternative substance to water*. Water-resource stress related to quantity and/or quality shortfalls will dominate future political agendas. Water shortages increase the probability for international conflict, endanger public health, reduce agricultural productivity, and damage life-supporting ecological systems. For the 21st century, a transition to a new approach is required, away from large, centralized structures toward decentralized, community-based strategies, focused on demand management and efficient technologies.

Desalination

Desalination of seawater to augment diminishing groundwater supplies is becoming increasingly important as a freshwater source. More than 12,000 desalination plants are now in operation worldwide, and plant construction is expected to increase 140% between 2009 and 2017, amounting to some $60 billion in investments. Approximately 50% of all desalination plants are in the Middle East. Desalination is an alternative to further groundwater mining and saltwater intrusion under Saudi Arabia; in fact, 30 desalination plants currently supply 70% of the country's drinking water needs (Figure 23a). In the United States, along the coast of southern California and in Florida, desalination is slowly increasing in use.

The Tampa–St. Petersburg area in Florida took a giant step forward with the opening of its own Tampa Bay desalination plant, which produces 25 MGD, about 10% of the region's drinking water supply, making it the largest in the United States. This output is about 12% of the production at the Jabal plant in Saudi Arabia. The seawater intake is from the Big Bend Power Station's cooling water discharge. The Tampa Bay plant produces drinking water through a series of filters to remove algae and particles and a reverse-osmosis process where the water is forced through semipermeable membranes (Figure 23b).

(a) Saudi Arabia

(b) Tampa Bay, Florida

FIGURE 23 **Water desalination.**
(a) Freshwater is supplied to Saudi Arabia from the Jabal water desalination plant along the Red Sea. (b) The Tampa Bay desalination plant adds 25 MGD to the region's water resources through filtration and reverse osmosis processes. [(a) Liaison Agency. (b) Tampa Bay Water.]

In Sydney, Australia, a reverse-osmosis desalination plant opened in 2010. The $17 billion Kurnell plant supplies about 15% of the region's water needs. Some 67 wind turbines supply energy needs for the operation.

Water Supply in the United States

The U.S. water supply derives from surface and groundwater sources that are fed by an average daily precipitation of 4200 BGD (billion gallons a day). That sum is based on an average annual precipitation value of 76.2 cm (30 in.) divided evenly among the 48 contiguous states (excluding Alaska and Hawai'i).

The 4200 billion gallons of average daily precipitation mentioned are unevenly distributed across the country and unevenly distributed throughout the year. For example, New England's water supply is so abundant that only about 1% of available water is consumed each year. The same is true in Canada, where the resource greatly exceeds that in the United States.

Figure 24 shows how the U.S. supply of 4200 BGD is distributed. Viewed daily, the national water budget has two general outputs: 71% actual evapotranspiration (ACTET) and 29% surplus (SURPL). The 71% actual evapotranspiration involves 2970 BGD of the daily supply. It passes through nonirrigated land, including farm crops and pasture, forest and browse (young leaves, twigs, and shoots), and nonagricultural vegetation. Eventually, it returns to the atmosphere to continue its journey through the hydrologic cycle. The remaining 29% surplus is what we directly use.

Note that groundwater is considered part of surface water because it is linked to surface supplies. In 2005, about 67% of fresh groundwater withdrawals were for irrigation and 18% for public supply water needs. Just six states accounted for 50% of withdrawals: California, Texas, Nebraska, Arkansas, Idaho, and Florida (where more than half of the public supply water is from groundwater).

The surplus 1230 BGD is runoff, available for withdrawal, consumption, and various instream uses.

- *Nonconsumptive uses*, sometimes called **withdrawal**, or *offstream use*, remove water from the supply, use it, and then return it to the same supply. Nonconsumptive water is used by industry, agriculture, and municipalities and in steam–electric power generation. A portion of the water withdrawn is consumed.
- **Consumptive uses** remove water from a stream, but do not return it, so it is not available for a second or third use. Some consumptive examples include water that evaporates or is vaporized in steam–electric plants.
- *Instream* uses are those that use streamflow in the channel, without removing it: Examples include navigation, wildlife and ecosystem preservation, waste dilution and removal, hydroelectric power production, fishing, and recreation.

When water returns to the system, water quality usually is altered—water is contaminated chemically with pollutants, or waste, or thermally with heat energy. In Figure 24, this portion of the budget is returned to runoff and eventually the ocean. This wastewater represents an opportunity to extend the resource through reuse.

Contaminated or not, returned water becomes a part of all water systems downstream. An example is New Orleans, the last city to withdraw municipal water from the Mississippi River. New Orleans receives diluted and mixed contaminants added throughout the entire Missouri–Ohio–Mississippi River drainage. This includes the effluent from chemical plants, runoff from millions of acres of farm fields treated with fertilizer and pesticides, treated and untreated sewage, oil spills, gasoline leaks, wastewater from thousands of industries, runoff from urban streets and storm drains, and turbidity from countless construction sites and from mining, farming, and logging activities. Abnormally high cancer rates among citizens living along the Mississippi River between Baton Rouge and New Orleans have led to the ominous label "Cancer Alley" for the region. The infamous "muck" that covered the region when the levees broke in 2005 contained some of this in its brew.

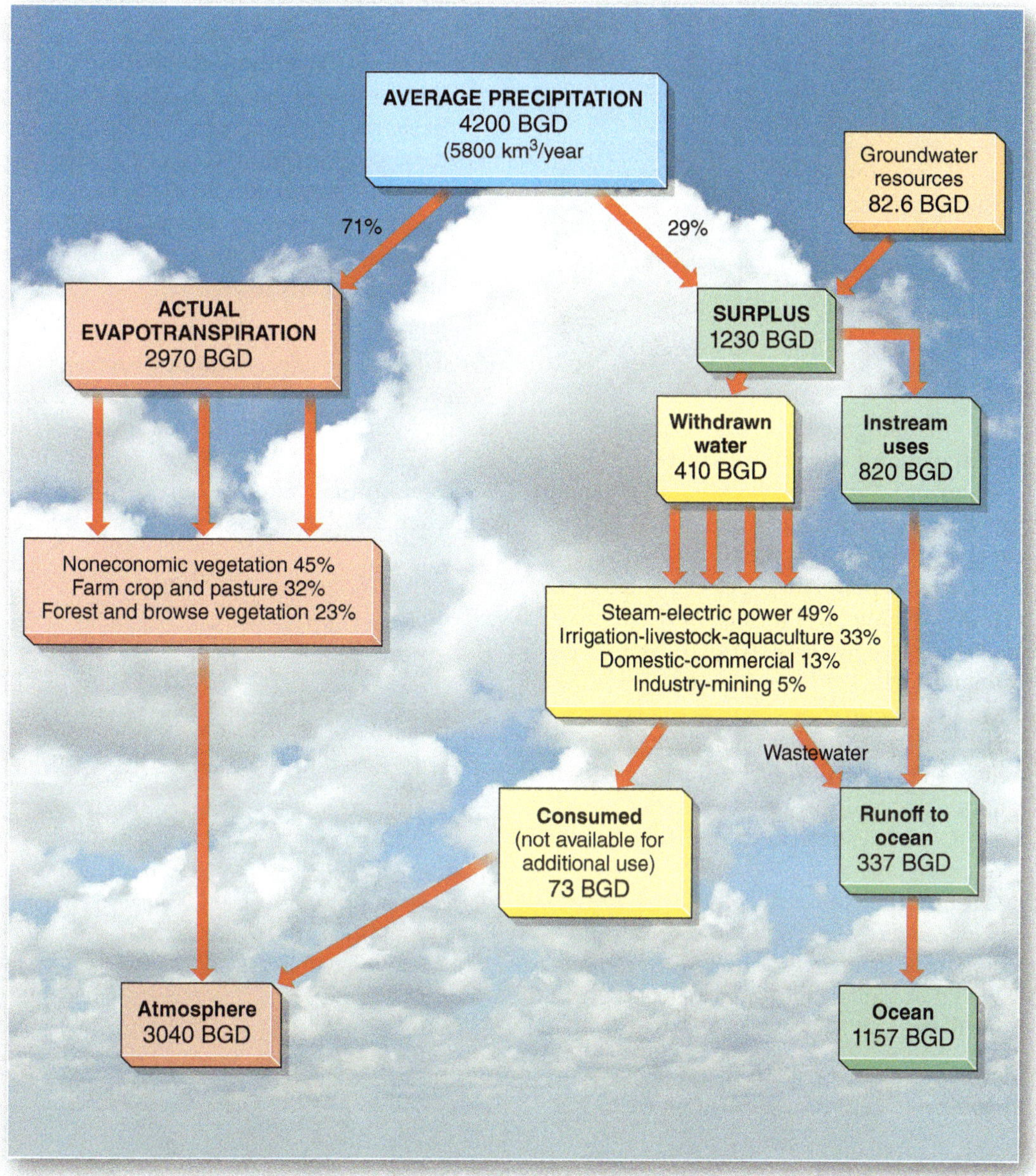

FIGURE 24 U.S. water budget.
Daily water budget for the contiguous 48 states in billions of gallons a day (BGD). [Data from Joan Kenny, Nancy Barber, Susan Hutson, Kristin Linsey, John Lovelace, and Molly Maupin, *Estimated Use of Water in the United States in 2005* (Denver, CO: USGS Circular 1344, 2005)—the latest year for which data are available. Background image by Bobbé Christopherson.]

The estimated U.S. withdrawal of water for 2005 was 410 BGD, almost three times the usage rate in 1940, double that in 1950, but a decrease of 5% since the peak year of 1980. A shift in emphasis from supply-side to demand-side planning, pricing, and management produced these efficiencies. Total per capita use was 1367 gal/day in 2005. For studies of water use in the United States and the U.S. Geological Survey's (USGS's) *Estimated Use of Water in the U.S. in 2005* (available as a free download), see http://water.usgs.gov/public/watuse/.

GEO REPORT 6 *The water it takes for food and necessities*

Simply providing the variety of food we enjoy requires voluminous water. For example, 77 g (2.7 oz) of broccoli requires 42 L (11 gal) of water to grow and process; producing 250 ml (8 oz) of milk requires 182 L (48 gal) of water; producing 28 g (1 oz) of cheese requires 212 L (56 gal); producing 1 egg requires 238 L (63 gal); and producing a 113-g (4-oz) beef patty requires 2314 L (616 gal). And then there are the toilets, the majority of which still flush approximately 4 gal of water. Imagine the spatial complexity of servicing the desert city of Las Vegas, with 150,000 hotel rooms times the number of toilet flushes per day; of providing all support services for 38 million visitors per year, plus 38 golf courses. One hotel confirms that it washes 14,000 pillowcases a day.

CRITICAL THINKING 3

That next glass of water

You have no doubt had several glasses of water between when you awoke this morning and the time you are reading these words. Where did this water originate? Obtain the name of the water company or agency, determine whether it is using surface or groundwater to meet demands, and check how the water is metered and billed. If your state or province requires water-quality reporting, obtain a copy of this analysis of your tap water from the water supplier.

Future Considerations

When precipitation is budgeted, the limits of the water resource become apparent. How can we satisfy the growing demand for water? Water availability per person declines as population increases, and individual demand increases with economic development, affluence, and technology. Thus, world population growth since 1970 reduced per capita water supplies by a third. Also, pollution limits the water-resource base, so that even before *quantity* constraints are felt, *quality* problems may limit the health and growth of a region.

The international aspect of the water-resource problem is illustrated by the 200 major river drainage basins in the world. One hundred and forty-five countries possess territory within an international river drainage basin—truly a global commons.

Working Group II, in its report entitled *Impacts, Adaptation, and Vulnerability*—part of the Intergovernmental Panel on Climate Change's *Fourth Assessment Report* (2007)—concluded that global climate change and greenhouse warming will cause added water problems:

> By mid-century, annual average river runoff and water availability are projected to increase 10–40% at high latitudes and in some wet tropical areas, and decrease by 10–30% over some dry regions at mid-latitudes and in the dry tropics, some of which are presently water-stressed areas. . . . Drought-affected areas will likely increase in extent. . . . In the course of the century, water supplies stored in glaciers and snow cover are projected to decline, reducing water availability in regions supplied by meltwater from major mountain ranges, where more than one-sixth of the world population currently lives.

Clearly, cooperation is needed, yet we continue toward a water crisis without a concept of a *world water economy* as a frame of reference. The geospatial question is this: When will more international coordination begin, and which country or group of countries will lead the way to sustain future water resources? The soil-water-budget approach detailed in this chapter is a place to start.

GEOSYSTEMS CONNECTION

In this chapter, we looked at water resources through a water-balance approach, using a systems view that considers both water supply and water demand. The ongoing drought in the southwestern United States brings the need for such a water-budget strategy to the forefront. With water resources as the ultimate output of the water–weather system, we shift to climate and climate change. Examination of world climates completes the journey beginning with solar energy flowing through the atmosphere to Earth's surface and then to the outputs of temperature and wind and ocean circulation, to water, weather, and water resources, and finally to climate.

KEY LEARNING CONCEPTS REVIEW

- ***Describe*** the origin of Earth's waters, ***define*** the quantity of water that exists today, and ***list*** the locations of Earth's freshwater supply.

Water molecules came from within Earth over a period of billions of years, in the **outgassing** process. Thus began endless cycling of water through the hydrologic system of evaporation–condensation–precipitation. Water covers about 71% of Earth. Approximately 97% of it is salty seawater, and the remaining 3% is freshwater—most of it frozen.

The present volume of water on Earth is estimated at 1.36 billion km³ (326 million mi³), an amount achieved roughly 2 billion years ago. This overall steady-state equilibrium might seem in conflict with the many changes in sea level that have occurred over Earth's history, but is not. **Eustasy** refers to worldwide changes in sea level and relates to the change in volume of water in the oceans. The amount of water stored in glaciers and ice sheets explains these changes as *glacio-eustatic* factors. At present, sea level is rising because of increases in the temperature of the oceans and the record melting of glacial ice.

outgassing
eustasy

1. Approximately where and when did Earth's water originate?
2. If the quantity of water on Earth has been quite constant in volume for at least 2 billion years, how can sea level have fluctuated? Explain.
3. Describe the locations of Earth's water, both oceanic and fresh. What is the largest repository of freshwater at this time? In what ways is this distribution of water significant to modern society?
4. Why would climate change be a concern, given this distribution of water?
5. Why might you describe Earth as the water planet? Explain.

- ***Illustrate*** the hydrologic cycle with a simple sketch, and ***label*** it with definitions for each water pathway.

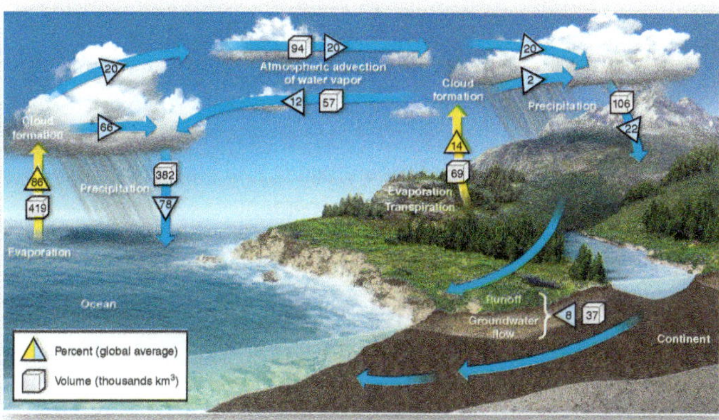

The **hydrologic cycle** is a model of Earth's water system, which has operated for billions of years from the lower atmosphere to several kilometers beneath Earth's surface. Water soaks into the subsurface through **infiltration**, or penetration of the soil surface. It further permeates soil or rock through vertical movement called **percolation.**

hydrologic cycle
infiltration
percolation

6. Sketch and explain a simplified model of the complex flows of water on Earth—the hydrologic cycle.
7. What are the possible routes that a raindrop may take on its way to and into the soil surface?
8. Compare precipitation and evaporation volumes from the ocean with those over land. Describe advection flows of moisture and countering surface and subsurface runoff.

- ***Relate*** the importance of the water-budget concept to your understanding of the hydrologic cycle, water resources, and soil moisture for a specific location.

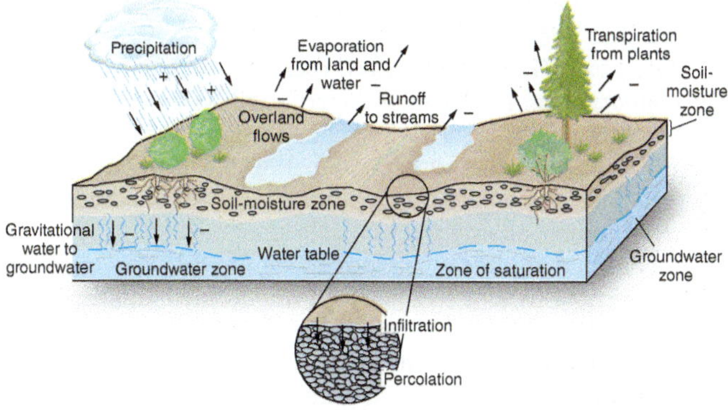

A **soil-water budget** can be established for any area of Earth's surface by measuring the precipitation input and the output of various water demands in the area considered. Understanding both the supply of the water resource and the natural demands on the resource is essential to sustainable human interaction with the hydrologic cycle. Streams represent only a tiny fraction of all water (1250 km³, or 300 mi³), the smallest volume of any of the freshwater categories. Yet streams represent four-fifths of all the water we use. Groundwater is the largest potential freshwater source in the hydrologic cycle and is tied to surface supplies.

soil-water budget

9. How might an understanding of the hydrologic cycle in a particular locale or the soil-moisture budget of a site assist you in assessing water resources? Give some specific examples.

- ***Construct*** the water-balance equation as a way of accounting for the expenditures of the water supply, and ***define*** each of the components in the equation and its specific operation.

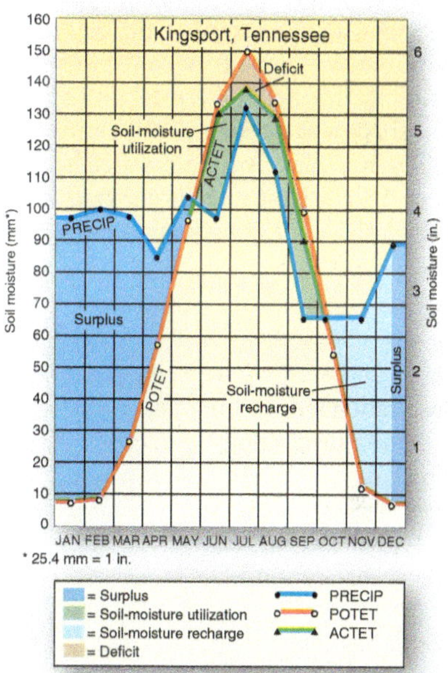

The moisture supply to Earth's surface is **precipitation** (PRECIP, or P), arriving as rain, sleet, snow, and hail. Precipitation is measured with a **rain gauge. Evaporation** is the net movement of free water molecules away from a wet surface into air. **Transpiration** is the movement of water through plants and back into the atmosphere; it is a cooling mechanism for plants. Evaporation and transpiration are combined into one term—**evapotranspiration.** The ultimate demand for moisture is **potential evapotranspiration** (POTET, or PE), the amount of water that *would* evaporate and transpire under optimum moisture conditions (adequate precipitation and adequate soil moisture). Evapotranspiration is measured with an **evaporation pan** (*evaporimeter*) or the more elaborate **lysimeter.**

Unsatisfied POTET is a **deficit** (DEFIC). By subtracting DEFIC from POTET, we determine **actual evapotranspiration,** or ACTET. Ideally, POTET and ACTET are about the same, so that plants have sufficient water. If POTET is satisfied and the soil is full of moisture, then additional water input becomes **surplus** (SURPL), which may puddle on the surface, flow across the surface toward stream channels, or percolate underground through the soil. The *overland flow* to streams includes precipitation and groundwater flows into river channels to make up the **total runoff** from the area.

A "savings account" of water that receives recharge deposits and provides for utilization withdrawals as water-balance conditions change is the **soil-moisture storage**, ΔSTRGE. This is the volume of water stored in the soil that is accessible to plant roots. In soil, *hygroscopic water* is inaccessible because it is a molecule-thin layer that is tightly bound to each soil particle by hydrogen bonding. As available water is utilized, soil reaches the **wilting point** (all that remains is unextractable water). **Capillary water** is generally accessible to plant roots because it is held in the soil by surface tension and hydrogen bonding between water and soil. Almost all capillary water that remains in the soil is **available water** in soil-moisture storage. After water drains from the larger pore spaces, the available water remaining for plants is termed **field capacity**, or storage capacity. When soil is saturated after a precipitation event, surplus water in the soil becomes **gravitational water** and percolates to groundwater. As **soil-moisture utilization** removes soil water, the plants work harder to extract the same amount of moisture, whereas **soil-moisture recharge** is the rate at which needed moisture enters the soil.

The texture and the structure of the soil dictate available pore spaces, or **porosity**. The soil's **permeability** is the degree to which water can flow through it. Permeability depends on particle sizes and the shape and packing of soil grains.

Drought does not have a simple water-budget definition; rather, it can occur in at least four forms: *meteorological drought*, *agricultural drought*, *hydrologic drought*, and/or *socioeconomic drought*.

precipitation
rain gauge
evaporation
transpiration
evapotranspiration
potential evapotranspiration
evaporation pan
lysimeter
deficit
actual evapotranspiration
surplus
total runoff
soil-moisture storage
wilting point
capillary water
available water
field capacity
gravitational water
soil-moisture utilization
soil-moisture recharge
porosity
permeability

10. Explain the meaning of this statement: "The soil-water budget is an assessment of the hydrologic cycle at a specific site."
11. What are the components of the water-balance equation? Construct the equation, and place each term's definition below its abbreviation in the equation.
12. Compare the annual water-balance data for Kingsport, Tennessee; Ottawa, Ontario; and Phoenix, Arizona. What differences do you see in the components? What similarities? What does this tell you about local water resources in each area?
13. Explain how to derive actual evapotranspiration (ACTET) in the water-balance equation.
14. What is potential evapotranspiration (POTET)? How do we go about estimating this potential rate? What factors did Thornthwaite use to determine this value?
15. Explain the operation of soil-moisture storage, soil-moisture utilization, and soil-moisture recharge. Include discussion of the field capacity, capillary water, and wilting point concepts.
16. In the case of silt-loam soil from Figure 11, roughly what is the available water capacity? How is this value derived?
17. Describe the four types of drought. Use the Internet to locate at least three different regions of the world currently experiencing drought. Were you previously aware of these droughts? Why do you think media coverage of drought seems lacking?
18. How would you describe the water budget of the Colorado River? What was the basis of agreements regarding distribution of the river's water? Provide an overview of current conditions of the Colorado River system in light of the ongoing drought, regional climate change, and increasing water demands from a growing population.

- ***Describe*** the nature of groundwater, and ***define*** the elements of the groundwater environment.

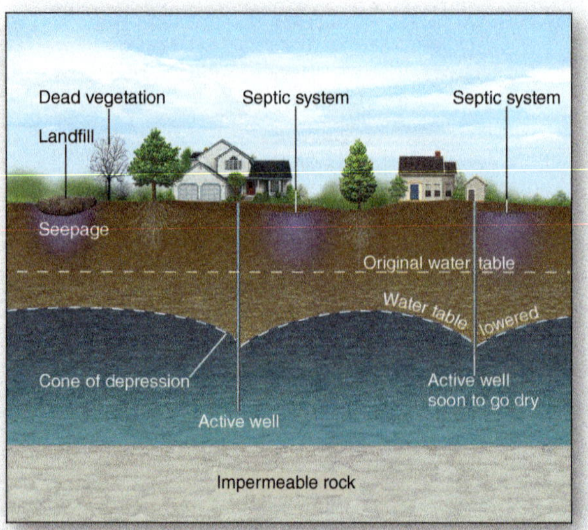

Groundwater is a part of the hydrologic cycle, but it lies beneath the surface beyond the soil-moisture root zone. Groundwater does not exist independently because its replenishment is tied to surface surpluses. Excess surface water moves through the **zone of aeration**, where soil and rock are less than saturated. Eventually, the water reaches the **zone of saturation**, where the pores are completely filled with water. The upper limit of the water that collects in the zone of saturation is the **water table**; it is the contact surface between the zones of saturation and aeration.

The *permeability* of subsurface rocks depends on whether they conduct water readily (higher permeability) or tend to obstruct its flow (lower permeability). They can even be impermeable. An **aquifer** is a rock layer that is permeable to groundwater flow in usable amounts. An **aquiclude** (aquitard) is a body of rock that does not allow water in usable amounts.

A **confined aquifer** is bounded above and below by impermeable layers of rock or sediment. An **unconfined aquifer** has a permeable layer on top and an impermeable one beneath. The **aquifer recharge area** extends over an entire unconfined aquifer. Water in a confined aquifer is under the pressure of its own weight, creating a pressure level to which the water can rise on its own, the *potentiometric surface*, which can be above ground level. Groundwater confined under pressure is **artesian water**; it may rise up in wells and even flow out at the surface without pumping if the head of the well is below the potentiometric surface.

As water is pumped from a well, the surrounding water table within an unconfined aquifer will experience **drawdown**, or become lower, if the rate of pumping exceeds the horizontal flow of water in the aquifer around the well. This excessive pumping causes a **cone of depression**. Aquifers frequently are pumped beyond their flow and recharge capacities, a condition known as **groundwater mining**.

groundwater
zone of aeration
zone of saturation
water table
aquifer
aquiclude
confined aquifer
unconfined aquifer
aquifer recharge area
artesian water
drawdown
cone of depression
groundwater mining

19. Are groundwater resources independent of surface supplies, or are the two interrelated? Explain your answer.
20. Make a simple sketch of the subsurface environment, labeling zones of aeration and saturation and the water table in an unconfined aquifer. Then add a confined aquifer to the sketch.
21. At what point does groundwater utilization become groundwater mining? Use the High Plains aquifer example to explain your answer.
22. What is the nature of groundwater pollution? Can contaminated groundwater be cleaned up easily? Explain. What is hydrofracking and how does it impact groundwater?

- ***Evaluate*** the U.S. water budget, and ***identify*** critical aspects of present and future freshwater supplies.

The world's water supply is distributed unevenly over Earth's surface. To meet demand, some areas will need to rely on water

supplied from sources other than runoff. **Desalination** of a water resource involves the removal of organics, debris, and salinity from seawater through distillation or reverse osmosis. This processing yields potable water for domestic uses.

In the United States, water surpluses are used in several ways. *Nonconsumptive uses*, called water **withdrawal** or *offstream use*, remove water from the supply, use it, and then return it to the stream. **Consumptive uses** remove water from a stream, but do not return it, so the water is not available for a second or third use. *Instream* uses do not remove water from the stream channel; examples are recreation and hydropower production. Americans in the 48 contiguous states withdraw approximately one-third of the available surplus runoff for irrigation, industry, and municipal uses.

desalination
withdrawal
consumptive use

23. Describe the principal pathways involved in the water budget of the contiguous 48 states. What is the difference between withdrawal and consumptive use of water resources? Compare these with instream uses.
24. Briefly assess the status of world water resources. What challenges exist in meeting the future needs of an expanding population and growing economies?
25. If wars in the 21st century are predicted to be about water availability in quantity and quality, what action could we take to understand the issues and avoid the conflicts?

MasteringGEOGRAPHY™

Visit http://www.masteringgeography.com/ for several figure animations, satellite loops, self-study quizzes, flashcards, visual glossary, case studies, career links, text reference maps, RSS Feeds, and an ebook version of *Elemental Geosystems.* Included are many geography web links to interesting Internet sources that support this chapter.

Climate Systems and Climate Change

Climate Systems and Climate Change

Published studies confirm increases of intense weather events and severe flooding episodes during the last three decades, part of the overall trend of changing climate. This Minnesota scene is just a day after a record tornado outbreak in June 2010. Beams of sunlight (crepuscular rays) stream from the edges of a cumulonimbus cloud. [Bobbé Christopherson.]

KEY LEARNING CONCEPTS

After reading the chapter, you should be able to:

- ***Define*** climate and climatology, and ***explain*** the difference between climate and weather.
- ***Review*** the principal components of climate, and ***relate*** the development of climate classification systems.
- ***Describe*** the principal climate classification categories, and ***locate*** these regions on a world map.
- ***Explain*** the precipitation and moisture efficiency criteria used to determine the arid and semiarid climates.
- ***Explain*** the causes and potential consequences of climate change, and ***outline*** future climate patterns from forecasts.

A Look at Puerto Rico's Climate at A Larger Scale

Examining the small-scale maps in this text, such as the world climates map in Figure 7, where the map scale is 1 inch equals 1650 miles, you see generalizations. On a larger-scale map of an island such as Puerto Rico, we can see more climatic detail and response to local elevation and orientation to trade winds. The variations in climate are reflected in the changes in vegetation, as you can see in the photos in Figure GN 1.

Puerto Rico is centered between the Greater and Lesser Antilles island chains, separating the Atlantic Ocean and the Caribbean Sea. The island is nearly rectangular, stretching 65 km (40 mi) north and south and 180 km (112 mi) east and west. Puerto Rico is an official territory of the United States, sharing the same currency and president and having nonvoting representation in Congress.

Across Puerto Rico, all months average above 18°C (64.4°F), qualifying it as tropical. The 18th parallel runs along Puerto Rico's south coast, positioning it to receive trade winds from the northeast. The mountains of the Cordillera Central, rising to 1338 m (4389 ft), divide Puerto Rico lengthwise, and the Sierra de Luquillo in the east, rising to 650 m (2133 ft), are home to the tropical rain forest of El Yunque National Forest. The northern and eastern slopes intercept moisture brought by the trade winds; note the annual rainfall totals in these areas. This is in contrast to the southern slopes and flatlands in the rain shadow.

On the map, you see the extent of tropical rain forest climates, where precipitation exceeds 6 cm (2.4 in.) every month. The mountains of the Cordillera Central add an orographic component to the climate, increasing annual precipitation. In the leeward south, we find a tropical monsoon climate where precipitation is less than 6 cm for 3 to 5 months during the year. Ponce and the south coast have a tropical savanna climate, where rainfall for 6 months is less than 6 cm (2.4 in.), and feature an acacia–savanna landscape, as shown in Figure GN 1. With this closer look in mind, we shift our perspective to examine climate categories across the globe. ■

San Juan, 150.9 cm

El Yunque National Forest, 508 cm

Pico del Este, 434.5 cm

Near Ponce, 69.7 cm

North of Adjuntas, 198.3 cm

FIGURE GN 1
Climates, representative photos, and rainfall data. What do you see in the photos that indicate differences in annual rainfall? Annual rainfall totals in centimeters (1 cm = 0.3937 in.; 1 in. = 2.54 cm). [All photos by Bobbé Christopherson.]

Earth experiences an almost infinite variety of *weather* at any given time and place. But, if we consider the weather over many years, including its variability and extremes, a pattern emerges that constitutes **climate**. Think of climatic patterns as dynamic rather than static, owing to the fact that we are witnessing climate change. Climate is more than a consideration of simple averages of temperature and precipitation. Today, climatologists know that intriguing global-scale linkages exist in the Earth–atmosphere–ocean system. For instance, strong monsoonal rains in West Africa are correlated with the development of intense Atlantic hurricanes.

Climatologists, among other scientists, are analyzing global climate change—record-breaking global average temperatures, glacial ice melt, drying soil-moisture conditions, changing crop yields, the spread of infectious disease, changing distributions of plants and animals, declining coral reef health and fisheries, and the thawing of high-latitude lands and sea ice. Climatologists are concerned about observed changes in the global climate, as these are occurring at a pace not evidenced in the records of the past millennia. Climate and natural vegetation shifts during the next 50 years could exceed the total of all changes since the peak of the last ice-age episode, some 18,000 years ago. Geographer/scientist Jack Williams summarized the issue:

> By the end of the 21st century, large portions of the Earth's surface may experience climates not found at present, and some 20th-century climates may disappear. . . . Novel climates are projected to develop primarily in the tropics and subtropics. . . . Disappearing climates increase the likelihood of species extinctions and community disruption for species endemic to particular climatic regimes, with the largest impacts projected for poleward and tropical montane regions.*

We need to realize that the climate map and climate designations we study in this chapter are not fixed, but are on the move as temperature and precipitation relationships shift.

In this chapter: Climates are so diverse that no two places on Earth's surface experience exactly the same climatic conditions; in fact, Earth is a vast collection of microclimates. However, broad similarities among local climates permit their grouping into climatic regions.

Many of the physical elements of the environment, link together to explain climates. Here we survey the patterns of climate using a series of sample cities and towns. We use a simplified classification system based on physical factors that help answer the "why" question—Why are climates in certain locations? Though imperfect, this method is easily understood and is based on a widely used classification system devised by climatologist Wladimir Köppen (pronounced KUR-pen).

Climatologists use powerful computer models to simulate changing complex interactions in the atmosphere, hydrosphere, lithosphere, and biosphere. This chapter concludes with a discussion of climate change and its vital implications for society.

*J. W. Williams, S. T. Jackson, and J. E. Kutzbach, "Projected distributions of novel and disappearing climates by 2100 AD," *Proceedings of the National Academy of Sciences* 104 (April 3, 2007): 5739.

Classifying Earth's Climates

Climatology, the study of climate and its variability, analyzes long-term weather patterns over time and space and the controls that produce Earth's diverse climatic conditions. One type of climatic analysis locates areas of similar weather statistics and groups them into **climatic regions**. Observed patterns grouped into regions are at the core of climate classification.

Climate Systems: A Review

The climate where you live may be humid with distinct seasons, or dry with consistent warmth, or moist and cool—almost any combination is possible. Some places have rainfall totaling more than 20 cm (8 in.) each month, with monthly average temperatures remaining above 27°C (80°F) year-round. Other places may be rainless for a decade at a time. A climate may have temperatures that average above freezing every month, yet still threaten severe frost problems for agriculture. Students reading this text in Singapore experience precipitation every month, ranging from 13.1 to 30.6 cm (5.1 to 12.0 in.), or 228.1 cm (89.8 in.) during an average year, whereas students at the university in Karachi, Pakistan, measure only 20.4 cm (8 in.) of rain over an entire year.

Table 1 provides a review of the primary components of climate, which work together to determine climatic conditions. Figure 1 shows the worldwide distribution of precipitation, our moisture supply. Simply relating the two principal climatic components—temperature and precipitation—reveals general climate types, such as tropical deserts (hot and dry), polar ice sheets (cold and dry), and equatorial rain forests (hot and wet). Temperature and precipitation patterns, plus other weather factors, provide the key to climate classification.

Climates greatly influence *ecosystems*, the natural, self-regulating communities formed by plants and animals in their nonliving environment. On land, the basic climatic regions determine to a large extent the location of the world's major ecosystems. These regions, called *biomes*, include forest, grassland, savanna, tundra, and desert. Plant, soil, and animal communities are associated with these biomes. Because climate cycles through periodic change, it is never really stable; therefore, ecosystems should be thought of as being in a constant state of adaptation and response. The present

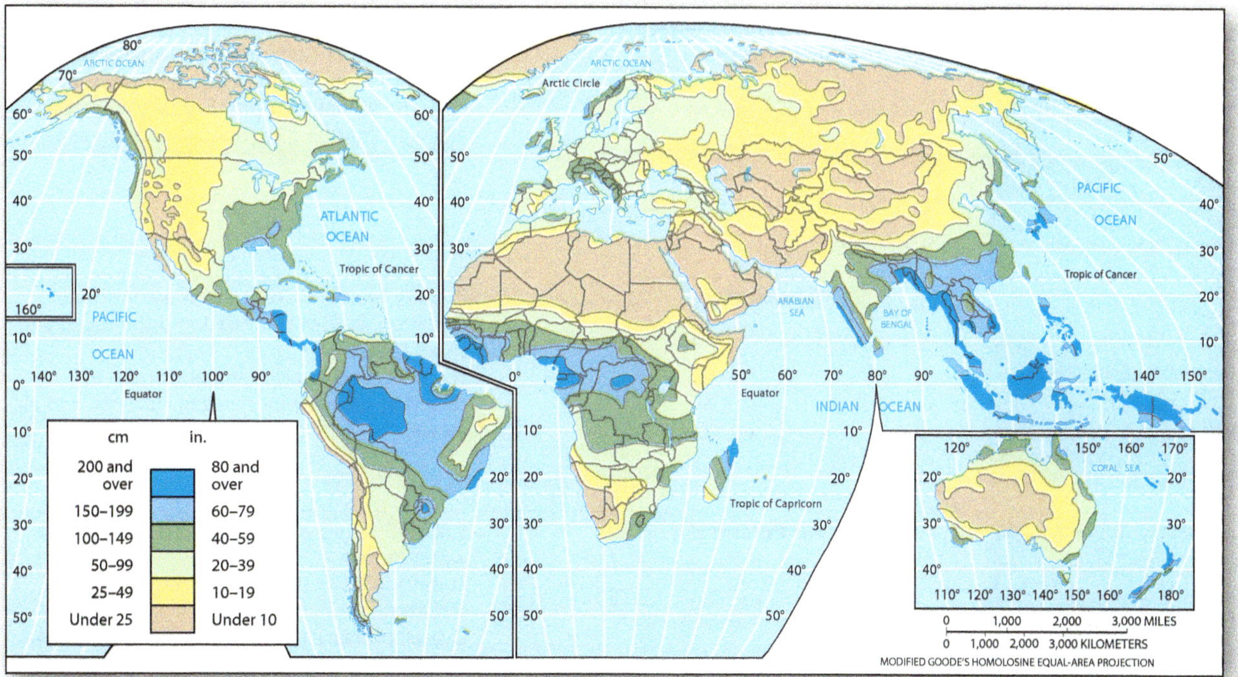

FIGURE 1 Worldwide average annual precipitation.
The causes that produce these patterns should be recognizable to you: temperature and pressure patterns; air mass types; convergent, convectional, orographic, and frontal lifting mechanisms; and the general energy availability that decreases toward the poles.

global climatic warming trend is producing changes in plant and animal distributions.

Classification Types and Categories

Classification is the process of ordering or grouping data or phenomena into related classes. Such generalizations are important organizational tools in science and are especially useful for the spatial analysis of climatic regions. A climate classification based on *causative* factors—for example, the interaction of air masses—is a **genetic classification**. This approach explores the "why" question as to the mix of climatic ingredients in certain locations. A climate classification based on *statistics* or other data determined by measurement of observed effects is an **empirical classification**.

Climate classifications based on temperature and precipitation are examples of the empirical approach. One empirical classification system, published by C. W. Thornthwaite, identified moisture regions using aspects of the water-balance approach and vegetation types. Another empirical system is the widely recognized Köppen climate classification, designed by Wladimir Köppen (1846–1940), a German climatologist and botanist. His classification work began with an article on heat zones in 1884 and continued throughout his career. The first wall map showing world climates, coauthored with his student Rudolph Geiger, was introduced in 1928 and soon was widely adopted. Köppen continued to refine it until his death.

As we devise spatial categories and boundaries, we must remember that boundaries really are transition zones of gradual change. The trends and overall patterns of boundary lines are more important than their precise placement, especially with the small scales generally used for world maps.

For our classification—a compromise between genetic and empirical systems—we focus on temperature and precipitation measurements and, for the desert areas, moisture efficiency as well as on causal factors that produce these climates. Six basic climate categories and their regional types provide the structure for our discussion in this chapter:

GEO REPORT 1 *Ancient thinking on climate classifications*

The ancient Greeks simplified their view of world climates into three zones: The "torrid zone" referred to warmer areas south of the Mediterranean; the "frigid zone" was to the north; and the area where they lived was labeled the "temperate zone," which they considered the optimum climate. They believed that travel too close to the equator or too far north would surely end in death. But the world is a diverse place, and Earth's myriad climatic variations are more complex than these simple views.

TABLE 1 Principal Components of Earth's Climate System

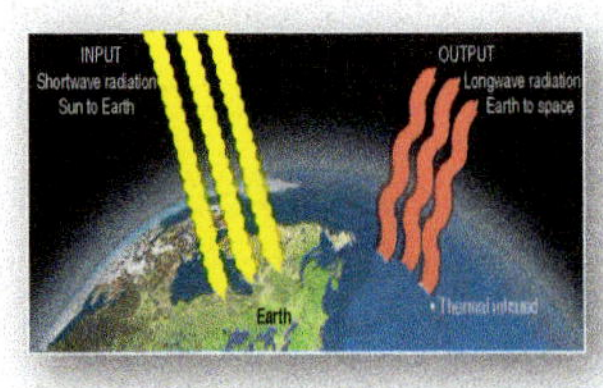	**Insolation**	Incoming solar radiation is the energy input for the climate system; insolation varies by latitude, as well as diurnally (daily) and seasonally with changing day length and sun angle.
	**Temperature**	Primary temperature controls are latitude, elevation, land-water heating differences, and cloud cover. The pattern of world temperatures is affected by global winds, ocean currents, and air masses.
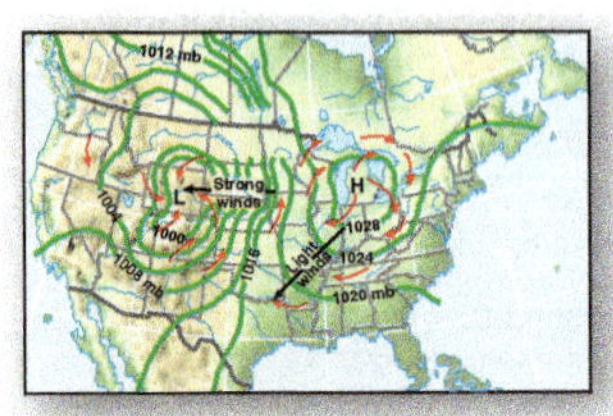	**Air Pressure**	Subtropical highs create areas of permanent water deficit. Equatorial lows create consistently wet climates. Overall pressure patterns influence atmospheric circulation and movement of air masses.
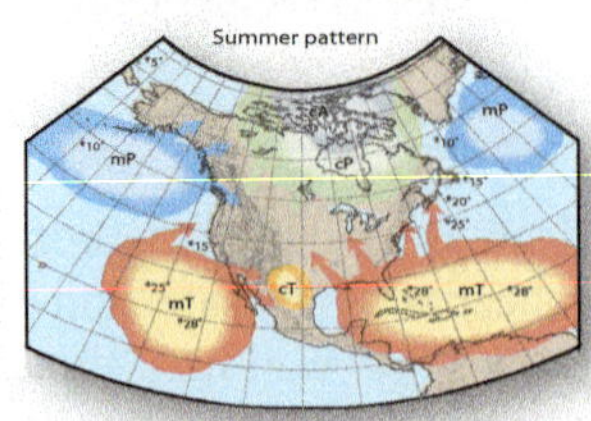	**Air Masses**	Vast bodies of homogeneous air form over oceanic and continental source regions. Location and physical characteristics of air masses are important.
	**Precipitation**	Moisture is represented by precipitation in all its forms. The hydrologic cycle transfers moisture through Earth's climate system.

- Tropical (tropical latitudes)
  rain forest (rainy all year)
  monsoon (6 to 12 months rainy)
  savanna (less than 6 months rainy)
- Mesothermal (midlatitudes, mild winters)
  humid subtropical (hot to warm summers)
  marine west coast (warm to cool summers)
  Mediterranean (dry summers)

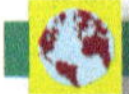

GEO REPORT 2 *Boundary considerations and changes under way*

The boundary between mesothermal and microthermal climates is sometimes placed along the isotherm where the coldest month is −3°C (26.6°F) or lower. That might be an accurate criterion for Europe, but for conditions in North America, the 0°C (32°F) isotherm is considered more appropriate. The difference between the 0°C and −3°C isotherms covers an area about the width of the state of Ohio. In Figure 2, you see the 0°C boundary used.

Climate change means these statistical boundaries are shifting. The Intergovernmental Panel on Climate Change (IPCC; discussed later in this chapter) predicts a 150- to 550-km (90- to 350-mi) range of possible poleward shift of climatic patterns in the midlatitudes during this century. Such change in climate would place Ohio, Indiana, and Illinois within climate regimes now experienced in Arkansas and Oklahoma. As you examine North America in Figure 2, use the graphic scale to get an idea of the magnitude of these potential shifts.

- Microthermal (mid and high latitudes, cold winters)
  humid continental (hot to warm, mild summers)
  subarctic (cool summers to very cold winters)
- Polar (high latitudes and polar regions)
  tundra (high latitude or high elevation)
  ice caps and ice sheets (perpetually frozen)
  polar marine (moderate polar climate)
- Highland (high elevations at all latitudes)

Only one climate category is based on moisture efficiency as well as temperature:

- Dry (permanent moisture deficits)
  arid deserts (tropical, subtropical hot and midlatitude cold)
  semiarid steppes (tropical, subtropical hot and midlatitude cold)

Figure 2 presents a world climate map. The following sections describe specific climates, organized around each of the main climate categories listed previously. An opening box at the beginning of each climate section gives (1) a simple description of the climate category and causal elements that are in operation and (2) a world map showing distribution and the featured representative cities. The names of the climates appear in italics in the chapter.

Selected cities represent each climate category, with their information on a **climograph**, a graph that shows monthly temperature and precipitation for a station. Also included are the location coordinates, average annual temperature, total annual precipitation, elevation, and location map for each city. Along the top of each climograph are the dominant weather features that are influential in that climate.

Discussions of the soils, vegetation, and major terrestrial biomes that fully integrate these global climate patterns are beyond the scope of this chapter.

CRITICAL THINKING 1

Finding your climate

Using Figure 2, locate your campus and your birthplace, and find the climate description. For these places, obtain monthly precipitation and temperature data. Briefly describe the information sources you used: library, Internet, teacher, and phone calls to state and provincial climatologists. Now, to refine your assessment of climate for the two locations, work through the Köppen climate criteria that established the climate classification for your two cities.

Tropical Climates (tropical latitudes)

Tropical climates, the most extensive, occupy about 36% of Earth's surface, including both ocean and land areas. The tropical climates straddle the equator from about 20° N to 20° S, roughly between the Tropics of Cancer and Capricorn—thus, the name. Tropical climates stretch northward to the tip of Florida and south-central Mexico, central India, and Southeast Asia and southward to northern Australia, Madagascar, central Africa, and southern Brazil. These climates truly are winterless. Important causal elements include

- Consistent daylength and insolation input, which produce consistently warm temperatures;
- Effects of the intertropical convergence zone (ITCZ), which brings rains as it shifts seasonally with the high Sun; and
- Warm ocean temperatures and unstable maritime air masses.

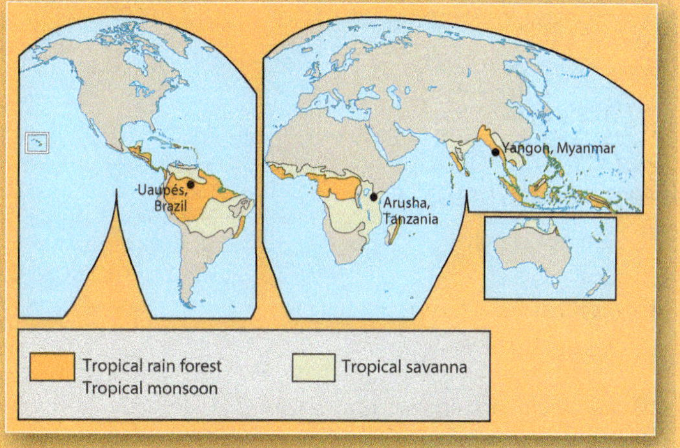

Tropical climates have three distinct regimes: *tropical rain forest* (ITCZ present all year), *tropical monsoon* (ITCZ present 6 to 12 months), and *tropical savanna* (ITCZ present less than 6 months).

Tropical Rain Forest Climates

Tropical rain forest climates are constantly moist and warm. Convectional thunderstorms, triggered by local heating and trade-wind convergence, peak each day from mid-afternoon to late evening inland and earlier in the day where marine influence is strong along coastlines. Precipitation follows the migrating ITCZ. The ITCZ shifts northward and southward with the summer Sun throughout the year, but it influences *tropical rain forest* regions all year long. Not surprisingly,

(text continued after next figure)

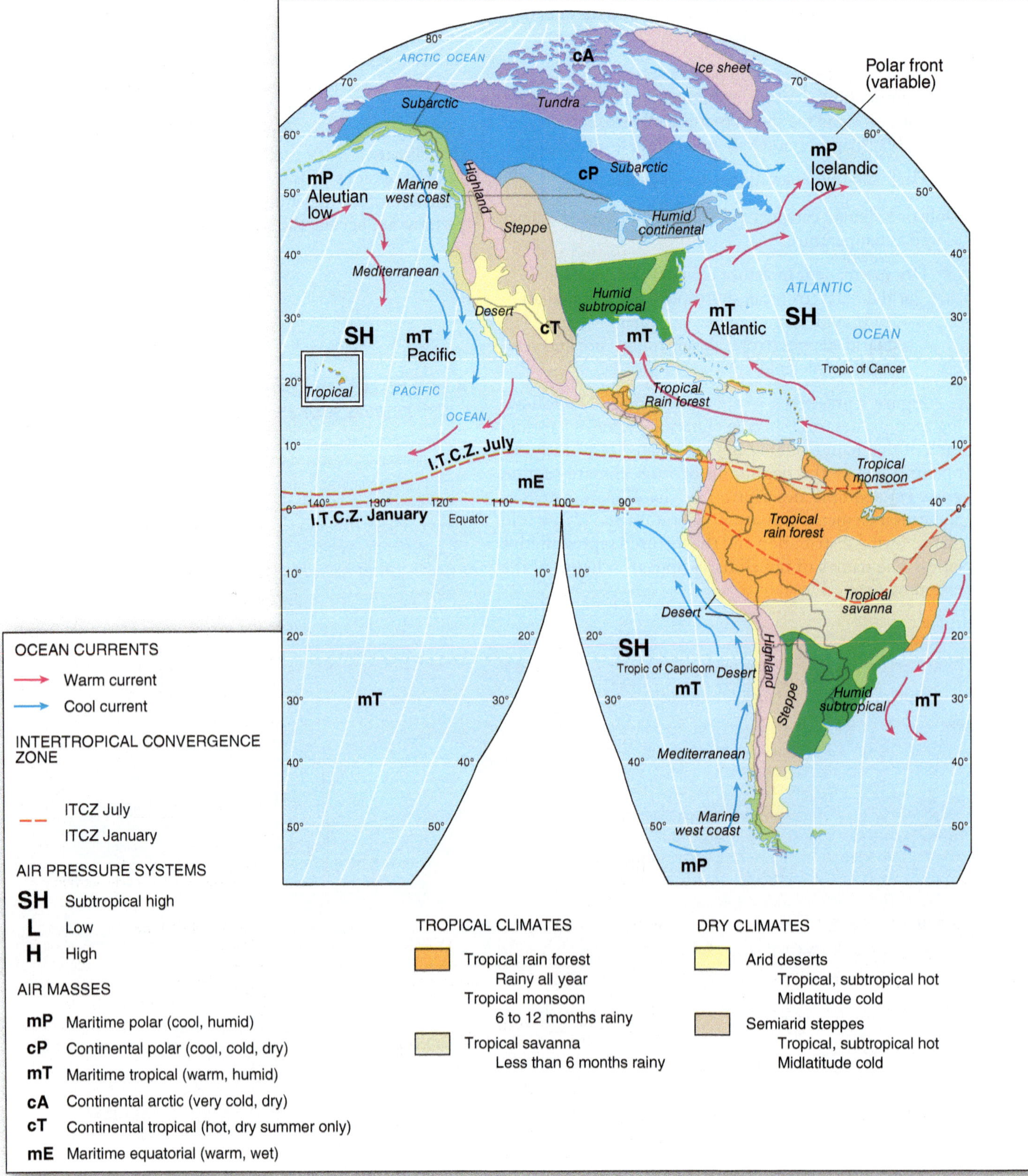

FIGURE 2 World climate classification.
Annotated on this map are selected air masses, nearshore ocean currents, pressure systems, and the January and July locations of the ITCZ. Use the colors in the legend to locate various climate types; some labels of the climate names appear in italics on the map to guide you.

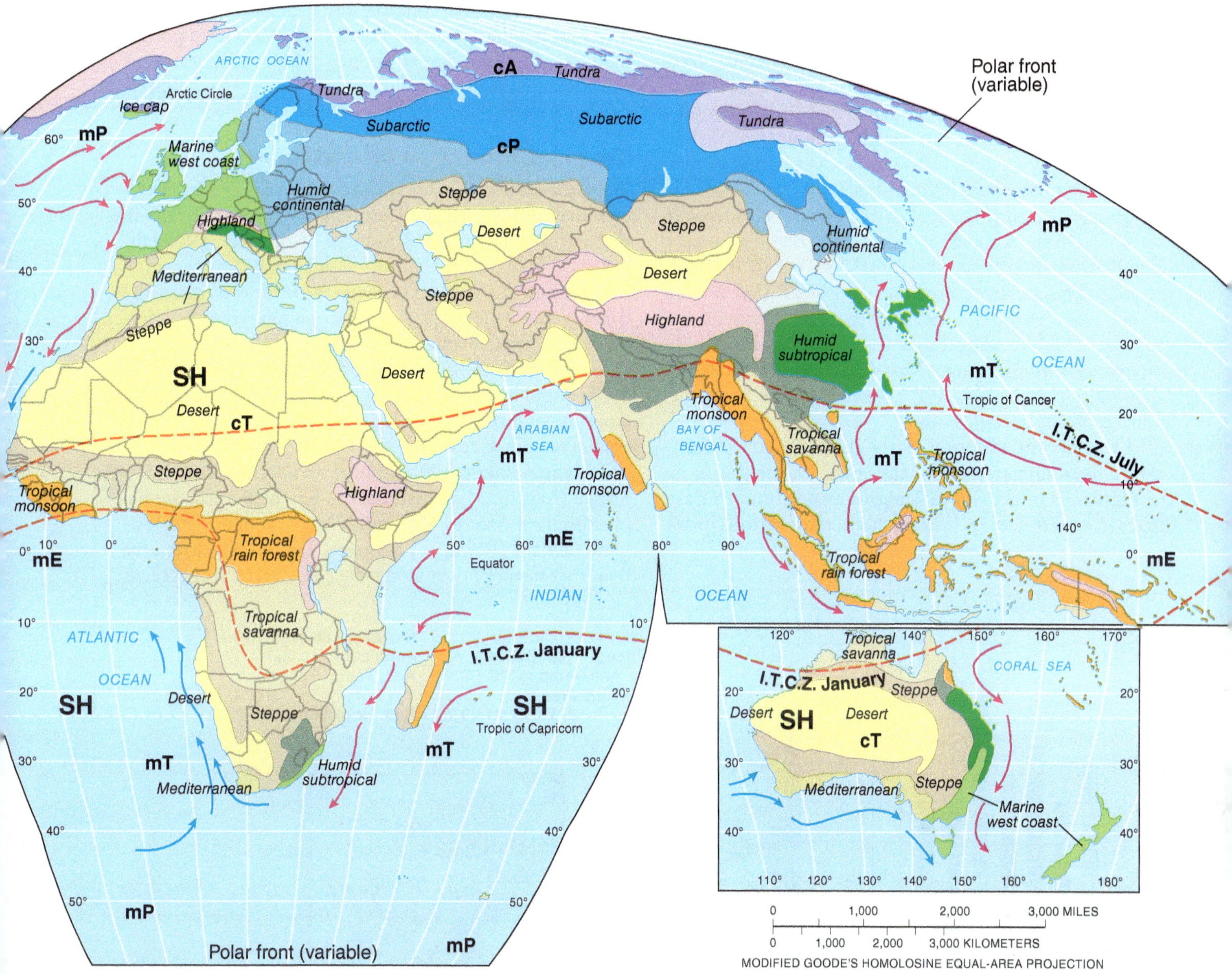

ARCTIC OCEAN
Arctic Circle
Ice cap
mP
Marine west coast
Tundra
cA
Subarctic
cP
Polar front (variable)
Humid continental
Highland
Mediterranean
Steppe
Desert
Humid continental
Highland
Humid subtropical
PACIFIC OCEAN
mT
Tropic of Cancer
I.T.C.Z. July
SH
cT
Tropical monsoon
ARABIAN SEA
BAY OF BENGAL
Tropical savanna
Tropical rain forest
mE
Equator
INDIAN OCEAN
ATLANTIC OCEAN
I.T.C.Z. January
Tropic of Capricorn
Humid subtropical
Polar front (variable)
CORAL SEA
Marine west coast

0 1,000 2,000 3,000 MILES
0 1,000 2,000 3,000 KILOMETERS
MODIFIED GOODE'S HOMOLOSINE EQUAL-AREA PROJECTION

MESOTHERMAL CLIMATES

- Humid subtropical — Moist all year, hot summer
- Humid subtropical — Winter-dry, hot to warm summers
- Marine west coast — Moist all year, warm to cool summers
- Mediterranean — Summer dry, hot to warm summers

MICROTHERMAL CLIMATES

- Humid continental — Hot summers: moist all year; Asian winter-dry
- Humid continental — Mild summers: moist all year; Asian winter-dry
- Subarctic regions — Cool summers
- Subarctic regions — Very cold winters

POLAR CLIMATES HIGHLANDS

- Tundra
- Ice cap and ice sheets; Highland temperature effects

Animation
Global Climate Maps, World Map References

water surpluses are enormous, creating the world's greatest stream discharges in the Amazon and Congo River basins.

High rainfall sustains lush evergreen broadleaf tree growth, producing Earth's equatorial and tropical rain forests. The leaf canopy is so dense that little light diffuses to the forest floor, leaving the ground surface dim and sparse in plant cover. Dense surface vegetation occurs along riverbanks, where light is abundant.

Uaupés, Brazil (Figure 3), is characteristic of *tropical rain forest*. On the climograph, you can see that the lowest-precipitation month receives nearly 15 cm (6 in.) and the annual temperature range is barely 2 C° (3.6 F°). In all such climates, the diurnal (day-to-night) temperature range exceeds the annual average minimum–maximum (coolest to warmest) range: Day–night temperatures can range more than 11 C° (20 F°), more than five times the annual monthly average range.

The only interruption in the distribution of *tropical rain forest* climates across the equatorial region is in the highlands of the South American Andes and in East Africa (see Figure 2). There, higher elevations produce lower temperatures; Mount Kilimanjaro is less than 4° south of the equator, but at 5895 m (19,340 ft), it has permanent glacial ice on its summit (although this ice is nearly gone due to increasing air temperatures). Such mountainous sites fall within the *highland* climate category.

Tropical Monsoon Climates

Tropical monsoon climates feature a dry season that lasts 1 or more months. Rainfall brought by the ITCZ falls in these areas from 6 to 12 months of the year. (Remember, the ITCZ affects the *tropical rain forest* climate region throughout the year.) The dry season occurs when the convergence zone is not overhead. Yangon, Myanmar (formerly Rangoon, Burma), is an example of this climate type, as illustrated by the climograph and photograph in Figure 4. Mountains prevent cold air masses from central Asia from moving over Yangon, resulting in its high average annual temperatures.

About 480 km (300 mi) north in another coastal city, Sittwe (Akyab), Myanmar, on the Bay of Bengal, annual precipitation rises to 515 cm (203 in.) compared to Yangon's 269 cm (106 in.). Therefore, Yangon is a drier area than that farther north along the coast, but it still exceeds

(a)

Station: Uaupés, Brazil
Lat/long: 0° 08′ S 67° 05′ W
Avg. Ann. Temp.: 25°C (77°F)
Total Ann. Precip.: 291.7 cm (114.8 in.)
Elevation: 86 m (282.2 ft)
Population: 10,000
Ann. Temp. Range: 2 C° (3.6 F°)
Ann. Hr of Sunshine: 2018

(b)

FIGURE 3 Tropical rain forest climate.
(a) Climograph for Uaupés, Brazil. (b) The rain forest along the Rio Negro River, Amazonas state, Brazil. [Gerard & Margi Moss/Photolibrary.]

the 250-cm annual precipitation criterion in use for the tropical monsoon classification.

Tropical monsoon climates lie principally along coastal areas within the *tropical rain forest* climatic realm and experience seasonal variation of wind and precipitation. Evergreen trees grade into thorn forests on the drier margins near the adjoining savanna climates.

Tropical Savanna Climates

Tropical savanna climates exist poleward of the *tropical rain forest* climates. The *Geosystems Now* photo from Ponce, Puerto Rico is such a region. The ITCZ reaches these climate regions for about 6 months or less of the year as it migrates with the summer Sun. Summers are wetter than winters because convectional rains accompany the shifting ITCZ when it is overhead. This produces a notable dry condition when the ITCZ is farthest away and high pressure dominates. Thus, POTET (natural moisture demand) exceeds PRECIP (natural moisture supply) in winter, causing water-budget deficits.

Temperatures vary more in *tropical savanna* climates than in *tropical rain forest* regions. The *tropical savanna* regime can have two temperature maximums during the year because the Sun's direct rays are overhead twice—before and after the summer solstice in each hemisphere as the Sun moves between the equator and the tropics. Dominant grasslands with scattered trees, drought resistant to cope with the highly variable precipitation, characterize the *tropical savanna* regions.

Arusha, Tanzania, is a *tropical savanna* city (Figure 5). This metropolitan area of more than 1,368,000 people is near the grassy plains of the Serengeti, a heavily visited national park that hosts one of the largest annual mammal migrations in the world. Temperatures are consistent with tropical climates, despite the elevation (1387 m) of the station. Note the marked dryness from June to October, which defines changing dominant pressure systems rather than annual changes in temperature. This region is near the transition to the drier *desert hot steppe* climates to the northeast.

ITCZ
Subtropical high
Subtropical high
Precipitation in centimeters (inches)
Temperature °C (°F)
J F M A M J J A S O N D
Month

(a)

Station: Yangon, Myanmar*
Lat/long: 16° 47′ N 96° 10′ E
Avg. Ann. Temp.: 27.3°C (81.1°F)
Total Ann. Precip.: 268.8 cm (105.8 in.)
Elevation: 23 m (76 ft)
Population: 6,000,000
Ann. Temp. Range: 5.5 C° (9.9 F°)

*(Formerly Rangoon, Burma)

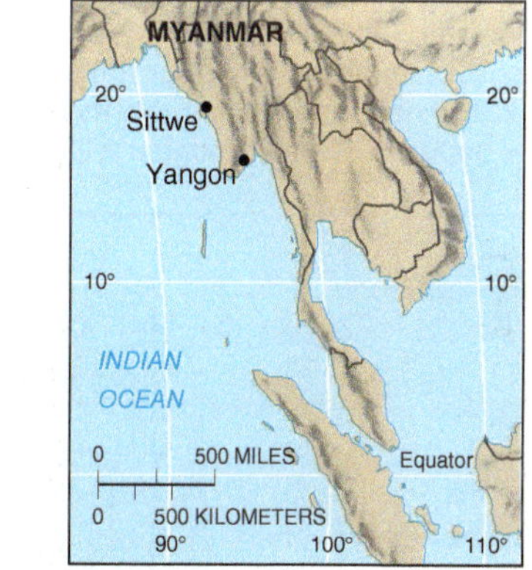

(b)

FIGURE 4 Tropical monsoon climate.
(a) Climograph for Yangon, Myanmar (formerly Rangoon, Burma); city of Sittwe also noted on map. (b) Mixed monsoonal forest and scrub characteristic of the region in eastern India. [shaileshnanal/Shuttershock.]

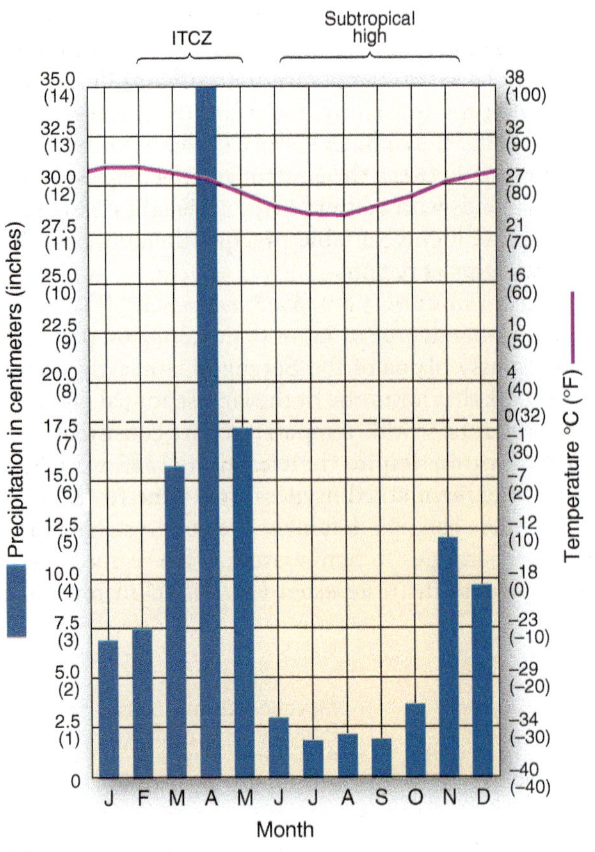

Station: Arusha, Tanzania
Lat/long: 3° 24′ S 36° 42′ E
Avg. Ann. Temp.: 26.5°C (79.7°F)
Total Ann. Precip.: 119 cm (46.9 in.)
Elevation: 1387 m (4550 ft)
Population: 1,368,000
Ann. Temp. Range: 4.1 C° (7.4 F°)
Ann. Hr of Sunshine: 2600

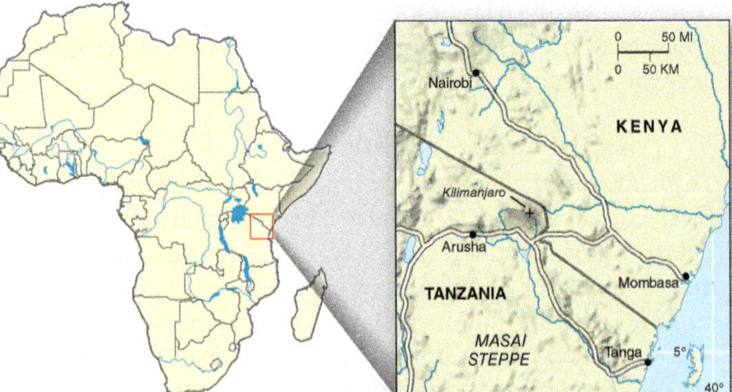

(b)

FIGURE 5 Tropical savanna climate.
(a) Climograph for Arusha, Tanzania; note the intense dry period. (b) Characteristic landscape in the Ngorongoro Conservation Area, Tanzania, near Arusha, with plants adapted to seasonally dry water budgets. [Blaine Harrington III/Corbis.]

Mesothermal Climates (midlatitudes, mild winters)

Mesothermal, meaning "middle temperature," describes these warm and temperate climates, where true seasonality begins. More than half the world's population resides in these mesothermal climates, which occupy about 27% of Earth's land and sea surface—the second largest percentage behind the tropical climates.

The mesothermal climates, and nearby portions of the microthermal climates (cold winters), are regions of great weather variability, for these are the latitudes of greatest air mass interaction. Causal elements include

- Latitudinal effects on insolation and temperature, as summers transition from hot to warm to cool moving poleward from the tropics.
- Shifting of maritime and continental air masses, as they are guided by upper-air westerly winds
- Migration of cyclonic (low-pressure) and anticyclonic (high-pressure) systems, bringing changeable weather conditions and air mass conflicts; and
- Effects of sea-surface temperatures on air mass strength: Cooler temperatures along west coasts weaken air masses, and warmer temperatures along east coasts strengthen air masses.

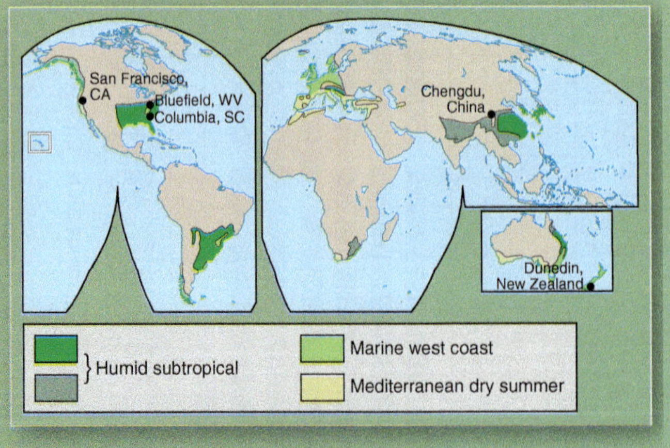

Mesothermal climates are humid, except where subtropical high pressure produces dry-summer conditions. Their four distinct regimes based on precipitation variability are *humid subtropical hot-summer* (moist all year), *humid subtropical winter-dry* (hot to warm summers, in Asia), *marine west coast* (warm to cool summers, moist all year), and *Mediterranean dry-summer* (warm to hot summers).

Humid Subtropical Climates

Humid subtropical hot-summer climates either are moist all year or have a pronounced winter-dry period, as occurs in eastern and southern Asia. Maritime tropical air masses generated over warm waters off eastern coasts influence *humid subtropical hot-summer* climates during summer. This warm, moist, unstable air produces convectional showers over land. In fall, winter, and spring, maritime tropical and continental polar air masses interact, generating frontal activity and frequent midlatitude cyclonic storms. These two mechanisms produce year-round precipitation. Overall, precipitation averages 100–200 cm (40–80 in.) a year. Columbia, South Carolina, is characteristic of this climate, which is found across the southeastern United States (Figure 6).

Humid subtropical winter-dry climates are related to the winter-dry, seasonal pulse of the monsoons. They extend poleward from *tropical savanna* climates and have a summer month that receives 10 times more precipitation than their driest winter month.

A representative station in Asia is Chengdu, China. Figure 7 demonstrates the strong correlation between precipitation and the high-summer Sun. In May 2008, this city and the surrounding region were hit with a magnitude 7.9 earthquake, with many strong aftershocks, causing widespread damage, killing 85,000 people, and injuring nearly 400,000 people (Figure 7b). This was the worst earthquake to strike China since the 1976 Tangshan quake that killed 250,000 people.

The habitability of the *humid subtropical hot-summer* and *humid subtropical winter-dry* climates and their ability to sustain populations are borne out by the concentration of people in north-central India, the bulk of China's 1.3 billion people, and the many who live in climatically similar portions of the United States. However, the intense summer rains of the Asian monsoon can produce flooding in India and Bangladesh. In the U.S. Southeast, dramatic thunderstorms are common and tornado occurrences each year are breaking records.

Marine West Coast Climates

Marine west coast climates, featuring mild winters and cool summers, dominate Europe and other middle- to high-latitude west coasts (see Figure 2). In the United States, these climates, with their cooler summers, are in contrast to the *humid subtropical hot-summer* climate of the Southeast.

Maritime polar air masses—cool, moist, unstable—dominate *marine west coast* climates. Weather systems forming along the polar front and maritime polar air masses move into these regions throughout the year, making weather quite unpredictable. Coastal fog, annually totaling 30 to 60 days, is a part of the moderating marine influence. Frosts are possible and tend to shorten the growing season.

Marine west coast climates are unusually mild for their latitude. They extend along the coastal margins of the Aleutian Islands in the North Pacific, cover the southern third of Iceland in the North Atlantic and coastal Scandinavia, and dominate the British Isles. Many of us might find it hard to imagine that such high-latitude locations can have average monthly temperatures above freezing throughout the year. Unlike in Europe, where the *marine west coast* regions are extensive, mountains in Canada, Alaska, Chile, and Australia restrict this climate to coastal environs. The climograph for Dunedin, New Zealand, demonstrates the moderate temperature patterns and the annual temperature range for a *marine west coast* city in the Southern Hemisphere (Figure 8).

An interesting anomaly occurs in the eastern United States. In portions of the Appalachian highlands, increased elevation lowers summer temperatures in the surrounding *humid subtropical hot-summer* climate, producing a *marine west coast* cooler summer. The climograph for Bluefield, West Virginia (Figure 9), reveals *marine west coast* temperature and precipitation patterns, despite its location in the East. Vegetation similarities between the Appalachians and the Pacific Northwest have enticed many emigrants from the East to settle in these climatically familiar environments in the Northwest.

Mediterranean Dry-Summer Climates

The *Mediterranean dry-summer* climate designation specifies that at least 70% of annual precipitation occurs during the winter months. This is in contrast to the majority of the world, which experiences summer-maximum precipitation. Across the planet during summer months, shifting cells of subtropical high pressure block moisture-bearing winds from adjacent regions. This shifting of stable, warm to hot, dry air over an area in summer and away from that area in winter creates a pronounced dry-summer and wet-winter pattern. For example, in summer the continental tropical air mass over the Sahara in Africa shifts northward over the Mediterranean region and blocks maritime air masses and cyclonic storm tracks.

Worldwide, cool offshore ocean currents (the California Current, Canary Current, Peru Current, Benguela Current, and West Australian Current) produce stability in overlying air masses along west coasts, poleward of subtropical high pressure. The world climate map (see Figure 2) shows *Mediterranean dry-summer* climates along the western margins of North America, central Chile, and the southwestern tip of Africa as well as across southern Australia and the Mediterranean Basin—the climate's namesake region. Examine the offshore currents along each of these regions on the world climate map.

Coastal maritime effects moderate the climate of San Francisco, California, producing a cool summer (Figure 10). The transition to a hot summer occurs no more than 24–32 km (15–20 mi) inland from San Francisco.

The *Mediterranean dry-summer* climate brings summer water-balance deficits. Winter precipitation recharges soil moisture, but water use usually exhausts soil moisture by

(text continued after figures)

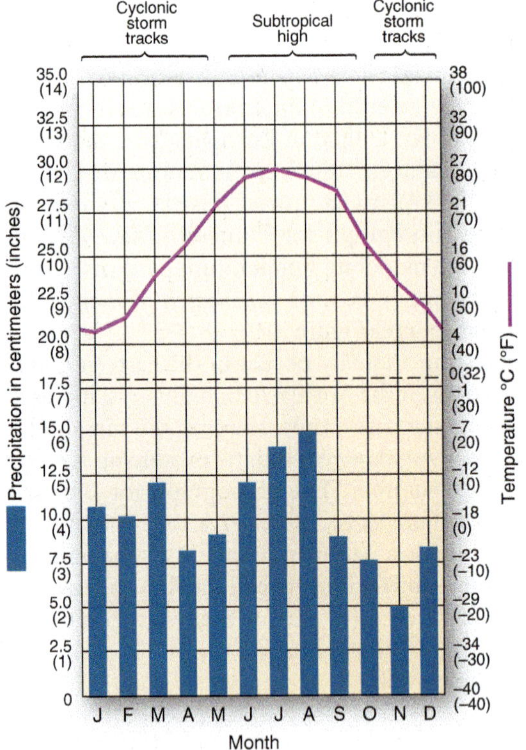

(a)

Station: Columbia, South Carolina
Lat/long: 34° N 81° W
Avg. Ann. Temp.: 17.3°C (63.1°F)
Total Ann. Precip.: 126.5 cm (49.8 in.)
Elevation: 96 m (315 ft)
Population: 116,000
Ann. Temp. Range: 20.7 C° (37.3 F°)
Ann. Hr of Sunshine: 2800

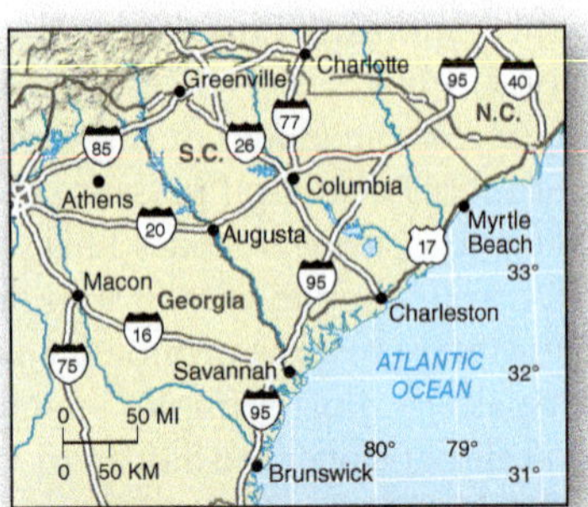

(b)

FIGURE 6 Humid subtropical hot-summer climate, rainy all year.
(a) Climograph for Columbia, South Carolina. Columbia receives seasonal cyclonic storm activity and summer convection showers within maritime tropical air. (b) The mixed evergreen forest of cypress and pine, with water lilies in southern Georgia. [Bobbé Christopherson.]

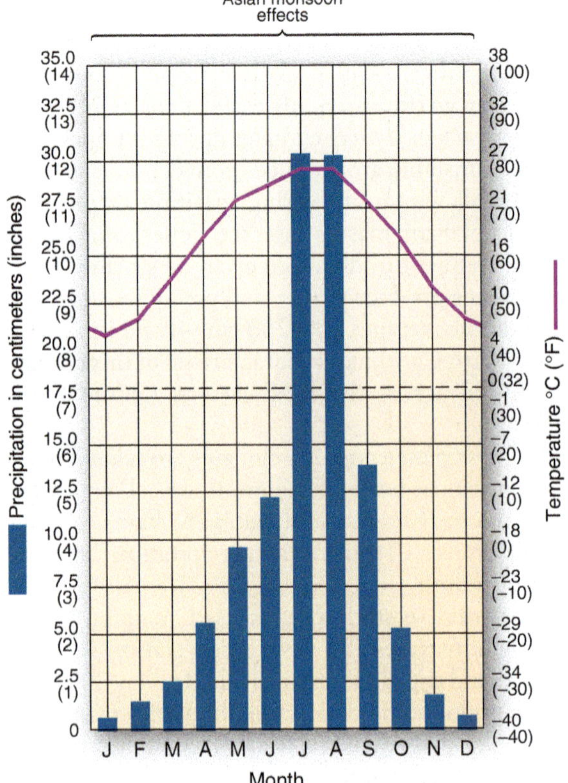

(a)

Station: Chengdu, China
Lat/long: 30° 40′ N 104° 04′ E
Avg. Ann. Temp.: 17°C (62.6°F)
Total Ann. Precip.: 114.6 cm (45.1 in.)
Elevation: 498 m (1633.9 ft)
Population: 2,500,000
Ann. Temp. Range: 20 C° (36 F°)
Ann. Hr of Sunshine: 1058

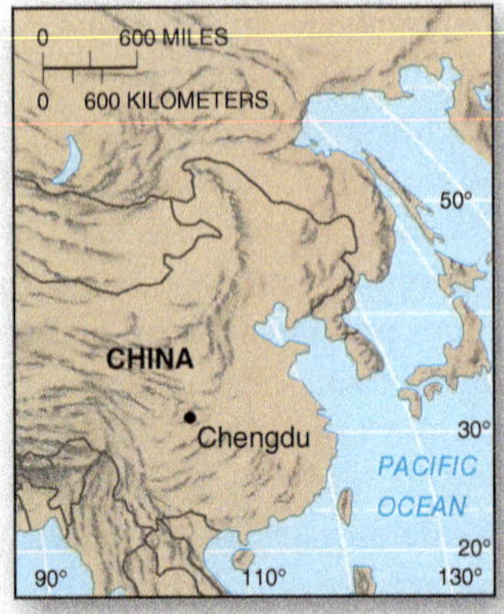

(b)

FIGURE 7 Humid subtropical winter-dry climate.
(a) Climograph for Chengdu, China. Note the summer-wet monsoonal precipitation. (b) People flee high-rise buildings following a major earthquake in Chengdu. [Photo courtesy of *China Daily*.]

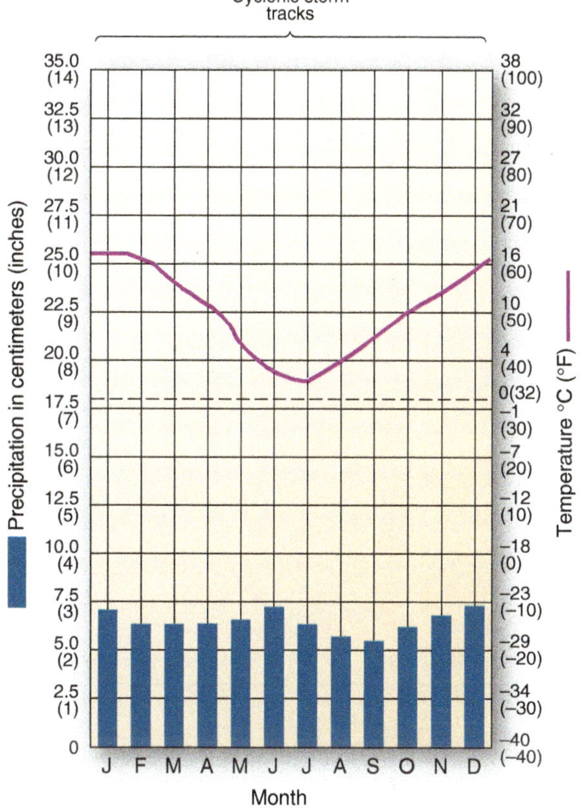

Station: Dunedin, New Zealand
Lat/long: 45° 54′ S 170° 31′ E
Avg. Ann. Temp.: 10.2°C (50.3°F)
Total Ann. Precip.: 78.7 cm (31.0 in.)
Elevation: 1.5 m (5 ft)
Population: 120,000
Ann. Temp. Range: 14.2 C° (25.5 F°)

(a)

(b)

FIGURE 8 A Southern Hemisphere marine west coast climate. (a) Climograph for Dunedin, New Zealand. (b) Meadow, forest, and mountains on South Island, New Zealand. [Photo by Brian Enting/Photo Researchers, Inc.]

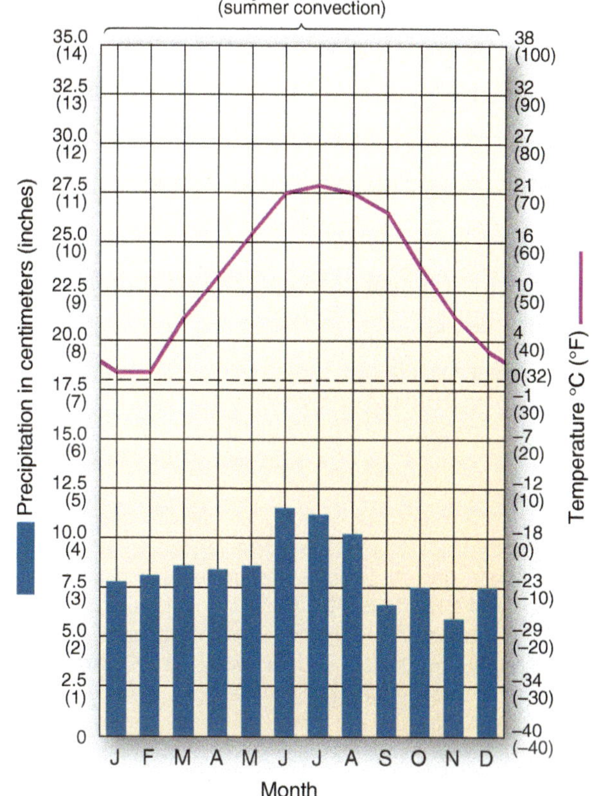

Station: Bluefield, West Virginia
Lat/long: 37° 16′ N 81° 13′ W
Avg. Ann. Temp.: 12°C (53.6°F)
Total Ann. Precip.: 101.9 cm (40.1 in.)
Elevation: 780 m (2559 ft)
Population: 11,000
Ann. Temp. Range: 21 C° (37.8 F°)

(a)

(b)

FIGURE 9 Marine west coast climate in the Appalachians of the eastern United States.
(a) Climograph for Bluefield, West Virginia. (b) Characteristic mixed forest in Appalachia in winter. [Author.]

late spring. Large-scale agriculture requires irrigation, although some subtropical fruits, nuts, and vegetables are uniquely suited to these conditions. Natural vegetation features a hard-leafed, drought-resistant variety known locally as *chaparral* in the western United States.

Microthermal Climates (mid and high latitudes, cold winters)

Humid microthermal climates have a winter season with some summer warmth. Here the term *microthermal* means cool temperate to cold. Approximately 21% of Earth's land surface is influenced by these climates, equaling about 7% of Earth's total surface.

These climates occur poleward of the mesothermal climates and experience great temperature ranges related to continentality and air mass conflicts. Temperatures decrease with increasing latitude and toward the interior of continental landmasses and result in intensely cold winters. In contrast to moist-all-year regions (northern tier across the United States and Canada, eastern Europe through the Ural Mountains) is the winter-dry association with the Asian dry monsoon and cold air masses across the region.

In Figure 2, note the absence of microthermal climates in the Southern Hemisphere. Because the Southern Hemisphere lacks substantial landmasses, microthermal climates develop only in highlands. Important causal elements include

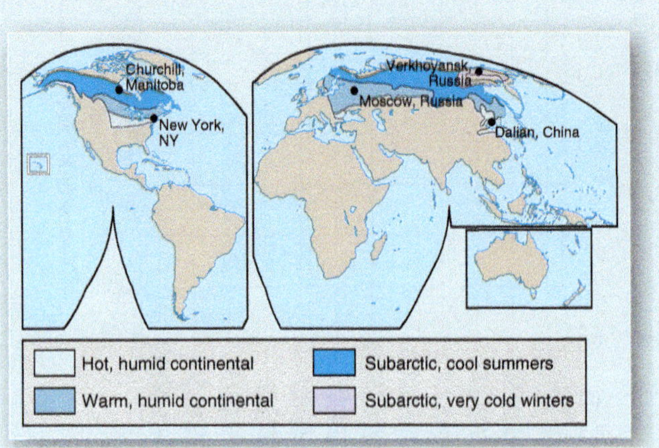

- Increasing seasonality (daylength and Sun altitude) and greater temperature ranges (daily and annually);
- Latitudinal effects on insolation and temperature: summers become cool moving northward, with winters becoming cold to very cold;
- Upper-air westerly winds and undulating Rossby waves, which bring warmer air northward and colder air southward for cyclonic activity, and convectional thunderstorms from maritime tropical air masses in summer;
- Continental interiors serving as source regions for intense continental polar air masses that dominate winter, blocking cyclonic storms; and
- An Asian winter-dry pattern associated with continental high pressure and related air masses, increasing from the Ural Mountains eastward to the Pacific Ocean.

Microthermal climates have four distinct regimes based on increasing cold with latitude and precipitation variability: *humid continental hot-summer* (Chicago, New York); *humid continental mild-summer* (Duluth, Toronto, Moscow); *subarctic cool-summer* (Churchill, Manitoba); and the formidable extremes of frigid *subarctic with very cold winters* (Verkhoyansk and northern Siberia).

Humid Continental Hot-Summer Climates

Humid continental hot-summer climates are differentiated by their annual precipitation distribution. In the summer, maritime tropical air masses influence both *humid continental moist-all-year* and *humid continental winter-dry* climates. In North America, frequent weather activity is possible between conflicting air masses—maritime tropical and continental polar—especially in winter. The climographs and photos for New York City and Dalian, China (Figure 11), illustrate these two hot-summer microthermal climates. The Dalian, China, climograph demonstrates a dry-winter tendency caused by the intruding cold continental air that forces dry monsoon conditions.

In the United States, the *humid continental hot-summer* region extends from the East Coast westward to about the 98th meridian (98° W in central Kansas) and the approximate location of the 51-cm (20-in.) *isohyet* (a line of equal precipitation). This climatic region is the location of corn, soybean, hog, feed crop, dairy, and cattle production. Farther west, lower precipitation receipts signal the dry climates discussed later in this chapter.

The region of milder summers poleward of these hot summer climates is in a climatic transition related to ongoing global climate change. Milder summers will become hotter as the boundary between these climatic subtypes shifts to higher latitudes. Such shifting of climatic boundaries and their related ecosystems is occurring worldwide.

Humid Continental Mild-Summer Climates

Agricultural activity remains important in the cooler microthermal climates and includes dairy, poultry, flax, sunflower,

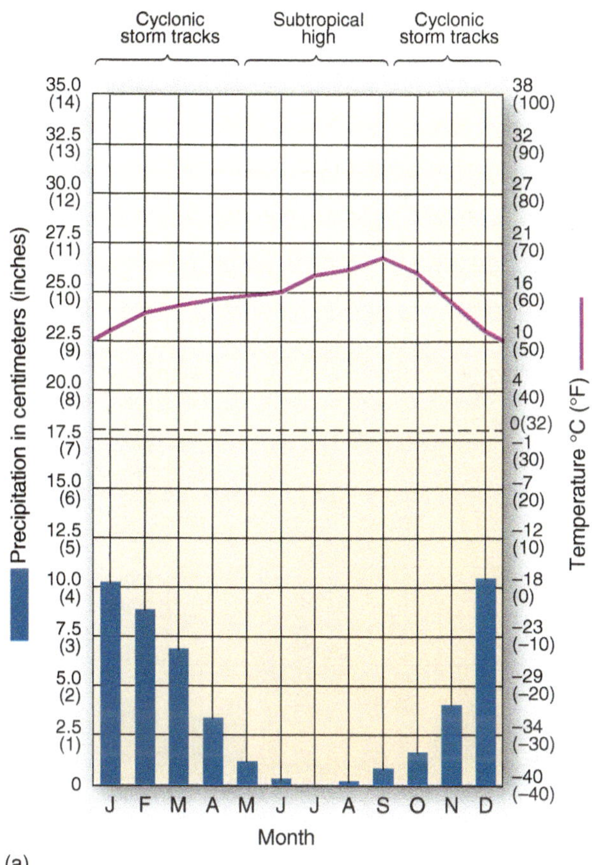

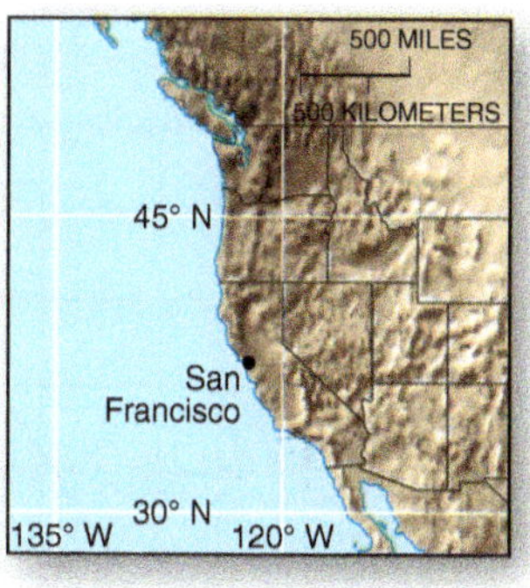

Station: San Francisco, California
Lat/long: 37° 37′ N 122° 23′ W
Avg. Ann. Temp.: 14.6°C (57.2°F)
Total Ann. Precip.: 56.6 cm (22.3 in.)
Elevation: 5 m (16.4 ft)
Population: 777,000
Ann. Temp. Range: 11.4 C° (20.5 F°)
Ann. Hr of Sunshine: 2975

(b)

FIGURE 10 Mediterranean climate, California.
(a) Climograph for San Francisco, California, with its cooler dry summer. (b) Central California Mediterranean landscape of oak savanna. [Bobbé Christopherson.]

sugar beet, wheat, and potato production. Frost-free periods range from fewer than 90 days in the north to as many as 225 days in the south. Overall, precipitation is less than in the hot-summer regions to the south; however, notably heavier snowfall is important to soil-moisture recharge when it melts. Various snow-capturing strategies are in use, including fences and tall stubble left standing after harvest in fields to create snowdrifts and thus more moisture retention in the soil.

A characteristic city of the humid continental mild-summer climate in the United States is Duluth, Minnesota. Figure 12 presents a climograph for Moscow, Russia, which is at 55° N, or about the same latitude as the southern shore of Hudson Bay in Canada.

The dry-winter aspect of the mild-summer climate occurs only in Asia, in a far-eastern area poleward of the winter-dry mesothermal climates. A representative *humid continental mild-summer* climate along Russia's east coast is Vladivostok, usually one of only two ice-free ports in that country.

Subarctic Climates

Farther poleward, seasonal change becomes greater. The short growing season is more intense during long summer days. The *subarctic* climates include vast stretches of Alaska, Canada, and northern Scandinavia with their cool summers and Siberian Russia with its very cold winters (Figure 13). Discoveries of minerals and petroleum reserves and the Arctic Ocean sea-ice losses have led to new interest in portions of these regions, such as the port expansion in Churchill (see Figure 13b).

Areas that receive 25 cm (10 in.) or more of precipitation a year on the northern continental margins and are covered by the so-called snow forests of fir, spruce, larch, and birch are the *boreal forests* of Canada and the *taiga* of Russia. These forests are in transition to the more open northern woodlands and to the tundra region of the far north. Forests thin out to the north when the warmest month drops below an average temperature of 10°C (50°F). During the decades ahead, the boreal forests will shift northward into the tundra in response to higher temperatures.

Precipitation and potential evapotranspiration both are low, so soils are generally moist and either partially or totally frozen beneath the surface, a phenomenon known as *permafrost*. The Churchill, Manitoba, climograph (Figure 13) shows average monthly temperatures below freezing for 7 months of

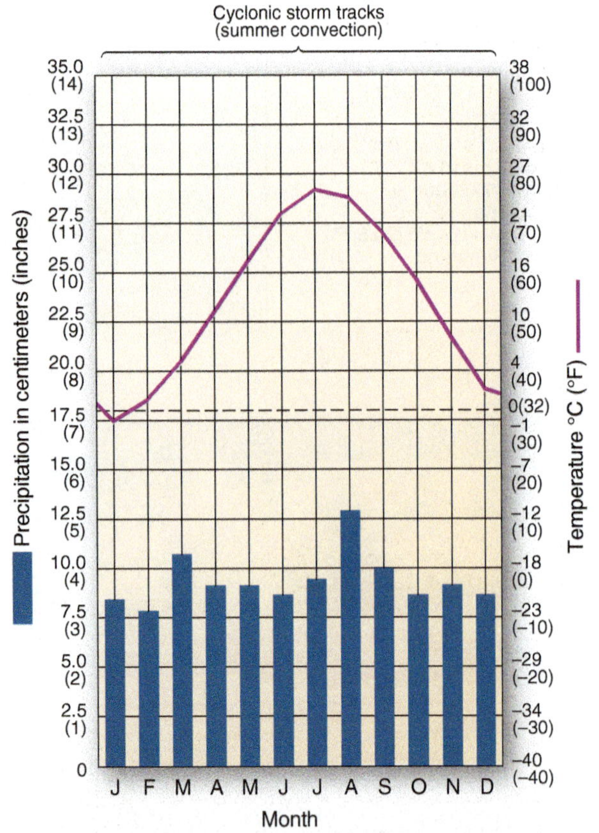

Station: New York, New York
Lat/long: 40° 46′ N 74° 01′ W
Avg. Ann. Temp.: 13°C (55.4°F)
Total Ann. Precip.: 112.3 cm (44.2 in.)
Elevation: 16 m (52.5 ft)
Population: 8,092,000
Ann. Temp. Range: 24 C° (43.2 F°)
Ann. Hr of Sunshine: 2564

(a)

Asian monsoon
effects

Precipitation in centimeters (inches)
Temperature °C (°F)
35.0 (14)
32.5 (13)
30.0 (12)
27.5 (11)
25.0 (10)
22.5 (9)
20.0 (8)
17.5 (7)
15.0 (6)
12.5 (5)
10.0 (4)
7.5 (3)
5.0 (2)
2.5 (1)
0
38 (100)
32 (90)
27 (80)
21 (70)
16 (60)
10 (50)
4 (40)
0(32)
−1 (30)
−7 (20)
−12 (10)
−18 (0)
−23 (−10)
−29 (−20)
−34 (−30)
−40 (−40)
J F M A M J J A S O N D
Month

Station: Dalian, China
Lat/long: 38° 54′ N 121° 54′ E
Avg. Ann. Temp.: 10°C (50°F)
Total Ann. Precip.: 57.8 cm (22.8 in.)
Elevation: 96 m (314.9 ft)
Population: 5,550,000
Ann. Temp. Range: 29 C° (52.2 F°)
Ann. Hr of Sunshine: 2762

(b)

(c)

(d)

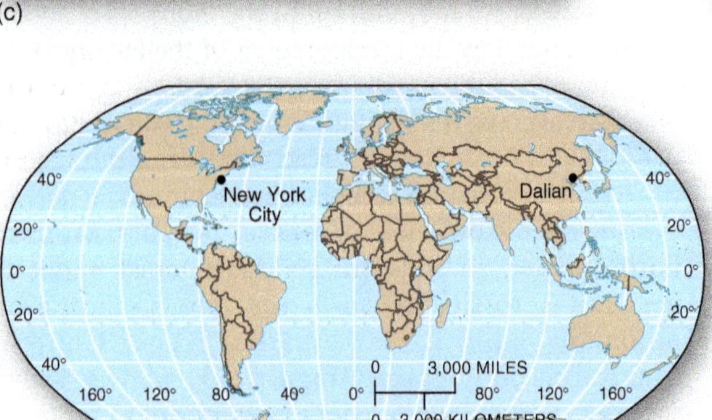

FIGURE 11 Humid continental hot-summer climates, New York and China.
Climographs for (a) New York City (humid continental hot-summer climate that is moist all year) and (b) Dalian, China (humid continental hot-summer climate that is dry in winter). (c) Belvedere Castle, 1872, in New York's Central Park; location of weather station from 1919 to 1960. (d) Dalian, China, cityscape and park in summer. [(c) Bobbé Christopherson. (d) Paul Louis Collection.]

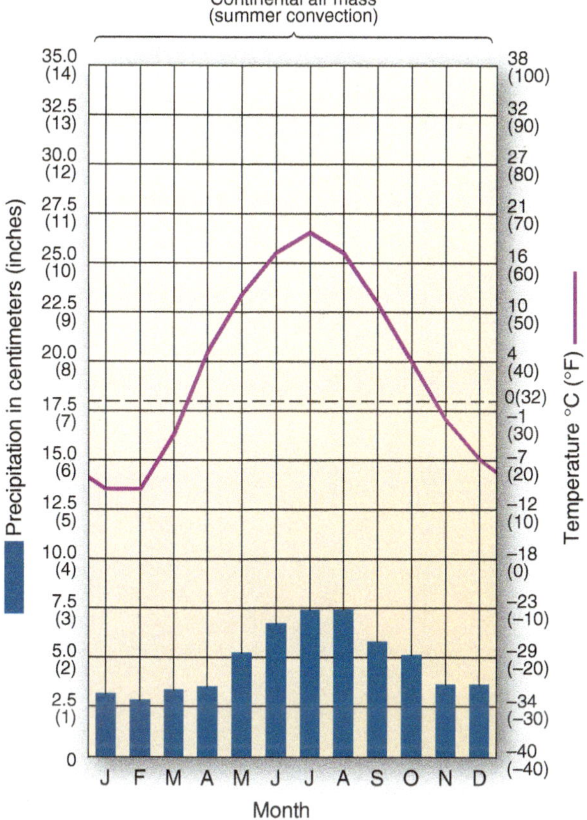

(a)

Station: Moscow, Russia
Lat/long: 55° 45′ N 37° 34′ E
Avg. Ann. Temp.: 4°C (39.2°F)
Total Ann. Precip.: 57.5 cm (22.6 in.)
Elevation: 156 m (511.8 ft)
Population: 11,460,000
Ann. Temp. Range: 29 C° (52.2 F°)
Ann. Hr of Sunshine: 1597

(b)

(c)

FIGURE 12 Humid continental mild-summer climate. (a) Climograph for Moscow, Russia. (b) Landscape between Moscow and St. Petersburg along the Volga River. (c) Winter scene of pathway through mixed forest near Brunswick, Maine, in the North American region with this climate type. [(b) Dave G. Houser/Corbis. (c) Bobbé Christopherson.]

the year, during which time light snow cover and frozen ground persist. High pressure dominates Churchill during its cold winter—this is the source region for the continental polar air mass. Churchill is representative of the *subarctic cool-summer* climate, with an annual temperature range of 40 C° (72 F°) and low precipitation of 44.3 cm (17.4 in.).

The *subarctic* climates that feature a dry and very cold winter occur only within Russia. The intense cold of Siberia and north-central and eastern Asia is difficult to comprehend, for these areas experience an average temperature lower than freezing for 7 months; minimum temperatures of below −68°C (−90°F) were recorded there. Yet summer maximum temperatures in these same areas can exceed 37°C (98°F).

An example of this extreme *subarctic climate with very cold winters* is Verkhoyansk, Siberia (Figure 14). For 4 months of the year, average temperatures fall below −34°C (−30°F). Verkhoyansk has probably the world's greatest annual temperature range from winter to summer: a remarkable 63 C° (113.4 F°). Winters feature brittle metals and plastics, triple-thick windowpanes, and temperatures that render straight antifreeze a solid.

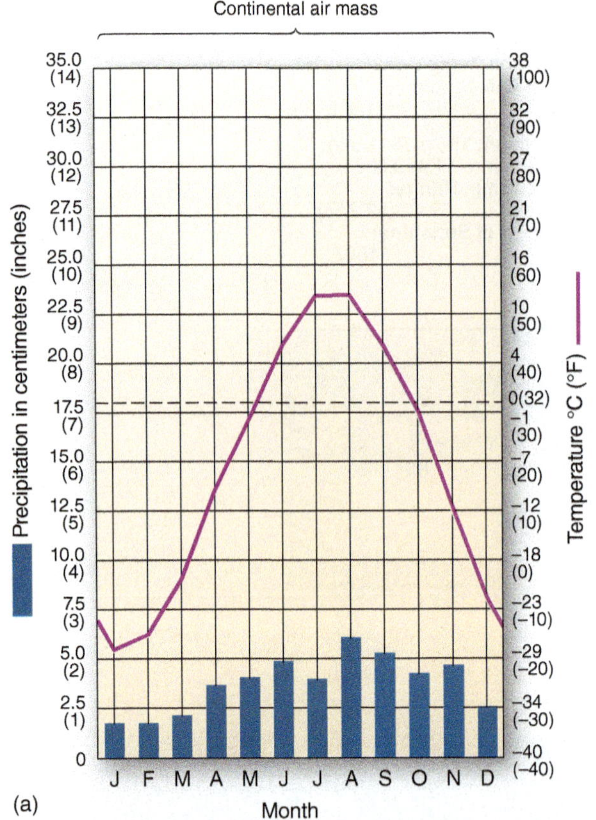

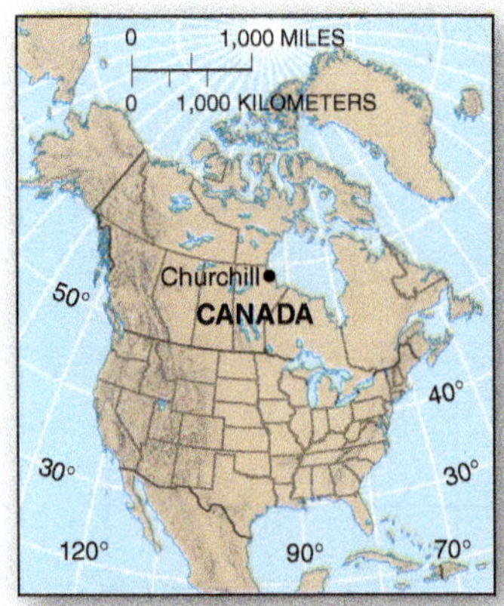

Station: Churchill, Manitoba
Lat/long: 58° 45′ N 94° 04′ W
Avg. Ann. Temp.: −7°C (19.4°F)
Total Ann. Precip.: 44.3 cm (17.4 in.)
Elevation: 35 m (114.8 ft)
Population: 1400
Ann. Temp. Range: 40 C° (72 F°)
Ann. Hr of Sunshine: 1732

(b)

FIGURE 13 Subarctic cool-summer climate.
(a) Climograph for Churchill, Manitoba. (b) Winter scene in Churchill showing the port facilities on Hudson Bay. [Bobbé Christopherson.]

Polar and Highland Climates

The polar climates have no true summer like that in lower latitudes. Dominating the South Pole is the Antarctic continent, surrounded by the Southern Ocean, whereas the North Pole region is the Arctic Ocean, surrounded by the continents of North America and Eurasia. Poleward of the Arctic and Antarctic Circles, daylength increases in summer until daylight becomes continuous, yet average monthly temperatures never rise above 10°C (50°F). These temperature conditions do not allow tree growth. Reasearch polar region temperature maps for January and July. Principal causal elements are the following:

- Low Sun altitude even during the long summer days, which is the principal climatic factor;
- Extremes of daylength between winter and summer, which determine the amount of insolation received;
- Extremely low humidity, producing low precipitation amounts—Earth's frozen deserts; and
- Surface albedo impacts, as light-colored surfaces of ice and snow reflect substantial energy away from the ground, thus reducing net radiation.

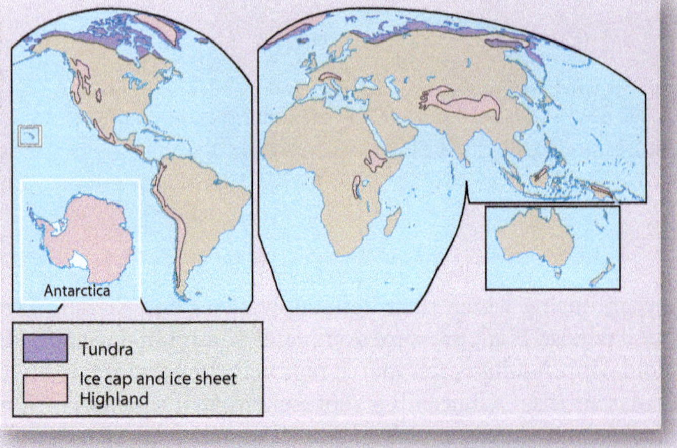

Polar climates have three regimes: *tundra* (high latitude or high elevation); *ice caps* and *ice sheets* (perpetually frozen); and *polar marine* (oceanic association, slight moderation of extreme cold).

Also in this climate category are *highland* climates. Even at low latitudes, the effects of elevation can produce tundra and polar conditions. Glaciers on tropical mountain summits attest to the cooling effects of altitude. *Highland* climates on the map follow the pattern of Earth's mountain ranges.

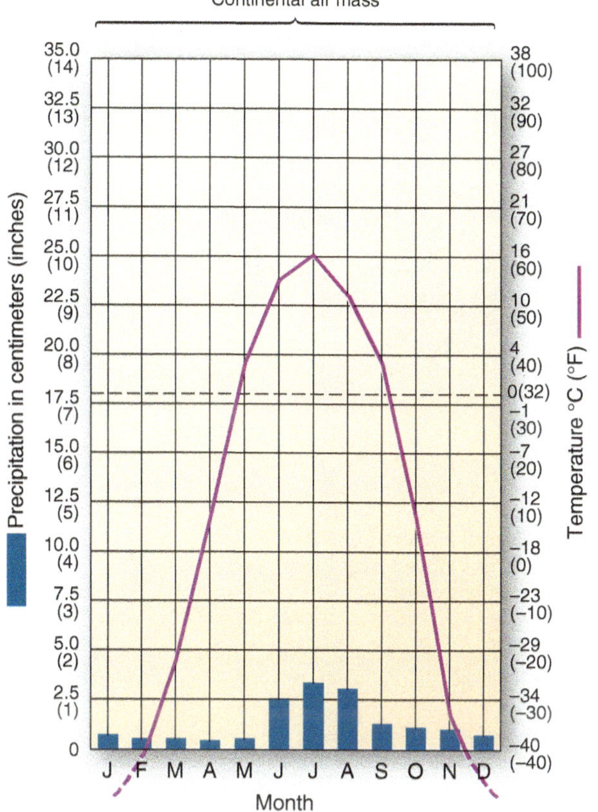

(a)

FIGURE 14 Extreme subarctic cold winter climate.
(a) Climograph for Verkhoyansk, Russia. (b) A summer scene in this unique continental location; the top layers of permafrost thaw, creating many ponds. [Dean Conger/Corbis.]

Station: Verkhoyansk, Russia
Lat/long: 67° 35′ N 133° 27′ E
Avg. Ann. Temp.: −15°C (5°F)
Total Ann. Precip.: 15.5 cm (6.1 in.)
Elevation: 137 m (449.5 ft)
Population: 1500
Ann. Temp. Range: 63 C° (113.4 F°)

(b)

Tundra Climates

In a *tundra* climate, land is under some snow cover for 8–10 months, with the warmest month above 0°C (32°F), yet never warming above 10°C (50°F). Because of elevation, the summit of Mount Washington in New Hampshire (1914 m, or 6280 ft) statistically qualifies as a highland *tundra* climate on a small scale. On a larger scale, approximately 410,500 km^2 (158,475 mi^2) of Greenland are ice-free, an area of tundra and rock about the size of California.

In spring when the snow melts, numerous plants appear—stunted sedges, mosses, flowering plants, and lichens—and persist through the short summer (Figure 15). Some of the dwarf willows (7.5 cm, or 3 in., tall) can exceed 300 years in age. Much of the area experiences permafrost and ground ice conditions; these are Earth's periglacial regions.

Global warming is bringing dramatic changes to the tundra. In parts of Canada and Alaska, registered temperatures as much as 5 to 10 C° (9 to 18 F°) above average are a regular occurrence, setting many records. As organic peat deposits in the tundra thaw, vast stores of carbon are released to the atmosphere, further adding to the greenhouse gas problem. Temperatures in the Arctic are warming at a rate twice that of the global average increase.

FIGURE 15 Greenland tundra.
Late September in East Greenland with fall colors and musk oxen. [Bobbé Christopherson.]

Tundra climates are strictly in the Northern Hemisphere, except for elevated mountain locations in the Southern Hemisphere and a portion of the Antarctic Peninsula.

(a)

(b)

FIGURE 16 Earth's ice sheets—Antarctica and Greenland.
These are Earth's frozen freshwater reservoirs. (a) In the Antarctic Sound, between Bransfield Strait and the Weddell Sea, mountains rise from the mist behind a flank of tabular icebergs. (b) Glaciers move toward the ocean into Davis Strait from West Greenland and the ice sheet on the horizon. [Bobbé Christopherson.]

Ice-Cap and Ice-Sheet Climates

Earth's two ice sheets cover the Antarctic continent and most of the island of Greenland. Thus, most of Antarctica and central Greenland fall within the *ice-sheet* climate, as does the North Pole, with all months averaging below freezing. These regions are dominated by dry, frigid air masses, with vast expanses that never warm above freezing. In fact, winter minimum temperatures in central Antarctica (July) frequently drop below the temperature of solid carbon dioxide or "dry ice" (–78°C, or –109°F).

The area of the North Pole is actually a sea covered by ice, whereas Antarctica is a substantial continental landmass. Antarctica is constantly snow-covered, but receives less than 8 cm (3 in.) of precipitation each year. However, Antarctic ice has accumulated to several kilometers deep and is the largest repository of freshwater on Earth. Data published in 2011 confirm that ice losses from both polar regions is continuing to occur at an accelerated rate.

Ice caps are smaller in extent than ice sheets, roughly less than 50,000 km^2 (19,300 mi^2), yet they completely bury the landscape like an ice sheet. The Vatnajökull ice cap in southeastern Iceland is an example.

Figure 16 shows two scenes of the repositories of multi-year ice on the West Antarctic and Greenland Ice Sheets. This ice contains a vast historical record of Earth's atmosphere. Within it, evidence of thousands of past volcanic eruptions from all over the world and ancient combinations of atmospheric gases lies trapped in frozen bubbles. Analyses of ice cores taken from Greenland and the latest one taken from Antarctica, push the climate record to 800,000 years before the present.

Polar Marine Climates

Polar marine climates are more moderate than other polar climates in winter, with no month below –7°C (20°F), yet they are not as warm as *tundra* climates. Because of marine influences, annual temperature ranges are low. This climate exists along the Bering Sea, on the southern tip of Greenland, and in northern Iceland, Norway, and the Southern Hemisphere, generally over oceans between 50° S and 60° S. Macquarie Island at 54° S in the Southern Ocean, south of New Zealand, is *polar marine*.

South Georgia Island, made famous as the place where Earnest Shackelton sought rescue help for him

FIGURE 17 South Georgia Island, a polar marine climate.
Here is the abandoned whaling station at Grytviken, South Georgia, processing more than 50,000 whales between 1904 and 1964, about a third of all whales processed on South Georgia among seven factories. The whales of the Southern Ocean were driven almost to extinction. [Bobbé Christopherson.]

and his men in 1916 after their failed Antarctic expedition (Figure 17), is *polar marine*. Although the island is in the Southern Ocean and part of Antarctica, the annual temperature range is only 8.5 C° (15.3 F°) between the seasons (the averages are 7°C in January and −1.5°C in July; 44.6°F and 29.3°F), with 7 months averaging slightly above freezing. Although cold at between 0°C and 4°C, the ocean temperatures moderate the climate despite its location at 54° S latitude. Average precipitation is 150 cm (59 in.), and it can snow during any month.

Dry Climates (permanent moisture deficits)

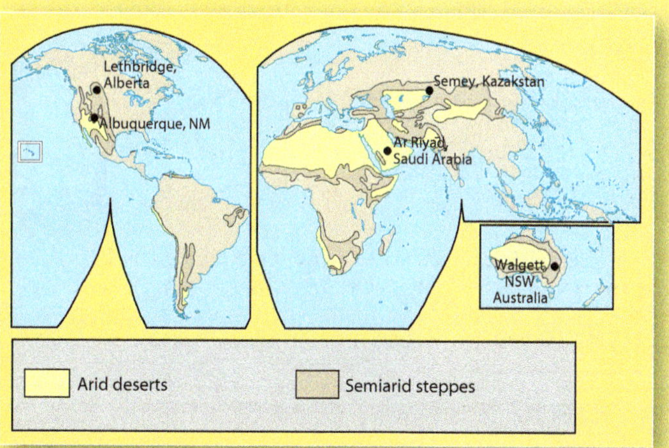

For understanding the dry climates, we consider moisture efficiency along with temperature. These dry regions occupy more than 35% of Earth's land area and are by far the most extensive climate over land. Sparse vegetation leaves the landscape bare; water demand exceeds the precipitation water supply throughout, creating permanent water deficits. The extent of these deficits distinguishes two types of dry climatic regions: *arid deserts*, where the precipitation supply is roughly less than one-half of the natural moisture demand; and *semiarid steppes*, where the precipitation supply is roughly more than one-half of natural moisture demand. (See specific annual and daily desert temperature regimes, including the highest record temperatures and surface energy budgets.)

Important causal elements in these dry lands include

- The dominant presence of dry, subsiding air in subtropical high-pressure systems;
- Location in the rain shadow (or leeward side) of mountains, where dry air subsides after moisture is intercepted on the windward slopes;
- Location in continental interiors, particularly central Asia, which are far from moisture-bearing air masses; and
- Shifting subtropical high-pressure systems, which produce semiarid steppes around the periphery of arid deserts.

Dry climates are distributed by latitude and the amount of moisture deficits in four distinct regimes: arid climates include *tropical, subtropical hot desert* and *midlatitude cold desert*; semiarid climates include *tropical, subtropical hot steppe* and *midlatitude cold steppe*.

Characteristics of Dry Climates

The world climate map in Figure 2 reveals the pattern of Earth's dry climates, which cover broad regions between 15° and 30° N and S latitude. In these areas, subtropical high-pressure cells predominate, with subsiding, stable air and low relative humidity. Under generally cloudless skies, these subtropical deserts extend to western continental margins, where cool, stabilizing ocean currents operate offshore and summer advection fog forms. The Atacama Desert of Chile, the Namib Desert of Namibia, the Western Sahara of Morocco, and the Australian Desert each lie adjacent to such a coastline (Figure 18).

Orographic lifting intercepts moisture-bearing weather systems to create rain shadows along mountain ranges that extend these dry regions into higher latitudes. Note these rain shadows in North and South America on the climate map. The isolated interior of Asia, far distant from any moisture-bearing air masses, also falls within the dry climate classification.

Dry climates are subdivided into deserts and steppes, which are distinguished by the amount of moisture deficit; deserts have greater moisture deficits than do steppes, but both have permanent water shortages. Important is whether precipitation falls principally in the winter with a dry summer, falls principally in the summer with a dry winter, or is evenly distributed. Winter rains are most effective because they fall at a time of lower moisture demand. Relative to temperature, the lower-latitude deserts and steppes tend to be hotter with less seasonal change than the midlatitude deserts and steppes, where mean annual temperatures are below 18°C (64.4°F) and freezing winter temperatures are possible.

A **steppe** is a regional term referring to the vast semiarid grassland biome of Eastern Europe and Asia (the equivalent biome in North America is shortgrass prairie, and in Africa, the savanna). In this chapter, we use steppe in a climatic context; a steppe climate is considered too dry to support forest, but too moist to be a desert.

Tropical, Subtropical Hot Desert Climates

Tropical, subtropical hot desert climates are Earth's true tropical and subtropical deserts and feature annual average temperatures above 18°C (64.4°F). They generally are found on the western sides of continents, although Egypt, Somalia, and Saudi Arabia also fall within this

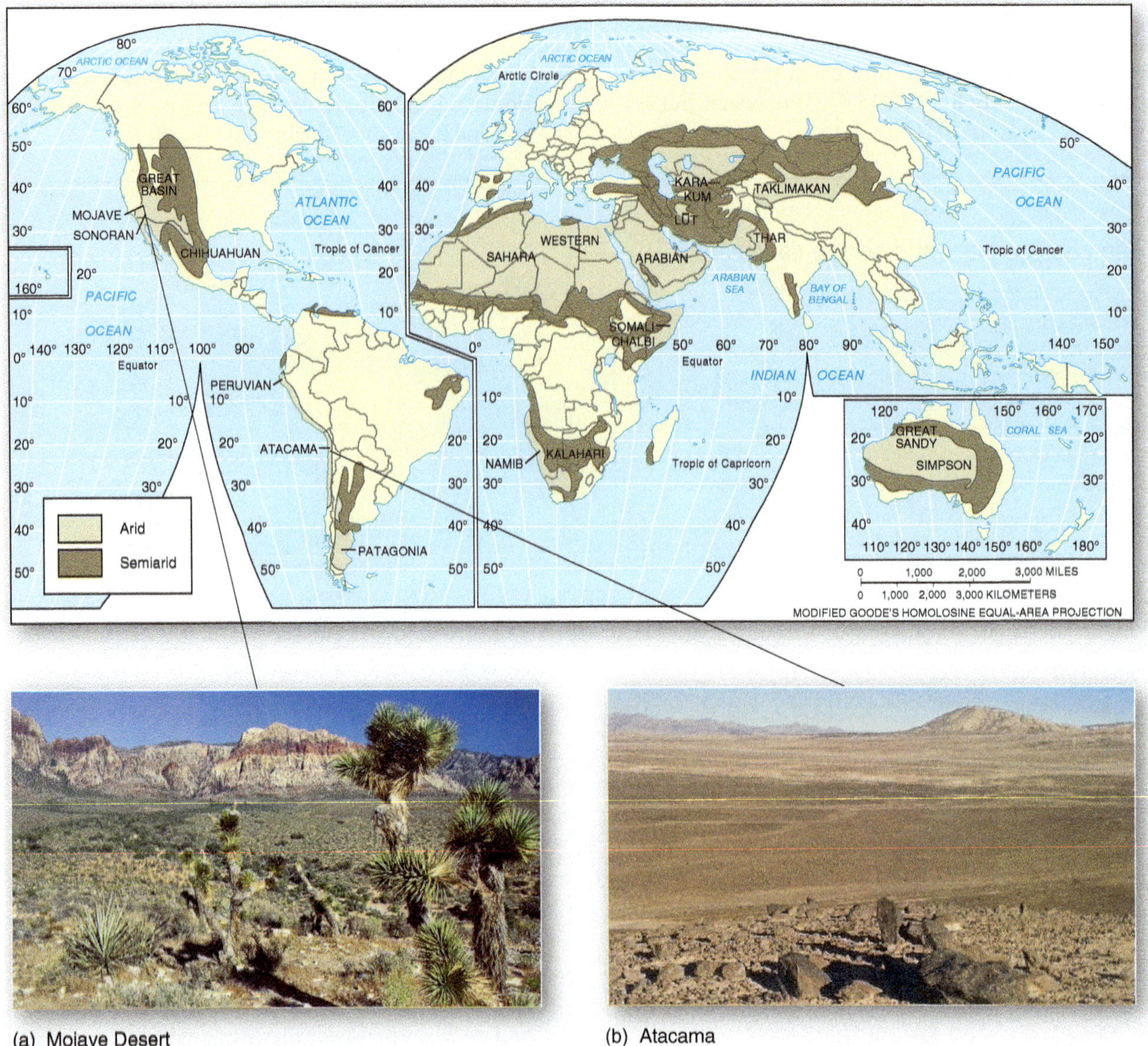

(a) Mojave Desert

(b) Atacama

FIGURE 18 Important deserts and steppes.
Worldwide distribution of arid desert and semiarid steppe climates. (a) Mojave Desert in the American Southwest. (b) Atacama Desert in subtropical Chile near Baquedano. [(a) Bobbé Christopherson. (b) Jacques Jangoux/ Photo Researchers, Inc.]

classification. Rainfall is from local summer convectional showers. Some regions receive almost no rainfall, whereas others may receive up to 35 cm (14 in.) of precipitation a year. A representative *subtropical hot desert* city is Ar Riyād (Riyadh), Saudi Arabia (Figure 19).

Along the Sahara Desert's southern margin in Africa is a drought-tortured region, the Sahel. Human populations suffered great hardship as desert conditions gradually expanded over their homelands. The process of desertification (expanding desert conditions) is an ongoing problem in many dry regions of the world.

In recent years, the media focused on the Iraq war and related political events. What seemed overlooked in many reports were the extremely hot summer air temperatures in Baghdad (located on the map in Figure 19), regularly reaching 50°C (122°F) and higher in the city. Such readings broke records for Baghdad in 2007. Baghdad records zero precipitation from May to September, as it is dominated by an intense subtropical high-pressure system. Keep these desert climates in mind as you follow events in the news.

Midlatitude Cold Desert Climates

Midlatitude cold desert climates cover only a small area: the countries along the southern border of Russia, the Taklimakan Desert, and Mongolia in Asia; the central third of Nevada and areas of the American Southwest, particularly at high elevations; and Patagonia in Argentina. Because of lower temperatures and lower moisture-demand values, rainfall must be low for a station to qualify as a *midlatitude cold desert* climate; consequently, total annual average rainfall is only about 15 cm (6 in.).

A representative station is Albuquerque, New Mexico, with 20.7 cm (8.1 in.) of precipitation and an annual average temperature of 14°C (57.2°F) (Figure 20). Note the

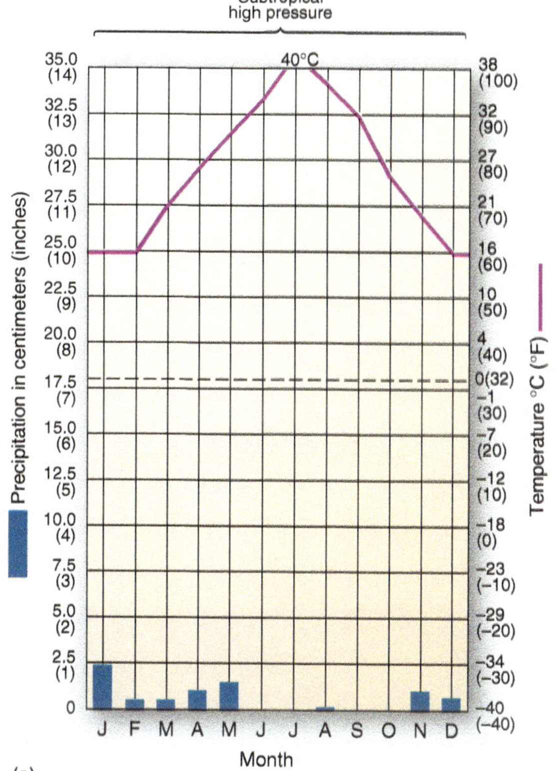

(a)

Station: Ar Riyāḍ (Riyadh), Saudi Arabia
Lat/long: 24° 42′ N 46° 43′ E
Avg. Ann. Temp.: 26°C (78.8°F)
Total Ann. Precip.: 8.2 cm (3.2 in.)
Elevation: 609 m (1998 ft)
Population: 5,024,000
Ann. Temp. Range: 24 C° (43.2 F°)

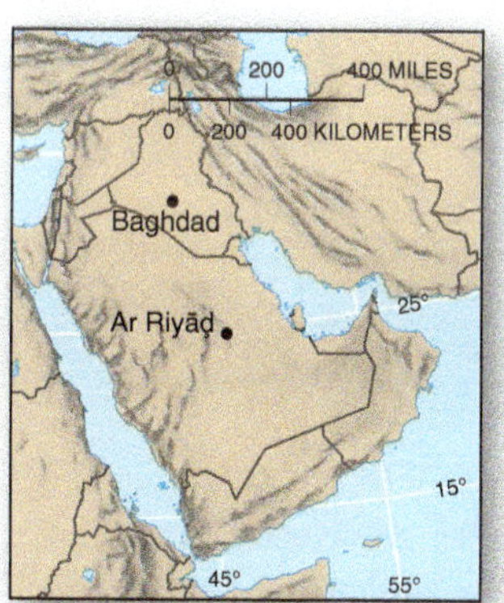

(b)

FIGURE 19 Tropical, subtropical hot desert climate.
(a) Climograph for Ar Riyāḍ (Riyadh), Saudi Arabia. (b) The Arabian desert landscape of Red Sands near Ar Riyāḍ. [Andreas Wolf/agefotostock;]

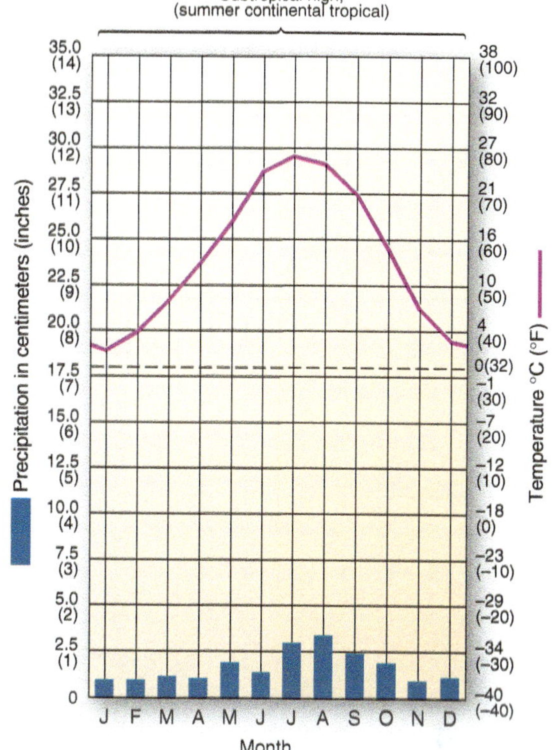

(a)

Station: Albuquerque, New Mexico
Lat/long: 35° 03′ N 106° 37′ W
Avg. Ann. Temp.: 14°C (57.2°F)
Total Ann. Precip.: 20.7 cm (8.1 in.)
Elevation: 1620 m (5315 ft)
Population: 522,000
Ann. Temp. Range: 24 C° (43.2 F°)
Ann. Hr of Sunshine: 3420

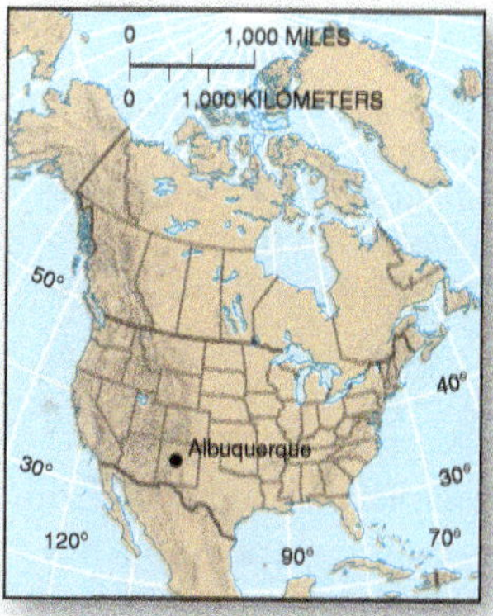

(b)

FIGURE 20 Midlatitude cold desert climate.
(a) Climograph for Albuquerque, New Mexico. (b) A winter scene near the New Mexico–Arizona border. [Bobbé Christopherson.]

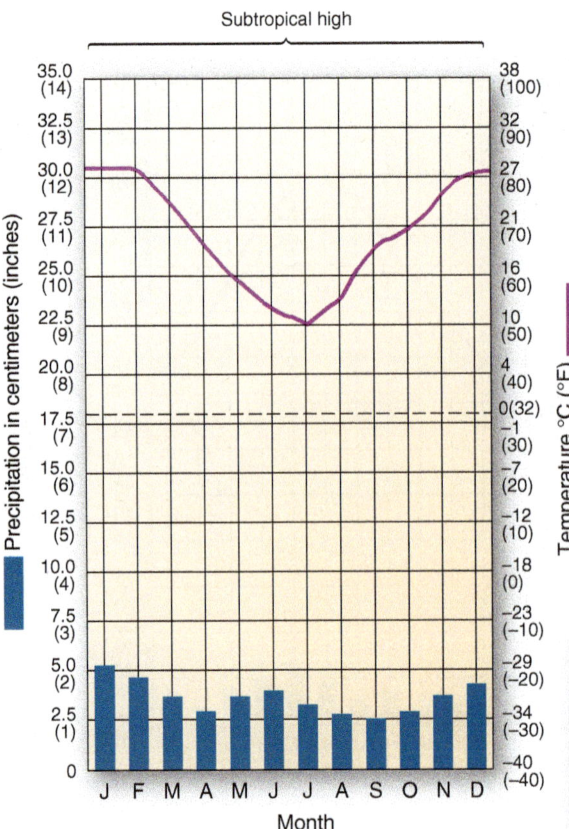

(a)

Station: Walgett, New South Wales, Australia
Lat/long: 30° S 148° 07′ E
Avg. Ann. Temp.: 20°C (68°F)
Total Ann. Precip.: 45.0 cm (17.7 in.)
Elevation: 133 m (436 ft)
Population: 8200
Ann. Temp. Range: 17 C° (31 F°)

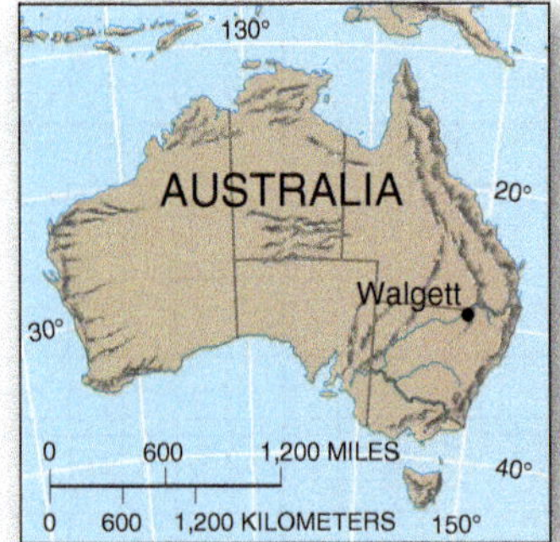

(b)

FIGURE 21 (a) **Tropical, subtropical hot steppe climate.**
Climograph for Walgett, New South Wales, Australia. (b) Vast plains characteristic of north-central New South Wales. [Prisma/SuperStock.]

precipitation increase from summer convectional showers on the climograph. See the end-of-chapter photos and caption for more on this region and climate change.

Tropical, Subtropical Hot Steppe Climates

Tropical, subtropical hot steppe climates generally exist around the periphery of hot deserts, where shifting subtropical high-pressure cells create a distinct summer-dry and winter-wet pattern. Average annual precipitation in *subtropical hot steppe* areas is usually below 60 cm (23.6 in.). Walgett, in interior New South Wales, Australia, provides a Southern Hemisphere example of this climate (Figure 21). This climate is seen around the Sahara's periphery and in the Iran, Afghanistan, Turkmenistan, and Kazakhstan region.

Midlatitude Cold Steppe Climates

The *midlatitude cold steppe* climates occur poleward of about 30° latitude and the *midlatitude cold desert* climates. Such midlatitude steppes are not generally found in the Southern Hemisphere. As with other dry climate regions, rainfall in the steppes is widely variable and undependable, ranging from 20 to 40 cm (7.9 to 15.7 in.). Not all rainfall is convectional, for cyclonic storm tracks penetrate the continents; however, most storms produce little precipitation.

Figure 22 presents a comparison between Asian and North American *midlatitude cold steppe* climates. Consider Semey (Semipalatinsk) in Kazakstan, with its greater temperature range and more evenly distributed precipitation, and Lethbridge, Alberta, with its lesser temperature range and summer maximum convectional precipitation.

GEO REPORT 3 *Climate science and the UNFCCC*

Relative to coordinating climate change science, the UNFCCC was set in motion at the 1992 Earth Summit in Rio de Janeiro. The lead body is the Conference of the Parties (COP), maintained by the 192 countries that ratified the UNFCCC Treaty. Meetings are held annually. For updates, see http://unfccc.int/2860.php. The 2011 gathering, *COP-17*, is in Durban, South Africa.

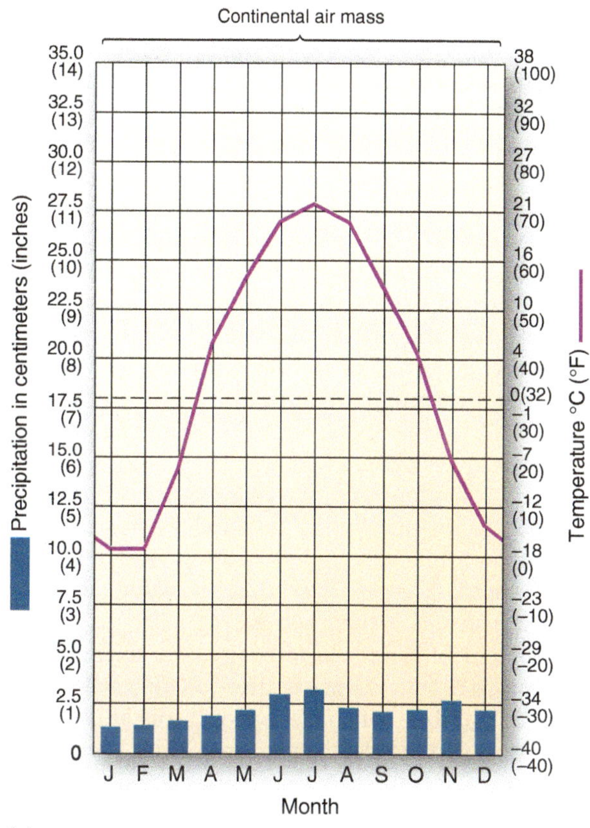

(a)

Station: Semey (Semipalatinsk), Kazakhstan
Lat/long: 50° 21′ N 80° 15′ E
Avg. Ann. Temp.: 3°C (37.4°F)
Total Ann. Precip.: 26.4 cm (10.4 in.)
Elevation: 206 m (675.9 ft)
Population: 270,500
Ann. Temp. Range: 39 C° (70.2 F°)

(b)

Continental air mass (summer convection) (winter cP air mass)

(c)

Station: Lethbridge, Alberta
Lat/long: 49° 42′ N 110° 50′ W
Avg. Ann. Temp.: 2.9°C (37.3°F)
Total Ann. Precip.: 25.8 cm (10.2 in.)
Elevation: 910 m (2985 ft)
Population: 73,000
Ann. Temp. Range: 24.3 C° (43.7 F°)

(d)

FIGURE 22 Midlatitude cold steppe climates, Kazakhstan and Canada. (a) Climograph for Semey (Semipalatinsk) in Kazakhstan. (b) Aerial view of Semey and the Ertis River. (c) Climograph for Lethbridge in Alberta. (d) Grain elevators highlight an Alberta, Canada, landscape. [(b) Dinara Sagatova. (d) Design Pics RF/Getty Images.]

Global Climate Change

Let us begin this important section with a bottom line. We have learned that carbon dioxide is the principal gas causing Earth's natural greenhouse effect, resulting in a warming trend in the atmosphere. We've seen the rise in CO_2 as measured since 1958 at the Mauna Loa station in Hawai'i. The annual emissions of CO_2 to the atmosphere have been increasing at about 3.0% per year since 2000. Recall that increasing greenhouse gases absorb longwave radiation, delaying losses of heat energy to space.

Using ice cores, scientists have reconstructed Earth's atmospheric history, including levels of atmospheric gases such as CO_2. The 800,000-year climate record from the Antarctic Dome-C ice core revealed that CO_2 levels in the atmosphere ranged between 100 ppm and 300 ppm—never over 300. The ice core data indicate that atmospheric CO_2 has never changed 30 ppm upward or downward during a period of less than 1000 years. Yet today, we see that atmospheric CO_2 rose 30 ppm in only the last 12 years.

You can check the data and see what the level of CO_2 is during the month when you are working on this chapter (ftp://ftp.cmdl.noaa.gov/ccg/co2/trends/co2_mm_mlo.txt). May and October are the highest and lowest months, respectively, for CO_2 readings during the year due to seasonal vegetation changes. CO_2 levels in January 2011 were 4 ppm higher than those in January 2010 and May 2011 was at 394 ppm; therefore, the forecast is for continued increases.

As the concentration of CO_2 in the atmosphere has increased, so has the average surface temperature of Earth (Figure 23). Record-high global temperatures have dominated the past two decades—for both land and ocean and for both day and night. Scientists think that we are already in the danger zone and that to avoid irreversible ice-sheet and species loss, we must avoid crossing the 450 ppm threshold for maximum CO_2. You can do the math using the rate of accelerated growth in emissions for the past 10 years to find out when we might reach this threshold. Further, to obtain climate stability, scientists tell us that we should implement policies to return the level of CO_2 to 350 ppm.* This is the bottom line based on actual levels of the principal greenhouse gas.

In the field of **paleoclimatology**, the science that studies past climates, scientists use not only ice cores, but also a number of other proxy, or substitute, indicators for climate reconstruction. Data from lake

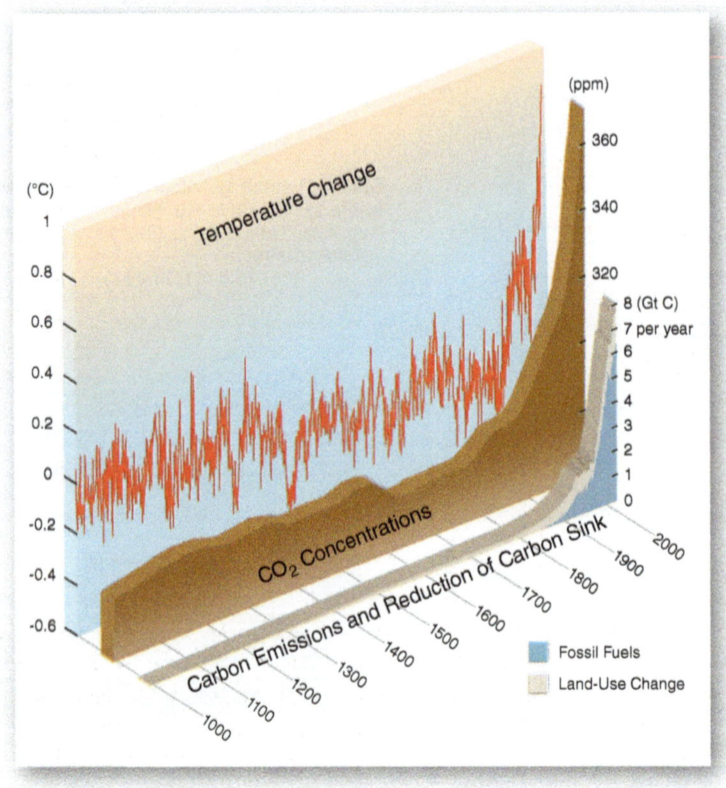

FIGURE 23 A thousand years of records and the covariance of carbon dioxide and temperature. Carbon emissions, CO_2 concentrations, and temperature change correlate over the past 1000 years. This graph was prepared before the record-setting temperatures of 2005. By May 2011, CO_2 levels were at 394 ppm. Earth systems are in record territory. [Illustration from ACIA, *Impacts of a Warming Arctic* (London: Cambridge University Press, 2004), p. 2. Used by permission of ACIA.]

and ocean sediments, coral reefs, ancient pollen, and tree-ring density, among others, point to the present time as the warmest in the last 120,000 years. These proxy indicators also suggest that the increase in temperature during the 20th century is *very likely*** the largest in any century over the past 1000 years (Figure 23). Earth is less than 1 C° (1.8 F°) from equaling the highest average temperature of the past 125,000 years. This warming trend is *very likely* due to a buildup of greenhouse gases from the burning of fossil fuels (coal, oil, natural gas); about 94% of CO_2 emissions come from the combustion of fossil fuels and the rest from cement manufacturing and other industries.

Significant climatic change has occurred on Earth in the past and most certainly will occur in the future. Humans can do nothing about long-term climatic influences that cycle Earth through swings from ice ages to warmer periods. However, our global society must address short-term changes that are influencing global temperatures within the life span of present generations. This is especially true since these changes are due to human activities—an anthropogenic forcing of climate. Article 2 of the United Nations Framework Convention on Climate Change (UNFCCC), signed in 1992, commits countries to stabilize greenhouse gases at levels that will "prevent dangerous anthropogenic interference with the climate system."

The fact that climate change is occurring is an accepted consensus among mainstream scientists. Determining the accelerating rate of this change is essential. In geologic time, changes in the environment occurred over millions of years, whereas elements of climate change today are happening in the span of decades. This rate of change affects the amount of time available for physical and biological systems to adapt. This rate is a key factor in the five "Reasons for Concern" developed by the IPCC in its *Assessment Reports* on global climate change and updated by the lead authors in "Assessing dangerous climate change through an update of the IPCC 'Reasons for Concern'" [*Proceedings of the National Academy of Sciences* 106, 11 (March 17, 2009): 4133–4137].

*Among many sources, see J. Hansen et al., "Target atmospheric CO_2: Where should humanity aim?" *Open Atmospheric Science Journal* 2 (March 2008): 217–231; and K. Zickfeld, M. Eby, H. D. Matthews, and A. J. Weaver, "Setting cumulative emissions targets to reduce the risk of dangerous climate change," *Proceedings of the National Academy of Sciences* 106, 38 (September 22, 2009): 16129–16134.

**As a standard scientific reference on climate change, the IPCC uses the following to indicate levels of confidence: *Virtually certain* > 99% probability of occurrence; *Extremely likely* > 95%; *Very likely* > 90%; *Likely* > 66%; *More likely than not* > 50%; *Unlikely* < 33%; *Very unlikely* < 10%; and *Extremely unlikely* < 5%.

"Reasons for Concern"

Figure 24 summarizes the five "Reasons for Concern" developed by IPCC scientists. As you explore climate change, perhaps this framework can assist you in organizing your approach. The IPCC "Reasons for Concern" are

- **Risks to Unique and Threatened Systems**—Risks include irreversible losses to physical systems (e.g., glaciers, coral reefs, lakes, barrier islands, small islands) and biological systems (e.g., biodiversity hotspots, mangroves, ecosystem migrations, species extinctions), among others.
- **Risks of Extreme Weather Events**—Risks include extreme event magnitude and frequency increases; intense precipitation and floods; tropical cyclone and tornado intensity increases; heat waves; droughts; and wildfires, among others.
- **Uneven Distribution of Climate Change Impacts**—Impacts are greatest in low-latitude and less-developed countries and for circumpolar Arctic indigenous peoples; disparity occurs among economic classes of people; range and seasonality of disease vectors and health impacts tend to affect lower-latitude countries.
- **Aggregate Impacts and Damages**—Effects are combined to assess total monetary damage and lives changed or lost; few poor or developing countries have the financial, technical, or institutional base to support adaptation.

GEO REPORT 4 *Professional consensus on climate change*

The American Association for the Advancement of Science (AAAS) reported in "The Scientific Consensus on Climate Change," by Naomi Oreskes [*Science* 306, 5702 (December 3, 2004): 1686], the results of a survey of all 928 climate-change papers published between 1993 and 2003 and concluded: "Remarkably, none of the papers disagreed with the consensus position."

The Association of American Geographers (AAG; 11,000 members) passed the *AAG Resolution Requesting Action on Climate Change* in 2006. This resolution places the AAG in line with other professional organizations and many national academies of sciences, now on record for action to slow rates of climate change. The American Meteorological Society (AMS; 13,000 members) published its *AMS Statement on Climate Change* in 2007. The American Physical Society (APS; 46,000 members) adopted its *APS National Policy on Climate Change* in 2007, declaring that "human causes of climate change are well understood and beyond dispute." The Geological Society of America (GSA; 22,000 members) adopted its strong "Climate Change Statement" that global climate has warmed and that human activities (greenhouse gases) account for it.

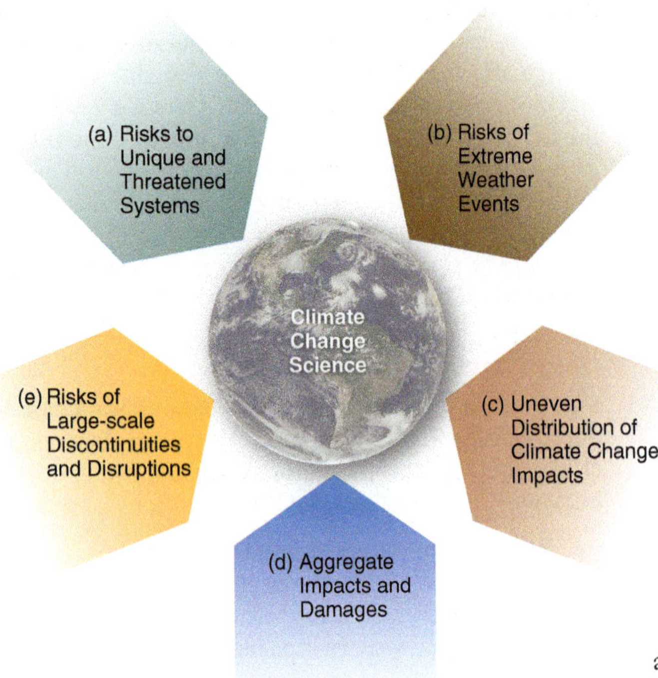

FIGURE 24 Summary of IPCC's five "Reasons for Concern" as they each inform climate-change science. [(1) IPCC, 2001, *Third Assessment Report* , Working Group II, Chapter 19 of *Vulnerability to Climate Change and Reasons for Concern: A Synthesis* (pp. 911–967); (2) IPCC, 2007, *Fourth Assessment Report*, Working Group II, *Assessing Key Vulnerabilities and the Risk from Climate Change* (pp. 779–810); (3) Joel Smith and Stephen Schneider, "Assessing dangerous climate change through an update of the IPCC 'Reasons for Concern'," *Proceedings of the National Academy of Sciences* 106, 11 (March 17, 2009): 4133–4137.]

- **Risks of Large-Scale Discontinuities and Disruptions**—Abrupt and dramatic system responses occur at thresholds in systems that fluctuate above and below an average, yet show a trend over time—a dynamic equilibrium. As conditions change, the system can no longer maintain that operational level and spasms to a new equilibrium; that moment is a "tipping point." Resulting disruptions include the melting of mountain glaciers, Greenland and West Antarctic ice-sheet losses, ocean acidification, permafrost melt and CO_2 liberation, and rapid sea-level rise, among others.

The 2009 International Scientific Conference on Climate Change reached conclusions that reinforce the "Reasons for Concern" in part:

- "The worst-case IPCC projections, or even worse, are being realized";
- "Emissions are soaring, projections of sea-level rise are higher than expected";
- "The acceleration of Greenland's and Antarctica's ice losses of mass are very clearly in evidence in satellite images"; and
- "Inaction is inexcusable, weaker emissions targets for 2020 increases the risk of crossing numerous tipping points."*

Table 2 presents a sampling of major scientific organizations and web sites dealing with climate-change topics and reports. You can find additional links on our *MasteringGeography* web site.

*Summarized in E. Kintisch, "Global warming: Projections of climate change go from bad to worse, scientists report," *Science* 323, 5921 (March 20, 2009): 1546–1547.

Climate-Change Measurements

Assessing and understanding global climate change requires a number of different measurements, some of which necessitate a combination of different data types and sources. Measurements of temperature and greenhouse gases are critical in helping scientists understand present climatic changes and their causes.

Temperature Trends As stated earlier, the field of paleoclimatology has become an indispensible tool for placing present changes in the context of thousands of years. A closer look at temperature change during the past century is in Figure 25. The graph plots observed annual land-surface air temperatures and 5-year mean temperatures from 1880 through 2010. The record year for warmth for land-surface temperatures is tied between 2010 and 2005, with 2007, 2009, and 1998 the second, third, and fourth warmest. For the Southern Hemisphere, 2009 was the warmest in the modern record. The decade of 2001–2010 was the warmest decade in the entire record.

The map in Figure 25b uses the same base period as the graph (1951–1980) to give you an idea of temperature anomalies across the globe for 2010. Refer to temperature anomaly maps for several decades. Note the Arctic region through Hudson Bay, Canada, where new records for land and water temperatures and sea-ice melt were set. Anomalies exceeding 3.5 C° (6.3 F°) were measured in the Canadian Arctic and the Antarctic Peninsula. On the *MasteringGeography* web site, you can watch a movie of temperature anomalies from 1881 to 2006 and observe the warming patterns over this time span.

Scientists are determining the difference between *forced fluctuations* (human-caused) and *unforced fluctuations* (natural) as a key to predicting future climate trends. Figure 26 shows a comparison of climate models, which include natural forcing (shaded blue area) and anthropogenic forcing (shaded pink area) for the globe. The black line on the graph plots observations from 1906 to 2005. Clearly, only those coupled climate models that include

TABLE 2 Sources of Information for Global Climate-Change Research

United Nations Environment Programme	http://www.unep.ch/
World Meteorological Organization	http://www.wmo.ch/
World Climate Research Programme	http://wcrp.wmo.int/
Global Climate Observing System	http://gosic.org/ios/GCOS-main-page.htm
Intergovernmental Panel on Climate Change	http://www.ipcc.ch/
Arctic Council	http://www.arctic-council.org/
Arctic Climate Impact Assessment	http://www.acia.uaf.edu/
Arctic Monitoring and Assessment Program	http://www.amap.no/
Conservation of Arctic Flora and Fauna	http://www.caff.is/
International Arctic Science Committee	http://arctic-council.org/observer/iasc
U.S. Global Change Research Program	http://www.globalchange.gov.
U.S. Environmental Protection Agency	http://www.epa.gov/climatechange/
Goddard Institute for Space Studies	http://www.giss.nasa.gov/
Global Hydrology and Climate Center	http://www.ghcc.msfc.nasa.gov
National Climate Data Center	http://www.ncdc.noaa.gov/
National Environmental Satellite, Data, and Information Service	http://www.nesdis.noaa.gov/
NASA Global Climate Change	http://climate.nasa.gov/
NWS Climate Prediction Center	http://www.cpc.ncep.noaa.gov/
Climate Institute	http://www.climate.org/
Pew Center on Global Climate Change	http://www.pewclimate.org/
National Ice Center	http://www.natice.noaa.gov/
National Snow and Ice Data Center	http://nsidc.org/
National Center for Atmospheric Research	http://www.ncar.ucar.edu/
Canada's Action on Climate Change	http://www.climatechange.gc.ca/
British Antarctic Survey	http://www.antarctica.ac.uk/
International Union for the Conservation of Nature and Natural Resources	http://www.iucn.org/
World.org 100 Top Climate Change Sites	http://www.world.org/weo/climate

human factors accurately simulate increasing temperatures. Solar variability and volcanic output alone do not explain the increase. The primary anthropogenic input to Earth's climate system is increased amounts of greenhouse gases.

Greenhouse Gases Carbon dioxide and water vapor are the principal radiatively active gases causing Earth's natural greenhouse effect. *Radiatively active* gases include atmospheric gases, such as carbon dioxide (CO_2), methane (CH_4), nitrous oxide (N_2O), chlorofluorocarbons (CFCs), and water vapor, which absorb and radiate longwave energy. Figure 27 plots changes in three of these greenhouse gases over the past 10,000 years.

Methane (CH_4) is increasing at a rate even faster than carbon dioxide. In ice cores, methane levels never topped 750 parts per billion (ppb) in the past 800,000 years, yet in

GEO REPORT 5 ***The IPCC and the Nobel Peace Prize***

The IPCC, formed in 1988, is an organization operating under the United Nations Environment Programme (UNEP) and the World Meteorological Organization (WMO) and is the scientific organization coordinating global climate-change research, climate forecasts, and policy formulation. In 2007, the IPCC shared the Nobel Peace Prize with former Vice-President Albert Gore for their two decades of work raising understanding and awareness of global climate-change science.

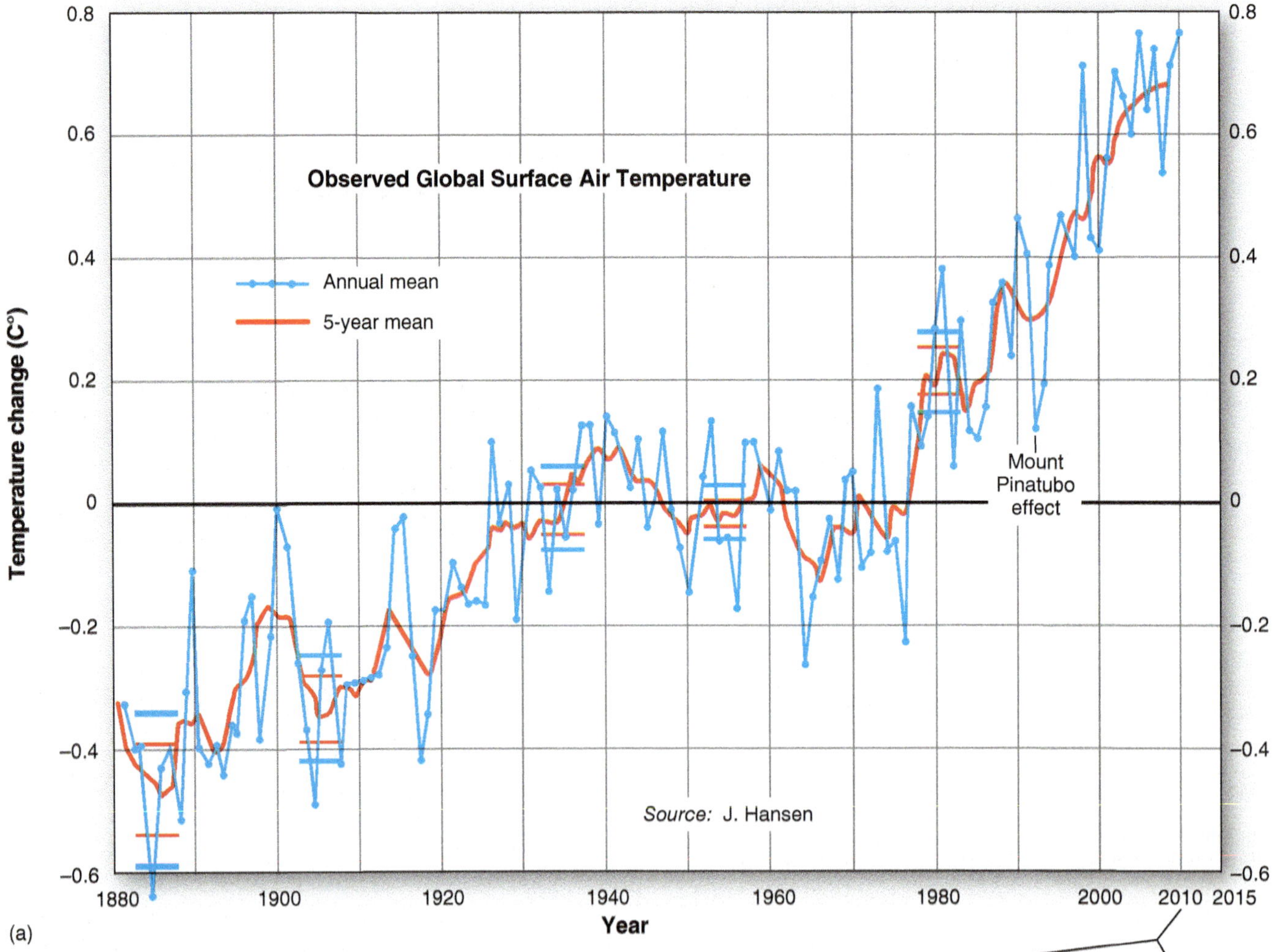

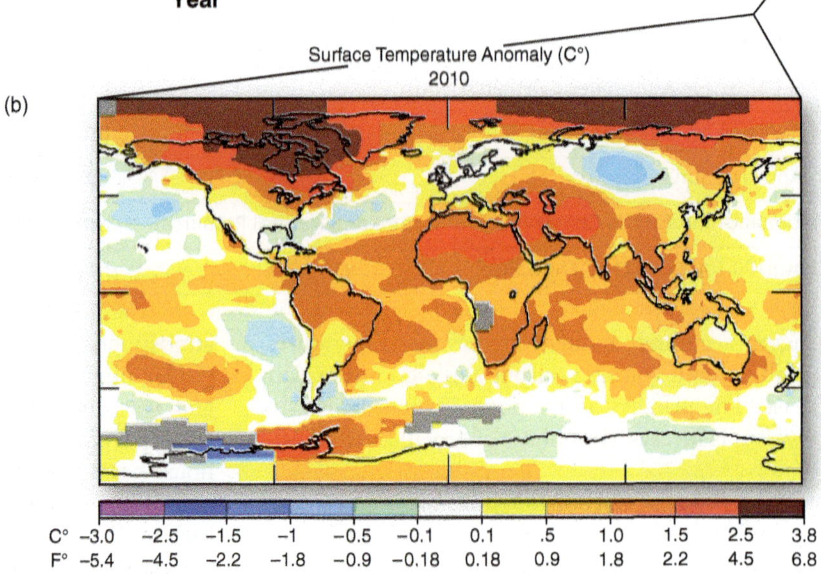

(a)

(b)

MG Animation Global Warming, Climate Change

FIGURE 25 Global temperature trends.
(a) Global land-surface air temperature trends from 1880 to 2010. The 0 baseline represents the 1951–1980 global average. Comparing average temperature anomalies and 5-year mean temperatures gives a sense of overall trends. (b) Temperature anomalies for 2010. The coloration represents C° departures from the base period 1951–1980. [(a), (b) Data courtesy of Dr. James Hansen, GISS/NASA, and NCDC/NOAA.]

China leads the world in CO_2 emissions

Over the past several years, China took the lead for carbon dioxide emissions, with the United States a close second. China, with 19.5% of global population, produces 4.6 tons per person, whereas the United States, with 4.5% of world population, is at 19.8 tons of CO_2 emissions per person. Clearly, per capita CO_2 emissions in the United States are far above an average person in China produces.

Figure 27 we see present levels at 1780 ppb. We are at an atmospheric concentration of methane far higher than at any time in the past 800 millennia.

Methane is generated by such organic processes as digestion and rotting in the absence of oxygen (anaerobic processes). About 50% of the excess methane comes from bacterial action in the intestinal tracts of livestock and from organic activity in flooded rice fields. Burning of vegetation causes another 20% of the excess, and bacterial action inside the digestive systems of termite populations also is a significant source. Methane is thought responsible for at least 19% of the total atmospheric warming.

Nitrous oxide (N_2O) is the third most important greenhouse gas that is forced by human activity—up 17% in atmospheric concentration since 1750 and now higher than at any time in the past 10,000 years (Figure 27). Fertilizer use increases the processes in soil that emit nitrous oxide, although more research is needed to fully understand the relationships. CFCs and other halocarbons also contribute to global warming. CFCs absorb longwave energy missed by carbon dioxide and water vapor in the lower troposphere.

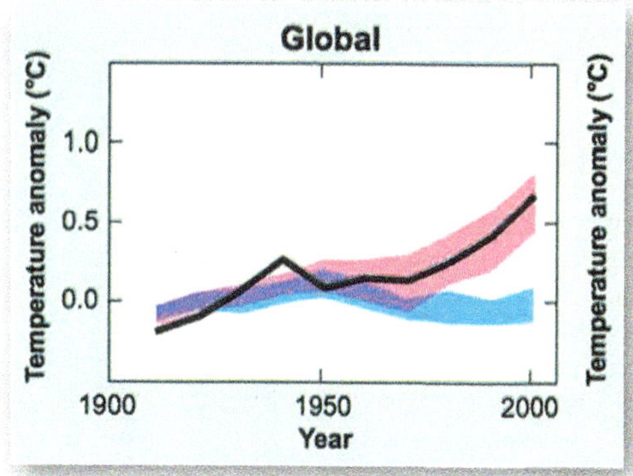

FIGURE 26 Explaining global temperature changes. Computer models accurately track observed temperature change (black line) when they factor in human-forced influences on climate (pink shading). Solar activity and volcanoes do not explain the increases (blue shading). [IPCC, Working Group I, *Fourth Assessment Report: Climate Change 2007: The Physical Science Basis* (Geneva, Switzerland: IPCC Secretariat, February 2007), Fig. SPM-4, p. 11.]

CRITICAL THINKING 2

The forcing element of fuel economy

Transportation is the major sector producing carbon dioxide emissions. In effect since 1975 in the United States, corporate average fuel economy (CAFÉ) requirements for automobiles are presently set at 27.7 mpg (8.55 L/100 km). For light trucks (including SUVs), these requirements were set at 22.2 mpg in 2007 (10.6 L/100 km) and changed to 23.5 in 2010. In Figure 2.1, examine the higher standards in all the other countries sampled.

A 10-mile-per-gallon increase in efficiency could save more than a million barrels of oil per day, or more than half of U.S. imports from the Persian Gulf states, making a 35-mpg goal for 2020 quite appealing. Increased numbers of drivers and driving will negate some of these savings, making the solution more complex than just having more-fuel-efficient cars and trucks. Study the graph, and explain the relative inefficiency of U.S. vehicles. Why are U.S. fuel standards about half those of the European Union and so far below the standard enforced in China? Why is having higher CAFÉ standards such a hard sell, given the price of fuel and all the problems involved with importing oil (conflicts, oil spills, balance of trade deficits) and drilling for oil? How do we communicate the upfront savings in money for drivers and the improved air quality that higher standards would bring?

FIGURE 2.1 Fuel economy standards for selected countries.
[Adapted from IPCC, *Fourth Assessment Report: Climate Change 2007: Mitigation and Climate Change* (Geneva, Switzerland: IPCC Secretariat, February 2007), Fig. 5.18, p. 373.]

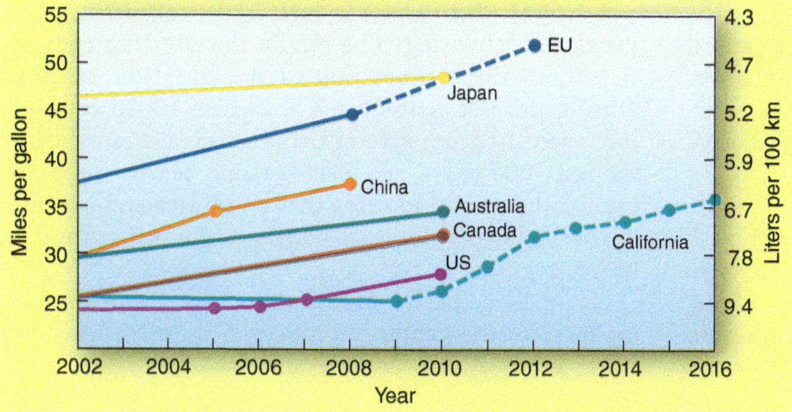

Climate Models and Forecasts

In addition to actual measurements of climatic elements and the paleoclimatic records, scientists use computer models to run climate-forecasting programs. The scientific challenge in understanding climate change is to sense climatic trends in what is essentially a nonlinear, chaotic natural system. Imagine the tremendous task of building a computer model of all climatic components and programming these linkages over different time frames and at various scales.

Using mathematical models originally established for forecasting weather, scientists developed a complex computer climate model known as a **general circulation model (GCM)**. At least a dozen established GCMs are now in operation around the world. Submodel programs for the atmosphere, ocean, land surface, cryosphere, and biosphere operate within the GCM. The most sophisticated models couple atmosphere and ocean submodels and are known as *Atmosphere–Ocean General Circulation Models (AOGCMs)*.

The first step is defining a manageable portion of Earth's climatic system for study. Climatologists create dimensional "grid boxes" that extend from beneath the ocean to the tropopause, in multiple layers (Figure 28). Resolution of these boxes in the atmosphere has greatly improved, and they are now sized at 180 km (112 mi) in the horizontal and 1 km (0.6 mi) in the vertical; in

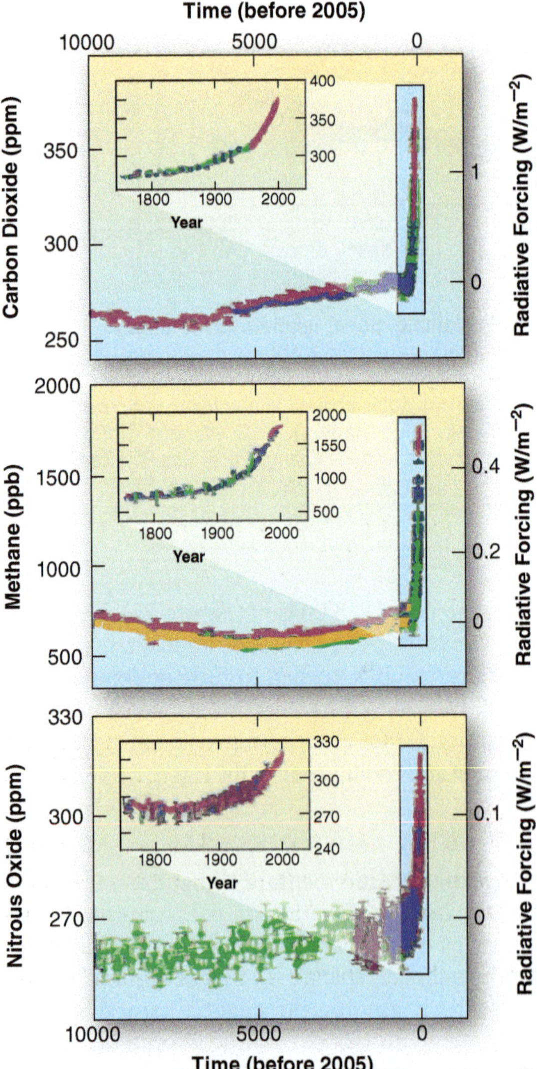

FIGURE 27 Greenhouse gas changes over the last 10,000 years. Ice-core and modern data show the trends in carbon dioxide, methane, and nitrous oxide over the last 10,000 years. We are living in unique territory on these graphs. To update, during May 2011, CO_2 passed the 394 ppm level, CH_4 was at 1780 ppb, and N_2O approached 330 ppb. [IPCC, Working Group I, *Fourth Assessment Report: Climate Change 2007: The Physical Science Basis* (Geneva, Switzerland: IPCC Secretariat, February 2007), Fig. SPM-1, p. 3.]

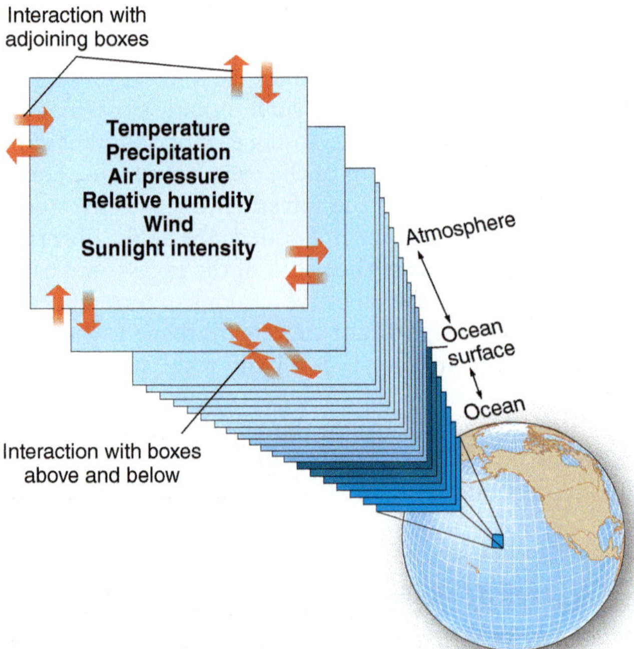

FIGURE 28 A general circulation model scheme. Temperature, precipitation, air pressure, relative humidity, wind, and sunlight intensity are sampled in myriad grid boxes. In the ocean, sampling is limited, but temperature, salinity, and ocean current data are considered. The interactions within a grid layer and between layers on all six sides are modeled in a general circulation model program.

the ocean, the boxes use the same horizontal and a vertical resolution of about 200 to 400 m (650–1300 ft). Analysts deal not only with the climatic components within each grid layer, but also with the interaction among the layers on all sides.

Temperature Scenarios A comparative benchmark among the operational GCMs is *climatic sensitivity* to doubling of carbon dioxide levels in the atmosphere. GCMs do not predict specific temperatures, but they do offer various scenarios of global warming. GCM-generated maps correlate well with the observed global warming patterns experienced since 1990.

The 2007 IPCC *Fourth Assessment Report*, using a variety of GCM forecast scenarios, predicted a range of average surface warming for this century. Figure 29 illustrates six of these scenarios, each with its own assumptions of economics, population, degree of global cooperation, and greenhouse gas emission levels. The orange line is the simulation experiment where greenhouse gas emissions are held at 2000 values with no increases. The gray bars give you the best estimate and likely ranges of outcomes—for example, from a "low forecast" in B1 to a "high forecast" in A1FI. Even the "B" scenario represents a significant increase in global land and ocean temperatures and will produce consequences.

Sea-Level Changes Sea-level rise is occurring, and the rate accelerating. The rate in the late 20th century was about three times that of the late 19th century. During the last century, sea level rose 10–20 cm (4–8 in.), a rate 10 times greater than the average rate during the last 3000 years. Sea level is rising because of melting ice sheets and glaciers that add water and because of thermal expansion that occurs as the ocean absorbs heat energy and warms.

The 2007 IPCC forecast scenarios for global mean sea-level rise this century are already being exceeded. New

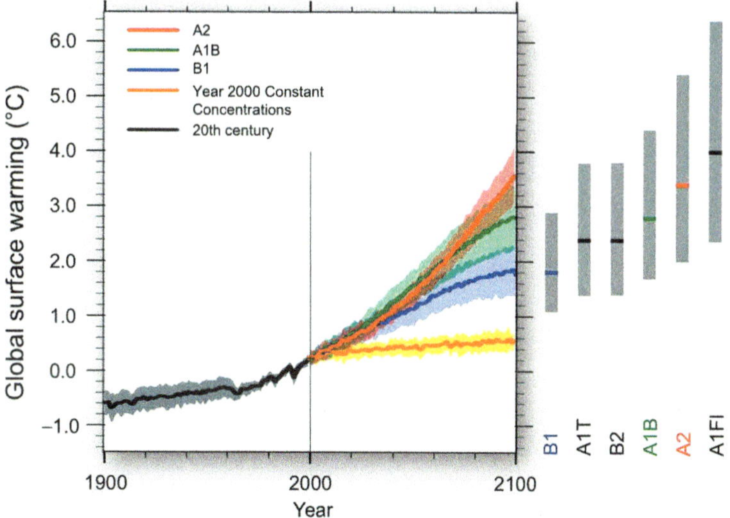

FIGURE 29 Model scenarios for surface warming.
Ranging from business as usual, lack of international cooperation, and continuation of the use of fossil fuels (A2FI) to a low-emission scenario (B1), each scenario spells climatic catastrophe to some degree. Holding emissions at the 2000 concentration (orange line plot) results in the least temperature impacts. [Graph from IPCC, Working Group I, *Fourth Assessment Report: Climate Change 2007: The Physical Science Basis* (Geneva, Switzerland: IPCC Secretariat, February 2007), Fig. SPM-5, p. 14.]

measurements of Greenland's ice-loss acceleration and Antarctic ice losses were not within the time frame for the 2007 report. Scientists are considering at least a 1.4-m (4.6-ft) "high case" for estimates of sea-level rise sometime this century as more realistic, given Greenland's present losses coupled with mountain glacial ice losses worldwide. Remember that a 0.3-m rise in sea level would produce a shoreline retreat of 30 m (98 ft) on average. Here is the concern:

> The data now available raise concerns that the climate system, in particular sea level, may be responding more quickly than climate models indicate. ... The rate of sea-level rise for the past 20 years is 25% faster than the rate of rise in any 20-year period in the preceding 115 years.... Since 1990 the observed sea-level has been rising faster than the rise projected by models.*

These increases would continue beyond 2100 even if greenhouse gas concentrations were stabilized today.

A quick survey of world coastlines shows that even a moderate rise could bring change of unparalleled proportions. At stake are the river deltas, lowland coastal farming valleys, and low-lying mainland areas, all contending with high water, high tides, and higher storm surges. Particularly tragic social and economic consequences will affect small island states, which are unable to adjust within their present country boundaries—disruption of biological systems, loss of biodiversity, reduction in water resources, and evacuation of residents are among the impacts.

The future may bring both internal and international migration of affected human populations, spread over decades, as people move away from coastal flooding caused by the sea-level rise—a 1-m rise will displace 130 million people. Presently, there is no body of world law that covers "environmental refugees."

"No Regrets"

Reading through all this climate-change science must seem pretty "heavy." Instead, think of this information as empowering and as motivation to take action—personally, locally, regionally, nationally, and globally.

The IPCC declared that "no regrets" opportunities to reduce carbon dioxide emissions are available in most countries and are defined as follows:

> No regrets options are by definition greenhouse gas emissions reduction options that have negative net costs, because they generate direct and indirect benefits that are large enough to offset the costs of implementing the options.

Benefits that equal or exceed their cost to society include reduced energy cost, improved air quality and health, reduction in tanker spills and oil imports, and deployment of renewable and sustainable energy sources, with the growth of new related business opportunities,

*S. Rahmstorf et al., "Recent climate observations compared to projections," *Science* 316, 5825 (May 4, 2007): 709.

among others. This holds true without even considering the benefits of slowing the rate of climate change.

For Europe, scientists determined that carbon emissions could be reduced to less than half the 1990 level by 2030, at a negative cost. A study by the U.S. Department of Energy's national laboratories found that we could meet the Kyoto Protocol carbon emission reduction targets with negative overall costs (cash benefit savings) ranging from –$7 to –$34 billion a year. Of course, one key to "no regrets" is untapped energy-efficiency and conservation potentials.

The most comprehensive economic analysis is *The Economics of Climate Change: The Stern Review*, prepared by Nicholas Stern for the British government (Cambridge, England: Cambridge University Press, 2007). This report concluded as follows:

- There is still time to avoid the worst impacts of climate change if we take strong action now.
- Climate change could have very serious impacts on growth and development. The costs of stabilizing the climate are significant, but manageable; delay would be dangerous and much more costly.
- Action on climate change is required across all countries, and it need not cap the aspirations of growth in rich and poor countries.
- A range of options exists to cut emissions; strong, deliberate policy action is required to motivate their use.
- Climate change demands an international response, based on shared understanding of long-term goals and agreement on frameworks for action.

CRITICAL THINKING 3

Thinking through an action plan to reduce human climate forcing

Many external factors force climate, as you can see in Figure 3.1. Let us work with the chart to see how the variables influence climate-change decisions.

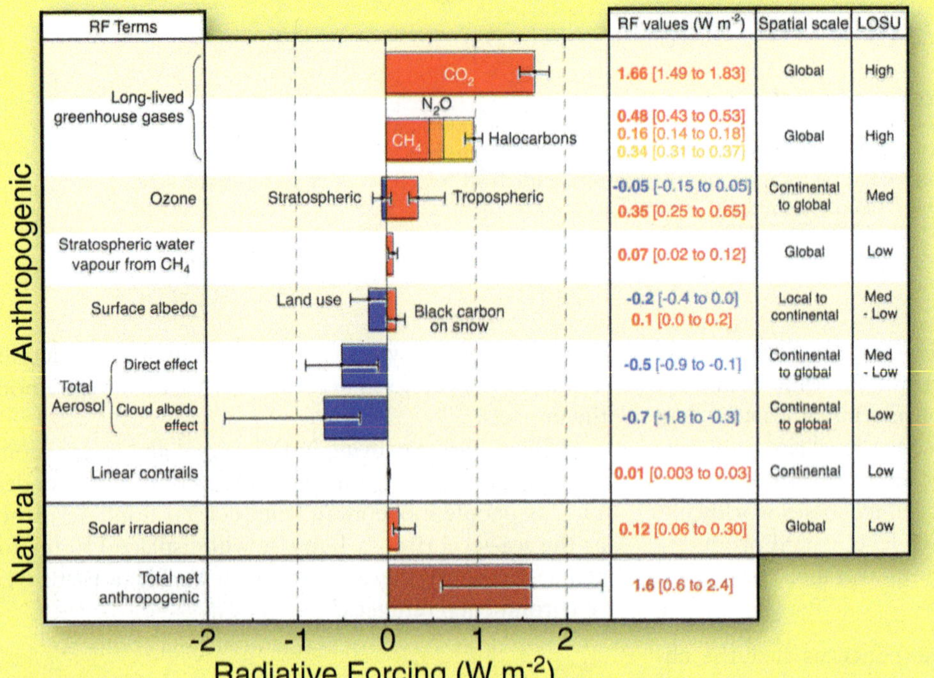

FIGURE 3.1 Analysis of radiative forcing of temperatures.
[IPCC, Working Group I, *Fourth Assessment Report: Climate Change 2007: The Physical Science Basis* (Geneva, Switzerland: IPCC Secretariat, February 2007), Figure SPM-2, p. 4, and Figure 2.20, p. 203.]

The estimates of radiative forcing (RF) in watts-per-square-meter units are given on the x-axis (horizontal axis). In the far-right column, LOSU refers to "level of scientific understanding." Those bars that extend to the right of the "0" value (in red, orange, and yellow) indicate warming, or *positive forcing*, such as "long-lived greenhouse gases." Bars that go to the left of the "0" value (in blue) indicate cooling, or *negative forcing*, such as cloud-albedo effect. Each bar also includes an estimate of the uncertainty range.

Assume you are a policy maker with a goal of reducing the rate of climate change—that is, reducing positive radiative forcing of the climate system. What strategies do you suggest to alter the extent of the columns and adjust the mix of elements that cause temperature increases? Assign priorities to each suggested strategy to denote the most- to least-effective strategies in moderating climate change. Brainstorm and discuss your strategies with others.

GEOSYSTEMS CONNECTION

Climate classification categories give us a portrait of energy and moisture and of solar insolation and surface energy budgets and provide a baseline that we can use to track changing climatic boundaries, given climate change.

KEY LEARNING CONCEPTS REVIEW

■ ***Define*** climate and climatology, and ***explain*** the difference between climate and weather.

Climate is a synthesis of weather phenomena at many scales, from planetary to local, in contrast to weather, which is the condition of the atmosphere at any given time and place. Earth experiences a wide variety of climatic conditions that can be grouped by general similarities into climatic regions. **Climatology** is the study of climate and attempts to discern similar weather statistics and identify **climatic regions**.

climate
climatology
climatic regions

1. Define climate and compare it with weather. What is climatology?
2. Explain how a climatic region synthesizes climate statistics.

■ ***Review*** the principal components of climate, and ***relate*** the development of classification systems.

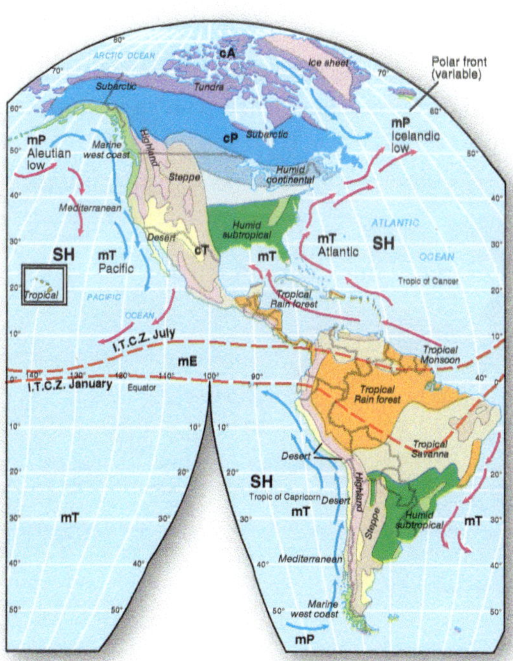

Climatic inputs include insolation (pattern of solar energy in the Earth–atmosphere environment), temperature (sensible heat energy content of the air), precipitation (the supply of moisture), air pressure (varying patterns of atmospheric density), and air masses (regional-sized homogeneous units of air). **Classification** is the process of ordering or grouping data in related categories. A **genetic classification** is one based on causative factors, such as the interaction of air masses. An **empirical classification** is one based on statistical data, such as temperature or precipitation. This text analyzes climate using aspects of both approaches, with a map based on climatological elements.

classification
genetic classification
empirical classification

3. How do radiation receipts, temperature, air-pressure inputs, and precipitation patterns interact to produce climate types? Give an example from a humid environment and one from an arid environment.
4. Evaluate the relationships among a climatic region, an ecosystem, and a biome.
5. What are the differences between a genetic and an empirical classification system?
6. What are some of the climatological elements used in classifying climates? Why is each of these used? Use the approach on the climate classification map in Figure 2 in preparing your answer.

■ ***Describe*** the principal climate classification categories, and ***locate*** these regions on a world map.

Keep in mind that temperature and precipitation are measurable results produced by interacting elements of weather and climate. These data are plotted on a **climograph** to display the characteristics of the climate.

World climates are grouped into six basic categories. Temperature and precipitation considerations form the basis of five climate categories and their regional types:

- Tropical (tropical latitudes)
  rain forest (rainy all year)
  monsoon (6 to 12 months rainy)
  savanna (less than 6 months rainy)
- Mesothermal (midlatitudes, mild winters)
  humid subtropical (hot to warm summers)
  marine west coast (warm to cool summers)
  Mediterranean (dry summers)
- Microthermal (mid and high latitudes, cold winters)
  humid continental (hot to warm, mild summers)
  subarctic (cool summers to very cold winters)
- Polar (high latitudes and polar regions)
  tundra (high latitude or high elevation)
  ice caps and ice sheets (perpetually frozen)
  polar marine (moderate polar climate)
- Highland (high elevations at all latitudes)

Only one climate category is based on moisture efficiency as well as temperature:

- Dry (permanent moisture deficits)
  arid deserts (tropical, subtropical hot and midlatitude cold)
  semiarid steppes (tropical, subtropical hot and midlatitude cold)

  climograph

7. List and discuss each of the principal climate categories. In which one of these general types do you live? Which category is the only type associated with the annual distribution and amount of precipitation?
8. What is a climograph, and how is it used to display climatic information?
9. Which of the major climate types occupies the most land and ocean area on Earth?
10. Characterize the tropical climates in terms of temperature, moisture, and location.
11. Using Africa's tropical climates as an example, characterize the climates produced by the seasonal shifting of the ITCZ with the high Sun.
12. Mesothermal climates occupy the second largest portion of Earth's entire surface. Describe their temperature, moisture, and precipitation characteristics.
13. Explain the distribution of the *humid subtropical hot-summer* and *Mediterranean dry-summer* climates at similar latitudes and the difference in precipitation patterns between the two types. Describe the difference in vegetation associated with these two climate types.
14. Which climates are characteristic of the Asian monsoon region?
15. Explain how a *marine west coast* climate can occur in the Appalachian region of the eastern United States.
16. What role do offshore ocean currents play in the distribution of the *marine west coast* climates? What type of fog is formed in these regions?
17. Discuss the climatic conditions for the coldest places on Earth outside the poles.

- ***Explain*** the precipitation and moisture efficiency criteria used to determine the arid and semiarid climates.

The dry climates of the tropics and midlatitudes consist of arid deserts and semiarid steppes. In arid deserts, precipitation (the natural water supply) is less than one-half of natural water demand. In *semiarid steppes*, precipitation is more than one-half of natural water demand. A **steppe** is a regional term referring to the vast semiarid grassland biome of Eastern Europe and Asia.

steppe

18. In general terms, what are the differences among the four desert classifications? How are moisture and temperature distributions used to differentiate these subtypes?
19. Relative to the distribution of arid and semiarid climates, describe at least three locations where they occur across the globe and the reasons for their presence in these locations.

- ***Explain*** the causes and potential consequences of climate change, and ***outline*** future climate patterns from forecasts.

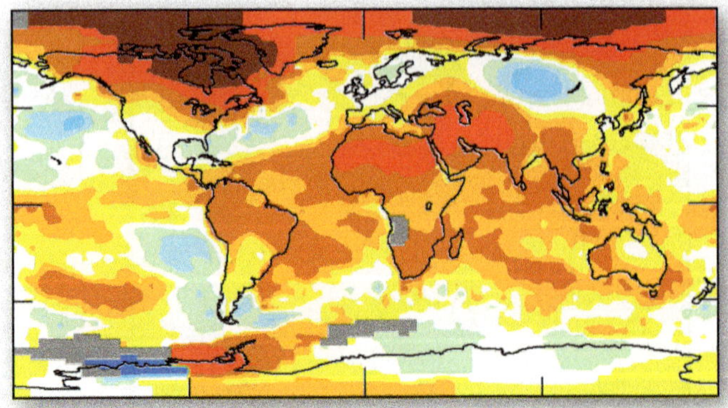

Various activities of present-day society are producing climatic changes, particularly a global warming trend. The highest average annual temperatures experienced since the advent of instrumental measurements have dominated the last 25 years. The scientific consensus is that climate change is related to the anthropogenic impacts that are enhancing the greenhouse effect.

Natural climatic variability over the span of Earth's history is the subject of **paleoclimatology**. A **general circulation model (GCM)** forecasts climate patterns and is providing greater capability and accuracy than in the past. People and their political institutions can use GCM forecasts to formulate policies aimed at reducing unwanted climate change.

paleoclimatology
general circulation model (GCM)

20. Explain climate forecasts. How do general circulation models (GCMs) produce such forecasts?

21. Describe the potential climatic effects of global warming on polar and high-latitude regions. What are the implications of these climatic changes for persons living at lower latitudes?

22. How is climatic change affecting agricultural and food production? Natural environments? Forests? The possible spread of disease?

23. What are the actions being taken at present to delay the effects of global climate change? What is the Kyoto Protocol? What is the current status of the U.S. government action on the protocol?

MasteringGEOGRAPHY™

Visit **http://www.masteringgeography.com/** for several figure animations, satellite loops, self-study quizzes, flashcards, visual glossary, case studies, career links, text reference maps, RSS Feeds, and an ebook version of *Elemental Geosystems*. Included are many geography web links to interesting Internet sources that support this chapter.

In New Mexico west of Santa Fe, near Los Alamos, in the Bandelier National Monument and Jemez Mountains (photo at about 2300 m, 7545 ft, elevation), climate change impacts are forcing out ponderosa pines as drought and bark beetles take their toll—replaced by juniper–piñon pine trees. In response, wildfires are increasing as temperatures rise and precipitation and soil-moisture decline (see photo of remote weather monitoring station that is tracking change). Over half the Monument burned in 1977, 1996, 2000, and 2007. Fires struck the area near Los Alamos and nearby mountains in June 2011 (see inset photo). Such climate–forest interactions are forecasted to accelerate in the coming decades. [Photos by Author.]

The Dynamic Planet

The Dynamic Planet

Pico de Fogo volcano, in the Cape Verde Islands in the Atlantic Ocean, rises to 2830 m (9285 ft). An eruption from the small vent cone on the slopes of Pico (stained with sulfur compounds) happened in 1995. This forced the evacuation of the village Chã das Caldeiras, located in the crater of the larger volcano Chã, which last erupted in 1637. Farming, including some vineyards and coffee, is done in the volcanic soils; homes are built with blocks of basaltic rock. [Bobbé Christopherson.]

KEY LEARNING CONCEPTS

After reading the chapter, you should be able to:

- ***Distinguish*** between the endogenic and exogenic systems, ***determine*** the driving force for each, and ***explain*** the pace at which these systems operate.
- ***Diagram*** Earth's interior in cross section, and ***describe*** each distinct layer.
- ***Illustrate*** the geologic cycle, and ***relate*** the rock cycle and rock types to endogenic and exogenic processes.
- ***Describe*** Pangaea and its breakup, and ***relate*** several physical proofs that crustal drifting is continuing today.
- ***Portray*** the pattern of Earth's major plates, and ***relate*** this pattern to the occurrence of earthquakes, volcanic activity, and hot spots.

Earth's Migrating Magnetic Poles

In this chapter, we journey to the center of Earth and study Earth's core, divided between a solid inner core and a dense, but fluid outer core. Earth's magnetic field is principally generated by motions in this outer core. Consider the north geographic pole—the axial pole centered where the meridians of longitude converge. This is *true north* and is a fixed point. However, Earth's magnetic field is focused at a different set of poles, which move at a measurable rate.

Before the Global Positioning System (GPS) was in widespread use, people relied on the compass to find direction. On a compass, the needle points to the *North Magnetic Pole* (NMP). At this pole on Earth's surface, the magnetic field is directed vertically downward, the magnetic dip. This is the observed magnetic pole, located and mapped by magnetic surveys.

When the compass needle indicates the NMP, this is not the same as the geographic pole, or true north. Based on the location where you are measuring with the compass, there could be an angular distance in degrees between the NMP and true north. This is the magnetic declination.

In 2008, north of San Francisco, California, the declination was 15° west. However, at the junction of the Iowa, Missouri, and Illinois borders the declination was 0°; in other words, the NMP and true north were aligned. In Boston, the declination was 15° east. To get true north from your compass reading, you add or subtract the declination accordingly. Isogonal maps plot lines of equal magnetic declination. Most topographic maps give you this information in a corner legend, but it is only accurate for the date the map was printed. Why? The NMP is on the move.

As the magnetic field of Earth changes, the NMP slowly drifts across the Canadian Arctic. The NMP moved 1100 km (685 mi) just this past century. Presently the NMP is moving northwest toward Siberia at approximately 50 km (31 mi) per year, and since 2007, the rate of movement has increased to 55–60 km (34–37 mi) per year. The observed positions for 1831–2012 are mapped in Figure GN 1. Each day the actual magnetic pole migrates in a small oval pattern around the average locations given on the map. The Geological Survey of Canada (GSC) tracks the motion of the NMP and the pole's location (see http://gsc.nrcan.gc.ca/geomag/nmp/northpole_e.php), a collaborative effort with the Bureau de Recherches Géologiques et Minières in France.

In 2012, the NMP is near 85.9° N by 147° W in the Canadian Arctic. Its antipode, or opposite pole, is the South Magnetic Pole (SMP), which lies off the coast of Wilkes Land, Antarctica. The SMP moves separately from the NMP and is presently headed northwest at just 5 km (3.1 mi) per year. This chapter discusses the changing intensity of Earth's magnetic field and how the field periodically reverses polarity. Earth's magnetic field affects animal migration. Birds and turtles, among others, can read magnetic declination. ■

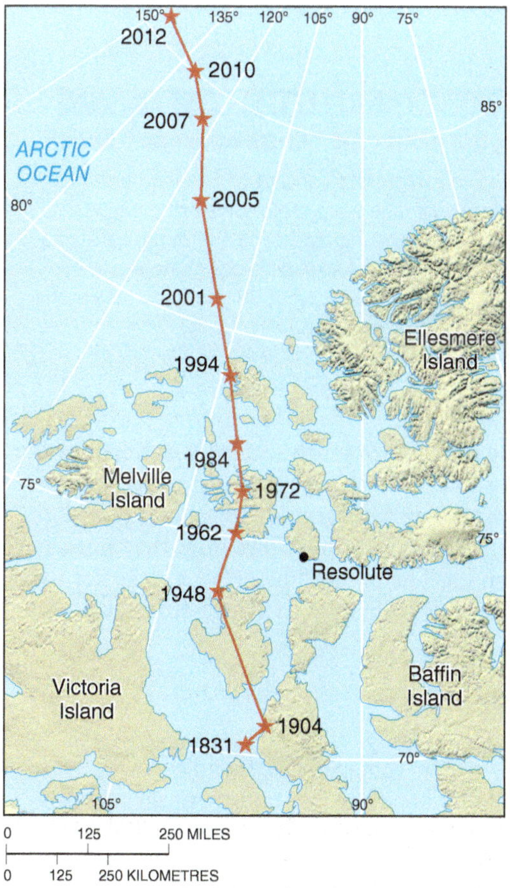

FIGURE GN 1 North Magnetic Pole movement, 1831 to 2012.

TABLE GN 1 Approximate North Magnetic Pole Coordinates, 2001 to 2015

Year	Latitude (°N)	Longitude (°W)
2001	81.3	110.8
2002	81.6	111.6
2003	82.0	112.4
2004	82.3	113.4
2005	82.7	114.4
2006	83.9	119.9
2007	84.4	121.7
2008	84.2	124.9
2009	84.9	131.0
2010	85.0	132.6
2011	85.1	134.0
2012	85.9	147.0
2015 prediction	86.1	153.0

Discoveries have revolutionized our understanding of Earth systems science and how continents and oceans came to be arranged as they are. A new era of understanding is emerging, combining various sciences within the study of physical geography. Events such as the March 2011 earthquake and tsunami that devastated Japan turn world attention to the spatial sciences for explanation. One task of physical geography is to explain the spatial implications of all this new information and real-world applications.

In this chapter: Earth's interior is organized as a core surrounded by roughly concentric shells of material. It is unevenly heated by the radioactive decay of unstable elements. A rock cycle produces three classes of rocks through igneous, sedimentary, and metamorphic processes. Internal processes—coupled with the rock cycle, hydrologic cycle, and tectonic cycle—result in a varied crustal surface, featuring irregular fractures, extensive mountain ranges both on land and on the ocean floor, drifting continental and oceanic crust, and frequent earthquakes and volcanic events. All of this movement of material results from *endogenic* forces within Earth—the subject of this chapter.

The Pace of Change

The **geologic time scale** is a summary timeline of all Earth history, shown in Figure 1. It reflects currently accepted names of time intervals for each segment of Earth's history, from vast *eons* through briefer *eras*, *periods*, and *epochs*. Present thinking places Earth's age at about 4.6 billion years, with the Moon about 30 million years younger, formed when a Mars-sized object struck the early Earth.

The time scale depicts two important kinds of time: *relative* (what happened in what order) and *absolute* (actual number of years before the present). Also on the geologic time scale, see the labels denoting the six major extinctions of life forms in Earth history. Rather than being complete extinctions, think of some of these spasms in planetary life as significant depletions. These range from 440 million years ago (m.y.a.) to the ongoing present-day episode caused by modern civilization.

Relative time is the sequence of events, based on the relative positions of rock strata above or below each other. Relative time is based on the important general principle of *superposition*, which states that *rock and sediment always are arranged with the youngest beds "superposed" toward the top of a rock formation and the oldest at the base, if they have not been disturbed*. The study of these sequences is *stratigraphy*. Thus, relative time places the Precambrian at the bottom (beginning) of the time scale and the Holocene (today) at the top. Important time clues—namely, *fossils*, the remains of ancient plants and animals—lie embedded within these strata. Since approximately 4.0 billion years ago, life has left its evolving imprint in the rocks.

Scientific methods such as radiometric dating determine *absolute time*, the actual "millions of years ago" shown on the time scale. These absolute ages permit scientists to actively update geologic time, refining the time-scale sequence and lending greater accuracy to relative dating sequences. For more on the geologic time scale, see http://www.ucmp.berkeley.edu/exhibit/geology.html.

Holocene is the name given to the youngest epoch in the geologic time scale, consisting of the last 11,500 years since the retreat of the continental glaciers. Because of the impact of human society on planetary systems, discussion is under way about designating a new name for the human epoch. A proposal is to call this time the *Anthropocene*.

However, when would such a time begin? Some think the beginning of the Industrial Revolution in the 18th century is the starting point, whereas others think an appropriate time is some 5000 years ago, when Asians began flooding rice fields that released methane gas into the atmosphere. Or perhaps 8000 years ago is a better chronology with the spread of domesticated crops, widespread clearing of forests, and the human use of fire to modify environments. Human impacts on the atmosphere began at the roots of civilization.

CRITICAL THINKING 1
Thoughts about an "Anthropocene" Epoch

Take a moment to explore this concept of naming our human epoch in the geologic time scale. Determine some arguments for such a change considering landscape alteration, deforestation, and climate change. If we were to designate the late Holocene as the Anthropocene, what do you think the criteria for the beginning date should be?

A guiding principle of Earth science is **uniformitarianism**, which assumes that *the same physical processes active in the environment today have been operating throughout geologic time*. For example, if streams carve valleys now, they must have done so 500 m.y.a. The phrase "the present is the key to the past" describes this principle. Evidence from exploration

GEO REPORT 1 Radioactive dating and Earth time

Radiometric dating of Earth materials involves the steady decay of certain atoms. An atom contains protons and neutrons in its nucleus. Certain forms of atoms called isotopes have unstable nuclei; that is, the protons and neutrons do not remain together indefinitely. As particles break away and the nucleus disintegrates, radiation is emitted, and the atom decays into a different element—this process is *radioactivity*. This provides the steady time clock needed to measure the age of ancient rocks, since the decay rates for different isotopes are determined precisely. Scientists compare the amount of original isotope in the sample with the amount of decayed end product in the sample to determine the date the rock formed.

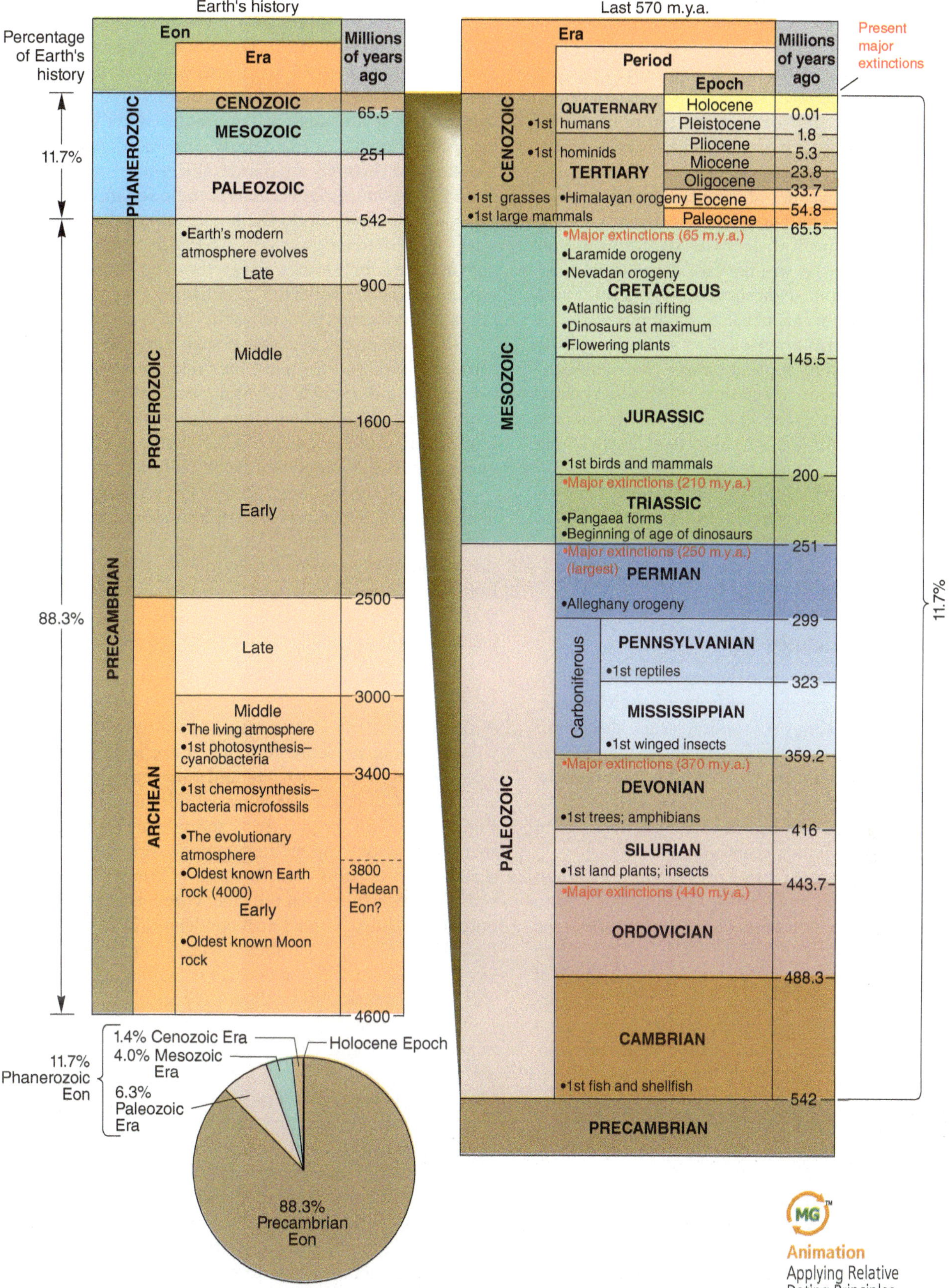

MG Animation
Applying Relative Dating Principles

FIGURE 1 Geologic time scale, showing highlights of Earth's history.
The six major extinctions or depletions of life forms are shown in red. The sixth extinction episode is under way at the present time. In the column to the left and the pie chart, note that 88.3% of geologic time occurred during the Precambrian Eon. Dates appear in m.y.a. (million years ago). [Data and update from Geological Society of America and *Nature* 429 (May 13, 2004): 124–125.]

and from the landscape record of volcanic eruptions, earthquakes, and exogenic processes supports uniformitarianism. The concept was first proposed by James Hutton in his *Theory of the Earth* (1795) and was later amplified by Charles Lyell in *Principles of Geology* (1830).

Within the principle of uniformitarianism, catastrophic events such as massive landslides, earthquakes, volcanic episodes, extraterrestrial asteroid impacts, and sometimes recurring episodes of mountain building punctuate geologic time. Vast superfloods occurred as ice-blocked lakes tore through their frozen dams in the later days of the last ice age, as was the case with glacial Lake Missoula, which left evidence across a broad region. These localized catastrophic events occur as small interruptions in the generally uniform processes that shape the slowly evolving landscape. Here the *punctuated equilibrium* concept (interruptions occur in the flow of events; systems jump to new operation levels) studied in the life sciences and paleontology might apply to aspects of Earth's long developmental history.

We start our journey deep within the planet. A knowledge of Earth's internal structure and energy is key to understanding the surface.

Earth's Structure and Internal Energy

Along with the other planets and the Sun, Earth is thought to have condensed and congealed from a nebula of dust, gas, and icy comets about 4.6 billion years ago. Until recently, the oldest known surface rocks on Earth were thought to be in northwestern Canada. The Acasta Gneiss is a 3.96-billion-year-old formation; the nearby Slave Province rocks date to 4.03 billion years old. Rocks from Greenland date to 3.8 billion years old.

Detrital zircons (particles of preexisting zirconium silica oxides that formed rock) in Western Australia date to between 4.2 and 4.4 billion years old and are possibly the oldest materials in Earth's crust. Research in 2008 found mineral grains in the Nuvvuagittuq greenstone belt of northern Quebec, Canada, that date to 4.28 billion years old. These discoveries tell us something significant: Earth was forming continental crust at least 4 billion years ago, during the Archean Eon. Although not an official designation, note the Hadean Eon in Figure 1, the proposed name for the period before the Archean.

As Earth solidified, gravity sorted materials by density. Heavier substances such as iron gravitated slowly to its center, and lighter elements such as silica slowly welled upward to the surface and became concentrated in the crust. Consequently, Earth's interior is sorted into roughly concentric layers, each one distinct in either chemical composition or temperature. Heat energy migrates outward from the center by conduction and by physical convection in the more fluid or plastic layers in the mantle and nearer the surface.

Our knowledge of Earth's *internal differentiation* into these layers is acquired entirely through indirect evidence because we are unable to drill more than a few kilometers into Earth's crust. For example, when an earthquake sends shock waves through the planet, the cooler areas, which generally are more rigid, transmit these **seismic waves** at a higher velocity than do the hotter areas, where seismic waves are slowed to lower velocity. Plastic zones simply do not transmit some seismic waves; they absorb them. Some seismic waves are reflected as densities change, whereas others are refracted, or bent, as they travel through Earth.

Thus, the distinctive ways in which seismic waves pass through Earth and the time they take to travel between two surface points help seismologists deduce the structure of Earth. This is the science of *seismic tomography*, as if Earth is subjected to a kind of CAT scan with every earthquake. Figure 2 is a model of Earth's interior.

On the *MasteringGeography* web site, you will find a map illustrating the dimensions of Earth's interior compared with surface distances in North America to give you a sense of size and scale. An airplane flying from Anchorage, Alaska, to Fort Lauderdale, Florida, would travel the same distance as that from Earth's center to its surface. The last 30 km of that journey represent the thickness of Earth's crust.

Earth's Core and Magnetism

A third of Earth's entire mass, but only a sixth of its volume, lies in its dense core. The **core** is differentiated into two regions—*inner core* and *outer core*—divided by a transition zone several hundred kilometers wide (see Figure 2b). The inner core is thought to be solid iron that is well above the melting temperature of iron at the surface, but remains solid because of tremendous pressure. Scientists think that the inner core formed before the outer core, shortly after Earth condensed. The iron is not pure, but probably is combined with silicon, and possibly oxygen and sulfur. The outer core is molten, metallic iron with lighter densities than the inner core.

The fluid outer core generates at least 90% of Earth's magnetic field and the magnetosphere that surrounds and protects Earth from solar wind and cosmic radiation. One hypothesis explains that circulation in the outer core converts thermal and gravitational energy into magnetic energy, producing Earth's magnetic field. The locations of the north and south magnetic poles are surface expressions of Earth's magnetic field and migrate as plotted on the map in *Geosystems Now* for this chapter.

An intriguing feature of Earth's magnetic field is that its polarity sometimes fades to zero and then returns to full

Earth on the scales

How much does our planet weigh? A revised estimate of Earth's mass, or weight, calculated in 2000 set its weight at 5.972 sextillion metric tons (5972 followed by 18 zeros).

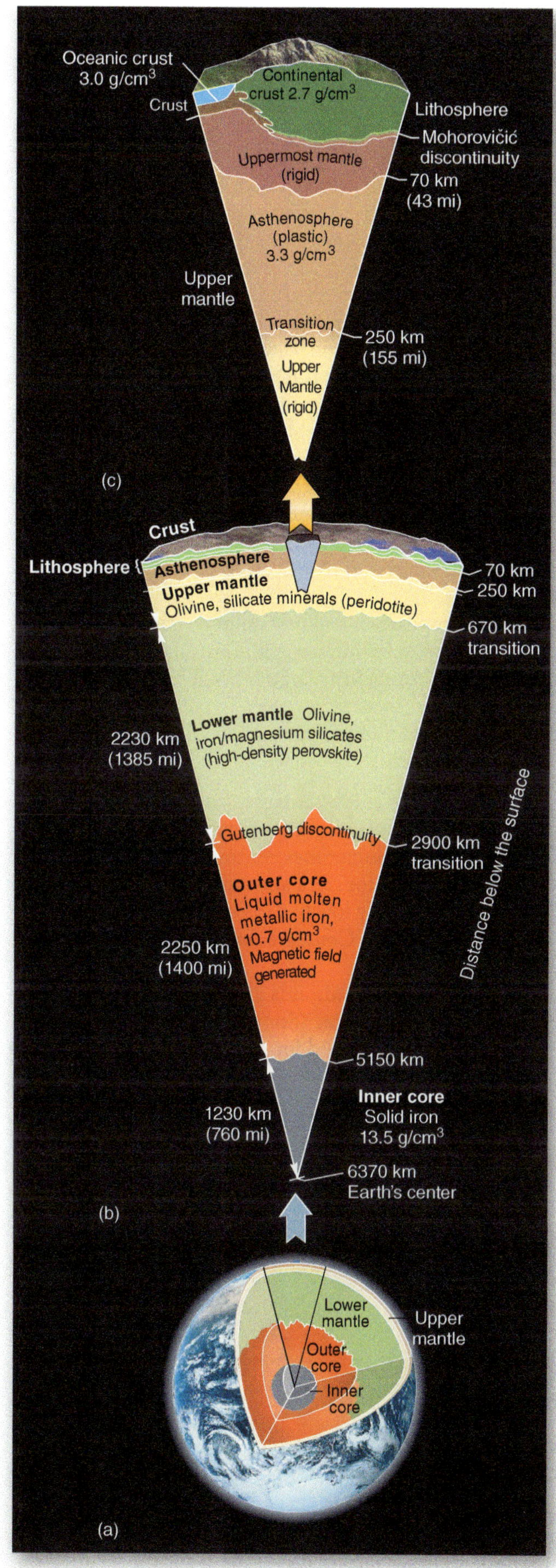

FIGURE 2 **Earth in cross section.**
(a) Cutaway showing Earth's interior. (b) Earth's interior in cross section, from the inner core to the crust. (c) Detail of the structure of the lithosphere and its relation to the asthenosphere. (For comparison to the densities noted, the density of water is 1.0 g/cm³, and that of mercury, a liquid metal, is 13.0 g/cm³.) [Photo from NASA.]

MG Notebook Distances from Earth's Core to Crust

strength, with the NMP and SMP reversed. In the process, the field does not blink on and off, but instead diminishes slowly to low intensity, perhaps 25% strength, and then rapidly regains full power. This **geomagnetic reversal** has taken place nine times during the past 4 million years and hundreds of times over Earth's history. During the transition interval of low strength, Earth's surface receives higher levels of cosmic radiation and solar particles, but note that past reversals do not correlate with species extinctions. The evolution of life has weathered many of these transitions.

The average period of a magnetic reversal is about 500,000 years; several hundred documented occurrences varied from as short as 20,000 to 30,000 years to 50 million years. Transition periods of low intensity last from 1000 to 10,000 years. The last reversal was 790,000 years ago, preceded by a transition ranging from 2000 years in length along the equator to 10,000 years in the midlatitudes. Given present rates of magnetic field decay over the last 150 years, we are perhaps 1000 years away from entering the next phase of field changes, although there is no expected pattern to use to forecast the timing. An apparent trend in recent geologic time is toward more frequent reversals. Why does this happen?

The reasons for these magnetic reversals are unknown. However, the spatial patterns they create at Earth's surface are a key tool in understanding the evolution of landmasses and the movements of the continents. When new iron-bearing rocks solidify from molten material (lava) at Earth's surface, the small magnetic particles in the rocks align according to the orientation of the magnetic poles at that time. As the rocks cool and solidify, this alignment locks in place. When Earth is with weak polarity in its magnetic field, a random pattern of magnetism in crustal rock results.

All across Earth, rocks of the same age bear an identical record of magnetic reversals in the form of measurable magnetic "stripes" in any magnetic material they contain, such as iron particles. These stripes illustrate global patterns of changing magnetism. Matching segments allow scientists to reassemble past continental arrangements. Later in this chapter, we see the importance of these magnetic reversals.

Earth's Mantle

Figure 2b shows a transition zone several hundred kilometers wide at an average depth of about 2900 km (1800 mi), dividing Earth's outer core from its mantle. This zone is a *discontinuity*, or a place where physical differences occur between adjoining regions in Earth's interior. Scientists at the California Institute of Technology analyzed more than 25,000 earthquakes and determined that this transition area, called the *Gutenberg discontinuity*, is uneven, with ragged peak-and-valley-like formations. Experts think that this zone of rough texture and low velocity creates some of the motion in Earth's mantle.

The lower and upper **mantle** represents about 80% of Earth's total volume. The mantle is rich in oxides of iron and magnesium and in silicates (FeO, MgO, and SiO_2), which are dense and tightly packed at depth, grading to lesser densities toward the surface. A broad transition zone of several hundred kilometers, centered between 410 and 660 km (255–410 mi) below the surface, separates the upper mantle from the lower mantle. The entire mantle experiences a gradual temperature increase with depth and a stiffening due to increased pressures. The denser lower mantle is thought to contain a mixture of iron, magnesium, and silicates, with some calcium and aluminum. One hypothesis states that a tremendous amount of water is bound up with minerals in the mantle.

The upper mantle divides into three fairly distinct layers: upper mantle, asthenosphere, and uppermost mantle, shown in Figure 2c. The uppermost mantle is a high-velocity zone just below the crust where seismic waves transmit through a rigid, cooler layer. This uppermost mantle, along with the crust, makes up the **lithosphere**, approximately 45–70 km (28–43 mi) thick.

Below the lithosphere, from about 70 km down to 250 km (43 mi to 155 mi), is the **asthenosphere**, or plastic layer (from the Greek *asthenos*, meaning "weak"). It contains pockets of increased heat from radioactive decay and is susceptible to slow convective currents in these hotter, less dense materials.

Because of its dynamic condition, the asthenosphere is the least rigid region of the mantle, with densities averaging 3.3 g/cm^3 (or 3300 kg/m^3). About 10% of the asthenosphere is molten in uneven patterns and hot spots. The resulting slow movement in this zone disturbs the overlying crust and creates tectonic activity—the folding, faulting, and general deformation of surface rocks.

Earth's Lithosphere and Crust

The lithosphere includes the **crust** and uppermost mantle to about 70 km (43 mi) in depth (Figure 2c). An important internal boundary between the crust and the high-velocity portion of the uppermost mantle is another discontinuity, called the **Mohorovičić discontinuity**, or **Moho** for short. It is named for the Yugoslavian seismologist who determined that seismic waves change at this depth due to sharp contrasts of materials and densities.

Figure 2c illustrates the relation of the crust to the rest of the lithosphere and the asthenosphere below. Crustal areas beneath mountain masses extend deep, perhaps to 50–60 km (31–37 mi), whereas the crust beneath continental interiors averages about 30 km (19 mi) in thickness. Oceanic crust averages only 5 km (3 mi). The crust is only a fraction of Earth's overall mass. Drilling through the crust and Moho discontinuity (the crust–mantle boundary) into the uppermost mantle remains an elusive scientific goal.

The longest-lasting deep-drilling attempt is on the northern Kola Peninsula near Zapolyarny, Russia, 250 km north of the Arctic Circle—the *Kola Borehole*. Twenty years of high-technology drilling (1970–1989) produced a hole 12.23 km deep (7.6 mi, or 40,128 ft), purely for exploration and science. Crystalline rock 1.4 billion years old at 180°C (356°F) was reached. (See an analysis log at http://www.icdp-online.de/.) A record holder for depth for a gas well is in Oklahoma; it was stopped at 9750 m (32,000 ft) when the drill bit ran into molten sulfur.

Oceanic crust is thinner than continental crust and is the object of several drilling attempts. Over the past 40 years, the Integrated Ocean Drilling Program (IODP) completed about 1700 bore holes, yielding 160 km of sediment and rock cores and more than 35,000 samples for researchers. Much of this science windfall helped put together the puzzle of geologic time and plate tectonics. See http://www.oceandrilling.org/ for the IODP home page information.

Japan's *Chikyu*, the largest deep-ocean drilling ship, began work in 2007. The ship is the first capable of high-latitude drilling in the Arctic (Figure 3). The *Chikyu* is "riserless" in that it uses seawater as the primary drilling fluid. It can drill to 7 km, more than three times the capability of the drilling ship *JOIDES Resolution*, operated by the United States and now converted to riserless operational status.

The composition and texture of continental and oceanic crusts are quite different, and this difference is a key to the concept of drifting continents. The oceanic crust is denser than the continental crust. In collisions, the denser oceanic material plunges beneath the lighter, more buoyant continental crust.

- *Continental crust* is essentially **granite**; it is crystalline and high in silica, aluminum, potassium, calcium, and sodium. (Sometimes continental crust is called *sial*, shorthand for *si*lica and *al*uminum.) Continental crust is relatively low in density, averaging 2.7 g/cm^3 (or 2700 kg/m^3). Compare this with other densities given in Figure 2.
- *Oceanic crust* is **basalt**; it is granular and high in silica, magnesium, and iron. (Sometimes oceanic crust is called *sima*, shorthand for *si*lica and *ma*gnesium.) It

FIGURE 3 Ocean drilling ship.
The new *Chikyu* research ship began drilling core samples from the ocean floor in 2007. [IODP.]

is denser than continental crust, averaging 3.0 g/cm^3 (or 3000 kg/m^3).

Buoyancy is the principle that something less dense, such as wood, floats in something denser, such as water. The principles of buoyancy and balance were combined in the 1800s into the important principle of **isostasy**, which explains certain vertical movements of Earth's crust.

Think of Earth's crust as floating on the denser layers beneath, much as a boat floats on water. Where the load is greater, owing to glaciers, sediment, or mountains, the crust tends to sink, or ride lower in the asthenosphere. Without that load (for example, when a glacier melts), the crust rides higher, in a recovery uplift known as *isostatic rebound.* Thus, the entire crust is in a constant state of compensating adjustment, or isostasy, slowly rising and sinking in response to its burdens, as it is pushed and dragged and pulled over the asthenosphere (Figure 4). An interesting development in Alaska relates this concept of isostatic rebound and climate change.

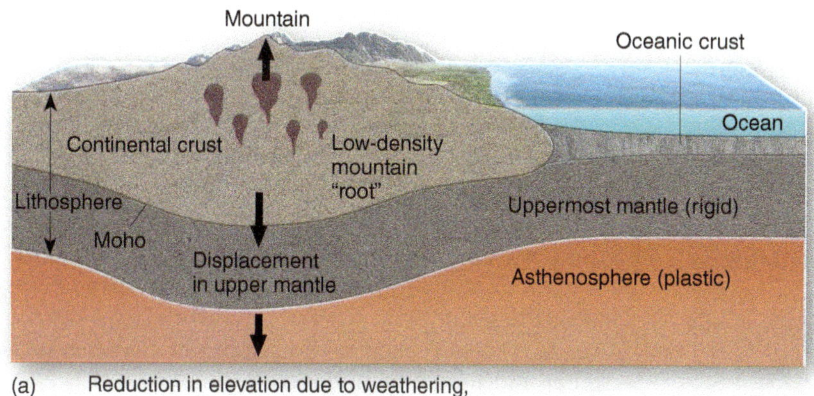

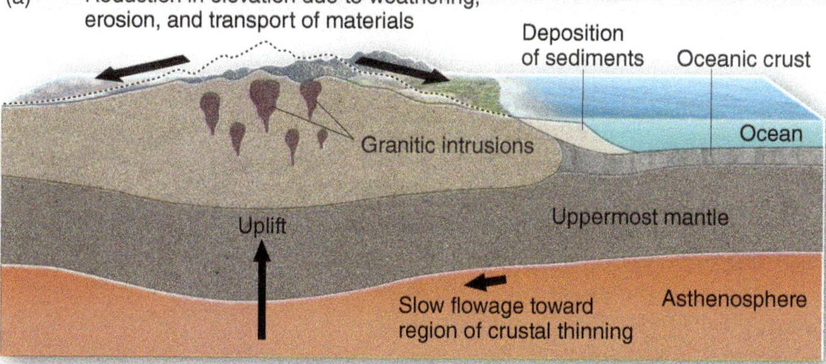

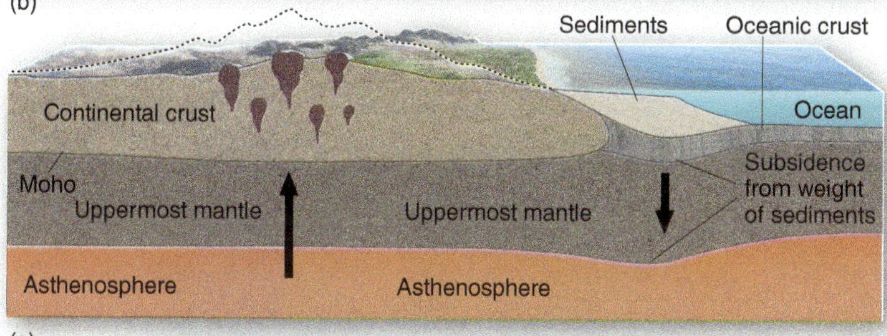

FIGURE 4 Isostatic adjustment of the crust. Earth's entire crust is in a constant state of compensating adjustment, as suggested by the sequential stages in (a) through (c): (a) The mountain mass slowly sinks, displacing mantle material. (b) Because of the loss of mass through erosion and transportation, the crust isostatically adjusts upward, and sediments accumulate in the ocean. (c) As the continent thins and rises, the heavy sediment load offshore begins to deform the lithosphere beneath the ocean. (d) The melting of ice from the last ice age and losses of overlying sediments are thought to produce an ongoing isostatic uplift of portions of the Sierra Nevada batholith. [Bobbé Christopherson.]

The retreat of glacial ice following the last ice-age cycle unloaded much weight off the crust in Alaska. Researchers from the Geophysical Institute at the University of Alaska–Fairbanks, using an array of GPS receivers, measured isostatic rebound of the crust following glacial ice losses. They expected to find a slowed rate of crustal rebound in southeastern Alaska, as compared to the more rapid response in the distant past when the ice first retreated.

Instead, they detected some of the most rapid vertical motion on Earth, averaging about 36 mm (1.42 in.) per year. Scientists attribute this isostatic rebound to the loss of modern glaciers in the region, especially the areas from Yakutat Bay and the Saint Elias Mountains in the north, through Glacier Bay, Juneau, and on south through the inland passage. This rapid rebound is attributable to climate change—causing glacial melt and retreat over the past 150 years—and correlates with record warmth across Alaska.

Earth's crust, an irregular, brittle layer, is the outermost shell, residing restlessly on a dynamic and diverse interior. Let us examine the processes at work on this crust and the variety of rock types that compose the landscape.

The Geologic Cycle

Earth's crust is in an ongoing state of change, being formed, deformed, moved, and broken down by physical, chemical, and biological processes. While the endogenic (internal) system is at work building landforms, the exogenic (external) system is busily wearing them down. This vast give-and-take at the Earth–atmosphere–ocean interface is the **geologic cycle**. It is fueled from two sources—Earth's internal heat and solar energy from space—influenced by the ever-present leveling force of Earth's gravity.

Figure 5 illustrates the geologic cycle. As you can see in the figure, the geologic cycle is composed of three principal cycles—hydrologic, rock, and tectonic. The *hydrologic cycle*, along the top of Figure 5, through erosion, transportation, and deposition, processes Earth materials with the chemical and physical action of water, ice, and wind. The *rock cycle* produces the three basic rock types found in the crust—igneous, metamorphic, and sedimentary. The *tectonic cycle* brings heat energy and new material to the surface and recycles material, creating movement and deformation of the crust.

The Rock Cycle

Only eight natural elements compose 98.5% of Earth's crust, and only two of these—oxygen and silicon—account for 74.3% (Table 1). Oxygen is the most reactive gas in the lower atmosphere, readily combining with other elements. For this reason, the percentage of oxygen is higher in the crust than the 21% concentration in the atmosphere. The internal differentiation process, in which less dense elements migrate toward the surface, explains the relatively large percentages of lightweight elements such as silicon and aluminum in the crust.

Earth's elements combine to form minerals. A **mineral** is an inorganic, or nonliving, natural compound having a specific chemical formula and usually possessing a crystalline structure. The combination of elements and the crystal structure give each mineral its characteristic hardness, color, density, and other properties. For example, the common mineral *quartz* is silicon dioxide, SiO_2, and has a distinctive six-sided crystal. *Mineralogy* is the study of the composition, properties, and classification of minerals. (See http://webmineral.com/.)

TABLE 1 Common Elements in Earth's Crust

Element	Percentage of Earth's Crust by Weight
Oxygen (O)	46.6
Silicon (Si)	27.7
Aluminum (Al)	8.1
Iron (Fe)	5.0
Calcium (Ca)	3.6
Sodium (Na)	2.8
Potassium (K)	2.6
Magnesium (Mg)	2.1
All others	1.5
Total	100.00

Note: A quartz crystal (SiO_2) consists of Earth's two most abundant elements, silicon (Si) and oxygen (O). Inset photo from *Laboratory Manual in Physical Geology,* 3rd ed., R. M. Busch, ed. © 1993 by Macmillan Publishing Co.

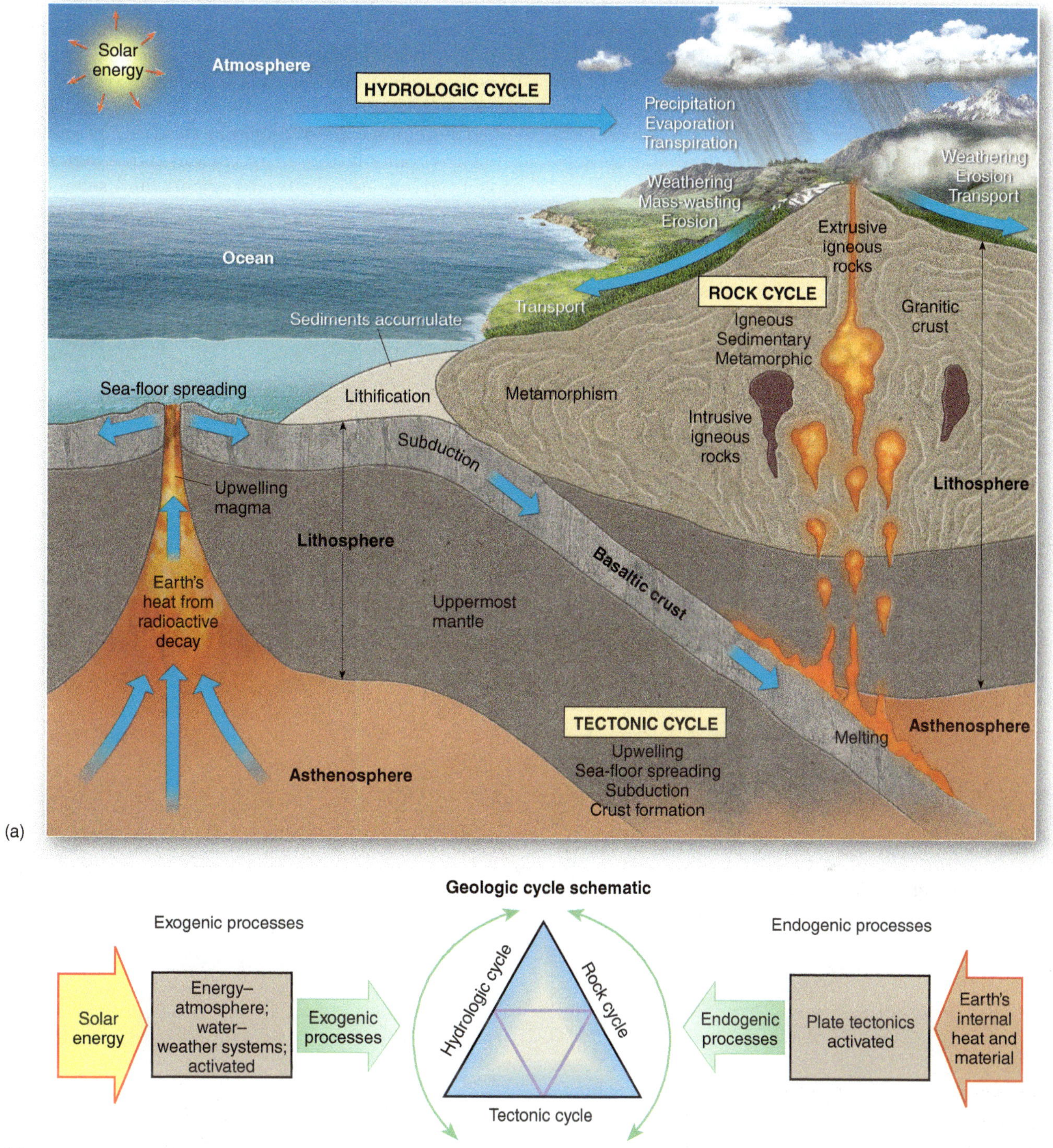

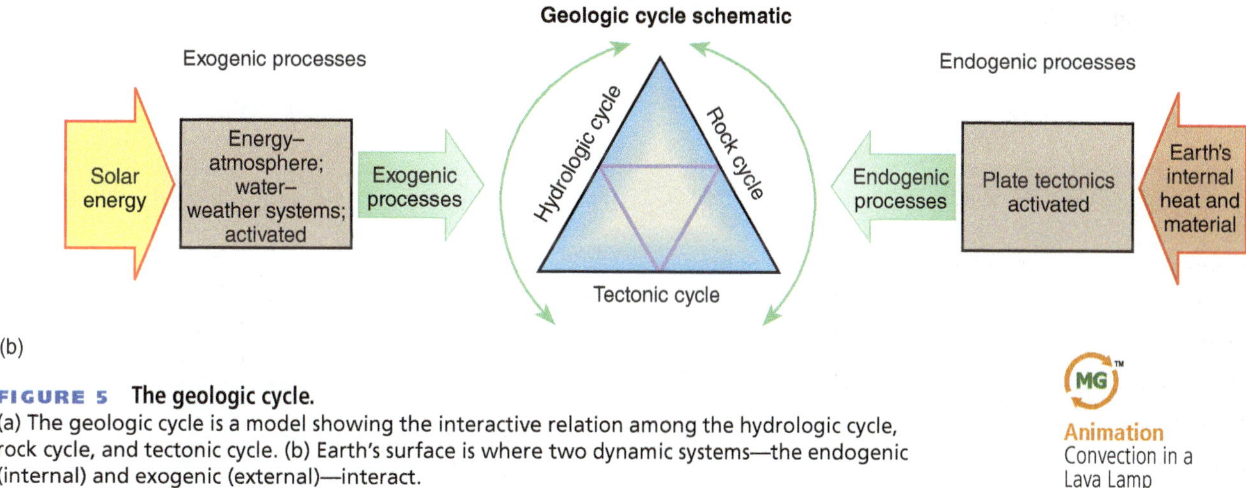

FIGURE 5 The geologic cycle.
(a) The geologic cycle is a model showing the interactive relation among the hydrologic cycle, rock cycle, and tectonic cycle. (b) Earth's surface is where two dynamic systems—the endogenic (internal) and exogenic (external)—interact.

MG™ **Animation** Convection in a Lava Lamp

One of the most widespread mineral families on Earth is the *silicates* because silicon and oxygen are so common and because they readily combine with each other and with other elements. Roughly 95% of Earth's crust is made up of silicates. This mineral family includes quartz, feldspar, clay minerals, and numerous gemstones. Several other groups of minerals are important: *Oxides* are minerals in which oxygen combines with metallic elements; *sulfides* and *sulfates* are minerals in which sulfur compounds combine with metallic elements; and *carbonates* feature carbon in combination with oxygen and other elements such as calcium, magnesium, and potassium.

A **rock** is an assemblage of minerals bound together (such as granite, a rock containing three minerals), or a mass of a single mineral (such as rock salt), or undifferentiated material (such as the noncrystalline glassy obsidian), or even solid organic material (such as coal). Thousands of different rocks have been identified. All can be sorted into one of three kinds, depending on the processes that formed them: *igneous* (melted), *sedimentary* (from settling out), and *metamorphic* (altered). Figure 6 illustrates these three processes and the interrelations among them that constitute the **rock cycle**.

Igneous Processes

An **igneous rock** is one that solidifies and crystallizes from a molten state. Familiar examples are granite, basalt, and rhyolite. Igneous rocks form from **magma**, which is molten rock beneath the surface (hence the name *igneous*, which means "fire-formed" in Latin). Magma is fluid, highly gaseous, and under tremendous pressure. Either it *intrudes* into crustal rocks, cooling and hardening below the surface to form **intrusive igneous rock**, or it *extrudes* onto the surface as **lava** and cools to form **extrusive igneous rock**, such as basalt.

The cooling history of an igneous rock—how fast it cooled and how steadily its temperature dropped—determines its crystalline physical characteristics, or crystallization. Igneous rocks range from coarse-grained (slower cooling, with more time for larger crystals to form) to fine-grained or glassy (faster cooling).

Igneous rocks make up approximately 90% of Earth's crust, although sedimentary rocks (sandstone,

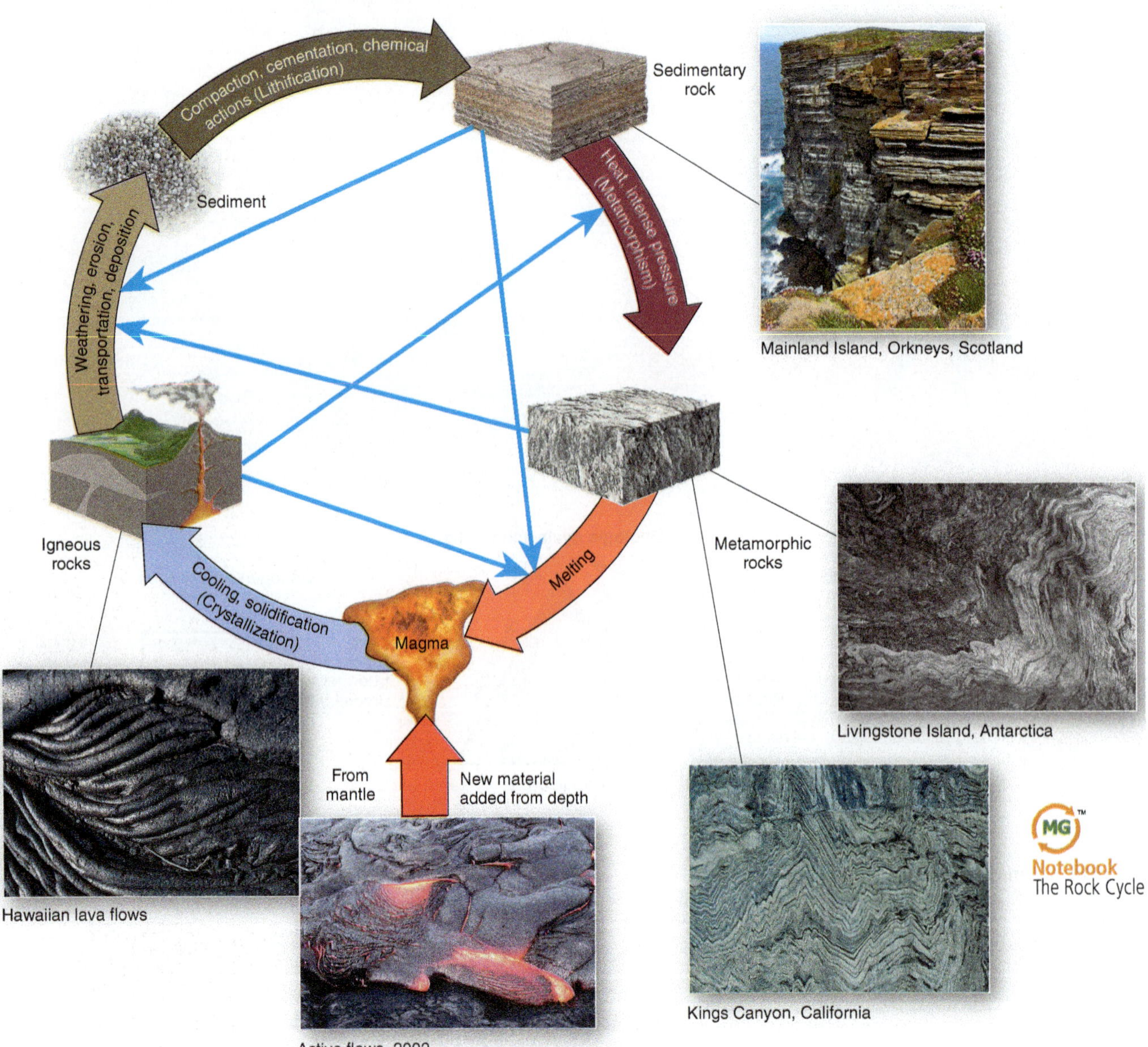

FIGURE 6 **The rock cycle.**
A rock-cycle schematic demonstrates the relation among igneous, sedimentary, and metamorphic processes. The arrows indicate that each rock type can enter the cycle at various points and be transformed into other rock types. Insolation input powers aspects of weathering, erosion, and transport systems. [Photos by Bobbé Christopherson.]

shale, limestone), soil, or oceans frequently cover them. Figure 7 illustrates a variety of intrusive and extrusive igneous rock types and landforms.

Intrusive igneous rock that cools slowly in the crust forms a **pluton**, a general term for any intrusive igneous rock body, regardless of size or shape. The Roman god of the underworld, Pluto, is the namesake. The largest pluton form is a **batholith**, defined as an irregular-shaped mass with a surface greater than 100 km^2 (40 mi^2) (Figure 8a). Batholiths form the mass of many large mountain ranges—for example, the Sierra Nevada batholith in California (see Figure 4d), the Idaho batholith, and the Coast Range batholith of British Columbia and Washington State.

Smaller plutons include the magma conduits of ancient volcanoes that have cooled and hardened. Those that form parallel to layers of sedimentary rock are *sills*; those that cross layers of the rock they invade are *dikes*. You see these two forms in Figure 7 at Petermann Island, Antarctica. Magma also can bulge between rock strata and produce a lens-shaped body, a *laccolith*, a type of sill. In addition, magma conduits themselves may solidify in roughly cylindrical forms that stand starkly above the landscape when

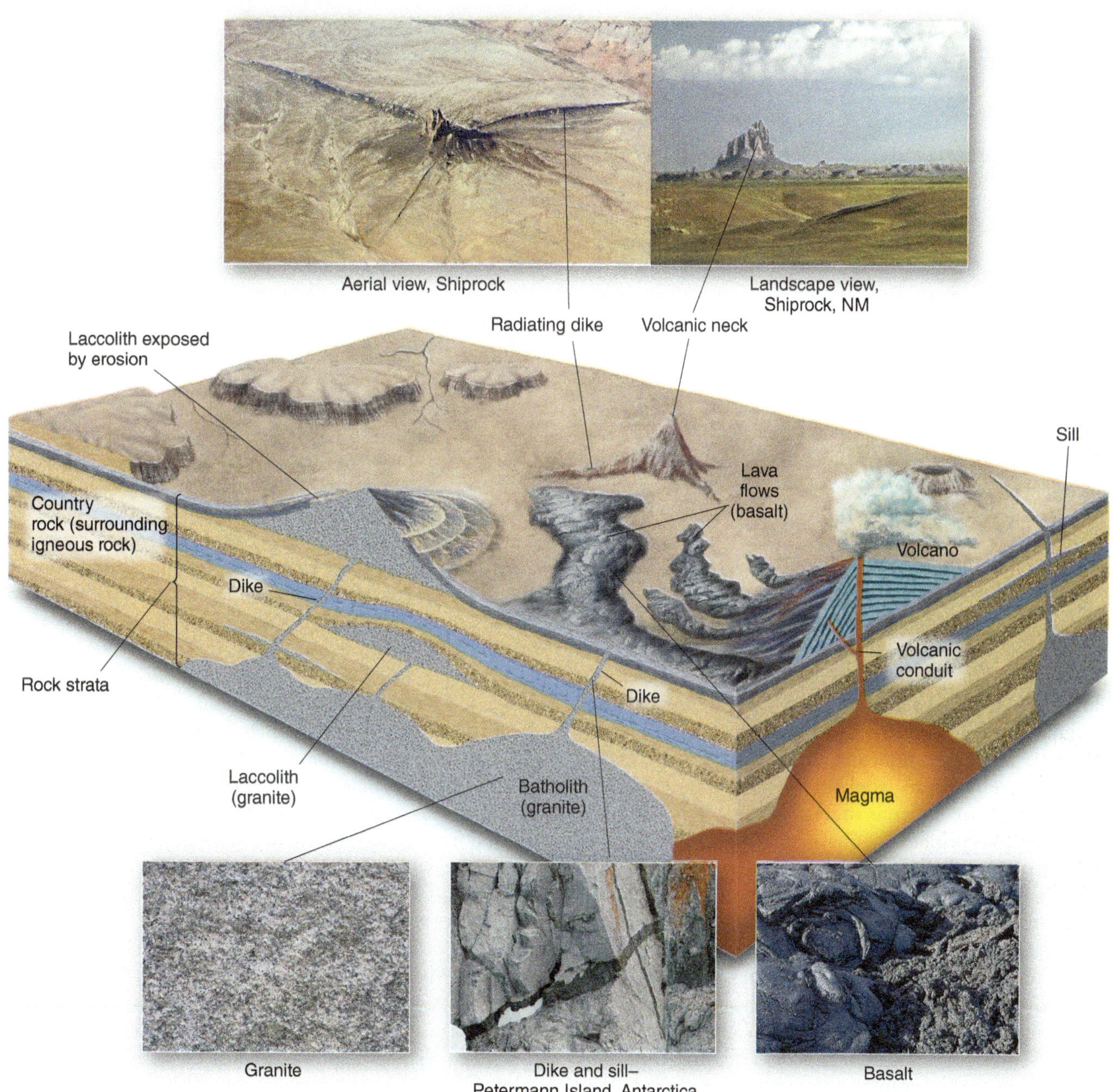

FIGURE 7 Igneous rock types and landforms.
The variety of igneous rocks, both intrusive (below the surface) and extrusive (on the surface), and associated landforms. Inset photographs show samples of granite (intrusive), basalt (extrusive), and other igneous forms. [Photos of rock samples and aerial by Bobbé Christopherson; surface photo of Shiprock volcanic neck by author.]

FIGURE 8 Intrusive and extrusive igneous rocks.
(a) Exposed intrusive granite, part of a batholith. (b) Basaltic lava flows on Hawai'i. The glowing opening is a skylight into an active lava tube where molten lava flows; the shiny surface is where lava recently flowed out of the skylight. [Bobbé Christopherson.]

finally exposed by weathering and erosion. Shiprock *volcanic neck* in New Mexico is such a feature, rising 518 m (1700 ft) above the surrounding plain, as suggested by the art in Figure 7 and shown in the inset photos; note the radiating dikes in the aerial photo. Weathering action of air, water, and ice can expose all of these intrusive forms.

Volcanic eruptions and flows produce extrusive igneous rock (Figure 8b).

Sedimentary Processes

Solar energy and gravity drive the process of *sedimentation*, with water as the principal transporting medium. Existing rock is disintegrated and dissolved by weathering, picked up and moved by erosion and transportation, and deposited along river, beach, and ocean sites, where burial initiates the rock-forming process. The formation of **sedimentary rock** involves **lithification** processes of cementation, compaction, and a hardening of sediments.

Most sedimentary rocks derive from fragments of existing rock or organic materials. Bits and pieces of former rocks—principally quartz, feldspar, and clay minerals—erode and then are mechanically transported by water, ice (glacial action), wind, and gravity. They are transported from "higher-energy" sites, where the carrying medium has the energy to pick up and move them, to "lower-energy" sites, where the material is dumped.

Some minerals, such as calcium carbonate, dissolve into solution and form sedimentary deposits by precipitating from those solutions to form rock. This is an important process in both the oceanic and the karst (weathered limestone) environments.

The layered strata of sedimentary rocks form an important record of past ages. **Stratigraphy** is the study of the sequence (superposition), thickness, and spatial distribution of strata. These sequences yield clues to the age and origin of the rocks. Figure 9a shows a sandstone sedimentary rock in a desert landscape. Note the multiple layers in the formation and how differently they resist weathering processes. The climatic history of this rock's formation environment is disclosed in the stratigraphy. Figure 9c shows sedimentary rock strata on Mars that imply water deposition of sediments sometime in the distant Martian past.

The two primary sources of sedimentary rocks are *clastic sediments*, formed from the mechanically transported fragments of older rock, and *chemical sediments*, formed from the dissolved minerals in solution, some having organic origins. Clastic sediments range in size from boulders to microscopic clay particles, which then lithify to become rock; sandstone is an example. Chemical sedimentary rocks are formed from dissolved minerals, transported in solution and chemically precipitated from solution (they are essentially nonclastic). The most common chemical sedimentary rock is **limestone**, which is lithified calcium carbonate, derived from inorganic and organic sources. A similar form is *dolomite*, which is lithified calcium–magnesium carbonate, $CaMg(CO_3)_2$. Limestone from marine organic origins is most common; it is biochemical—derived from shell and bone produced by biological activity (see inset photo in Figure 9b). Once formed, these rocks are vulnerable to chemical weathering, which produces unique landforms.

Chemical sediments from inorganic sources are deposited when water evaporates and leaves behind a residue of salts. These *evaporites* may exist as common salts, such as gypsum or sodium chloride (table salt). Chemical deposition also occurs in the water of natural hot springs from chemical reactions between minerals and oxygen. This is a sedimentary process related to *hydrothermal activity*. An

(a)

(b)

(c) Martian sedimentary formations

Sandstone

Limestone

FIGURE 9 Sedimentary rock types.
(a) Sandstone formation with sedimentary strata subjected to differential weathering; note weaker underlying siltstone, leaving a balanced rock above. (b) A limestone landscape, formed by chemical sedimentary processes, in south-central Indiana; inset samples have whole shells and some clasts (parts) cemented together. (c) Ancient sediment deposition is evident in the Martian western Arabia Terra (8° N and 7° W). [(a), (b), Inset photos by Bobbé Christopherson. (c) *Mars Global Surveyor*, NASA/JPL/ Malin Space Science Systems.]

example is the massive deposit of travertine, a form of calcium carbonate, at Mammoth Hot Springs in Yellowstone National Park (Figure 10a).

Hydrothermal activity also occurs on the ocean floor along the rift valleys formed by sea-floor spreading. These "black smokers" belch dark clouds of hydrogen sulfides, minerals, and metals that hot water (in excess of 380°C, or 716°F) leached from the basalt. In contact with seawater, metals and minerals precipitate into deposits (Figure 10b). Along the Mid-Atlantic Ridge, one region of hydrothermal activity has 30- to 60-m (98- to 198-ft) towering-chimney vents of calcium carbonate that are at least 30,000 years old and still active.

Metamorphic Processes

Any rock, either igneous or sedimentary, may be transformed into a **metamorphic rock** by going through profound physical or chemical changes under pressure and increased temperature. (The name *metamorphic* comes from a Greek word meaning "to change form.") Metamorphic rocks generally are more compact than the original rock and therefore are harder and more resistant to weathering and erosion (Figure 11).

Several conditions can cause metamorphism. Most common is when subsurface rock is subjected to high temperatures and high compressional stresses over millions of years. Igneous rocks become compressed during collisions between slabs of Earth's crust (see the discussion of plate tectonics later in this chapter). Sometimes rocks simply are crushed under great weight when a crustal area is thrust beneath other crust. In another setting, igneous rocks may be sheared and stressed along earthquake fault zones, causing metamorphism.

Metamorphic rocks comprise the ancient roots of mountains. Exposed at the bottom of the inner gorge of the Grand Canyon in Arizona, a Precambrian (Archean) metamorphic rock, the Vishnu Schist, is a remnant of such a mountain root (Figure 11b). Despite the fact that the schist is harder than steel, the Colorado River has cut down into the uplifted Colorado Plateau, exposing and eroding these ancient rocks.

(a)

(b)

FIGURE 10 Hydrothermal deposits.
(a) Mammoth Hot Springs, Yellowstone National Park, is an example of a hydrothermal deposit principally composed of travertine ($CaCO_3$), deposited as a chemical precipitate from heated spring water as it evaporated. (b) Hydrothermal vents with black smokers rise along the Mid-Atlantic Ridge. [(a) Author. (b) Scripps Institution of Oceanography/University of California, San Diego.]

(a)

(b)

FIGURE 11 Metamorphic rocks.
(a) A metamorphic rock outcrop in Greenland, the Amitsoq Gneiss, at 3.8 billion years old, is one of the oldest rock formations on Earth. (b) Precambrian Vishnu Schist makes up these rock cliffs in the inner gorge of the Grand Canyon in northern Arizona. These metamorphic rocks lie beneath many layers of sedimentary rocks deep in the continent. [(a) Photo by Kevin Schafer/Photolibrary/Peter Arnold, Inc. (b) Author.]

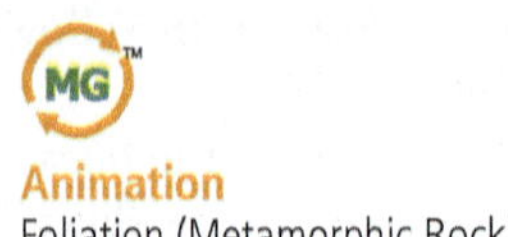

Animation
Foliation (Metamorphic Rock)

Another metamorphic condition occurs when sediments collect in broad depressions in Earth's crust and, because of their own weight, create enough pressure in the bottommost layers to transform the sediments into metamorphic rock, a process of *regional metamorphism*. Also, molten magma rising within the crust may "cook" adjacent rock, a process of *contact metamorphism*.

Metamorphic rocks may be changed both physically and chemically from the original rocks. Table 2 lists some metamorphic rock types, their parent rocks, and their resultant textures. If the mineral structure demonstrates a particular alignment after metamorphism, the rock is *foliated*, and some minerals may appear as wavy striations (streaks or lines) in the new rock. The four inset photographs demonstrate foliated and nonfoliated textures. Which form do you see—foliated or nonfoliated—in Figure 11a or in the far-right inset photo of metamorphic rock from Livingston Island in Figure 6?

On the Isle of Lewis (Outer Hebrides), northwest of the Scottish coast, people constructed the Standing Stones of Calanais (Callanish) beginning approximately 5000 years ago (Table 2, far-right inset). These ancient people used the 3.1-billion-year-old metamorphic Lewisian gneiss and arranged the monument with the foliations aligned vertically. The standing stone in the photo is about 3.5 m (11.5 ft) tall.

TABLE 2 Metamorphic Rocks

Parent Rock	Metamorphic Equivalent	Texture
Shale (clay minerals)	Slate	Foliated
Granite, slate, shale	Gneiss	Foliated
Basalt, shale, peridotite	Schist	Foliated
Limestone, dolomite	Marble	Nonfoliated
Sandstone	Quartzite	Nonfoliated

Note: Slate and Gneiss photos by Bobbé Christopherson; Marble and Foliated photos from *Laboratory Manual in Physical Geology*, 3rd ed., R. M. Busch, ed. © 1993 by Macmillan Publishing Co.

You see how the rock-forming processes yield the igneous, sedimentary, and metamorphic materials of Earth's crust. Next, we look at how vast *tectonic processes* press, push, and drag portions of the crust in large-scale movements, causing the continents to *drift*.

Plate Tectonics

Have you ever looked at a world map and noticed that a few of the continental landmasses appear to have matching shapes like pieces of a jigsaw puzzle—particularly South America and Africa? The incredible reality is that the continental pieces once did fit together. Continental landmasses not only migrated to their present locations, but also continue to move at speeds up to 6 cm (2.4 in.) per year. We say that the continents are *adrift* because convection currents in the asthenosphere and upper mantle are dragging them around. The key point is that the arrangement of continents and oceans we see today is not permanent, but is in a continuing state of change.

A continent, such as North America, is actually a collage of crustal pieces that migrated from elsewhere to form the landscape we know. Through a historical chronology, let us trace the discoveries that led to the plate tectonics theory—a major revolution in Earth systems science.

A Brief History

As early mapping gained accuracy, some observers noticed the symmetry among continents, particularly the fit between South America and Africa. Abraham Ortelius (1527–1598), a geographer, noted the apparent fit of some continental coastlines in his *Thesaurus Geographicus* (1596). In 1620, English philosopher Sir Francis Bacon noted gross similarities between the edges of Africa and South America (although he did not suggest that they had drifted apart). Benjamin Franklin wrote in 1780 that the crust must be a shell that can break and shift by movements of fluid below. Others wrote—unscientifically—about such apparent relationships, but it was not until much later that a valid explanation came forward.

In 1912, German geophysicist and meteorologist Alfred Wegener publicly presented in a lecture his idea that Earth's landmasses migrate. His book *Origin of the Continents and Oceans* appeared in 1915. Today, Wegener is regarded as the father of this concept, which he first called *continental drift*. Scientists at the time were unreceptive to Wegener's revolutionary proposal. Thus, a great debate began, lasting almost 50 years until a scientific consensus developed that Wegener was right after all.

Wegener thought that all landmasses formed one supercontinent approximately 225 m.y.a., during the Triassic Period. **Pangaea** is the name he gave this one landmass, meaning "all Earth" (see Figure 15b). Although his initial model kept the landmasses together too long and his proposal included an incorrect driving mechanism for the moving continents, Wegener's arrangement of Pangaea and its breakup was correct.

To come up with his Pangaea fit, Wegener studied the geologic record represented in the rock strata, the fossil record, and the climatic record for the continents. He concluded that South America and Africa correlated in many complex ways. He decided that the large midlatitude coal deposits, which date to the Permian and Carboniferous Periods (251–354 m.y.a.), exist because these regions once were nearer the equator and therefore covered by lush vegetation that became coal.

As modern scientific capabilities built the case for continental drift, the 1950s and 1960s saw a revival of interest in Wegener's concepts and, finally, confirmation. Aided by an avalanche of discoveries, the plate tectonics theory today is universally accepted as an accurate model of the way Earth's surface evolves.

Tectonic, from the Greek *tektonikùs*, meaning "building" or "construction," refers to changes in the configuration of Earth's crust as a result of internal forces. **Plate tectonics** include the processes of upwelling of magma; lithospheric plate movements; sea-floor spreading and lithospheric subduction; earthquakes; volcanic activity; and lithospheric deformation such as warping, folding, and faulting.

Sea-Floor Spreading

The key to establishing the theory of continental drift was a better understanding of the seafloor. The seafloor has a remarkable feature: an interconnected worldwide mountain chain, forming a ridge some 64,000 km (40,000 mi) in extent and averaging more than 1000 km (600 mi) in width. How did this global mountain chain get there?

In the early 1960s, geophysicist Harry H. Hess proposed **sea-floor spreading** as the mechanism that builds this mountain chain and drives continental movement. Hess said that these submarine mountain ranges were **mid-ocean ridges** and the direct result of upwelling flows of magma from hot areas in the upper mantle and asthenosphere and perhaps from the deeper lower mantle. Hess and Robert S. Dietz proposed that old seafloor sinks back into the Earth's mantle at deep ocean trenches and in subduction zones where plates collide.

Today, scientists know that mid-ocean ridges occur at divergent plate boundaries, where plates are moving apart. As the seafloor spreads, magma rises and accumulates in magma chambers beneath the centerline of the ridge (Figure 12a). Some of the magma rises and erupts through fractures and small volcanoes along the ridge, forming new seafloor (see Figure 12b). As the plates continue to move apart, more magma rises from below to fill the gaps. Scientists now think that this upward movement of material beneath an ocean ridge is a consequence of seafloor spreading rather than the cause.

Figure 12d shows a portion of the Mid-Atlantic Ridge where the system surfaces at Thingvellir, Iceland. The rifts indicate the spreading movement at the boundary of the North American plate along one side and the Eurasian plate on the other.

Geomagnetism Earlier we discussed the history of reversals in Earth's magnetic field. The chronology of these reversals proved to be a fundamental piece of the plate tectonics puzzle by providing scientists with ages for materials on the ocean floor.

As the seafloor spreads and new seafloor generates, magnetic particles in the lava orient with the magnetic field in force at the time the lava cools and hardens. The particles become locked in this alignment as part of the new seafloor, creating an ongoing magnetic record in the crust of Earth's polarity.

Figure 13 illustrates such a record from the Mid-Atlantic Ridge south of Iceland. The colors denote the alternating magnetic polarization preserved in the minerals of the oceanic crust. Note the mirror images that develop on either side of the rift as a result of the nearly symmetrical spreading of the seafloor; the relative ages of the rocks increase with distance from the ridge. Combining Earth's magnetic-field reversals with other measurements allowed scientists to determine the age of the seafloor.

The youngest crust anywhere on Earth is at the spreading centers of the mid-ocean ridges, and with increasing distance from these centers, the crust gets steadily older (Figure 14). The oldest seafloor is in the western Pacific near Japan, dating to the Jurassic Period. Note on the map in the figure the distance between this basin and its spreading center in the South Pacific, west of South America.

Overall, the seafloor is relatively young; nowhere is it more than 208 million years old—remarkable when you remember that Earth's age is 4.6 billion years. The reason is that oceanic lithosphere is short-lived—the oldest sections, farthest from the mid-ocean ridges, are slowly plunging beneath continental crust along Earth's deep oceanic trenches. The discovery that the seafloor is young demolished earlier thinking that the oldest rocks would be found there.

Subduction of the Lithosphere

In contrast to the upwelling zones along the mid-ocean ridges are the areas of descending lithosphere elsewhere. On the left side of Figure 12a, note how one plate is diving, or being dragged, beneath another into the mantle. Recall that the basaltic ocean crust has a density of 3.0 g/cm^3, whereas continental crust averages a lighter 2.7 g/cm^3. As a result, when continental crust and oceanic crust slowly collide, the denser ocean floor will grind beneath the lighter continental crust, thus forming a **subduction zone**.

The world's deep ocean trenches coincide with these subduction zones and are the lowest features on Earth's surface. Deepest is the Mariana Trench near Guam, which descends below sea level to –11,030 m (–36,198 ft); next deepest is the Tonga Trench, also in the Pacific, which drops to –10,882 m (–35,702 ft).

Subduction occurs at convergent plate boundaries, where plates are colliding. The subducting slab of crust exerts a gravitational pull on the rest of the plate—an important driving force in plate motion. The subducted portion travels down into the asthenosphere, where it remelts and eventually is recycled as magma, rising again toward the surface through deep fissures and cracks in crustal rock. Volcanic mountains such as the Andes in South America and the Cascade Range from northern California to the Canadian border form inland of these subduction zones as a result of rising plumes of magma, as suggested in Figure 12a. Sometimes the diving plate remains intact for hundreds of kilometers, whereas at other times it can break into large pieces, thought to be the case under the Cascade Range with its distribution of volcanoes.

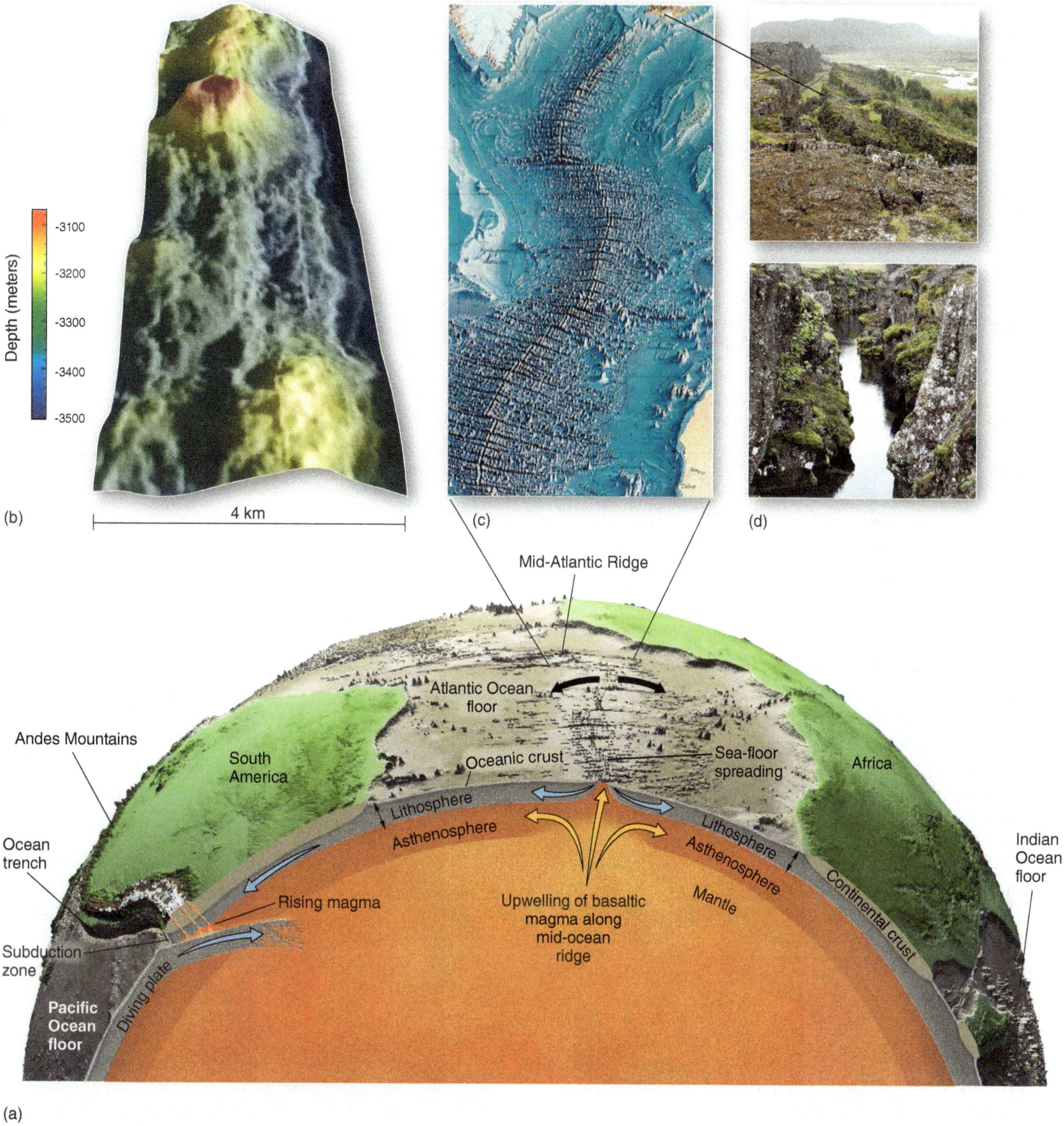

FIGURE 12 Crustal movements.
(a) Sea-floor spreading, upwelling currents, subduction, and plate movements, shown in cross section. Arrows indicate the direction of the spreading. (b) A 4-km-wide image of the Mid-Atlantic Ridge showing linear faults, a volcanic crater, a rift valley, and ridges. The image was taken by the TOBI (towed ocean-bottom instrument) at approximately 29° N latitude. (c) Detail from ocean-floor map. (d) The mid-Atlantic rift surfaces through Iceland. [(b) Image courtesy of D. K. Smith, Woods Hole Oceanographic Institute. (c) Office of Naval Research. (d) Bobbé Christopherson.]

Animation
Sea-Floor Spreading, Subduction

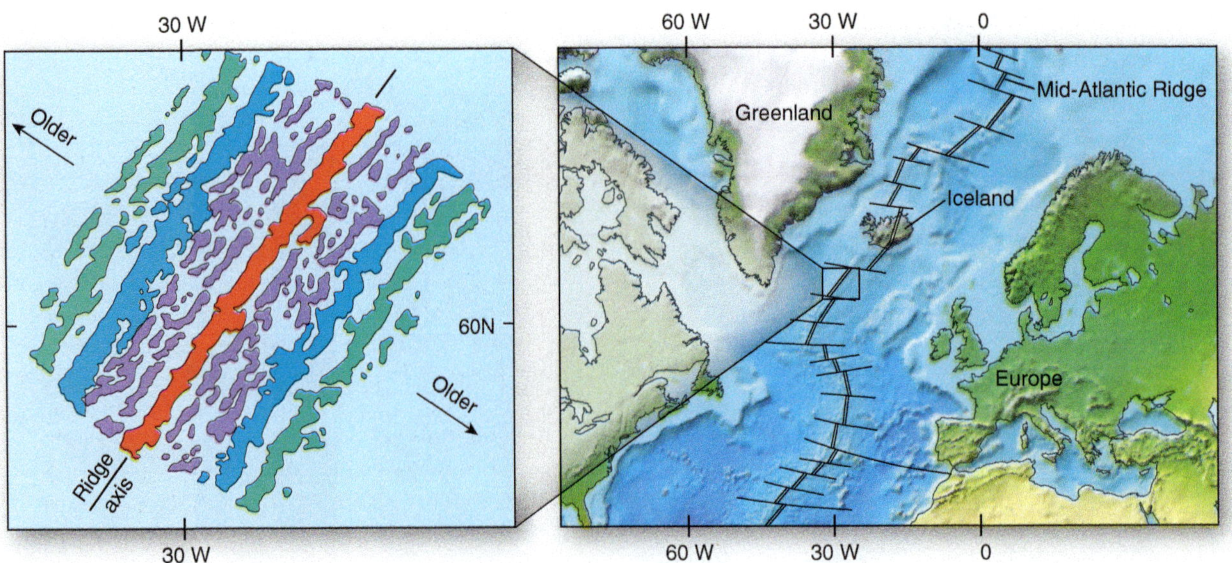

FIGURE 13 Magnetic reversals recorded in the seafloor.
Magnetic reversals recorded in the seafloor south of Iceland along the Mid-Atlantic Ridge. [Adapted from J. R. Heirtzler, S. Le Pichon, and J. G. Baron, *Deep-Sea Research* 13, © 1966, Pergamon Press, p. 247.]

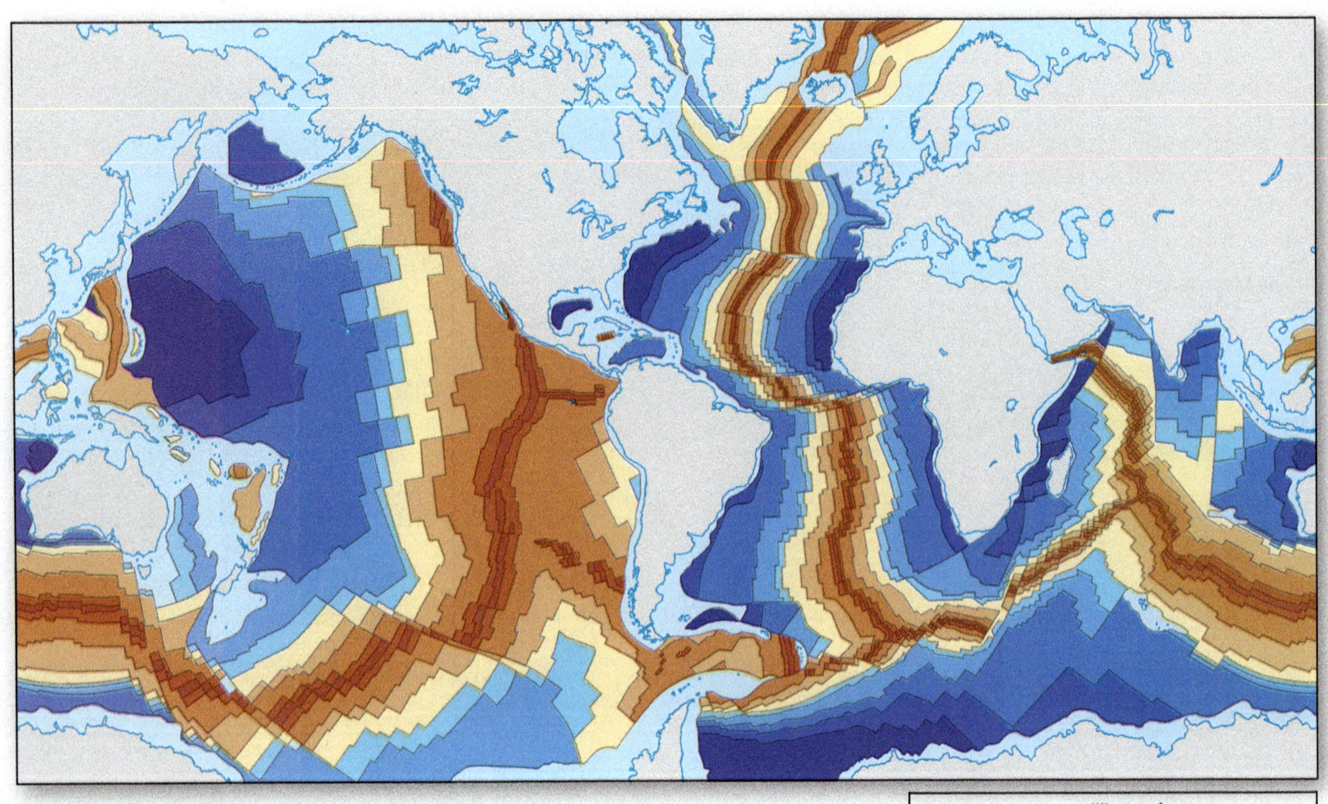

FIGURE 14 Relative age of the oceanic crust.
Compare the dark-red color near the East Pacific Rise in the eastern Pacific Ocean with the same dark-red color along the Mid-Atlantic Ridge. What does the difference in width tell you about the rates of plate motion in the two locations? [Adapted from *The Bedrock Geology of the World* by R. L. Larson, *et al.*, © 1985, W. H. Freeman and Company.]

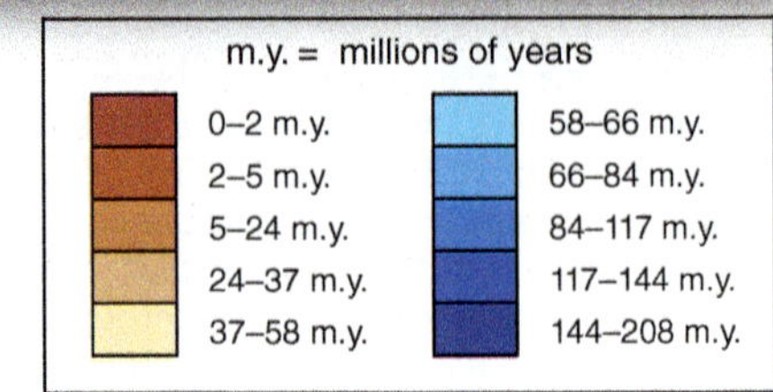

The fact that spreading ridges and subduction zones are areas of earthquake and volcanic activity provides important proof of plate tectonics. Now, using current scientific findings, let us go back and reconstruct the past and Pangaea.

The Formation and Breakup of Pangaea

The supercontinent of Pangaea and its subsequent breakup into today's continents represent only the last 225 million years of Earth's 4.6 billion years, or only the most recent 1/23 of Earth's existence. During the remaining 22/23 of geologic time, previous supercontinents may have existed. The landmasses as we know them were unrecognizable.

Figure 15 shows the arrangement of the continents beginning with (a) the pre-Pangaea arrangement of 465 m.y.a. (during the Middle Ordovician Period) and moving to (b) an updated version of Wegener's Pangaea, 225–200 m.y.a. (Triassic–Jurassic Periods); (c) the configuration that occurred by 135 m.y.a. (the beginning of the Cretaceous Period), including the continents of Gondwana and Laurasia; (d) the arrangement 65 m.y.a. (shortly after the beginning of the Tertiary Period); and (e) the present arrangement in modern geologic time (the late Cenozoic Era).

Earth's present crust is divided into at least 14 plates, of which about half are major and half are minor in terms of area (Figure 16). Literally hundreds of smaller pieces and perhaps dozens of microplates that migrated together make up these broad plates. The arrows in the figure indicate the direction in which each plate is presently moving, and the length of the arrows suggests the relative rate of movement during the past 20 million years. On the *MasteringGeography* web site, you can manipulate a similar animated map to feature the speed arrows, or the plates, with or without the landmasses.

An illustration of the seafloor also is helpful in identifying the plate boundaries in the following discussion. You might try correlating the features illustrated in Figure 16 with a seafloor map.

II CRITICAL THINKING 2

Tracking your location since Pangaea

Using the maps in this chapter, determine your present location relative to Earth's crustal plates. Now, using Figure 15b, approximately identify where your present location was 225 m.y.a.; express it in a rough estimate using the equator and the longitudes noted on the map.

Plate Boundaries

The boundaries where plates meet clearly are dynamic places, although slow-moving within human time frames. The block diagrams in Figure 16 show the three general types of motion and interaction that occur along the boundary areas:

- *Divergent boundaries* are characteristic of sea-floor spreading centers, where upwelling material from the mantle forms new seafloor and lithospheric plates spread apart—a constructional process. The spreading makes these zones of tension. An example noted in the figure is the divergent boundary along the East Pacific Rise, which gives birth to the Nazca plate (moving eastward) and the Pacific plate (moving northwestward). Whereas most divergent boundaries occur at mid-ocean ridges, a few occur within continents themselves. An example is the Great Rift Valley of East Africa, where crust is rifting apart.
- *Convergent boundaries* are characteristic of collision zones, where areas of continental and oceanic lithosphere collide. These are zones of compression and crustal loss—a destructional process. Examples include the subduction zones off the west coast of South and Central America, along the Aleutian trenches, and along the east coast of Japan, where the magnitude 9.0 quake struck in 2011; areas where two plates of continental crust collide, such as the collision zone between India and Asia; and areas where oceanic plates collide, such as along the deep trenches in the western Pacific Ocean.
- *Transform boundaries* occur where plates slide laterally past one another at right angles to a sea-floor spreading center, neither diverging nor converging and usually with no volcanic eruptions. These are the right-angle fractures stretching across the mid-ocean ridge system worldwide.

Related to plate boundaries, another piece of the tectonic puzzle fell into place in 1965 when University of Toronto geophysicist Tuzo Wilson first described the nature of transform boundaries and their relation to earthquake activity. All the spreading centers on Earth's crust feature these perpendicular scars. Some are a few hundred kilometers long; others, such as those along the East Pacific Rise, stretch out 1000 km or more (over 600 mi).

Across the entire ocean floor, spreading-center mid-ocean ridges are the location of *transform faults*. These faults generally are parallel to the direction in which the plate is moving, and the resulting fracture zone is active only along the fault section between ridges of spreading centers. Along transform faults, the motion is one of horizontal displacement—no new crust is formed or old crust subducted.

The famous San Andreas fault system in California, where continental crust has overridden a transform system, exhibits this type of motion. The fault that triggered the 1995 Kobe earthquake in Japan also has this type of horizontal motion.

Earthquake and Volcanic Activity

Plate boundaries are the primary location of earthquake and volcanic activity, and the correlation of these phenomena is an important aspect of plate tectonics. The massive earthquakes that hit Haiti, Chile, New Zealand, and Japan in 2010 and 2011 and the 2010 volcanic eruption in Iceland focused world attention on these principles.

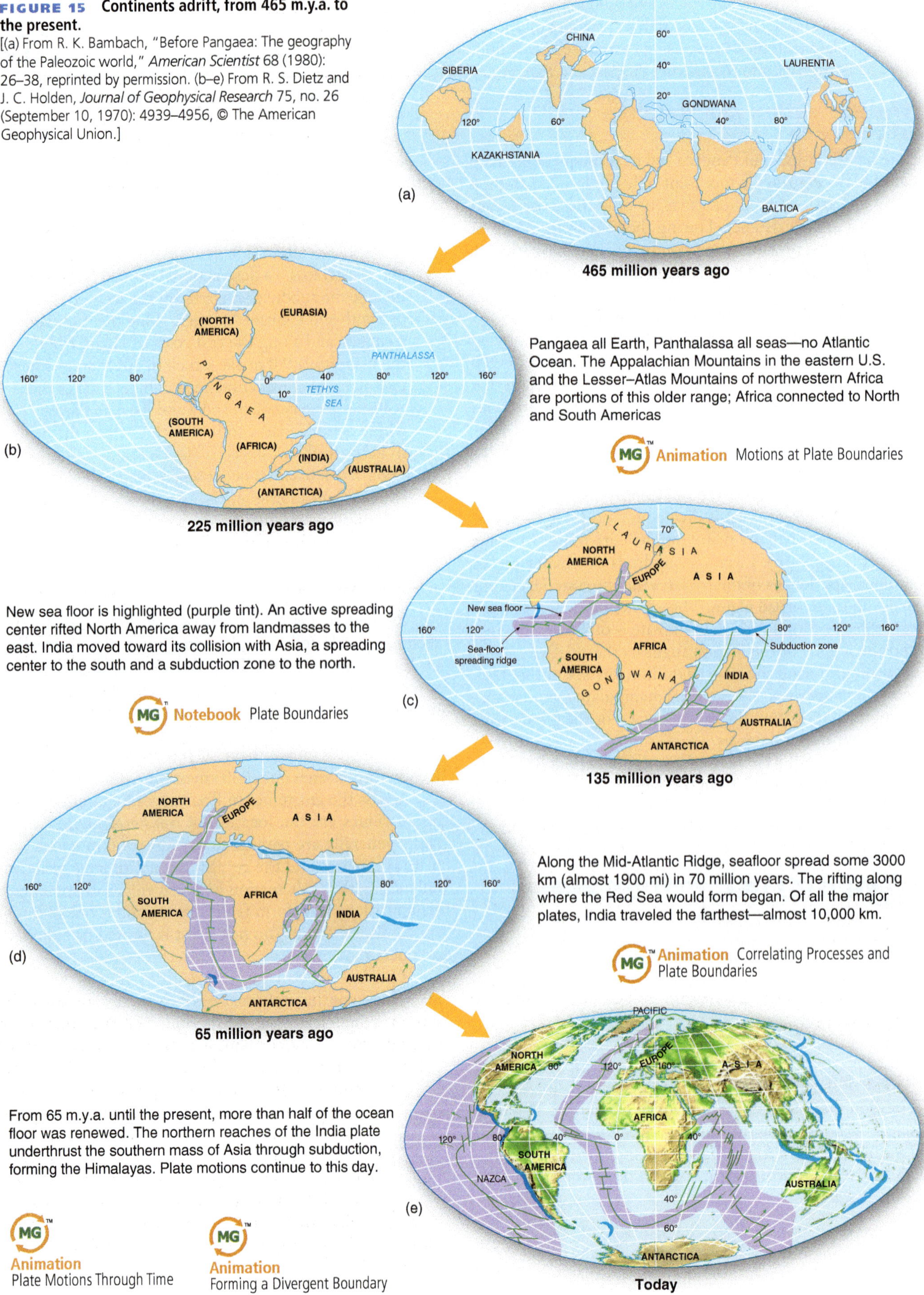

FIGURE 15 Continents adrift, from 465 m.y.a. to the present.
[(a) From R. K. Bambach, "Before Pangaea: The geography of the Paleozoic world," *American Scientist* 68 (1980): 26–38, reprinted by permission. (b–e) From R. S. Dietz and J. C. Holden, *Journal of Geophysical Research* 75, no. 26 (September 10, 1970): 4939–4956, © The American Geophysical Union.]

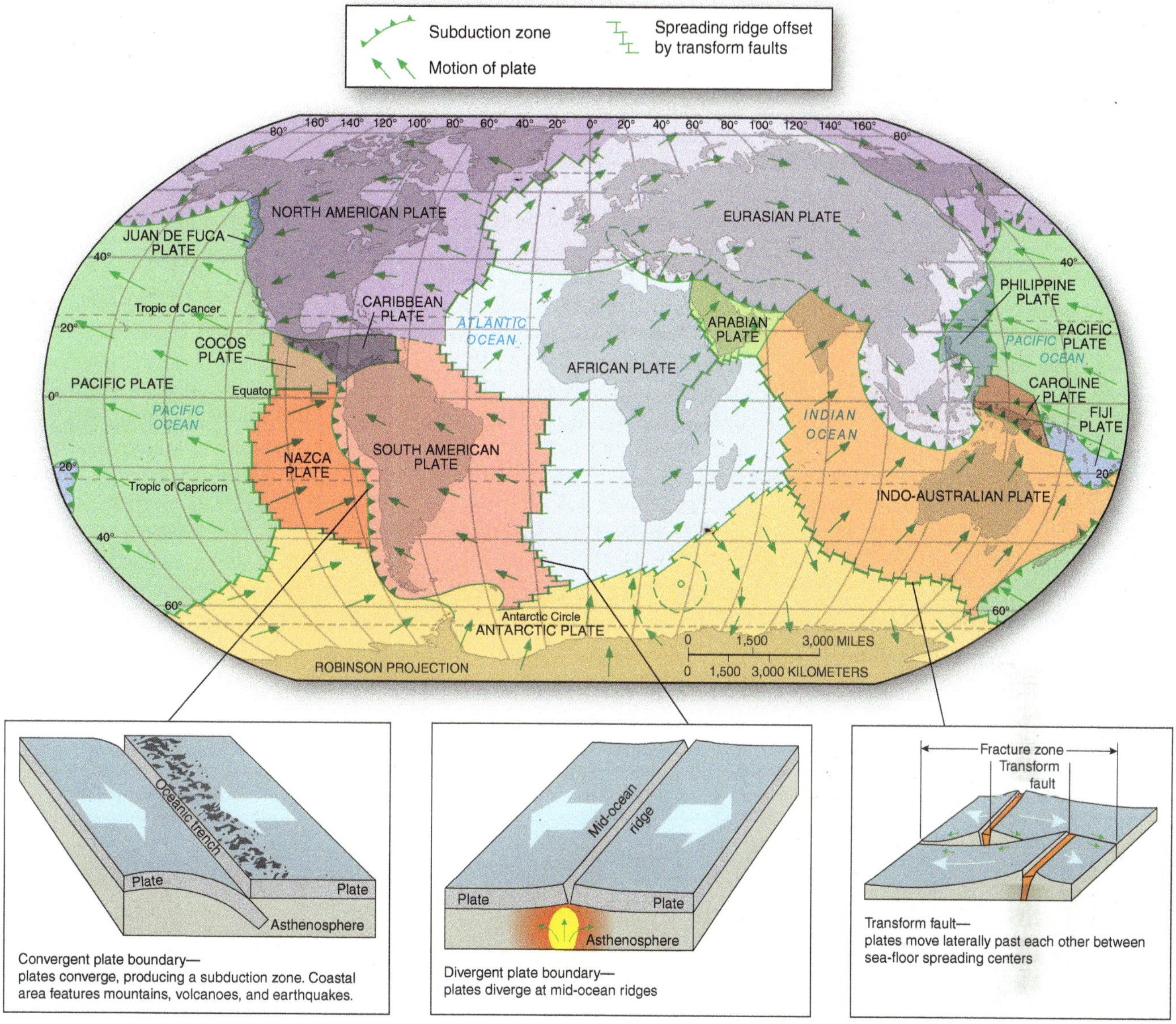

Convergent plate boundary—
plates converge, producing a subduction zone. Coastal area features mountains, volcanoes, and earthquakes.

Divergent plate boundary—
plates diverge at mid-ocean ridges

Transform fault—
plates move laterally past each other between sea-floor spreading centers

FIGURE 16 Earth's major lithospheric plates and their movements. Each arrow represents 20 million years of movement. The longer arrows indicate that the Pacific and Nazca plates are moving more rapidly than are the Atlantic plates. Compare the length of these arrows with those purple areas on Figure 15. [Adapted from U.S. Geodynamics Committee, National Academy of Sciences and National Academy of Engineering.]

Animation India Collision with Asia

Figure 17 maps earthquake zones, volcanic sites, hot spots, and plate motion. The "ring of fire" surrounding the Pacific Basin, named for the frequent incidence of volcanoes, is evident. The subducting edge of the Pacific plate thrusts deep into the crust and mantle and produces molten material that makes its way back toward the surface. The upwelling magma forms active volcanoes along the Pacific Rim. Such processes occur similarly at plate boundaries throughout the world.

Hot Spots

A dramatic aspect of Earth's internal dynamics is the estimated 50 to 100 **hot spots** across Earth's surface. These are individual sites of upwelling material, arriving at the surface in tall plumes from the mantle or rising from near the surface, that produce thermal effects in groundwater and crust. Some of these sites can be developed for geothermal power (Focus Study 1). Hot spots occur beneath both oceanic and continental crust. Some hot spots are anchored deep in the stiff lower mantle, tending to remain fixed relative to migrating plates; others appear to be above plumes that move themselves or shift with plate motion. Thus, the area of a plate that is above a hot spot is locally heated for the brief geologic time it is there (a few hundred thousand or million years).

FOCUS STUDY 1

Heat from Earth—Geothermal Energy and Power

A tremendous amount of endogenic energy flows from Earth's interior toward the surface. Temperatures at the base of Earth's crust range from 200°C to 1000°C (392°F to 1800°F). Convection and conduction transport this geothermal energy in enormous quantities from the mantle to the crust, yet geothermal power development is limited in extent to certain locations (Figure 1.1).

What Is Geothermal Energy?

Geothermal energy is produced when pockets of magma and hot portions of the crust heat groundwater. This energy is transmitted to the surface by heated water or steam accessed through the drilling of wells. For an effective *underground thermal reservoir* to form, an aquifer must have high porosity and high permeability that allows heated water to move freely through connecting pore spaces. Ideally, this aquifer should heat groundwater from 180°C to 350°C (355°F to 600°F) and be accessible to drilling within 3 km (1.9 mi) of the surface, although 6- to 7-km (3.7- to 4.3-mi) depths are workable.

Geothermal energy literally refers to heat from Earth's interior, whereas *geothermal power* relates to specific applied strategies of geothermal electric or geothermal direct. *Geothermal electric* uses steam, or hot water that flashes to steam, to drive a turbine-generator. In *geothermal direct*, hot water is used to heat and cool buildings using a heat-exchange system; to heat greenhouses, soil, and swimming pools; and for manufacturing processes and aquaculture, among many other uses.

Geothermal Power Production

The first geothermal electricity-generating station—built in Larderello, Italy, in 1904—has operated continuously since 1913 with an installed capacity of 360 MWe (megawatts electric). Today, geothermal applications are in use in 30 countries, through some 200 plants, producing an output of 8000 MWe and direct heat of 12,000 MWt (megawatts

(a)

(b)

FIGURE 1.1 Surface geothermal activity in Iceland.
(a) This is the original Geysir, in Haukadalur, Iceland, from which we derive the name for all other geysers on Earth; historical accounts of Geysir's activity date back to A.D. 1294. (b) The popular Blue Lagoon Spa is filled with hot geothermal waters. The Svartsengi power plant is in the distance in this geothermal field on the Reykjavík Peninsula, Iceland. The plant's name means "Black Meadow," referring to the extensive lava beds throughout this region. [Bobbé Christopherson.]

The Pacific plate moved across a hot, upward-erupting plume over the last 80 million years, creating a string of volcanic islands stretching northwestward away from the hot spot. This hot spot produced, and continues to form, the Hawaiian–Emperor Islands chain (Figure 18). Thus, the ages of the islands and seamounts (submarine mountains that do not reach the surface) in the chain increase northwestward from the island of Hawai'i, as you can see from the ages marked in the figure. The oldest island in the Hawaiian part of the chain is Kaua'i, approximately 5 million years old; today, it is weathered and eroded into deep canyons and valleys.

To the northwest of this active hot spot in Hawai'i, the island of Midway rises as a part of the same system. From there, the Emperor seamounts follow northwestward until they reach about 40 million years in age. At that point, this linear island chain shifts direction northward. This bend in the chain is now thought to be from both movement in the thermal). In Reykjavík, Iceland, the majority of space heating (87%) and some of the electrical production (18%) are geothermal. The Svartsengi power plant (40 MWe) on the Reykjavík Peninsula is an example of such a modern facility (Figure 1.1b). In the same area, a large array of wells collects heat from hot water and pumps it to the city for geothermal direct applications.

In the Paris Basin, France, some 25,000 residences are heated using geothermal direct 70°C (158°F) water. In the Philippines, almost 30% of total electrical production is generated with geothermal energy. The top six countries for installed geothermal electrical generation are the United States, Philippines, Italy, Mexico, Indonesia, and Japan. Worldwide operational capacity is 8933 MWe of a potential estimated to be in excess of 80,000 MWe and hundreds of thousands of MWt. The Geysers Geothermal Field in northern California (so named despite the lack of any geysers in the area) began production in 1960, increased to a peak in 1989 of 1967 MWe, and lowered to a present capacity of 1070 MWe. By the mid-1990s, the field contained some 600 wells, with an average well depth of 2500 m (8200 ft).

Geothermal power capacity of some 2800 MWe is operating in California, Hawai'i, Nevada, and Utah, with a new 185-MWe plant proposed in the desert near Brawley, California. Figure 1.2 maps low-, medium-, and high-temperature known geothermal resource areas (KGRAs) in the United States. About 300 cities are within 8 km (5 mi) of a KGRA. The Department of Energy has identified about 9000 potential development sites. For more information, see http://www1.eere.energy.gov/geothermal/, http://geothermal.marin.org/, http://www.geothermal.org/, or http://smu.edu/geothermal/.

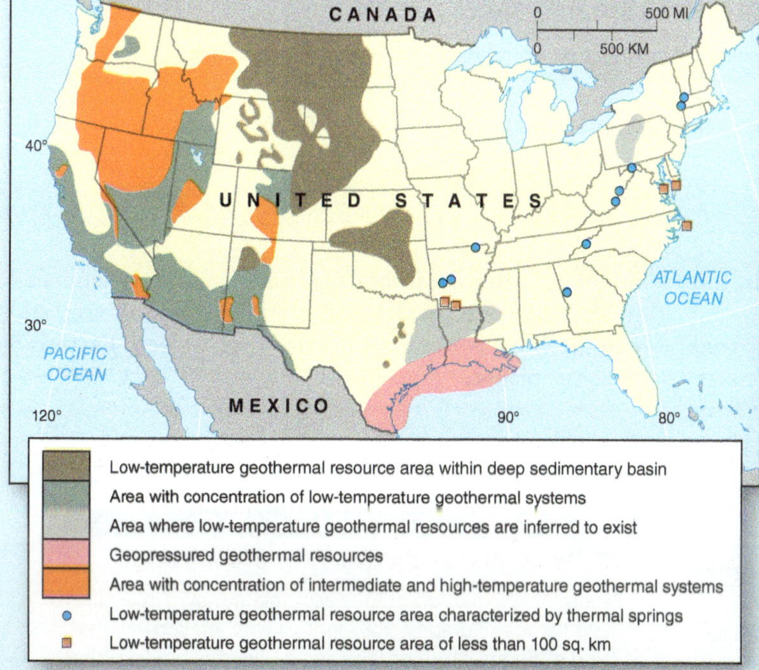

FIGURE 1.2 Known geothermal resource areas.
Geothermal resources in the conterminous United States. [Map courtesy W. A. Duffield *et al.*, *Tapping the Earth's Natural Heat*, USGS Circular 1125, 1994, p. 35.]

plume and a possible change in the plate motion itself. The old thinking that the plumes remained fixed relative to the migrating plate has been revised. At the northernmost extreme, the seamounts that formed about 80 m.y.a. are now approaching the Aleutian Trench, where they eventually will be subducted beneath the Eurasian plate. Perhaps

GEO REPORT 3 *A lot of basalt in Hawai'i*

A mass of basalt forms the island of Hawai'i. From seafloor to summits, it contains about 40,000 km³ (9600 mi³) of basalt, which is enough to cover the states of Massachusetts, Connecticut, and Rhode Island to a depth of 1 km.

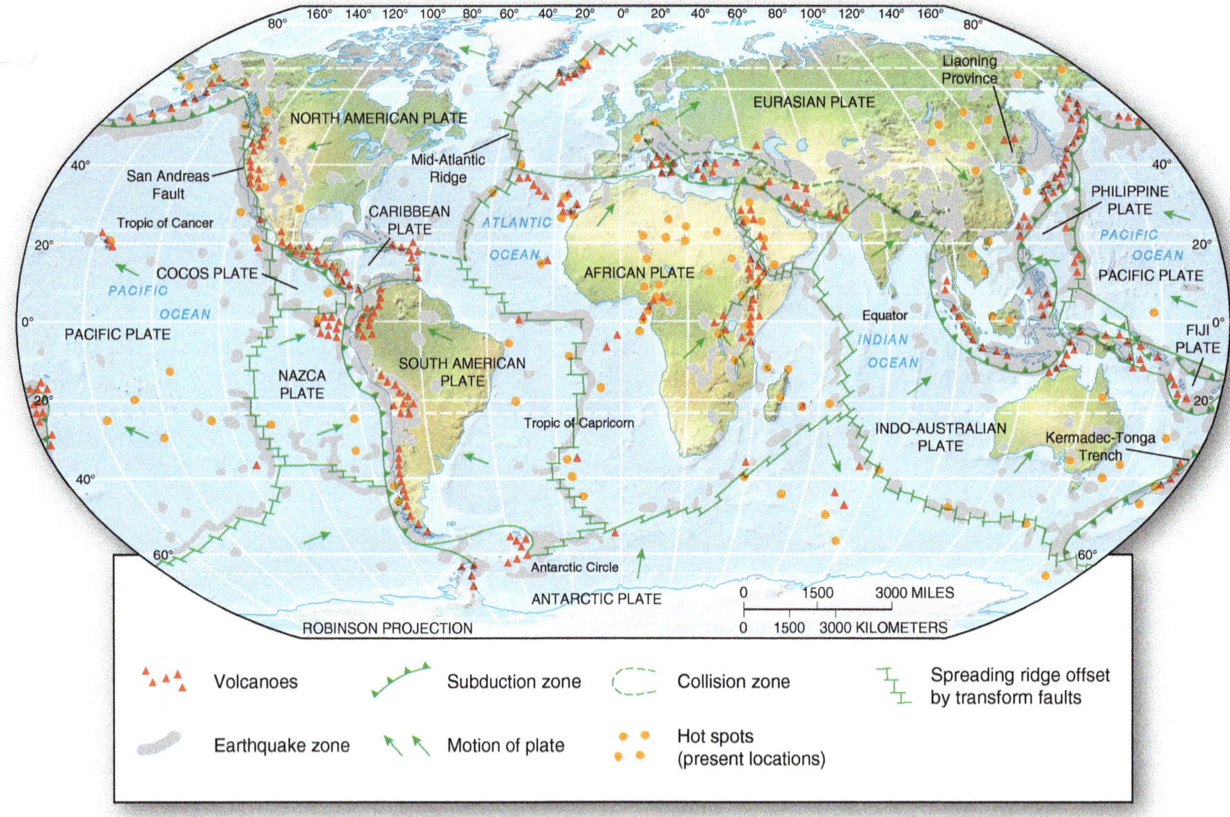

FIGURE 17 Earthquake and volcanic activity locations.
Earthquake and volcanic activity in relation to major tectonic plate boundaries and principal hot spots. [Earthquake, volcano, and hot spot data adapted from USGS.]

some 80 million years hence, the Hawaiian Islands, too, will slowly disappear into the trench. Aloha!

The big island of Hawai'i, the newest, actually took less than 1 million years to build to its present stature. The island is a huge mound of lava, melded from several sea-floor fissures through five volcanoes, rising from the seafloor 5800 m (19,000 ft) to the ocean surface. From sea level, its highest peak, Mauna Kea, rises to an elevation of 4205 m (13,796 ft). This total height of almost 10,000 m (32,800 ft) represents the highest mountain on Earth if measured from the seafloor.

The youngest island in the Hawaiian chain is still a seamount. It rises 3350 m (11,000 ft) from its base, but is still 975 m (3200 ft) beneath the ocean surface. Even though this new island will not experience the tropical Sun for about 10,000 years, it is already named Lo'ihi (noted on the map).

Iceland is a result of an active hot spot sitting astride a mid-ocean ridge—visible on the different maps and images of the seafloor. It is an excellent example of a segment of mid-ocean ridge rising above sea level. This hot spot has generated enough material to form Iceland, and eruptions continue from deep in the mantle, as happened in 2010. As a result, Iceland is still growing in area and volume. This is further evidence that, indeed, Earth is a dynamic planet.

II CRITICAL THINKING 3

How fast is the Pacific plate moving?

Relative to the motion of the Pacific plate shown in Figure 18 (note the map's graphic scale in the lower-left corner), the island of Midway formed 27.7 m.y.a. over the hot spot that is active under the southeast coast of the big island of Hawai'i today. Given the scale of the map, roughly determine the average annual speed of the Pacific plate in centimeters per year for Midway to have traveled this distance. Given your calculation for the plate speed and assuming the directions of movement remain the same, approximately how many years will it take the remnants of Midway to reach 50° N in the upper-left corner of the map?

Alaska
Aleutian Islands
Hawaii
Aleutian Islands
Meiji Seamount
Emperor Seamounts
Hawaiian-Emperor bend
Hawaiian Ridge
Hawaii
0 1000 MILES
0 1000 KILOMETERS
50°
40°
30°
20°
160°
180°
160°
140°
120°
Suiko Seamount (**59.6**)
Nintoku Seamount (**56.2**)
Jingu Seamount (**55.4**)
Ojin Seamount
Koko Seamount (**48.1**)
Kimmei Seamount
Yuryaku Seamount
Abbott Seamount (**38.7**)
Daikakuji Seamount
Direction of Pacific plate movement
Midway (**27.7**)
Kure
Pearl and Hermes Reef
Laysan (**20.0**)
Gardner Pinnacles
Northampton Bank
Necker (**10.3**)
Nihoa
La Perouse Pinnacle
The islands and seamounts in the chain are progressively younger toward the southeast.
Kaua'i (**5.1**)
O'ahu (**2.6**)
Ni'ihau
Maui (**1.3**)
Moloka'i
Lāna'i
Hawai'i (**0.4**)
Hot spot location
Lō'ihi (newest forming future island)
= Exposed island
0 250 500 MILES
0 250 500 KILOMETERS
50°
40°
30°
20°
170°
180°
170°
160°

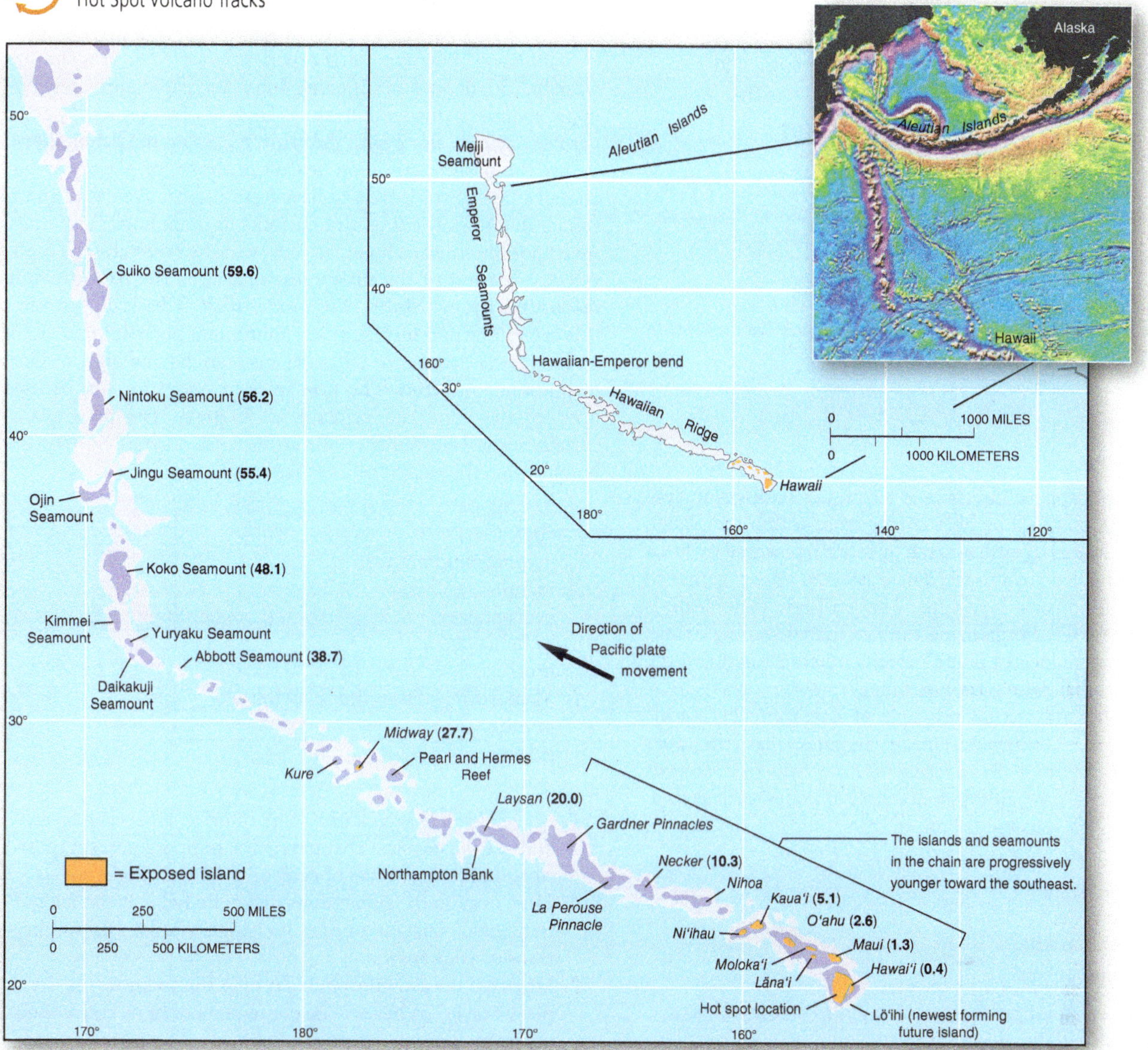

(a)

FIGURE 18 Hot spot tracks across the North Pacific.
Hawai'i and the linear volcanic chain of islands known as the Emperor Seamounts. (a) The islands and seamounts (undersea volcanoes) in the chain are progressively younger toward the southeast. Ages, in m.y.a., are shown in parentheses. Note that Midway Island is 27.7 million years old, meaning that the site was over the plume 27.7 m.y.a. (b) Lo'ihi is forming 975 m (3200 ft) beneath the Pacific Ocean off South Point; presently a seamount, it is growing into the next Hawaiian island. [(a) After D. A. Clague, "Petrology and K–Ar (Potassium–Argon) ages of dredged volcanic rocks from the western Hawaiian ridge and the southern Emperor seamount chain," *Geological Society of America Bulletin* 86 (1975): 991; inset from global gravity anomaly map image, Scripps Institution of Oceanography. (b) Bobbé Christopherson.]

(b) Lō'ihi is off South Point

Beginning with the internal structure of Earth, we tracked the flow of energy toward the surface. Owing to these internal dynamics, the crust is forced about, and gravity pulls on heavier elements. Plate tectonics is the science studying these continent-sized migrating pieces of crust that can move on a collision course with other plates. Earth's present surface map is the result of these vast forces and motions. The surface expressions of all this energy and matter in motion are: the stress and strain of folding, faulting, and deformation; the building of mountains; and the sometimes dramatic activity of earthquakes and volcanoes.

■ ***Distinguish*** between the endogenic and exogenic systems, ***determine*** the driving force for each, and ***explain*** the pace at which these systems operate.

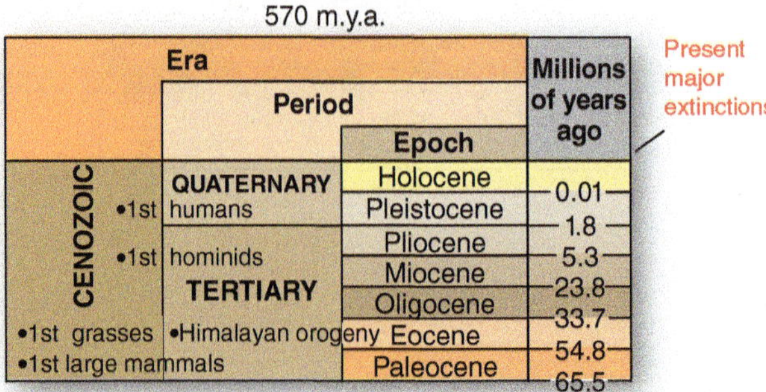

The Earth–atmosphere interface is where the **endogenic system** (internal), powered by heat energy from within the planet, interacts with the **exogenic system** (external), powered by insolation and influenced by gravity. These systems work together to produce Earth's diverse landscape. The **geologic time scale** is an effective device for organizing the vast span of geologic time. It depicts the sequence of Earth's events (relative time) and the approximate actual dates (absolute time).

The most fundamental principle of Earth science is **uniformitarianism**. Uniformitarianism assumes that the *same physical processes active in the environment today have been operating throughout geologic time*, although dramatic episodes, such as massive landslides or volcanic eruptions, can interrupt the flow of events, leading to a state of *punctuated equilibrium*.

endogenic system
exogenic system
geologic time scale
uniformitarianism

1. To what extent is Earth's crust active at this time in its history?
2. Define the endogenic and the exogenic systems. Describe the driving forces that energize these systems.
3. How is the geologic time scale organized? What is the basis for the time scale in relative and absolute terms? What era, period, and epoch are we living in today?
4. Contrast the uniformitarianism and punctuated equilibrium models for Earth's development.

■ ***Diagram*** Earth's interior in cross section, and ***describe*** each distinct layer.

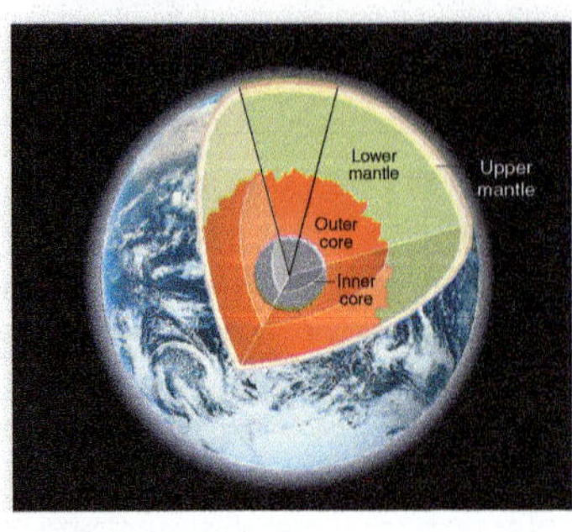

We have learned about Earth's interior from indirect evidence—the way its various layers transmit **seismic waves**. The **core** is differentiated into an inner core and an outer core, divided by a transition zone. Earth's magnetic field is generated almost entirely within the outer core. Polarity reversals in Earth's magnetism are recorded in cooling magma that contains iron minerals. The patterns of **geomagnetic reversal** frozen in rock help scientists piece together the story of Earth's mobile crust.

Beyond Earth's core lies the **mantle**, differentiated into lower mantle and upper mantle. It experiences a gradual temperature increase with depth and stiffening due to increased pressures. The upper mantle is divided into three fairly distinct layers. The uppermost mantle, along with the crust, makes up the **lithosphere**. Below the lithosphere is the **asthenosphere**, or *plastic layer*. It contains pockets of increased heat from radioactive decay and is susceptible to slow convective currents in these hotter materials. An important internal boundary between the **crust** and the high-velocity portion of the uppermost mantle is the **Mohorovičić discontinuity**, or **Moho**. *Continental crust* is basically **granite**; it is crystalline and high in silica, aluminum, potassium, calcium, and sodium. *Oceanic crust* is **basalt**; it is granular and high in silica, magnesium, and iron. The principles of buoyancy and balance produce the important principle of **isostasy**. Isostasy explains certain vertical movements of Earth's crust, such as isostatic rebound when the weight of ice is removed.

seismic wave
core
geomagnetic reversal
mantle
lithosphere
asthenosphere
crust
Mohorovičić discontinuity (Moho)
granite
basalt
isostasy

5. Make a simple sketch of Earth's interior, label each layer, and list the physical characteristics, temperature, composition, and range of size of each on your drawing.
6. How does Earth generate its magnetic field? Is the magnetic field constant, or does it change? Explain the implications of your answer.
7. Describe the asthenosphere. Why is it also known as the plastic layer? What are the consequences of its convection currents?
8. What is a discontinuity? Describe the principal discontinuities within Earth.
9. Define isostasy and isostatic rebound, and explain the crustal equilibrium concept.
10. Diagram the uppermost mantle and crust. Label the density of the layers in grams per cubic centimeter. What two types of crust were described in the text in terms of rock composition?

■ ***Illustrate*** the geologic cycle, and ***relate*** the rock cycle and rock types to endogenic and exogenic processes.

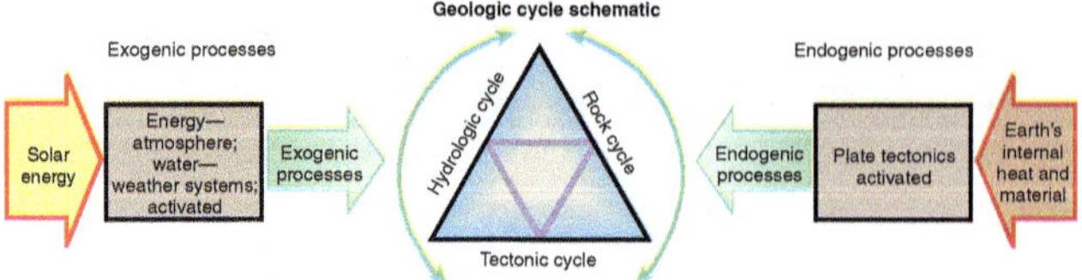

The **geologic cycle** is a model of the internal and external interactions that shape the crust. A **mineral** is an inorganic natural compound having a specific chemical formula and possessing a crystalline structure. A **rock** is an assemblage of minerals bound together (such as granite, a rock containing three minerals), or it may be a mass of a single mineral (such as rock salt).

The geologic cycle comprises three cycles: the *hydrologic cycle*, the *tectonic cycle*, and the **rock cycle**. The rock cycle describes the three principal rock-forming processes and the rocks they produce. **Igneous rocks** form from **magma,** which is molten rock beneath the surface. Magma either *intrudes* into crustal rocks, cools, and hardens, forming **intrusive igneous rock**, or *extrudes* onto the surface, forming **extrusive igneous rock** such as **lava**. Intrusive igneous rock that cools slowly in the crust forms a **pluton**. The largest pluton form is a **batholith**.

Lithification is the cementation, compaction, and hardening of sediments into **sedimentary rocks.** These layered strata form important records of past ages. **Stratigraphy** is the study of the sequence (superposition), thickness, and spatial distribution of strata, which yield clues to the age and origin of the rocks. Clastic sedimentary rocks are derived from the fragments of weathered rocks. Chemical sedimentary rocks are formed from dissolved minerals in solution; the most common is **limestone,** which is lithified calcium carbonate, $CaCO_3$.

Any rock, either igneous or sedimentary, may be transformed into a **metamorphic rock** by going through profound physical or chemical changes under pressure and increased temperature.

geologic cycle
mineral
rock
rock cycle
igneous rock
magma
intrusive igneous rock
lava
extrusive igneous rock
pluton
batholith
sedimentary rock
lithification
stratigraphy
limestone
metamorphic rock

11. Illustrate the geologic cycle, and define each component: rock cycle, tectonic cycle, and hydrologic cycle.
12. What is a mineral? A mineral family? Name the most common minerals on Earth. What is a rock?
13. Describe igneous processes. What is the difference between intrusive and extrusive types of igneous rocks?
14. Characterize both coarse- and fine-grained textures; how is this related to the cooling history of the rock?
15. Briefly describe sedimentary processes and lithification. Describe the sources and particle sizes of sedimentary rocks.
16. What is metamorphism, and how are metamorphic rocks produced? Name some original parent rocks and their metamorphic equivalents.

■ ***Describe*** Pangaea and its breakup, and ***relate*** several physical proofs that crustal drifting is continuing today.

The present configuration of the ocean basins and continents is the result of *tectonic processes* involving Earth's interior dynamics and crust. Alfred Wegener coined the phrase *continental drift* to describe his idea that the crust is moved by vast forces within the planet. **Pangaea** was the name he gave to a single assemblage of continental crust some 225 m.y.a. that subsequently broke apart. Earth's lithosphere is fractured into huge slabs or plates, each moving in response to gravitational pull and to flowing currents in the mantle that create frictional drag on the plate. The all-encompassing theory of **plate tectonics** includes **sea-floor spreading** along **mid-ocean ridges** and denser oceanic crust diving beneath lighter continental crust along **subduction zones**.

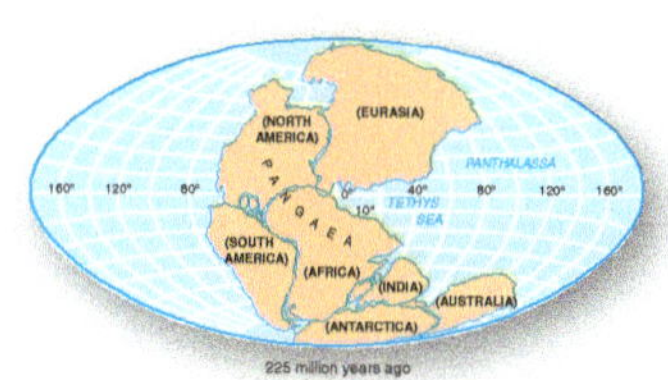

Pangaea
plate tectonics
sea-floor spreading
mid-ocean ridge
subduction zone

17. Briefly review the history of the theory of continental drift, sea-floor spreading, and the all-inclusive plate tectonics theory. What was Alfred Wegener's role?
18. Define upwelling, and describe related features on the ocean floor. Define subduction, and explain the process.
19. What was Pangaea? What happened to it during the past 225 million years?
20. Characterize the three types of plate boundaries and the actions associated with each type.

■ ***Portray*** the pattern of Earth's major plates, and ***relate*** this pattern to the occurrence of earthquakes, volcanic activity, and hot spots.

Occurrences of often-damaging earthquakes and volcanoes are correlated with plate boundaries. Three types of plate boundaries form: divergent, convergent, and transform. Along the offset portions of mid-ocean ridges, horizontal motions produce *transform faults*.

As many as 50 to 100 **hot spots** exist across Earth's surface, where plumes of magma—some anchored in the lower mantle, others originating from shallow sources in the upper mantle—generate a flow upward. **Geothermal energy** literally refers to heat from Earth's interior, whereas *geothermal power* relates to specific applied strategies of geothermal electric or geothermal direct applications.

hot spot
geothermal energy

21. What is the relation between plate boundaries and volcanic and earthquake activity?
22. What is the nature of motion along a transform fault? Name a famous example of such a fault.

Visit **http://www.masteringgeography.com/** for several figure animations, satellite loops, self-study quizzes, flashcards, visual glossary, case studies, career links, text reference maps, RSS Feeds, and an ebook version of *Elemental Geosystems*. Included are many geography web links to interesting Internet sources that support this chapter.

Tectonics, Earthquakes, and Volcanism

Tectonics, Earthquakes, and Volcanism

The scarred ocean floor is clearly visible: sea-floor spreading centers marked by oceanic ridges that stretch over 64,000 km (40,000 mi), subduction zones indicated by deep oceanic trenches, and transform faults slicing across oceanic ridges. [*World Ocean Floor* by Bruce C. Heezen and Marie Tharp, 1977, Office of Naval Research.]

KEY LEARNING CONCEPTS

After reading the chapter, you should be able to:

- ***Describe*** first, second, and third orders of relief, and ***relate*** examples of each from Earth's major topographic regions.
- ***Describe*** the several origins of continental crust, and ***define*** displaced terranes.
- ***Explain*** compressional processes and folding, and ***describe*** four principal types of faults and their characteristic landforms.
- ***Relate*** the three types of plate collisions associated with orogenesis, and ***identify*** specific examples of each.
- ***Explain*** the nature of earthquakes, including their characteristics, measurement, fault mechanics, and forecasting methods.
- ***Distinguish*** between an effusive and an explosive volcanic eruption, and ***describe*** related landforms, using specific examples.

GEOSYSTEMS NOW

The San Jacinto Fault Connection

The San Jacinto fault is an active earthquake fault in southern California. It is part of the San Andreas fault system, which is made up of hundreds of horizontally moving faults. These faults are produced by the relative motion of the northwestward-moving Pacific plate against the southeastward-moving North American plate; some 5 cm (2 in.) per year of motion builds stress and accumulated strain. The San Jacinto fault runs from north of the Mexican border to the "Inland Empire" of San Bernardino, somewhat parallel to the Elsinore fault, which continues on into Orange County, and the Whittier fault, which crosses into Los Angeles. Numerous other related faults lace through the region with this same alignment (Figure GN 1).

From the small inland communities in the Mohave Desert to the sprawling coastal population centers of metropolitan Los Angeles, the people of southern California live with earthquakes. One overriding question for everyone is, "When will the 'Big One' occur?" The U.S. Geological Survey (USGS) regards the San Jacinto fault as capable of an M 7.5 quake ("M" is the abbreviation for *moment magnitude* and refers to an earthquake rating scale discussed in this chapter). The San Jacinto fault's relation to the Elsinore, Whittier, and other fault lines in the San Andreas system indicates the potential for major earthquakes across the metropolitan southern California landscape.

An M 7.5 would release almost 30 times more energy than that produced by the 1994 Northridge earthquake—thus, a major quake compared to a strong quake. Remember, the Northridge quake remains the most costly in terms of property damage in U.S. history.

Scientific evidence regarding the nature of faulting and crustal movement suggests that a major earthquake may be preceded by a number of small earthquakes in an area. Recent evidence points to a "wavelike pattern" of small quakes as rupturing spreads along the fault plane. The latest earthquake activity along the San Jacinto and Elsinore faults may be following this pattern.

Records show that at least six quakes have occurred along the San Jacinto fault in the last 50 years: an M 5.8 and M 6.5 in 1968, an M 5.3 in 1980, and an M 5.0 in 2005. Then an M 4.1 hit February 13, 2010, about 40 km (25 mi) south of Palm Springs. The largest of the sequence was the M 7.2 El Mayor–Cucapah quake on April 4, 2010, some 65 km south-southeast of El Centro, in Baja, Mexico. An aftershock of M 5.7 occurred on June 15.

The April quake transferred strain to the San Jacinto fault, with large clusters of aftershocks toward the north in the fault structure. Continuing the pattern, an M 5.4 quake hit along the San Jacinto fault on July 7, 2010, the Borrego quake, with aftershocks again spread to the northwest. If strain is moving northward along the system, then there should be much concern. A network of 100 global positioning system (GPS) stations monitors any crustal change across the region that might indicate an upcoming earthquake. More on earthquake forecasting is ahead in this chapter.

As said so many times in this text, such a situation adds to the importance of Earth systems science and physical geography toward education of the public to ensure proper planning, zoning, and preparation. Zoning could block new construction in particularly vulnerable areas and promote the retrofitting of poorly built infrastructure. A great quake along the San Jacinto and related faults should not be a surprise, but should be anticipated with adaptation and mitigation actions in place. ■

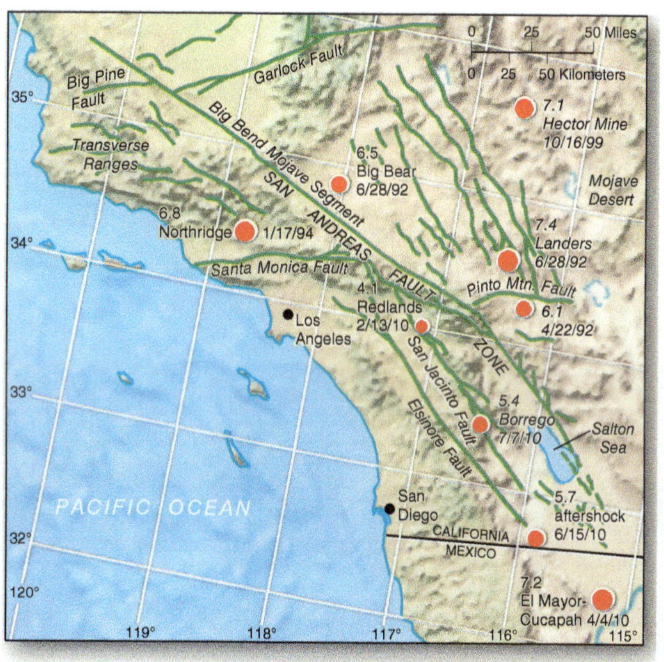

FIGURE GN 1 Southern California seismic map.

Earth's endogenic systems produce flows of heat and material toward the surface to form crust. Ongoing processes produce continental landscapes and oceanic sea-floor crust, sometimes in dramatic episodes. Earth's physical systems move to the front pages whenever an earthquake strikes or after one of the nearly 50 volcanic eruptions a year that threaten a city.

In Haiti and Chile in 2010 and in New Zealand and Japan in 2011, the world was again riveted to images of massive earthquakes as unstable plate boundaries snapped into new positions. The quake along northeastern Honshu Island produced a devastating tsunami, an estimated 30,000 deaths, and an estimated USD $325 billion in damage (Figure 1). More on these recent events is in Focus Study 1 in this chapter.

Volcanic eruptions pose threats to the lives and property of those who live in proximity to the hazard. Earth systems science is providing analysis and warnings to affected populations as never before. For instance, in April 2010 the Eyjafjallajökull volcano in southern Iceland erupted (see Figure 22). Previously, this mountain had erupted in 1821 and 1823. The ash cloud rose to 10,660 m (35,000 ft) and quickly dispersed toward Europe and commercial airline corridors. Airspace was closed for five days, canceling more than 100,000 flights. When flights resumed, routes were changed to avoid lingering ash. Because this eruption was essentially horizontal in the lower atmosphere, there was not a climate signature in Earth's atmosphere, as occurred from Mount Pinatubo in 1991 and its vertical blast, which caused a brief temperature lowering.

In this chapter: We examine processes that construct Earth's surface and create world structural regions. Tectonic processes deform, recycle, and reshape Earth's crust. These processes occur sometimes in dramatic episodes, but most often in slow, deliberate motions that build the landscape. Continental crust has been forming throughout most of Earth's 4.6-billion-year existence.

The arrangement of continents and oceans, the origin of mountain ranges, the topography of the land and the seafloor, and the locations of earthquake and volcanic activity are all evidence of our dynamic Earth. Principal seismic and volcanic zones occur along plate boundaries and hot-spot locations, thus linking plate tectonics to the potential devastation of earthquakes and to the local threats of major volcanic eruptions and their attendant global climatic impact.

We begin our look at tectonics and volcanism on the ocean floor, hidden from direct view. The map that opens this chapter is a striking representation, laying the foundation for this chapter and subsequent study. Try to correlate this sea-floor illustration with maps of crustal plates and plate boundaries.

CRITICAL THINKING 1

Ocean floor tectonics tour

Using the chapter-opening map, follow the ocean ridge and spreading center known as the East Pacific Rise northward as it trends beneath the west coast of the North American plate, disappearing under earthquake-prone California. Locate the continents, the offshore-submerged continental shelves, and the expanse of the sediment-covered abyssal plain on the map.

On the floor of the Indian Ocean, you see the wide track along which the Indian plate traveled northward to its collision with the Eurasian plate. Vast deposits of sediment cover the Indian Ocean floor, south of the Ganges River and to the east of India. Sediments derived from the Himalayan Range blanket the floor of the Bay of Bengal (south of Bangladesh) to a depth of 20 km (12.4 mi). These sediments result from centuries of soil erosion in the land of the monsoons.

In the Pacific, a chain of islands and seamounts marks the hot-spot track on the Pacific plate from Hawai'i to the Aleutians. Visible as dark trenches are subduction zones south and east of Alaska and Japan and along the western coast of South and Central America. Follow the Mid-Atlantic Ridge spreading center the full length of the Atlantic to where it passes through Iceland, sitting astride the ridge. Take time with this map.

FIGURE 1 Earthquake and tsunami damage in Japan.
Damage scene 4 days after the March 11, 2011, quake and tsunami in Ofunato, Japan, north of Sendai. [U.S. Navy photo by Specialist 1st Class M.M. Bradley.]

Earth's Surface Relief

Relief refers to vertical elevation differences in the landscape. Examples include the low relief of Nebraska and Saskatchewan, the medium relief of foothills along mountain ranges, and the high relief of the Rockies and Himalayas. The undulating form of Earth's surface, including its relief, is **topography**, portrayed so effectively on topographic maps—the lay of the land.

The relief and topography of Earth's landforms played a vital role in human history: High mountain passes both protected and isolated societies, ridges and valleys dictated transportation routes, and vast plains necessitated developing faster methods of communication and travel. Earth's topography has stimulated human invention and spurred adaptation.

Crustal Orders of Relief and Hypsometry

For convenience of description, geographers group the landscape's topography into three *orders of relief*. These orders classify landscapes by scale, from vast ocean basins and continents down to local hills and valleys. The first order of relief is the coarsest level of landforms, consisting of the continents and oceans. **Continental landmasses** are those portions of crust that reside above or near sea level, including the undersea continental shelves along the coastlines. **Ocean basins**, featured in the chapter-opening map illustration, are entirely below sea level. Approximately 71% of Earth is covered by water.

The second order of relief is the intermediate level of landforms, for both continental and ocean-basin features. Continental features in the second order of relief include mountain masses, plains, and lowlands. A few examples are the Alps, Canadian and American Rockies, west Siberian lowland, and Tibetan Plateau. The great rock "shields" that form the heart of each continental mass are of this second order. In the ocean basins, the second order of relief includes continental rises, slopes, abyssal plains, mid-ocean ridges, submarine canyons, and oceanic trenches (subduction zones)—all visible in the sea-floor illustration that opens this chapter.

The third and most detailed order of relief includes individual mountains, cliffs, valleys, hills, and other landforms of smaller scale. These features are identifiable as local landscapes.

Modern computers, satellite radar, and tools such as GPS for determining location and elevation assist in studying Earth's relief and topography. Scientists put elevation data in digital form for computer manipulation and display in *digital elevation models (DEMs)*. Since 2000, the Shuttle Radar Topography Mission (SRTM) has surveyed almost 80% of Earth's land surface. Figure 2 features two of these images showing second and third orders of relief. For more information and the SRTM Gallery, see http://www2.jpl.nasa.gov/srtm/mission.htm.

(a) Kamchatka Peninsula

(b) Panama Canal and local landscape

FIGURE 2 Second and third orders of relief. SRTM images portray second orders of relief on the Kamchatka Peninsula, Russia (a), and third orders of relief along the Panama Canal (b). [Shuttle Radar Topography Mission, courtesy of JPL/NGA/NASA–CalTech.]

Other examples are the digitized shaded relief map of the United States prepared by the USGS and the related map combining topography and geology. Available at the USGS web site titled "A Tapestry of Time and Terrain," this composite map offers a detailed color illustration of land surfaces and the ages of underlying formations (see http://tapestry.usgs.gov/).

Figure 3 is a *hypsographic curve* (from the Greek *hypsos*, meaning "height") that shows the distribution of Earth's surface by area and elevation in relation to sea level. Relative to Earth's diameter of 12,756 km (7926 mi), the surface is of low relief—only about 20 km (12.5 mi) from highest peak to lowest oceanic trench. For perspective, Mount Everest is 8.8 km (5.5 mi) above sea level, and the Mariana Trench is 11 km (6.8 mi) below sea level.

GEO REPORT 1 ***Mount Everest at new heights***

In 1999, climbers determined a new height for Mount Everest using direct GPS placement on the mountain's icy summit. Everest's new elevation of 8850 m (29,035 ft) is close to the previous official measure of 8848 m (29,028 ft) set in 1954 by the Survey of India. GPS readings also indicated that the Himalayas are moving northeastward at a rate up to 6 mm (0.25 in.) per year, as the mountain range is being driven farther into Asia by plate tectonics—the continuing collision of Indian and Asian landmasses.

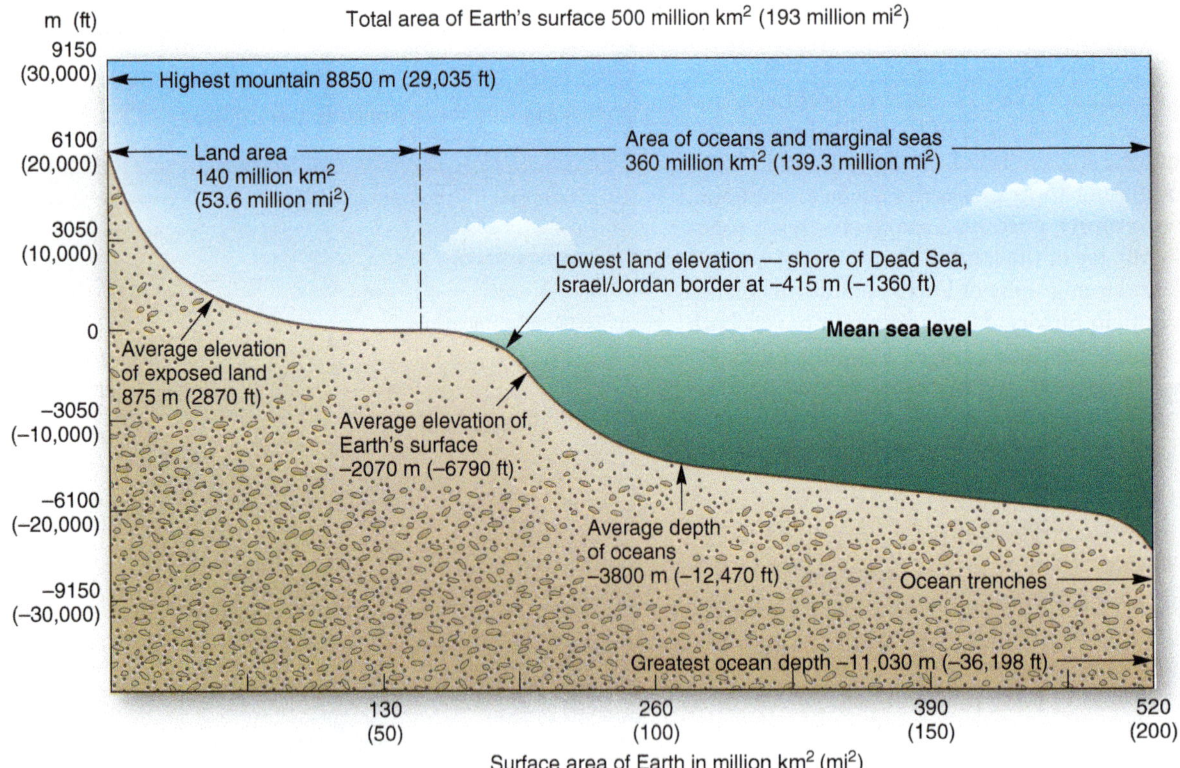

FIGURE 3 Earth's hypsometry.
Hypsographic curve of Earth's surface area and elevation as related to mean sea level. From the highest point above sea level (Mount Everest) to the deepest oceanic trench (Mariana Trench), Earth's overall relief is almost 20 km (12.5 mi).

The average elevation of Earth's solid surface is actually under water: –2070 m (–6790 ft) below mean sea level. The average elevation for exposed land is only 875 m (2870 ft). For the ocean depths, the average elevation is –3800 m (–12,470 ft). From this description you can see that, on the average, the oceans are much deeper than continental regions are high. Overall the underwater ocean basins, ocean floor, and submarine mountain ranges form Earth's largest "landscape."

Earth's Topographic Regions

The three orders of relief can be further generalized into six topographic regions: plains, high tablelands, hills and low tablelands, mountains, widely spaced mountains, and depressions (Figure 4). An arbitrary elevation or descriptive limit that is in common use defines each type of topography (see the map legend).

Four of the continents possess extensive *plains*, areas with local relief of less than 100 m (325 ft) and slope angles of 5° or less. Some plains have high elevations of more than 600 m (2000 ft); in the United States, the high plains attain elevations above 1220 m (4000 ft). The Colorado Plateau, Greenland, and Antarctica are notable *high tablelands* (the latter two composed of ice), with elevations exceeding 1520 m (5000 ft). *Hills* and *low tablelands* dominate Africa.

Mountain ranges, characterized by local relief exceeding 600 m (2000 ft), occur on each continent. Earth's relief and topography are undergoing constant change as a result of processes that form crust.

II CRITICAL THINKING 2

Scaling topographic regions to your area

Using the topographic regions map in Figure 4, assess the region within 100 km (62 mi) and 1000 km (620 mi) of your campus. Describe the topographic character and the variety of relief within these two regional scales. You may want to consult local maps and atlases in your analysis or *Google Earth*. Do you perceive that this type of topographic region influences lifestyles? Economic activities? Transportation? Was it influential in the history of the region?

Crustal Formation

How did Earth's continental crust form? What gave rise to the three orders of relief just discussed? Earth's surface is a battleground of opposing processes: On the one hand, tectonic activity, driven by our planet's internal energy, builds crust; on the other hand, the exogenic processes of weathering and erosion, powered by the Sun through the actions of air, water, waves, and ice, tear down crust. Consider the compression as Africa and Saudi Arabia crush northeastward into the Persian Gulf and Iran, while exogenic energy fuels a massive dust storm.

Tectonic activity generally is slow, requiring millions of years. Endogenic processes result in gradual uplift and new landforms, with major mountain building occurring along plate boundaries. These uplifted crustal regions are

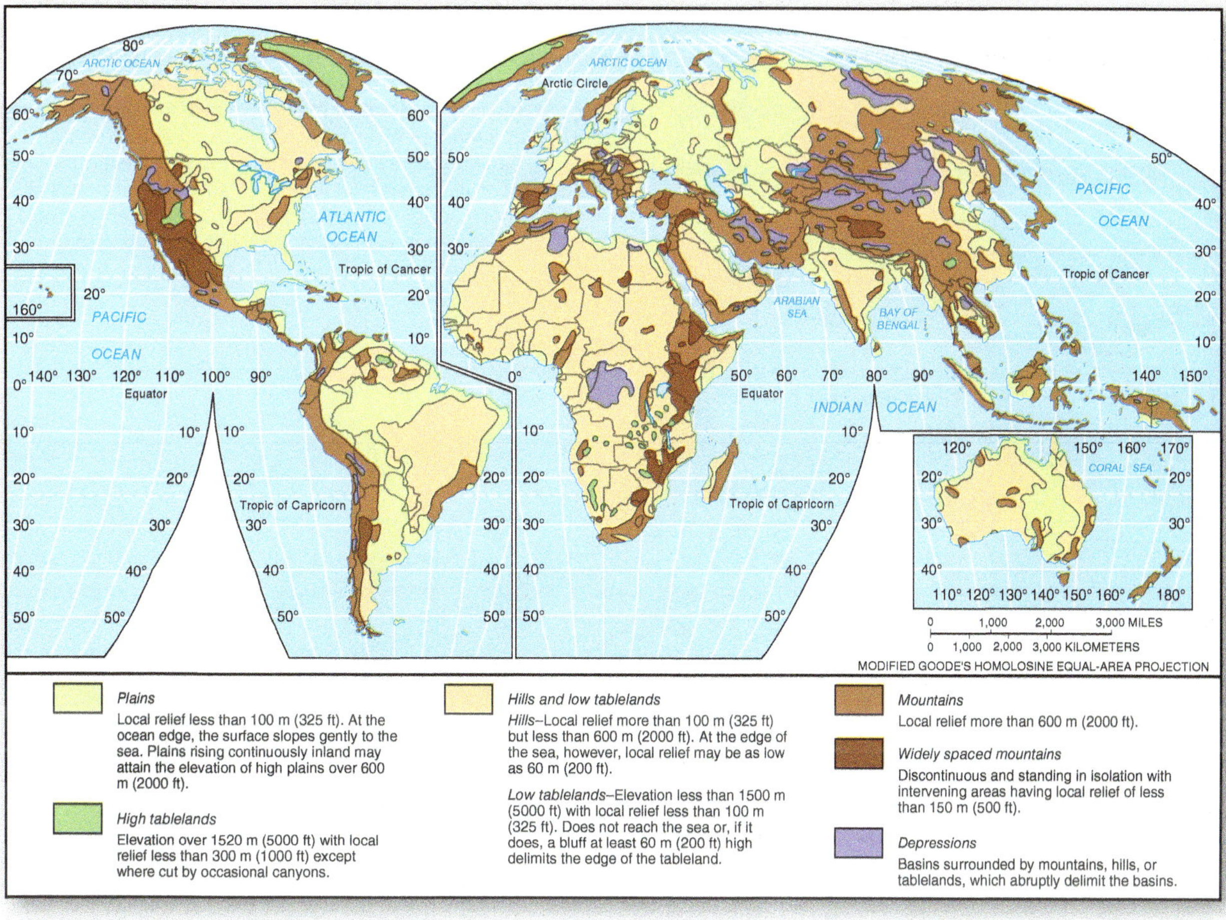

ARCTIC OCEAN
Arctic Circle
ATLANTIC OCEAN
PACIFIC OCEAN
Tropic of Cancer
Equator
Tropic of Capricorn
ARABIAN SEA
BAY OF BENGAL
INDIAN OCEAN
CORAL SEA
0 1,000 2,000 3,000 MILES
0 1,000 2,000 3,000 KILOMETERS
MODIFIED GOODE'S HOMOLOSINE EQUAL-AREA PROJECTION
Plains
Local relief less than 100 m (325 ft). At the ocean edge, the surface slopes gently to the sea. Plains rising continuously inland may attain the elevation of high plains over 600 m (2000 ft).
High tablelands
Elevation over 1520 m (5000 ft) with local relief less than 300 m (1000 ft) except where cut by occasional canyons.
Hills and low tablelands
Hills–Local relief more than 100 m (325 ft) but less than 600 m (2000 ft). At the edge of the sea, however, local relief may be as low as 60 m (200 ft).
Low tablelands–Elevation less than 1500 m (5000 ft) with local relief less than 100 m (325 ft). Does not reach the sea or, if it does, a bluff at least 60 m (200 ft) high delimits the edge of the tableland.
Mountains
Local relief more than 600 m (2000 ft).
Widely spaced mountains
Discontinuous and standing in isolation with intervening areas having local relief of less than 150 m (500 ft).
Depressions
Basins surrounded by mountains, hills, or tablelands, which abruptly delimit the basins.

FIGURE 4 Earth's topographic regions.
Compare the map and legend to the world physical map inside the back cover of this text. [After R. E. Murphy, "Landforms of the world," *Annals of the Association of American Geographers* 58, 1 (March 1968). Adapted by permission.]

quite varied, but we think of them in three general categories, all discussed in this chapter:

- Residual mountains and stable continental cratons, formed from inactive remnants of ancient tectonic activity;
- Tectonic mountains and landforms, produced by active folding, faulting, and crustal movements; and
- Volcanic features, formed by the surface accumulation of molten rock from eruptions of subsurface materials.

Thus, several distinct processes operate in concert to produce the continental crust we see around us.

Continental Shields

All continents have a nucleus of ancient crystalline rock on which the continent "grows" with the addition of crustal fragments and sediments. This nucleus is the *craton*, or heartland region, of the continental crust. Cratons generally have been eroded to a low elevation and relief. Most date to the Precambrian and can be more than 2 billion years old. The lack of basaltic components in these cratons offers a clue to their stability. The lithosphere is thicker in cratonic regions, which consist of crust and the lithospheric uppermost mantle, than it is beneath younger portions of continents and oceanic crust.

A **continental shield** is a region where a craton is exposed at the surface. Figure 5 shows the principal areas of exposed shields and a photo of the Canadian shield in Québec. Layers of younger sedimentary rock surround these shields and appear quite stable over time. Examples of such a stable platform are the region that stretches from east of the Rockies to the Appalachians and northward into central and eastern Canada, a large portion of China, eastern Europe to the Ural Mountains, and portions of Siberia.

On the *MasteringGeography* web site, you will find a map of seven world structural regions that possess distinctive types of landscapes, grouped because of their shared physical characteristics. As you examine the map, identify the continental shield at the heart of each landmass. Continental platforms composed of younger sedimentary deposits surround these areas. Various mountain chains, rifted regions, and isolated volcanic areas are also noted on the map.

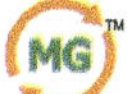

MG™ Notebook World Structural Regions and Major Mountain Systems

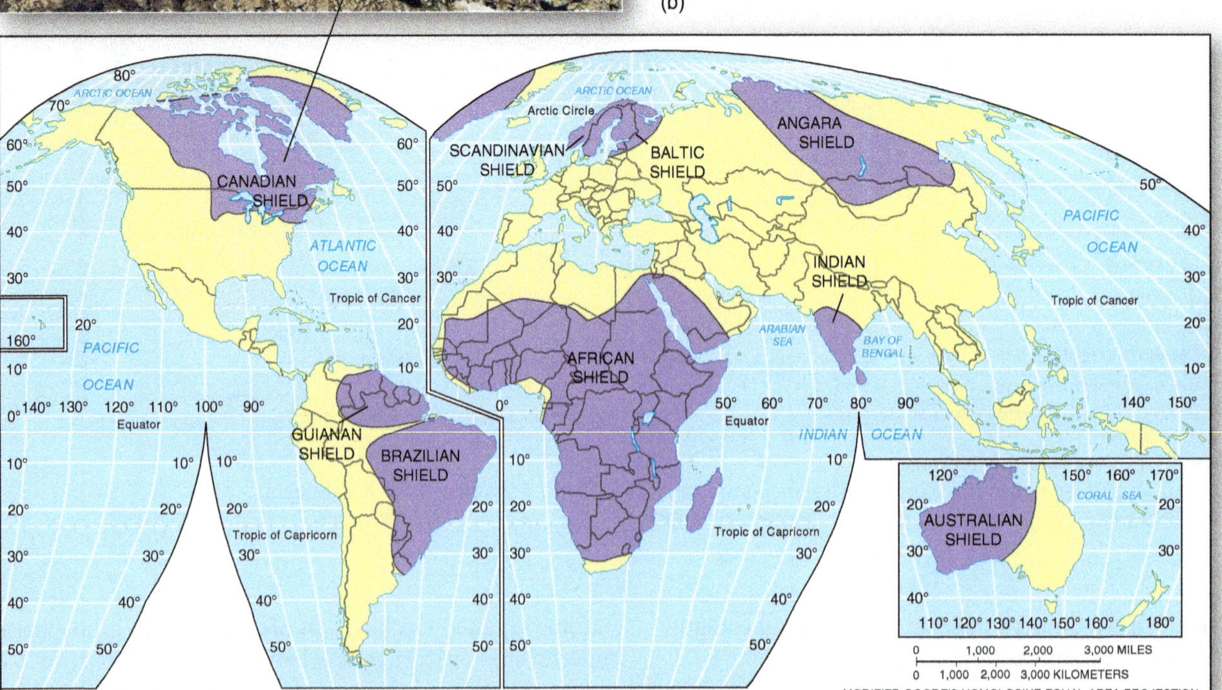

(b)

(a)

FIGURE 5 Continental shields.
(a) Portions of major continental shields exposed by erosion. Adjacent portions of these shields remain covered by younger sedimentary layers. (b) Canadian shield landscape in northern Québec, stable for hundreds of millions of years, stripped by past glaciations and marked by intrusive igneous dikes (magmatic intrusions). **Can you see evidence in the photo of directional flow of the continental glaciers?** [(a) After R. E. Murphy, "Landforms of the world," *Annals of the Association of American Geographers* 58, 1 (March 1968). Adapted by permission. (b) Bobbé Christopherson.]

Building Continental Crust and Terranes

The formation of continental crust is complex and takes hundreds of millions of years. It involves the entire sequence of sea-floor spreading and formation of oceanic crust, its later subduction and remelting, and its subsequent rise as new magma, all summarized in Figure 6.

To understand this process, study Figure 6 and the inset photos. Begin with the magma that originates in the asthenosphere and wells up along the mid-ocean ridges. Basaltic magma is formed from minerals in the upper mantle that are rich in iron and magnesium. Such magma contains less than 50% silica and has a low-viscosity (thin) texture—it tends to flow. This mafic material rises to erupt at spreading centers and cools to form new basaltic seafloor, which spreads outward to collide with continental crust along its far edges. This denser oceanic crust plunges beneath the lighter continental crust, into the mantle, where it remelts. The new magma then rises and cools, forming more continental crust, in the form of intrusive granitic igneous rock.

As the subducting oceanic plate works its way under a continental plate, it takes with it trapped seawater and sediment from eroded continental crust. The remelting incorporates the seawater, sediments, and surrounding crust into the mixture. As a result, the magma, generally called a *melt*, which migrates upward from a subducted plate, contains 50%–75% silica and aluminum (called *andesitic* or *silicic*, depending on silica content). The melt has a high-viscosity (thick) texture—it tends to block and plug conduits to the surface.

Bodies of such silica-rich magma may reach the surface in explosive volcanic eruptions, or they may stop short and become subsurface intrusive bodies in the crust, cooling slowly to form granitic crystalline plutons such as batholiths. Note that this composition is quite different from that of the magma that rises directly

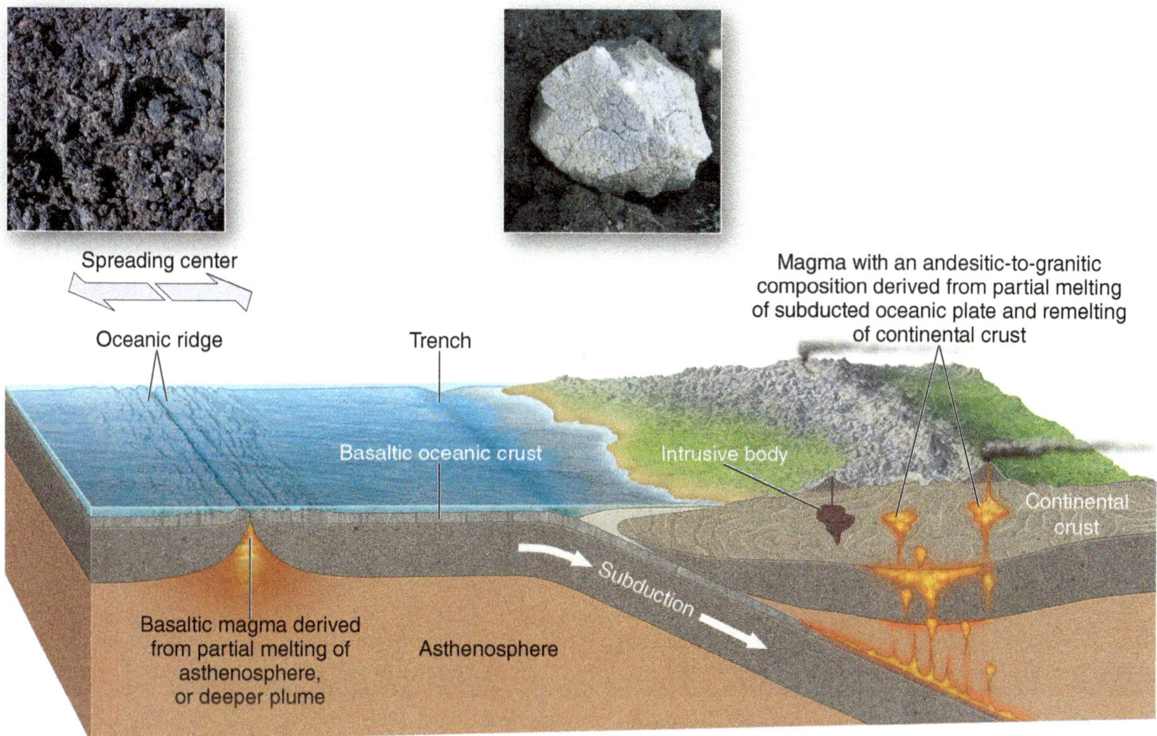

FIGURE 6 Crustal formation.
Material from the asthenosphere upwells along sea-floor spreading centers. Basaltic ocean floor is subducted beneath lighter continental crust, where it melts, along with its cargo of sediments, water, and minerals. This melting generates magma, which makes its way up through the crust to form igneous intrusions and extrusive eruptions. The dacite volcanic bomb (lighter rock on right, higher in silica) is from Mount St. Helens, and the basalt rock (darker rock on left, lower in silica) is from Hawai'i. What does this coloration tell you about the rocks' history and composition? [Bobbé Christopherson.]

from the asthenosphere at sea-floor spreading centers. In these processes of crustal formation, you can literally follow the cycling of materials through the tectonic cycle.

Each of Earth's major lithospheric plates actually is a collage of many crustal pieces acquired from a variety of sources. Crustal fragments of ocean floor, curving chains (or arcs) of volcanic islands, and other pieces of continental crust all have been forced against the edges of continental shields and platforms. These slowly migrating crustal pieces, which have become attached or accreted to the plates, are **terranes** (not to be confused with *terrain*, which refers to the topography of a tract of land). These displaced terranes, sometimes called *microplate* or *exotic terranes*, have histories different from those of the continents that capture them. They are usually framed by fault-zone fractures and differ in rock composition and structure from their new continental homes.

In the region surrounding the Pacific, accreted terranes are particularly prevalent. At least 25% of the growth of western North America can be attributed to the accretion of at least 50 terranes since the early Jurassic Period (190 million years ago). A good example is the Wrangell Mountains, which lie just east of Prince William Sound and the city of Valdez, Alaska. The *Wrangellia terranes*—a former volcanic island arc and associated marine sediments from near the equator—migrated approximately 10,000 km (6200 mi) to form the Wrangell Mountains and three other distinct formations along the western margin of the continent. A map of these terranes is on the *MasteringGeography* web site.

The Appalachian Mountains, extending from Alabama to the Maritime Provinces of Canada, possess bits of land once attached to ancient Europe, Africa, South America, Antarctica, and various oceanic islands. The discovery of terranes, made only in the 1980s, demonstrates one of the ways continents are assembled.

Crustal Deformation

Rocks, whether igneous, sedimentary, or metamorphic, are subjected to powerful stress by tectonic forces, gravity, and the weight of overlying rocks. Figure 7 shows three types of stress: *tension* (stretching), *compression* (shortening), and *shear* (twisting or tearing).

Strain is how rocks respond to stress. Strain is expressed in rocks by *folding* (bending) or *faulting* (breaking). Think of stress as a force and the resulting strain as the deformation in the rock. Whether a rock bends or breaks depends on several factors, including composition and how much pressure is on the rock. An important quality is whether the rock is *brittle* or *ductile*. The patterns created by these processes are clearly visible in the landforms we see today,

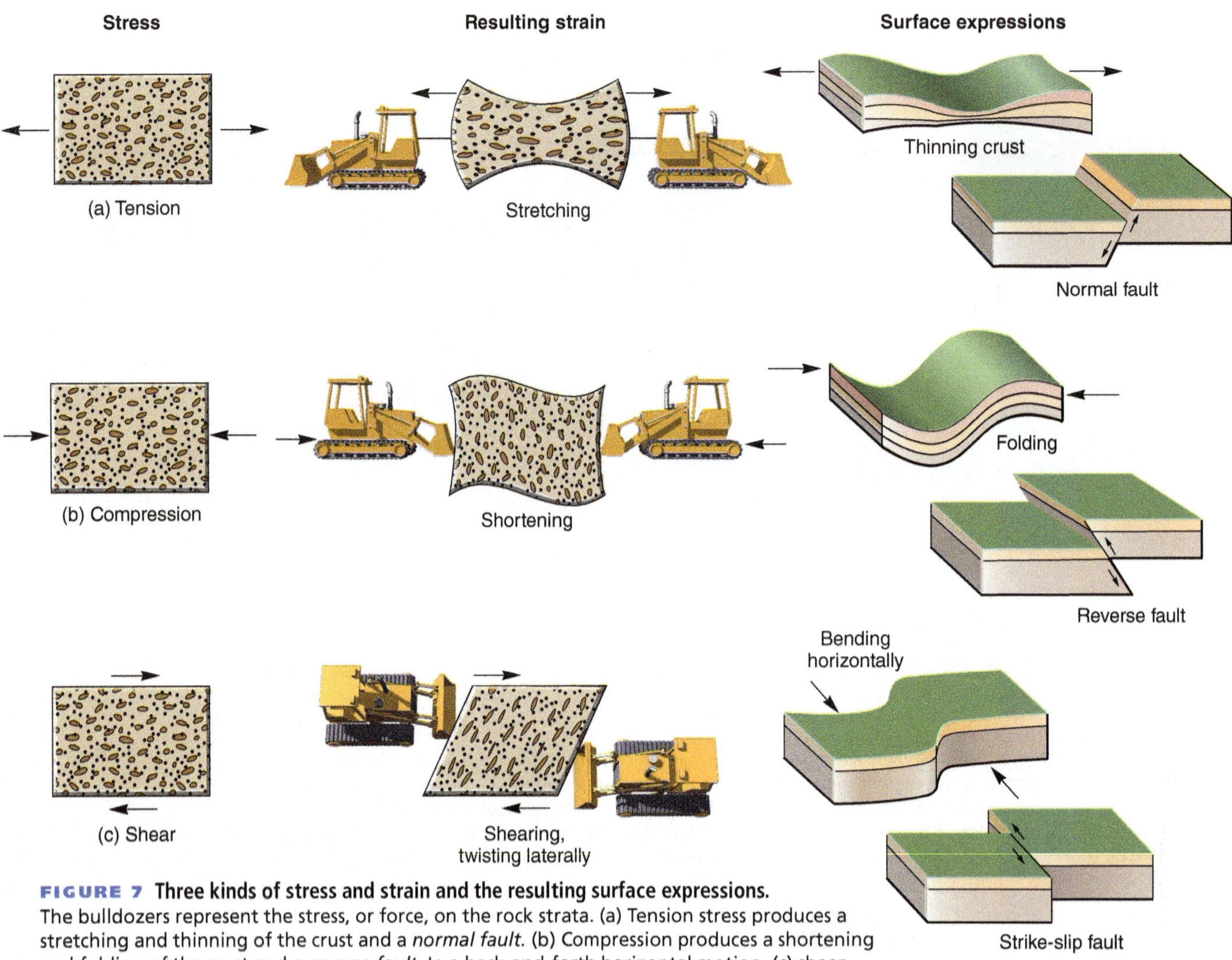

FIGURE 7 Three kinds of stress and strain and the resulting surface expressions. The bulldozers represent the stress, or force, on the rock strata. (a) Tension stress produces a stretching and thinning of the crust and a *normal fault*. (b) Compression produces a shortening and folding of the crust and a *reverse fault*. In a back-and-forth horizontal motion, (c) shear stress produces a bending of the crust and, on breaking, a *strike-slip fault*.

especially in mountain areas. Figure 7 illustrates each type of stress and the resulting strain and surface expressions that develop.

Folding and Broad Warping

When rock strata that are layered and flat are subjected to compressional forces, they become deformed (Figure 8). Convergent plate boundaries intensely compress rocks, deforming them in a process known as **folding**. As an analogy, if we take sections of thick fabric, stack them flat on a table, and then slowly push on opposite ends of the stack, the cloth layers will bend and rumple into folds similar to those shown in Figure 8a.

If we then draw a line down the center axis of a resulting ridge and a line down the center axis of a resulting trough, we see how the names of the folds are assigned. Along the *ridge* of a fold, layers *slope downward away from the axis*, forming an **anticline**. In the *trough* of a fold, however, layers *slope downward toward the axis*, resulting in a **syncline**.

If the axis of either type of fold is not "level" (horizontal, or parallel to Earth's surface), the fold axis then *plunges*, inclined (dipped down) at an angle. Knowledge of how folds are angled to Earth's surface and where they are located is important for the petroleum industry. For example, petroleum geologists know that oil and natural gas collect in the upper portions of anticlinal folds in permeable rock layers such as sandstone.

Figure 8a further illustrates the landforms that result from the effects of weathering and other exogenic processes in folded landscapes:

- A residual *synclinal ridge* may form within a syncline because different rock strata offer greater resistance to weathering processes. An actual synclinal ridge is exposed dramatically in an interstate highway road cut in Figure 8b.
- Compressional forces often push folds far enough that they actually overturn upon their own strata (*overturned anticline*).
- Further stress eventually fractures the rock strata along distinct lines, and some overturned folds are thrust upward, causing a considerable shortening of the original strata (*thrust fault*). Areas of intense stress, compressional folding, and faulting are visible in a road cut where the San Andreas fault in southern California passes beneath the Antelope Valley Freeway (Figure 8c).

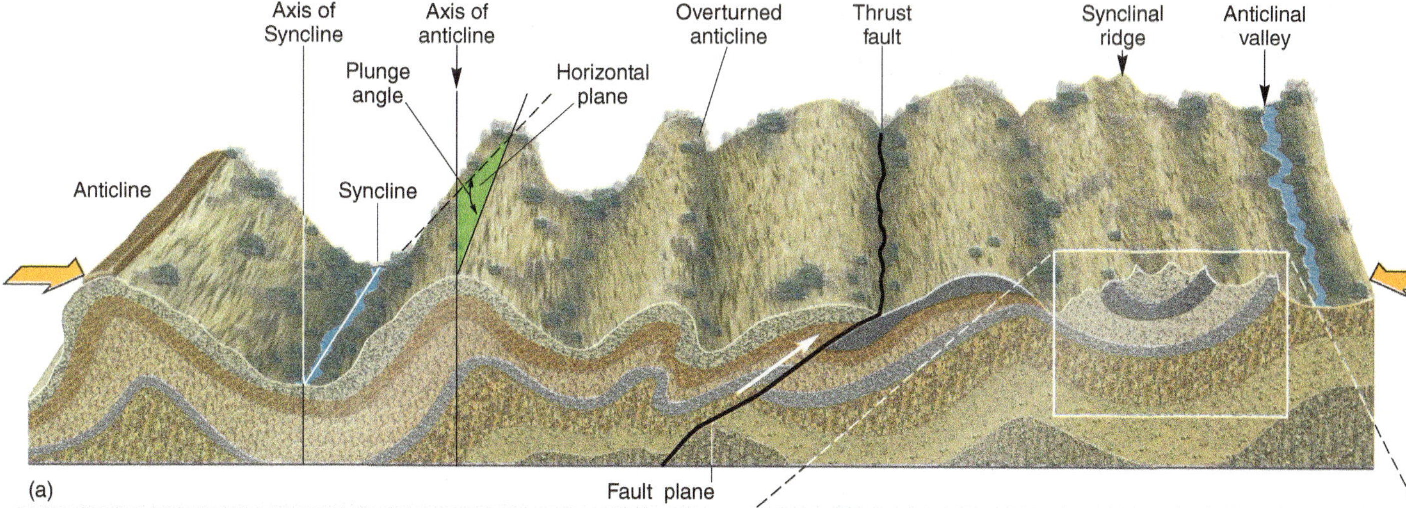

(c) Folded strata along San Andreas fault

(b) Synclinal ridge, western Maryland

FIGURE 8 Folded landscapes.
(a) Folded landscape and the basic types of fold structures. (b) A road cut exposes a synclinal ridge in western Maryland. This syncline is a natural outdoor classroom, and the state of Maryland built an interpretive center with a walkway above the highway. (c) Folding, squeezing, and uplift from strong compressional and shearing forces show well in a road cut along the San Andreas fault zone, beside the Antelope Valley Freeway. [(b) Mike Boroff/Photri-Microstock. (c) Bobbé Christopherson.]

The Canadian Rocky Mountains, the Appalachian Mountains, and areas of the Middle East illustrate the complexity of folded landscapes. Satellites allow us to view many of these structures from an orbital perspective, as in Figure 9, north of the Persian Gulf in the Zagros Mountains of Iran. This area was a dispersed terrane that separated from the Eurasian plate. However, the collision produced by the northward push of the Arabian block is now shoving this terrane back into Eurasia and forming an active margin known as the Zagros crush zone, a continuing collision more than 400 km (250 mi) wide. In the satellite image, anticlines form the parallel ridges; active weathering and erosion processes are exposing the underlying strata.

In addition to the rumpling of rock strata just discussed, broad warping actions affect Earth's continental crust. These actions produce similar up-and-down bending of strata, but the bends are far greater in extent than those produced by folding. Warping forces include mantle convection, isostatic adjustment such as that caused by the weight of previous ice loads across northern Canada, and crustal swelling above an underlying hot spot. Warping features can be small, individual, foldlike structures called *basins* and *domes* (Figure 10a and b). They can also range up to regional features the size of the Ozark Mountain complex in Arkansas and Missouri, the Colorado Plateau in the West, the Richat Dome in Mauritania, or the Black Hills of South Dakota (Figure 10c and d).

Faulting

A freshly poured concrete sidewalk is smooth and strong. But stress the sidewalk by driving heavy equipment over it, and the resulting strain might cause a fracture. Pieces on either side of the fracture may move up, down, or horizontally depending on the direction of stress. Similarly, when rock strata are stressed beyond their ability to remain a

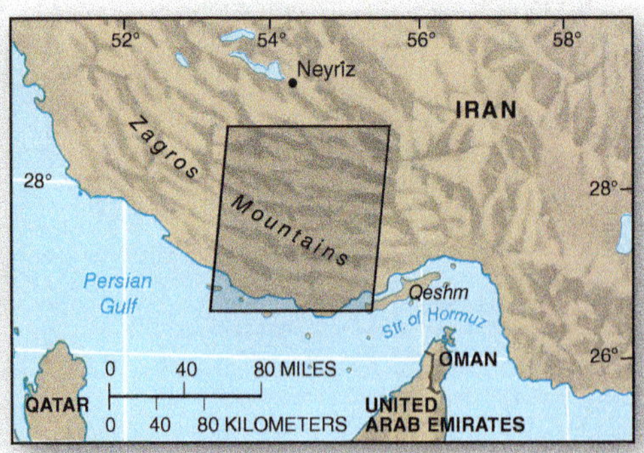

FIGURE 9 Folding in the Zagros crush zone, Iran.
The Zagros Mountains are a product of the Zagros crush zone between the Arabian and Eurasian plates, where the northward push of the Arabian block is causing the folded mountains shown. [NASA.]

solid unit, they express the strain as a fracture. Rocks on either side of the fracture displace relative to the other side in a process known as **faulting**. Thus, *fault zones* are areas where fractures in the rock demonstrate crustal movement. At the moment of fracture, a sharp release of energy occurs, producing an **earthquake** or *quake*.

The fracture surface along which the two sides of a fault move is the *fault plane*. The names of the three basic types of faults, illustrated in Figure 11, are based on the tilt and orientation of the fault plane. A normal fault forms when rocks are pulled apart by tensional stress. A thrust or reverse fault results when rocks are forced together by compressional stress. A strike-slip fault forms when rocks are torn by lateral-shearing stress.

When forces pull rocks apart, the tension causes a **normal fault**, or *tension fault*. When the break occurs, rock on one side moves vertically along an inclined fault plane (Figure 11a). The downward-shifting side is the *hanging wall*; it drops

(text continued after figures)

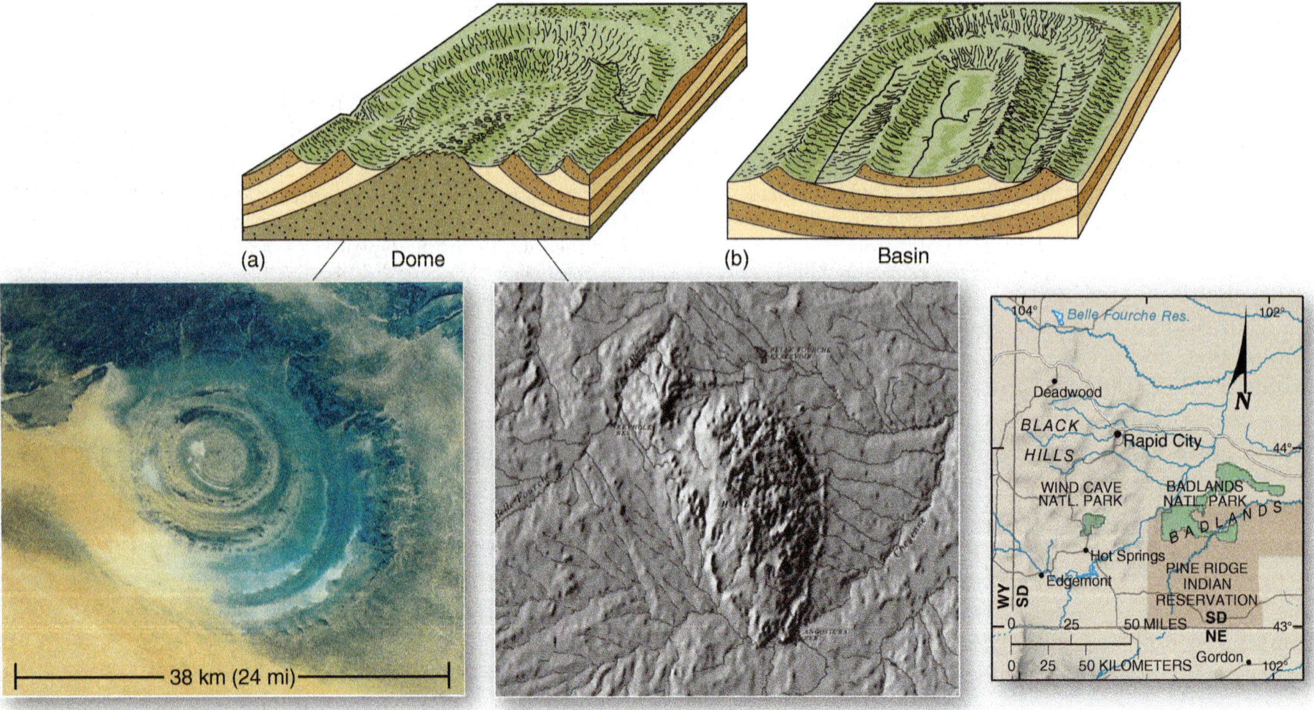

(c) Richat dome, Mauritania

(d) Black Hills, South Dakota

FIGURE 10 Domes and basins.
(a) An upwarped dome. (b) A structural basin. (c) The Richat Dome structure of Mauritania. (d) The Black Hills of South Dakota are a dome structure, shown here on a digitized relief map. [(c) *Terra* ASTER image, NASA/GSFC/MITI. (d) From USGS DEM I-2206, 1992.]

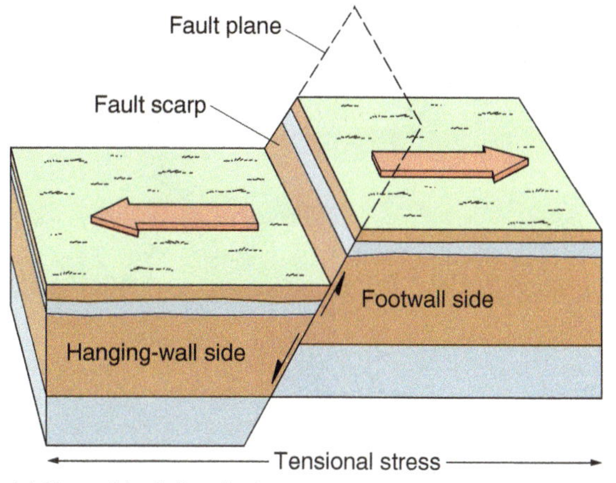

(a) Normal fault (tension)

(a) California and Utah

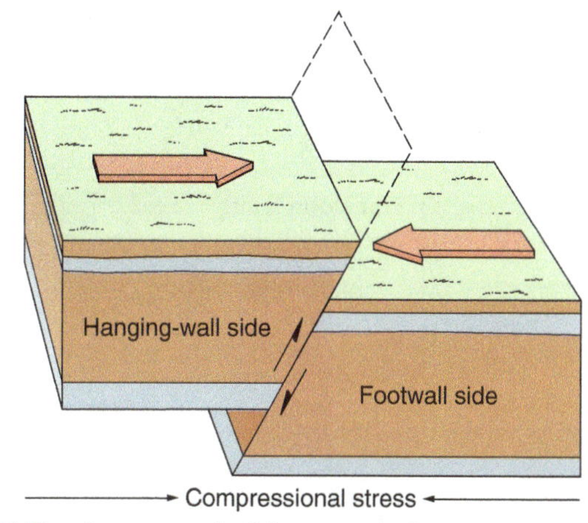

(b) Thrust or reverse fault (compression)

(b) British Columbia

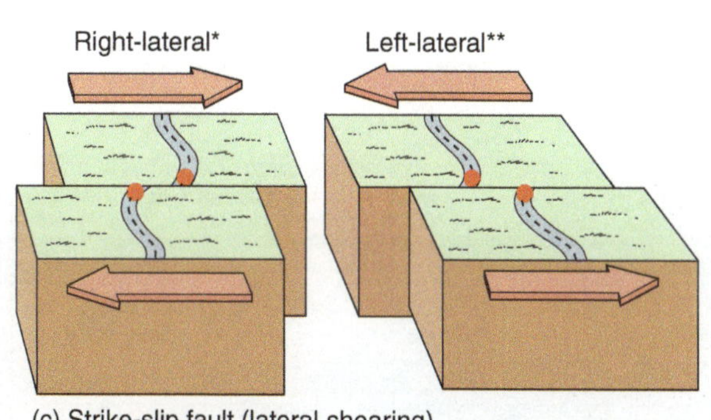

(c) Strike-slip fault (lateral shearing)

* Viewed from either dot on each road, movement to opposite side is *to the right*.
** Viewed from either dot on each road, movement to opposite side is *to the left*.

(c) San Andreas Fault

FIGURE 11 Types of faults.
(a) A normal fault produced by tension in the crust, visible along the edge of mountain ranges in California and along the Wasatch Front in Utah. (b) A thrust, or reverse fault produced by compression in the crust, visible in these offset strata in coal seams and volcanic ash in British Columbia. (c) A strike-slip fault produced by lateral shearing, clearly seen looking southeast along the San Andreas fault rift zone; arrows show relative motion. Can you find the San Andreas fault on the satellite image? Look for a linear rift stretching from southeast to northwest, at the edge of the coastal mountains and the San Joaquin Valley. Use the arrows as guides. [(a) Bobbé Christopherson. (b) Fletcher and Baylis/Photo Researchers, Inc. (c) Photo: Kevin Schafer/Photolibrary/Peter Arnold, Inc.; image: *Terra* MISR image NASA/GSFC/JPL.]

Animation
Fault Types, Transform Faults, Plate Margins

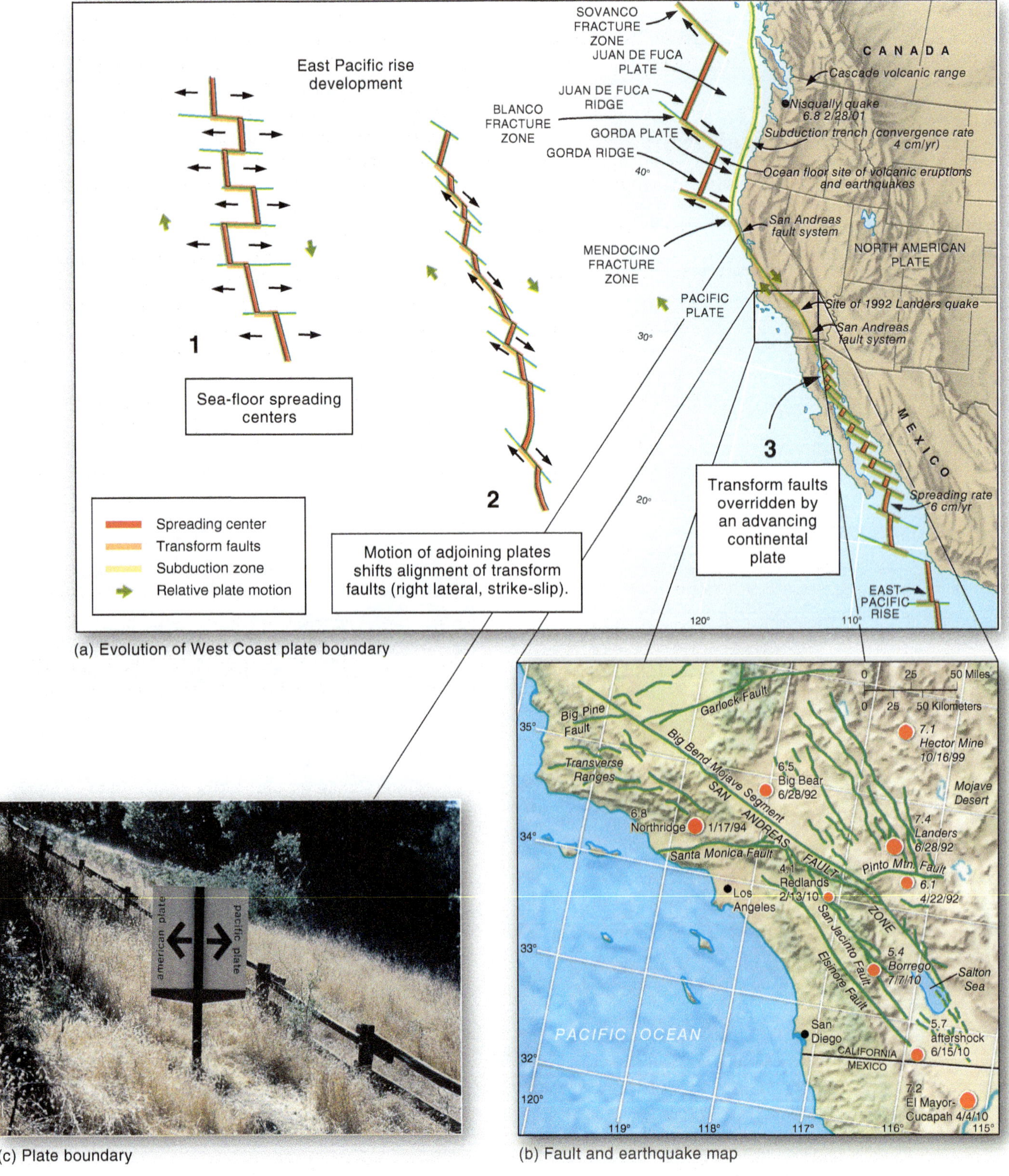

(a) Evolution of West Coast plate boundary

(c) Plate boundary

(b) Fault and earthquake map

FIGURE 12 San Andreas fault formation.
(a) Formation of the San Andreas fault system as a series of transform faults in three successive stages. (b) Enlargement shows the portion of southern California where the 1992 Landers, 1994 Northridge (Reseda), 1999 Hector Mine, and 2010 Redlands, Borrego, and El Mayor earthquakes occurred. Note the January 2001 M 6.8 Nisqually quake, in Washington State, related to the subduction zone offshore on map (a). (c) Trail sign near the epicenter of the 1906 San Francisco earthquake roughly marks the Pacific–North American plate boundary, Marin County, Point Reyes National Seashore, California. [(c) Author.]

relative to the *footwall block*. The exposed fault plane sometimes is visible along the base of faulted mountains, where individual ridges are truncated by the movements of the fault and appear as triangular facets at the ends of the ridges. A cliff formed by faulting is commonly called a *fault scarp*, or *escarpment*.

Compressional forces associated with converging plates force rocks to move *upward* along the fault plane. This is a **reverse fault**, or *compression fault* (Figure 11b). On the surface, it appears similar to a normal fault, although more collapse and landslides may occur from the hanging wall component. In England, when miners worked along a reverse fault, they would stand on the lower side (footwall) and hang their lanterns on the upper side (hanging wall), giving rise to these terms.

If the fault plane forms a low angle relative to the horizontal, the fault is termed a **thrust fault**, or *overthrust fault*, indicating that the overlying block has shifted far over the underlying block (see Figure 8, "Thrust fault"). Place your hands palms-down on your desk, with fingertips together, and slide one hand up over the other—this is the motion of a low-angle thrust fault, with one side pushing over the other.

In the Alps, several such overthrusts have resulted from compressional forces of the ongoing collision between the African and Eurasian plates. Beneath the Los Angeles Basin, overthrust faults produce a high risk of earthquakes and caused many quakes in the 20th century, including the $30 billion 1994 Northridge earthquake. These blind (unknown until they rupture) thrust faults beneath the Los Angeles region remain a major earthquake threat.

If movement along a fault plane is horizontal, such as produced along a transform fault, it forms a **strike-slip fault** (Figure 11c). The movement is *right-lateral* or *left-lateral* depending on the motion perceived when you observe movement on one side of the fault relative to the other side.

Although strike-slip faults do not produce cliffs (scarps), as do the other types of faults, they can create linear rift valleys. This is the case with the San Andreas fault system of California. The rift valley is clearly visible in Figure 11c, where the edges of the North American and Pacific plates are grinding past one another as a result of transform-fault movement.

The evolution of the San Andreas fault system is shown in Figure 12. Note in the figure how the East Pacific rise developed as a spreading center with associated transform faults (1), while the North American plate was progressing westward after the breakup of Pangaea. Forces then shifted the transform faults toward a northwest–southeast alignment along a weaving axis (2). Finally, the western margin of North America overrode those shifting transform faults (3).

In *relative* terms, the motion along this series of transform faults is right-lateral, whereas in *absolute* terms, the North American plate is still moving westward. Consequently, the San Andreas system is a series of faults that are *transform* (associated with a former spreading center), *strike-slip* (horizontal in motion), and *right-lateral* (one side is moving to the right relative to the other side).

Faulted Landscapes Across some landscapes pairs of faults act in concert forming distinctive terrain. The term **horst** applies to upward-faulted blocks; **graben** refers to downward-faulted blocks (Figure 13a). The Great Rift Valley of East Africa, associated with crustal spreading, is an example of such a horst and graben landscape. This rift extends northward to the Red Sea, which fills the

FIGURE 13 Faulted landscapes.
(a) Pairs of faults produce a horst-and-graben landscape. (b) The Red Sea occupies a down-dropped block that is part of the rift system through East Africa, a graben. Note that the locator map is aligned in same direction as the astronaut photo with north toward the lower left. [(b) NASA *Gemini*.]

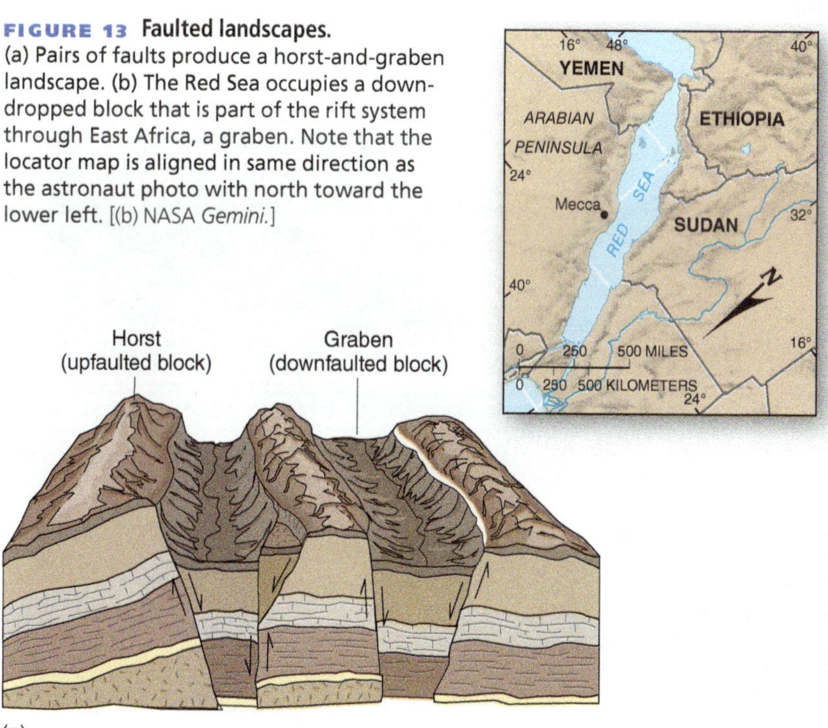

rift formed by parallel normal faults (Figure 13b). Lake Baikal in Siberia is also a graben. This lake basin is the deepest continental "rift valley" on Earth and continues to widen at an average rate of about 2.5 cm (1 in.) per year. Another example, among many, is the Rhine graben, through which the Rhine River flows in Europe.

A physiographic province is a large region that is identified by several geologic or topographic traits. In the U.S. interior west, the **Basin and Range Province** is distinct for its north–south trending mountains. Formed by combinations of faults, these roughly parallel mountains and valleys are aligned pairs of normal faults, an example of a horst-and-graben landscape (Figure 14a and b).

The underlying driver for the formation of this landscape is the westward movement of the North American plate; the faulting results from tensional forces caused by uplifting and thinning of the crust. Basin-and-range relief is abrupt, and rock structures are angular and rugged. As the ranges erode, transported materials accumulate to great depths in the basins, gradually producing extensive plains. The basins' elevations average roughly 1200–1500 m (4000–5000 ft) above sea level, with mountain crests rising higher by another 900–1500 m (3000–5000 ft).

Death Valley, California, is the lowest of these basins, with an elevation of –86 m (–282 ft). However, to the west of the valley, the Panamint Range rises to 3368 m (11,050 ft) at Telescope Peak—almost 3.5 vertical kilometers (2.2 mi) of desert mountain relief.

Several other landforms are associated with basin-and-range topography. In Figure 14c and d, note the **bolson** label, indicating a slope-and-basin area between the crests of two adjacent ridges in a dry region of internal drainage. Figure 14c also identifies a *playa*, an area of salt crust left behind by evaporation in a bolson or valley.

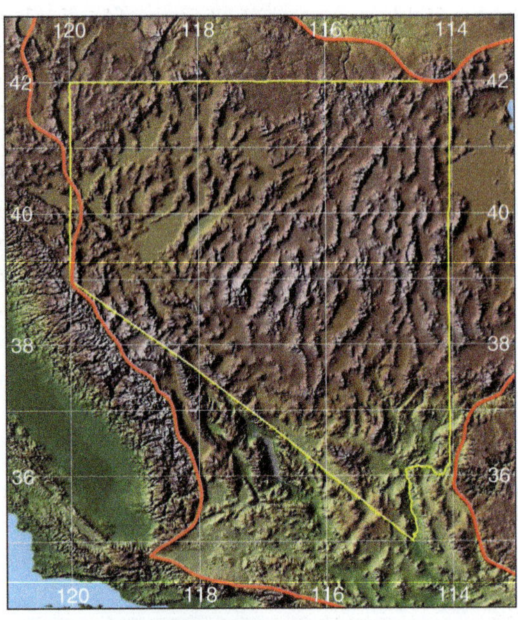

(a) Basin and range topography

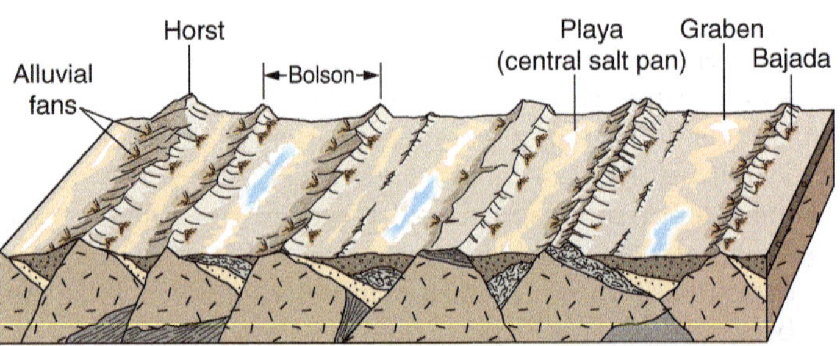

(b) Basin and range structure

(c) Death Valley bolson

(d) Nevada playas

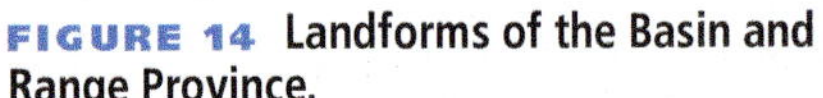

FIGURE 14 Landforms of the Basin and Range Province.
(a) DEM shaded relief map with the Basin and Range Province within the red outline. (b) Parallel faults produce a series of ranges and basins, including bolsons. Infrequent precipitation events leave alluvial fan deposits at the mouths of canyons; coalesced alluvial fans join to form a bajada. (c) Death Valley features parallel mountain ranges and a central playa. (d) Playas in two basins. [(a) GSFC/NASA. (c) Author. (d) Bobbé Christopherson.]

Mountain Building

The geologic term for mountain building is **orogenesis**, literally meaning the birth of mountains (*oros* comes from the Greek for "mountain"). An *orogeny* is a mountain-building episode, occurring over millions of years. It can occur through large-scale deformation and uplift of the crust. An orogeny may include the capture of migrating exotic terranes, addition by accretion to the continental margins, or the intrusion of granitic magmas to form plutons. The net result of this accumulating material is a thickening of the crust. The granite plutons often become exposed by erosion following uplift. Uplift is the final act of an orogenic cycle of mountain building. Earth's major chains of folded and faulted mountains, called *orogens*, are remarkably well correlated with the plate tectonics model.

No orogeny is a simple event; many involve previous developmental stages dating back far into Earth's past, and the processes are ongoing today. Major mountain ranges, and the latest related orogenies that caused them, include the following:

- Appalachian Mountains and the folded Ridge and Valley Province of the eastern United States and Canadian Maritime Provinces—*Alleghany orogeny*, 250–300 million years ago (m.y.a.), associated with the collision of Africa and North America;
- Rocky Mountains of North America—*Laramide orogeny*, 40–80 m.y.a.; third mountain-building episode, beginning 170 m.y.a., including the *Sevier orogeny*;
- Sierra Nevada and Klamath Mountains of California—*Nevadan orogeny*, with faulting 29–35 m.y.a. and older batholithic intrusion emplacements dating back 80 to 180 million years;
- Alps of Europe—*Alpine orogeny*, 2–66 m.y.a., principally in the Tertiary Period and continuing to the present across southern Europe and the Mediterranean, with many earlier episodes (see Figure 15); and
- Himalayas of Asia—*Himalayan orogeny*, 45–54 m.y.a., beginning with the collision of the India and Eurasia plates and continuing to the present.

Two major mountain systems on Earth are the Cordilleran System in North and South America and the Eurasian-Himalayan System, which stretches from the Alps across Asia to the Himalayas. Go to the *MasteringGeography* web site to view a map of world structural regions, including these mountain systems.

Types of Orogenesis

Figure 16 illustrates three types of tectonic activity that cause orogenesis along convergent plate margins. Figure 16a shows *oceanic plate–continental plate collision orogenesis*. This type of convergence is now occurring along the Pacific coast of the Americas and has formed the Andes, the Sierra of Central America, the Rockies, and other western mountains. We see folded sedimentary formations, with intrusions of magma forming granitic plutons at the heart of these mountains. Their buildup has been augmented by capturing displaced terranes, accreted during collision with the continental mass. Also note the associated volcanic activity inland from the subduction zone, the

Animation
Plate Boundaries

FIGURE 15 European Alps.
Western (France), central (Italy), and eastern (Austria) segments make up the crescent shape of the Alps. Complex overturned faults and crustal shortening due to compressional forces occur along convergent plates. The Alps are some 1200 km (750 mi) in length, occupying 207,000 km^2 (80,000 mi^2). Note the snow coverage in this December image. [*Terra* MODIS image, NASA/GSFC.]

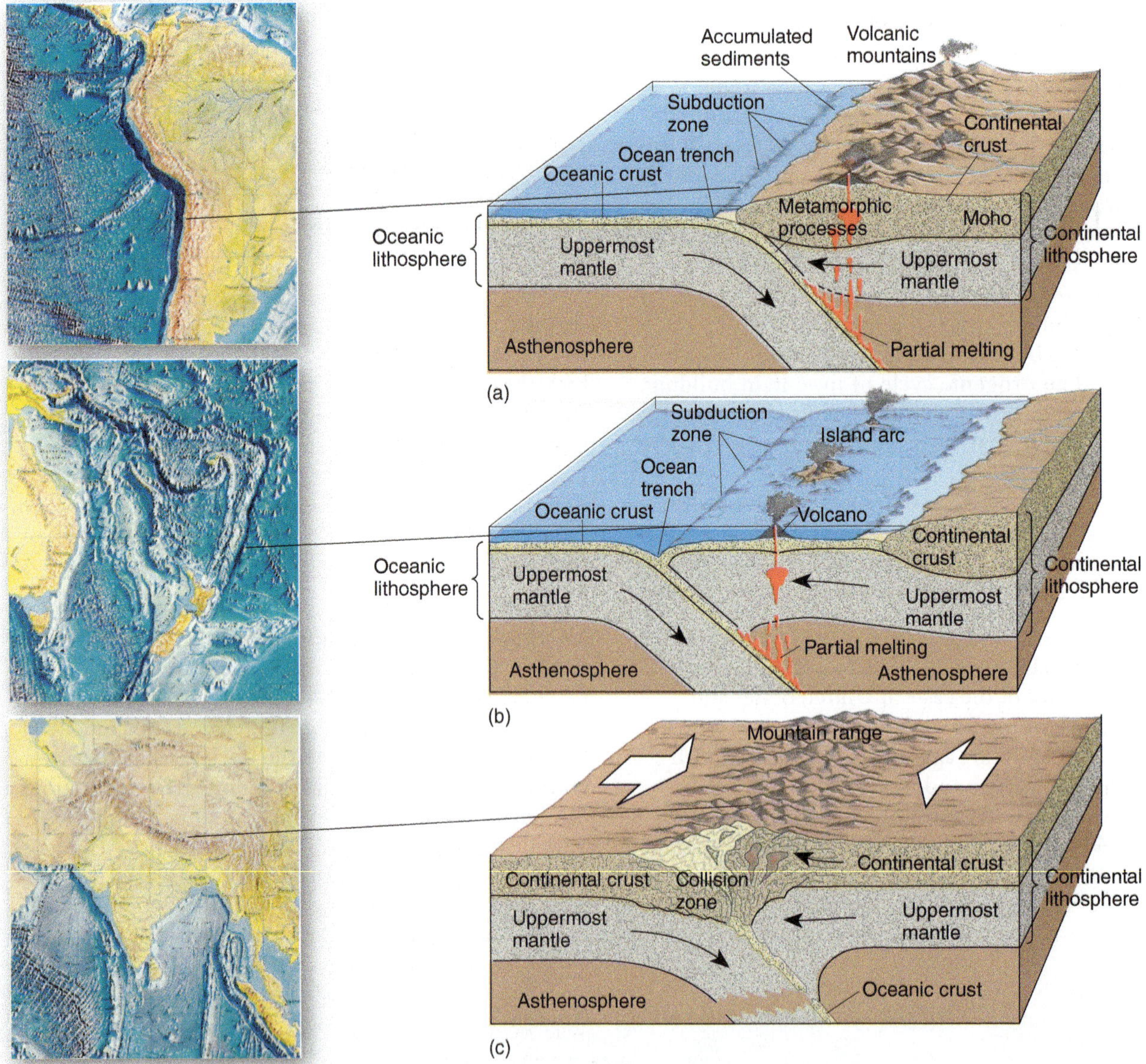

FIGURE 16 Three types of orogenesis caused by plate convergence. Mountain building can be caused by (a) oceanic plate–continental plate collisions (example: Nazca plate–South American plate collision and subduction); (b) oceanic plate–oceanic plate collisions (example: New Hebrides Trench near Vanuatu, 16° S, 168° E); and (c) continental plate–continental plate collision (example: Indian plate and Eurasian landmass collision and resulting Himalayan Mountains). Can you identify other mountains associated with plate convergence on the chapter-opening map? [(a)–(c) Inset maps from B. Heezen & Marie Tharp, Office of Naval Research.]

eruption of flood (plateau) basalts (see Figure 26), and the development of composite volcanoes (see Figure 29).

In *oceanic plate–oceanic plate collision orogenesis* (Figure 16b), plate convergence can produce either simple or more complex volcanic island arcs, such as Indonesia and Japan, which include deformation and metamorphism of rocks and granitic intrusions. These processes formed the chains of island arcs and volcanoes that continue from the southwestern Pacific to the western Pacific, the Philippines, the Kurils, and on through portions of the Aleutians.

Both collision types—(a) oceanic plate–continental plate and (b) oceanic plate–oceanic plate—are active around the Pacific Rim. Both are thermal in nature because the diving plate melts and migrates back toward the surface as molten rock. The region of active volcanoes and earthquakes around the Pacific is known as the *circum-Pacific belt* or, more popularly, the *ring of fire*.

The mechanism for *continental plate–continental plate collision orogenesis* is mechanical; large masses of continental crust are subjected to intense folding, overthrusting, faulting, and uplifting (Figure 16c). The converging plates crush and deform both marine sediments and basaltic oceanic crust. The formation of the European Alps is a result of such compression forces and includes considerable crustal shortening, forming great overturned folds, called *nappes*.

The collision of India with the Eurasian landmass, producing the Himalayas, is estimated to have shortened the overall continental crust by as much as 1000 km (about 600 mi) and to have produced telescoping sequences of thrust faults at depths of 40 km (25 mi). The Himalayas feature the tallest above-sea-level mountains on Earth, including all 10 of Earth's highest peaks.

As India moves northeastward at about 2 m (6.6 ft) a year, the disruption created by this plate collision has reached far under China, causing frequent earthquakes. As evidence of this ongoing strain, the January 2001 quake in Gujarat, India, was along a shallow thrust fault that gave way under the pressure of the northward-pushing Indian plate. More than 1 million buildings were destroyed or damaged during this event. Again, a 40-km (25-mi) segment of the 2500-km (1553-mi) fault zone that marks the plate boundary snapped in October 2005, when an M 7.6 quake hit the Kashmir region of Pakistan, killing more than 83,000 people.

The Grand Tetons and the Sierra Nevada

The Sierra Nevada of California and the Grand Tetons of Wyoming are examples of recent stages of mountain building. Each is a *tilted-fault-block* mountain range, in which a normal fault on one side of the range has produced a tilted mountain landscape of dramatic relief (Figure 17). Magma intruded into those blocks, slowly cooling to form granitic cores of coarsely crystalline rock. After tremendous tectonic uplift and the removal of overlying material through weathering, erosion, and transport, those granitic masses are now exposed in each mountain range. In some areas, these batholiths were previously covered by more than 7500 m (25,000 ft) of overlying material.

Recent research in the Sierra Nevada disclosed that some of the uplift was isostatic, caused by the erosion of overburden and the loss of melting ice mass following the last ice age some 18,000 years ago. The accumulation of sediments in the adjoining valley to the west depressed the crust, thus further enhancing relief in the landscape.

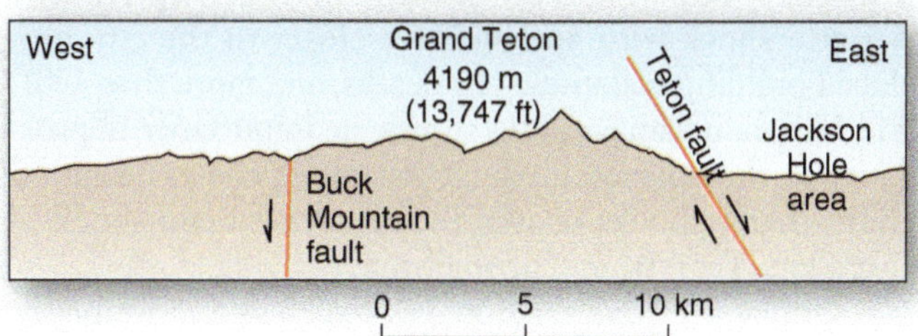

FIGURE 17 Tilted-fault block.
The Teton Range in Wyoming is an example of a tilted-fault block, a range of scenic beauty featuring a 2130-m (7,000-ft) rugged relief between Jackson Hole and the summits. The Grand Teton is the highest peak in the range at 4190 m (13,747 ft). [Author.]

The Appalachian Mountains

The eroded, fold-and-thrust belt of the eastern United States and southeastern Canada has origins dating to the formation of Pangaea and the collision of Africa and North America (250–300 m.y.a.). The complexity of the Alleghany orogeny derives from at least two earlier orogenic cycles of uplift and the accretion of several captured terranes.

Linked during the Pangaea collision and now separated by an ocean, the mountain ranges on either side of the Atlantic Ocean share both structure and composition. In fact, the Lesser (or Anti-) Atlas Mountains of Mauritania and northwestern Africa were connected to the Appalachians at some time in the past, but the mountains embedded in the African plate rafted apart from the Appalachians.

The Appalachian Mountain region comprises several landscape subregions (refer to the locator map in Figure 18): the Ridge and Valley Province (elongated sequences of folded sedimentary rock); the Blue Ridge Province (principally of crystalline rock, highest where North Carolina, Virginia, and Tennessee converge); the Piedmont (hilly to gentle terrain along most of the eastern and southern margins of the mountains); the east coastal plain (from gentle hills to flat plains that extend to the coast); and the Canadian Maritime Provinces.

Figure 18 displays the linear folds of the Appalachian system. Note how *water gaps* form where rivers cut through dissected ridges. These important breaks in the rugged landscape greatly influenced migration, settlement patterns, and the diffusion of cultural traits in the 1700s. The initial flow of people, goods, and ideas was guided by this topography. The Susquehanna River in east-central Pennsylvania is one watercourse that interrupts the ridges and valleys of the Appalachians.

Earthquakes

Crustal plates do not glide smoothly past one another. Instead, tremendous friction exists along plate boundaries. The *stress* (a force) of plate motion builds *strain* (a deformation) in the rocks until friction is overcome and the sides along plate boundaries or fault lines suddenly break loose. The two sides of the fault plane then lurch into new positions, moving from centimeters to several meters, and release enormous amounts of seismic energy into the surrounding crust. This energy radiates throughout the planet, diminishing with distance, but sufficient enough to register on instruments worldwide.

In 2007, southern Sumatra, Indonesia, was hit with M 8.4 and M 7.8 quakes, near the same plate boundary

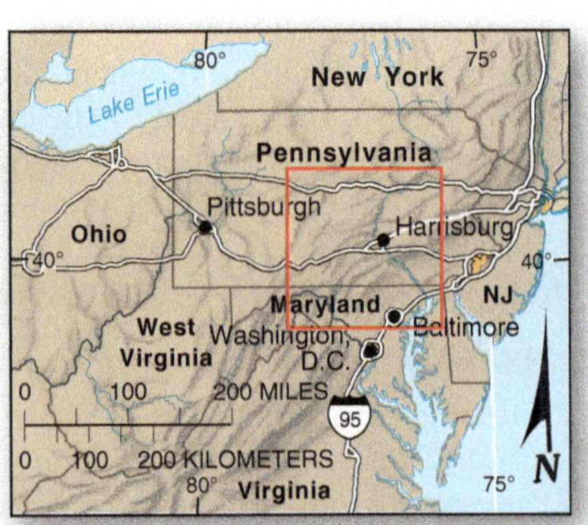

(b) Little and Line Mountains

(a) Appalachian Mountains

FIGURE 18 The Appalachian Mountains.
(a) Appalachian Mountain region from Pennsylvania south through Maryland, Virginia, and West Virginia in a *Terra* image from October 11, 2000, showing true fall colors. The highly folded nature of this entire region is clearly visible in the satellite image. (b) The folded Little and Line Mountains end at the Susquehanna River, along the left edge of this aerial photo, following a light March snowfall. [(a) *Terra* MODIS image, NASA/GSFC. (b) Bobbé Christopherson.]

where four other quakes greater than M 7.9 had occurred since 1998. At this boundary, the Australian plate moves northeast, subducting beneath the Sunda plate on which Sumatra rides, at a relative speed of 6.6 cm/year (2.6 in./year). This is where the M 9.1 Sumatra–Andaman earthquake struck December 26, 2004, triggering the devastating Indian Ocean tsunami; the quake and seismic wave took 228,000 lives. For complete listings of these and other earthquakes, go to http://earthquake.usgs.gov/earthquakes/.

What are the mechanisms that produce such dramatic tectonic events? Why do most quakes strike in total surprise, such as in New Zealand and Japan in 2011?

Focus, Epicenter, Foreshock, and Aftershock

The subsurface area along a fault plane, where the motion of seismic waves is initiated, is the *focus*, or hypocenter, of an earthquake (see the labels in Figure 19). The area at the surface directly above the focus is the *epicenter.* Shock waves produced by an earthquake radiate outward through the crust from the focus and epicenter. Some of the seismic waves are conducted throughout the planet to distant instruments. Scientists explore Earth's interior using these seismic wave patterns and the nature of their transmission through the layers of the planet.

A *foreshock*, which precedes the main shock, also is possible. The pattern of foreshocks is now regarded as an important consideration in the forecasting effort. An *aftershock* may occur after the main shock, sharing the same general area of the epicenter; some aftershocks rival the main tremor in magnitude. For instance, in New Zealand an M 7.1 quake struck in September 2010 with an epicenter 45 km (30 mi) from Christchurch causing USD $2.7 billion and no deaths. Seventeen days later a 6.3 aftershock with an epicenter closer to the city produced building collapses, 350 deaths, and more than USD $15 billion in damage. This shows the importance of proximity to the epicenter, which was along the easternmost limit of aftershocks related to the earlier main shock, at just 6 km (3 mi) from Christchurch.

Unlike previous earthquakes—such as San Francisco in 1906, when the plates shifted a maximum of 6.4 m (21 ft) relative to each other—no fault plane or rifting was evident at the surface in the 1989 Loma Prieta, California, area. Instead, the fault plane suggested in Figure 19 shows the two plates moving horizontally approximately

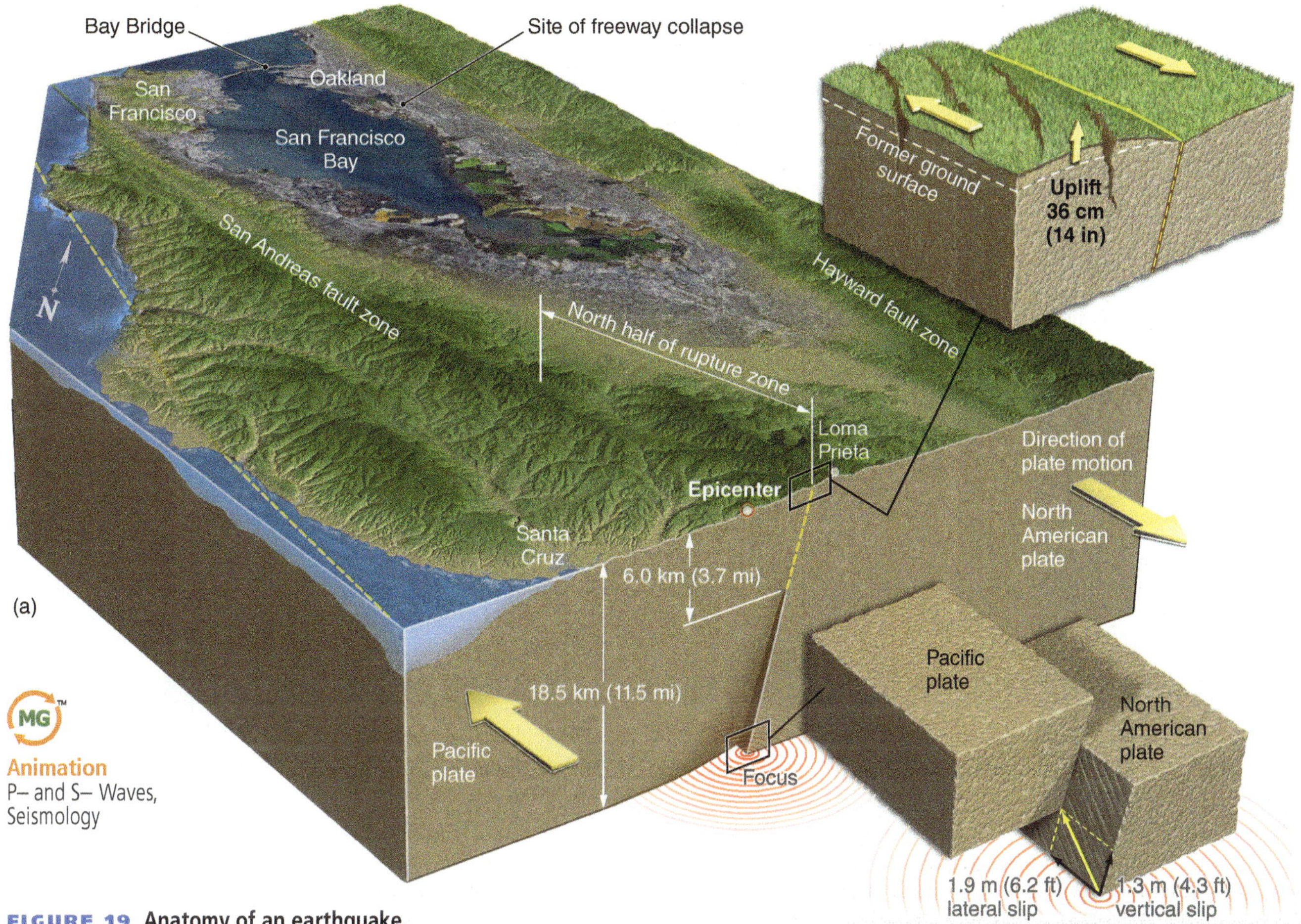

MG Animation
P– and S– Waves, Seismology

FIGURE 19 Anatomy of an earthquake.
(a) The fault plane solution for the 1989 Loma Prieta, California, earthquake shows the lateral and vertical (thrust) movements occurring at depth. There was no surface expression of this fault plane. (b) Section failure in the San Francisco–Oakland Bay Bridge. [(a) After USGS. (b) Courtesy of California Department of Transportation.]

2 m (6 ft) past each other deep below the surface, with the Pacific plate thrusting 1.3 m (4.3 ft) upward. This vertical motion is unusual for the San Andreas fault and indicates that this portion of the San Andreas system is more complex than previously thought. Damage totaled $8 billion, 14,000 people were displaced from their homes, 4000 were injured, and 63 were killed.

Earthquake Intensity and Magnitude

Tectonic earthquakes are those quakes associated with faulting. A worldwide network of more than 4000 **seismograph** instruments records vibrations transmitted as waves of energy throughout Earth's interior and in the crust. Using these devices and actual observations, scientists rate earthquakes on two kinds of scales: a *qualitative* damage intensity scale and a *quantitative* magnitude-of-energy-released scale.

A damage *intensity scale* is useful in classifying and describing damage to terrain and structures after an earthquake. Earthquake damage intensity is rated on the arbitrary *Mercalli scale*, a Roman-numeral scale from I to XII, representing "barely felt" to "catastrophic total destruction." It was designed in 1902 and modified in 1931. Table 1 shows this scale and the number of quakes in each category that are expected each year. The strongest earthquake thought to have struck was the M 9.6 in Chile in 1960, producing Mercalli XII damage. The fault-line break in the crust extended over 1000 km (629 mi) in that quake.

In 1935, Charles Richter designed a system to estimate earthquake magnitude. In this method, a seismograph located at least 100 km (62 mi) from the epicenter of the quake records the amplitude of seismic waves. The measurement is then charted on the **Richter scale**. The relation of magnitude to energy released is still a useful feature of his scale.

TABLE 1 Magnitude, Intensity, and Frequency of Earthquakes

Description	Effects on Populated Areas	Moment Magnitude Scale	Modified Mercalli Scale	Number per Year*
Great	Damage nearly total	8.0 and higher	XII	1
Major	Great damage	7–7.9	X–XI	17
Strong	Considerable-to-serious damage to buildings; railroad tracks bent	6–6.9	VIII–IX	134
Moderate	Felt-by-all, with slight building damage	5–5.9	V–VII	1,319
Light	Felt-by-some to felt-by-many	4–4.9	III–IV	13,000 (estimated)
Minor	Slight, some feel it	3–3.9	I–II	130,000 (estimated)
Very minor	Not felt, but recorded	2–2.9	None to I	1,300,000 (estimated)

Source: USGS, Earthquake Information Center.
* Based on observations since 1990.

The Richter scale is logarithmic: Each whole number on it represents a 10-fold increase in the measured wave amplitude. Translated into energy, each whole number signifies a 31.5-fold increase in energy released. Thus, a magnitude of 3.0 on the Richter scale represents 31.5 times more energy than a 2.0 and 992 times more energy than a 1.0. The Richter scale has since become more quantitative. Revision was needed because the scale did not properly measure or differentiate between quakes of high intensity. Seismologists wanted to know more about what they call the *seismic moment* to understand a broader range of possible motions during an earthquake.

The **moment magnitude scale**, in use since 1993, is more accurate for large earthquakes than is Richter's *amplitude magnitude* scale. Moment magnitude considers the amount of fault slippage produced by the earthquake, the size of the surface (or subsurface) area that ruptured, and the nature of the materials that faulted, including how resistant they were to failure. The new scale considers extreme ground acceleration (movement upward), which the Richter amplitude magnitude method underestimated.

A reassessment of past quakes has increased the rating of some and decreased that of others. As an example, the 1964 earthquake at Prince William Sound in Alaska had an amplitude magnitude of 8.6, but on the moment magnitude scale, it increased to an M 9.2. Note that Table 2 includes more earthquakes for the period following 1960 than for the years before 1960. This is not because earthquake frequency has increased; rather, it reflects an effort to include recent events that affected increased population densities in vulnerable areas.

The National Earthquake Information Center in Golden, Colorado, reports earthquake epicenters. For references, see http://earthquake.usgs.gov/regional/neic/ and the National Geophysical Data Center at http://www.ngdc.noaa.gov/hazard/. Focus Study 1 offers more details on the quakes of 2010 and 2011.

The Nature of Faulting

We earlier described types of faults and faulting motions. The specific mechanics of how a fault breaks remain under study, but **elastic-rebound theory** describes the basic process. Generally, two sides along a fault appear to be locked by friction, resisting any movement despite the powerful forces acting on the adjoining pieces of crust. Stress continues to build strain along the *fault plane* surfaces, storing elastic energy like a wound-up spring.

(text continued after Focus Study 1)

GEO REPORT 2 ***Large earthquakes affect the entire Earth system***

Scientific evidence is mounting that Earth's largest earthquake events have a global influence. The 2004 Sumatra–Andaman earthquake appears to have affected fault strengths and global seismicity as changes in measured stress and strain increased. Related to this was an unusual increase in M 8.0 and higher quakes after 2004.

An M 7.9 quake near Denali National Park, Alaska, was the largest on Earth in 2002. This quake triggered far-reaching effects: more than 200 small earthquakes in Yellowstone, seismic crustal waves that were felt in Texas, and altered water tables and well water in Pennsylvania. As happened with the 2004 quake, the 2011 quake in Japan caused Earth's axial tilt to shift several centimeters and the redistribution of mass shortened daylength by 1.8 millionths of a second, as calculated by the Jet Propulsion Laboratory of the National Aeronautics and Space Administration (NASA). Earth, indeed, behaves as a vast tectonic system.

TABLE 2 A Sampling of Significant Earthquakes*

Year	Date	Location	Number of Deaths	Mercalli Intensity	Moment Magnitude (Richter)
1556	Jan. 23	Shaanxi Province, China	830,000	**	**
1737	Oct. 11	Calcutta, India	300,000	**	**
1812	Feb. 7	New Madrid, Missouri	Several	XI–XII	~7.0–8.1
1857	Jan. 9	Fort Tejon, California	**	X–XI	**
1886	Aug. 31	Charleston, South Carolina	**	IX	6.7
1906	Apr. 18	San Francisco, California	3,000	XI	7.7 (8.25)
1923	Sept. 1	Kwanto, Japan	143,000	XII	7.9 (8.2)
1939	Dec. 27	Erzincan, Turkey	40,000	XII	7.6 (8.0)
1960	May 22	Southern Chile	5,700	XII	9.6 (8.6)
1964	Mar. 28	Southern Alaska	131	X–XII	9.2 (8.6)
1970	May 31	Northern Peru	66,000	**	7.9 (7.8)
1971	Feb. 9	San Fernando, California	65	VII–IX	6.7 (6.5)
1976	July 28	Tangshan, China	250,000	XI–XII	7.4 (7.6)
1978	Sept. 16	Iran	25,000	X–XII	7.8 (7.7)
1985	Sept. 19	Mexico City, Mexico	7,000	IX–XII	8.1 (8.1)
1988	Dec. 7	Armenia–Turkey border	30,000	XII	6.8 (6.9)
1989	Oct. 17	Loma Prieta (near Santa Cruz, California)	63	VII–IX	7.0 (7.1)
1994	Jan. 17	Northridge (Reseda), California	66	VII–IX	6.8
1995	Jan. 17	Kobe, Japan	5,500	XII	6.9
1999	Aug. 17	Izmit, Turkey	17,100	VIII–XI	7.4
2001	Jan. 26	Gujarat state, India	19,998	X–XII	7.7
2002	Nov. 3	Near Denali National Park, Alaska	1	X	7.9
2003	Dec. 26	Bam, Iran	30,000	X–XII	6.9
2004	Dec. 26	Northern Sumatra (west coast)	228,000+***	X–XII	9.3
2005	Oct. 8	Kashmir region, Pakistan	83,000+	X–XII	7.6
2008	May 12	Chengdu, China	87,000+	X–XII	7.9
2010	Jan. 12	Port-Au-Prince, Haiti	223,000	X–XII	7.0
2010	Feb. 27	Maule, Chile	521	IX–XI	8.8
2010	Sept. 4	Christchurch, New Zealand	350	X–XII	7.1
2011	Feb. 21	Christchurch, New Zealand	166	VI–VIII	6.3
2011	Mar. 11	Tohoku/Sendai, Japan	30,000****	X–XII	9.0

* Note that earthquakes are not on an increase; rather, the list reflects a greater sample for recent years.
** Data not available.
*** Estimated deaths in 11 countries from the quake and resulting tsunami that traveled across the Indian Ocean.
**** Combined deaths from earthquake and tsunami.

FOCUS STUDY 1

Earthquakes in Haiti, Chile, and Japan: A Comparative Analysis

Let us take a summary look at three quakes that struck in 2010 and 2011. As we compare, use this information to further your understanding of the relation of plate tectonics and quake occurrences. Table 1.1 summarizes these three events, whereas Table 2 details significant earthquakes in history.

The first setting was the impoverished country of Haiti, January 12, 2010, just before 5 P.M., when an M 7.0 earthquake struck. The epicenter was 15 km (10 mi) southwest of the capital. Seven minutes later an aftershock of M 6.0 continued the tragedy. More than 223,000 people died, with 300,000 injuries. Almost 300,000 houses were destroyed or damaged. Total damage exceeded the country's $14 billion gross domestic product (GDP).

The fault plane solution—that is, the orientation of the fault plane and the direction of slip motion—determined that the Caribbean plate moved eastward relative to the North American plate's westward shift, in a horizontal strike-slip motion along a 50-km section of the Enriquillo–Plaintain Garden fault. Having this fault segment snap added more stress to the eastern segment of the fault, which is some 600 km in length. The entire fault system is accumulating elastic energy at the same rate as the section that broke in the quake. Port-Au-Prince was destroyed in 1751, 1770, and 2010.

Six weeks later the Nazca plate, moving eastward beneath the westward-moving South American plate, suddenly shifted, generating an M 8.8 quake southwest of Santiago, near Maule, Chile. This is near Concepción and the epicenter of the greatest earthquake of the 20th century, the M 9.6 that hit in 1960. Some of the fault-slip zone from that record quake matched areas for this February 27, 2010, event. Damage exceeded $30 billion, compared to Chile's GDP of $45 billion. The deaths of 521 people and the injuries to 12,000 marked the human dimension. At least two tsunami were generated, arriving in Hilo, Hawai'i, about 15 hours later, each only a meter in height.

The fault plane solution here was a subduction zone earthquake. This area of convergence and subduction is moving at a relative speed of 7 m (23 ft) per century. Damage across Chile was reduced by strict building codes that went into effect in 1985.

Japan rocked on the afternoon of March 11, 2011, when an M 9.0 quake struck at 5:46 UTC (12:46 A.M. EST). Off the northeast coast of Honshu Island, the focus was at a depth of 32 km (19.9 mi) along the subduction boundary between the converging North American and Pacific plates—this was the Tohoku earthquake along the Japan Trench. The epicenter surface expression was at 38.3° N 142.4° E—about 370 km (230 mi) northeast of Tokyo. Imagine an area some 338 km (N–S) by 150 km (210 mi by 93 mi) thrust faulting and abruptly lifting 30–40 m (98–131 ft) and displacing the ocean above it. The nearest coastal city is Sendai (Figure 1.1).

The westward-moving Pacific plate is pulled and dives beneath the North American plate east of the Japan Trench at a rate averaging 83 mm/year

TABLE 1.1 Summary of Three Major Earthquakes in 2010 and 2011

Location, date, and local time	Map	Moment magnitude*	Focus depth	Epicenter distance to nearest city	Type of fault motion	Tectonic plate location
Port-Au-Prince, Haiti Jan. 12, 2010 4:53 P.M.	Haiti (Port-Au-Prince)	M 7.0	13 km (8 mi) Ocean	15 km (10 mi) southwest from Port-Au-Prince	Strike-slip fault	Transform boundary: Caribbean plate moving eastward with respect to the North America plate
Maule, Chile Feb. 27, 2010 3:34 A.M.	Chile (Maule)	M 8.8	35 km (22 mi) Ocean	95 km (60 mi) from Santiago	Thrust fault at subduction zone	Convergent boundary: Nazca plate subducting beneath South American plate
Tohoku, Honshu, Japan Mar. 11, 2011 2:46 P.M.	Honshu, Japan (Sendai)	M 9.0	32 km (20 mi) Ocean	129 km (80 mi) from Sendai	Thrust fault at subduction zone	Convergent boundary: Pacific plate subducting beneath North American plate

* Reported by USGS.

Note: Inset maps from B. Heezen & Marie Tharp, Office of Naval Research.

FIGURE 1.1 Search efforts complicated by tsunami and radiation threat.
Fire trucks line up along what was a city street in Sukuiso, Japan, 6 days after the quake and tsunami. Radiation dangers from the Fukushima nuclear power station disaster delay the search for casualties. [U.S. Navy photo, Specialist 3rd Class D. McCord.]

FIGURE 1.2 Tsunami moves ashore, overwhelming Iwanuma, Japan.
Houses, cars, and city debris are carried kilometers inland over farmlands. Iwanuma is 20 km south of Sendai and 30 km north of the Fukushima Daiichi nuclear plants. [Kyodo News Photo/Reuters Pictures.]

Human dimension	Damage Cost (USD)
222,570 killed, 300,000 injured, 1.3 million displaced	$25 billion
521 killed, 12,000 injured, 800,000 displaced	$30 billion
~30,000 deaths	~$325 billion

(3.5 in./year). On the ocean-floor map that begins this chapter you can see several microplates that form this complex plate boundary.

Foreshocks began about 48 hours before the main quake, whereas several hundred aftershocks continued for weeks, registering between M 5.0 and M 7.0, with a high of M 7.1. The number of people killed will probably never be known, but an estimate of 30,000 is suggested by the known dead and missing as of summer 2011. Damage estimates from the quake and tsunami are at USD $325 billion.

This tremendous energy then radiated across the Pacific Ocean in a massive tsunami. The deep coastal embayments along the coast of Honshu magnify tsunami energy and make this region particularly vulnerable. This reality makes the coastal siting of six nuclear reactors at the Fukushima Daiichi plant, south of Sendai, a poor planning decision. The quake and tsunami damaged cooling systems, and subsequent hydrogen explosions destroyed secondary containment structures, leading to three reactor cores melting through their foundations and massive radiation releases to the land, atmosphere, and ocean.

The tsunami averaged 10 m (33 ft) at Miyagi. Where the wave entered the narrow Ofunate harbor, wave heights reached nearly 30 m (98 ft) as it funneled up the valley 3 km (1.8 mi). Even Japan's strict hazard preparedness standards were of no avail as the deep, swift wave traveled inland (Figure 1.2). The Pacific Tsunami Warning System alerted the countries around the Pacific basin. Damage occurred on Maui and Hawai'i and in the harbors of Crescent City and Santa Cruz on the California coast.

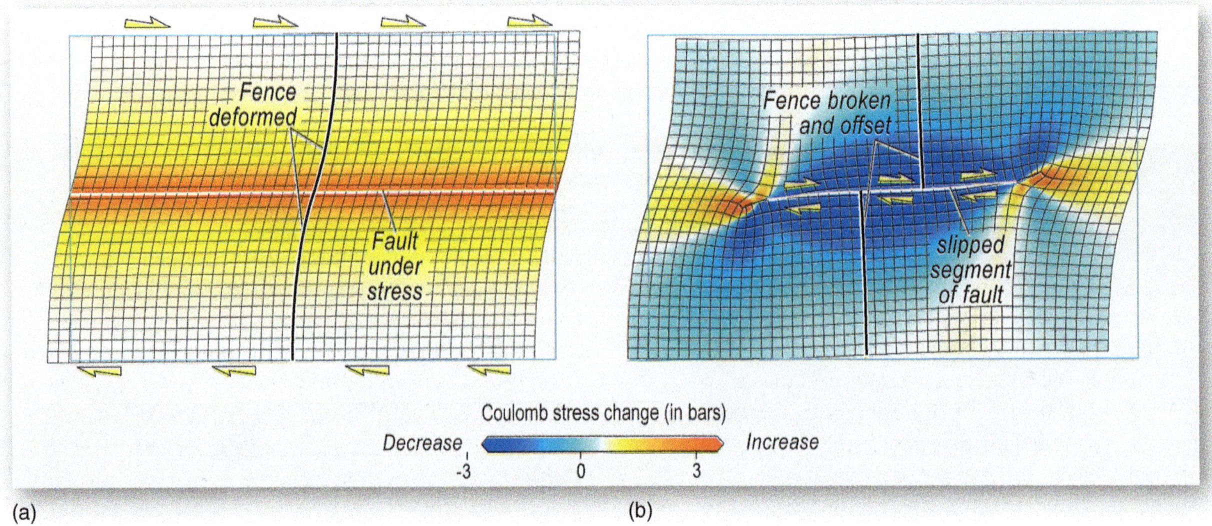

FIGURE 20 Buildup and release of stress and strain along a fault system. The elastic-rebound mechanism applies to strike-slip faults such as the San Andreas system of faults in California, North Anatolian fault in Turkey, Enriquillo fault in Haiti, and Nojima fault zone near Kobe, Japan. Note the fence that crosses the fault line. This stress continues to build to the break point, the two sides snap into new positions, strain is released, and the fence no longer forms a continuous property line. The segments of the fault that remain locked now have added strain. A coulomb is a unit of shear-stress failure overcoming friction and resistance to movement; the color scale ranges from blue (decreased stress) to red (increased stress). [Illustrations courtesy of Serkan Bozkurt, USGS.]

Animation
Elastic Rebound

When the strain buildup finally exceeds the frictional lock, both sides of the fault abruptly move to a condition of less strain, releasing a burst of mechanical energy.

Think of the fault plane as a surface with irregularities that act as sticking points, preventing movement, similar to two pieces of wood held together by drops of glue of different sizes rather than an even coating of glue. Research scientists at the USGS and the University of California identify these small areas of high strain as *asperities*. They are the points that break and release the sides of the fault.

If the fracture along the fault line is isolated to a small asperity break, the quake will be small in magnitude. Clearly, as some asperities break (perhaps recorded as small foreshocks), the strain increases on surrounding asperities that remain intact. Thus, small earthquakes in an area may be precursors to a major quake. However, if the break involves the release of strain along several asperities, the quake will be greater in extent and will involve the shifting of massive amounts of crust. The latest evidence points to a wavelike pattern, as rupturing spreads along the fault plane, rather than the entire fault surface giving way at once.

The buildup and release of stress and strain accumulate as the two sides of the fault attempt to move laterally past one another, yet remain locked (Figure 20). Stress forces continue to build strain until it overwhelms the frictional sticking points and the two sides snap violently and at great speed into new positions—an earthquake hits.

Earthquake Prediction and Planning

The map in Figure 21 plots the earthquake hazards for the United States. These occurrences give some indication of relative risk by region. The challenge is to discover how to predict the *specific time and place* for a quake in the short term in these regions of past earthquake experience.

How do you forecast an earthquake? One approach is to examine the history of each plate boundary and determine the frequency of past earthquakes, the study of *paleoseismology*. Paleoseismologists construct maps that provide an estimate of expected earthquake activity based on past

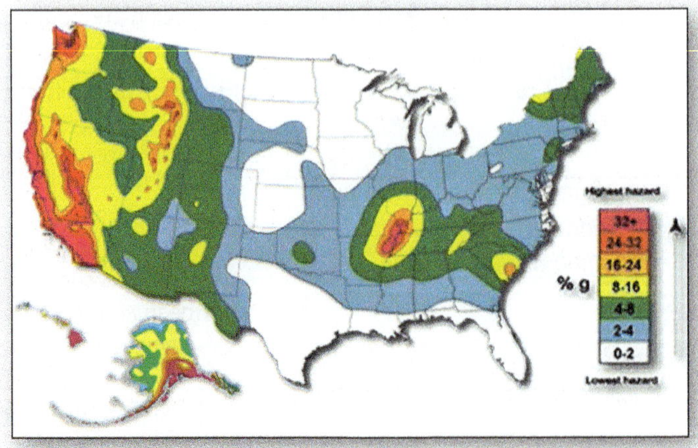

FIGURE 21 Earthquake hazard map for the United States. Earthquake ground accelerations having a 10% probability of being topped in the next 50 years. Acceleration is expressed as a percentage of 1 g (gravity), with red being the highest shaking. Active seismic regions include the West Coast, the Wasatch Front of Utah northward into Canada, the central Mississippi Valley, the southern Appalachians, and portions of South Carolina, upstate New York, and Ontario. [USGS; see http://eqhazmaps.usgs.gov/.]

performance. An area that is quiet and overdue for an earthquake is a *seismic gap*; such an area possesses accumulated strain. The area along the Aleutian Trench subduction zone had three such gaps until the great 1964 Alaskan earthquake filled one of them. The areas around San Francisco and northeast and southeast of Los Angeles represent other such gaps along the San Andreas fault system.

A second approach to forecasting is to observe and measure phenomena that might precede an earthquake. *Dilitancy* refers to the slight increase in volume of rock produced by small cracks that form under stress and accumulated strain. The affected region may tilt and swell in response to strain. Tiltmeters measure these changes in suspect areas. Another indicator of dilitancy is an increase in radon (a naturally occurring, slightly radioactive gas) dissolved in groundwater. At present, earthquake hazard zones have thousands of radon monitors taking samples in test wells.

In the absence of effective forecasting weeks, months, or years ahead, earthquake warning systems can be useful. Following the 1989 Loma Prieta earthquake near San Francisco, freeway-repair workers were linked to a broadcast system that gave them 20-second alerts of aftershocks from distant epicenters. In southern California, the USGS is coordinating a Southern California Seismographic Network (SCSN; http://www.scsn.org/) to correlate 350 instruments for immediate earthquake location analysis and disaster coordination. Also, for the southern California region, see http://earthquake.usgs.gov/regional/sca/.

The most intensely studied seismic area in the world is along the San Andreas fault outside Parkfield, California. The area features tiltmeters, gas-monitoring wells, and a newly completed drill hole where instruments are placed in the fault at a depth between 2 km and 3 km (1.2 mi and 1.9 mi)—the San Andreas Fault Observatory at Depth (SAFOD). The goal is to sample material that is in the subsurface area of fault slippage.

Synthetic-aperture radar images also measure movement along the San Andreas fault zone. These images track even the slightest movements in the buildup to a quake as well as the activity of aftershocks.

In the San Francisco Bay Area, the present forecast predicts a 62% chance of an M 6.7, or higher, striking between 2000 and 2030 along the San Andreas system of faults. Added to this is a 14% chance of a significant earthquake occurring along some yet unknown fault. Adding to the risk is the extent of landfill in the Bay Area, where about half the original bay is now filled and occupied with buildings. In an earthquake, such fill fails in a process of liquefaction, where shaking brings water to the surface and liquefies the soil.

Someday accurate earthquake forecasting may be a reality, but several questions remain: How will humans respond to a forecast? Can a major metropolitan region be evacuated for short periods of time? Can a city relocate after a disaster to an area of lower risk? Actual implementation of an action plan to reduce death, injury, and property damage from earthquakes is difficult. The political environment adds complexity, since the potential socioeconomic impact of earthquake prediction on an urban community involves negative economic impacts in the period before the quake hits. Imagine a chamber of commerce, bank, real estate agent, tax assessor, or politician that would welcome an earthquake prediction and such negative publicity for one's city. These factors work against effective prediction and planning.

A valid and applicable generalization is that *humans and their institutions seem unable or unwilling to perceive hazards in a familiar environment*. In other words, we tend to feel secure in our homes and communities, even if they are sitting on a quiet fault zone. Such an axiom of human behavior certainly helps explain why large populations continue to live and work in earthquake-prone settings. Similar questions also can be raised about populations in areas vulnerable to floods, droughts, hurricanes, and coastal storm surges and in settlements on barrier islands. See the Natural Hazards Center at the University of Colorado at http://www.colorado.edu/hazards/index.html.

Volcanism

Volcanic eruptions across the globe remind us of Earth's internal energy. Ongoing eruption activity matches plate tectonic activity. A few recent eruptions, among many, include Mount Merapi (Indonesia), Eyjafjallajökull (Iceland), Kīlauea (Hawai'i), Soufriere Hills on Montserrat (Lesser Antilles), Mount Etna (Sicily, Italy), Nyamuragira (Democratic Republic of the Congo), several on the Kamchatka Peninsula (Russia; see Figure 2), Rabaul (Papua New Guinea), Grímsvötn (Iceland), Axial Summit and the Jackson Segment (sea-floor spreading center off the coast of Oregon), and Shishaldin (Unimak Island, Alaska; see Figure 30).

GEO REPORT 3 ***Northridge classes held in the outdoors***

Students and faculty at California State University–Northridge, in the San Fernando Valley of southern California, were near the epicenter of the most devastating earthquake in U.S. history in terms of property damage—$30 billion in destruction across the region. The quake was caused by one of the many low-angle thrust faults that underlie the Los Angeles region. The January 17, 1994, Northridge (Reseda) earthquake, an M 6.8, and more than 10,000 aftershocks caused approximately $350 million in damage to campus buildings 2 weeks before the beginning of spring classes. The semester began just 3 weeks late in 450 temporary trailers. Geography professors taught some class sessions outdoors for a brief time. Amazingly, graduation was still held in May.

FIGURE 22 The Eyjafjallajökull eruption in Iceland, May 10, 2010. Ash plume rises to between 5 and 6 km (3.1 and 3.7 mi). [*Aqua*, MODIS sensor NASA/GSFC.]

The Eyjafjallajökull eruption on April 13, 2010, was notable because its ash forced the 5-day closure of European airspace, grounding some 100,000 flights (Figure 22). Iceland's Meteorological Office monitored the effusive eruption with its 56-station seismic network, implemented with risk assessment and evacuation plans in 1999. Such subglacial eruptions do produce floodwaters and sometimes explosive reactions between meltwater and lava. No large cities were threatened. The region near the volcano is mainly rural farm and pasture land.

Over 1300 identifiable volcanic cones and mountains exist on Earth, although fewer than 600 are active (have had at least one eruption in recorded history). In an average year, about 50 volcanoes erupt worldwide, varying from modest activity to major explosions. An index to the world's volcanoes is at http://vulcan.wr.usgs.gov/Volcanoes/framework.html, and the National Museum of Natural History Global Volcanism Program lists information for more than 8500 eruptions at http://www.nmnh.si.edu/gvp/. For links to volcano observatories worldwide, check http://www.geo.mtu.edu/volcanoes/links/observatories.html.

Eruptions in remote locations and at depths on the seafloor go largely unnoticed, but the occasional eruption of great magnitude near a population center makes headlines. North America has about 70 volcanoes (mostly inactive) along the western margin of the continent. Mount St. Helens in Washington State is a famous active example (see Focus Study 2).

Volcanic Features

A **volcano** forms at the end of a central vent or pipe that rises from the asthenosphere and upper mantle through the crust into a volcanic mountain. A **crater**, or circular surface depression, usually forms at or near the summit. Magma rises and collects in a magma chamber deep below the volcano until conditions are right for an eruption. This subsurface magma emits tremendous heat; in some areas, it boils groundwater, as seen in the thermal springs and geysers of Yellowstone National Park and elsewhere in the world—geothermal energy.

Lava (molten rock), gases, and **pyroclastics**, or *tephra* (pulverized rock and clastic materials of various sizes ejected violently during an eruption), pass through the vent to the surface and build the volcanic landform. Flowing basaltic lava takes two principal forms, both named in Hawaiian terms (Figure 23). One form, called **aa**, is rough and jagged with sharp edges. This texture happens because the lava loses trapped gases, flows slowly, and develops a thick skin that cracks into the jagged surface. Another principal lava texture that is more fluid than aa is **pahoehoe**. As this lava flows, it forms a thin crust that develops folds and appears "ropy," like coiled, twisted rope. Both forms can come from the same eruption, and sometimes pahoehoe will become aa as the flow progresses. Other types of basaltic magma are described later in this section.

The fact that lava can occur in many different textures and forms accounts for the varied behavior of volcanoes and the different landforms they build. In this section, we look at five volcanic landforms and their origins: cinder cones, calderas, shield volcanoes, flood basalts, and composite volcanoes.

A **cinder cone** is a small, cone-shaped hill usually less than 450 m (1500 ft) high, with a truncated top formed

(a) Aa

(b) Pahoehoe

FIGURE 23 Two types of basaltic lava—Hawaiian examples, close up. (a) A rough, sharp-edged lava, aa is said to get its name from the sounds people make if they attempt to walk on it. The gold-colored strands are clumps of natural spun glass formed by the lava as it blew out into the air—called *Pele's hair*. (b) Pahoehoe forms ropy chords in twisted folds. [Bobbé Christopherson.]

FIGURE 24 Many cinder cones on Ascension Island. Ascension Island is a massive composite volcano that rises over 3000 m (9842 ft) from the ocean floor, with 858 m above sea level. It is classified as inactive. [Bobbé Christopherson.]

from cinders that accumulate during moderately explosive eruptions. Cinder cones are made of pyroclastic material and *scoria* (cindery rock, full of air bubbles). For example, about 100 cinder cones and craters are found on the Ascension Islands, located about 8° S latitude in the Atlantic Ocean (Figure 24).

A **caldera** (Spanish for "kettle") is a large, basin-shaped depression. It forms when summit material on a volcanic mountain collapses inward after an eruption or other loss of magma. A caldera may fill with rainwater, as it did in beautiful Crater Lake in southern Oregon.

The Long Valley caldera (Figure 25), near the California–Nevada border, was formed by a powerful volcanic eruption 760,000 years ago. The oval caldera is about 15 by 30 km (9 by 19 mi) long in a north–south direction at an elevation of 2000 m (6500 ft). About 1200 tons of carbon dioxide are coming up through the soil in the old caldera each day, killing about 170 acres (69 ha) of forest in six different areas. The source is active and moving magma at a depth of some 3 km (1.86 mi). These gas emissions signal volcanic activity and are useful indicators of potential eruptions. For updates, see http://lvo.wr.usgs.gov/.

On Fogo Island in the Cape Verde Islands (15° N 24.5° W), the Cha caldera opens to the sea on the eastern side. The best farmland is in the caldera, so the people choose to live and work there. Eruptions began in 1995 along the flank of Pico do Fogo, destroying farmland and forcing the evacuation of 5000 people. The population returned to work the volcanic soils and to develop the beginnings of an ecotourism business when the eruption sequence subsided. Grape vines were planted in the basaltic soil for local wine production.

Location and Types of Volcanic Activity

The location of volcanic mountains on Earth is a function of plate tectonics and hot-spot activity. Volcanic activity occurs in three settings (with representative examples):

- Along subduction boundaries at continental plate–oceanic plate convergence (such as Mount St. Helens and Kliuchevskoi, Siberia) or oceanic plate–oceanic plate convergence (Philippines and Japan).
- Along sea-floor spreading centers on the ocean floor (Iceland on the Mid-Atlantic Ridge and off the coast of Oregon and Washington) and along areas of rifting on continental plates (the rift zone in East Africa).
- At hot spots, where individual plumes of magma rise to the crust (such as Hawai'i and Yellowstone National Park).

Figure 26 illustrates these three settings for volcanic activity, which you can compare with active volcano sites and plate boundaries.

During a single eruption, a volcano may behave in several different ways. The primary factors in determining an eruption type are (1) the magma's chemistry, which is related to its source, and (2) the magma's viscosity. Viscosity is the magma's resistance to flow ("thickness"), ranging from low viscosity (very fluid) to high viscosity (thick and flowing slowly). We consider two types of eruptions—effusive and explosive—and the characteristic landforms they build.

Effusive Eruptions

Effusive eruptions are the relatively gentle ones that produce enormous volumes of lava annually on the seafloor and in places such as Hawai'i and Iceland. These direct eruptions from the asthenosphere and upper mantle produce a low-viscosity magma that is fluid and cools to form a dark, basaltic rock low in silica (less than 50% silica) and rich in iron and magnesium. Gases readily escape from this magma because of its low viscosity, adding to a gentle **effusive eruption** that pours out on the surface, with relatively small explosions and few pyroclastics. However, dramatic fountains of basaltic lava sometimes shoot upward, powered by jets of rapidly expanding gases.

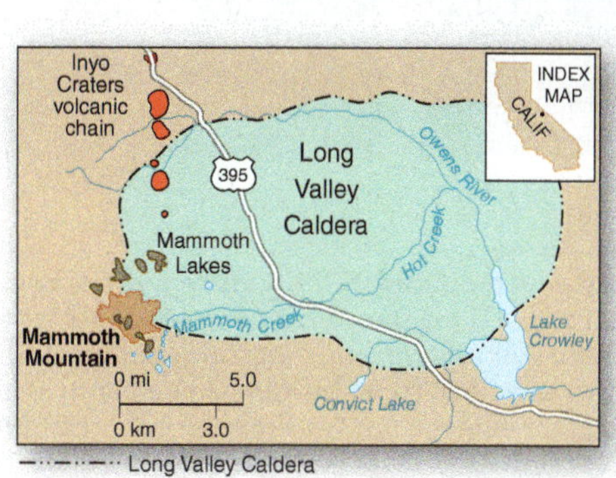

FIGURE 25 Forest death from CO_2 emission, Long Valley caldera, California. A warning sign signals the danger from CO_2 gassing up through soils from subsurface magma and related volcanic activity. The hazard has killed one person to date. [Bobbé Christopherson.]

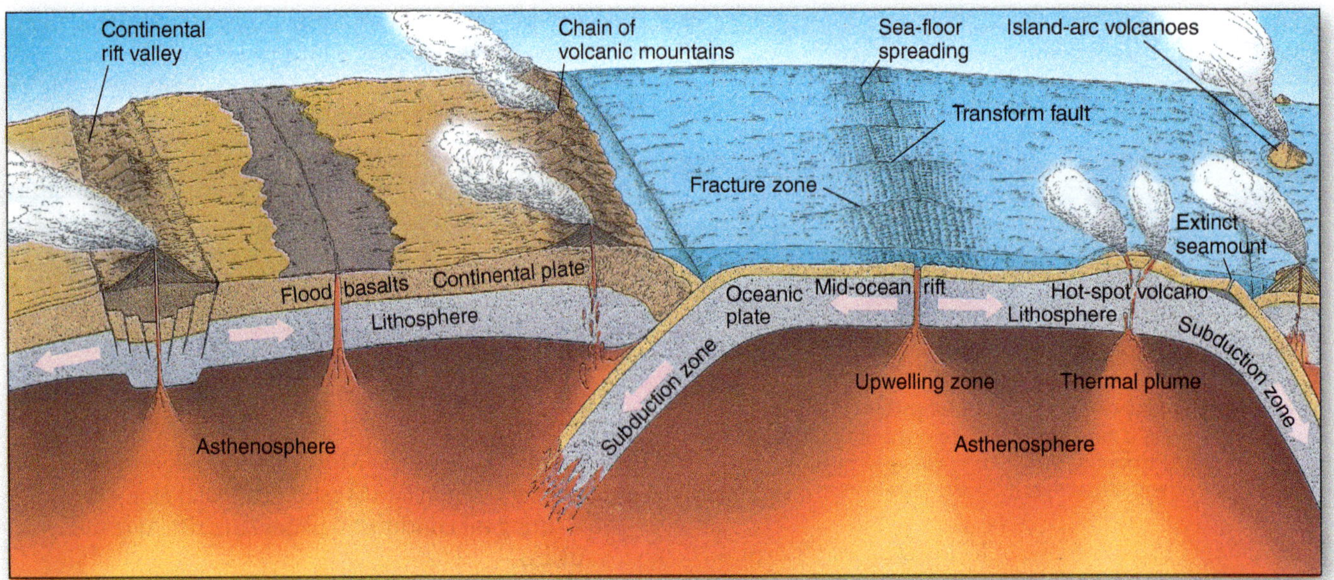

FIGURE 26 Tectonic settings of volcanic activity.
Magma rises and lava erupts from rifts, through crust above subduction zones, and where thermal plumes at hot spots break through the crust. [Adapted from U.S. Geological Survey, *The Dynamic Planet* (Washington, DC: Government Printing Office, 1989).]

Animation
Forming Types of Volcanoes

An effusive eruption may come from a single vent or from the flank of a volcano, through a side vent. If such vents form a linear opening, they are *fissures*; these sometimes erupt in a dramatic *curtain of fire* (sheets of molten rock spraying into the air). Rift zones capable of erupting tend to converge on the central crater, or vent, as they do in Hawai'i. The interior of such a crater, often a sunken caldera, may fill with low-viscosity magma during an eruption, forming a molten lake, which then may overflow, sending lava downslope in dramatic rivers and falls of molten rock.

On the island of Hawai'i, the continuing Kīlauea eruption is the longest in recorded history, having been active since January 3, 1983 (Figure 27). Although this eruption is located on the slopes of the massive Mauna Loa volcano, scientists have determined that Kīlauea has its own magma plumbing system down some 60 km into Earth, allowing it to produce more lava than any other vent in recorded history. To date, the eruption has produced 3.1 km^3 (0.7 mi^3) of lava, covering 117 km^2 (45 mi^2). During 1989–1990, lava flows from Kīlauea actually consumed several visitor buildings in the Hawai'i Volcanoes National Park. Beginning in

FIGURE 27 Kīlauea landscape.
(a) Aerial photo of the newest land on the planet produced by the massive flows of basaltic lavas from the Kīlauea volcano, Hawai'i Volcano National Park. In the distance, ocean water quenches the intense 1200°C (2200°F) lava on contact, producing steam and hydrochloric acid mist. This entire area is slowly slipping toward the sea. (b) Dramatic Hawaiian active lava flows form the Kamoamoa bench as it builds into the sea. The glowing lava is clearly visible through the steam. Even at the safe distance of this aerial photo, the radiated heat from the lava flow is incredible to feel. [Bobbé Christopherson.]

May 2002, an aggressive eruption sequence intensified, flowing over 14 km (7 mi) of the Chain of Craters Road and continuing for several years to send streams of lava to the ocean (Figure 27b).

Pu'u O'o is the active crater on Kīlauea and is presently continuing to erupt. In 2007, a portion of Pu'u O'o crater's west side collapsed, filled with lava, and collapsed again (Figure 28)—see http://hvo.wr.usgs.gov/. In March 2011, a new rift formed west of the crater and lava redirected away from former flows to the ocean.

A typical mountain landform built from effusive eruptions is gently sloped, gradually rising from the surrounding landscape to a summit crater. The shape is similar in outline to a shield of armor lying face up on the ground and therefore is called a **shield volcano**. The shield shape and size of Mauna Loa in Hawai'i are distinctive when compared with Mount Rainier in Washington, which is a different type of volcano (explained shortly) and the largest in the Cascade Range (Figure 29).

The height of the Mauna Loa shield is the result of successive eruptions, flowing one on top of another. Mauna Loa is one of five shield volcanoes that make up the island of Hawai'i. At least 1 million years were needed to accumulate its mass. Mauna Kea is slightly taller, but Mauna Loa is the most massive single mountain on Earth.

In another volcanic setting, effusive eruptions send material out through hot spots or elongated fissures, such as a continental rift valley, forming extensive sheets of basaltic lava on the surface (see Figure 26). The Columbian Plateau of the northwestern United States, some 2–3 km thick (1.2–1.8 mi), is the result of the eruption of **flood basalts**, sometimes called *plateau basalts*.

Explosive Eruptions

Volcanic activity inland from subduction zones produces the infamous explosive volcanoes. Magma produced by the melting of subducted oceanic plate and other materials is thicker (more viscous) than magma that forms effusive volcanoes. It is 50%–75% silica and high in aluminum; consequently, it tends to block the magma conduit. The blockage traps and compresses gases, causing pressure to build for a possible **explosive eruption**, such as Mount St. Helen (Focus Study 2).

(a)

(b)

(c)

FIGURE 28 Dynamic and active Pu'u O'o, at Kīlauea, Hawai'i. (a) The cracked and faulted crater of Pu'u O'o in 1999. Note the changes that happened (b) by 2007 and (c) by 2011. Portions of the crater wall collapsed in summer 2007, refilled with lava, and collapsed again. Active lava continues to fill the crater from the spatter cones. [(a) Bobbé Christopherson. (b), (c) USGS Hawaiian Volcano Observatory.]

Slow slip events across Kīlauea's south flank

The entire south flank of the Kīlauea volcano is in a long-term motion toward the ocean, along a low-angle fault at a rate of about 7 cm (2.75 in.) per year—see the area in Figure 27a. GPS units, tiltmeters, and small earthquakes mark the slow movement. In February 2010, in one 36-hour period, a slow slip event of 3 cm (1.18 in.) occurred, accompanied by a flurry of small earthquakes. A bench collapse or failure of this new basaltic landscape into the sea is possible, but the eventual outcome of these slow slip events is unknown. In March 2011, lava flows to the ocean changed as new eruptions began west of Pu'u O'o.

FOCUS STUDY 2

The 1980 Eruption of Mount St. Helens

Quiet since 1857, Mount St. Helens awoke in March 1980, with a sharp earthquake registering an M 4.1. The first eruptive outburst occurred a week later, beginning with an M 4.5 quake and continuing with a thick black plume of ash and the development of a small summit crater. Ten days later, after scientists hurriedly placed instruments around the volcano, the first volcanic earthquake, called a *harmonic tremor*, registered. Harmonic tremors are slow, steady vibrations, unlike the sharp releases of energy associated with tectonic earthquakes and faulting. These vibrations indicated that magma was on the move within the mountain.

Also developing was a massive bulge on Mount St. Helens' north side, indicating the direction of the magma flow within the volcano. A bulge represents the greatest risk from a composite volcano, for it could signal a potential lateral burst through the bulge and across the landscape.

Early on Sunday, May 18, the area north of the mountain was rocked by an M 5.0 quake, the strongest to date. The mountain, with its distended 245-m (800-ft) bulge, was shaken, but nothing happened. Then a second quake, at M 5.1, hit a few minutes later, loosening the bulge and launching the eruption. David Johnston, a volcanologist with the USGS, was only 8 km (5 mi) from the mountain, servicing instruments, when he saw the eruption begin. He radioed headquarters in Vancouver, Washington, saying "Vancouver, Vancouver, this is it!" He perished in the eruption. For a continuously updated live picture of Mount St. Helens from Johnston's approximate observation point and other specifics, go to http://www.fs.fed.us/gpnf/volcanocams/msh/. The camera is mounted below the roofline at the Johnston Ridge Observatory, which is open to the public.

As the contents of the mountain exploded, a surge of hot gas (about 300°C, or 570°F), steam-filled ash, pyroclastics, and a *nuée ardente* (rapidly moving, very hot, explosive ash and incandescent gases) moved northward, hugging the ground and traveling at speeds up to 400 kmph (250 mph) for a distance of 28 km (17 mi).

The slumping north face of the mountain produced the greatest landslide witnessed in recorded history; about 2.75 km^3 (0.67 mi^3) of rock, ice, and trapped air, all fluidized with steam, surged at speeds approaching 250 kmph (155 mph). Landslide materials traveled for 21 km (13 mi) into the valley, blanketing the forest, covering a lake, and filling the rivers below. A series of photographs, taken at 10-second intervals from the east looking west, records this sequence (Figure 2.1). The eruption continued with intensity for 9 hours, first clearing out old rock from the throat of the volcano and then blasting new material for days.

As destructive as such eruptions are, they also are constructive, for this is the way in which a volcano eventually builds its height. Before the eruption, Mount St. Helens was 2950 m (9677 ft) tall; the eruption blew away 418 m (1370 ft). Today, Mount St. Helens is building a lava dome within its crater. The thick lava rapidly and repeatedly plugs and breaks in a series of lesser dome eruptions that may continue for several decades. The several lava domes are more than 300 m (1000 ft) high, so a new mountain is being born from the eruption of the old.

The lava dome is covered with a dozen survey benchmarks and several tiltmeters to monitor the status of the volcano. Swarms of minor earthquakes along the north flank of the mountain began in November 2001, marking this mountain as still unstable. Dome eruptions of varying intensities occurred through 2007. Intensive scientific research and monitoring has paid off, as every eruption since 1980 was successfully forecasted from days to as long as 3 weeks in advance, with the exception of one small eruption in 1984.

More than three decades have passed, yet strong interest in the area continues; scientists and more than 1 million tourists visit the Mount St. Helens Volcanic National Monument each year. For more information, see the Cascades Volcano Observatory at http://vulcan.wr.usgs.gov/.

The attention drawn to Mount St. Helens over these three decades is deserved, especially when you think of the status of volcanic science 30 years ago, before cell phones, laptops, and GPS technology. A recent paper summarizes this well:

> The eruption remains a seminal historical event—studying it and its aftermath revolutionized the way scientists approach the field of volcanology. Not only was the eruption spectacular, but also it occurred in daytime, at an accessible volcano, in a country with the resources to transform the disaster into scientific opportunity, amid a transformation in digital technology. Lives lost and the impact of the eruption on people and infrastructure downstream and downwind made it imperative for scientists to investigate events and work with communities to lessen losses from future eruptions.*

[Images & Volcans/Photo Researchers, Inc.]

*J. W. Vallance et al., "Mount St. Helens: A 30-year legacy of volcanism," *EOS, Transactions* (American Geophysical Union), May 11, 2010, p. 169.

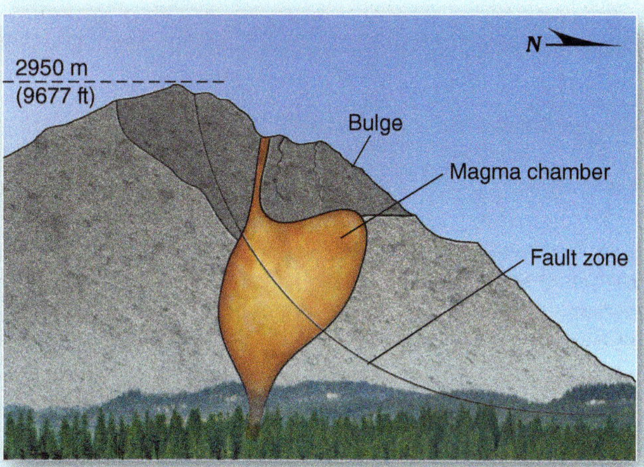

FIGURE 2.1 The Mount St. Helens eruption sequence and corresponding schematics.
[Photo sequence by Keith Ronnholm.]

Animation Debris Avalanche and Eruption of Mount St. Helens

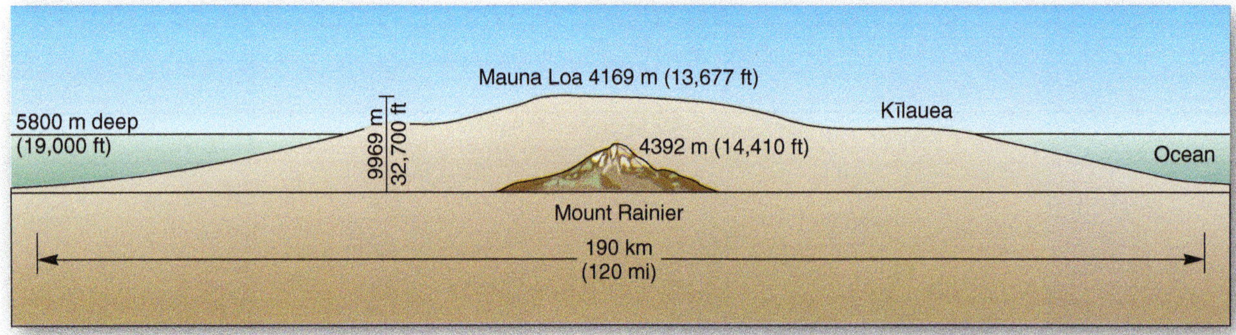

FIGURE 29 Shield and composite volcanoes compared. Comparison of Mauna Loa in Hawai'i, a shield volcano, and Mount Rainier in Washington State, a composite volcano. Their strikingly different profiles signify their different tectonic origins. Note the gently sloped shield shape in the inset photo. [After U.S. Geological Survey, *Eruption of Hawaiian Volcanoes* (Washington, DC: Government Printing Office, 1986). Inset photo by Bobbé Christopherson.]

From this magma, a lighter dacitic rock forms at the surface, as illustrated in the comparison in Figure 6. Unlike the volcanoes in Hawai'i Volcanoes National Park, where tourists gather at observation platforms or hike out across the cooling lava flows to watch the relatively calm effusive eruptions, these explosive volcanoes do not invite close inspection and can explode with little warning.

The term **composite volcano** describes these explosively formed mountains. (They are sometimes called *stratovolcanoes* because they are built up in alternating layers of ash, rock, and lava, but shield volcanoes also can exhibit a stratified structure, so *composite* is the preferred term.) Composite volcanoes tend to have steep sides, are more conical in shape than shield volcanoes, and therefore are also known as *composite cones*. If a single summit vent erupts repeatedly, a remarkable symmetry may develop as the mountain grows in size, as demonstrated by Mount Orizaba in Mexico, Mount Shishaldin in Alaska (Figure 30), Mount Fuji in Japan, Mount Mayon in the Philippines, and the pre-1980-eruption shape of Mount St. Helens in Washington.

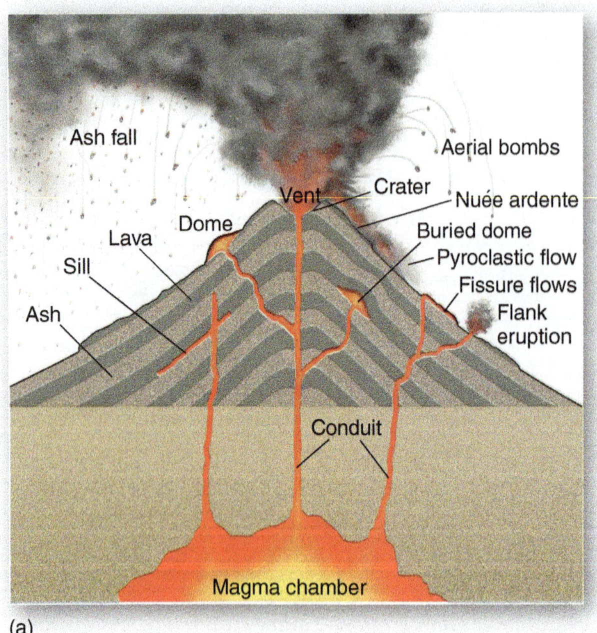

FIGURE 30 A composite volcano.
(a) A typical composite volcano with its cone-shaped form in an explosive eruption. (b) Mount Shishaldin, Unimak Island in the eastern Aleutian Islands, Alaska, is a 2857-m (9372-ft) composite volcano. It is shown here during a 1995 eruption; it was active through 2001. [(b) Photo courtesy of AeroMap U.S., Inc., Anchorage, Alaska.]

Probably the most studied and photographed composite volcano on Earth is Mount St. Helens, located 70 km (45 mi) northeast of Portland, Oregon, and 130 km (80 mi) south of the Tacoma–Seattle area. Mount St. Helens is the youngest and most active of the Cascade Range of volcanoes, which form a line from Mount Lassen in California to Mount Meager in British Columbia. The Cascade Range is the product of the Juan de Fuca sea-floor spreading center off the coast of northern California, Oregon, Washington, and British Columbia and the plate subduction that occurs offshore, as identified in the upper right of Figure 12a. Focus Study 2 details the highly publicized 1980 eruption of Mount St. Helens.

Owing to its chemical makeup and high viscosity, rising magma in a composite volcano forms a plug near the surface. The blockage causes tremendous pressure to build, keeping the trapped gases compressed and liquefied. When the blockage can no longer hold back this pressurized inferno, an explosion equivalent to megatons of TNT blasts the top and sides off the mountain. This type of eruption produces much less lava than effusive eruptions, but larger amounts of *pyroclastics*, which include volcanic *ash* (<2 mm, or <0.08 in., in diameter), dust, cinders, *lapilli* (up to 32 mm, or 1.26 in., in diameter), *scoria* (volcanic slag), pumice, and *aerial bombs* (explosively ejected blobs of incandescent lava). A *nuée ardente*, French for "glowing cloud," is an incandescent, hot, turbulent gas, ash, and pyroclastic cloud that can jet across the landscape in an eruption.

Mount Pinatubo Eruption In June 1991, after 600 years of dormancy, Mount Pinatubo in the Philippines erupted. The summit of the 1460-m (4795-ft) volcano exploded, devastating many surrounding villages and permanently closing Clark Air Force Base, operated by the United States. Fortunately, scientists from the USGS and local scientists accurately predicted the eruption. A timely evacuation of the surrounding countryside saved thousands of lives, but 800 people were killed.

Although volcanoes are regional events, their spatial implications can be worldwide. The single volcanic eruption of Mount Pinatubo was significant to the global environment. Here is a summary of its effects:

- 15–20 million tons of ash and sulfuric acid mist were blasted into the atmosphere, concentrating at an altitude of 16–25 km (10–15.5 mi).
- 12 km³ (3.0 mi³) of material were ejected and extruded by the eruption (12 times the volume from Mount St. Helens).
- 60 days after the eruption, a thin, spreading aerosol cloud affected about 42% of the globe (from 20° S to 30° N).
- Colorful twilight and dawn skies were observed worldwide.
- An increase in atmospheric albedo of 1.5% (4.3 W/m²) occurred.
- An increase in the atmospheric absorption of insolation followed (2.5 W/m²).
- A decrease in net radiation at the surface and a lowering of Northern Hemisphere average temperatures of 0.5 C° (0.9 F°) were measured.
- Atmospheric scientists and volcanologists were able to study the eruption aftermath using satellite-borne orbiting sensors and general-circulation-model computer simulations.

Volcano Forecasting and Planning

The USGS and the Office of Foreign Disaster Assistance operate the Volcano Disaster Assistance Program (VDAP). For a listing of more than two dozen projects, see http://vulcan.wr.usgs.gov/Vdap/framework.html. The need for such a program is evident in that over the past 30 years, volcanic activity has killed 29,000 people, forced more than 800,000 to evacuate their homes, and caused more than $3 billion in damage. The program was established after 23,000 people died in the eruption of Nevado del Ruiz, Colombia, in 1985. The U.S. VDAP is in place to help local scientists with eruption forecasts by setting up mobile volcano-monitoring systems at the most-threatened sites.

An effort such as this led to the life-saving evacuation of 60,000 people hours before Mount Pinatubo exploded. In addition, satellite remote sensing is helping VDAP to monitor eruption cloud dynamics, atmospheric emissions and climatic effects, and lava and thermal measurements; to make topographic measurements; to estimate volcanic hazard potential; and to enhance geologic mapping—all in an effort to better understand our dynamic planet. Integrated seismographic networks and monitoring are making possible early warning systems.

Go to http://vulcan.wr.usgs.gov/Photo/volcano_cams.html to access "volcano cams" positioned around the world, allowing 24-hour surveillance of many volcanoes. Be sure to note whether it is day or night for the location you are checking.

GEOSYSTEMS CONNECTION

Here we discussed the crust-building processes of Earth's endogenic systems. Earth's surface topography results from formation and deformation processes powered by radioactive-decay heat radiating from Earth's interior. Mountain building, earthquakes, and volcanism are the resulting outputs of these systems. Contrast this to the exogenic system, where solar energy and gravity empower weathering, erosion, and deposition through the agents of water, wind, waves, and ice. These processes reduce relief and the landscape.

KEY LEARNING CONCEPTS REVIEW

■ ***Describe*** first, second, and third orders of relief, and ***relate*** examples of each from Earth's major topographic regions.

Tectonic forces generated within the planet dramatically shape Earth's surface. **Relief** is the vertical elevation difference in a local landscape. The undulating physical surface of Earth, including relief, is **topography**. Convenient descriptive categories are termed *orders of relief*. The coarsest level of landforms includes the **continental landmasses** and **ocean basins**; the finest comprises local hills and valleys.

relief	continental landmass
topography	ocean basin

1. How does the map of the ocean floor in the chapter-opening illustration exhibit the principles of plate tectonics? Briefly analyze.
2. What is meant by an order of relief? Give an example from each order.
3. Explain the difference between relief and topography.

■ ***Describe*** the several origins of continental crust, and ***define*** displaced terranes.

A continent has a nucleus of ancient crystalline rock called a *craton*. A region where a craton is exposed is a **continental shield**. As continental crust forms, it is enlarged through accretion of dispersed **terranes**. An example is the *Wrangellia terrane* of the Pacific Northwest and Alaska.

continental shield	terrane

4. What is a craton? Relate this structure to continental shields and platforms, and describe these regions in North America.
5. What is a migrating terrane, and how does it add to the formation of continental landmasses? Using the map on the *MasteringGeography* web site, briefly describe the journey and destination of the Wrangellia terrane.

■ ***Explain*** compressional processes and folding, and ***describe*** four principal types of faults and their characteristic landforms.

Folding, broad warping, and faulting deform the crust and produce characteristic landforms. Compression causes rocks to deform in a process known as **folding**, during which rock strata bend and may overturn. Along the *ridge* of a fold, layers *slope downward away from the axis*, which is an **anticline**. In the *trough* of a fold, however, layers *slope downward toward the axis;* this is a **syncline**.

When rock strata are stressed beyond their ability to remain a solid unit, they express the strain as a fracture. Rocks on either side of the fracture are displaced relative to the other side in a process known as **faulting**. Thus, *fault zones* are areas where fractures in the rock demonstrate crustal movement. At the moment of fracture, a sharp release of energy, an **earthquake** or *quake*, occurs.

When forces pull rocks apart, the tension causes a **normal fault**, sometimes visible on the landscape as a scarp, or escarpment. Compressional forces associated with converging plates force rocks to move upward, producing a **reverse fault**. A low-angle fault plane is referred to as a **thrust fault**. Horizontal movement along a fault plane that produces a linear rift valley is a **strike-slip fault**. In the U.S. interior west, the **Basin and Range Province** is an example of aligned pairs of normal faults and a distinctive horst-and-graben landscape. The term **horst** is applied to upward-faulted blocks; **graben** refers to downward-faulted blocks. A **bolson** is the slope-and-basin area between mountain ridges in this type of arid region.

folding	thrust fault
anticline	strike-slip fault
syncline	horst
faulting	graben
earthquake	Basin and Range Province
normal fault	bolson
reverse fault	

6. Diagram a simple folded landscape in cross section, and identify the features created by the folded strata.
7. Define the four basic types of faults. How are faults related to earthquakes and seismic activity?
8. How did the Basin and Range Province evolve in the western United States? What other examples exist of this type of landscape?

■ ***Relate*** the three types of plate collisions associated with orogenesis, and ***identify*** specific examples of each.

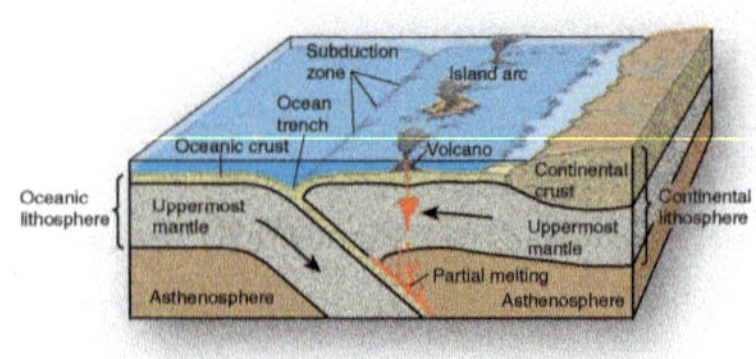

Orogenesis is the birth of mountains. An orogeny is a mountain-building episode, occurring over millions of years, that thickens continental crust. It can occur through large-scale deformation and uplift of the crust. It also may include the capture and cementation of migrating terranes to the continental margins and the intrusion of granitic magmas to form plutons.

Oceanic plate–continental plate collision orogenesis is now occurring along the Pacific coast of the Americas and has formed the Andes, the Sierra of Central America, the Rockies, and other western mountains. *Oceanic plate–oceanic plate* collision orogenesis produces either simple or more complex volcanic island arcs such as Japan, the Philippines, the Kurils, and portions of the Aleutians. The region around the Pacific contains expressions of each type of collision in the *circum-Pacific belt*, or the *ring of fire*. *Continental plate–continental plate* collision orogenesis is quite mechanical; large masses of continental crust, such as the Himalayan Range, are subjected to intense folding, overthrusting, faulting, and uplifting.

orogenesis

9. Define orogenesis. What is meant by the birth of mountain chains?
10. Name some significant orogenies.
11. Identify on a map several of Earth's mountain chains. What processes contributed to their development?
12. How are plate boundaries related to episodes of mountain building? Explain how different types of plate boundaries produce differing orogenic episodes and different landscapes.
13. Relate tectonic processes to the formation of the Appalachians and the Alleghany orogeny.

■ ***Explain*** the nature of earthquakes, including their characteristics, measurement, fault mechanics, and forecasting methods.

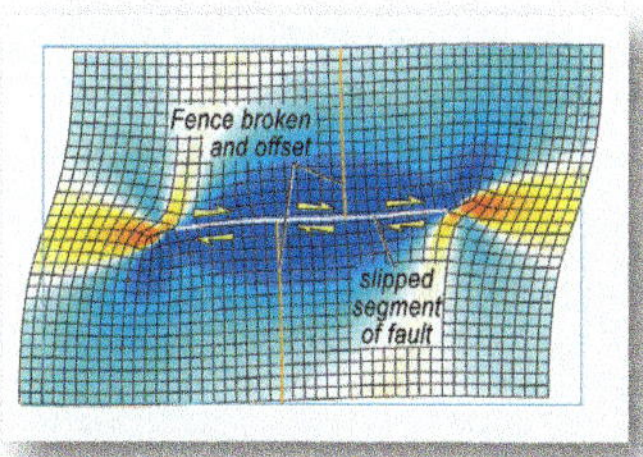

Earthquakes generally occur along plate boundaries; major ones can be disastrous. Earthquakes result from faults, which are under continuing scientific study. Earthquake prediction and improved planning are active concerns of *seismology*, the study of earthquake waves and Earth's interior. Seismic motions are measured with a **seismograph**.

Charles Richter developed the **Richter scale**, a measure of earthquake magnitude. A more precise and quantitative scale that assesses the *seismic moment* is now used, especially for larger quakes; this is the **moment magnitude scale**. The specific mechanics of how a fault breaks are under study, but the **elastic-rebound theory** describes the basic process. In general, two sides along a fault appear to be locked by friction, resisting any movement. This stress continues to build strain along the fault surfaces, storing elastic energy like a wound-up spring. When energy is released abruptly as the rock breaks, both sides of the fault return to a condition of less strain.

seismograph	moment magnitude scale
Richter scale	elastic-rebound theory

14. What is the relationship between an epicenter and the focus of an earthquake? Give an example from the Loma Prieta, California, earthquake.
15. Differentiate among the Mercalli, moment magnitude, and amplitude (Richter) scales. How are these used to describe an earthquake? Reference some recent quakes in your discussion.
16. How do the elastic-rebound theory and asperities help explain the nature of faulting? In your explanation, relate the concepts of stress (force) and strain (deformation) along a fault. How does this lead to rupture and earthquake?
17. Describe the San Andreas fault and its relationship to ancient sea-floor spreading movements along transform faults.
18. How are paleoseismology and the seismic gap concept related to expected earthquake occurrences?
19. What do you see as the biggest barrier to effective earthquake prediction?

■ ***Distinguish*** between an effusive and an explosive volcanic eruption, and ***describe*** related landforms, using specific examples.

A **volcano** forms at the end of a central vent or pipe that rises from the asthenosphere through the crust into a volcanic mountain. A **crater**, or circular surface depression, usually forms at the summit. Areas where magma is near the surface may heat groundwater, producing *geothermal energy*.

Eruptions produce **lava** (molten rock), gases, and **pyroclastics** (pulverized rock and clastic materials ejected violently during an eruption) that pass through the vent to openings and fissures at the surface and build volcanic landforms. Basaltic lava flows occur in two principal textures: **aa**, rough and sharp-edged lava, and **pahoehoe**, smooth, ropy folds of lava. Volcanic activity produces landforms such as a **cinder cone**, a small hill, or a large basin-shaped depression sometimes caused by the collapse of a volcano's summit, forming a **caldera**.

Volcanoes are of two general types, based on the chemistry and the viscosity of the magma involved. An **effusive eruption** produces a **shield volcano** (such as Kīlauea in Hawai'i) and extensive deposits of **flood basalts**, or plateau basalts. Magma of higher viscosity leads to an **explosive eruption** (such as Mount Pinatubo in the Philippines), producing a **composite volcano**. Volcanic activity has produced some destructive moments in history, but constantly creates new seafloor, land, and soils.

volcano	caldera
crater	effusive eruption
lava	shield volcano
pyroclastics	flood basalt
aa	explosive eruption
pahoehoe	composite volcano
cinder cone	

20. What is a volcano? In general terms, describe some related features.
21. Where do you expect to find volcanic activity in the world? Why?
22. Compare effusive and explosive eruptions. Why are they different? What distinct landforms are produced by each type? Give examples of each.
23. Describe several recent volcanic eruptions, such as in Hawai'i and Iceland. What is the present status in each place? Specifically, what changes are occurring in Hawai'i?

Visit **http://www.masteringgeography.com/** for several figure animations, satellite loops, self-study quizzes, flashcards, visual glossary, case studies, career links, text reference maps, RSS Feeds, and an ebook version of *Elemental Geosystems*. Included are many geography web links to interesting Internet sources that support this chapter.

The Oceans, Coastal Systems, and Wind Processes

The Oceans, Coastal Systems, and Wind Processes

Tsunami waves break over a protective wall onto the streets of Miyako, Iwate Prefecture, in northeastern Japan, triggered by a catastrophic M 9.0 earthquake, March 11, 2011. Buildings, cars, houses, and victims were carried far inland. Miyako is about 120 km (75 mi) north of the quake epicenter and 200 km (125 mi) north of the Fukushima Daiichi nuclear power plant disaster. There is more on this in *Geosystems Now*. [REUTERS/Mainichi Shimbun.]

KEY LEARNING CONCEPTS

After reading the chapter, you should be able to:

- ***Describe*** the chemical composition and physical structure of the ocean.
- ***Identify*** the components of the coastal environment, including mean sea level, and ***explain*** the actions of tides.
- ***Describe*** wave motion at sea and near shore, and ***explain*** coastal straightening and coastal landforms.
- ***Describe*** barrier beaches and islands and their hazards as they relate to human settlement.
- ***Assess*** living coastal environments: corals and coastal wetlands.
- ***Describe*** eolian erosion, including deflation, abrasion, and the resultant landforms.
- ***Describe*** eolian transportation, and ***explain*** eolian depositional landforms, including the major classes of sand dunes.

Tsunami Warnings, Past and Present

Walking inland from the coast of northeast Honshu Island, Japan, one finds stone tablets rising from the ground, some up to 3 m (10 ft) tall, and covered with calligraphy (photo and information at http://coastalcare.org/2011/04/tsunami-warnings-written-in-stone/). These tsunami stones contain warnings about where not to build because of the danger of seismic sea waves—the dreaded tsunami. Some of the stones date back 6 centuries; others date to when two tsunami hit the region in the late 19th century. The stones, which number in the hundreds, seem to shout, "Don't build houses below this point."

A *tsunami* is a set of ocean waves caused by a large, abrupt disturbance of the seafloor. As with earthquakes and floods, human hazard perception often becomes difficult over time and in familiar environments. In Japan, as elsewhere, the 20th century progressed and people forgot about the tsunami stones. Coastal population and settlement increased, and nuclear power stations were built just steps from the beach. Then on March 11, 2011, the Tohoku/Sendai earthquake produced a tsunami that refreshed the ancient stone-tablet warnings.

In this modern era in Japan, tsunami warnings came immediately. Eight to 10 minutes after the quake, the first tsunami wave hit the northeastern coast of Honshu, the closest shoreline to the earthquake's epicenter. Tsunami wave heights averaged 10 m (33 ft) in some areas and reached 30 m (98 ft) in narrow harbors. At Ofunato, the tsunami traveled 3 km (1.8 miles) inland; waves reached 10 km inland (6.2 miles) in other areas.

Seawalls and breakwaters designed for high waves generated by typhoons and tsunami protect about 40% of the country's coastline. However, deep coastal embayments magnify tsunami energy and make this region particularly vulnerable. In Kamaishi during the March 11 event, the $1.5 billion tsunami seawall was breached by a 5-m (15-ft) tsunami wave, submerging the city center—similar scenes were repeated in other coastal cities.

The quake and tsunami damaged cooling systems at six nuclear reactors at the Fukushima Daiichi plant, situated along the coast south of Sendai; three of the reactors experienced core meltdowns within a few days. Subsequent hydrogen explosions destroyed three secondary containment structures, leading to massive radiation releases to the land, atmosphere, and ocean. Cleanup will take years, with radiation fallout adding to the difficulty.

Nine minutes after the initial earthquake, the Pacific Tsunami Warning Center (PTWS) issued tsunami warnings to the Pacific islands and distant continents. This first step is initiated when a seismic station detects a significant quake or landslide underwater. Deep-ocean sensors register a change in pressure associated with an ocean disturbance; data is relayed to a surface buoy and then transmitted via satellite to the PTWS. This second step is the Deep-ocean Assessment and Reporting of Tsunamis (DART), a 32-station network in the Pacific (Figure GN 1). Over the next hour. tsunami forecasts and warnings continued, including wave-height predictions (Figure GN 2).

FIGURE GN 1 One of NOAA's DART buoys. The sea-surface buoy is anchored above a bottom pressure recorder, the two linked by acoustic telemetry for real-time communication. The buoy transmits readings from the sea-floor recorder to land-based surface stations through the *Iridium* satellite system. The National Geophysical Data Center is the data archive for DART. [NOAA.]

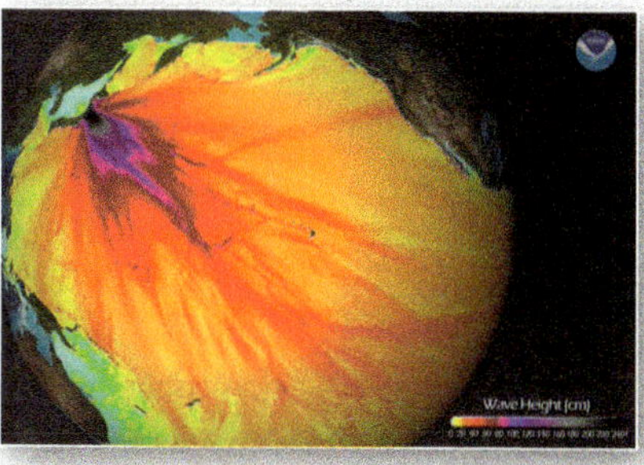

FIGURE GN 2 NOAA tsunami wave height prediction. [NOAA.]

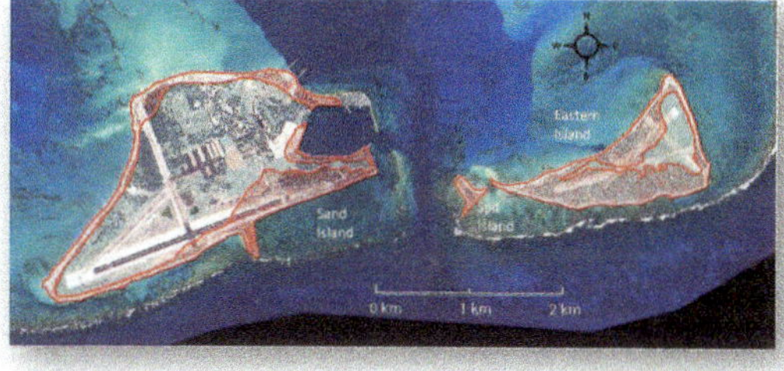

FIGURE GN 3 Tsunami reaches Midway. A tsunami overwashes portions of Sand and Eastern Islands in the Midway Islands (the sea-covered areas noted with red outlines and shading). [U.S. Fish and Wildlife Service, DOI.]

Sea-floor topography guides and deflects long-wavelength tsunami energy. As it moved across the Pacific, the tsunami overwashed portions of the Midway Islands 4 hours after the quake (Figure GN 3). Oahu, Maui, and Hawai'i were impacted with 1-m waves 7 hours after the quake. Waves 2.1 m (7 ft) high struck northern and central California about 12 hours after the quake, causing several million dollars in damage to harbors, boats, and piers. Waves 30 to 70 cm (1.0 to 2.3 ft) high arrived at New Zealand.

The tsunami warnings generally failed to help the Japanese during this huge wave event, for people had too little time to flee from vulnerable coastal areas. However, the warnings were effective in preparing other regions for the waves. Yet, despite warnings in Hawai'i and along the U.S. mainland, people arrived along shorelines with cameras in hand to capture images of the incoming danger. All this brings to mind the warnings on the ancient tsunami stones. ■

Walk along a shoreline and you witness the dramatic interaction of Earth's vast oceanic, atmospheric, and lithospheric systems. At times, the ocean attacks the coast in a stormy rage of erosive power; at other times, the moist sea breeze, salty mist, and repetitive motion of the water are gentle and calming. The coastlines are areas of dynamic change and beauty.

Commerce and access to sea routes, fishing, and tourism prompt many people to settle near the ocean. A scientific assessment estimates that about 40% of Earth's population lives within 100 km (62 mi) of coastlines. In the United States, about 50% of the people live in areas designated as *coastal* (this includes the Great Lakes).

Therefore, an understanding of coastal processes and landforms is important to nearly half the world's population. And because these processes along coastlines often produce dramatic change, they are essential to consider in planning and development. A World Resources Institute study found as much as 50% of the world's coastlines at some risk of loss through erosion and rising sea level or disruption from pollution. The National Ocean Service coordinates many scientific activities related to the ocean; information is available at http://www.nos.noaa.gov/.

The ocean is a vast ecosystem, intricately linked to life on the planet and to life-sustaining systems in the atmosphere, the hydrosphere, and the lithosphere. Oceans act as a vast buffering system, absorbing excess atmospheric carbon dioxide and thermal energy; yet the system is overwhelmed with the rate of change over the past several decades. The first meeting of the Conference on the Ocean Observing System for Climate took place in St. Raphael, France, in 1999; the second meeting occurred 10 years later in Venice, Italy. The program noted the profound changes that had transpired in the ocean system over those 10 years and set a goal for a new physical and carbon ocean-observing system by 2015—see http://www.oceanobs09.net/.

Wind is an agent of geomorphic change along coastlines as well as in other environments. Although wind's ability to erode, transport, and deposit materials is small compared to that of water and ice, wind processes can move significant quantities of sand and shape landforms.

In this chapter: We begin with a brief look at our global oceans and seas. We discuss the physical and chemical properties of seawater. Our coverage of coastal systems includes discussions about tides, waves, coastal erosion, and depositional landforms such as beaches and barrier islands. Important organic processes produce corals, salt marshes, and mangroves. A systems framework of specific inputs (components and driving forces), actions (movements and processes), and outputs (results and consequences) organizes our discussion of coastal processes. We then examine wind processes, including wind erosion and the resulting landforms. We conclude with a look at wind deposition, including sand dunes and sand seas.

Global Oceans and Seas

The ocean is one of Earth's last great scientific frontiers and is of great interest to geographers. Remote sensing from orbiting spacecraft and satellites, aircraft, surface vessels, and submersibles is providing a wealth of data and a new capability to understand the oceanic system. We can track the pattern of sea-surface temperatures and ocean currents, both surface and deep. The world's oceans and their area, volume, and depth are readily available. The locations of oceans and major seas are mapped and listed alphabetically in Figure 1.

Chemical Composition of Seawater

Water is the "universal solvent," dissolving at least 57 of the 92 elements found in nature. In fact, most natural elements and the compounds they form are found in the seas as dissolved solids, or *solutes*. Thus, seawater is a solution, and the concentration of dissolved solids is **salinity**.

The ocean remains a remarkably homogeneous mixture. The ratio of individual salts does not change, despite minor fluctuations in overall salinity. In 1874, the British HMS *Challenger* sailed around the world taking surface and depth measurements and collecting samples of seawater. Analyses of those samples first demonstrated the uniform composition of seawater.

Ocean Chemistry Ocean chemistry is a result of complex exchanges among seawater, the atmosphere, minerals, bottom sediments, and living organisms. In addition, significant flows of mineral-rich water enter the ocean through hydrothermal (hot water) vents in the ocean floor. These vents are the "black smokers," noted for the dense, black, mineral-laden water that spews from them. The uniformity of seawater results from complementary chemical reactions and continuous mixing—after all, the ocean basins interconnect, and water circulates among them.

Seven elements account for more than 99% of the dissolved solids in seawater. They are (with their ionic form) chlorine (as chloride, Cl^-), sodium (as Na^+), magnesium (as Mg^{2+}), sulfur (as sulfate, SO_4^{2-}), calcium (as Ca^{2+}), potassium (as K^+), and bromine (as bromide, Br^-). Seawater also contains dissolved gases (such as carbon dioxide, nitrogen, and oxygen), suspended and dissolved organic matter, and a multitude of trace elements.

Commercially, only sodium chloride (common table salt), magnesium, and bromine are extracted in any significant amount from the ocean. Future mining of minerals from the seafloor is technically feasible, although it remains uneconomical.

Average Salinity: 35‰ There are several ways to express salinity (dissolved solids by volume) in seawater, using the worldwide average value:

- 3.5% (% parts per hundred)
- 35,000 ppm (parts per million)

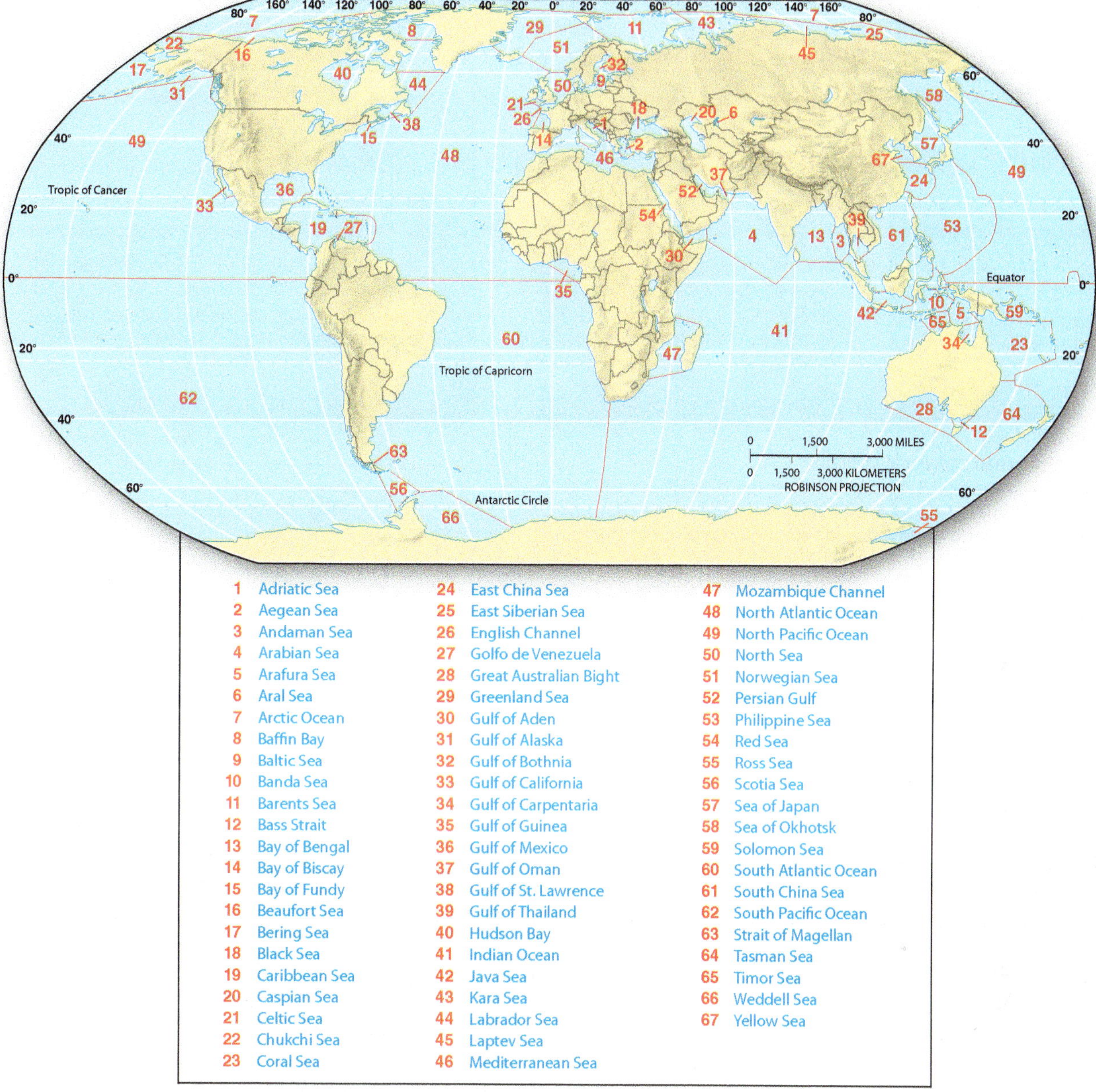

FIGURE 1 Principal oceans and seas of the world.
A sea is generally smaller than an ocean and is near a landmass; sometimes the term refers to a large, inland, salty body of water. Match the alphabetized name and number with its location on the map.

- 35,000 mg/l
- 35 g/kg
- 35‰ (‰ parts per thousand), the most common notation

Salinity worldwide normally varies between 34‰ and 37‰; variations are attributable to atmospheric conditions above the water and to the volume of freshwater inflows. In equatorial water, precipitation is great throughout the year, diluting salinity values to 34.5‰ (slightly lower than average). In subtropical oceans—where evaporation rates are greatest because of the influence of hot, dry, subtropical high-pressure cells—salinity is more concentrated, increasing to 36‰. In these regions, salinity is rising as increased evaporation rates rise with temperature.

The term **brine** is applied to water that exceeds the average of 35‰ salinity. **Brackish** applies to water that is less than 35‰ salts. In general, oceans are lower in salinity near landmasses because of freshwater runoff and river discharges. Extreme examples include the Baltic Sea (north of Poland and Germany) and the Gulf of Bothnia (between Sweden and Finland), which average 10‰ or less salinity because of heavy freshwater runoff and low evaporation rates.

In contrast, the Sargasso Sea, within the North Atlantic subtropical gyre, averages 38‰. The Persian Gulf has a salinity of 40‰ as a result of high evaporation rates in a nearly enclosed basin. Deep pockets, or "brine lakes," along the floor of the Red Sea and the Mediterranean Sea register up to a salty 225‰.

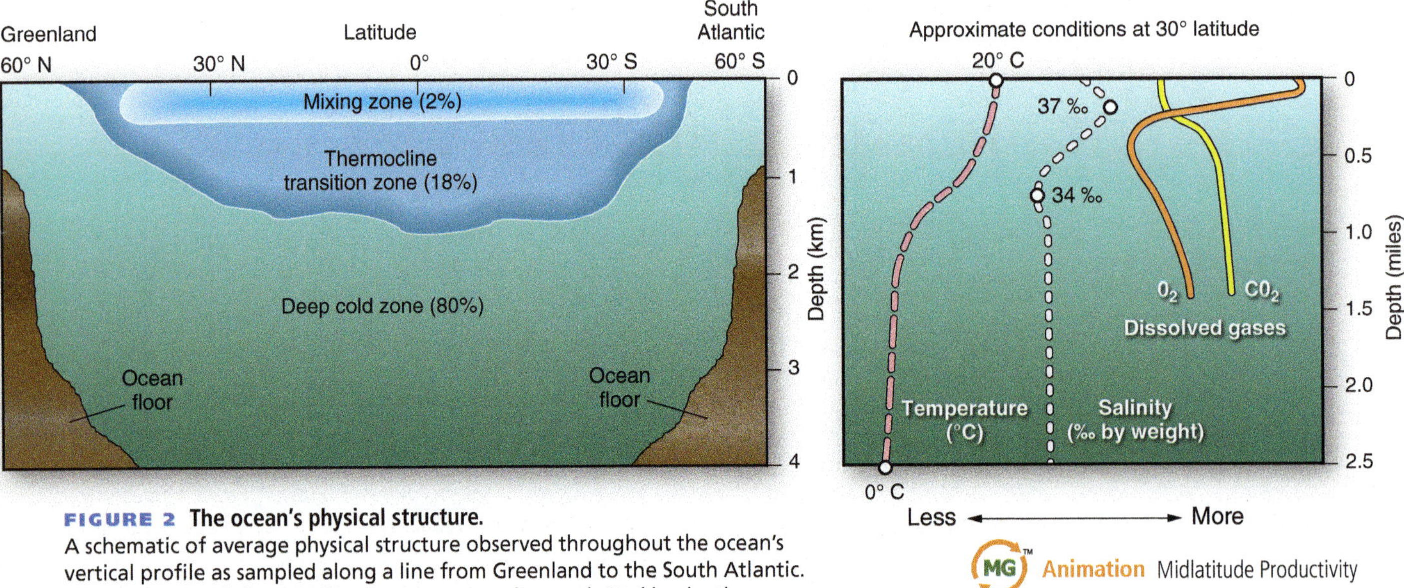

FIGURE 2 The ocean's physical structure.
A schematic of average physical structure observed throughout the ocean's vertical profile as sampled along a line from Greenland to the South Atlantic. Temperature, salinity, and dissolved gases are shown plotted by depth.

MG™ Animation Midlatitude Productivity

The ocean reflects conditions in Earth's environment. As an example, the high-latitude oceans have been freshening over the past decade, as mentioned earlier in this chapter. Another change under way is oceanic acidification, taking place as the ocean absorbs excess carbon dioxide from the atmosphere—acidity is increasing rapidly.

Hydrolysis forms carbonic acid in the seawater, resulting in a lowering of the ocean pH—an acidification. A more acid ocean will cause certain marine organisms such as corals and some plankton to have difficulty maintaining external calcium carbonate structures. pH could decrease by −0.4 to −0.5 units this century; the ocean's average pH today is 8.2. The scale is logarithmic, so a decrease of 0.1 equals a 30% increase in acidity. Oceanic biodiversity and food webs will respond to this change in unknown ways.

The dissolved solids remain in the ocean, but the water recycles endlessly through the hydrologic cycle, driven by energy from the Sun. The water you drink today may have water molecules in it that not long ago were in the Pacific Ocean, in the Yangtze River, in groundwater in Sweden, or airborne in the clouds over Peru.

Physical Structure of the Ocean

The basic physical structure of the ocean is layered, as shown in Figure 2. The figure also graphs four key aspects of the ocean, each of which varies with increasing depth: average temperature, salinity, dissolved carbon dioxide, and dissolved oxygen.

The ocean's surface layer is warmed by the Sun and is wind-driven. Variations in water temperature and solutes are blended rapidly in a *mixing zone* that represents only 2% of the oceanic mass. Below the mixing zone is the *thermocline transition zone*, a region more than 1 km deep of decreasing temperature gradient that lacks the motion of the surface. Friction at these depths dampens the effect of surface currents. In addition, colder water temperatures at the lower margin tend to inhibit any convective movements.

From a depth of 1–1.5 km (0.6–0.9 mi) to the ocean floor, temperature and salinity values are quite uniform. Temperatures in this *deep cold zone* are near 0°C (32°F). Water in the deep cold zone does not freeze, however, because of its salinity and the intense pressures at those depths; seawater freezes at about −2°C (28.4°F) at the surface. Generally, the coldest water is along the bottom. Now let us shift to the edge of the sea and examine Earth's coastlines.

Coastal System Components

Earth's surface features, such as mountains and crustal plates, were formed over millions of years. However, most of Earth's coastlines are relatively new, existing in their present state as the setting for continuous change. The land, ocean, atmosphere, Sun, and Moon interact to produce tides, currents, waves, erosional features, and depositional features along the continental margins.

Inputs to the coastal environment include many elements you may have already studied:

The Mediterranean Sea is getting saltier

The Mediterranean Sea is warming at a faster rate than the oceans. Increased salinity and temperatures are occurring in the deep layers, below 600 m (1968 ft) to the sea bed. Saltier conditions change the water density and cause net outflows past the Strait of Gibraltar, thus blocking natural mixing with the Atlantic Ocean. As climate changes, warming is disrupting the natural mixing in such water bodies.

- *Solar energy* input drives the atmosphere and the hydrosphere. A conversion of insolation to kinetic energy produces prevailing winds, weather systems, and climate.
- *Atmospheric winds*, in turn, generate ocean currents and waves, key inputs to the coastal environment.
- *Climatic regimes*, which result from insolation and moisture, strongly influence coastal geomorphic processes.
- The *nature of coastal rock* and coastal geomorphology are important in determining rates of erosion and sediment production.
- *Human activities* are an increasingly significant input to coastal change.

All these inputs occur within the ever-present influence of gravity's pull—not only from Earth, but also from the Moon and the Sun. Gravity provides the potential energy of position for materials in motion and produces the tides. A dynamic equilibrium among all these components produces coastline features of infinite variety and beauty.

The Coastal Environment and Sea Level

The coastal environment is the **littoral zone**, from the Latin word, *litoris*, for "shore." Figure 3 illustrates the littoral zone and includes specific components discussed later in the chapter. The littoral zone spans some land as well as water. Landward, it extends to the highest waterline that occurs on shore during a storm. Seaward, it extends to where water is too deep for storm waves to move sediments on the seafloor—usually around 60 m, or 200 ft, in depth. The specific contact line between the sea and the land is the *shoreline*, although this line shifts with tides, storms, and sea-level adjustments. The *coast* continues inland from high tide to the first major landform change and may include areas considered to be part of the coast in local usage.

Because the level of the ocean varies, the littoral zone naturally shifts position from time to time. A rise in sea level causes submergence of land, whereas a drop in sea level exposes new coastal areas. In addition, uplift and subsidence of the land itself initiate changes in the littoral zone.

Sea level is an important concept. Every elevation you see in an atlas or on a map is referenced to mean sea level. Yet this average sea level changes daily with the tides and over the long term with changes in climate, tectonic plate movements, and glaciation. Thus, *sea level* is a relative term. At present, no international system exists to determine exact sea level over time. The Global Sea Level Observing System (GLOSS) is an international group actively working on sea-level issues and is part of the larger Permanent Service for Mean Sea Level, which you can find at http://www.pol.ac.uk/psmsl/programmes/.

Mean sea level (MSL) is a value based on average tidal levels recorded hourly at a given site over many years. MSL varies spatially because of ocean currents and waves, tidal variations, air temperature, pressure differences and wind patterns, ocean temperature variations, slight variations in Earth's gravity, and changes in oceanic volume.

At present, the overall U.S. MSL is calculated at approximately 40 locations along the coastal margins of the continent. These sites are being upgraded with new equipment in the Next Generation Water Level Measurement System, using next-generation tide gauges, specifically along the U.S. and Canadian Atlantic Coast, Bermuda, and the Hawaiian Islands. The *NAVSTAR* satellites of the Global Positioning System (GPS) make possible the correlation of data within a network of ground- and ocean-based measurements.

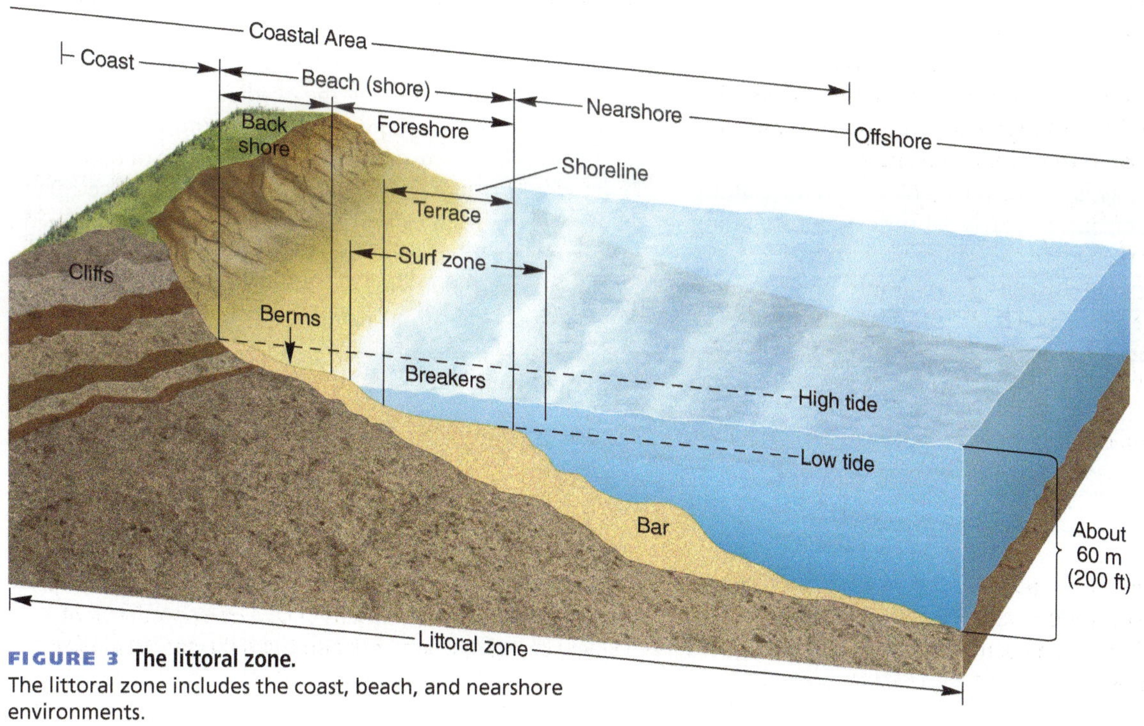

FIGURE 3 The littoral zone.
The littoral zone includes the coast, beach, and nearshore environments.

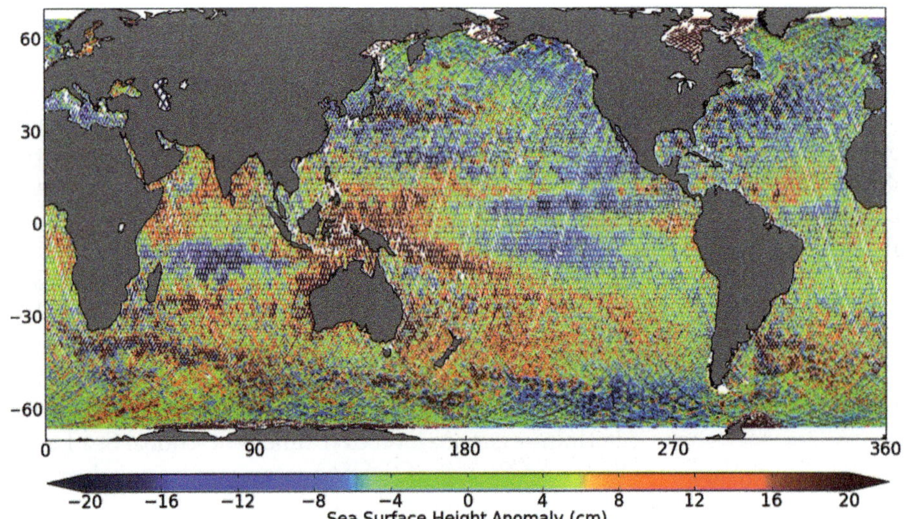

FIGURE 4 Sea-surface heights for April 16 to 26, 2011. Sea-surface height anomalies noted by the color scale are given in centimeters above or below Earth's geoid from the *Jason-1* and *Jason-2* altimeter missions. Data are near real-time, usually available within 7 hours of acquisition. The overall sea-surface relief portrayed in the image is about 2 m (6.6 ft). The maximum sea level is in the western Pacific Ocean (darkest reds). The minimum is around Antarctica (blue and purple). [Satellite data JPL/NASA.]

Changes in Sea Level

Over the long term, sea-level fluctuations expose a range of coastal landforms to tidal and wave processes. As average global temperatures cycle through cold or warm climatic spells, the quantity of ice locked up in the ice sheets of Antarctica and Greenland and in hundreds of mountain glaciers can increase or decrease and result in sea-level changes accordingly. At the peak of the most recent Pleistocene glaciation, about 18,000 B.P. (years before the present), sea level was about 130 m (430 ft) lower than it is today. On the other hand, if Antarctica and Greenland ever became ice-free (if their ice sheets fully melted), sea level would rise at least 65 m (215 ft) worldwide.

Just 100 years ago sea level was 38 cm (15 in.) lower along the coast of southern Florida. Venice, Italy, has experienced a rise of 25 cm (10 in.) since 1890. During the last century, average sea level rose 10–20 cm (4–8 in.), a rate 10 times higher than the average rate during the last 3000 years. Since 1930, sea-level rise has continued at an increasing rate, with some variability explained by global dam construction and artificial reservoir impoundments of water. The present sea-level rise is spatially uneven, as is MSL; for instance, the rate along the coast of Argentina is nearly 10 times the rate along the coast of France.

Remote sensing by the *Jason-1* and the *Jason-2/Ocean Surface Topography Mission* satellites tracks changing sea level (see http://climate.nasa.gov/; click on "Sea Level Viewer"). Instruments aboard these satellites are able to map ocean-surface topography to within a few centimeters, producing maps of ocean warming and sea-level trends over time (Figure 4). Recent data show a 4.5-cm (1.7-in.) rise in global MSL from 1993 to 2008. About 50% is attributed to thermal expansion produced by higher water temperatures. The balance of sea-level rise is from worldwide losses in glacial ice and losses from the Greenland and West Antarctic Ice Sheets.

The 2007 Intergovernmental Panel on Climate Change (IPCC) forecast for global MSL rise this century, given regional variations, is a range from 0.18 to 0.59 m (7.1 to 23.2 in.). However, the 2006–2009 measurements of Greenland's ice loss were not included in the forecasts, and data suggest an acceleration of ice melt. Scientists are carefully monitoring the growing instability in the West Antarctic Ice Sheet as well. A fair working estimate for sea-level rise this century now stands at 1.0 to 1.4 m (3.28 to 4.6 ft); the state of California is using a rise of 1.4 m in its planning models.

Given these trends and the predicted climatic changes ahead, sea level will continue to rise and be potentially devastating for many coastal locations. A rise of only 0.3 m (1 ft) would cause shorelines worldwide to move inland an average of 30 m (100 ft). This elevated sea level would inundate valuable real estate along coastlines all over the world. Some 20,000 km^2 (7800 mi^2) of land along North American shores alone would be drowned, at a staggering loss of trillions of dollars. A 95-cm (3.1-ft) sea-level rise could inundate 15% of Egypt's arable land, 17% of

Sea level varies along the U.S. coastline

Sea level varies along the full extent of North American shorelines. The mean sea level (MSL) of the U.S. Gulf Coast is about 25 cm (10 in.) higher than that of Florida's east coast, which is the lowest in North America. MSL rises northward along the eastern coast, being 38 cm (15 in.) higher in Maine than in Florida. Along the U.S. western coast, MSL is higher than Florida's by about 58 cm (23 in.) in San Diego and by about 86 cm (34 in.) in Oregon. Overall, North America's Pacific Coast MSL averages about 66 cm (26 in.) higher than the Atlantic Coast MSL. For the United States, see Sea Levels Online at http://tidesandcurrents.noaa.gov/sltrends/sltrends.shtml.

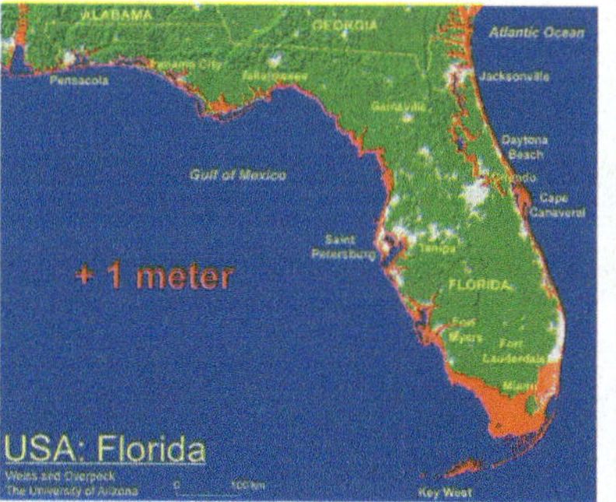

FIGURE 5 Coastal inundation caused by a 1-m (3.28-ft) rise in sea level.
Along three portions of U.S. coastline, scientists at the University of Arizona using USGS digital elevation data produced these maps to show a 1-m sea-level rise and its impact. [Maps prepared by Weiss and Overpeck, Environmental Studies Laboratory, Department of Geosciences, University of Arizona. Used by permission.]

Bangladesh, and many island countries and communities. However, uncertainty exists in these forecasts.

The University of Arizona's Environmental Studies Laboratory prepared a dramatic map series related to rising sea level. Using digital elevation model (DEM) data, the scientists plotted 1-m to 6-m increases in sea level and the amount of coastal inundation (Figure 5). As you examine the three maps, consider what adjustments to human settlement will be required.

CRITICAL THINKING 1

Thinking through a rising sea level

Based on coastal inundation shown in Figure 5, what is your assessment of southern Louisiana if sea level rises 1 m? What is the region's future? Go to the web site where these maps were created, http://www.geo.arizona.edu/dgesl/; click on "maps susceptible to sea level rise"; and proceed to select a coastal area of interest to you. Initially, enter a 1-m rise and examine the map generated. Try other values. Briefly analyze what you find. Certainly, any calculations of the costs of slowing fossil-fuel burning to lower emissions of greenhouse gases should be balanced against damage estimates from such coastal inundation. What do you think?

Coastal System Actions

The coastal system is the scene of complex tidal fluctuation, winds, waves, ocean currents, and the occasional impact of storms. These forces shape landforms ranging from gentle beaches to steep cliffs, and they sustain delicate ecosystems.

Tides

Tides are complex twice-daily oscillations in sea level, ranging worldwide from barely noticeable to several meters. They are experienced to varying degrees along every ocean shore around the world. Tidal action is a relentless energy agent for geomorphic change. As tides flood (rise) and ebb (fall), the daily migration of the shoreline landward and seaward causes significant changes that affect sediment erosion and transportation.

Tides are important in human activities, including navigation, fishing, and recreation. Tides are especially important to ships because the entrance to many ports is limited by shallow water, and thus high tide is required for passage. Tall-masted ships may need a low tide to clear overhead bridges. Tides also exist in large lakes, but because the tidal range is small, tides are difficult to distinguish from changes caused by wind. Lake Superior, for instance, has a tidal variation of only about 5 cm (2 in.).

Causes of Tides Tides are produced by the gravitational pull of both the Sun and the Moon. Recall Earth's relation to the Sun and Moon and the reasons for the seasons. The Sun's influence is only about half that of the Moon's because of the Sun's greater distance from Earth, although it is a significant force. Figure 6 illustrates the relation among the Moon, the Sun, and Earth and the generation of variable tidal bulges on opposite sides of the planet.

The gravitational pull of the Moon tugs on Earth's atmosphere, oceans, and lithosphere. The same is true for the Sun, to a lesser extent. Earth's solid and fluid surfaces all experience some stretching as a result of this gravitational pull. The stretching raises large *tidal bulges* in the atmosphere (which we can't see), smaller tidal bulges in the ocean, and very slight bulges in Earth's rigid crust. Our concern here is the tidal bulges in the ocean.

Gravity and inertia are essential elements in understanding tides. *Gravity* is the force of attraction between two bodies. *Inertia* is the tendency of objects to stay still if motionless or to keep moving in the same direction if in motion. The gravitational effect on the side of Earth facing the Moon or Sun is greater than that experienced by the far side, where inertial forces are slightly greater. In effect, from this inertial point of view, as the nearside water and Earth are drawn toward the Moon and Sun, the farside water is left behind because of the slightly weaker gravitational pull. This arrangement produces the two opposing tidal bulges on opposite sides of Earth.

Tides appear to move in and out along the shoreline, but they do not actually do so. Instead, Earth's surface rotates into and out of the relatively "fixed" tidal bulges as Earth changes its position in relation to the Moon and Sun. Every 24 hours and 50 minutes, any given point on Earth rotates through two bulges as a direct result of this

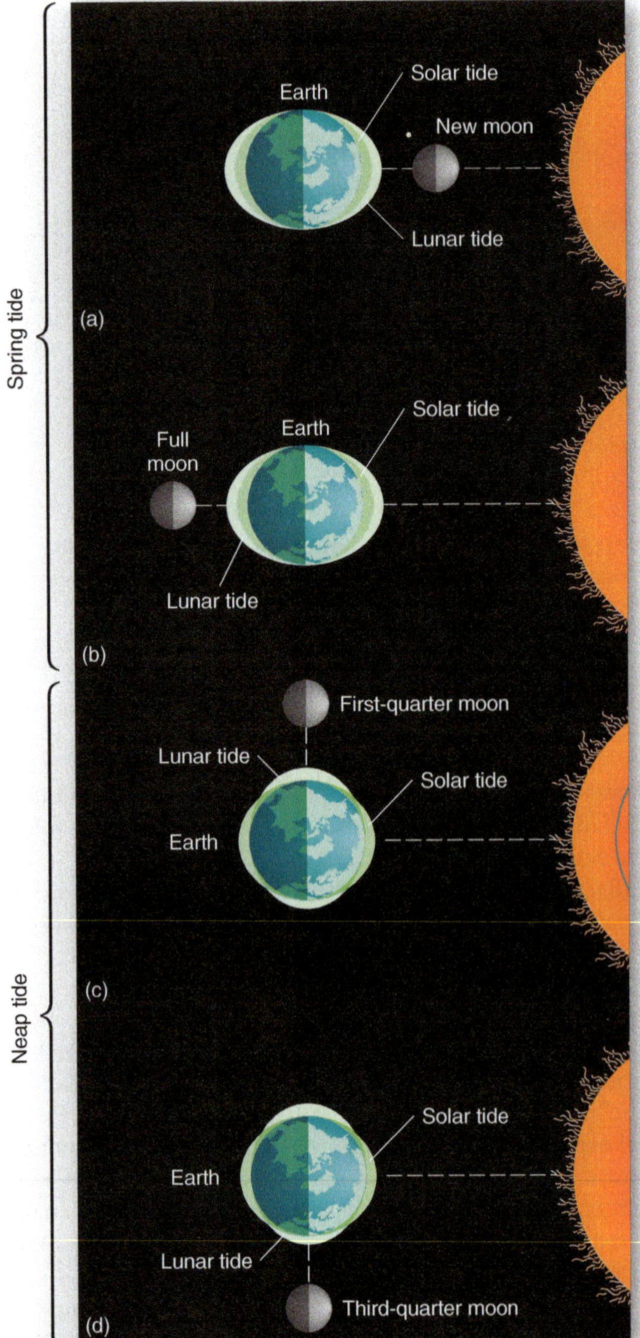

FIGURE 6 The cause of tides. Gravitational relations of the Sun, the Moon, and Earth combine to produce spring tides (a, b) and neap tides (c, d). (Tides are greatly exaggerated for illustration.)

rotational positioning. Thus, every day, most coastal locations experience two high (rising) tides, known as *flood tides*, and two low (falling) tides, known as *ebb tides*. The difference between consecutive high and low tides is considered the *tidal range*.

Spring and Neap Tides The combined gravitational effect of the Sun and Moon is strongest in the conjunction alignment and results in the greatest tidal range between high and low tides, known as *spring tides*. (Spring means to "spring forth"; it has no relation to the season of the year.)

Figure 6b shows the other alignment that gives rise to spring tides, when the Moon and Sun are at *opposition*. In this arrangement, the Moon and Sun cause separate tidal bulges, affecting the water nearest to each of them. In addition, the left-behind water resulting from the pull of the body on the opposite side augments each bulge.

When the Moon and Sun are neither in conjunction nor in opposition, but are more or less in the positions shown in Figure 6c and d, their gravitational influences are offset and counteract each other, producing a lesser tidal range known as *neap tide*. (*Neap* means "without the power of advancing.")

Tides also are influenced by other factors, including ocean-basin characteristics (size, depth, and topography), latitude, and shoreline shape. These factors cause a great variety of tidal ranges. For example, some locations may experience almost no difference between high and low tides. The highest tides occur when open water is forced into partially enclosed gulfs or bays. The Bay of Fundy in Nova Scotia records the greatest tidal range on Earth, a difference of 16 m (52.5 ft) (Figure 7a, b). For more on tides and tide prediction and a complete listing of links, see http://ocean.peterbrueggeman.com/tidepredict.html.

Tidal Power The fact that sea level changes daily with the tides suggests an opportunity: Could these predictable flows be harnessed to generate electricity? The answer is yes, given the right conditions. Bays and estuaries tend to focus tidal energy, concentrating it in a smaller area than in the open ocean. This provides an opportunity to construct a dam with water gates, locks to let ships through, and turbines to generate power.

Only 30 locations in the world are suited for tidal power generation. At present, only 3 are producing electricity. Two are outside North America—a 4-megawatt-capacity station in Russia in operation since 1968 (at Kislaya-Guba Bay on the White Sea) and a facility in France operating since 1967 (on the Rance River estuary on the Brittany coast). The tides in the Rance estuary fluctuate up to 13 m (43 ft), and power production has been almost continuous there, providing an electrical-generating capacity of a moderate 240 megawatts (about 20% of the capacity of Hoover Dam).

The third area is the Bay of Fundy in Nova Scotia, Canada. At one of several favorable sites on the bay, the Annapolis Tidal Generating Station was built in 1984. Nova Scotia Power Incorporated operates this 20-megawatt plant (Figure 7c). According to the Canadian government, tidal power generation at ideal sites is economically competitive with fossil-fuel plants.

Waves

Friction between moving air (wind) and the ocean surface generates undulations of water in **waves**. Waves travel in groups of *wave trains*. Waves vary widely in scale: On a small scale, a moving boat creates a wake of small waves; at a larger scale, storms generate large groups of wave trains. At the extreme is the wind wake produced by the presence of the Hawaiian Islands, traceable westward across the

(a)

(b)

(c)

FIGURE 7 Tidal range and tidal power.
Tidal range is great in some bays and estuaries, such as Halls Harbor near the Bay of Fundy at flood tide (a) and ebb tide (b). (c) The flow of water between high and low tide is ideal for turning turbines and generating electricity, as is done at the Annapolis Tidal Generating Station, near the Bay of Fundy in Nova Scotia. [(a)–(c) Bobbé Christopherson.]

Pacific Ocean surface for 3000 km (1865 mi). The islands disrupt the steady trade winds and produce related surface temperature and wind changes.

A stormy area at sea is a *generating region* for large wave trains, which radiate outward in all directions. The ocean is crisscrossed with intricate patterns of these multidirectional waves. The waves seen along a coast may be the product of a storm center thousands of kilometers away.

Regular patterns of smooth, rounded waves, the mature undulations of the open ocean, are **swells.** As waves leave the generating region, wave energy continues to run in these swells, which can range from small ripples to very large flat-crested waves. A wave leaving a deep-water generating region tends to extend its wavelength horizontally for many meters. Tremendous energy occasionally accumulates to form unusually large waves. One moonlit night in 1933, the U.S. Navy tanker *Ramapo* reported a wave in the Pacific higher than its mainmast, at about 34 m (112 ft)!

As you watch waves in open water, it appears that water is migrating in the direction of wave travel, but only a slight amount of water is actually advancing. It is the *wave energy* that is moving through the flexible medium of water. Water within a wave in the open ocean is simply transferring energy from molecule to molecule in simple cyclic undulations; these are *waves of transition* (Figure 8). Individual water particles move forward only slightly, forming a vertically circular pattern.

The diameter of the paths formed by the orbiting water particles decreases with depth. As a deep-ocean wave approaches the shoreline and enters shallower water (10–20 m, or 30–65 ft), the orbiting water particles are vertically restricted. This restriction causes more-elliptical, flattened orbits to form near the bottom. This change from circular to elliptical orbits slows the entire wave, although more waves continue arriving. The result is closer-spaced waves, growing in height and steepness, with sharper wave crests. As the crest of each wave rises, a point is reached when its height exceeds its vertical stability, and the wave falls into a characteristic **breaker**, crashing onto the beach (Figure 8b).

In a breaker, the orbital motion of transition gives way to elliptical *waves of translation*, in which both energy and water move toward shore. The slope of the shore determines wave style. Plunging breakers indicate a steep bottom profile, whereas spilling breakers indicate a gentle, shallow bottom profile. In some areas, unexpected high waves can arise suddenly. Learning to recognize severe wave conditions is a good idea before you venture along the shore in these areas.

When the backwash of water flows to the ocean from the beach in a concentrated column, usually at a right angle to the line of breakers, it is a *rip current*. A person caught in one of these can be swept offshore, but usually only a short distance. These brief, short torrents of water can be dangerous (Figure 8c).

As various wave trains move along in the open sea, they interact by *interference*. These interfering waves sometimes align, so that the wave crests and troughs from one wave train are in phase with those of another. When this in-phase condition occurs, the height of the waves is amplified, sometimes dramatically. The resulting "killer waves" or "sleeper waves" can sweep in unannounced and overtake unsuspecting victims. Signs along portions of the California, Oregon, Washington, and British Columbia coastline

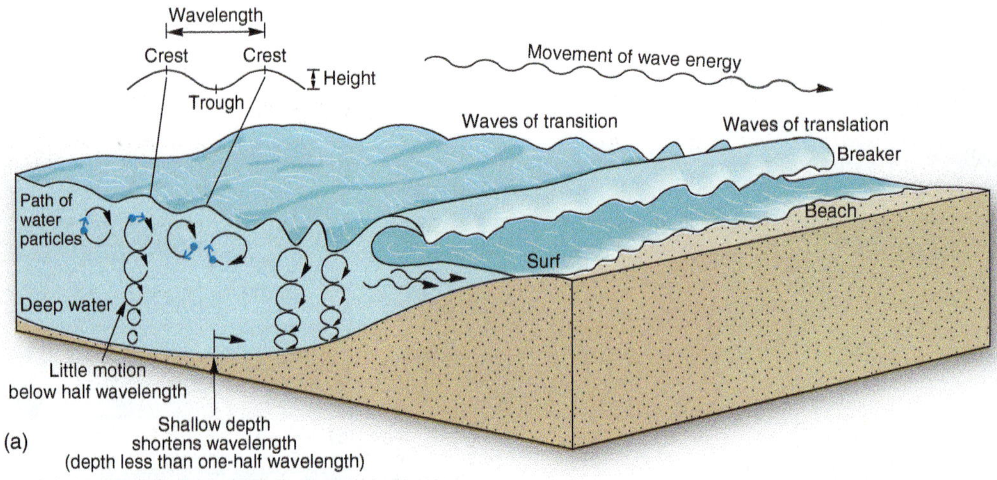

(b)

(c)

FIGURE 8 Wave formation and breakers.
(a) The orbiting tracks of water particles change from circular motions and swells in deep water (waves of transition) to more elliptical orbits near the bottom in shallow water (waves of translation). (b) Cascades of waves attack the shore along Baja California, Mexico. (c) A dangerous rip current interrupts approaching breakers. Note the churned-up water where the rip current enters the surf. [Bobbé Christopherson.]

Animation
Wave Motion/Wave Refraction

warn beachcombers to watch for "killer waves." In August 2009, despite warnings from park rangers, a person was killed as several giant waves hit Acadia National Park on the coast of Maine. Hurricane Bill in the Atlantic was the source of the wave energy. In contrast, out-of-phase wave trains will dampen wave energy at the shore. When you observe the breakers along a beach, the changing beat of the surf actually is produced by the patterns of *wave interference* that occurred in far-distant areas of the ocean.

Wave Refraction In general, wave action tends to straighten a coastline. Where waves approach an irregular coast, they bend around headlands, which are protruding landforms generally composed of resistant rocks (Figure 9). The submarine topography refracts, or bends, approaching waves. The refracted energy is focused around headlands and dissipates energy in coves, bays, and the submerged coastal valleys between headlands. Thus, headlands receive the brunt of wave attack along a coastline. This **wave refraction** redistributes wave energy, so that different sections of the coastline vary in erosion potential, with the long-term effect of straightening the coast.

Figure 10 shows waves approaching the coast at a slight angle, for they usually arrive at some angle other than parallel. As the waves enter shallow water, they are

GEO REPORT 3 ***Sea-wave amplification kills***

On March 3, 2010, a large cruise ship in the western Mediterranean Sea, off the coast of Marseilles, France, was struck by three surprise waves about 7.9 m (26 ft) in height. Two passengers were killed and many injured as waves shattered windows, flooding parts of the ship's interior. Rescue personnel took the injured to hospitals in Barcelona, Spain. Scientists are studying what causes such abnormal waves, which tend to happen in open ocean; elements include strong winds and wave interference.

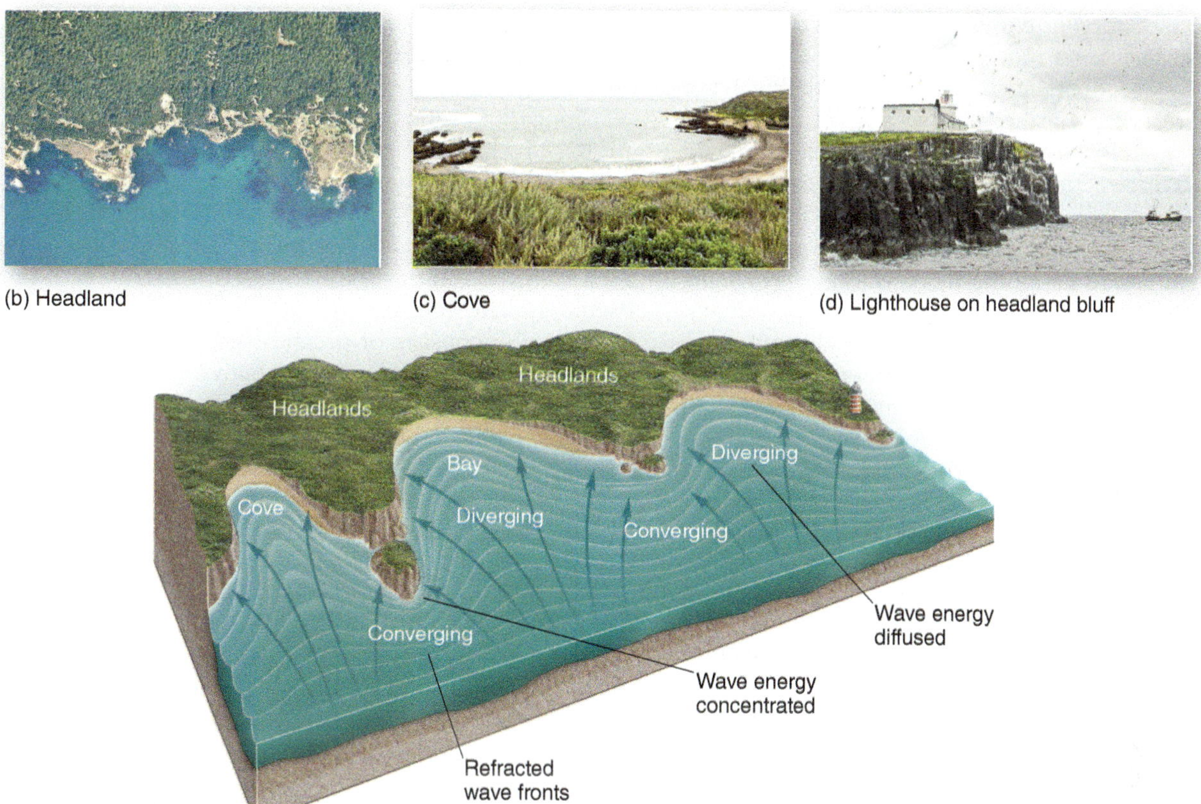

FIGURE 9 Coastal straightening.
(a) The process of coastal straightening is brought about by wave refraction. Wave energy is concentrated as it converges on headlands (b) and is diffused as it diverges in coves and bays (c). (d) Headlands are frequent sites for lighthouses such as the Farne light on Farne Island, England. At least six species of birds in thousands of nesting pairs are on the island, including Atlantic Puffins, Kittiwakes, and Arctic Terns. [Bobbé Christopherson.]

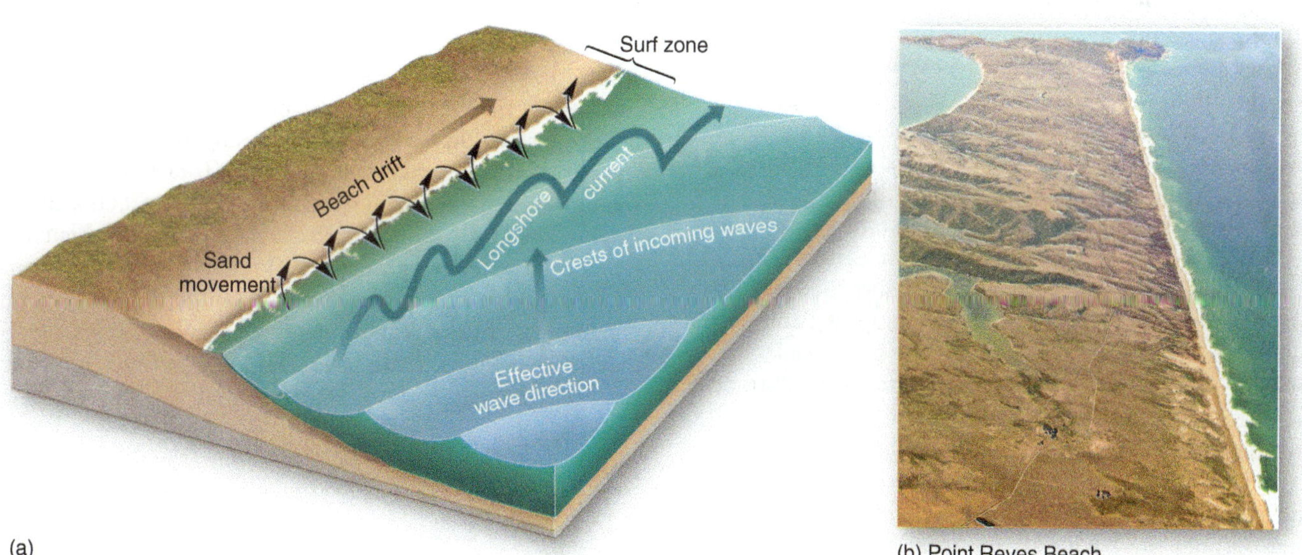

FIGURE 10 Longshore current and beach drift.
(a) Longshore currents are produced as waves approach the surf zone and shallower water. Longshore drift and beach drift result as substantial volumes of material are moved along the shore. (b) Processes at work along Point Reyes Beach, Point Reyes National Seashore, California (aerial view to the south). [Bobbé Christopherson.]

Animation
Beach Drift, Coastal Erosion

refracted as the shoreline end of the wave slows. The wave portion in deeper water moves faster in comparison, thus producing a current parallel to the coast, zigzagging in the prevalent direction of the incoming waves. This **longshore current**, or *littoral current*, depends on wind direction and resultant wave direction. A longshore current is generated only in the surf zone and works in combination with wave action to transport large amounts of sand, gravel, sediment, and debris along the shore as *longshore drift*, or **littoral drift**, the more comprehensive term.

Particles on the beach also are moved along as *beach drift*, shifting back and forth between water and land with each *swash* and *backwash* of surf. Individual sediment grains trace arched paths along the beach. You have perhaps stood on a beach and heard the sound of myriad sand grains and seawater in the backwash of surf. These dislodged materials are available for transport and eventual deposition in coves and inlets and can represent a significant volume.

Tsunami, or Seismic Sea Wave An occasional wave that momentarily, but powerfully influences coastlines is the tsunami. Japanese for "harbor wave," **tsunami** is named for its devastating effect when its energy is focused in harbors. Revisit this chapter's opening photo and this chapter's *Geosystems Now*, to see tsunami-related damage in Japan and the tsunami as it moves inland. Often, tsunami are reported incorrectly as "tidal waves," but they have no relation to the tides. Sudden, sharp motions in the seafloor, caused by earthquakes, submarine landslides, or eruptions of undersea volcanoes, produce tsunami. Thus, they properly are *seismic sea waves*.

A large undersea disturbance usually generates a solitary wave of great wavelength. Tsunami generally exceed 100 km (60 mi) in wavelength (crest to crest) but are only a meter (3 ft) or so in height. They travel at great speeds in deep-ocean water—velocities of 600–800 kmph (375–500 mph) are not uncommon—but often pass unnoticed on the open sea because their great wavelength makes the rise and fall of water hard to observe.

As a tsunami approaches a coast, however, the shallow water forces the wavelength to shorten. As a result, the wave height may increase up to 15 m (50 ft) or more. Such a wave has the potential to devastate a coastal area, causing property damage and death. For example, in 1992 the citizens of Casares, Nicaragua, were surprised by a 12-m (39-ft) tsunami that took 270 lives. A 1998 Papua New Guinea tsunami, launched by a massive undersea landslide of some 4 km^3 (1 mi^3), killed 2000. During the 20th century, records show 141 damaging tsunami and perhaps 900 smaller ones, with a total death toll of about 70,000.

Hawai'i is vulnerable to tsunami because of its position in the open central Pacific, surrounded by the ring of fire that outlines the Pacific Basin. As an example, a tsunami produced near the Philippines would reach Hawai'i in 10 hours. The U.S. Army Corps of Engineers has reported 41 damaging tsunami in Hawai'i during the past 142 years—statistically, 1 every 3.5 years. Because tsunami travel such great distances so quickly and are undetectable in the open ocean, accurate forecasts are difficult and occurrences are often unexpected.

For nations surrounding the Pacific, tsunami warnings are issued whenever seismic stations detect a significant quake or landslide underwater, where it might generate a tsunami. This system was refined in 2004 with the Deep-ocean Assessment and Reporting of Tsunamis (DART), a tsunami hazard-mitigation network of 39 stations in the Pacific, Indian, and Atlantic Oceans (see Figure GN 1). Each station consists of pressure sensors on the ocean floor with accompanying surface buoys. When a tsunami triggers the DART sensors, regional warning centers issue bulletins to affected regions. (See http://www.ndbc.noaa.gov/dart/dart.shtml for more information.)

On December 26, 2004, an M 9.3 earthquake (fourth largest in a century) struck off the west coast of northern Sumatra, triggering a massive tsunami across the Indian Ocean—the Sumatra–Andaman earthquake and tsunami. No warning system was in place when this occurred. The earthquake trigger was the continuing underthrust of the Indo-Australian plate beneath the Burma plate along the Sunda Trench subduction zone. Imagine the island of Sumatra springing up about 13.7 m (45 ft) in elevation! You can find this oceanic trench on a map of the ocean floor, stretching along the coast of Indonesia in the eastern Indian Ocean Basin.

Radar images from four Earth-orbiting satellites at the time clearly show the tsunami wave energy traveling across the Indian Ocean. In Figure 11, we see two of these images, one at 2:05 hours and the other at 7:10 hours after the event. Energy from this tsunami wave actually traveled several times around the global ocean basins before settling down. With Earth's mid-ocean mountain chain acting as a guide, related large waves arrived at the shores of Nova Scotia, Antarctica, and Peru.

Geophysicists even picked up slight changes in Earth's rotation speed (which was slowed by 3 microseconds) and a shift in the North Pole location by 2.5 cm (1 in.) in response to this event. A similar shift occurred during the 2011 Japan quake and tsunami. Total deaths from the Indonesian quake and tsunami exceeded 150,000, and a final count may never be known. In response to this tsunami, the Indian Ocean Tsunami Warning and Mitigation System was created as part of the ongoing United Nations tsunami warning system project (see http://itic.ioc-unesco.org/ for more information). For NOAA's tsunami research program, see http://nctr.pmel.noaa.gov/.

Coastal System Outputs

As you can see, coastlines are active places, with energy and sediment being continuously delivered to a narrow environment. The action of tides, currents, wind, waves, and changing sea level produces a variety of erosional and depositional landforms. We look first at erosional coastlines, such as the U.S. West Coast, and then at depositional coastlines, such as

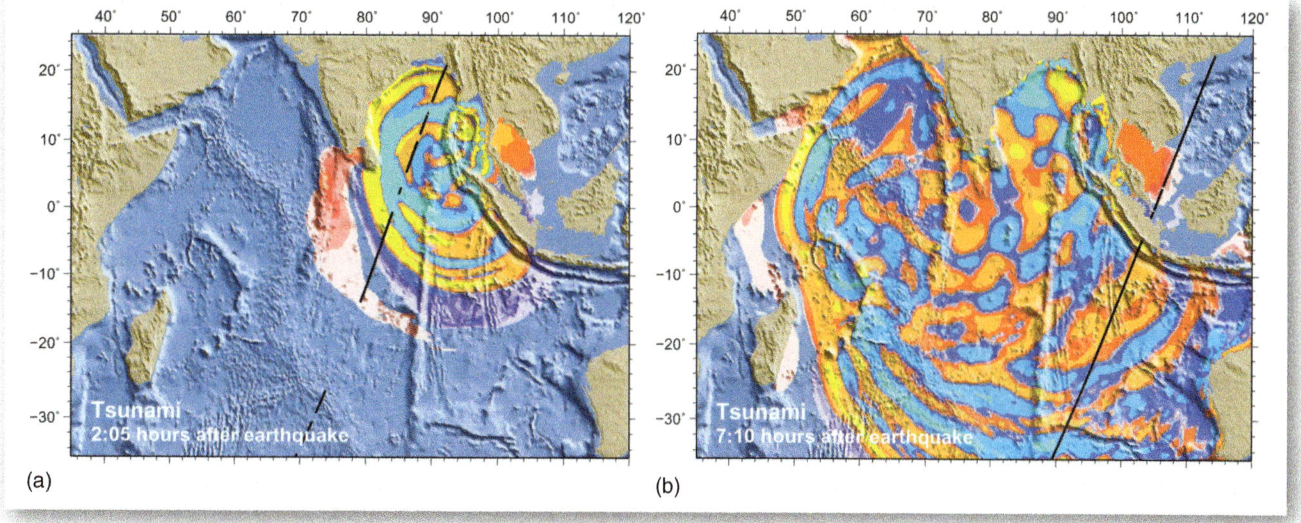

FIGURE 11 Satellites track tsunami waves across the Indian Ocean, 2004. (a) A *Jason-1* image 2 hours after the M 9.3 earthquake showing wave heights of 60 cm (24 in.) radiating outward from the epicenter off Sumatra. (b) The *Geosat Follow On* (*GFO*) satellite radar captured the wave patterns 7 hours and 10 minutes after the earthquake. [NOAA, Laboratory for Satellite Altimetry.]

the U.S. East and Gulf Coasts. In this era of rising sea level, coastlines are becoming even more dynamic.

Coastal Erosion

The active margin of the Pacific Ocean along North and South America is a typical erosional coastline. *Erosional coastlines* tend to be rugged, of high relief, and tectonically active, as expected from their association with the leading edge of drifting lithospheric plates (review plate tectonics). Figure 12 presents features commonly observed along an erosional coast. Within this erosional setting, depositional processes can occur, producing depositional landforms.

Sea *cliffs* are formed by the undercutting action of the sea. As indentations slowly grow at water level, a sea cliff becomes notched and eventually will collapse and retreat (Figure 12e). Other erosional forms evolve along cliff-dominated coastlines, including *sea caves*, *sea arches*, and *sea stacks*. As erosion continues, arches may collapse, leaving isolated stacks in the water (Figure 12b, d).

Wave action can cut a horizontal bench in the tidal zone, extending from a sea cliff out into the sea. Such a structure is a **wave-cut platform**, or *wave-cut terrace*. If the relation between the land and sea level has changed over time, multiple platforms or terraces may rise like stair steps back from the coast. These marine terraces are remarkable indicators of a changing relation between the land and sea, with some terraces more than 370 m (1200 ft) above sea level. A tectonically active region, such as the California coast, has many examples of multiple wave-cut platforms, which at times can be unstable and vulnerable to failure (Figure 12 c, f).

Coastal Deposition

Depositional coasts generally are along land of gentle relief, where sediments from many sources are available. Such is the case with the Atlantic and Gulf coastal plains of the United States, which lie along the relatively passive, trailing edge of the North American lithospheric plate. Yet erosional processes and inundation influence depositional coasts, particularly during storm activity.

Figure 13 illustrates characteristic landforms deposited by waves and currents. One notable depositional landform is the **barrier spit**, which consists of material deposited in a long ridge extending out from a coast. It partially crosses and blocks the mouth of a bay. A classic barrier spit is Sandy Hook, New Jersey (south of New York City). Such barrier spit formations are also found at Point Reyes (Figure 13c) and Morro Bay (Figure 13d), in California.

If a spit grows to completely cut off the bay from the ocean and form an inland lagoon, it becomes a **bay barrier**, or *baymouth bar*. Spits and barriers are made up of materials that have been eroded and transported by *littoral drift* (considered beach drift and longshore drift combined). For much sediment to accumulate, offshore currents must be weak, since strong currents carry material away before it can be deposited. Tidal flats and salt marshes are characteristic low-relief features wherever tidal influence is greater than wave action. As noted earlier, if these deposits completely cut off the bay from the ocean, an inland **lagoon** forms. A **tombolo** occurs when sediment deposits connect the shoreline with an offshore island or sea stack by accumulating on an underwater wave-built terrace (Figure 13a).

Not all the beaches of the world are composed of sand, for they can be made up of shingles (beach gravel) and shells, among other materials (Figure 13b). Let us examine these transient coastal deposits in more detail—let's go to the beach.

Beaches Of all the depositional landforms along coastlines, beaches probably are the most familiar. Beaches vary

FIGURE 12 Erosional coastal features.
(a) Characteristic coastal erosional landforms: (b) headlands and an arch, Ascension Island, Atlantic Ocean; (c) wave-cut platforms near Bixby Bridge, Cabrillo Highway, California; (d) stacks and headlands, Gough Island, Southern Ocean; (e) notched cliff, Bjørnøya (Bear Island), Barents Sea; and (f) collapsing cliffs and failing houses. [Bobbé Christopherson.]

in type and permanence, especially along coastlines dominated by wave action. Technically, a **beach** is that place along a coast where sediment is in motion, deposited by waves and currents. Material from the land temporarily resides on the beach while it is in active transit along the shore. You probably have experienced a beach at some time, along a seacoast, a lakeshore, or even a stream. Perhaps you have even built your own "landforms" in the sand, only to see them washed away by the waves: a lesson in erosion.

On average, the beach zone spans the area from about 5 m (16 ft) above high tide to 10 m (33 ft) below low tide (see Figure 3). However, the specific definition varies greatly along individual shorelines. Worldwide, quartz (SiO_2) dominates beach sands because it resists weathering and therefore remains after other minerals are removed. In volcanic areas, beaches are derived from wave-processed lava. Hawai'i and Iceland, for example, feature some black-sand beaches.

Many beaches, such as those in southern France and western Italy, lack sand and are composed of pebbles and cobbles—a type of *shingle beach*. Some shores have no beaches at all; scrambling across boulders and rocks may be the only way to move along the coast. The coasts of Maine and portions of Canada's Atlantic Provinces are classic examples. These coasts, composed of resistant granite rock, are scenically rugged and have few beaches.

FIGURE 13 Depositional coastal features.
Characteristic coastal depositional landforms: barrier spits, lagoons, tombolos, and beaches. (a) The Limantour barrier spit nearly blocks the entrance to Drakes Estero, along Point Reyes. (b) A barrier spit forms Morro Bay, with the sound opening to the sea near 178-m (584-ft) Morro Rock, a volcanic plug. (c) A tombolo at Point Sur along the central California coast, where sediment deposits connect the shore with an island. (d) A shell beach deposited by the ocean. [Bobbé Christopherson.]

A beach acts to stabilize a shoreline by absorbing wave energy, as is evident by the amount of material that is in almost constant motion (see "Sand movement" in Figure 10a). Some beaches are stable. Others cycle seasonally: They accumulate during the summer; are moved offshore by winter storm waves, forming a submerged bar; and are redeposited onshore the following summer. Protected areas along a coastline tend to accumulate sediment, which can lead to large coastal sand dunes. Prevailing winds often drag such coastal dunes inland, sometimes burying trees and highways.

Maintaining Beaches Changes in coastal sediment transport can disrupt human activities—beaches are lost, harbors are closed, and coastal highways and beach houses can be inundated with sediment. Thus, people use various strategies to interrupt littoral drift and beach drift. The goal is either to halt sand accumulation or to force accumulation in a desired way through construction of engineered structures, or "hard" shoreline protection.

Figure 14 illustrates common approaches: a *groin* to slow drift action along the coast, a *jetty* to block material from harbor entrances, and a *breakwater* to create a zone of

MG™ **Animation** Coastal Stabilization Structures

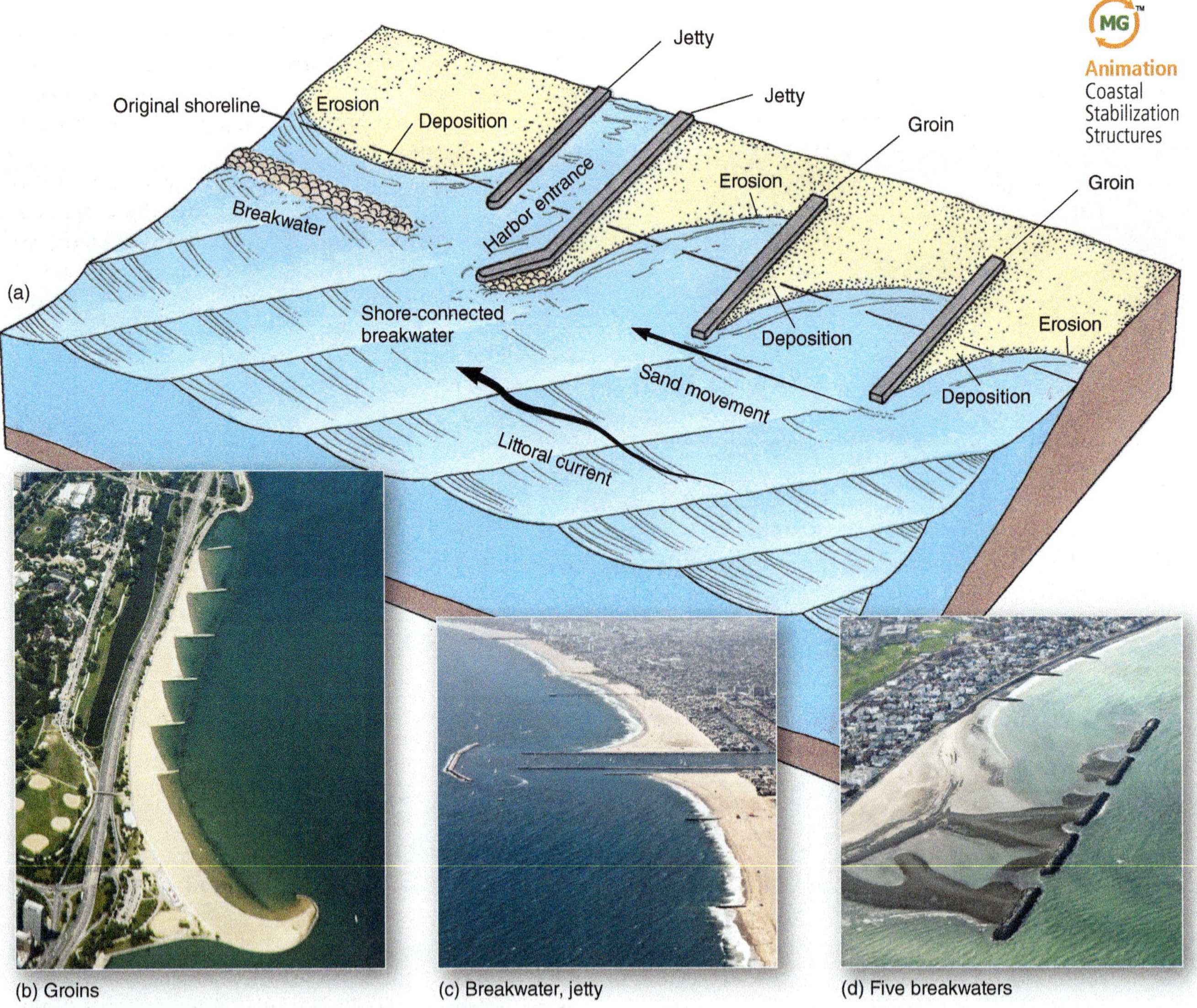

(b) Groins (c) Breakwater, jetty (d) Five breakwaters

FIGURE 14 Interfering with the littoral drift of sand.
(a) Various constructions attempt to control littoral drift and beach drift along a coast: breakwater, jetty, and groin. Aerial photographs of coastal constructions: (b) Note the disruption of sediment movement by each groin along the coast of Lake Michigan, north of Chicago; (c) a breakwater and jetties protect the entrance to Marina del Rey, California; (d) the Five Sisters breakwaters in Winthrop, Massachusetts (near Boston)—note coarse gravels and sand accumulating in bars behind the breakwaters since their construction in the 1930s. [Bobbé Christopherson.]

still water near the coastline. However, interrupting the littoral drift that is the natural replenishment for beaches may lead to unwanted changes in sediment distribution downcurrent. Careful planning and impact assessment should be part of any strategy for preserving or altering a beach.

In contrast to the term *hard structures*, the hauling of sand to replenish a beach is considered "soft" shoreline protection. *Beach nourishment* refers to the artificial replacement of sand along a beach. Through such efforts, a beach that normally experiences a net loss of sediment will be "nourished" with new sand. Years of human effort and expense to build beaches can be erased by a single storm, however.

The city of Miami, Florida, and surrounding Dade County have spent almost $70 million since the 1970s in a continuing effort to rebuild their beaches. Sand is transported to the replenishment area from a source area. To maintain a 200-m-wide (660-ft-wide) beach, planners determine net sand loss per year and set a schedule for replenishment. In Miami Beach, an 8-year replenishment cycle is maintained.

Unforeseen environmental impact may accompany the addition of sand to a beach, especially if the sand is from an unmatched source, in terms of its ecological traits. If the new sands do not physically and chemically match the existing varieties, disruption of coastal marine life is possible. More than $2 billion has been spent from New York to Florida to date to replenish beaches, with costs over the next 10 years forecast to be billions more. For more on beach nourishment, see http://www.csc.noaa.gov/beachnourishment/;

for basics, go to http://www.brynmawr.edu/geology/geomorph/beachnourishmentinfo.html.

Barrier Beach Formation Barrier chains are long, narrow, depositional features, generally of sand, that form offshore roughly parallel to the coast. Common forms are **barrier beaches** and the broader, more extensive landforms called **barrier islands**. Tidal variation in the area usually is moderate to low, with adequate sediment supplies coming from nearby coastal plains. Figure 15 illustrates the many features of barrier chains, using North Carolina's famed Outer Banks as an example, including Cape Hatteras, across Pamlico Sound from the mainland. The area presently is designated as one of 10 national seashore reserves supervised by the National Park Service.

On the landward side of a barrier formation are tidal flats, marshes, swamps, lagoons, coastal dunes, and beaches, visible in Figure 15. Barrier beaches appear to adjust to sea level and may naturally shift position from time to time in response to wave action and longshore currents. A break in a barrier forms an inlet that connects a bay with the ocean. The name *barrier* is appropriate, for these formations take the brunt of storm energy and actually shield the mainland. Various hypotheses exist to explain the formation of barrier islands. They may begin as offshore bars or low ridges of submerged sediment near shore and then gradually migrate toward shore as sea level rises.

FIGURE 15 Barrier island chain.
Landsat image of barrier island chain along the North Carolina coast. You can see key depositional forms: spit, island, beach, lagoon, and inlet. A sound is a large inlet of the ocean; Pamlico Sound is an example. The Cape Hatteras lighthouse was moved inland in 1999; photos are on the *MasteringGeography* web site. [*Terra* MODIS image, NASA/GSFC.]

Barrier beaches and islands are quite common worldwide, lying offshore of nearly 10% of Earth's coastlines. Examples are found off Africa, India's eastern coast, Sri Lanka, Australia, and Alaska's northern slope as well as offshore in the Baltic and Mediterranean Seas. Earth's most extensive chain of barrier islands is along the U.S. Atlantic and Gulf Coasts, extending some 5000 km (3100 mi) from Long Island to Texas and Mexico.

Barrier Island Vulnerabilities and Hazards Because many barrier islands seem to be migrating landward, they are an unwise choice for home sites or commercial building. Nonetheless, they are a common choice, even though they take the brunt of storm energy. The hazard represented by the settlement of barrier islands was made graphically clear when Hurricane Hugo assaulted South Carolina in 1989. In the Charleston area, Hugo swept away beachfront houses, barrier island developments, and millions of tons of sand; the hurricane destroyed up to 95% of the single-family homes in one community. The southern portion of one island was torn away. With increased development and continuing real estate appreciation, each future storm can be expected to cause ever-increasing capital losses.

The barrier islands off the Louisiana shore are disappearing. They are affected by subsidence resulting from the compaction of Mississippi delta sediments, deflation from the pumping of oil and gas reserves, a changing sea level that is rising at 1 cm (0.4 in.) per year in the region, and an increase in tropical storm intensity. In 1998, Hurricane Georges destroyed large tracts of the Chandeleur Islands, located 30 to 40 km (19 to 25 mi) from the Louisiana–Mississippi Gulf Coast, leaving the mainland with reduced protection (Figure 16). Louisiana's increasingly exposed wetlands are disappearing at the rate of 65 km^2 (25 mi^2) per year. Hurricane Katrina (2005) alone removed this amount of wetlands and swept away most of the remaining Chandeleur Islands. The regional office of the U.S. Geological Survey predicts that in a few decades the barrier islands may be gone.

Along the Bolivar Peninsula, a barrier spit near Galveston on the Texas Gulf Coast, beach erosion rates average 2 m (6.5 ft) per year as sea level continues to rise. Hurricane Ike struck Galveston Island, Bolivar Peninsula, and the Texas–Louisiana Gulf Coast in September 2008. The barrier island urbanization was devastated as $30 billion in structures were swept away along with more than 195 lives. You will find photos of the peninsula and the damage from Hurricane Ike on the *MasteringGeography* web site. Surveys found 80% to 95% of homes were destroyed.

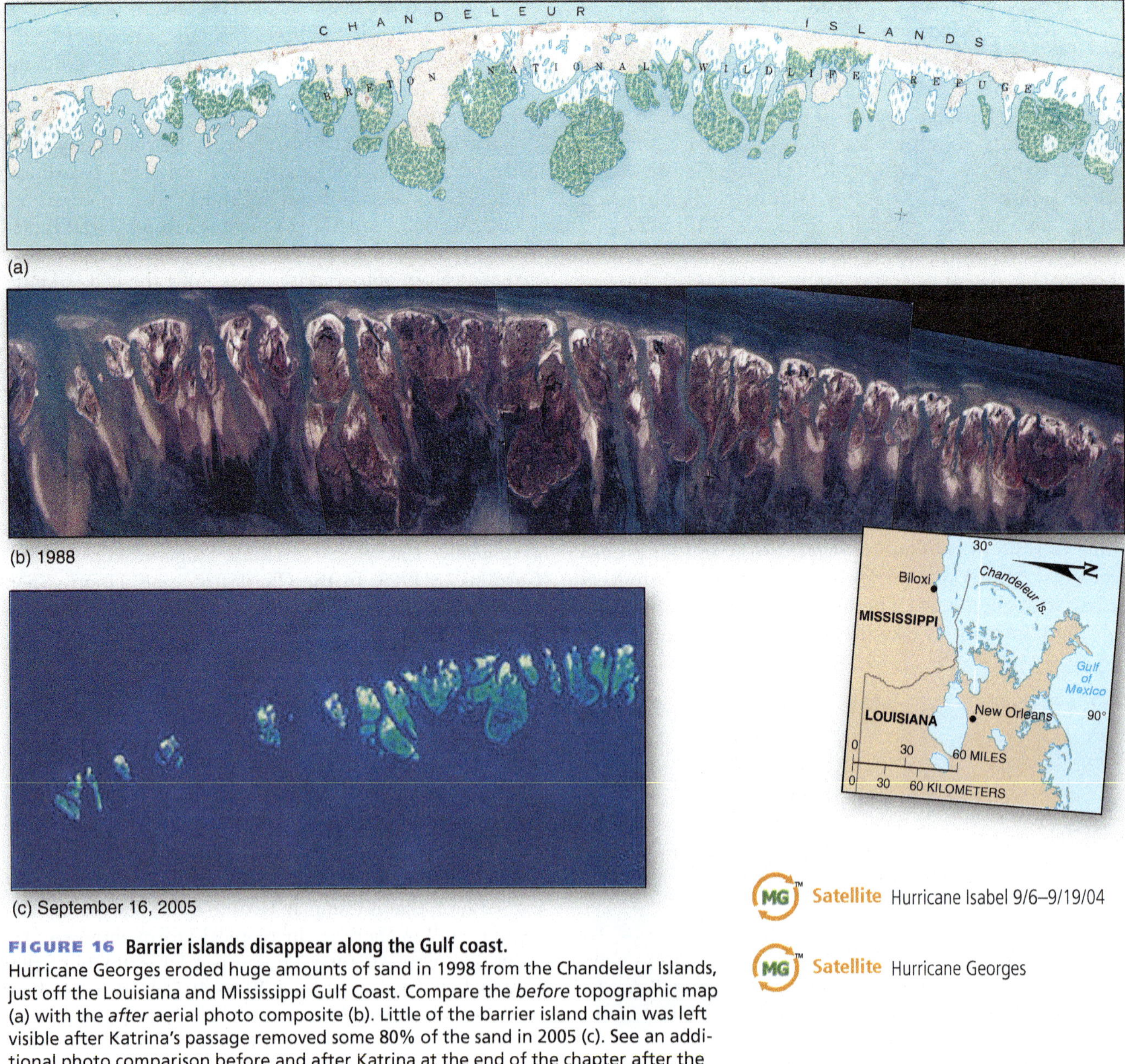

FIGURE 16 Barrier islands disappear along the Gulf coast.
Hurricane Georges eroded huge amounts of sand in 1998 from the Chandeleur Islands, just off the Louisiana and Mississippi Gulf Coast. Compare the *before* topographic map (a) with the *after* aerial photo composite (b). Little of the barrier island chain was left visible after Katrina's passage removed some 80% of the sand in 2005 (c). See an additional photo comparison before and after Katrina at the end of the chapter after the summary and review. The sand inventory loss is huge. [(a) USGS. (b) Aerial Data Service, Earth Imaging. (c) USGS Hurricane Impact Studies.]

MG™ **Satellite** Hurricane Isabel 9/6–9/19/04

MG™ **Satellite** Hurricane Georges

We are approaching a time when most barrier islands will be developed and occupied (Figure 17). Barrier islands and coastal beaches do migrate over time. Houses that were more than a mile from the sea in the Hamptons along the southeastern shore of Long Island, New York, are now within only 30 m (100 ft) of it. The time remaining for these homes can be quickly shortened by a single hurricane or by a sequence of storms. Hurricane Earl in 2010 passed close to these coastal environments, causing sand inventory losses.

Despite our understanding of beach and barrier island migration, the effect of storms, and warnings from scientists and government agencies, coastal development proceeds. Society behaves as though beaches and barrier islands are stable, fixed features or as though they can be engineered to be permanent. Experience has shown that severe erosion generally cannot be prevented. Focus Study 1 presents the basics for a sustainable approach to shoreline planning.

A reasonable conclusion seems to be that the key to protective environmental planning and zoning is to *allocate responsibility and cost in the event of a disaster*. An ideal system places a hazard tax on land, based on assessed risk, and restricts the government's responsibility to fund reconstruction or an individual's right to reconstruct on frequently damaged sites. Comprehensive mapping of erosion-hazard areas would help avoid the ever-increasing costs from recurring disasters.

CRITICAL THINKING 2

What seems to be a reasonable conclusion, however. . . .

This chapter includes the following statement: "A reasonable conclusion seems to be that the key to protective environmental planning and zoning is to *allocate responsibility and cost in the event of a disaster*."

What do you think about this as a policy statement? How would you approach implementing such a strategy? What special interests might oppose such an approach? What response would you expect from city government or business interests? From banking or the real estate industry? In what way could you use geographic information systems (GIS) to survey, assess, list owners, and follow taxation status for a vulnerable stretch of coastline?

FIGURE 17 Barrier island subdivisions. The town of Barnegat Light abruptly stops where Long Beach Island is protected in Barnegat Lighthouse State Park, New Jersey. The protected area is almost entirely composed of replenished sand. [Bobbé Christopherson.]

Biological Processes: Coral Formations

Not all coastlines form by purely physical processes. Some form as the result of biological processes, such as coral growth. A **coral** is a simple marine animal with a small, cylindrical, saclike body called a *polyp*; it is related to other marine invertebrates, such as anemones and jellyfish. Corals secrete calcium carbonate ($CaCO_3$) from the lower half of their bodies, forming a hard, calcified external skeleton.

Corals live in a *symbiotic* relationship with algae: They live together in a mutually helpful arrangement, each dependent on the other for survival. Corals cannot photosynthesize, but they do obtain some of their own nourishment. Algae perform photosynthesis and convert solar energy to chemical energy in the system, providing the coral with about 60% of its nutrition and assisting the coral with the calcification process. In return, corals provide the algae with nutrients. Coral reefs are the most diverse marine ecosystems. Preliminary estimates of coral species place the number at a million worldwide, yet, as in most ecosystems in water or on land, biodiversity is declining in these communities.

Figure 18 shows the distribution of living coral formations. Corals mostly thrive in warm tropical oceans, so the difference in ocean temperature between the western coasts and eastern coasts of continents is critical to their distribution. Western coastal waters tend to be cooler, thereby discouraging coral activity, whereas eastern coastal currents are warmer and thus enhance coral growth.

Living colonial corals range in distribution from about 30° N to 30° S. Corals occupy a very specific ecological zone: 10- to 55-m (30- to 180-ft) depth, 27‰–40‰ salinity, and 18°C to 29°C (64°F to 85°F) water temperature. Their upper threshold is 30°C (86°F); above that temperature, the corals begin to bleach and die. Corals require clear, sediment-free water and consequently do not locate near the mouths of sediment-charged freshwater streams. For example, note the lack of these structures along the U.S. Gulf Coast. Corals have low genetic diversity worldwide and long generation times, which together mean that corals are slow to adapt and vulnerable to changing conditions.

However, an interesting exception to these environmental parameters for corals is the unique species of cool corals that exist in cold, dark water and deep ocean, at temperatures as low as 4°C (39°F) and in depths to 2000 m (6562 ft), well beyond the expected range. Scientists study these remarkable oddities, which do not rely on algae, but harvest nutrients from plankton and particulate matter.

Coral Reefs Corals exist as both solitary and colonial formations. The colonial corals produce enormous structures. Their skeletons accumulate, forming coral rock. Through many generations, live corals near the ocean's surface build on the foundation of older coral skeletons, which, in turn, may rest upon a volcanic seamount or some other submarine feature built up from the ocean floor. *Coral reefs* form by this process. Thus, a coral reef is a biologically derived sedimentary rock. It can assume one of several distinctive shapes.

In 1842, Charles Darwin hypothesized an evolution of reef formation. He suggested that, as reefs develop around

(text continued after Focus Study 1)

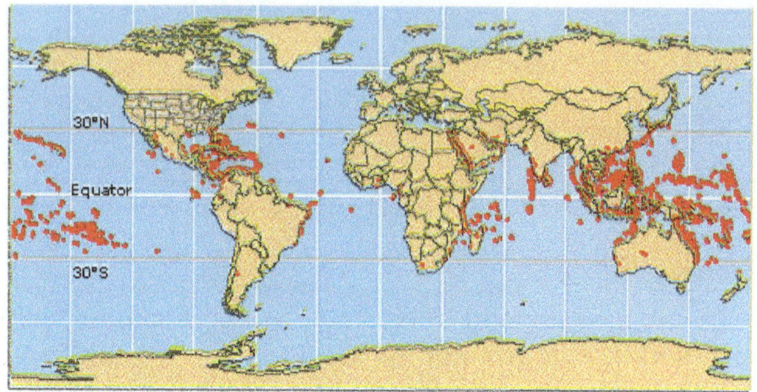

FIGURE 18 Worldwide distribution of living coral formations. The red dots represent major stony-reef coral colonies and include prolific reef growth and atoll formation. Colonial corals range in distribution from about 30° N to 30° S. [NOS/NOAA, 2008.]

FOCUS STUDY 1

An Environmental Approach to Shoreline Planning

Coastlines are places of wonderful opportunity, such as ecosystem preservation, recreation, and development. They also are zones of specific constraints and are vulnerable to shoreline processes. Poor understanding of this resource and a lack of environmental analysis often go hand in hand, surrounded by intense developmental pressures for economic gain.

For example, Cape Cod, Massachusetts, is a narrow coastal sandy peninsula composed of glacial outwash and morainal deposits. With much of its land protected as part of the Cape Cod National Seashore Reserve in 1961, Cape Cod is still subject to extensive human impacts and aggressive coastal processes. Urbanization along the cape has developed in a patchwork in and around protected areas, making a complex mix of private and public jurisdiction, land use, and plans (Figure 1.1).

Settlements outside the reserve are vulnerable to sea-level rise, storm surges, and saltwater intrusion into groundwater systems. Houses and businesses are barely above sea level and use septic systems with leach fields for waste disposal. These systems and most structures will be increasingly vulnerable to future sea-level rise. See http://pubs.usgs.gov/of/2002/of02-233/ for a report on the concept of coastal vulnerability along Cape Cod. Scientists are working to better understand this dynamic environment. Proper planning and thinking about the future are difficult as various stakeholders defend their positions.

Beaches and Dunes—Where to Build?

In his book *Design with Nature*, the late ecologist and landscape architect Ian McHarg discusses the New Jersey shore. He shows how proper understanding of a coastal environment could have avoided problems from major storms and coastal development. Figure 1.2 illustrates the New Jersey shore from ocean to back bay. Let us walk across this landscape and discover how it should be treated under ideal conditions. Remember that much of this applies to coastal areas elsewhere.

We begin our walk at the water's edge and proceed across the beach. Sand beaches are the primary natural defense against the ocean; they act as bulwarks against the pounding of a stormy sea. The shoreline tolerates recreation, but not construction, because of its shifting, changing nature during storms, daily tidal fluctuations, and the potential effects of rising sea level. Beaches are susceptible to pollution and require environmental protection to control nearshore dumping of dangerous materials.

Walking inland, we encounter the primary dune. Even more sensitive than the beach, it is fragile, easily disturbed, and vulnerable to erosion, and it cannot tolerate the passage of people trekking to the beach. Some vegetation is present, but it has only a small effect on sand stabilization. Carefully controlled access points to the beach should be designated, and restricted access should be enforced. (See two examples of beach stabilization in Figure 26.)

The trough behind the primary dune is relatively tolerant of limited recreation and building. The plants send roots down to fresh groundwater reserves and anchor the sand in the process. Thus, if construction should inhibit the surface recharge of that water supply, the natural protective ground cover could die and destabilize the environment. Or subsequent saltwater intrusion might contaminate well water. Clearly, groundwater resources and the location of recharge aquifers must be considered in planning. The continuing use of septic sewage systems in the trough is not sustainable.

Behind the trough is the secondary dune, a second line of defense against the sea. It, too, is tolerant of some use, yet is vulnerable to destruction. Next is the backdune, more suitable for development than any zone between it and the sea. Further inland are the bayshore and the bay, where no dredging or filling and only limited dumping of treated wastes and toxics should be permitted. This zone is tolerant of intensive recreation. In reality, of course, the opposite of such careful assessment and planning prevails.

FIGURE 1.1 Vulnerable coastal settlements along Beach Point on Cape Cod, Massachusetts. [Bobbé Christopherson.]

FIGURE 1.2 Coastal environment and planning along the New Jersey shore.
(a) A planning perspective from ocean to bay. Note letters on the illustration that identify photo locations. (b) Light truck and SUV tracks in the protected Island Beach State Park. These vehicles are banned from developed stretches of beach. (c) Houses once distant from the surf are hit by waves. Sand is brought in to strengthen defenses. (d) Development along the primary dunes—an amusement park— challenges the natural setting. (e) The primary dune in a somewhat natural state. (f) An undeveloped trough behind the primary dune. (g) The former trough, paved and developed, barely above high-tide levels. (h) Development and commerce in the bayshore and bay. [(a) After *Design with Nature* by Ian McHarg. Copyright © 1969 by Ian L. McHarg. Adapted by permission. (b)–(h) Bobbé Christopherson.]

Science and Political Reality

Before an intensive government study of the New Jersey shore was completed in 1962, no analysis of coastal hazards had been done outside of academic circles. What is common knowledge in science classrooms and laboratories still has not filtered through to financial, developmental, and real estate interests. As a result, on the New Jersey shore and along much of the Atlantic and Gulf Coasts, improper development of the fragile coastal zone (primary dunes, trough, and secondary dunes) led to extensive destruction during storms in 1962, 1992, 2004, and 2005, and a near miss in 2010, among other times.

Scientists estimate that the U.S. Atlantic and Gulf coastlines will continue to erode—in some cases, tens of meters in a few decades. Society should reconcile ecology and economics if these coastal environments are to be sustained, especially in a time of increased storm intensity and sea-level rise.

a volcanic island and the island itself gradually subsides, equilibrium is maintained between the subsidence of the island and the upward growth of the corals. This idea, generally accepted today, is portrayed in Figure 19. Note the specific examples of each reef stage: *fringing reefs* (platforms of surrounding coral rock), *barrier reefs* (reefs that enclose lagoons), and *atolls* (circular, ring-shaped reefs).

Earth's most extensive fringing reef is the Bahamian platform in the western Atlantic (Figure 19c), covering some 96,000 km^2 (37,000 mi^2). Look at the composite *Terra* and *GOES* image of the Western Hemisphere on the half-title page of *Elemental Geosystems*. Can you spot the Bahama coral platform? The largest barrier reef, the Great Barrier Reef along the shore of the state of Queensland, Australia, exceeds 2025 km (1260 mi) in length, is 16–145 km (10–90 mi) wide, and includes at least 700 coral-formed islands and keys (coral islets or barrier islands).

Coral Bleaching Coral reefs may experience a phenomenon known as *bleaching*, which occurs as normally colorful corals turn stark white by expelling their own nutrient-supplying algae. Exactly why the corals eject their symbiotic partner is unknown, for without algae the corals die. Scientists are currently tracking this worldwide phenomenon, which is occurring in the Caribbean Sea and the Indian Ocean as well as off the shores of Australia, Indonesia, Japan, Kenya, Florida, Texas, and Hawai'i.

Possible causes include local pollution, disease, sedimentation, changes in ocean salinity, and increasing oceanic acidity. One acknowledged cause is the warming of sea-surface temperatures, linked to greenhouse warming of the atmosphere. In *Status of Coral Reefs of the World: 2000*, a report from the Global Coral Reef Monitoring Network, warmer water was found to be a greater threat to corals than local pollution or other environmental problems (see http://www.coris.noaa.gov/).

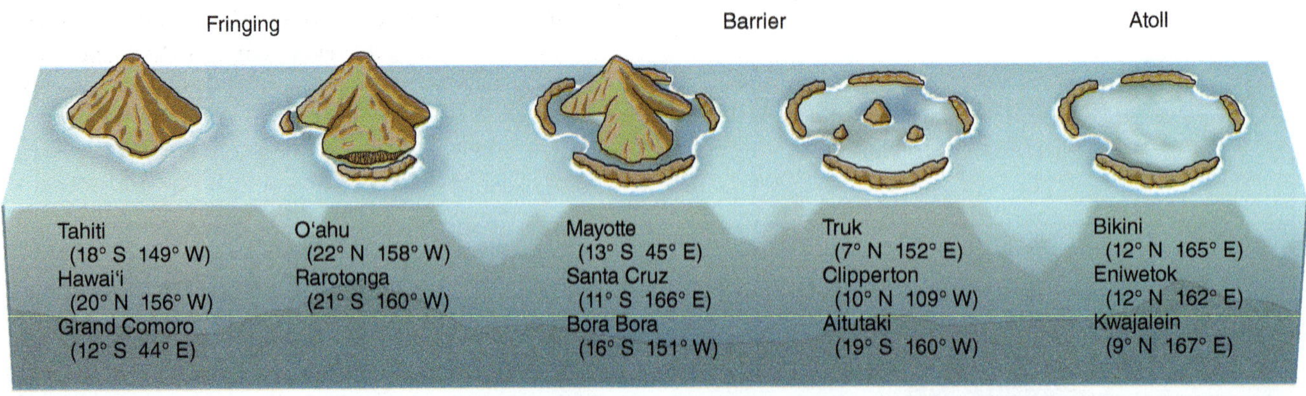

(a)

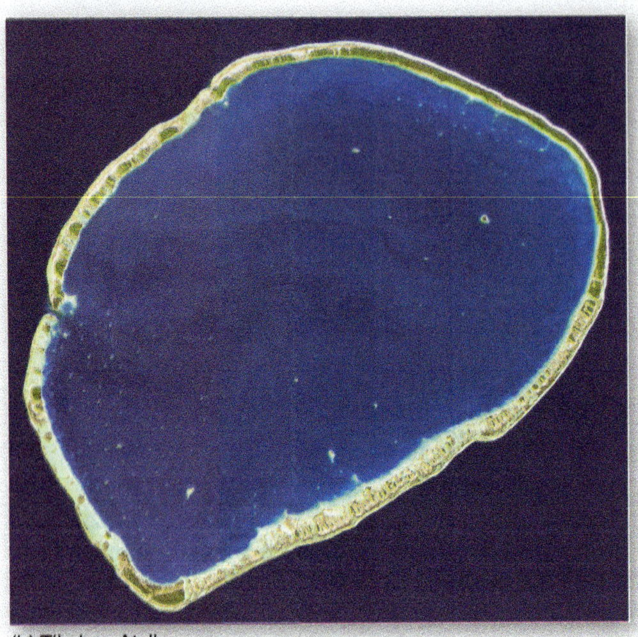

(b) Tikehau Atoll

(c) Bahamian coral platform

FIGURE 19 Coral forms.
(a) Common coral formations in a sequence of reef growth formed around a subsiding volcanic island: fringing reefs, barrier reefs, and an atoll. (b) Satellite image of the Tikehau Atoll, French Polynesia; note the airport runway and village in the far south (15° S 148° 10′ W). (c) The Bahamas: The lighter areas feature ocean depths to 10 m (33 ft); the darker blues indicate depths dropping off to 4000 m (13,100 ft). [(a) After D. R. Stoddart, *The Geographical Magazine* 63 (1971): 610. (b) *EO-1* image, NASA. (c) *Terra* image, NASA/GSFC.]

Although a natural process, coral bleaching is now occurring at an unprecedented rate as average ocean temperatures climb higher, thus linking the issue of climate change to the health of all living coral formations. By the end of 2000, approximately 30% of reefs were lost, with much of the die-off related to the record El Niño event of 1998. In 2010, scientists reported one of the most rapid and severe coral bleaching and mortality events on record near Aceh, Indonesia, on the northern tip of the island of Sumatra. Some species declined 80% in just a few months, in response to sea-surface temperature anomalies across the region. Many of these corals previously were resilient to other ecosystem disruptions, such as the Sumatra–Andaman tsunami in 2004.

As sea-surface temperatures continue to rise, forecasts state that coral losses will continue. For more information and Internet links, see http://www.usgs.gov/coralreef.html and the Global Coral Reef Monitoring Network at http://www.gcrmn.org/.

FIGURE 20 Coastal salt marsh.
Salt marshes are productive ecosystems commonly occurring poleward of 30° latitude in both hemispheres. This is Gearheart Marsh, part of the Arcata Marsh system on the Pacific Coast in northern California. [Bobbé Christopherson.]

II CRITICAL THINKING 3

Exploring corals

Under "Destinations" in Chapter 12 of the *Mastering Geography* web site, go to the link called "Coral Reefs." Sample some of the links on this page. Do you find any information about the damage to and bleaching of coral reefs reported in 1998 or at present? In which places in the world is bleaching being reported? Are the suspect causes presented here mentioned in "Bleaching Hot Spots" or any of the "Coral Reef Alliance" references?

Coastal Wetlands

Some coastal areas have great *biological productivity* (plant growth; spawning grounds for fish, shellfish, and other organisms) stemming from trapped organic matter and sediments. Such a rich coastal marsh environment can greatly outproduce a wheat field in raw vegetation per acre. Thus, coastal marshes can support rich wildlife habitats. Unfortunately, these wetland ecosystems are quite fragile and are threatened by human development.

Wetlands are saturated with water enough of the time to support *hydrophytic vegetation* (plants that grow in water or wet soil). Wetlands usually occur on poorly drained soils. Geographically, they occur not only along coastlines, but also as northern bogs (peatlands with high water tables), as potholes in prairie lands, as cypress swamps (with standing or gently flowing water), as river bottomlands and floodplains, and as arctic and subarctic environments that experience permafrost during the year. Coastal wetlands are of two general types—salt marshes and mangrove swamps. In the Northern Hemisphere, **salt marshes** tend to form north of the 30th parallel, whereas **mangrove swamps** form equatorward from that parallel in the Eastern and Western Hemispheres. This distribution is dictated by the occurrence of freezing conditions, which control the survival of mangrove seedlings. Roughly the same latitudinal limits apply in the Southern Hemisphere.

Coastal wetlands have many important functions, one of which is to buffer coastlines from storm surges associated with hurricanes. On the *MasteringGeography* web site, you will find a discussion of the impacts of wetland removal, storm surge, and rising sea level on Bayou LaFourche in southern Mississippi.

Salt marshes usually form in estuaries and behind barrier beaches and spits. An accumulation of mud produces a site for the growth of *halophytic* (salt-tolerant) plants. This vegetation then traps additional alluvial sediments and adds to the salt marsh area. Because salt marshes are in the intertidal zone (between the farthest reaches of high and low tides), sinuous, branching channels are produced as tidal waters flood into and ebb from the marsh (Figure 20).

Sediment accumulation on tropical coastlines provides the site for mangrove trees, shrubs, and other small trees. The prop roots of the mangrove are constantly finding

GEO REPORT 4 ***Ocean acidification impact on corals***

An early study of increasing ocean acidification and its impact on corals occurred from 1991 to 1993 in *Biosphere 2*—the closed habitat experiment located north of Tucson, Arizona. The habitat suffered from high carbon dioxide levels, and the model ocean in *Biosphere 2* quickly absorbed massive amounts of the excessive carbon dioxide. The model ocean became more acidic, which, in turn, chemically attacked the corals in the ocean. This same process is now occurring in the global oceans as CO_2 levels rise—here in Biosphere 1—with much research focused on the effects of acidification on oceanic flora and fauna.

(a) Mangroves

(b) Mangrove ecosystem underwater

FIGURE 21 Mangroves.
(a) Mangroves at sunset in "Ding" Darling National Wildlife Refuge, Sanibel Island, Florida; you can see the roots above the water line. (b) Underwater mangrove roots form a habitat for numerous plants and animals in a specific ecosystem. [Bobbé Christopherson.]

new anchorages. The roots are visible above the waterline, but reach below the water surface, providing a habitat for a multitude of specialized life forms (Figure 21). Mangrove swamps often secure and fix enough material to form islands.

The World Resources Institute and the United Nations Environment Programme estimate that from preagricultural times to today, mangrove losses are running between 40% (examples, Cameroon and Indonesia) and nearly 80% (examples, Bangladesh and Philippines). Deliberate removal was a common practice by many governments in the early days of settlement because of a falsely conceived fear of disease or pestilence in these swamplands.

The Work of Wind

Wind is an agent of geomorphic change in coastal and desert environments. Like moving water, moving air causes erosion, transportation, and deposition of materials ranging from sand to snow. Moving air is a fluid and it behaves similarly, although it has a lower viscosity (it is less dense) than water. Although lacking the lifting ability of water, wind processes can modify and move quantities of materials along coastlines, in deserts, and elsewhere. Consistent local wind can prune and shape vegetation and sculpt ice and snow surfaces (Figure 22).

The work of wind is **eolian** (also spelled *aeolian*, for Aeolus, ruler of the winds in Greek mythology). The ability of wind to move materials is actually small compared

(a)

(b)

FIGURE 22 The work of wind.
(a) Wind-sculpted tree near South Point, Hawai'i. Nearly constant tradewinds keep this tree naturally pruned. (b) Blowing wind shapes ice in formations of sastrugi. Can you tell the direction of the prevailing winds looking at the ice? [Bobbé Christopherson.]

with that of other transporting agents such as water and ice because air is so much less dense than those other media. Yet, over time, wind accomplishes enormous work. British Army Major Ralph Bagnold, an engineering officer stationed in Egypt in 1925, was a pioneer in eolian research. Bagnold's often-cited work *The Physics of Blown Sand and Desert Dunes* was published in 1941. Bagnold studied the ability of wind to transport sand over the surface of a dune. He found that a steady wind of 50 kmph (30 mph) can move approximately one-half ton of sand per day over a 1-m-wide section of dune.

Eolian Erosion

Two principal wind-erosion processes are **deflation**, the removal and lifting of individual loose particles, and **abrasion**, the grinding of rock surfaces by the "sandblasting" action of particles captured in the air. Deflation and abrasion produce a variety of distinctive landforms and landscapes.

Deflation Deflation literally blows away loose or noncohesive sediment and works with rainwater to form a surface resembling a cobblestone street: a **desert pavement** that protects underlying sediment from further deflation and water erosion. Traditionally, deflation was regarded as a key formative process, eroding fine dust, clay, and sand and leaving behind a concentration of pebbles and gravel as desert pavement (Figure 23a).

Another hypothesis that better explains some desert pavement surfaces states that deposition of windblown sediments, not removal, is the formative agent. Windblown particles settle between and below coarse rocks and pebbles that are gradually displaced upward. Rainwater is involved as wetting and drying episodes swell and shrink clay-sized particles. The gravel fragments are gradually lifted to surface positions to form the pavement (Figure 23b). Desert pavements are so common that many provincial names are used for them—for example, *gibber plain* in Australia; *gobi* in China; and in Africa, *lag gravels* or *serir*, or *reg* desert if some fine particles remain.

Heavy recreational activity damages fragile desert landscapes, especially in the United States, where more than 15 million off-road vehicles are now in use. Such vehicles crush plants and animals; disrupt desert pavement, leading to greater deflation; and create ruts that easily concentrate sheetwash to form gullies.

Wherever wind encounters loose sediment, deflation may remove enough material to form basins known as **blowout depressions**. These depressions range from small indentations less than a meter wide up to areas hundreds of meters wide and many meters deep. Chemical weathering, although slow in arid regions owing to the lack of water, is important in the formation of a blowout, for it removes the cementing materials that give particles their cohesiveness. Large depressions in the Sahara Desert are at least partially formed by deflation. The enormous Munkhafad el Qaṭṭâra (Qaṭṭâra Depression), which covers 18,000 km^2 (6950 mi^2) just inland from the Mediterranean Sea in the Western Desert of Egypt, is now about 130 m (427 ft) below sea level at its lowest point.

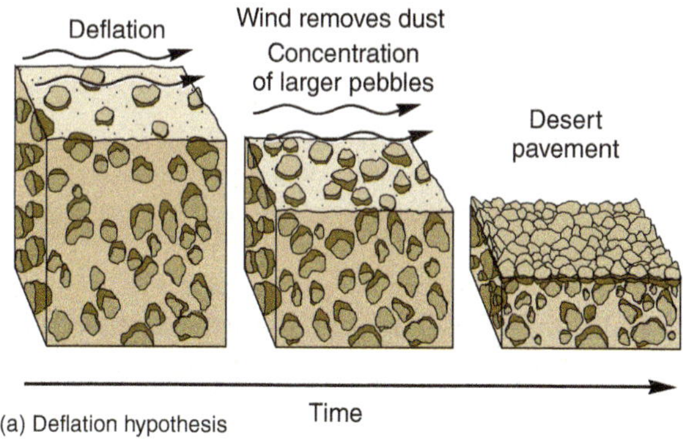

(a) Deflation hypothesis

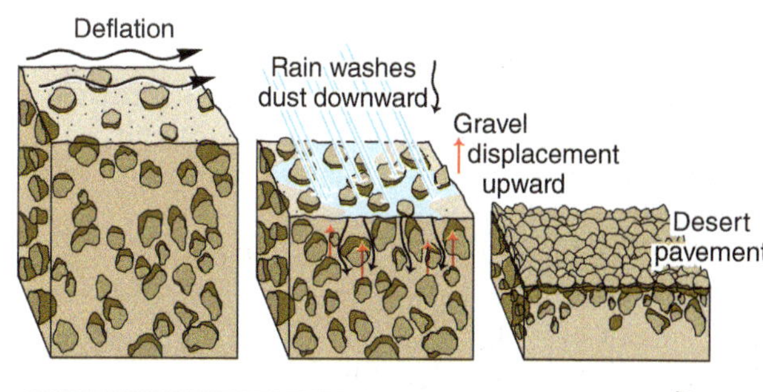

(b) Sediment-accumulation hypothesis

(c)

FIGURE 23 Desert pavement.
(a) Desert pavement may be formed when larger rocks and fragments are left after deflation and sheetwash remove finer dust, silt, and clays. (b) Other desert pavements seem to be formed by wind delivering fine particles that settle and wash downward; through cycles of swelling and shrinking, the gravels gradually migrate upward to form pavement. (c) A typical desert pavement. [Bobbé Christopherson.]

Abrasion You may have seen work crews sandblasting surfaces on buildings, bridges, or streets to clean them or to remove unwanted markings. Sandblasting uses a stream of compressed air filled with sand grains to quickly abrade a surface. Abrasion by windblown particles is nature's slower version of sandblasting, and it is especially effective at polishing exposed rocks when the abrading particles are hard and angular. Variables that affect the rate of abrasion include the hardness of surface rocks, wind velocity, and wind constancy. Abrasive action is restricted to the area immediately above the ground, usually no more than a meter or two in height, because sand grains are lifted only a short distance.

Rocks exposed to eolian abrasion appear pitted, fluted (grooved), or polished. They usually are aerodynamically shaped in a specific direction, according to the consistent flow of airborne particles carried by prevailing winds. Rocks that have such evidence of eolian erosion are **ventifacts** (literally, "artifacts of the wind"). On a larger scale, deflation and abrasion are capable of streamlining rock structures that are aligned parallel to the most effective wind direction, leaving behind distinctive, elongated ridges or formations called **yardangs**. These wind-sculpted features can range from meters to kilometers in length and up to many meters in height.

On Earth, some yardangs are large enough to be detected on satellite imagery. The Ica Valley of southern Peru contains yardangs reaching 100 m (330 ft) in height and several kilometers in length. Abrasion is concentrated on the windward end of each yardang, with deflation operating on the leeward portions (Figure 24). The Sphinx in Egypt was perhaps partially formed as a yardang, suggesting a head and body. Some scientists think this shape led the ancients to complete the bulk of the sculpture artificially with masonry.

Eolian Transportation

Atmospheric circulation can transport fine material, such as volcanic debris, fire soot and smoke, and dust, worldwide within days. Wind exerts a drag, or frictional pull, on surface particles until they become airborne, just as water in a stream picks up sediment (again, think of air as a fluid). The distance that wind is capable of transporting particles in suspension varies greatly with particle size. Only the finest dust particles travel significant distances, so the finer material suspended in a dust storm is lifted much higher than are the coarser particles of a sandstorm.

People living in areas of frequent dust storms are faced with infiltration of very fine particles into their homes and businesses through even the smallest cracks. People living in desert regions and along sandy beaches, where frequent sandstorms occur, contend with the sandblasting of painted surfaces and etched window glass.

Grain size is important in wind erosion. Intermediate-sized grains move most easily—it is the largest and the smallest sand particles that require the strongest winds to move. The large particles are heavier and thus require stronger winds. The small particles are difficult to move because they exhibit a mutual cohesiveness and because they usually present a smooth (aerodynamic) surface to the wind.

The term *saltation* can be used to describe movement of particles by water. The term also describes the wind transport of grains, usually larger than 0.2 mm (0.008 in.), along the ground. About 80% of wind transport of particles is accomplished by this skipping and bouncing action (Figure 25). Compared with fluvial transport, in which saltation is accomplished by hydraulic lift, eolian saltation is executed by aerodynamic lift, elastic bounce, and impact.

On impact, grains hit other grains and knock them into the air. Saltating particles crash into other particles, knocking them both loose and forward. This type of movement is **surface creep**, which slides and rolls particles too large for saltation and affects about 20% of the material transported by wind. Once in motion, particles continue to be transported by lower wind velocities. In a desert or along a beach, sometimes you can hear a slight hissing sound, almost like steam escaping, produced by the myriad saltating grains of sand as they bounce along and collide with surface particles.

Both human and natural sand erosion and transport from a beach are slowed by conservation measures such as the introduction of stabilizing native plants, the use of fences, and the restriction of pedestrian traffic to walkways (Figure 26). As human settlement encroaches on coastal dunes, sand transport becomes problematic.

Eolian Deposition

The smallest features shaped by individual saltating grains are ripples. Eolian ripples are similar to

(a)

(b)

FIGURE 24 A yardang.
(a) A small wind-sculpted rock formation located in Snow Canyon outside St. George, Utah.
(b) Consistent winds shape this exposed rock on Bear Island in the North Atlantic. The rock sits on a surface of patterned ground and periglacial features. [Bobbé Christopherson.]

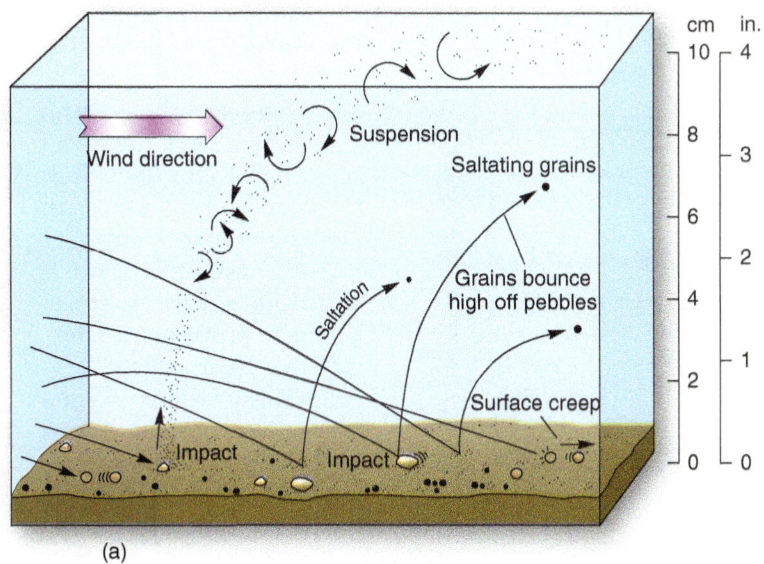

FIGURE 25 How the wind moves sand.
(a) Eolian suspension, saltation, and surface creep are transportation mechanisms. Compare with the saltation and traction that occur in another fluid, water. (b) Sand grains saltating along the surface in the Stovepipe Wells dune field, Death Valley, California. [Author.]

fluvial ripples, although the impact of saltating grains is slight in water. Ripples form in crests and troughs, positioned transversely (at a right angle) to the direction of the wind.

Many people know arid landscapes only from the movies, which leave the impression that most deserts are covered by sand. Instead, desert pavements predominate across most subtropical arid landscapes; only about 10% of desert areas are covered with sand. Sand grains generally are deposited as transient ridges or hills called dunes.

A **dune** is a wind-sculpted accumulation of sand. An extensive area of dunes, such as that found in North Africa, is characteristic of an **erg desert**, or **sand sea**. The Grand Erg Oriental in the central Sahara exceeds 1200 m (4000 ft) in depth and covers 192,000 km^2 (75,000 mi^2), comparable to the area of Nebraska. This sand sea has been active for more than 1.3 million years. Similar sand seas, such as the Grand Ar Rub'al Khālī Erg, are active in Saudi Arabia.

In eastern Algeria, the Issaouane Erg covers 38,000 km^2 (14,673 mi^2). Winds from varying directions produce star dunes with multiple slipfaces (Figure 27a). *Star dunes* are the mountainous giants of the sandy desert. They are pinwheel-shaped, with several radiating arms rising and joining to form a common central peak, where they approach 200 m (650 ft) in height. Some in the Sonoran Desert approach this size. In the image, you can also see some crescentic dunes, which suggest the region has

FIGURE 26 Preventing sand transport.
(a) Popham Beach State Park, Maine. Further erosion and transport of coastal dunes can be controlled by stabilizing strategies, such as planting native plants and confining pedestrian traffic to walkways. (b) Tufts of beach grass are planted to stabilize this coastal area in Atlantic City, New Jersey. One storm surge can erase such efforts. [Bobbé Christopherson.]

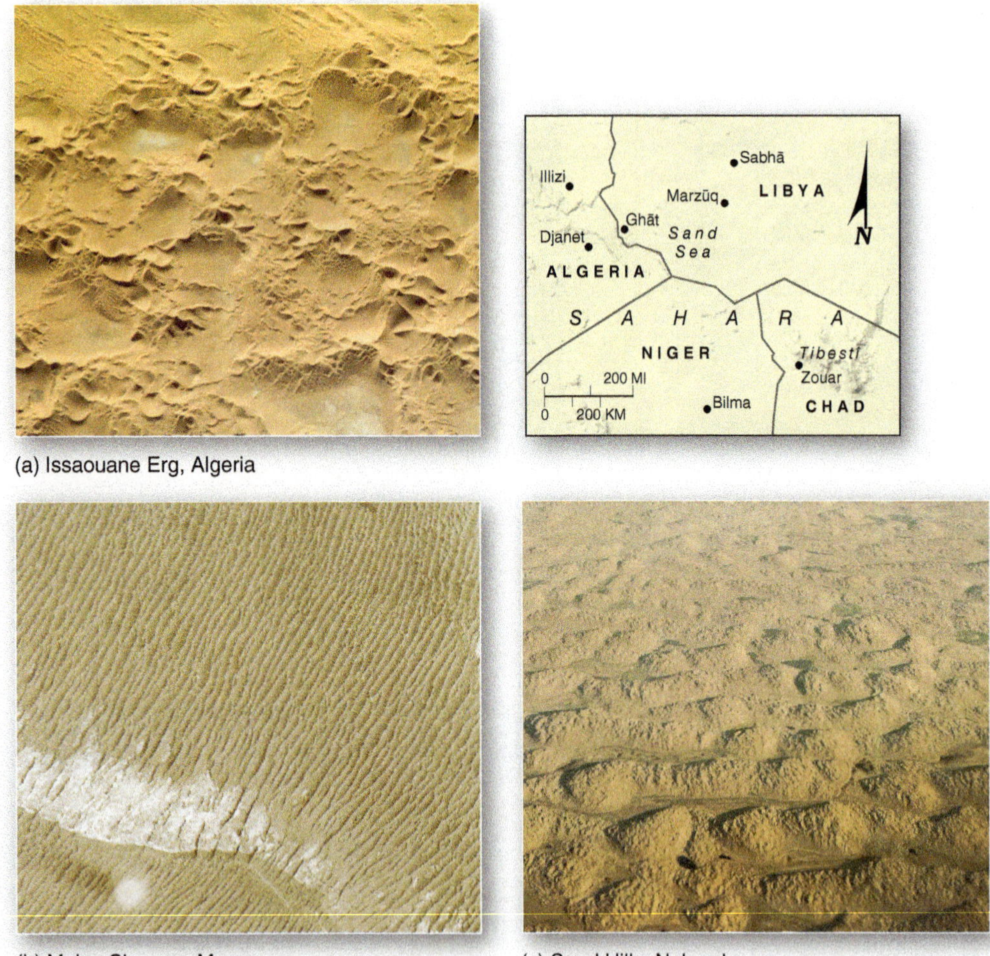

(a) Issaouane Erg, Algeria

(b) Melas Chasma, Mars

(c) Sand Hills, Nebraska

FIGURE 27 Seas of sand.
(a) The Issaouane Erg of eastern Algeria is a blend of principally star dunes, some barchan dunes, and linear dunes in the far upper-left—all disclose the prevailing wind history of the region. (b) Sand dunes are found on the Martian surface in the southern area of Melas Chasma in Valles Marineris. Note the dust devil in the lower left. The area covered is about 2 km wide. (c) Sand Hills, central Nebraska, sit atop the High Plains aquifer. These densely packed barchan dunes, inactive for at least 600 years, are fixed (stabilized) by vegetation. [(a) ISS astronaut photo, NASA/GSFC. (b) Mars Global Surveyor, Mars Orbiter Camera image courtesy of NASA/JPL/Malin Space Science Systems. (c) Bobbé Christopherson.]

experienced changing wind patterns over time, as they form from a single principal wind flow. Dunes are present on Mars as well as in semiarid areas such as the Great Plains of the United States (Figure 27b and c).

Dune Movement and Form Dune fields, whether in arid regions or along coastlines, tend to migrate in the direction of effective, sand-transporting winds. In this regard, stronger seasonal winds or winds from a passing storm may prove more effective than average prevailing winds. When saltating sand grains encounter small patches of sand, their kinetic energy (motion) is dissipated and they accumulate. As height increases above 30 cm (12 in.), a *slipface* and characteristic dune features form.

By studying the dune model in Figure 28, you can see that winds characteristically create a gently sloping *windward side* (stoss side), with a more steeply sloped slipface on the *leeward side*. A dune usually is asymmetrical in one or more directions. The angle of a slipface is the steepest angle at which loose material is stable—its *angle of repose*. Thus, the constant flow of new material makes a slipface, a type of *avalanche slope*. Sand builds up as it moves over the crest of the dune to the brink; then it avalanches, falling and cascading as the slipface continually adjusts, seeking its angle of repose (usually 30° to 34°). In this way, a dune migrates

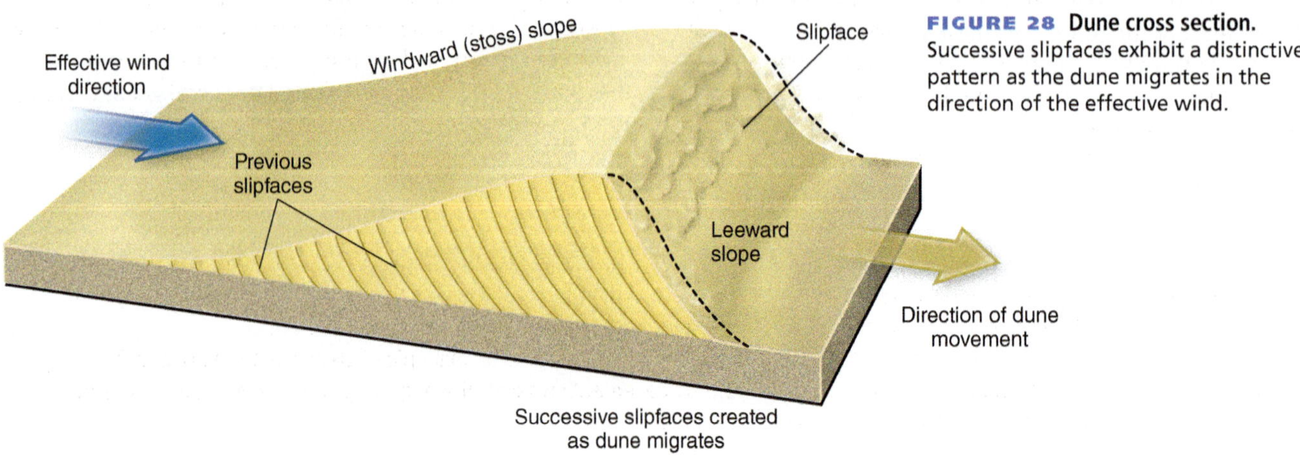

FIGURE 28 Dune cross section. Successive slipfaces exhibit a distinctive pattern as the dune migrates in the direction of the effective wind.

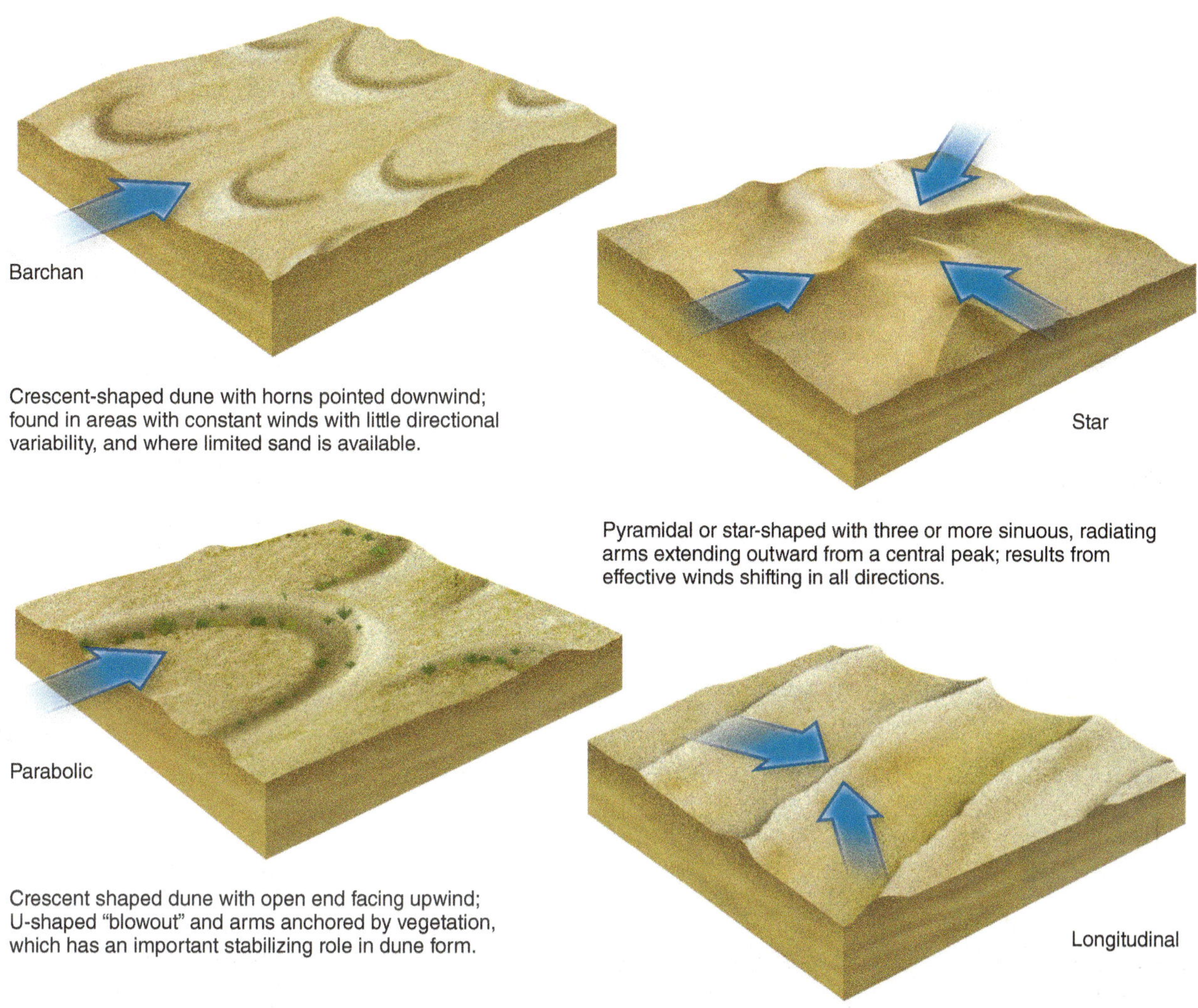

FIGURE 29 Major dune forms.
Arrows show wind direction. [Adapted from E. D. McKee, *A Study of Global Sand Seas*, USGS Professional Paper 1052 (Washington, DC: U.S. Government Printing Office, 1979).]

downwind, as suggested by the successive dune profiles in Figure 28.

Dunes have many wind-shaped styles that make classification difficult. We simplify dune forms into three classes—*crescentic* (crescent, curved shape), *linear* (straight form), and massive *star dunes*. Examples of each are in Figure 29 and detailed on the *MasteringGeography* web site. Active sand dunes cover about 10% of Earth's deserts. Dune fields are also present in humid climates, such as along coastal Oregon, the south shore of Lake Michigan, and the U.S. Gulf and Atlantic coastlines; in Europe; and elsewhere.

These same dune-forming principles and terms (for example, *dune* and *slipface*) apply to snow-covered landscapes. *Snow dunes* are formed as wind deposits snow in drifts. In semiarid farming areas, capturing drifting snow with fences and tall stubble left in fields contributes significantly to soil moisture when the snow melts.

GEO REPORT 5 Conflicts feed the sand seas

Military activities can threaten desert pavement. A serious environmental impact of the ongoing wars in Iraq and Afghanistan is the disruption of desert pavement by explosives and the movement of heavy vehicles. As thousands of square kilometers of stable desert pavement break apart, nearby cities and farms experience increased dust and sand invasions.

The Registan Desert of southern Afghanistan, south of the city of Kandahar, is an example of such a sand sea over a flat terrain. A result of drought conditions and war-disrupted desert pavement surfaces, the migrating sand is overtaking areas of sparse agricultural activity and has covered more than 100 villages.

Dune Lithification Patterns of cross bedding, or *cross stratification*, are sometimes present in desert sandstone, formed by lithification of ancient sand dunes. When such a dune was accumulating, sand cascaded down its slipface and distinct bedding planes (layers) were established that remained after the dune lithified (Figure 30). Ripple marks, animal tracks, and fossils also are found preserved in these sandstones.

FIGURE 30 Cross bedding in sedimentary rocks. The bedding pattern of cross stratification in this sandstone tells us about dune environments before lithification (hardening into rock). [Bobbé Christopherson.]

CRITICAL THINKING 4

The nearest eolian features

What eolian features are nearest to your present location? Are they coastal, lakeshore, or desert dunes? Which causative factors discussed in this chapter explain the location or form of these features? Are you able to visit the site?

GEOSYSTEMS CONNECTION

You probably have examined or will examine aspects of weathering, erosion and transportation, and deposition, through the agents of streams, waves, and wind. In this chapter, the systems approach moved you through coastal system inputs, actions, and outputs and analyzed the effects of wind processes. However, there are agents of change in the cryosphere and the ice environments on Earth: systems that are undergoing the highest rate of change as climates shift.

KEY LEARNING CONCEPTS REVIEW

- ***Describe*** the chemical composition and physical structure of the ocean.

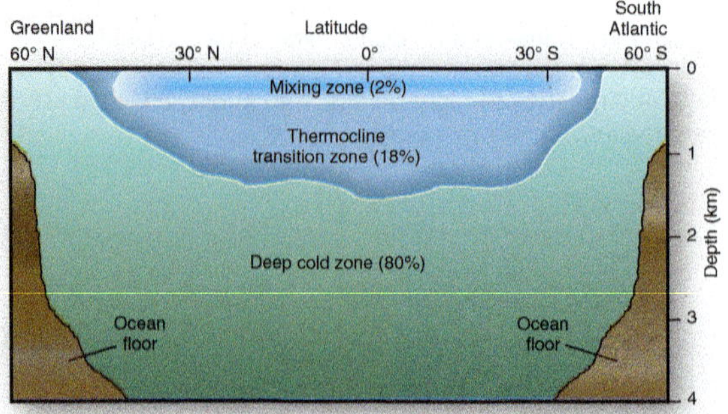

Water is the "universal solvent," dissolving at least 57 of the 92 elements found in nature. Seawater is a solution, and the concentration of dissolved solids is **salinity. Brine** exceeds the average 35‰ (parts per thousand) salinity; **brackish** applies to water that is less than 35‰. The ocean is divided by depth into the narrow mixing zone at the surface, the thermocline transition zone, and the deep cold zone.

salinity
brine
brackish

1. Describe the salinity of seawater: its composition, amount, and distribution.
2. Analyze the latitudinal distribution of salinity discussed in the chapter. Why is salinity less along the equator and greater in the subtropics?
3. What are the three general zones relative to physical structure within the ocean? Characterize each by temperature, salinity, dissolved oxygen, and dissolved carbon dioxide.

- ***Identify*** the components of the coastal environment, including mean sea level, and ***explain*** the actions of tides.

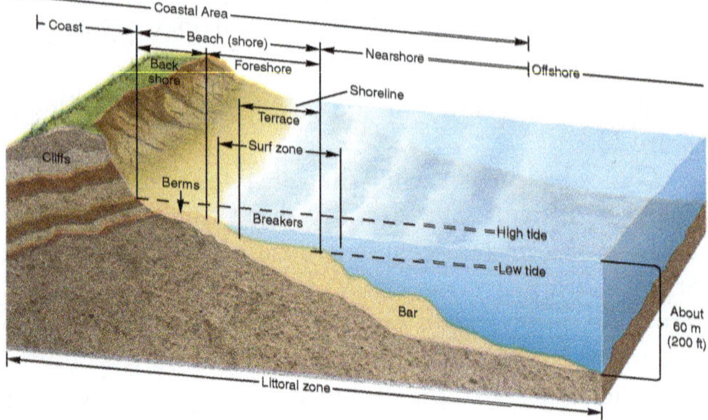

The coastal environment is the **littoral zone** and exists where the tide-driven, wave-driven sea confronts the land. Inputs to the coastal environment include solar energy, wind and weather, climatic variation, the nature of coastal geomorphology, and human activities.

Mean sea level (MSL) is based on average tidal levels recorded hourly at a given site over many years. MSL varies spatially because of ocean currents and waves, tidal variations, air temperature and pressure differences, ocean temperature variations, slight variations in Earth's gravity, and changes in oceanic volume. MSL worldwide is rising in response to global warming of the atmosphere and oceans.

Tides are complex daily oscillations in sea level, ranging worldwide from barely noticeable to many meters. Tides are produced by the gravitational pull of both the Moon and the Sun. Most coastal locations experience two high (rising) *flood tides* and two low (falling) *ebb tides* every day. The difference between consecutive high and low tides is the tidal range. *Spring tides* exhibit the greatest tidal range, when the Moon and the Sun are in either conjunction or opposition. *Neap tides* produce a lesser tidal range.

littoral zone
mean sea level (MSL)
tide

4. What are the key terms used to describe the coastal environment?
5. Define mean sea level. How is this value determined? Is it constant or variable around the world? Explain.
6. What interacting forces generate the pattern of tides?
7. What characteristic tides are expected during a new Moon or a full Moon? During the first-quarter and third-quarter phases of the Moon? What is meant by a flood tide? An ebb tide?
8. Explain briefly how tidal power would be utilized to produce electricity. Are there any sites doing this in North America? If so, briefly describe where they are and how they operate.

■ ***Describe*** wave motion at sea and near shore, and ***explain*** coastal straightening and coastal landforms.

Friction between moving air (wind) and the ocean surface generates undulations of water that we call **waves**. Wave energy in the open sea travels through water, but the water itself stays in place. Regular patterns of smooth, rounded waves—the mature undulations of the open ocean—are **swells**. Near shore, the restricted depth of water slows the wave, forming *waves of translation*, in which both energy and water actually move forward toward shore. As the crest of each wave rises, the wave falls into a characteristic **breaker**.

Wave refraction redistributes wave energy so that different sections of the coastline vary in erosion potential. Headlands are eroded, whereas coves and bays receive materials, with the long-term effect of straightening the coast. As waves approach a shore at an angle, refraction produces a **longshore current** of water moving parallel to the shore. This current produces the *longshore drift* of sand, sediment, gravel, and assorted materials. **Littoral drift** is transport of materials along the shore and a more comprehensive term. Particles move along the beach as *beach drift*, shifting back and forth between water and land. A **tsunami** is a seismic sea wave triggered by an undersea landslide or earthquake. It travels at great speeds in the open sea and gains height as it comes ashore, posing a coastal hazard.

An *erosional coast* features wave action that cuts a horizontal bench in the tidal zone, extending from a sea cliff out into the sea. Such a structure is a **wave-cut platform**, or *wave-cut terrace*. In contrast, *depositional coasts* generally are located along land of gentle relief, where depositional sediments are available from many sources. Characteristic landforms deposited by waves and currents are a **barrier spit** (material deposited in a long ridge extending out from a coast); a **bay barrier**, or *baymouth bar* (a spit that cuts off the bay from the ocean and forms an inland **lagoon**); a **tombolo** (where sediment deposits connect the shoreline with an offshore island or sea stack); and a **beach** (land along the shore where sediment is in motion, deposited by waves and currents).

wave
swell
breaker
wave refraction
longshore current
littoral drift
tsunami
wave-cut platform
barrier spit
bay barrier
lagoon
tombolo
beach

9. What is a wave? How are waves generated, and how do they travel across the ocean? Does the water travel with the wave? Discuss the process of wave formation and transmission.
10. Describe the refraction process that occurs when waves reach an irregular coastline. Why is the coastline straightened?
11. Define the components of beach drift, and the longshore current and longshore drift.
12. Explain how a seismic sea wave attains such tremendous velocities. Why is it given a Japanese name—tsunami?
13. What is meant by an erosional coast? What are the expected features of such a coast?
14. What is meant by a depositional coast? What are the expected features of such a coast?
15. How do people attempt to modify littoral drift? What strategies do they use? What are the positive and negative impacts of these actions?
16. Describe a beach—its form, composition, function, and evolution.
17. What success has Miami had with beach replenishment? Is it a practical strategy?

■ ***Describe*** barrier beaches and islands and their hazards as they relate to human settlement.

Barrier chains are long, narrow, depositional features, generally of sand, that form offshore roughly parallel to the coast. Common forms are **barrier beaches** and the broader, more extensive **barrier islands**. Barrier formations are transient coastal features,

constantly on the move, and they are a poor, but common, choice for development.

barrier beach
barrier island

18. On the basis of the information in the text and any other sources at your disposal, do you think barrier islands and beaches should be used for development? If so, under what conditions? If not, why not?
19. After Hurricane Hazel destroyed the Grand Strand off South Carolina in 1954, settlements were rebuilt; yet they were hit again by Hurricane Hugo 35 years later, in 1989. Why does this type of recurring damage happen to human populations?
20. What type of environmental analysis is needed for rational development and growth in a region like the New Jersey shore? Evaluate each element of the Jersey shore and the approach suggested to coastal hazards, planning, and protection in Focus Study 1 and in Figure 1.2.

- ***Assess*** living coastal environments: corals and coastal wetlands.

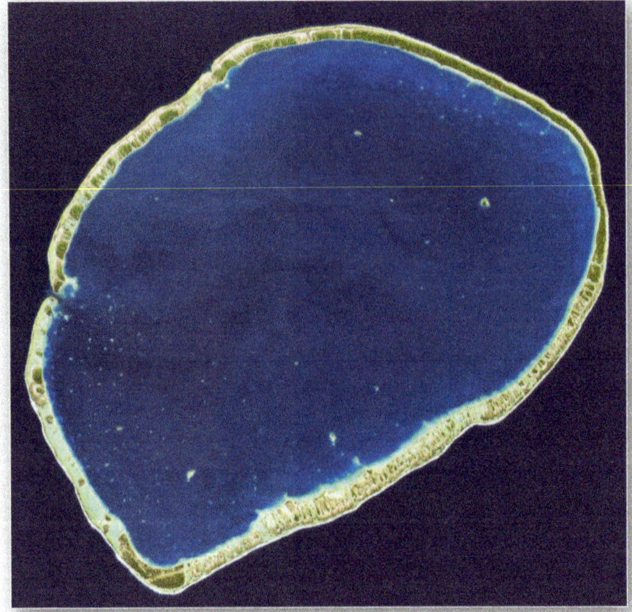

A **coral** is a simple marine invertebrate that forms a hard, calcified, external skeleton. Over generations, corals accumulate in large reef structures. Corals live in a *symbiotic* (mutually helpful) relationship with algae; each is dependent on the other for survival.

Wetlands are lands saturated with water that support specific plants adapted to wet conditions. Coastal wetlands form as **salt marshes** poleward of the 30th parallel in each hemisphere and as **mangrove swamps** equatorward of these parallels.

coral
wetland
salt marsh
mangrove swamp

21. How are corals able to construct reefs and islands?
22. Describe a trend in corals that is troubling scientists, and discuss some possible causes.
23. Why are the coastal wetlands poleward of 30° N and S latitude different from those that are equatorward? Describe the differences.

- ***Describe*** eolian erosion, including deflation, abrasion, and the resultant landforms.

Eolian processes modify and move sand accumulations along coastal beaches and deserts. Two principal wind-erosion processes are **deflation**, the removal and lifting of individual loose particles, and **abrasion**, the "sandblasting" of rock surfaces with particles captured in the air. Deflation literally blows away loose or noncohesive sediment and works with rainwater to form a surface resembling a cobblestone street: a **desert pavement** that protects underlying sediment from further deflation and water erosion. Wherever wind encounters loose sediment, deflation may remove enough material to form basins. Called **blowout depressions**, they range from small indentations less than a meter wide up to areas hundreds of meters wide and many meters deep. Rocks that bear evidence of eolian erosion are **ventifacts**. On a larger scale, deflation and abrasion are capable of streamlining rock structures, leaving behind distinctive rock formations or elongated ridges called **yardangs**.

eolian
deflation
abrasion
desert pavement
blowout depression
ventifact
yardang

24. Explain the term *eolian* and its application in this chapter. How would you characterize the ability of the wind to move material?
25. Who was Ralph Bagnold? What was his contribution to eolian studies?
26. Describe the erosional processes associated with moving air.
27. Explain deflation and provide an overview of each hypothesis on the processes that produce desert pavement.
28. How are ventifacts and yardangs formed by the wind?

■ ***Describe*** eolian transportation, and ***explain*** eolian depositional landforms, including the major classes of sand dunes.

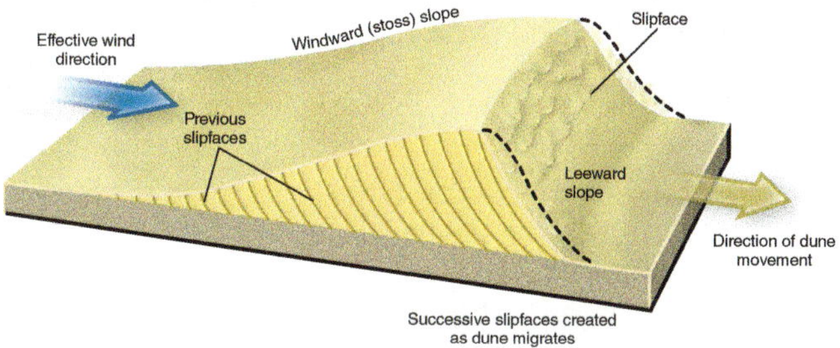

Wind exerts a drag or frictional pull on surface particles until they become airborne. The finer material suspended in a dust storm is lifted much higher than are the coarser particles of a sandstorm; only the finest dust particles travel significant distances. Saltating particles crash into other particles, knocking them both loose and forward. The motion of **surface creep** slides and rolls particles too large for saltation. In arid and semiarid climates and along some coastlines where sand is available, dunes accumulate. A **dune** is a wind-sculpted accumulation of sand. An extensive area of dunes, such as that found in North Africa, is characteristic of an **erg desert**, or **sand sea**. When saltating sand grains encounter small patches of sand, their kinetic energy (motion) is dissipated, and they start to accumulate into a dune. As height increases above 30 cm (12 in.), a steeply sloping *slipface* on the lee side and characteristic dune features are formed. Dune forms are broadly classified as *crescentic*, *linear*, and *star*.

surface creep
dune
erg desert
sand sea

29. Differentiate between a dust storm and a sandstorm.
30. What is the difference between eolian saltation and fluvial saltation?
31. Explain the concept of surface creep.
32. What is the difference between an erg desert and desert pavement? Which type is a sand sea? Are all deserts covered by sand? Explain.
33. What are the three classes of dune forms? Describe an example within each class. What do you think is the major shaping force for sand dunes?
34. Which form of dune is the mountain giant of the desert? What are the characteristic wind patterns that produce such dunes?

MasteringGEOGRAPHY™

Visit **http://www.masteringgeography.com/** for several figure animations, satellite loops, self-study quizzes, flashcards, visual glossary, case studies, career links, text reference maps, RSS Feeds, and an ebook version of *Elemental Geosystems.* Included are many geography web links to interesting Internet sources that support this chapter.

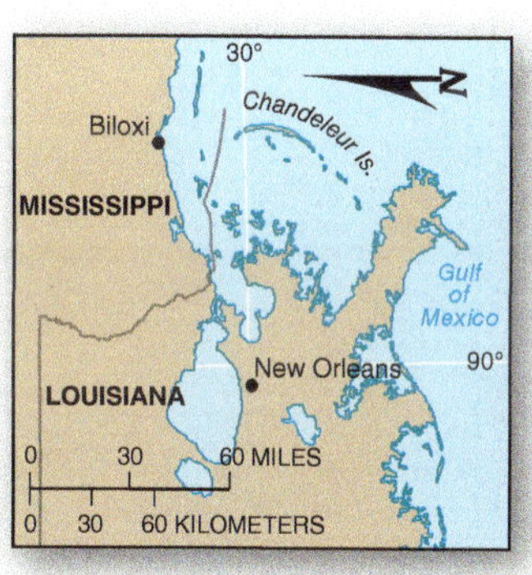

Another view of the Chandeleur Islands shown in Figure 16, in an aerial photo comparison between 2001 and two days after Hurricane Katrina, shows the devastation to the sand inventory in the Northern Chandeleur Islands. The yellow arrow points to the same location in each photo. [USGS Hurricane Impact Studies.]

Index

Page references followed by "f" indicate illustrated figures or photographs; followed by "t" indicates a table.

D

E

N

O

P

W

X

Y

Z